What Sorrows Labour in My Parent's Breast?

What Sorrows Labour in My Parent's Breast?

A History of the Enslaved Black Family

Brenda E. Stevenson

ROWMAN & LITTLEFIELD
Lanham • Boulder • New York • London

Published by Rowman & Littlefield
An imprint of The Rowman & Littlefield Publishing Group, Inc.
4501 Forbes Boulevard, Suite 200, Lanham, Maryland 20706
www.rowman.com

86-90 Paul Street, London EC2A 4NE

Copyright © 2023 by The Rowman & Littlefield Publishing Group, Inc.

All rights reserved. No part of this book may be reproduced in any form or by any electronic or mechanical means, including information storage and retrieval systems, without written permission from the publisher, except by a reviewer who may quote passages in a review.

British Library Cataloguing in Publication Information Available

Library of Congress Cataloging-in-Publication Data Available

978-1-4422-5216-5 (cloth)
978-1-4422-5217-2 (electronic)

For the African girl sold from Virginia to South Carolina and all her kin.

Contents

Acknowledgments ix

Introduction: The Black Family in the Public Imagination: What's Slavery and Slavery Scholarship Got to Do with It? 1

BEGINNINGS 37

1 Traditions from Whence They Came: Marriage and Family in Western/Central Africa at the Time of the Atlantic Slave Trade 39

2 The Colonial Enslaved Family: Foundations and Creations 79

3 Traditions of Resistance and Family from the Colonial Era Forward 129

THE ANTEBELLUM FAMILIAL EXPERIENCE 183

4 Antebellum Courtship and Marital Rituals 185

5 Antebellum Family Life 219

6 Death and Resurrection 273

Conclusion: Bob Samuels's American Family 301

Appendix A: Godfrey Family Units 309

Appendix B: Percentage of Households Per State with Enslaved People, 1860 319

Notes 323

Index 409

About the Author 429

Acknowledgments

Thank you, God, for my many blessings! Thank you, ancestors, for surviving the struggles and passing on the joy and beauty of life! I will be forever thankful to my parents, James and Emma Gerald Stevenson, for the beautiful family they gave me, one that includes my loving, supportive sisters, Beverly and Iris, my brother-in-law Carlton Harris, nieces, in-laws, southern cousins, and a host of caring friends. My adult life has been framed by my own marriage and family. My husband, Dr. James H. Cones III, is the absolute best. His family has been a treasure trove of love and acceptance. James has cared for me and taken care of me, and we continue to have wonderful adventures together. Our most wondrous labor is our daughter, the beautiful and brilliant Emma. She is the delight of my life.

Beyond God and family, my work as a social historian has been the center of my attention for many years now. These efforts, including this new book, would not have ever been possible without a host of generous, challenging, inspirational teachers, mentors, colleagues, students, and friends along with institutional support from multiple funding agencies.

Professor John W. Blassingame remains my most important mentor in all things related to the enslaved, and I am thankful that I had an opportunity to gain tremendously from his enviable intellect and careful supervision. Nancy Cott guided me on the path to studying women and has continued to support me over the decades. These are incredible gifts for which I am grateful. Ellen DuBois has both inspired and aided in my work in women's and gender history since we first became colleagues at UCLA. V. P. Franklin has been a constant and generous teacher, advisor, supporter, friend, and collaborator. Everyone should have a V. P. in their lives and careers. Gerald Jaynes, Darlene Clark Hine, Deborah White, Eric Foner, Arnold Rampersad, and David Barry Gaspar along with the late David Brion Davis and Paul Gaston have all contributed to my growth as a social historian and a scholar of Black people in early America. Generous colleagues are a special blessing. Stephen Aron and Ellen Dubois have been wonderful always. They, along with Ron Mellor, Scott Waugh, David Meyers, John Laslett, Teo Ruiz, Joan Waugh, Richard von Glahn, Eric Avila, Ivan Berend, M. Belinda Tucker, Claudia Mitchell Kernan, Roy Ritchie, Darnell Hunt, Charles Alexander, Cheryl Keyes, Claudia Bestor, Katherine Marino, Verna Abe, and Eboni Shaw have made up a campus community that I treasure at UCLA. New colleagues at Oxford, including Barbara Savage, Lyndal Roper, Charlene Villasenor Black, Meleisa Ono-George, William Whyte, Maggie Snowling, Stephen Tuck, and Jane Garnett have helped with that transition in the all-important year in which I completed the final draft. Colleagues-at-large and friends, particularly Sharla Fett, but also Lois Banner, Britta Waldschmidt-Nelson, Yemane Demissie, Roxani Margariti, Sharon Harley, Rosalyn Terborg-Penn, Pero Dagbovie, Catherine Clinton, Mary Ellen Carroll, Marvina White, Leslie Ebert, Robyn and Pam Cresswell, Paula Moya, Sandra Castaneda, Marta Vago, and Fr. Paul Vigil, make this work, which is sometimes painful and enraging, tolerable.

I too have been blessed with wonderful students, from whom I continue to learn. Some, long past receiving their degrees, remain close friends and collaborators. I especially treasure my ties with Marne Campbell, Jessica Millward, Daina Ramey Berry, Janira Teague, Jessica Harris, Susan Solt, Jakobi Williams, Yatta Kiazolu, Amber Withers, and Tsekani Browne. Some of them, along with more current students, have contributed tremendously to this project in their capacity as research assistants, in particular Marissa Jenrich, Janira Teague, and Kaitlin Boyd. I am especially thankful to Marissa, who has seen me through so much of the final stages—always pleasant, professional, generous, and intelligent.

Research assistants and other absolute necessities would not have been possible without the incredible support of funding agencies both at UCLA and Oxford and especially from external sources. This project benefited greatly from research funds made possible through the Nickoll Family Endowed Chair in History that I hold at UCLA. A UCLA sabbatical supplemented generous fellowship support from the John Simon Guggenheim Foundation, the American Academy in Berlin, the National Humanities Center, and the Center for Advanced Studies in the Behavioral Sciences that collectively provided essential time for research and writing. Sam Schuth, a research associate at the National Humanities Center and later the Swem Library at William and Mary, was very valuable in the early collection of documents. So too were guides, curators, and docents at numerous plantation sites and local museums in Virginia, North and South Carolina, Louisiana, Mississippi, Georgia, and Alabama. The staff at the Autry Museum of the American West aided with documents and artifacts from the Spanish American Empire and Texas. Jon Sisk at Rowman & Littlefield has waited patiently and graciously for the project to conclude. I am thankful for his trust in me and belief in this book.

Introduction

The Black Family in the Public Imagination: What's Slavery and Slavery Scholarship Got to Do with It?

On a steamy late July evening in 2016 in the city of brotherly love—Philadelphia—the most important Black family in US history was a central reference point. First Lady of the United States Michelle Obama spoke lovingly and provocatively of her family, her husband, President Barack Obama, and their daughters, Sasha and Malia, from the podium of the Democratic National Convention. This great nation, she reminded her audience, always has been about securing the future for its children and grandchildren—"about the love and hope and impossibly big dreams that we all have for our children."[1] Despite the pressures, responsibilities, threats, and privileges that she and the president had experienced since his election in 2008, as parents, she noted, they always stayed focused on the future, as it should unfold, for their children and those of the nation. Mrs. Obama then went on to link the twenty-first-century experiences of Sasha and Malia with those of other Black people at the turn of the nineteenth century, observing that her children had played freely (and with Secret Service protection) on the lawn of the White House, the presidential mansion that "was built by slaves" (and then worked in through several administrations).[2] It was a brilliant moment of historical contrast and context. Her reference to the service of Black Americans to the nation, symbolized in the building of the most iconic residence of the United States, reaffirmed the contested nature and public image of Black citizenship and family.

For many during the first Black president's two terms in the highest office in the land, Barack and Michelle Obama's family became America's first family. Regaled in an image-rich public persona that revealed a stable nuclear family headed by the world's leading patriarch and his beautiful, sophisticated, intelligent female partner with their two smart daughters—one already following in her parents' Ivy League footsteps to Harvard—no one in his or her right mind could argue that the Obama family was not a family to emulate, if not envy. But could this public, if not iconic, image of one "successful" Black family—for eight years the most important family in the world's most powerful nation—shift hundreds of years of critique and denunciation of African American kinship?

If one looked just a little closer at the Obamas, one also would see a family that had, in its previous generation, some characteristics that, historically, would have been publicly stigmatized rather than applauded. President Barack Obama "famously" grew up with an absent Black father, having had very little contact with Barack Sr. before his untimely death and virtually no relationship with his Kenyan half siblings and other paternal relations. At times during his childhood, the president also had an absent mother. When Ann Dunham was away, Obama's extended family, in the form of his maternal grandparents, took care of him. While his mother was a struggling single parent and student, she sometimes had to resort to using food stamps. President Obama's father practiced polygamy (he was already married to Kezia Obama when he wed Ann Dunham), and both of the president's parents had children with other persons.

Most social scientists of the earlier twentieth century would have argued that these are not the characteristics of the patriarchal nuclear family that the United States has memorialized and embraced across the generations as

Official Obama family portrait, c. 2011. Pete Souza / Via Getty Images.

"ideal." Absent father, food stamps, grandparent assistance, baby mamas and daddies—these were all traits employed, and still used, to vilify the Black family. These also were the "negative" characteristics of Black family life that then Senator Barack Obama sometimes pointed to when fashioning his "by the bootstraps" account of his life. Doing so, he painted himself as a champion of his own fate—a worthy citizen who proved his ability to lead by overcoming his own domestic dysfunction to gain an elite education, a double Ivy League–degreed wife, a Senate seat, and eventually the White House. His very personal family story did something else as well. It illustrated—for those who were inclined to understand African American family dynamics—important traditions of structural and parental role flexibility and other varied strategies that African American families devised to survive and, indeed, succeed.

Regardless of the deluge of public images of America's Black "first family," popular notions of the dysfunctional Black family in slavery, freedom, and contemporary society remain. Then Senator Obama too promoted this "dysfunctionality" thesis in his own speeches. Even while providing the nation with the example of his and Michelle's enviable family circle, Obama added credibility, without context, to the "absent male" trope. "Too many men are M.I.A." he told a Chicago church audience on Father's Day in 2008. "They have abandoned their responsibilities, acting like boys instead of men. And the foundations of our families are weaker because of it."[3] It was not hard to read between his lines. What Barack Obama was saying was that the Black family that he had formed with his wife was wonderful. And it was, like him, exceptional.

Assumptions of Black familial dysfunction, of course, center not just on an absent Black husband, father, and traditional breadwinner, but also on beliefs about an "outsized" presence of Black women in the Black family. African American women have been assailed as being too strong, too present, and too domineering, to the detriment of the "traditional" patriarchal role of men. Even Michelle Obama was subject to this kind of vilification from her husband's political enemies as well mainstream journalists. Alongside the obvious racist misogyny of those who branded her ugly and beast-like[4] and the infamous eroticized portrait of her as an enslaved woman with bare breasts on the cover of Spain's *Fuera de Serie* magazine,[5] there were the slew of insulting tweets, Facebook comments, and damning headlines in tabloids.[6] "Many people I talked to afterward found Michelle wondrous," the *New York Times*' Maureen Dowd, for example, wrote in an op-ed before Obama's first presidential election. "But others worried that her chiding was emasculating, casting her husband—under fire for lacking experience—as an undisciplined child."[7]

Conversely, Black women also have been attacked for not being faithful to their maternal role. The popular Mammy stereotype of the late nineteenth and

Obama gives Father's Day speech at Sunday service. David Banks / Via Getty Images.

early twentieth centuries was as famous for the enslaved woman's "absence" in her Black children's lives as it was for her supposed undying loyalty to and care of her captor's White family. Black women could be maternal, this image implied, but only when they had White children under their care. Later in the twentieth century and in the early twenty-first, the popularity of Mammy was superseded by the image of the deceptive Black vixen—the parasitic welfare queen and baby mama—who exploited her children for her own material well-being, not theirs.

Forty years before the public's embrace of First Lady Michelle Obama and her family, another woman from Chicago became identified with the American public's perspective of the Black family. She also had ties to the presidency. Linda Taylor, the infamous "welfare queen" of the Windy City, came to represent low-income Black mothers who purportedly benefitted from federal programs like Aid to Families with Dependent Children (AFDC). Ronald Reagan regaled in stories of Taylor during his failed 1976 presidential campaign. Reagan did not coin the phrase "welfare queen"; according to *Slate* journalist Josh Levin, the *Chicago Tribune* did.[8] Still, Reagan milked the story, and the phrase, for all it was worth in his bid to become president, partially through his campaign against welfare fraud.

The Black Family in the Public Imagination 5

Linda Taylor, c. 1974. Bettmann / Via Getty Images.

Linda Taylor, a name that was one of many aliases, appeared in press photos and stories as a mother accused of having bilked hundreds of thousands of dollars out of the welfare system that allegedly was being propped up by liberal Democrat politicians. Her criminal activities were not to support her children—two of whom had been found living in filth.[9] Rather, she was believed to have used the money to purchase expensive cars, furs, and other luxuries for herself. Even though the racial identity of Taylor remained ambiguous (she has been identified as African American, Caucasian, Asian, and mixed race), the public was left with the perception that she was of African descent. She, and her criminal antics, came to symbolize Black female household heads (on and not on welfare) and, by association, the dysfunctional Black family of twentieth-century urban America. This image, in turn, played into the centuries-old denunciation of Black people as generally inferior—culturally, physically, socially, morally, and intellectually. "Flawed" family structure and relations were, many argued, clear evidence of Black people's "natural" inequality with Whites.

The image of the "criminally negligent" "crack mom" added fuel to the twentieth-century fire. According to the racist, misogynist, class-biased "scientific" predictions of the time, crack-addicted mothers would effectively, and finally, put an end to the Black family as a member of the human family. "Can the Children Be Saved?" one *Newsweek* cover story rhetorically asked a doubtful nation.[10] From the onset of the crack cocaine epidemic in poor Black neighborhoods in urban America in the 1980s, scientists, physicians, and journalists maligned Black mothers who were addicts as responsible for irreparable damage to their unborn children and, by extension, to their communities and America's future society. The weak "science" underpinning notions of the severity to unborn children of crack cocaine exposure became popularized and institutionalized in social policy and law that resulted not only in the continued battering of Black motherhood but also the restriction of their maternal rights and even incarceration of some, to say nothing of the state's dehumanizing scrutiny and the media's public humiliation that these female parents suffered. "Crack Babies: The Worst Threat Is Mom Herself" headlined a 1989 *Washington Post* story.[11]

This type of public discourse also harmed affected children, labeling them in ways that relegated them to "unhuman." A *Rolling Stone* magazine story from 1990 carried a typical headline: "Childhood's End: What Life Is Like for Crack Babies—Babies born to crack-addicted mothers are like no others. Brain damaged in ways yet unknown, they're oblivious to any affection. How do you care for a baby who hates to be held?"[12] A 2019 editorial board article in the *New York Times* ("Slandering the Unborn") admitted that news organizations like its own helped to demonize "black women 'addicts' by erroneously reporting that they were giving birth to a generation of neurologically damaged children who were less than fully human and who would bankrupt the schools and social service agencies once they came of age."[13]

Not only "science" but much of social science seemed to support these negative theories about Black family life. Creating images of negligent male or female parents as the "problem" with Black families not only obscured the positive attributes of Black family life and Black parenting, but also hid the real assaults on Black family life fixed in our society's discriminatory laws, economic practices, cultural attitudes, and social customs.

Related stereotyping of the Black family was captured in headlines such as the one from the November 1983 *New York Times* article "Breakup of Black Families Imperils Gains of Decades"[14] and further popularized, even in the twenty-first century, in film, television, and music videos, with rap artists like Kanye West cashing in on his 2006 Grammy-winning multiplatinum anthem saluting slick "gold diggers" and a stream of movies that ridiculed Black motherhood, including the 2017 *Baby Mamas* from "motherland" Nigeria.[15]

Even the late-twentieth-century phenomenon of the *Cosby Show*, the most popular sitcom of the 1980s—featuring an upper-middle-class Black nuclear family with professional, attentive parents of high-achieving children and steeped in homages to Black music, literature, the visual arts, and HBCUs—could not persuade the public that the Black family was not deeply, internally damaged. Indeed, it was ironically (now convicted) Bill Cosby himself, who publicly "moralized" through outrageous "blaming the victim" tirades the "problems" of the modern Black family. In a series of speeches given in the 1990s and early 2000s, Cosby underscored the issues he believed plagued the family and laid the blame for it not on the systemic inequalities African Americans faced, but on Blacks themselves. The famed comedian and holder of a doctorate in education repeatedly derided working poor families for female parenting, what he believed was the lack of fiscal responsibility of those who engaged in conspicuous consumption, the use of Black vernacular speech and naming patterns, and the petty criminality of Black youth.[16] At the commemoration for the fiftieth anniversary of *Brown v. Board of Education*, for example, Cosby railed to continued applause:

> Fifty percent dropout rate, I'm telling you, and people in jail, and women having children by five, six different men. Under what excuse, I want somebody to love me, and as soon as you have it, you forget to parent. Grandmother, mother, and great grandmother in the same room, raising children, and the child knows nothing about love or respect of any one of the three of them. All this child knows is 'gimme, . . .' These people want to buy the friendship of a child . . . and the child couldn't care less. . . . And these people are not parenting. They're buying things for the kid. $500 sneakers, for what? They won't buy or spend $250 on Hooked on Phonics.[17]

Cosby certainly was not alone. But these kinds of public denunciations by him and other high-profile Americans, just as those found in scholarly circles and publications, collectively had significant, and negative, impact. They resulted in battles over welfare reform,[18] differential treatment and analyses of K–12 school performance, and the forced sterilization of Black females. As one journalist writing on eugenics noted: "By the mid-1960s the stage had been set. Both liberals and conservatives were questioning minority birth rates. Add to that the growing discussion about world population growth, and the result was that people who coerced or forced minorities into sterilization operations could easily justify their actions."[19] The mythology also has disproportionately criminalized Black youth—recall, for example, the 2014 "no angel" comment in the *New York Times* regarding Ferguson, Missouri, police shooting victim

Michael Brown[20]—and vilified Black life as having embraced a debilitating "culture of poverty."[21]

Family "dysfunction," critics insisted, undergirded the inability of Black Americans to take advantage of resources and opportunities that many other ethnically and racially defined groups eventually were able to embrace through assimilation of the "White" familial example. As noted African American family sociologist Robert Staples wrote, "The black family that does not meet the criteria of middle-class family behavior is *ipso facto* defined as a deviant type which should be studied as a pathological form of social organization."[22] Staples referred to what Walter Allen, in his brilliant assessment of twentieth-century social science scholarship, labeled the "cultural deviance" model.[23] "Cultural deviance" was one of three "distinct theoretical perspectives" that Allen delineated. The other two are "cultural equivalence," in which social scientists refused to recognize the "distinct cultural forms" of African Americans in general and African American families in particular; and the "cultural variance" viewpoint that underscored the varied socioeconomic constructs of Black and White life that meant differentiation in familial structure, function, and coping strategies.[24]

In the decades approaching the twenty-first century, some social scientists managed to shift their conclusions concerning the strengths and problems of the historic and contemporary African American family. Still, old stereotypes persisted. When asked why these images have remained so popular in one form or another in America's public imagination—besides perpetual and systemic racism—one response repeatedly offered is "Moynihan!"[25]

MOYNIHAN! HIS PREDECESSORS, RESPONDENTS, AND THEIR RELATIONSHIP TO BLACK FAMILY HISTORIOGRAPHY

"The evidence—not final, but powerfully persuasive—is that the Negro family in the urban ghettos is crumbling. A middle-class group has managed to save itself, but for vast numbers of the unskilled, poorly-educated, city working class the fabric of conventional social relationships has all but disintegrated."[26]

The collective image that emerged from the Moynihan Report of 1965, which largely consisted of summaries of at least two generations of social scientific observation and critique, proved to be a pernicious, and lingering, assault on the US Black family. The damaging appraisal was founded on the belief that the heteronormative, patriarchal, nuclear family comprised the ideal kin-based household for modern society and that any other manifestation of family life was to be eschewed. In particular, the presence of a patriarchal head (who is the breadwinner husband/father) was held up as a font of stability and the only legitimate foundation for the family and the nation. Without a strong patriarch at the helm, the prevailing sentiment implied, doom in the form of poverty, ignorance, immorality, and even criminality was inevitable. The twentieth-century Black family, many believed, lacked this strong patriarchal head. In its place was the African American wife and mother who served as a controlling matriarch.

The father was emasculated and often absent, while their children were poorly socialized, underperforming students caught in a culture and households that damned their futures, destining them to achieve no more than their parents. All were dregs on the welfare state and, altogether, neither a viable nor preferred part of American society.[27]

Culling the data on Black family structure in urban America, Daniel Patrick Moynihan asserted that what he labeled as the African American "tangle of pathology" derived from a long history of Black oppression that began with slavery and later was exacerbated by the poverty and instability of African American life during the long Jim Crow/Great Migration eras. After all, four million African Americans left slavery after 250 years of producing wealth and opportunity for others with no wealth and very few opportunities of their own. Only a small proportion of men, and an even smaller number of women, were skilled workers beyond the agricultural sector of the economy. Black ability to acquire the land, tools, and work animals to become independent farmers was practically nil. Less than 10 percent were literate. Rights constituted in law quickly, and often violently, faded within the generation that they were created. Regardless of these persistent systemic inequalities and inadequacies, Black men and women always created and clung to their marriages, families, and kinship networks, even if social scientists and popular commentators on Black life judged Black domesticity against a White standard. The indictment began with a flawed historiography.

This historical analysis initially was driven by the work of U. B. Phillips, a southerner who taught at Tulane, the University of Wisconsin, and then Yale. Phillips's slavery monographs, known for topical breadth and use of plantation records, characterized enslaved people as inferior and, therefore, as social, cultural and material beneficiaries, not victims, of slavery.[28] He wrongly described "the predominant plantation [slave] type," as "having an eagerness for society, music and merriment, a fondness for display whether of person, dress, vocabulary or emotion, a not flagrant sensuality, a receptiveness toward any religion whose exercises were exhilarating, a proneness to superstition, a courteous acceptance of subordination, an avidity for praise, a readiness for loyalty of a feudal sort, and last but not least, a healthy human repugnance toward overwork."[29]

"The Pain of the Absent Father," c. 2013. Rod Anderson, cartoon, *The Christian Post*, July 8, 2013.

    Phillips's description of the enslaved family was equally problematic since his focus was on the paternal nature of the White slaveholding family, and how those enslaved benefitted from that paternalism, instead of offering details of slave domesticity. The slave master, he instructed his readers, was the "head" of all families on his plantation, Black and White. Similarly, the plantation mistress was a feminine/motherly presence from whom all benefited.[30] Enslaved adult kin and parents, regardless of their gender, in other words, had no real importance to or impact on Black domesticity. Phillips's

"Marriage Fixes Everything," c. 2014. Barry Deutsch, cartoon, Ampersand: Political Cartoons by Barry Deutsch, March 21, 2014. Used with permission of the artist.

contributions to the canon of slavery studies soon were followed by a number of like-minded historical treatments.[31]

While some historians by mid-century were beginning to disagree with the Phillips school of analyses—particularly his contentions on the nature of White paternalism, their counterarguments also disproportionately denigrated the enslaved Black family. Frank Tannenbaum's 1946 comparative study, for example, concluded that slave regimes in North America and the British Caribbean, unlike those in Latin America, where the enslaved's humanity was recognized in state and Catholic Church law and proceedings, were the harshest in the "New World," with especially severe impact on the enslaved family.[32] "Under the law of most southern states," Tannenbaum asserted, "there was no regard for the Negro family, no question of the right of the owner to sell his slaves separately, and no limitation upon separating husband and wife, or child from its mother."[33] Others, including Brazilian historians

Gilberto Freyre and Emilia Viotti Da Costa, along with French anthropologist Roger Bastide, noted that a characteristic of slave social life was a "vast primitive promiscuity," particularly among the women, that undermined any stable family life.[34] Their analyses ignored the rampant sexual exploitation of enslaved females by members of their captors' families and supervisory staff as well as the sexual trafficking of enslaved girls and women as prostitutes, fancy girls, and concubines.[35]

One of the most influential works by a US historian that drew on Tannenbaum's analyses was Kenneth Stampp's 1956 *The Peculiar Institution*. The southern bondsman, Stampp concluded, "had no civil rights, no political rights, no claim to his time, no freedom of movement."[36] Accordingly, there really was little to be identified as the foundations for a familial household since "slaves, as chattels, could not make contracts," including a legal marital contract. The lack of this legal capacity meant that enslaved couples had access to one another and their children only at the leisure of their masters. "No state legislature ever seriously entertained the thought of encroaching upon the master's rights by legalizing slave marriage," Stampp explained. "On the contrary, these states guaranteed the rights of property in human chattels in every way feasible."[37] And it was not just the laws that hindered family development and stability, Stampp noted. It also was the lack of a stable African American "culture" that could support marital and familial development. "In Africa," Stampp asserted, "the Negroes had been accustomed to a strictly regulated family and a rigidly enforced moral code. But in America the disintegration of their social organization removed the traditional sanctions which had encouraged them to respect their old custom." As a result, "Here, as at so many other points, the slaves had lost their native culture without being able to find a workable substitute and therefore lived in a kind of cultural chaos."[38]

Stanley Elkins developed a related thesis in his 1959 monograph *Slavery: A Problem in American Institutional and Intellectual Life*. He proclaimed that the southern US plantation, like the Nazi concentration camp, operated as a "closed system" for enslaved Blacks. Plantations, Elkins theorized, produced Sambo personalities, manifest in the behavior of those enslaved people who identified more with the perspectives of their slaveholders and overseers than those of their own bonded families and communities. Elkins, who is quoted in the Moynihan Report, concluded that the lack of protection of enslaved people's marriage and family under law, coupled with slaveholders' financial incentives not to promote stable family life, resulted in tremendously impaired Black families. In their domestic units, a father was legally "unknown," a husband had "no rights to his marriage bed," and, as such, intimate relations were little more than "concubinage" while "motherhood [was only] clothed in the scant dignity of the breeding function."[39] This kind of critique of the enslaved Black family, particularly that of marriage, reduced the perceived social life of the race to one of promiscuity. It denied any notion of Black romance or familial commitment, but rather labeled adult familial relations as emotionally meaningless sexual liaisons.

EARLY TWENTIETH-CENTURY SOCIAL SCIENTISTS AND THE BLACK FAMILY

Moynihan, however, did not have to rely solely on historians for his analysis of the impact of US slavery on the Black family. He also drew on the work of, and collaborated with, other social scientists of his day. His "report" was a hodgepodge of their work, lacking the complete research context from which these monographs were produced.

The exceptional activist and intellectual of African American life and history W. E. B. Du Bois set some of the early standards for scholarly discourse on the Black family in his 1899 *Philadelphia Negro*[40] and particularly in his 1908 book *The Negro American Family*.[41] Du Bois emphasized differences in Black kinship units across rural and urban locales as well as class lines, linking both to education and wealth access. Significantly, Du Bois did not denounce all families that did not meet a White, middle-class ideal. He found merit in Black families living in the rural South as well as those that were poor or poorly educated. Rural Black families, he noted, were comprised mostly of "honest, decent people, with a fairly good standard of family morals," despite the "influence of the past." Only between 3 and 4 percent of families he encountered in his research, he added, were not residentially intact.[42]

Du Bois based most of his conclusions on primary research that Atlanta University colleagues and students conducted under the aegis of the Atlanta University Conference for the Study of Negro Problems (AU Conference). It was part of an ambitious scholarly agenda that Du Bois and other members of the American Negro Academy, such as sociologist and mathematician Kelly Miller, devised to provide documentary evidence on African American social, economic, and political issues.

The AU Conference also served as an intellectual forum where Black intellectuals could combat racist scholarship of the era, such as famed statistician Frederick L. Hoffman's highly influential 1896 study *Race Traits and Tendencies of the American Negro*.[43] According to Hoffman, not only was the Black race doomed for extinction, but it was also greatly flawed socially. Large sectors of the African American population, he asserted, were "unchaste" and therefore had only "irregular connections" and "inferior forms of marriage." Their relationships lacked "affection, admiration, [and] sympathy." As a result, couples even lacked the desire to bear and rear children, thereby leading, along with other factors such as a propensity for disease, to the race's eventual disappearance.[44]

Challenging Hoffman's conclusions, Du Bois drew on the work of Mary White Ovington, a White socialist, founding member of the NAACP, and social researcher who studied Black housing and un/employment in New York City. Ovington strongly correlated economic status with family stability, not ethnicity, conclusions that called to questions notions, like those of Hoffman and his eugenicist associates, that not only was the Black family doomed, it was doomed due to racial and cultural inferiority. Even though Ovington believed that economic difficulties were the most significant threat to Black family life, she was impressed with the attempts of urban poor Black families to create stable, nurturing households. According to Ovington, "the majority of Negro homes, like the majority of homes of all working people, are places where good and honest men and women are striving, often against great odds, to bring up their children to lead moral and useful lives."[45] Not only were the families of poor urban people, across racial and ethnic lines, similar, she argued, there also were obvious analogies between White and Black professional household structures and relations—again denying racial and cultural differences.[46]

Moynihan did not draw much on these analyses, but rather leaned toward those of Nathan Glazer and E. Franklin Frazier. Frazier, the first Black president of the American Sociological Association, along with Glazer provided quite fertile ground for Moynihan's theses. Indeed, the writings of Frazier and Glazer were linked, with Glazer even writing the foreword to Frazier's 1966 revised and abridged edition of *The Negro Family in the United States*.[47] Glazer also was tied intellectually and professionally to Moynihan, who contributed a chapter to Glazer's influential 1963 work *Beyond the Melting Pot: The Negroes, Puerto Ricans, Jews, Italians and Irish of New York City*.[48] Glazer likewise provided some of Moynihan's conclusions. Not surprisingly, *Beyond the Melting Pot* was similar in tone and assertion to Frazier's *The Negro Family in the United States*, particularly in its emphases on urban migrant poverty as a significant deterrent to Black family stability. Unlike those of Du Bois or Ovington, Glazer's findings focused more on barriers rather than the efforts of poor, urbanized African Americas to have a successful family life. "The Negro immigrant" to New York, Glazer wrote, "has not had the good fortune of arriving with useful skills and strong institutions, nor has he found a prosperous, well-organized community to help him."[49]

Glazer emphasized, quite profoundly, what he believed were Black cultural deficiencies and their negative social consequences. Not only did African Americans suffer from economic poverty, he argued, they were undermined as well by a "cultural poverty": "The Negro is only an American, and nothing else," Glazer asserted. "He has no values and culture to guard and protect."[50] As a result, a significant number of African American families did not have the same kind of cultural support for success and family stability as other mid-century urban migrants or immigrants.

Centering his research on Black households in 1960 Manhattan, Glazer offered in defense of his conclusions summary Black household statistics. "A quarter were headed by women," he wrote. "In contrast, less than one-tenth of the white households were headed by women. The rate of illegitimacy among Negroes is about fourteen or fifteen times that among whites."[51] Even though these conditions were not those of the majority, Glazer still characterized their "incidence" in Black families as "enormous" and a looming "threat."[52] These deficiencies, he further concluded, derived in large part from slavery. "The experience of slavery left as its most serious heritage a steady weakness in the Negro family. There was no marriage in the slave family. . . . There was no possibility of taking responsibility for one's children, for one had in the end no power over them."[53] Glazer's arguments were drawn in part from Frazier's decades earlier conclusions.

Frazier, in his 1938 edition of *The Negro Family*, set the tone for much of the intellectual discourse regarding the Black family that was to follow. *The Negro Family* responded in part to popular notions held during the first half of the twentieth century about the differences in Black and White family structure ("matriarchal" vs. "patriarchal"), marital status (cohabitation vs. contractual), and the legal standing of children (illegitimate vs. legitimate) that many believed were, collectively, proof of the "primitive" and inferior nature of Black people as a racial group. Frazier maintained instead that these obvious social differences were linked to survival mechanisms that African Americans contrived in face of the social, economic, and legal hardships that society imposed on them, both during the era of slavery and its aftermath. He supported his "nurture" thesis by offering not only what he believed was evidence of the US enslaved's almost immediate loss of traditional African cultures, but also examples of those of African descent not subjected to the typical harsh reality of slavery who had created families that were similar in structure and function to those of Whites.

Frazier's work did not recognize the cultural relativism theory of pioneering anthropologist Franz Boas.[54] Nor did it take into significant consideration earlier conclusions in Du Bois's *Black Folk Then and Now*,[55] Carter G. Woodson's *The African Background Outlined*,[56] or even published scholarship in Woodson's *Journal of Negro History* regarding the US enslaved experience and enslaved people's African cultural antecedents. Frazier was willing to acknowledge the presence of African cultural retentions elsewhere in the Black Atlantic, such as in South America and the Caribbean, but he unequivocally concluded that "African traditions and practices did not take root and survive in the United States."[57] With particular regard to the Black family, he added, "There is no reliable evidence that African culture has had any influence on its development."[58] And since the famed Black sociologist believed that Black family life was essential to African American advancement in contemporary US society, Frazier could not glean much about the structure and function of enslaved families that would be useful to maintain.

Black family structural and behavioral change had to be implemented, Frazier concluded, so that Black family life would be acceptable to the larger society. That is, Black familial characteristics had to conform to those of White, middle-class familial traits.[59] Frazier approved of the "strong attachment" that Black southern mothers had for their children, but disparaged sex and childbearing outside of marriage. He wholeheartedly disapproved of what he termed as Black "matriarchs" and their "irregular" marriages.[60] Black families living in the urban North, Frazier continued, were particularly plagued by absentee fathers and "loose sex behavior" due, in part, to domestic problems that southern migrant families brought with them from the South, including single mothers.[61] He failed to recognize the important presence in Black households of fathers (or paternal male kin) who might have resided with mothers and their children on a part-time basis and provided some financial contributions to their wives and children because they worked in distant locales or were temporarily incarcerated. These were two realities of post-Reconstruction Black life determined in large measure by institutionalized and commonplace economic and judicial racial discrimination still present, and affecting Black families today.[62] Likewise, neither Frazier, his contemporaries, nor many later twentieth-century social scientists remarked on the positive attributes female-headed households contributed to Black family life.[63]

Anthropologist Melville J. Herskovits challenged Frazier's thesis on African cultural retention. In his 1941 groundbreaking *The Myth of the Negro Past*, Herskovits took on not only Frazier, but other leading scholars.[64] "Negroes in the United States are not Africans," he conceded, "but they are the descendants of Africans. There is no more theoretical support for a hypothesis that they have retained nothing of the culture of their African forebears than for supporting that they remained completely African in their behavior."[65] However, Herskovits did remain somewhat ambivalent about the lingering influence of African cultures on enslaved persons' family relations. "It goes without saying that the plantation system," he asserted, "rendered the survival of African family types impossible . . . except in dilute form."[66] Still, he hinted at kinship system influences from Africa, including those that emphasized the importance of ancestors, shaped the relations between husband and wife, and advocated communal self-help. These traits, he noted, were "passed on as children were taught by their parents" and allowed by masters as long as they did not "impede the smooth functioning of the estates" or because enslaved persons protected them with secrecy.[67]

Scholars forcefully countered Herskovits's intervention. Swedish economist and sociologist Gunnar Myrdal, in his 1944 "comprehensive" study of the status of African American life in the United States, *An American Dilemma: The Negro Problem in Modern Democracy*, agreed with Frazier and Glazer that African social and cultural influences were not relevant to twentieth-century African American everyday household practices. Even in the face of long-term discrimination and segregation, Myrdal wrote, "Negro institutions are, nevertheless, similar to those of the white man. They show little similarity to African institutions."[68] The general "social pathology" of the African American, he noted alongside a long list of characteristics that he compiled, including the "instability of the Negro family," were, in his estimation, all derived from "caste pressures."[69] The "pragmatic" answer to these problems, he concluded, should be complete assimilation, *"to acquire the traits held in esteem by the dominant white Americans*. This will be the premise here."[70]

The Nobel Prize–winning Myrdal also wholeheartedly supported Frazier's conclusions regarding the impact of Black slavery on the contemporary Black family.[71] He accepted, without qualification, Frazier's contention that the enslaved family provided a weak and dysfunctional foundation for twentieth-century African Americans.[72] Franklin's 1938 *The Negro Family*, Myrdal generally asserted, "is such an excellent description and analysis of the American Negro family that it is practically necessary only to relate its conclusions to our context and to refer the reader to it for details."[73] But Myrdal was impressed with Fisk University sociologist Charles S. Johnson's claim in his 1934 *Shadow of the Plantation*[74] of a general lack of stigma in the Black Belt attached to common-law marriage and the overall significance of children in all families.[75] "The important thing," he added, "is that the Negro lower classes, especially in the rural South, have built up a type of family organization conducive to social health, even though the practices are outside the American tradition."[76]

African American social scientists St. Claire Drake and Horace R. Cayton, too, echoed some of Frazier's conclusions, particularly those regarding the familial instability of the urban Black lower class. In their massive 1945 study *Black Metropolis: A Study of Negro Life in a Northern City*, they linked this fragility largely to their place within the economy.[77] "There has never been sufficient economic opportunity," they concluded, "to permit the mass of Negro workers to acquire the material goods—housing, furniture, clothing, savings—for laying the basis for a middle-class way of life."[78] Cayton and Drake also insisted that the instability derived in part from a "legacy of slavery" and postslavery rural southern culture brought north by migrants.[79]

The "upper class," they insisted, were "'home-centered,' stressing an ordered and disciplined family life."[80] The middle class had great aspirations to do the same.[81] Among the lower class, however, the specter of the absent Black family man, whom they attributed to the "roving . . . masses of Negro men," prevented the "formation of stable, conventional, family units." Instead of male heads of households who took on the financial support of the family, "both husband and children come to look to their women as the ultimate source of support."[82]

Frazier, Glazer, Drake, and Cayton centered much of their attention on urban Black social life, while Du Bois and Johnson studied southern Black domestic life. Anthropologist Hortense Powdermaker based her influential 1939 study *After Freedom: A Cultural Study in the Deep South* on Black life in Indianola, Mississippi.[83] Her work further validated those of her early to mid-twentieth-century contemporaries. Powdermaker, too, made a distinction between middle/upper- and lower-class southern African American family structures and long-term stability. Behavioral scientists who observed Black family life in both urban and rural areas in the first half of the twentieth century, therefore, generally believed that socioeconomic class and diverse cultural designs, particularly the level to which African Americans assimilated middle-class European American familial ideals and structures, were important determinants of African American family structure and operation. They all assumed that there was a lingering influence of Black southern slavery and culture on the urban lower class, although they differed in their conclusions about the enduring influence of African cultural roots.

Moynihan also was influenced by Oscar Lewis's "subculture of poverty" thesis, more commonly known as the "culture of poverty." Lewis, an anthropologist whose early work centered on Native American, Mexican, and Puerto Rican families, first used this term in his 1959 *Five Families: Mexican Case Studies in the Culture of Poverty*.[84] It was not long before he and others began to attribute this "culture" to other working-poor groups residing in the United States, including African Americans. Lewis posited that while conditions of poverty often were "imposed by the state," some persons remained economically marginalized over generations because their families and communities had socialized them to do so. "The people in the culture of poverty have a strong feeling of marginality, of helplessness, of dependency, of not belonging," Lewis wrote. "In the United States, the culture of poverty of the Negroes has the additional disadvantage of racial discrimination."[85]

Communities affected by a culture of poverty were threatened by "delinquency, vice and violence" and had a "very low sense of history," low aspirations, and, as a result, indulged in "short-range hedonism."[86] They passed these "cultural traits" onto their children at a young age, Lewis insisted. "By the time slum children are age six or seven, they have usually absorbed the basic values and attitudes of their subculture and are not psychologically geared to take full advantage of changing conditions or increased opportunities in their lifetime."[87] Instead of families being the place where morals, values, and success are nurtured and taught to the next generation, families actually were the problematic site where failure, immorality, criminality, and pathos are cultivated. These ideas bolstered longstanding "scientific" notions of African Americans as a distinct and inferior group (or race) with no social institutions, including families, that had worthy qualities. Lewis's ideas provided important context for what became the "tangle of pathology" Moynihan detailed in his report.[88]

REFRAMING PERSPECTIVES ON THE BLACK FAMILY IN THE ERA OF THE CIVIL RIGHTS MOVEMENT AND BEYOND

Conclusions in the Moynihan Report that linked Black socioeconomic problems to a dysfunctional working-class Black family, although hardly novel, were not commonly discussed in the public. That all changed almost overnight when none other than President Lyndon Johnson previewed them in his 1965 commencement remarks at Howard University, the nation's premier historic Black institution of higher learning. Johnson's was a speech purportedly written in part by Moynihan himself.[89] He was careful to begin his speech with descriptions of celebratory aspects of Black life and achievement. Likewise, when he moved on to enumerate Black social and economic problems, such as high rates of joblessness, poverty, and an absence of the nuclear family, he cautiously placed the blame for these difficulties squarely outside the Black race or culture. They were due, he told his audience, to the historic oppression of Black Americans: "These differences are not racial differences. . . . They are solely and simply the consequence of ancient brutality, past injustice, and present prejudice . . . the devastating heritage of long years of slavery; and a century of oppression, hatred, and injustice."[90]

As a planned aid to his War on Poverty agenda, Johnson hoped his speech would "guilt" White listeners into supporting social initiatives that he wanted to propose, particularly job training and placement programs that were to benefit poor Black communities.[91] He believed the nation had a "glorious opportunity to end the one huge wrong of the American nation"—sustained Black oppression. "Freedom is not enough," he pronounced. "You do not take a person who for years has been hobbled by chains and liberate him,

President Lyndon B. Johnson at Howard University delivering the commencement address, June 4, 1965. Courtesy of Moorland Spingarn Research Center, Howard University.

bring him up to the starting line of a race, and then say, 'You are free to compete with all the others,' and still justly believe that you have been completely fair."[92]

Johnson's statements seemed particularly relevant because many, Black and White, thought that his progressive attitude and actions regarding mitigating the systemic oppression of Black America indicated his genuine commitment to change in the national racial dynamic. Still, there were others who regarded Johnson's words as a ripe opportunity to press their own, quite different, social agenda. When Johnson spoke of the "breakdown of the Negro family structure" and coupled it with the truism that "the family is the cornerstone of our society," those who wanted to assert that African Americans were a doomed and inferior race—even though Johnson had given quite a different assessment—believed that they had the proof they needed to document their biased views, and from the mouth of the sitting president no less.[93]

Moynihan's findings were soon being discussed widely in the national press, especially his contentions that seemed to document Black social dysfunction. Those opposed to the Black freedom movements and social welfare programs of the day found Monynihan's conclusions useful in their construction of "culture of poverty" arguments and as a ready defense when they faced "blame the victim" accusations. They especially found Moynihan's and Johnson's theses valuable in their ongoing opposition to the implementation of federal legislation (e.g., the Civil Rights Act of 1964 and the Voting Rights Act of 1965), Supreme Court decisions (e.g., *Brown v. Board of Education*, 1954), and the growing federal movement for "affirmative action" that was highly visible in 1961 when President John Kennedy issued Executive Order 10925, creating the Committee on Equal Employment Opportunity. Whatever Moynihan's intentions, and, for that matter, Johnson's, it would have been tremendously naive of either to believe that racially hostile elements of the national press and public, along with those opposed to the social changes the Civil Rights movement had wrought that were meant to usher in a more level playing field for Black Americans, would not use these ideas to their advantage.

Social scientists of the 1960s and the decades that followed found themselves agreeing with some of Moynihan's conclusions, while disagreeing with others. As it had for their predecessors, slavery, and the enslaved's family, as they perceived it, remained a touchstone for many social scientists trying to discern the nature and quality of Black familial life in the twentieth and twenty-first centuries[94] While historical studies from the first several decades of the twentieth century placed little value on the enslaved family's existence, function, and lingering influence, beginning in the 1970s slavery historians, particularly those who were social historians, concluded otherwise.

John Blassingame's 1972 *The Slave Community: Plantation Life in the Antebellum South*,[95] Eugene Genovese's *Roll, Jordan, Roll: The World the Slaves Made* (1974),[96] and Herbert Gutman's *The Black Family in Slavery and Freedom, 1750–1925* (1976)[97] fundamentally altered the scholarly discourse on the structure and nature of the enslaved family in the antebellum South. Even though previous scholars, such as John B. Cade in his 1935 groundbreaking article "Out of the Mouth of the Ex-Slaves," published in the *Journal of Negro History*,[98] spoke to the presence of functioning families as the enslaved themselves described their social lives, this was not the prevalent thesis. It really was not until the 1970s that the methodology of this new generation of slavery scholars, which centered more on the enslaved rather than the slaveholder, produced remarkably different conclusions from those of even two decades earlier. Blassingame, Genovese, Gutman, and others effectively destroyed the notion of a nonexistent or horribly dysfunctional family.

Revisionist historians' assertions about the structure and viability of the enslaved family derived from multiple sources and inspirations. Particularly important was recovering the voices of those who had been enslaved. Historians relied largely on eighteenth- and nineteenth-century autobiographical accounts, newspaper interviews, letters, a few diaries, 1930s Works Progress Administration (WPA) narratives of formerly enslaved persons, and the oral histories of earlier generations of their enslaved kin. These new monographs also benefited from their intellectual location in the relatively new social history that sought to identify personal and group power among the politically, economically, and socially marginalized. The visibility of African American agency in the Civil Rights and Black Power movements of the era, along with decolonization projects in the Black diaspora, also inspired a rethinking of the question of "agency" among the enslaved. Likewise, some desire to respond to the Moynihan Report's conclusions about Black familial dysfunction meant that scholars had to reconsider the historical analyses on the origins of the modern Black family—the family of the enslaved.

"The Southern plantation family was unique in the New World," Blassingame began his important chapter, "The Slave Family," "because it permitted the development of a monogamous slave family."[99] Written as a master's thesis when Blassingame was a student at Howard University before he took up his doctoral studies at Yale, his phenomenal monograph made note of essential differences between enslaved families and those of Whites and free Blacks. Nonetheless, he insisted that these differences did not diminish the importance of the domestic institution in, and to, the enslaved community. He asserted that a balanced adult sex ratio among southern antebellum captives had made heterosexual marriage partners available. The desire of the enslaved themselves for monogamous marriages, he noted, along with the religious beliefs of slaveholders and the benefits they believed they could derive from promoting stable slave families among their "property," led to widespread enslaved monogamy. Documenting a bevy of family-related behaviors, including slave courtship, marital difficulties, kinship, child-bearing, and child-rearing, Blassingame reconstituted the domestic lives of enslaved people intellectually, culturally, and practically. In so doing, he situated the enslaved family in close structural and functional proximity to that of modern White families.

The resulting logic was obvious: If sociologists, anthropologists, and other social scientists believed the modern Black family was so distinct as to garner a label of "dysfunctional," then that dysfunctionality and its distinctions were not historically linked to the enslaved family. "The family, while it had no legal existence in slavery, was in actuality one of the most important survival methods for the slaves," Blassingame concluded. In his well-documented estimation, the enslaved realized much in family life, including "companionship, love, sexual gratification, sympathetic understanding of his sufferings; he learned how to avoid punishment, to cooperate with other Blacks, and to maintain his self-esteem."[100] Blassingame was particularly drawn to the idea of a "present" *not* "absent" Black male family head. There was something of a gender role "democracy" in the enslaved family—an egalitarianism—he asserted. Still, husbands and fathers seemed determined to acquire patriarchal status and authority within their homes, and believed that wives and mothers should take on the gendered roles of helpmeet, cook, comforter, nurse, and childcare provider. In return, the enslaved woman, Blassingame concluded, could expect, and certainly desired, her husband to serve as the family head by disciplining their children, providing supplemental material support, and giving her family love, devotion, protection, and attention.

Blassingame's work clearly signaled a fundamental break from the older historiography. Genovese, who published his monumental study of antebellum enslaved life, *Roll, Jordan Roll*, two years later, embraced both the older thesis of planter paternalism and revisionist assertions of Black agency and familial importance among enslaved people. Like Blassingame, he was especially interested in documenting that Black male agency as protector and provider for the family was a norm, rather than an exception, in the enslaved family. Genovese's enslaved man was a patriarch—a weakened version of a White patriarch, given the controls of his master, but a patriarch nonetheless. When one thinks of the harm that enslaved men faced to protect their wives, Genovese argued, "the wonder is not that more black men did not defend their women but that so many did."[101] Genovese went on to assert, "Slave men provided for their families to a greater extent than has been appreciated. . . . The men took pride in their effort."[102] Collectively, "Many men and women resisted the 'infantilization,' 'emasculation' and 'dehumanization' inherent in the system's aggression against the slave family."[103] Resistance, he concluded, "provided black people with solid norms of family life and [gender] role differentiation. . . . The slaves from their own experience had come to value a two-parent, male-centered household."[104]

Published in 1976, Gutman's *The Black Family in Slavery and Freedom, 1750–1925*, reiterated the Blassingame and Genovese theses regarding the stable nature of the enslaved Black family, the prescribed gender roles of men and women within their domestic households, and the crucial similarities of the Black family, even the enslaved Black family, to that of Whites. Gutman admits his motivation in the opening page of his tome. "This volume," he wrote, "was stimulated by the bitter public and academic controversy surrounding Daniel P. Moynihan's *The Negro Family in America: The Case for*

National Action (1965)."[105] He, too, wanted to question one of the Moynihan Report's influential theses, the conclusion drawn from E. Franklin Frazier's description of the working-class Black family as a "tangle of pathology." With such a mandate, Gutman set out not only to set the record straight on the Black family, enslaved and free, but also to document Black familial traditions that mirrored those of middle-class Whites, most notably long-term marriages with a nuclear structure.

Culling plantation slave inventories, marriage registration records of the newly freed, manuscript census records, enslaved and freed people's naming patterns, and narrative accounts, Gutman made a strong case for his conclusions. Like his revisionist peers, Gutman asserted that the social problems Moynihan described linked to matriarchal families with absent male heads was not a result of the enslaved experience. "Upon their emancipation," he concluded, most . . . ex-slave families had two parents, and most older couples had lived together in long-lasting unions."[106]

During the next several decades, many slavery scholars supported the conclusions of Blassingame, Genovese, and Gutman, regardless of the broader topics in which they embedded their assent. Among them were those pioneering historians of women in slavery, and Black women more broadly. Political activist and scholar Angela Davis in her groundbreaking work *Women, Race and Class* (1981)[107] and historians Jacqueline Jones in *Labor of Love, Labor of Sorrow: Black Women, Work, and the Family from Slavery to the Present* (1985),[108] Deborah Grey White in *Ar'n't I a Woman? Female Slaves in the Plantation South* (1985),[109] and Elizabeth Fox Genovese in *Within the Plantation Household: Black and White Women of the Old South* (1988),[110] for example, all agreed with some of these findings.

They did so while also carving out an essentialist place for Black women in their enslaved households, pointing to a matrifocal emphases. Davis explained the vital importance of the bonded Black woman to enslaved families outside the narrow confines of monogamy and the nuclear structure. White, to her credit, offered conclusions that, at their base, eroded some support for the revisionist assertions. In the first complete research monograph published on enslaved Black women in the antebellum South, she documented the indispensable importance of the enslaved mother and wife to the enslaved family, an importance she connected to their African cultural heritage.[111]

Not only did these female revisionist scholars reclaim the place of enslaved women in the Black family that had been diminished by earlier historians, they also addressed the historical eroticization and masculinization of enslaved women that had caused social critics to deem them as immoral and psychological burdens for the Black family and community"[112] The popular triptych of toxic Black womanhood—"Mammy," "Jezebel," and "Sapphire"—still imprints criticism of female roles in African American family life today. One need only consider public criticism of Michelle Obama to understand how even the most elite African American women still cannot escape this vilification.[113]

Many late-twentieth-century scholars of the enslaved family supplied additional modifications to the Blassingame-Genovese-Gutman model, but fundamentally accepted the theses of nuclear family prevalence.[114] Other historians, however, perceived some differences when they examined colonial enslaved familial experiences, particularly those scholars of the Chesapeake colonies of Virginia and Maryland. Some, like Allen Kulikoff, asserted that enslaved family life did not rely on long-term single marriages or nuclear residential and functional structures.[115]

There also emerged varying views by scholars of the antebellum decades. Jo Ann Manfra and Robert Dykstra discovered that antebellum families in the Upper South had a significant record of marital breakage and serial marriage, evidence that challenged the thesis of the prevalence of monogamy.[116] Writing on Virginia as well, in what was described as "post-revisionist" analysis, I found widespread matrifocal family residences and a sustained significance of extended enslaved families, rather than the dominant nuclear "ideal" and/or reality.[117]

My 1996 monograph *Life in Black and White: Family in the Slave South* presented compelling evidence from colonial and antebellum Virginia that many enslaved people's families did not have a nuclear structure or "core," and there was not enough evidence that nuclear families were enslaved people's familial ideal. Marrying within one's ethnic group or with similar cultural/linguistic backgrounds; matrifocality (not matriarchy!); polygamy; single parents; abroad spouses; one-, two-, and three-generational households; all male-domestic residences related through blood, marriage, fictive kinship, and occupations; and single- and mixed-gender sibling dwellings—these, along with monogamous marriages and coresidential nuclear families, all comprised the familial experiences of Virginia's enslaved, the largest (and oldest) Black enslaved population in the colonial and antebellum South. Beneath this impressive record of diversity, however, lay an extended, flexible family household—flexible in membership, structure, and member responsibility. Indeed, the extended family across the generations of the enslaved was the most consistent and clearly identifiable family type and ideal. It was the extended family that provided its members with nurture, education, socialization, material support, recreation, and survival/resistance strategies when the enslaved experienced the domestic chaos slaveholders regularly imposed.[118]

Scholars of Black family life in other parts of the Atlantic confirmed the importance of matrifocality, whether in extended or nuclear families. B. W. Higman, in a 1978 study on the Trinidadian enslaved population of the early nineteenth century, vigorously asserted the importance of kinship and similarities between his sample and southern enslaved families due, he surmised, in part, because of the likenesses of the slaveholding patterns (comparatively small in relation to the large estates of most Caribbean enslaved societies) and the African ethnicities they represented.[119] Higman found that most family household types were comprised of mothers and children. Nuclear families (dual-gender parents and children) were the next most significant type.[120] But, Higman noted, most Africans arrived from groups that were either extended or polygynous. The presence of nuclear family in Trinidad probably was either a "building block" for these kinship styles or a pressured adaptation.[121] Likewise, historian Marietta Morrissey in 1989 stated that "Caribbean slaves formed many family types—nuclear, female-headed, extended and polygamous."[122] Barbara Bush, in her groundbreaking 1990 study *Slave Women in Caribbean Society, 1650–1838*, concluded similarly.[123]

Ira Berlin's 1998 monograph *Many Thousands Gone: The First Two Centuries of Slavery in North America* asserted that enslaved people were part of extended families that spread from the quarter to across the nearby countryside.[124] He also noted that Upper South enslaved families had residential patterns somewhat different from those of the low country, where the sizes of the plantations of the latter made a residential enslaved family a far greater possibility in the low country than in the Chesapeake of Virginia and Maryland.[125] This was, of course, until the domestic slave trade of the antebellum era moved more and more men, women, and adolescents to the even Lower South and Southwest, without much consideration of family ties.[126]

The same year of Berlin's publication, another massive monograph that took up the question of the enslaved family appeared: Philip Morgan's *Slave Counterpoint: Black Culture in the Eighteenth-Century Chesapeake and Lowcountry*.[127] Like Blassingame, Genovese, Gutman, and others, Morgan argued that for South Carolina, the "two-parent family form predominated," but also noted that the "single-parent and extended households became more numerous over time."[128] Regarding the Upper South, Morgan agreed with Kulikoff and me that there was much more diversity due to the smaller sizes of the holdings and work units and, subsequently, the greater practice of abroad marriages. "By the late eighteenth century," he concluded, "the most common household form for slaves appears to have been a two-parent one in the low-country and a single-parent one in the Chesapeake."[129] This "single parent" typically was female and was supported by an abroad husband as well as extended and fictive kin. As Morgan wrote, "The development of extended households on large estates in both regions constituted a major improvement in slaves' lives."[130]

CONTEMPORARY WORKS

The historiography of the enslaved family has moved forward, even if public opinion has not, with less emphasis placed on the Black family's exact structure. Broader research studies on slavery typically have some focus on the importance of the enslaved family to its constituents, none more impressive than Richard Dunn's massive *A Tale of Two Plantations: Slave Life and Labor in Jamaica and Virginia* (2014), with its copious demographic appendices that detailed expansive family membership and relations on the plantations he surveyed across their two centuries of operations at two very different sites of the institution.[131]

Other scholars writing social and gendered histories of the enslaved in the past few decades have continued to include family as a significant part of their analyses. Some have done so by probing family relations, problems, and triumphs through biographies; others, by focusing particularly on women's roles. Darlene Clark Hine and Rosalyn Terborg Penn's *Encyclopedia of Black Women in America* (1993),[132] along with Daina Ramey Berry and Deleso Alford's *Enslaved Women in America* (2012)[133] and Clark Hine and Kathleen Thompson's collaboration *A Shining Thread of Hope: The History of Black Women in America* (1998),[134] have provided readers of all intellectual stripes essential introductions to Black female life in America that prove to be both inspirational and instructive regarding the roles of Black women in the family and vice versa. Likewise, Berry and Kali Gross's *A Black Women's History of the United States* (2020)[135] explains the underlying connection between misconceptions of the enslaved family, particularly how we understand the roles of females in kinship groups, with the lingering myths of a "dysfunctional" Black family of the twentieth and twenty-first centuries. Important as well has been Wilma King's *Stolen Childhood* (1998), which centers on enslaved youth, reiterating the importance of children to enslaved families and the care kin provided their most vulnerable members.[136]

Margaret Washington in *Sojourner Truth's America* (2011)[137] excavated her subject's enslaved family life, setting an excellent example that has been followed by others. Jessica Millward's *Finding Charity's Folk: Enslaved and Free Black Women in Maryland* (2015)[138] detailed, in particular, the transition from slavery to freedom pursued by enslaved women who then went on to reconstitute their families and to contribute to free Black community formation. Earlier, Jane Landers pioneered this kind of analysis for Africans and African-descended people residing in Spain's North American site of settler colonialism in *Black Society in Spanish Florida* (1999), and more recently Tiya Miles's *The Dawn of Freedom: A Chronicle of Slavery and Freedom in the City of the Straits* (2018) contributed to this tradition in her discussion as a site of enslavement for both Africans and Indigenous peoples mapped onto two European colonial empires (French and British) before it became a part of the United States.[139]

Erica Nelson Dunbar's *Never Caught: The Washingtons' Relentless Pursuit of Their Runaway Slave, Ona Judge* (2018)[140] astutely exposed Ona Judge's familial connections and concerns while enslaved in Virginia and how she found a place for herself, including marriage and motherhood, as a self-emancipated woman. Certainly, the descriptions of the family lives of those enslaved persons claimed by the most elite Whites in the society, like Martha Washington's Ona, have produced some important and insightful descriptions of kinship times among captive domestics. Together, Annette Gordon Reed's Pulitzer Prize–winning *The Hemings of Monticello: An American Family* (2009) and Lucia Stanton's *"Those Who Labor for my Happiness": Slavery at Thomas Jefferson's Monticello* (2012)[141] offered illuminating details of family life on Thomas Jefferson's plantation. Elizabeth Dowling Taylor's bestseller *A Slave in the White House: Paul Jennings and the Madisons* (2012), in which the author had the good fortune to be able to draw directly on the published account of Paul Jennings himself (*A Colored Man's Reminiscences of James Madison*, 1865), is an example of one of the best of these works, providing much about the interior thoughts and lives of Jennings and his skilled family and enslaved associates, particularly their struggles to remain with their kin and to gain freedom.[142]

Most of these works underscore the importance of family and its inner and evolving nature in multiple and complex contexts as well as the impetus for seeking the emotional, physical, and cultural releases that family provided. They tend to have centered on "elite" domestics, but other works demonstrate that family was as precious to the field bondsperson as to the domestic or skilled worker. Moreover, they exposed the varied contributions that women and men made to family life.

Family protected by the prize of freedom is a theme taken on explicitly by Marissa Fuentes in her methodologically important *Dispossessed Lives: Enslaved Women, Violence and the Archive* (2018), William Thomas in *A Question of Freedom: The Families Who Challenged Slavery from the Founding of the Nation to the Civil War* (2020), Jessica Marie Johnson in her roundly lauded *Wicked Flesh: Black Women, Intimacy and Freedom in the Atlantic World* (2020), Vanessa Holden in her timely study *Surviving Southampton: African American Women and Resistance in Nat Turner's Community* (2021), and Camilla Cowling in her work on Latin America, *Conceiving Freedom: Women of Color, Gender and the Abolition of Slavery in Havana and Rio de Janeiro* (2013).[143] Similarly, Heather Williams's *Help Me to Find My People: The African American Search for Family Lost in Slavery* (2016) offered compelling evidence of the tremendous efforts that newly freed people mounted to find, reclaim, and reconnect with family members lost to the domestic slave trade, while Tera Hunter's *Bound in Wedlock: Slave and Free Black Marriage in the 19th Century* (2019) provided her readers with a close recounting of the importance of marriage to free, freed, and enslaved black people in the nation in the nineteenth century while Daina Ramey Berry reminded her readers in *The Price for their Pound of Flesh: The Value of the Enslaved from Womb to Grave, in the Building of A Nation* (2017) that despite the enslaver's determination to commodify every aspect of the black body, they could not diminish or erase bondspeople's sense of their "soul value."[144]

Most of these latter research monographs have not only deepened our understanding of enslaved families and those individuals who comprised them, but also assisted in the general advance of methodological praxis by addressing the difficulties of trying to conceive and produce such studies given the silence, distortion, and indeed violence of "traditional" archival sources. These efforts are an extension of the labor of dedicated archivists and historians of the early twentieth century, such as Carter G. Woodson, John B. Cade and Susie Byrd, who sought to provide Black derived oral and written documents to support emerging scholars of Black life as well as the work of revisionist scholars of the 1970s and 1980s who fought against the denigration of these Black sources by a biased academy, using them to create the first substantial cohort of studies from the perspective of the enslaved.[145] An essential hallmark of efforts to understand the interior lives of the enslaved also was found in Nell Irwin Painter's groundbreaking *Soul Murder and Slavery* (1993).[146] Contemporary scholars of historical method as applied to Black life such as Millward, Berry, Miles, Fuentes, Johnson, Hunter, Holden, and Williams have drawn on these earlier interventions along with using their monographs, in part, to demonstrate ways to excavate Black subjectivities by locating archival bias, actively reading against that bias, asking different questions of familiar sources, creating voices from composites, and employing methods of intersectionality and what the literary/cultural scholar Saidiya Hartman has titled "critical fabulation."[147]

What Sorrows Labour in my Parents' Breast? takes into consideration this important history of the history of the enslaved Black family, drawing on these works and engaging in the discourse that has been a part of this scholarly trajectory while moving forward. It is meant to uniquely capture as comprehensively as possible the ways that enslaved Africans and their descendants defined, experienced, valued, and maintained kinship. It is an ambitious study that extends from the beginnings of European colonial exploitation in North America until the era of the American Civil War. These "beginnings" include not just the "20 and odd" pirated Africans who so famously arrived in the British colonial outpost of Virginia in 1619. They also include a summary of marriage and family life in some of the

Indigenous communities of the Africans taken captive and early family formation among those Africans whom the Spanish, French, and Dutch brought to North America. It begins, continues, and ends with the destined-to-be-heard Black narrative voice.

Bethany Veney's determined march to freedom and family was laborious, frustrating, and dangerous. Like the millions of enslaved Black people in North America across three centuries who dared to defy law, custom, "science," and the White elite's claim to their ownership, Bethany grew up knowing the necessity of family along with the agony of its loss. Even before adolescence, her freedom dreams were fed by her desire to have a family that could not be taken away from her and that could actually thrive from its own labor. Decades later, Bethany told her autobiographer that she "sometimes tried to picture what my life might have been could I have been set free" during early adolescence and had the opportunity to work hard and save, buy a home, plant a garden, and bring "my sisters and brothers to share with me these blessings of freedom."[148] Before she actually could do so, the realities of an enslaved life "happened"—her mother, Charlotte, died; her siblings, daughter, and husband were given or sold away; and Bethany, too, was sold and rented out multiple times. Refusing to resign her or her family's fate to one determined by others hostile to Black people's very humanity, Bethany eventually found a way to flee bondage, leaving the Blue Ridge Mountains of Virginia in 1858 and managing to carry her young son Joe with her. Unfortunately, Joe became ill and died soon after their self-emancipation, rendering another "great [familial] affliction" for her to withstand.[149]

After the Civil War, Bethany worked hard to reunite her kin, or at least those she could still find. On her first trip back to Virginia, she retrieved her daughter Charlotte along with Charlotte's husband and child. She managed three more trips back, bringing sixteen additional members of her kinship network north to Massachusetts.[150] For her, there was no freedom without family. Even more profoundly, one simply could not exist without family—whether memory, fantasy, or reality.

Abdul Rahman Ibrahima ibn Sori shared Bethany's conviction that family was essential to one's purpose. Ibrahima, unlike Bethany, born an elite. He was a wealthy, well educated, multilingual, royal Fulbe emir, warrior, husband, and father of a two-year-old son when he was captured in Guinea in the late 1780s and transported to New Orleans and then to Spanish-held Natchez, where a middling Mississippi cotton famer bought him for $930. Ibrahima's father, who had been ruler of Futa Jalon, provided Ibrahima (one of thirty-three sons by four wives) with a magnificent education—enrollment in rigorous mosque schools, an English tutor, and study almost one thousand miles from his home at the heralded intellectual center Timbuktu. Ibrahima spoke not only multiple African languages but also Arabic and English.[151]

Bethany Veney, Manuscripts, Archives and Rare Books Division, Schomburg Center for Research in Black Culture, The New York Public Library, Sc Rare 326.92-V.

Ibrahima's life, obviously, would never be the same once he arrived in America. Three persona-defining elements, however, remained visible even in the monumental diminishment of Ibrahim's personal power: his allegiance to Islam, his impressive intellect, and, of course, the abiding significance of family. After several years enslaved, Ibrahima remarried. Isabella, a newly arrived woman on the farm who already was a mother to at least one and perhaps three children, became his wife. The two soon began to have children together, nine in total.[152] Knowing well the frightful insecurity of having a captive family, Ibrahima risked his own long sought-after freedom and return to his African home—a possibility only through the miraculous intercession

Abdul Rham,an Ibrahima ibn Henry Inman, *Sketch of Abduhl Rahhahman,* illustration, c. 1833-1834, Prints and Photographs Division, Library of Congress, LC-USZ62-39606.

of no less than President John Adams, Secretary of State Henry Clay, and the sultan of Morocco—in order to earn money so that he could liberate his American family. Ibrahima and Isabella eventually were successful in traveling to Liberia and freeing two of their sons, along with their son's families. His other children, and their descendants, remained enslaved.[153] Ibrahima himself died soon after his arrival in West Africa, never physically making it back to his family of origin. For him, family—however small the portion—was worth risks, even life-threatening, freedom-forfeiting risks.

Several decades before Bethany Veney's birth in 1813 or Prince Ibrahima's death in 1829, the famed African poet Phillis Wheatley expressed

Phillis Wheatley. Scipio Moorhead, *Phillis Wheatley, Negro Servant to Mr. John Wheatley, of Boston*, engraving, c. 1773, Rare Book and Special Collections Division, Library of Congress, LC-USZ62-40054.

the compelling sentiment of the absolute value of family. In one of her published poems, the line "What sorrows labour in my parents' breast?" probed the existential crisis she was certain her West African parents suffered after she was "snatched" from them as a small child at the height of the Atlantic slave trade. Her parents' loss was the mirror image of her own, and those of millions of others stolen and lost to family. What are parents without their children? What were children like Phillis without their parents?

The trope of the missing Black family has lived large in the ambitious research designs of scholars, the critical imagination of the public, and the caustic decisions of policy makers. The reality, however, is that even through the pain and loss brought on by centuries of slavery and systemic racialized inequalities of all sorts, Black people wanted to and were able to create family ties that fostered humanity, assured survival, and even undergirded postemancipation progress across the generations. We know this because of their created texts spoken, written, sang, sewed, prayed, drummed, joked, woven, carved, cried, and danced into a living, evolving, enduring archive that is the source of this book.

What Sorrows Labour in My Parent's Breast? largely progresses chronologically, with recurring themes that underscore the multifaceted realities of loss, recovery, resilience, and resistance embedded in Black captives' desire to experience family life despite their capture, sale, exile, exploitation, abuse, and enslavement. Particular attention is given to the ways in which enslaved people experienced and voiced their experiences of marriage and kinship through lenses of gender, generation, location, labor status, legal statutes, and common racialist practice. *What Sorrows Labour in My Parents' Breast?* exposes the complex, often vulnerable stages, structures, and functions of *the* vitally important Black institution as it evolved and survived under the extreme subversion and surveillance that the institution of slavery, and its benefactors, relentlessly imposed. There are two major sections. The first three chapters constitute Beginnings; the latter three, The Antebellum Familial Experience.

In Beginnings, "Traditions from Whence They Came: Marriage and Family in Western/Central Africa at the Time of the Atlantic Slave Trade" reviews family life and kinship patterns in western and western central Africa that would have informed North American captives' fundamental attachment to family as the basis for their social and humanistic identities, as well as their ideals and practices of marriage, family, and domesticity. While it is not certain what exact traditional kinship and gender ideals and obligations, household structures, or marital and parenting practices came to be manifest in family and community life of enslaved peoples, this chapter provides a window into that rich diversity, and the similarities, that captives took with them and had available to draw on and negotiate with one another across ethnic lines when faced with the challenging social, cultural, and legal circumstances enslavers imposed.

"The Colonial Enslaved Family: Foundations and Creations" explores the experience of family life for Black enslaved people forced to reside in the competing colonial North American spaces claimed by the Dutch, French, Spanish, and British. It allows the reader a close look at the praxis of kinship initiation and re-creation among enslaved Africans from the point of capture and collection on the coast of Africa, through the Middle Passage, and, once they arrived and were redistributed, along the colonial frontiers of North America. Black sociosexual companionship, marriage, and family ties emerged and took hold against the backdrop, and oppositional to the grain, of developing legal, governance, economic, and cultural structures that colonial settlers, entrepreneurs, political agents, and other stakeholders imposed. Africans in America created family ties not only because kinship was essential to their indigenous lives and cultures, but also as resistance to the founding of systemic racist institutions and attitudes by European settlers who claimed to own them.

"Traditions of Resistance and Family from the Colonial Era Forward" describes in detail the tremendous efforts Black enslaved family members put forward to protect their kinship relations both during and after this period of national significance. It documents that by the time of the American Revolution, the bonded Black family in its many manifestations (nuclear, matrifocal, extended, blended, communal, fictive) was firmly established as a vital social, cultural, material, and psychological resource for enslaved Africans and African Americans. But it was one under constant threat and assault. This abuse did not go unanswered. While White patriots in the mainland British colonies fought for their freedom from England, "owned" Black men and women continued their relentless efforts to gain protection and liberty for themselves and their kin. The American Revolution (as did other armed incursions) posed ripe opportunities for tens of thousands of bondspeople to seek and win freedom for themselves and their families. But enslaved people hardly waited for *that* revolution. They carried out endless acts of resistance, rebellion, and personal revolutions *for* and with family before, during, and after the American Revolution created a slaveholding nation that would become the largest in the Atlantic world.

The antebellum period from 1820 to 1860 comprised the key era of the United States as a slave society. Following the reduction in slave territory during the early national period, there was a time of immense territorial expansion. The Black enslaved population doubled from two million people in 1820 to very near four million in 1860. Most, like Bethany Veney, would not be able to spend their enslaved lives residing with their families of birth or of creation once they reached adolescence. The lucrative and efficient domestic slave trade relegated enslaved men, women, and children as easily available, movable, and liquidable property. Marital unity and family integrity were hardly ever the priority of those who claimed to own Black people. African American enslaved families nonetheless persisted under the most arduous material, psychological, and physical circumstances. How did men and women, the elderly, and children—all members of families—fare in, and because of, the domestic slave trade? How did they manage to maintain some kinship ties, create new ones, and hold themselves accountable to their ideals—not their captors' ideals—of family?

The Antebellum Familial Experience begins with "Antebellum Courtship and Marital Rituals." This chapter is about the ritualistic and real attitudes and practices of enslaved adults who committed themselves to love, romance, and marriage. It surveys courtship attitudes and behaviors, the traits that adults desired and despised in a partner, the negotiations with family and captors regarding one's choice for a spouse, and the various kinds of ceremonies (or not) that signified one's marital commitment.

"Antebellum Family Life" explores a wide swath of topics related to the enslaved family experience during the cotton boom decades, including child-rearing and socialization of youth to enslaved labor routines, family obligations and racial etiquette, along with familial food culture, recreation, housing and household composition, religious and medicinal practices, and the familial roles and experiences of the elderly. Discussion of their lifeways are set against the backdrop of the devastating impact of the domestic slave trade that repeatedly disrupted families, even the same family several times, as one after another—parent, sibling, spouse, child, aunt, uncle, friend—was sold, rented, inherited, moved, or given away.

The final chapter, "Death and Resurrection," describes various meanings of death and the possibility—for some, the certainty—of return and resurrection beyond the captivity of enslavers. It describes the gendered roles that families and community members assumed in burial and memorialization, the diversity of these events, and their cultural context. It continues with a glance into what life was like after the Civil War, when enslaved peoples gained their "freedom," surveying efforts of familial resurrection, re-creation, survival, and progress against the backdrop of emancipation's varied meanings and experiences.

BEGINNINGS

Chapter 1

Traditions from Whence They Came

Marriage and Family in Western/ Central Africa at the Time of the Atlantic Slave Trade

INTRODUCTION

The famed eighteenth-century poet Phillis Wheatley was an orphan from the time she was taken from her family and forced into the Atlantic slave trade. Traffickers in Africans brought Phillis to North America in 1761, at the height of the largest forced migration of people in the known history of the planet. Records indicate that Phillis, one of several "small Negroes," arrived on the slave ship that she would be named for. Her trader was the wealthy merchant Timothy Fitch of Medford, Massachusetts. An advertisement for the shipment appeared in a local Boston paper on July 30, 1761:

> To be Sold, A Parcel of Likely Negroes, imported from Africa, enquire of John Avery at his House, next door to the White-Horse, or at a Store adjoining the said Avery's Distill House, at the South-End near the South Market: Also if any Persons have any Negro Men, strong and hearty, tho not of the best morral character, which are proper Subjects for Transportation, may have an Exchange for small Negroes.[1]

Phillis was young, female, small, and with the appearance of a "sickly" disposition, dressed only in dirty carpets wrapped around her waist; Fitch certainly had no guarantee that anyone would purchase her. Phillis, however, finally did become the chattel of John Wheatley, a Boston shipping merchant, city official, and prominent businessman and landholder who had a reputation as a master tailor. John Wheatley resided in Boston, which meant that Phillis would continue to grow up bound in an urban, northern seaport city where enslaved people might not have been extensive in number, but where African slavery clearly was accepted. Indeed, Massachusetts initially led the way in

Map of local slave trade in West Africa. Homann Erben, Jean Baptiste Bourguignon D' Anville, and R. De Marchais, Gvinea propria, nec non Nigritiæ vel Terræ Nigrorvm maxima pars: geographis hodiernis dicta utraque Æthiopia inferior, & hujus quidem pars australis. Norimbergæ: Homannianorum Heredum, 1743, Map, Library of Congress, Geography and Map Division, World Digital Library.

the northern British mainland colonies in slave ownership and investment in the slave trade. In the 1620s, Samuel Maverick became the first known resident of that colony to own Black captives. Early colonists imported Africans and captured Native Americas whom they exchanged for Black bondspeople in the British Caribbean.

Regardless of what family relations Phillis might have been able to acquire or was forced into once she reached North America, she remained aware that she had been part of a family in her West African homeland. What might her family have been like? And what conditions might have resulted in her becoming part of the Atlantic slave trade, forced to leave them behind for the remainder of her life?

Although Phillis's ethnicity is uncertain, it is widely believed that she came from the Senegambia region of West Africa.[2] Some suggest that her ethnic origin was Wolof because of a memory she had of her mother pouring water libations at the daily rise of the sun—a ceremony attributed to the Wolof.[3] Wolof were one of the dominant ethnic groups in the Senegambia,[4] with a language and culture that many of other ethnicities from that same region shared.[5] Phillis's generation of Senegambians would not have been the very first enslaved by Europeans. Still, the Portuguese traded for them as early as the fifteenth century, selling them in Lisbon and to other parts of the Iberian Peninsula. Paintings from that time and place often depict Africans, some enslaved, others who had gained their freedom, working in Portuguese cities and seaports.[6] Forced to convert to Catholicism, members of this Ladino community eventually became among the first to be enslaved in the Americas.[7"]

During the two hundred years before Phillis was enslaved, the Portuguese and Spanish sold large numbers of bonded Senegambians, including Wolofs, to sites in their American colonial empires, such as Brazil, Peru, Ecuador, Colombia, Venezuela, Mexico, and the Spanish Caribbean.[8] Many first arrived in the Portuguese colony of Cape Verde, off the West African coast, before shipment further west to the Americas. Traders exchanged slave cargoes for salt, rum, cotton textiles, and other goods. Despite an early reputation of rebelliousness,[9] many slaveholders preferred Senegambians because they perceived them to have unusual "intelligence, strength, resiliency, temperament, and musicality."[10] By the eighteenth century, Senegambians were highly desired in the colonies that would become the United States, where potential slaveowners considered them good workers and producers of workers. They believed Wolof women were not only beautiful, elegant, and intelligent, but also very fertile. Indeed, these females were so highly prized that colonial Spanish planters in Louisiana were willing to pay higher prices for Wolof women than for Wolof men.[11]

SLAVERY IN AFRICA BEFORE THE ATLANTIC TRADE

The Atlantic Black slave trade was part of an ageless global practice of human bondage. Slavery has existed in almost every place on Earth where people have lived—the precontact Americas, Europe, Asia, the Middle East, and Africa. Indeed, slavery existed in much of Africa, and Africans of many ethnicities were subject to enslavement by political, military, and/or cultural "enemies" long before the onset of the Atlantic slave trade that would bring an estimated 12.5 to 15 million Black men, women, and children to the "New World."

Even before the first millennium, young Ethiopian men (as bonded warriors) and women and girls (valued for their beauty and enslaved in harems) were part of a flourishing Arab trade in eastern Africa. West Africans and even western central Africans also became part of this lucrative exchange of "goods." Along with ivory, gold, and salt, Arab traders carried them west as far as the Persian Gulf and beyond. By the eighth century CE, in particular, a thriving Muslim trade moved bonded persons from sub-Saharan Africa to the Persian Gulf and, by the tenth century CE, to Asia.[12] This trade's center was in the Libyan Desert, where captives moved along slave routes through Timbuktu, Kano, Bornu, and Wadaj.[13] The majority were females purchased to be domestics and concubines. Jewish traders also operated in these regions.[14] The important West African kingdoms of Ghana, Mali, and Songhai practiced some forms of bondage too.[15] By the mid-nineteenth century, Muslim traders traveled as far inland in Africa as the upper Congo and Lake Victoria, selling captives in Zanzibar, Turkey, Iraq, Iran, and Arabia. Likewise, Kongolese society had slavery and the Hausa exercised the institution from the fourteenth century.[16]

In Igboland, located in southeastern Nigeria, persons could be enslaved for a number of criminal offenses, including murder, incest, sorcery, and theft. Others derived their status from warfare with political, or "foreign," enemies or because of a personal or family member's debt.[17] Kagne and Margru, both Mende girls, became pawns locally to guarantee their fathers' debts. They became captives in the Atlantic trade when the debts went unpaid. Their shipmates, Fahidzhin-na, Shu-le, and Kwong, were enslaved because of adultery.[18] Ukawsaw Gronniosaw (later called James Albert), a Muslim prince from Bornou, was captured and sold by a ruler in the Gold Coast who feared that Ukawsaw, who was traveling through his kingdom without permission or diplomatic license, was a spy sent by his family to prepare for future war.[19]

Of course, the practice of slavery over large expanses of time, across such vast landscapes, and among such diverse cultural groups varied tremendously. Still, there were similarities. Most captives in pre-European-contact Africa were women and children. The bondsperson's value typically derived from their skills and marketability and usually brought "prestige" to the household that claimed them. Enslaved persons largely experienced a lesser social, material, and legal status than free people; were subject to heightened surveillance; and had little control over their movements and personal lives. Many worked in agriculture, livestock, and construction. Others were craftsmen, domestics, eunuchs, body servants, porters, traders, musicians, soldiers, miners, concubines, market helpers, and cloth makers. Some even held government and court offices.[20]

The consequences of slavery for the families of those bonded in Africa also varied, oftentimes along gender lines. Enslaved women, for example, typically were important assets within a western/central African household not only because of their labor but also because of their ability to produce children. Free males sometimes married them. Doing so meant that these men did not have to deliver a bride-price to the woman's family, since these females usually were not part of a recognized kin group that would have required this obligation. It also meant that in matrilineal societies, like the Akan or Kongo, men could have control of the children these women bore, instead of the brothers of their legal wives. Once enslaved women were married and part of a kinship group, they could become assimilated into the society in which they had been enslaved. Those who were enslaved as children might have been treated similar to members of the household, although the tasks they had to perform typically were lowlier than those of free youth and, like the experience of Olaudah Equiano, they could be sold away without warning. In some societies, such as those in Dahomey and Ivory Coast, children of enslaved women and free men took the free status of their fathers.[21] Even if enslaved women or children were not adopted into their captors' kin network, an enslaved family that remained the property of a free family across the generations tended to experience improved status over time.

Both males and females could own bonded people. As the wives and concubines of powerful men during the era of the Atlantic slave trade, as well as having high status in their own right, some African females acquired captives. Likewise, free women traders along the western African coastline down to Luanda held and sold people. Small numbers of enslaved women, like some enslaved men, also found a way to acquire bonded people, particularly if they were close to gaining their own freedom and with their slaveholders' permission.

Once the Atlantic slave trade began in the fifteenth century, those Africans who already had the status of bondsperson and who had not yet been incorporated into a free family kin group typically were the first traded to the Europeans. Like other enslaved people across time and space, most Africans did not become captives among their own "nation" or ethnic/cultural groups, but rather began that status as captives of war. Adahoonzou, a king in Dahomey for example, explained of his participation in the eighteenth-century trade of Africans to the Americas that those whom he and others traded were prisoners of war who, if not sold as bondspeople, would have been put to death.[22]

Western/central Africans who were enslaved within their own groups usually were being punished for a crime, debt, or immorality. Olaudah Equiano, who served as a captive in Virginia and the Caribbean, explained that in his Igbo homeland, a person could be enslaved for crime or adultery.[23] Olaudah also noted that some leaders took great pains to ascertain the origins of captives before they allowed slavers to take their human cargo through their territory. "Sometimes indeed we sold slaves to them," he admitted, "but they were only prisoners of war, or such among us as had been convicted of kidnapping, or adultery, and some other crimes, which we esteemed heinous."[24]

Olaudah's depiction of African slavery purportedly was drawn from his observations as part of a slaveholding family as well as his own bondage in West Africa before he became a captive in the Americas. His experiences while enslaved before crossing the Atlantic indicate some of the assorted ways in which African enslavers employed their bound workers. He worked primarily as a domestic, as an assistant to artisans, and in agricultural ventures. His first was a goldsmith who occupied Olaudah in multiple ways—as his helper, as a domestic for his wives and children, and as an assistant to the cook. Olaudah noted that he was "used extremely well," even though he still tried to escape. This family sold him to a rich woman. In her household, he served as companion to a boy about his age. His captor, Olaudah reported, treated him well, even better than his first master. As an elite bondsperson in this well-established household, Olaudah, too, had bondspeople who attended him. Before meals, other captives were tasked to "wash" and "perfume" him. Olaudah's enslaver also granted him, as the senior of the two boys, the privilege of eating and drinking first. "Indeed every thing here, and all their treatment of me," he wrote, "made me forget that I was a slave," and he believed that he had been adopted as part of their family.[25] It was a short-lived fantasy. After two months, his holder sold him.[26]

THE SLAVE TRADE FROM AFRICA TO THE AMERICAS

Many European countries including the Portuguese, Dutch, Spanish, French, British, and Swedes, along with African entities from Senegambia south through the western central areas of the continent and beyond, participated in the long-term and lucrative complex of businesses that comprised the African slave trade to the Americas. African captives represented a tremendous diversity of peoples from areas that now form the modern-day nations of Morocco, Senegal, the Gambia, Guinea, Guinea Bissau, Ghana, Sierra Leone, Ivory Coast, Liberia, Benin, Nigeria, Burkina Faso, Mali, Cameroon, Gabon, Angola, Congo, the Democratic Republic of Congo, Zaire, and Madagascar.[27] Historians believe that the largest of those exported came from western central Africa, followed by the Bights of Benin and Biafra. Others were from the Gold Coast, Senegambia, Madagascar, Ivory Coast, Liberia, and Sierra Leone.[28] This trade affected not just Africa, Europe, and the Americas but nearly every continent, producing a truly global enterprise foundational to the development of the modern world.

Traditions from Whence They Came 45

Slave traders in Goree, Senegal, Eighteenth Century Jacques Grasset Saint-Sauveur, *After a drawing by Labrousse: Slave trade on Goree Island (Cap Verde, Senegal)*, from "Encyclopédie des voyages," Inv. 75.7168. Musée du Quai Branly - Jacques Chirac/Paris/France. © RMN-Grand Palais / Art Resource, New York.

The trade from Africa to Europe, and later inclusive of the Caribbean and the Americas, began slowly, initially focused on the Portuguese seeking gold and ivory. European obsession with these items led to sites in West Africa being dubbed the "Gold Coast" and "Ivory Coast," the latter being a name that still exists today. However, a growing momentum in intercontinental trade derived from an increasing focus on African captives for the unfree labor markets that were the underpinnings of the expanding American mercantile economies in agriculture, mining, livestock, lumber, and creole bondspeople. From the late fifteenth century through the sixteenth, the Portuguese exported almost two thousand Africans per year.[29]

By the seventeenth century, European interests in the slave trade had spread far beyond the Iberian Peninsula, and purchases increased by a multiple of five. Over the next hundred years, traders took an average of fifty thousand Africans annually to the Americas, reaching a peak of approximately eighty thousand per year in the 1780s.[30] Very few captives remained in family groups.

Preadolescent African youths were unusual in the slave trade, and young girls like Phillis Wheatley were even more rare. Still, as the prices for enslaved Africans rose in eighteenth-century British America, so, too, did the number of captive children, particularly boys.[31] The most valued were males from their teens to about thirty years old. Timothy Fitch spoke for most traders when he instructed his captain: "Now in Regard to your purchasing Slaves, you'l Observe to get as few Girl Slaves as Possible & as many Prime Boys as you Can."[32]

Slave traders exchanged African people for multiple luxury and everyday use items, including South Asian cowrie shells that served as currency in parts of West Africa, brass and pewter, iron bars, glass beads, firearms, liquors, and grains. Eighteenth-century captive Broteer Furro, whom his purchaser renamed Venture Smith, recalled that he was sold on the Gold Coast for calico cloth and four gallons of rum.[33] Olaudah Equiano remembered that one of his purchasers paid 172 cowrie shells for him.[34] A list of goods Timothy Fitch sent to trade was somewhat customary—weapons, ammunition, rum, tobacco, sugar, flour, and bread.[35]

Monopolistic enterprises such France's Compagnie de Senegal, the Dutch West India Company, and the British Royal African Company controlled much of the trade during the seventeenth and eighteenth centuries, but certainly not all of it. African rulers and traders were accomplished businessmen and women in their own right. "Pirates" and private dealers also commanded some of the trade from its outset. As the profits increased, stakeholder rivalries intensified. With the support of the royal houses of Europe who commissioned these companies, they were able to build and maintain massive fortresses called "castles" and smaller barracoons along the West African coastline that operated as holding cells for captives and living and business quarters for all others invested in some aspect of the trade. The Gold Coast had as many as forty of these structures, including the massive Cape Coast Castle, constructed by the Portuguese beginning in the late fifteenth century. Command of these fortresses, with their massive and heavily armed military forces, meant some protection from would-be European interlopers, the resistance of those taken, and attacks from uncooperative locals.

As the numbers traded increased over time, so, too, did the violent methods of acquisition. African chiefs, rulers, and appointed middlemen who had managed to orchestrate much of the trade through their control of European access to west/central African coastlines and inland markets began to lose their localized monopolies through warfare with neighboring groups and an escalation of unauthorized raids. Captives such as Equiano often found themselves kidnapped and sold, first to other Africans and then eventually to Atlantic traders. Abdul Rahman Ibrahim ibn was a Fulani Muslim commander and cleric in his father's kingdom when he and his army were viciously attacked and many killed. Their enemies traded the survivors to Mandingos who sold them to a British slave trading ship bound for the Americas.[36]

The Atlantic slave trade destroyed millions of western and western central African families, unraveling and weakening indigenous African communities, political entities, and economies. Regardless of their ethnic or national affiliations or their final destination in the Americas, husbands and wives, parents and children, grandparents, aunts, uncles, and cousins rarely accompanied each other to the same New World destinations. Only about a half million arrived in British North America. Brazil claimed the largest number of African arrivals—roughly four million. Large shipments went as well to other European colonial settler societies in the Americas, particularly the Caribbean, with much smaller numbers to Europe.[37] First the Portuguese and then the Dutch controlled the trade in the earliest eras of activity, but the British dominated at its eighteenth-century peak—earning the incredibly dubious distinction of delivering the majority of enslaved Africans to the New World.[38] Forced to leave family members and the environmental underpinnings of their cultures behind, enslaved men, women, and children still brought with them their memories of and allegiances to their ways of life, including kinship and community structures and rituals.

MARRIAGE AND FAMILY IN WESTERN/ WESTERN CENTRAL AFRICA

Diversity in African cultural groups was expressed in a variety of complex family styles, structures, internal dynamics, and rituals. Religious practices and beliefs had substantial influence on all aspects of family life, as did many other social, political, and economic frameworks. Africans who became captives in the Atlantic slave trade expressed cultural elements from their indigenous communities, but also recognized, to some extent, the languages, religious practices, and family styles of fellow captives among them. Olaudah Equiano, for example, was quite aware of cultural distinctions between his Igbo peoples and those of other cultural groups he encountered as he was traded from the African hinterland to the coast. Writing of one group that seemed particularly different in their practices from his, Olaudah noted: "All the nations and people I had hitherto passed through resembled our own in their manners, customs, and language; but I came at length to a country, the inhabitants of which differed from us in all those particulars. I was very much struck with this difference, especially when I came among a people who did not circumcise and ate without washing their hands."[39] Olaudah added that their women were not as modest as Igbo females because they "ate, and drank, and slept, with their men" and, most surprisingly, seemed to have no rituals or sacrificial events (religion) that he recognized. He also was astonished by their pointed, filed teeth and markings of ornamentation on their bodies. Although they wanted to mark him in this way, Olaudah refused.[40] His cultural alienation from these people also was driven by their adoption of some aspects of European culture—cooking in iron pots and using European cutlasses, along with one-on-one combat techniques.[41]

Despite the cultural variation captives experienced and observed in one another, they easily recognized that family, nonetheless, was the essential determinant of one's identity, shared regardless of a person's age, gender, class, language, religion, or other cultural attributes. Adult kin, particularly parents, welcomed their children into their families with distinct naming rituals, taught them how to identify other kin or ethnic community members physically and culturally, socialized them to be responsible members of their kinship groups, and ritually initiated them into adult life. Likewise, specific rituals ushered a deceased ancestor to the next realm of their existence, but not out of contact with living family members. Ancestors remained important members of kinship groups, relied upon and honored for their continued protection and guidance.

Marriage and blood/lineal descent stood at the core of one's identity and African family life. John Mbiti noted that "for African peoples, marriage is the focus of existence. It is the point where all the members of a given community meet: the departed, the living and those yet to be born. All the dimensions of time here, and the whole drama of history is repeated, renewed and revitalized."[42] This central familial event meant that everyone who reached adulthood was expected to marry and to have children. To do so was not just one's hope and privilege as a member of a family, but a social, economic, and religious duty. Each generation was expected to reproduce itself by having children so that the family would extend both forward in time through new generations and backward through their ancestors.[43] "Marriage and procreation in African communities," Mbiti added, "are a unity: without procreation marriage is incomplete."[44]

Marriage preparations across western/central African cultures were extensive and heavily ritualized. These significant demarcations in a person's development began with birth—not only physical birth, but also religious initiation so that the person could be part of their family and community. Typically, children reaching puberty endured rites that constituted "the birth of the young people into the state of maturity and responsibility."[45] Among those people who did not practice such initiation rituals, young people's family members socialized them, throughout their childhood, to eventually take on adult roles within their communities and kinship groups. Intimate histories of these customs and beliefs, passed down through oral traditions, dance, music, ceremonies, and practices, remained relevant for those sold into the slave trade and their descendants in the Americas.

Lineages traditionally determined through direct ancestral descent to which family a child belonged at birth. Clans also were a form of familial identity, but usually were larger than lineages, and the exact line of descent was less clear.[46] Some groups, such as the Kongo in western central Africa and the Akan of the Gold Coast, two groups that were large minorities among enslaved people in the Americas, were matrilineal—tracing kinship alliance to a single female ancestor. Children born to these marriages "belonged" to their mother's family. Their maternal uncle, rather than their father, was their male guardian. Others who arrived in the Americas—including the Igbo and Yoruba of the Bights of Benin and Biafra, and the Mende peoples of Sierra Leone—came from patrilineal societies. Unilateral descent, however, did not mean family members did not have close ties to kin members not directly related to that particular ancestor. Moreover, there were examples of extended families derived from kin relations with those descended from both one's mother and one's father, such as among the Yako of southeastern Nigeria, who had both matrilineal and patrilineal clans.[47] No matter the gendered line of descent, being part of a particular lineage meant that "possessive rights over the children belong entirely to the lineage and . . . within the lineage the individual has his most important duties and also his most significant rights," including one's support and inherited property."[48]

African captives came from groups who practiced both monogamy and polygamy. Yet even among those where polygamy flourished, only men who could financially support more than one wife and their offspring were supposed to practice it. In many of these societies, first wives had to approve of their husbands seeking an additional spouse. Venture Smith recalled that his father had two wives, but his mother separated from him when he went to acquire another wife without first consulting her.[49] Multiple wives signaled a man's extraordinary wealth, and those persons who practiced polygamy believed, in part, that it increased a family's ability to care collectively for its members and prevented male adultery.[50] Different societal and cultural practices also meant a diversity of ages at which one was first betrothed or could marry, marital rituals, conditions of marriage dissolution, gender prescriptions, childrearing conventions, elderly and ancestral positionality, and rules of endogamy and exogamy.

African kinship ideals, patterns, and experiences were not static but, like all aspects of African cultures that will be addressed in this book, took on a range of changes from the subtle to the dramatic over the long history of the slave trade. It also is important to note that descriptions of African kinship patterns also can vary, sometimes greatly, according to who is reporting this information—practitioners, ethnographers, travelers, missionaries, or historians. The discussion presented here draws on all these sources as they were reported at the time. Despite these challenges, the next several sections attempt to describe what comprised family membership and how family functioned in those places from which the majority of enslaved Africans were taken before they were forced to travel to North America. It would be from some of these kinship traditions that Africans would draw when they quickly began to re-create families as captives. These beliefs, ideals, and practices were particularly important among those peoples who were residentially clustered with others of similar cultural background.

Senegambia (Wolof, Serer, Mandinka, Fula, Etc.)

Phillis Wheatley's cultural affiliation with Wolof, Mandingo, or another Senegambian group placed her among many who were Islamic in faith (along with lingering pre-Islamic, animistic practices) and whose kinship groups were hierarchical, patriarchal, and patrilineal. Phillis might have been raised in a nuclear family, but it would have been unusual for her not to have had sustained contact with extended kin through both parents. If her father was well-off, he may have practiced polygamy, and Phillis probably would have had numerous siblings.[51]

What is certain is that her capture and enslavement in Boston removed Phillis from an indigenous African community rich in religious, familial, and oral traditions. Senegambians were known for their musicians and griots who practiced oral/artistic traditions, including socialization through stories and proverbs. Even though she was young when taken, Phillis shared in this tradition as a poet. We also know that women and men had distinct familial and communal roles. Phillis's mother and female kin would have taught her to be deferential to elders and to male authority, including her husband; to recognize and respect the class structure of their society; and to value and enhance her physical beauty. Females typically worked as agriculturalists, enriching their families and communities with their labor in corn, millet, and sometimes rice. Among artists, men were musicians and women were dancers. Girls sometimes were promised to marry before puberty but could not marry before reaching physical adolescence.[52] Men married later in order to be able

Traditions from Whence They Came 51

Senegal Woman and Her Son. David Boliat, *Femme Wolof portant son enfant*, Print, c. 1853, General Research Division, The New York Public Library.

to afford to establish a household.[53] Phillis's mother also would have made certain, as her child reached the age to marry, that Phillis's suitors were honorable, kind, and generous. Despite maternal input, however, it would have been Phillis's father who decided whom she married. Wolof peoples typically did not marry across class lines.[54] Both parents also would have been concerned that her husband was not closely related through blood, a taboo in many western/western central African cultures. The Wolof, however, did marry cross-cousins, a practice linked to the importance of compatibility and the belief that such marriages provided motivation for the couple to be well-behaved and treat each other well. Men sometimes resorted to the use of magic to win a woman's hand in marriage, but they were expected to impress their beloved and her family with a series of gifts.[55] Slavery was a part of their society, but it impacted family life quite differently from the ways it configured Black domestic life in the Americas. Freeborn Senegambian men, for example, could marry female descendants of enslaved people and their children would be free. So, too, was a bondswoman once she married a free man. Freeborn women, however, could not marry bondsmen or their descendants.[56]

According to the narrative about the early eighteenth-century family life of Ayuba Suleiman Diallo (later called Job Ben Solomon), who was from Bondu in Senegal and was a Fulbe, females married as young adolescents but remained veiled with their husbands for three years after marriage, in keeping with expected feminine modesty. Diallo was enslaved in Maryland thirty years before Phillis was captured. He first married in his homeland when he was fifteen years old; his wife was eleven. Among the Muslim Senegambians, the father of the potential groom decided when his son was ready to marry and then requested the right for him to marry a female who had the appropriate respect for gender prescriptions. The first wife chosen was the most important in polygamous societies, since her behavior, labor, childrearing practices, and relationship with her husband set the pattern for any additional wives the husband might acquire. If the potential bride's father agreed, the two patriarchs determined the details of the couple's marriage initiation, including the amount of property received from the groom's family. The father of the bride gave this property to her as her dowry. Diallo noted, "All Things being concluded on, the two Fathers and the young Man go to the Priest, and declare their Agreement; which finishes the Marriage."[57]

The series of events constituting the wedding included ritualized play in which the bride's female relations tried to prevent the groom from taking her away from them. The groom had to ply his intended's reluctant kin with gifts and secure one of his friends to remove his fiancée safely. Eventually, the groom could claim his bride and take her to their marital home. This convention indicated the importance of the bride to her family and their fear of "a breach of family solidarity" when she left her family of birth to reside with her husband and his family.[58] When there was more than one wife, the husband had to avoid conflict among them by dividing his time and attentions equally. Divorce was possible, but not for insignificant reasons. Male prerogatives meant that when a bride left her husband, she did so without the benefit of her dowry, was viewed as "scandalous," and could not marry another man in her community. If the husband divorced a wife, however, she could keep her dowry and remarry.[59]

As in most African cultures, children were prized members of Senegambian families. Indeed, many married primarily to have children. "The most important part of the 'value' of a woman is her child-bearing capacity," one expert noted. "If the woman proves to be barren, in many tribes her kin either return the marriage payment or provide another woman to bear children."[60] Male children were circumcised, but there is not strong evidence that females of Phillis's generation were. Familial rituals were important markers of maturation and change in children's relationship to their kinship group and community. For example, at the child's age of seven days, family and associates would have gathered at Phillis's father's home for her naming ceremony, orchestrated by the community's holy man. He was responsible for writing Phillis's Wolof name both on wood and a piece of paper. The child was washed in clear water, and the paper with her name written on it was rolled up and placed around her neck. This "name necklace" remained until the writing disappeared. The ceremony also included a feast sponsored by the child's father, who was responsible for providing a cow or sheep for participants to eat, part of which was reserved for the community's poor.[61]

Senegambian fathers, significantly, were responsible for passing on skills and knowledge to their sons. Ayuba Sulieman Diallo was the grandson of the former king of Futa, and his father was the high priest. The latter prepared Diallo to be a priest, teaching him the requisite Arabic and Koranic scriptures. Adult sons, in turn, aided their fathers with their work. Diallo, for example, served as a sub-priest to his father and traded for him in distant markets. Slavery, even sale to Europe and the Americas, would not have been an oddity at the time or place of Phillis's birth.

Mende/Temme

Household heads of the patrilineal and polygamous Mende of Sierra Leone and that vicinity usually were the eldest community males and priests.[62] Women exercised some social and political power and could even serve as chiefs.[63] Preparation for marriage, in part, meant initiation into gender-specific societies that prepared Mende youth for adulthood: Poro for males and Sande for females. These organizations taught gendered rituals, responsibilities, and ideal behavior. The Sande made certain that females learned the traditions of feminine hygiene, how to enhance and display one's beauty, the duties of motherhood, and how to live harmoniously within Mende society. The Sande masquerade celebrated female beauty and power—the only fully female masquerade in western/western central Africa in which females took on the personae of spirits. One could not marry without having taken part in these initiations.[64]

The Poro prepared Mende boys to attend to the needs of their spouses, families, and communities. Through training and ritualized initiation in physically isolated areas of nearby bush, elder men taught them how to provide and prepare their own food, how to complete rigorous work assignments, and the details of local law, custom, and ritual. They learned to hunt and fish, clear farmland, cultivate rice, and build and create tools, arts, and crafts such as baskets and nets. As social anthropologist K. L. Little explained, "To a large extent, the social life of the Poro bush approximates the social life of the larger community. In essence, the boys learn their roles as men in a miniature world of their own."[65]

As Mende girls approached puberty, their initiation into the Sande (very similar to the Bondu secret society in the Temne, who lived adjacent)[66] began and was sustained over several years, interspersed with periods of normal activity. During their training, they remained physically isolated, residing in a nearby wooded area. Elder Sande members assigned their charges new names and taught them ritual songs, dances, and family care, including their duties to children, husbands, family elders, and ancestors. They learned how to grow, harvest, and cook rice, corn, and other crops as well as to fish and prepare meats. As adults, women were expected to respect elders, to be modest and chaste, and to avoid contact with men until marriage. Nuptials occurred soon after completion of their period of instruction. Initiation into Sande also included clitoral circumcision. This entire process helped to build bonds between a cohort of Mende girls and their teachers, bonds that remained even if they left their villages after marriage.[67]

At the conclusion of initiation, both males and females wore gender-specific adult clothing. Men donned long cloths that covered most of their bodies, while women wore cloths wrapped from the waist down.[68] Mende girls and women, as well as some males, adorned themselves with necklaces, bracelets, and anklets made from string, beads, and shells. Tattoos cut into chests, torsos, and arms were popular. Males also enhanced their physical attractiveness by filing and extracting their teeth in various patterns. (Recall that Olaudah remarked on how this practice seemed so odd to him.) When one Mende male in North America was asked why he had sharpened his teeth so they stuck pointedly out of his mouth, he replied quickly, "to make the ladies love him."[69] Once their initiation into the Sande was complete and the bride-price accepted, females went to be with their bridegrooms.[70] Bau, a nineteenth-century enslaved man, was a rice farmer with a wife and three children before being kidnapped and shipped to the Americas. He explained that he had given ten pieces of cloth, a goat, a gun, and mats made by his mother to his bride's family when he married.[71]

While the Poro and Sande societies taught boys and girls how to assume their roles as adults in Mende communities, the Humoi society, headed by a woman, enforced the "rules of marriage and mating."[72] Among the Mende, Humoi society members, comprised of male and female divisions, regulated exogamy guidelines that determined who (according to one's family affiliations) one could or could not marry or engage with in sexual relations. Some of these rules forbade men from sexual relations with close patrilineal kin, the near family of any woman with whom he had been intimate, any female with whom his brothers had had relations, or a woman who had breastfed him.[73] These rules also barred men from sexual relations with females before they reached puberty and women who were pregnant or were nursing. No one was allowed to have sexual relations in the bush. Male siblings could not sit on the bed of female siblings, and vice versa. Men found guilty of "criminal connection" with women could be enslaved. The numerous and complex rules regarding proper sexual behavior also included restrictions regarding sexual hygiene. Women, for example, could not visit their parents on the same day that they had sexual relations, nor could they speak to or visit with any family member or member of the man's family until they washed after sexual activity. They also had to wash before touching food.[74]

Akan Peoples

Ashanti kinship groups, the largest ethnicity among the Akan in the Gold Coast, were matrilineal. According to famed anthropologist Meyer Fortes, their "lineage consists of all the descendants of both sexes by a known genealogy of a single known ancestress in the unbroken female line."[75] They lived together on the land ancestrally associated with them, and their lineage head (an elder male) was responsible for their well-being. This elder received bride-price payments for those lineage females marrying, had the final say on divorces, and presided at funerals.[76] Females headed some households, consisting of the female leader, her sisters, and all their children and sometimes their grandchildren. Despite being matrilineal, Akan families had close affiliation with their paternal line(s) of relations and had particular expectations of fathers and other males. Many male-headed households included their wives, their offspring, and perhaps a female in-law and her children.[77]

There usually was a relatively large amount of gendered social equality in families. Lineage heads sometimes had elder female assistants who helped to settle disputes and supervised female socialization, including attending to girls' moral training and organizing their puberty rituals.[78] Women were not politically or socially superior to men, but there was the Akan Queenmother (*ohemmaa*), a person of royal matrilineal descent chosen by both male and female senior lineage members. She and her court of very elite women could wield tremendous power, particularly over other females. Queenmothers supervised the moral lessons elder women gave to female members. They attended familial ceremonies, including those that ritualized weddings, birth, and puberty.[79] Queenmothers also addressed local social problems and crimes, such as rape, that affected women and men, and intervened in marital disputes, including accusations of adultery.[80] A few managed to become king when no "suitable" male heir to the throne was available.[81]

Like other western/central Africans, Akan peoples highly prized children. Family members considered it a great tragedy and shame not to have them.[82] Likewise, those women who bore many children garnered exceptional praise. The Ashanti believed that the closest tie within a family was between the mother and her children, and most children were born in their mother's birth home. There, the expectant mother had the benefit of care by her own mother and female kin. To be born there also tied the child to the mother's lineage.[83] The mother's brother served as the child's guardian, as is often the case in matrilineal societies. Maternal grandmothers also helped a great deal with rearing of grandchildren, allowing the mother to continue her agricultural work. Very young children, however, accompanied their mother to work, and they slept together. Mothers provided their children with food and clothing and were expected to make great sacrifices for them. They actively socialized their female children. Children were trained to convey respect and obedience and to be affectionate. Sons had to provide materially for their mothers.[84] Fathers established child paternity by naming the child on the eighth day after its birth and by caring for it.[85] Fathers, like mothers, also provided food and clothing. They were disciplinarians and especially were responsible for their sons' moral and civic upbringing.[86]

Akan girls married when they reached puberty, indicated both by the beginning of menses and the size of their breast. Their society expected female abstinence prior to marriage. In preparation for a girl's potential betrothal, older female kin accompanied her to a stream of water and administered ritual bathing. They also called on local deities to certify that she was prepared to marry. In some locales, this ritual included adorning the would-be bride with special jewelry, such as a bracelet made of white cord with three beads—white, gold, and black—as an indicator of her new status. In other areas, women streaked the girl's body with white coloring and dressed her in the most beautiful clothing and jewelry available. Even poor families made every effort to adorn the potential bride's body elaborately. They dressed her in silk, trimmed her hair with gold, and placed strings of beads around her neck, arms, ankles, and waist. Once they had completely dressed her, female peers paraded the wife-to-be through the streets. They sang of her maidenhood and indicated her availability for marriage. If she had not been promised as a child, suitors approached her family to gain their permission to marry. Once her parents agreed and the appropriate property was given to the bride's family, a public notification of the marriage took place, often with much pomp and circumstance.[87]

The marriage ritual was accompanied by a feast at the bridegroom's home with music, wedding songs, and dancing. Following the marriage night, the bridegroom, satisfied that his bride was a virgin, adorned her head, shoulders, and torso with dried clay. She was then paraded publicly again, accompanied by other young women who sang her praises. Her life as a wife began the following day.[88] Wives did not necessarily reside continuously with their husbands, but rules of female sexual allegiance to husbands were strict, except for very elite women. Typically, married women spent much of their time with their own lineage kin.[89]

Igbo Peoples

Olaudah Equiano wrote eloquently and in great detail of his family life, even though his recollections came some thirty years after his kidnapping. His description reflected a mid-eighteenth-century elite status before African traders kidnapped and sold him and his sister. Igbo of Olaudah's generation were a patrilineal society, with fathers responsible for family governance. Olaudah's father also was an esteemed elder who had a role on their village's male governance council.

Marriage was an important transition in a person's life, marked by ritual as were other important events such as naming and circumcision. Parents decided who their children would marry and made the arrangements for them to do so when they were young. Polygamy was allowed, but Olaudah could not recall any man married to more than two women. Once they reached the point of marriage, a feast was held, and the couple presented themselves to their families, friends, and villages. "In the midst of all their friends," Olaudah declared, the new husband announces that his bride "is thenceforth to be looked upon as his wife and that no other person is to pay any addresses to her." The declaration was spread throughout the area and the wife then withdrew, later to be taken by her parents to her husband's home, where another feast with both families in attendance celebrated her arrival. The bride's parents relayed blessings on the couple. Then "they tie[d] round her waist a cotton string of the thickness of a goose-quill," that only married women could wear.[90] It was then that the bride truly was considered a married woman. Her dowry, Olaudah remembered, typically consisted of land, bondspeople, cattle, household goods and agricultural tools that both sets of parents and other friends and relations gave. The husband's parents also gifted property to the bride's family. This contribution, often termed brideprice or bride-wealth, was not always of great importance, as anthropologist A. R. Radcliffe-Brown noted, and it would be a mistake to think of it as a "payment" for the woman. This gift was used sometimes to "replace" the daughter in her family by obtaining a wife for a family member, usually a brother of the woman who had married. A daughter was replaced by a daughter-in-law, as sister by a wife or sister-in-law, since, after marriage, the bride belonged to her husband's family. Bride-price did seal a marriage, and once received, the bride's family could not reclaim her, or access to her children, unless there was a divorce and the bride-price returned.[91] It also helped to stabilize marriages because wives did not want their families to have to pay the bride-price back if their marriages failed.[92] After these ritualized and real exchanges occurred, a celebratory festival ensued with bonfires, dancing, and music.[93] Olaudah indicated that specific music, dancing, and "poetry" helped to communally solemnize and seal these important familial events. Certainly, marriages were considered essential to the social integrity of families, clans, and communities. The Igbo expected wives to remain faithful to their husbands. Women found guilty of adultery, Olaudah added, could receive very harsh punishments and even death.[94]

Family compounds comprised a series of houses that might be separated from others by a fence or moat. Household members included the male head, wives, children, and enslaved men, women, and children. The larger the household, the larger the cluster of buildings that collectively, Olaudah recalled, sometimes resembled a "village." The male head of the family and his wives could both have day and night houses, the latter used as sleeping quarters. A husband's day house typically included two rooms—one to accommodate guests and the other for visitation of family members. There often was another separate building where he and his male children slept. The day house of the family's head was the most prominent and stood in the center of the compound, with those of his wives and their young children located to the sides of it. Societal taboo also required that women reside in a "little house made for" when they had their menses. They returned to their usual home after making an "offering" and "purification."[95] Bondspeople and their families also lived inside the compound.[96] All family members worked as agriculturalists to support their households. Women also traded in local markets. Both men and women could be armed for battle when necessary.[97]

The Igbo also considered deceased ancestors as part of their families and believed them to be always present as their protectors. The living attended to ancestral spirits by pouring out libations and placing food on the ground for them, along with offerings of animal and fowl blood. Olaudah's own mother, he recounted, would visit the tomb of her deceased mother daily to provide offerings, "cries and lamentations."[98]

In West Africa, the Igbo lived near other ethnic groups, including the Hausa and Yoruba. Ukawsaw Gronniosaw was born in the Kingdom of

Bornou in northeastern Nigeria in about 1705. He may have been Hausa or Kanuri. Gronniosaw initially was enslaved at the age of fifteen on the Gold Coast, but later was sent to Barbados, where traders sold him twice to men who resided in New York City. Like the Senegambian Ayuba Sulieman Diallo (Job Ben Solomon), Gronniosaw was royalty—the grandson of a king—and raised as a Muslim.

In his autobiographical account, *A Narrative of the Most Remarkable Particulars in the Life of James Albert Ukawsaw Gronniosaw, An African Prince, As Related by Himself* (1770), he described family life in his home, where both blood and marriage defined one's kinship. Gronniosaw never forgot his family in Bornou, particularly his parents, his grandparents, and his favorite sister. His depictions of his West African family and community, again like those of Dialllo, are those of tight-knit, highly structured, stratified social and cultural institutions in which individuals knew their station and how to behave in it. In Gronniosaw's family, power located at the pinnacle of his family was held by his grandfather, the king, then flowed downward to his father, mother, older siblings, and finally to servants. His was a rich social world where children had to obey their elders and, in turn, parents and older kin supported their offspring materially and emotionally. Family members were close, and while children could not question their parents, mothers and fathers were not tyrants. As the youngest of six children, Gronniosaw felt particularly attached to his mother and believed she favored him. The values and behaviors of his larger Bornou community mirrored those of his family. Friends were supposed to be kind and loyal, while community members were expected to demonstrate public respect for operative political and social hierarchies. They worshipped and marked other important communal events together.[99]

Yoruba Peoples

Like the Igbo, the Yoruba were patrilineal and had other similar kinship traditions. Family, according to Yoruba scholar Oluwaseun Foluso Phillips, "was the most sacred and important institution among the Yoruba. "It is," he added, "the most effective agent of socialization where children are taught lessons in honor and shame to become an omoluabi (a well-rounded, honest, responsible, respectful, and respectable individual)."[100] Polygamy existed, and each wife had her own house in close proximity to her husband's quarters.[101] Males typically slept in the same quarters. Families were hierarchical, and adults, especially elders and ancestors, were respected and deemed responsible for the well-being of all members. As in most cultures, different family members were tasked with varied arenas of responsibility to kin and the larger society. The Father (*baba*) controlled much of the family business, including handling of disputes that might arise from adultery, infertility, personality, spousal incompatibility, and co-wife rivalry.[102] The eldest male (*baale*) sometimes was responsible for sorting out problems among extended family members. The *olorin* (local leaders) handled family disputes that raised awareness at the district level, while the king (*Oba*) and his council settled particularly onerous family difficulties.[103]

Former Alabama captive Kossuala (Cudjo Lewis) recalled of his Benin family and village that O-lo-loo-ay, his father, was not considered wealthy but did have three wives. The first wife helped to choose her husband's additional spouses. Adultery was forbidden and husbands were expected to protect their wives from harm.[104] Kossula's mother, Ny-fond-lo-loo, was the second wife and he was her only child. The other co-wives had a total of twelve children. He fondly remembered growing up in his compound and playing with his siblings—wrestling, running competitions, climbing fruit trees, and hunting. As he grew older, the elders taught the boys how to hunt, choose a camp site and to fight.[105]

Yoruba peoples regarded women highly, particularly their role as mothers. There were even some examples of female Yoruba kings.[106] The traditional elevated status of mothers was taught both privately and publicly. Public instruction was a part of western Yorubaland's significant ritual events—the Gelede masquerade. As specialist Babatunde Lawal remarked, Yoruba gelede society's purpose, in part, was to "maintain good gender relations by advocating respect for motherhood within a patrilineal culture." It was necessary to do so because "preservation of humanity depends on the role of the female as mother" and because mothers had special powers that needed to be harnessed for societal good.[107] In particular, Gelede recognized the spiritual forces that older women, "our mothers," commanded.[108]

Yoruba, like most western/central African cultural/language groups, placed very high regard on marriage as the center of domestic life. Marriage provided sexual gratification, children, their care, and one's economic well-being. It demonstrated that a person was socially responsible. It also expanded one's kin network, uniting at least two extended families, not just the bride and groom.[109] During the initiation of the marriage ritual, female members of the groom's family identified potential brides for his parents to consider.[110] In order for a man to marry, his parents had to present the would-be bride's parents with a proposition for betrothal, sometimes through an intermediary. Her parents then decided whether to accept the proposal, usually consulting a diviner to gain an additional perspective. Once the prospective bride's parents acquiesced, they met the suitor. In the case of polygamy, the senior wife often acted as the intermediary.[111]

Elite families betrothed their daughters when very young, and girls were expected to remain virgins until marriage. Grooms also wanted their brides

Gelede Body Mask. Yorùbá. Gelede Body Mask, 19th century. Benin, Africa. Wood, paint, 49 1/2 x 22 x 15 1/2 in. (125.7 x 55.9 x 39.4 cm). Brooklyn Museum, Gift of Corice and Armand P. Arman, 1999.129.

to have come from upstanding families and to be of good character; that is, they wanted their wives-to-be to be chaste, obedient, agreeable, fertile, and hardworking.[112] The local babalawo, or priest, set the day for the wedding, which was an elaborate, expensive affair for the wealthy; simple and quiet for others. The groom or his intermediary presented the bride's family with three gift installments of items that might include cloth, yams, cowrie shells (currency), and kola nuts. Their payments had to be completed before the marriage took place. The bride was decorated with "scarified designs" on her face and body—also financed by her groom—shortly before the nuptials took place.[113]

Female family members and friends accompanied the bride while singing special wedding songs to the groom's home, where the wedding feast was held. (Some groups also had separate feasting at the home of the bride and the home of the groom).[114] At the end of the first day of the feast, a female relative of the groom, or the senior wife, provided evidence of the bride's virginity. A negative finding could send her back to her family and cause the return of the groom's family gifts. (Later in the marriage, such a finding also could result in the husband's claim of bride-wealth and custody of their children.)[115] Otherwise, the marriage feast continued the following day.[116] In polygamous marriages, the new bride initially lived with the senior wife so that she could bond with her and learn through her example. She also could visit her own family occasionally during the day. In addition to his bride-wealth payment, the husband was obliged to provide his in-laws with labor, typically agricultural or construction, once or twice annually.[117]

Kongo Peoples

Kongo peoples and other persons from western central Africa mostly were matrilineal and, to some extent, matrilocal—husbands customarily resided with their wives' families.[118] Matrilineal descent groups among Kongo peoples were sometimes referred to as "kanda,"[119] but kin affiliation was more "flexible" than this term suggests. The kanda connected the living with their deceased ancestors and the land they claimed generationally for agricultural purposes.[120] Individual descent connection, when not related to land use, was bilateral: that is, from both maternal and paternal ancestry. This permitted one to consider half siblings as "brothers" or "sisters" and father's brothers to be treated as "fathers." Individuals took a father's first name as their second name, indicating the male parent's importance. By the sixteenth century, historian Anne Hilton noted, the effect of both the growing slave trade and Catholicism had begun to increase the importance of patrilineal descent. Religious change also impacted naming patterns and discouraged polygamy. The Catholic elite began to use as second names, for example, the surnames of Portuguese nobles. By the seventeenth century, the Kongo preferred cross-cousin marriages between persons related through their mother's or father's kinship lines.[121] From the late seventeenth through the eighteenth centuries—the height of the slave trade—the concept of the kanda regained great significance.[122]

The process of acquiring a wife remained mostly the same through much of the Atlantic trade eras, although certainly, as with the other peoples surveyed here, there were significant disruptions in marriage and family life—ritually and practically—as the numbers of young people siphoned off into transoceanic and overland bondage schemes increased. The groom, with the permission of his parents and those of his potential bride, presented her with a gift that signaled his intentions. He also might give a present, perhaps regional cloth or wine, to her father. The girl, who typically was thirteen to fifteen years old, then entered premarital seclusion: anywhere from two weeks to four months. Gifts from the groom and the bride's brother made known that both families had some "ownership" in any child born to the couple. Divorce was not difficult to acquire in temporary unions or "trial" marriages.[123] Formal marriages included more rituals and much heftier exchanges of property and were not easily ended.[124] This type of commitment also could mean that the wife and her children would remain with the husband's family, but the children still would have to go to their guardian (wife's brother) once they reached puberty.[125]

As in most African cultural groups, gender roles for married Kongolese couples extended to daily labor. In largely agricultural societies, men cleared the brush and cultivated tree crops while women planted, weeded, and harvested. Men also built houses, made cloth, sculpted, ran ironworks, hunted, and conducted long-distance trading. Women cooked, cared for children, and performed other domestic labor. When possible, they also dived for marketable seashells and boiled saltwater to produce salt.[126]

VIOLENT CAPTURE

Marriageable-aged women were the largest group of females violently captured and brought to the Americas. But some children, like Phillis Wheatley, were also taken. Few of them could hope to experience the family rituals that older females remembered even after their shipment across the Atlantic. Their memories instead remained centered on the brutal disruptions that carried them away from all the love, protection, and inclusion they knew at such a tender age.

Phillis's contemporary Chloe Spear recalled that White traders had been hiding in the bush and jumped out, capturing her and some friends while they played. "Not withstanding the piteous cries and tears of these poor defenceless children," her biographer explained, "they were arrested by cruel hands, put in to a boat, and carried to the dismal Slave Ship, which lay off a few miles in the river."[127] Who were these stolen children and adults, forcefully taken from their kin and communities? And how were the identities of those who managed to stay behind in Africa altered once their loved ones "disappeared" to the Americas?

Teme was a young Mende girl who resided in Sierra Leone with her mother, older brother, and sister when a group of men attacked their home at

CHLOE AND HER PLAYMATES TAKEN CAPTIVE BY THE SLAVE-DEALERS.

Chloe and Her Playmates Taken Captive by the Slave-Dealers "Chloe and Her Playmates Taken Captive by the Slave-Dealers," 1832, in *Memoir of Mrs. Chloe Spear, a Native of Africa, who was Enslaved in Childhood, and died in Boston, January 5, 1815...aged 65 years by a Lady of Boston* (Boston: James Loring, 1832), frontispiece image. Courtesy of Documenting the American South, Libraries of the University of North Carolina, Chapel Hill.

night and took them all as prisoners. She became a part of the famed *Amistad* "cargo" and did not see her relatives again. Others aboard, most of whom were Mende and sold out of the slave fort of Lomboko, told similar stories of capture. Kidnappers stole the boy Kali, for example, off the street, without his parents or siblings. Ngahoni, a married man with a child, was taken by four men while he worked in his rice field, as was Ba-u. Grabeau was caught while traveling; so, too, were Cinque and Bartu.[128]

Broteer Furro vividly recalled the brutality that accompanied his capture, at the age of six and a half years, and his eventual sale to Rhode Island traders. His father, Saugum Furro, a prince of the cattle-herding Dukandara tribe, had offered help to protect a weaker group from a marauding army of several thousand whom Europeans had hired to capture people. Hoping to avoid an attack, Saugum paid a hefty ransom to the interlopers, but to no avail. They killed Saugum, burned his villages, and took all surviving hostages—Broteer, his brothers Cundazoo and Soozaduko, and the other village members—as captives. This army of slavers continued their attacks against various villages until they reached the town of Anamaboo on the coast of present-day Ghana. There, the fortunes of the slaving army reversed, and the resident community captured all, placing them in the local English slave castle for sale.

These events of the family's demise and enslavement remained vivid, frightening memories. "They then came to us in the reeds, and the very first salute I had from them was a violent blow on the head with the fore part of a gun, and at the same time a grasp round the neck," Broteer wrote of his capture. He also witnessed his father's robbery and then vicious torture and murder.[129]

Boyrereau Brinch resided in the Niger River Valley in Mali when he was enslaved at about age fifteen or sixteen in 1758.[130] Slavers captured him and many of his companions on the shore of the river, where they had been swimming and enjoying a day of water sports. Until his taking, he had "devoted parents," who, on that occasion, had "delighted in [my] vivacity and agility." According to Boyrereau, thirty or forty of the "pale race of Vultures" "waylayed" them, captured eleven (he among them), gagged them to hush their "screams" and "lamentations," and carried them by boat down the river, away from any hope of rescue.[131]

Eliza Evans, who was enslaved in the nineteenth century in Alabama, was one of the recipients of her grandmother's oral memories of her Atlantic slave trade capture and enslavement. The story traveled with the family as they moved across time and place. Eliza's grandmother "Gigi" was "a little girl 'bout eight or nine years old" out foraging for wood as part of her family's feast preparation when she was taken by "white men who went slipping 'round and would capture or entice black folks onto their boats." She tried to scream out, but the thieves placed a "stick in her mouth," which held it open so she could not be heard. By the time they got her to the boat, she was "so tired out" she could not act to defend herself or to escape. Her Middle Passage was estimated at four months. A John Mixon purchased her in Alabama and renamed her Gracie.[132]

While Broteer's trip to the coast was by foot, others, like Eliza's grandmother and Chloe, arrived in canoes. No matter the manner in which they came to be at the slave castles strewn up and down the African Atlantic coastline, their path there was incredibly cruel and destructive. Most took the last sight of their homes and families at the time of their capture or on the way to the coast. Boyrereau arrived four days after his taking at the coast in a state of physical and mental exhaustion—dazed, starved, confused, and frightened. "Gloom and horror" accompanied him throughout his trip.[133] He was placed in a ship's hold with other screaming, crying men, women, and children, the latter placed in another space where they uniformly cried for food, drink, and their parents.

By night, the traders had divided the captives into smaller groups and separated Boyrereau from his comrades. The next day, the kidnappers sailed to a nearby trading post, where both African and European merchants continued the trade and social mingling that ended only when the local traders, too, were drugged and enslaved. Boyrereau recalled that all the while this was happening, he thought constantly of his family and the life he was being forced to leave. He certainly was not alone in his misery. Even a seven-year-old boy, named Guy by his slavers, who was a goat herder before his kidnapping, lamented that his small siblings would die from starvation without him at home to provide for them, since his father already had been captured. Guy died during the Middle Passage and was thrown overboard. So, too, was an infant born of a "princess."[134] Slavers disregarded all manner of family ties that their "cargo" treasured so immensely.

They did, however, take notice of whatever wealth their captives had. Slavers stole African victims' clothing, jewelry, and any other items thought to be of worth. Boyrereau noted that "every thing of value was taken from us, and instead of gold rings, bracelets of gold beads, chains and jewels, we had an old piece of sail cloth tied round our waists."[135] Traders also demanded that their captives work aboard the Middle Passage ships under threat of whippings, starvation, dehydration, and even death. This was the fate of one of Boyrereau's first friends at sea, a teenage girl named Gow who had been taken with her small brother, Thry. They had been sent by their father from their home in Guinea to be educated in Mali but were taken as captives while there. One of the ship's sailors, who was responsible for enforcing labor quotas, beat Gow to death with a whip in front of her brother and the rest of the captives when her work did not suit him. Before her death, Gow, Thry, and Boyrereau bonded over their shared traumas and fears: their loss of family, their starvation and burning thirst, their inability to keep up with the impossible work quotas they had been assigned, Gow's fear that her brother would be sold away from her, and how pained she was that the slavers had stolen the golden bracelet that her grandmother, on her deathbed, had given to her so that she would always remember her. The teen died mourning her family and fearing the fate of her little brother.[136] "Thry," Boyrereau recalled, "went and laid his head upon her neck and said, 'Come Gow, don't cry any more, come get up, don't go to sleep and leave me awake, because I am so lonesome I cannot bear it, do wake up.' He cried over her corpse some time and then went to sleep upon the dead body of his sister and protector."[137]

Kossuala Cudjo Lewis, one of the Africans on the *Clotilda*, believed to have been the last slave ship to arrive in the United States before the Civil War, was nineteen years old when he woke up to find his village on fire and under attack by male and female warriors. Kossuala traumatized not only by the destructive fire and the loss of his family, but also by the beheadings of those who resisted enslavement, including his own leader. Upon his king's refusal to submit to the king of Dahomey, Kossuala recalled, "One woman soldier step up wid de machete and chop off de head of de king, and pick it off de ground and hand it to de King of Dahomey. When I think 'bout day time I try not to cry no mo'," the former captive recalled in the 1930s. "My eyes dey stop cryin' but de tears runnee down inside me all de time. I see none my family."[138]

Ottobah Cugoano likewise offered a harrowing and heart-wrenching account of the deception and disappointment he endured as his captors brought him closer and closer to the African coast. To keep him calm and cooperative, they offered Ottobah the possibility that he could return home or that they would contact his relations so that he could be rescued. As they marched Ottobah closer to the slave castle, he began to see others in shackles arriving too, his hope giving way to extreme anxiety. "After I was ordered out," he explained, "the horrors I soon saw and felt, cannot be well described; I saw many of my miserable countrymen chained two and two, some hand-cuffed, and some with their hands tied behind." His emotional state declined even more once his kidnapper left him at the castle: "I saw him take a gun, a piece of cloth, and some lead for me," Ottobah recalled, "and then he told me that he must now leave me there, and went off. This made me cry bitterly, but I was soon conducted to a prison [the basement of the slave castle], for three days, where I heard the groans and cries of many, and saw some of my fellow-captives."[139]

Perhaps Ottobah believed his physical bondage and emotional devastation while being held the slave castle were the extent of this new horror that had come to define his life. They were not. He soon learned that this was only the beginning. Each step deeper and deeper into his new status as an enslaved person bound for the Americas presented a new layer of terror and dread. "But when a vessel arrived to conduct us away to the ship, it was a most horrible scene" he confessed. "There was nothing to be heard but the rattling of chains, smacking of whips, and the groans and cries of our fellow-men. Some would not stir from the ground, when they were lashed and beat in the most horrible manner."[140] From the initial fort where he was held captive, traders took Ottobah and his peers to Cape Coast Castle, from where other bondspersons were being boarded on nearby ships. Ottobah watched and waited for an opportunity to send word back to his family of his fate, with some hope that they would be able to help him. But no such chance arrived, even though he was kept on a ship for several weeks just off the Gold Coast. One can only imagine the growing anxiety, fear, anger, and depression settling on him. "And when we found ourselves at last taken away, death was more preferable than life," he concluded.[141] Ottobah especially mourned the loss of his family.

Cape Coast Castle. *Cape Coast Castle, and Forts William, Victoria, and McCarthy, Gold Coast,* mid-nineteenth century, Albert and Shirley Small Special Collections Library, University of Virginia.

"Let it suffice to say," he recalled, "that I was thus lost to my dear indulgent parents and relations, and they to me. All my help was cries and tears, and these could not avail, nor suffered long, till one succeeding woe and dread swelled up another."[142]

Those rare family members taken together faced the continual threat of division, either by death or violent separation, before they were sold in the Americas. Broteer faced final parting from his kin in the British-owned slave castle at Anomabo. Olaudah Equiano, who was a friend to Ottobah years later in London, remembered vividly his brutal capture at age eleven with his sister and their eventual separation: "One day, when all our people were gone out to their works as usual, and only I and my dear sister were left to mind the house, two men and a woman got over our walls, and in a moment seized us both," he noted. "And without giving us time to cry out, or make resistance, they stopped our mouths, and ran off with us into the nearest wood." The single emotional comfort Olaudah and his sister found "was in being in one another's arms' that night and bathing each other with tears." But that reprieve did not last long. Olaudah's autobiography revealed his great loss on the second night of their capture: "My sister and I were then separated, while we lay clasped in each other's arms. It was in vain that we besought them not to part us; she was torn from me, and immediately carried away, while I was left in a state of distraction not to be described. I cried and grieved continually; and for several days I did not eat anything but what they forced into my mouth."[143]

Olaudah miraculously met his sister again briefly before he came to the Americas, when they both were enslaved in West Africa. He never saw any other family members. Still, his desire and deep need for family did not cease. Even before he arrived on the African coast, he reached out to others to try to establish a fictive familial bond. There were two families in which he was enslaved before coming to the Americas that struck him as like his own linguistically, with comparable domestic tools and duties, a female captor who reminded him of his own mother, and children who were about his own age. In one such family, he admitted, after about two months, "I began to think I was to be adopted . . . and was beginning to be reconciled to my situation."[144] It was not to be.

The greatest harm Chloe Spear and her friends experienced after capture was their realization of the loss of their "tender" mothers and "avenging" fathers who could not come to "alleviate their wretchedness." They hardly could imagine returning to the pleasant familiarity of their place of birth, the affirmation of their communal recreation and ritual, or the "fond embraces of their parents and brothers and sisters."[145] As the other millions mourned deeply of their immeasurable losses, so, too, did these girls cry for themselves. Later, perhaps as did Phillis Wheatley, they realized the pain their families too must have experienced from the numbing "silence" imposed by the architects of the transatlantic trade—as Chole noted, "the bitter wailings of a bereft mother, the deep anxiety of an afflicted father, the tender lamentations and suffused eyes of brothers and sisters."[146]

Kossuala recalled marching in the hot sun to the coast with other captives, having left behind scenes of all those killed in his village and forced to travel with victorious warriors who took the bloody heads of those slain along as their trophies. "Some got two, three head," Kossuala added. "Oh Lor' I wish dey bury dem! I doan lak see my people head in de soldier hands; and de smell makee me so sick."[147] Arriving on the coast, slavers placed Kossuala and the other captives in a barracoon, each "nation" its own individual temporary barracks. Kossuala had never before seen the ocean or White people. These mysteries, however, did not keep most from trying to form relations with those of like condition. "We not so sad now," he noted, "and we all young folks so we play game and clam up de side de barracoon so we see whut goin' on outside." There they stayed for three weeks. Their cautious ease disappeared when they were examined by White buyers in preparation for the Middle Passage. Kossuala noted that the buyers were determined to purchase equal numbers of males and females. "Den we cry," he added, "we sad 'cause we doan want to leave the rest of our people in de barracoon. We all lonesome for our home. We doan know whut goin' become of us."[148]

MIDDLE PASSAGE HORRORS

Children typically stayed in a segregated room in the ship's hold with adult female captives. Some may have been the infants or toddlers of the enslaved women on board, while some mothers had been forced to leave their children behind. If Phillis Wheatley was Wolof, she may have been able to locate other females of her ethnicity on her slave ship, since Wolof females were some of the most highly represented among the ethnicities that were enslaved.[149]

Did Phillis find a surrogate mother among them? Imagine the seven-year-old without kin in the dark, filthy, foul-smelling, disease-ridden slave hold. Or think of her above deck watching the rough waves and the sharks that followed slave ships across the Atlantic, jostled about by the bored crew, witness to the unceremonious ocean dumping of the dead, dying, or resistant. Travelling the 3,850 miles from her Senegambian world to a British colonial Massachusetts seaport would have been a nightmare that she would never forget and from which she would never completely wake or recover.

Records indicate that Phillis's Middle Passage was especially inhumane. First, it was long. The round trip the *Phillis* took from Boston to Africa and back was 240 days in length. Second, it was deadly; one-fourth of the captives onboard died during the voyage.[150] Third, as a girl child—one of several youth on board—Phillis would have received less than the minimal rations of food, drinking water, shelter, or medical attention that the more valuable male children and adult men and women would have garnered. The women and men, and even the children, would not have been able to retain more than a few of their physical cultural indicators beyond their hairstyles and facial and body markings, except for any beaded necklaces or arm and ankle bracelets that they were able to keep. Very few, if any, would have had clothing to wear until they were closer to the New World ports of sale. Phillis was not old or strong enough to fend off violent assailants or predators. Is it any wonder that she remained "sickly" for some time after her arrival in Massachusetts? No doubt she was physically, psychologically, and spiritually traumatized from all that she had seen, heard, feared, and survived on her Atlantic voyage.

Meanwhile, the older male captive Kossuala struggled to be on the same boat as his friend, Keebie. Having accomplished this goal, he immediately faced another challenge—the shame of being stripped of his clothing. "I so shame! We come in de 'Merica soil naked and de people say we naked savage." He remembered his Middle Passage as a time of humiliation, anguished desire for his loved ones, physical darkness, bodily weakness driven by hunger, and great thirst, along with his great fear of the howling Atlantic.[151]

Few other captive narratives from the Atlantic slave trade included as detailed account of Middle Passage horrors as Olaudah Equiano's. His first experiences seeing, and being on, a slave ship, in conjunction with his first interactions with the British crew, convinced the eleven-year-old that he had entered hell, or, as he described it, "a world of bad spirits."[152] His reactions devolved quickly from "astonishment" to "terror." Within a few hours after he was brought aboard, the crew had thrown him up into the air, tried to drug him with alcohol, and placed him in the ship's hold. There, Olaudah entered a world he could never have imagined. With "the loathsomeness of the stench, and crying together," he admitted, "I became so sick and low that I was not able to eat, nor had I the least desire to taste any thing. I now wished for the last friend, death, to relieve me."[153]

Olaudah did not kill himself, but this was not the last time he thought of doing so. Those who tried and failed to die by suicide, he soon discovered, received harsh whippings and were forced to stay chained below. He found himself wishing for the "meanest" form of slavery in Africa rather than what he experienced with the British. This new type of bondage that he was sold into meant he was to be whipped with each assertion of his own will, even the refusal of food.[154] "On my refusing to eat," he explained, "one of them held me fast by the hands, and laid me across I think the windlass, and tied my feet, while the other flogged me severely. I had never experienced any thing of this kind before."[155]

Indeed, some crew members threatened those captives who would not or could not eat with even more violent punishments, whipping them hourly until they complied. Alexander Falconbridge, a physician who served on eighteenth-century slave ships, offered harrowing details of such treatments. "Upon the negroes refusing to take sustenance," he testified, "I have seen coals of fire, glowing hot, put on a shovel, and placed so near their lips as to scorch and burn them," with the threat of forcing them to swallow the hot coals. Falconbridge also wrote of a "certain captain" in the slave trade who "poured melted lead on such of the negroes as obstinately refused their food."[156] They were punished for not eating, but commonly, they did not have enough to eat. Captives suffered from a lack of food and water from the time of their capture. Olaudah, Boyrereau, and others documented that most usually they did not receive enough food and the water was contaminated. Sometimes they begged for the fish left after the crew had eaten but were refused. Those who tried to steal food again faced severe flogging.[157] Indeed, slavers withheld food as another way to control resistant captives. One bondsman, for example, who had been a judge in his village, pled the cause of those enslaved, particularly the difficult ordeal of the little children who had been taken from their families—"look at those little fatherless children, whom you kidnapped from their parents—hear their cries, behold their sufferings"—and of their families' grief at their losses—"think of the bewailing of their bereft parents." The ship's captain responded to his plea for freedom and family reunification with a reduction of rations to only water and multiple whippings for all the enslaved on the ship. Their forced starvation, amended after the third day with the addition of one biscuit per day, remained in place for six days.[158]

Sylvia King was taken as a grown woman. She recalled her sale on the other side of the Atlantic after being captured, drugged, and placed in a ship's hold. Many entered and remained in the Middle Passage completely nude because they had been forced to undress before they boarded the slave ships. This was only one of several great humiliations endured.[159] Once in New Orleans, King was forced "on the [auction] block" and again shamefully displayed. "We was all chained and dey strips all our clothes off and de folks what gwine buy us comes round and feels us all over," she noted. "Iffen any de niggers don't want to take dere clothes off, de man gits a long, black whip and cuts dem up hard."[160]

These memories—part of the post-traumatic stress African captives enslaved in the Americas suffered for the remainder of their lives and across the generations—recalled the sheer violence—physical, psychological, sexual, and sensory—and the incredible bereavements of family and community that they endured. Falconbridge documented that many bondspeople "lost their senses" even before boarding the ship, but still were forced to go. "It frequently happens," he explained, "that the negroes, on being purchased by the Europeans, become raving mad; and many of them die in that state; particularly the women."[161] Falconbridge added that "while I was one day ashore at Bonny Bight of Benin I saw a middle-aged stout woman . . . chained to the post of a black trader's door, in a state of furious insanity. . . . On board a ship in Bonny River, I saw a young negro woman chained to the deck, who had lost her senses soon after she was purchased and taken on board."[162] Olaudah wrote with devastating clarity about the filth that all of the captives lived in while on board the ship. The scent itself was enough to cause a person to faint. The stale air in the ship's hold added to the stench, as did the rank odor of the "necessary pots," which children like him had to be careful not to fall into and drown. The number of sweating bodies was so many that Olaudah indicated it was hard for one to even turn and there always was a sense that there was not enough air for one to breathe.

Sickness was everywhere. Crews callously threw dead bodies overboard. Crying women and children added to sensory traumas. So, too, of course, did their sexual abuse. Officer and sailors both had complete sexual access to captives. Many women arrived in the Americas pregnant from rapes that had occurred sometime after their capture.[163] According to Falconbridge, ships' crewmen and officers were "sometimes guilty of such brutal excesses as disgrace human nature."[164] Ottobah concurred. According to him, "it was common for the dirty filthy sailors to take the African women and lie upon their bodies." The captive men could not help them resist their rapes—they "were chained and pent up in holes."[165] Boyrereau concurred, adding that "the sailors who were not provided with mistresses, would force the women before the eyes of their husbands. A sailor one day, forced the wife of a slave, by the name of Blay, before his face." Blay tried to retaliate by plotting a shipboard revolt that would return the captives to their homelands, but instead was betrayed by the ship's interpreter and badly whipped.[166]

Almost two million Africans died during the Middle Passage from a number of conditions—dysentery, malaria, smallpox, dehydration, starvation, scurvy, physical abuse, suffocation, and suicide.[167] Historian Colin Palmer, analyzing just an eight-year window in the late seventeenth century, documented that nearly a quarter of the captives transported by the Royal African Company to British colonies in the Caribbean and North America died before reaching their destination.[168] Even as late as the early nineteenth century, some slave ships had at least one-third of their cargo dead by the time of arrival.[169] Others were sick or diseased when marched off the ships for their first sale. An 1807 South Carolina Court of Appeals case (*Furman v. Miller*) provided details of a man who purchased for $200 an African female who died about six weeks later. According to Furman and the examining physician he hired, the girl demonstrated signs of a prolonged illness, perhaps dropsy (enlarged heart), which the doctor attributed to her not getting enough exercise during the Middle Passage. He elaborated that she "had a fever and a cough," and "was swelled."[170]

It is something of a miracle that any of the captives survived, even though the trade in African bonded workers was profitable enough for ships' captains and their crews to try to maintain their cargoes' physical and psychological well-being, at least minimally. Timothy Fitch, owner of the *Phillis*, instructed his captains that he wanted his "cargo" treated well enough that they would fetch a good price. Writing to Captain Peter Gwin, who was on his 1760 voyage to Africa that would result in the capture of Phillis Wheatley, Fitch ordered him to "let your slaves be well lookd after & Carefully Tended." Gwin was to make certain that the captives had plenty of exercise on the upper deck, that he kept "up Thare Spirretts" and that he had plenty of rice and water for the trip. Keeping up "Spirretts" typically meant forcing Africans to dance and sing, even while shackled. Writing from the seventeenth-century slaver *Hannibal*, Thomas Phillips noted, "We often at sea in the evening would let the slaves come up into the sun to air themselves, and make them jump and dance for an hour or two."[171] Slave traders might have been more successful in maintaining the health of their captives if they fed them better. For all his supposed "precautions," Fitch supplied only ten weeks of provisions for a trip that took at least fifteen.[172]

Fitch's top priorities were his bottom line and the safety of his vessel and crew. With every voyage, there was a reasonable fear of captive revolt, which was a relatively common occurrence. Fitch warned his captains "to be constantly Upon your Gard Night & Day & Keep good Watch that you May Not be Cutt of by Your Own Slaves/tho Neavor So Few on Board Or that you are Not Taken by Sirprize by Boats fro the Shore which has often ben the Case."[173] Enslaved Africans longed for their freedom and acted to reclaim it at every step. The viciousness they endured during capture and Middle Passage reinforced their desire to escape. Miraculously, some were able to escape and return to their families. Others perished in their attempts.

Cinque, the famed Mende leader of the 1839 *Amistad* shipboard rebellion, testified that his abuse during the Middle Passage fueled his determination to fight for his freedom. According to his court affidavit, he was treated inhumanely, at first "driven by force and put on board said vessel," where his hands were "confined by irons," and then starved—with not half enough to eat or drink, only two potatoes and one plantain twice a day and half a teacup of water morning and evening. Crew members beat him on his head and taunted him with the threat that a "white man would eat them when they landed."[174] Olaudah Equiano also feared that Whites would eat him, as did Ottobah Cugoano, who wrote: "I saw several white people, which made me afraid that they would eat me, according to our notion, as children, in the inland parts of the country."[175] He, too, was part of a planned revolt that, unfortunately, was betrayed by a few female captives who had allied themselves with some of the sailors. Not all the women, Ottobah made certain to explain, were traitors. Indeed, it was the bonded women and boys, because they had more freedom of movement on the ship, who had been tasked with burning the ship during the attempted revolt. The crew killed several who were implicated in the plot.[176]

Could family or community develop among the captives in such harsh environments as the forced march, barracoon, slave castle, or slave ship? The challenges are obvious, but their psychological and physical comforts, to say nothing of their identities, were so embedded in familial identity and experiences for most western/central Africans that many made attempts to establish such relations when and where they could. These phenomena perhaps were especially so for young captives such as Phillis Wheatley, Chole Spear, Boyrereau Brinch, and Olaudah Equiano.

While we have no documentation describing Phillis's personal Middle Passage experiences, except for the horrifying mortality statistics and indicators of starvation from her particular voyage, Chloe's narrative certainly documents her intimacy with the girls with whom she was kidnapped and with whom she was able to remain throughout her Middle Passage. They all likely were taken care of by some of the captive women on the ship, allowing some kin-like attention. Likewise, Chloe's account revealed the great emotional pain she felt at her loss when her friends from home were sold in Philadelphia, while she was sent on to Boston.[177] Despondent, confused, and feeling hopeless, she, like others, contemplated suicide, "supposing that when she died, she should return to her country and friends."[178]

Olaudah's autobiography documents his attempts to remain with his family relations and, failing that, his desire to create kin-like relations with others. Once inside the slave ship's hold, his attempts reemerged. There, he found some of his "own nation" which "eased" his mind somewhat because they were able to explain to him that they all were going to another place to work. They, both males and females, undoubtedly formed the core of Olaudah's fictive kin group onboard the ship. This was not to last. Like Chole, Olaudah explained that once they arrived at their first American place of sale—Barbados—purchase by different buyers meant a loss of friendships and fictive kin that he had forged during Middle Passage: "I now totally lost the small remains of comfort I had enjoyed in conversing with my countrymen; the women too, who used to wash and take care of me, were all gone different ways, and I never saw one of them afterwards."[179] Kossuala recalled that when his group of captives first arrived and were bought by different persons, "we very sorry to be parted from one 'nother. We seventy days cross de water from de Affica soil, and now dey part us from one 'nother. Derefore we cry. Our grief so heavy look lak we cain stand it. I think maybe I die in my sleep when I dream about my mama."[180] Boyrereau also testified to this new misery—the loss of his fictive kin through sale. These were the people with whom he had sang, worked, cried, and been comforted, with whom he had figured out what was coming next in the horror that was their new enslaved lives and how to survive it.[181]

As Olaudah, Chole, Boyrereau, and others indicated, fictive kin relations did develop during the Middle Passage, as men and women shared information regarding their destinies and expected roles in the New World and as females took care of the ill and young among them. This was possible not only because of the seminal importance of family and community, but also because of the shared languages and cultures of many who found themselves bound together. Olaudah could speak with many of the captives he encountered and quickly learned the languages of the others.[182] "Family" communications would be different once he reached his place of enslavement.

Transshipments, such as those experienced by Chloe and Olaudah, also had meaning for those who had arrived at an earlier date but were sold again to another island or to North or South America or were forced back from one of the mainlands to the Caribbean. The trade to the sugar islands from mainland colonies typically resulted when an enslaved person was found guilty of a crime. Deemed too valuable to kill as punishment, they were sold by courts as convicts to other locations. The mulatto Lewis, for example, left whatever family and friends he had in Maryland in April 1692, when the court stayed his death penalty for being found guilty of theft in order to have him "bound for Barbadoes" where he was to be "sold and disposed of there to the most advantage."[183]

While most who survived the brutality of the Middle Passage suffered the loss of their African kin forever, there were a few examples of "elite" captives, particularly those who were slave traders themselves, who managed to return to their families of birth. Ayuba Suleiman Diallo (Job Ben Solomon) complained bitterly of his lack of community once he reached the Catholic Chesapeake colony of Maryland in the early 1730s. Chief among his concerns involved two important missing attributes of kinship and community: his capacity to communicate verbally with others and his ability to worship as a Muslim. Eventually, Diallo was able to locate and speak to a local African elder who knew the Jallof language, affording Diallo the opportunity to at least tell his story. Still, Diallo found little chance of forming a family or a community and did not want to do so. He only wanted to return to his family in Bundu (Senegal). His wealthy father had contacts in the Atlantic slave-trading world, affording Diallo the rare opportunity to be taken to England. There, he succeeded in raising money for his sale price (another rarity) and was able to return home—a miracle by any stretch of the African captive's imagination.[184]

Captain John Thompson of York County, Virginia, purchased captive Efik cousins Ephraim and Ancona Robin John, members of an elite slave trading family from Old Calabar (Nigeria), in 1767. Taken and shipped from the Bight of Benin, they were first sold to Dominica. From there, Ephraim and Ancona were transshipped to Charleston and bought by Thompson, whom they served as sailors and domestics on his schooner. Although the cousins had managed to stay together during their Middle Passage and transshipments to South Carolina and then Virginia, Thompson proved to be a cruel enslaver. There is little doubt that their ability to speak English, their familiarity with the slave-trading business, and certainly their Atlantic world family ties helped them to survive their bondage.[185]

Ayuba Suleiman Diallo (Job Ben Solomon). William Hoare of Bath, Ayuba Suleiman Diallo called Job Ben Solomon, Oil on Canvas, 1733, OM.762, Courtesy of Qatar Museums / Lusail Museum, Doha – Qatar.

Their kinship brought them relief and comfort; still, they experienced slavery as painful and frustrating. Ancona wrote that Thompson "would tie me up &whip me many times for nothing at al[l] then some times be Cause I could not Dress his Diner for him not understanding how to do it... he was exceeding badly man ever I saw."[186] Their five years in Virginia did not lessen the cousins' desire to return home. Their privileged lives in West Africa kept alive their strong belief that they would be able to do so. Soon after their enslaver's sudden death, they were recognized by African sailors from their home country who worked on the slave ship *Greyhound*, which was then in port. The *Greyhound*'s captain offered to take Ephraim and Ancona home if they could escape to his ship.[187]

They escaped, but their plan did not unfold as anticipated. On the way back to Old Calabar, the *Greyhound* stopped first in Bristol—one of England's most active slave-trading ports.[188] They described their second "Middle

Passage" as a "writched transport" of two weeks.[189] The cousins remained in England for two years, trying to claim their freedom through the assistance of a business partner of their family, Thomas Jones. Ephraim and Ancona's case eventually went before the English courts and was heard by Chief Justice Lord Mansfield. The court determined they were free. Both eventually traveled back to Old Calabar, but not before they were converted to Christianity. At least one of the cousins again became active in the slave trade as part of his family's business enterprises.[190]

It is the cruelest of ironies that many slave-trading families, European and African, benefited—and still benefit today—from the devastation, division, and destruction of so many western/central African families, and as a consequence, contemporary Black families in the Caribbean, the Americas, and the wider diaspora continue to have second-class citizenship and are subject to systemic discrimination across all aspects of their lives.

Chapter 2

The Colonial Enslaved Family
Foundations and Creations

When I think of home, I think of a place where there's love overflowing.[1]

EARLY BONDSPEOPLE AND FAMILY: THE 1619 EXAMPLE

Angela arrived in Virginia on the *Treasurer* during the summer of 1619. An Angolan woman, whose name at birth and the other details of her family life have been lost to history, she would have been one of the several African females brought to the first permanent British colony in North America. Family was narrowly possible for this first cohort of matrilineal descent Africans. Yet evidence indicates that marriages, families, and fictive kinship ties did develop.

In August 1619, two small groups of Africans, probably Kimbundu speakers from the Kingdom of Ndongo, arrived at Point Comfort on Virginia's southeastern coast.[2] They had started out together from Luanda as a group of 350 on the *São João Bautista*. Some two-thirds died in the Middle Passage. The *São João Bautista* had nearly reached its destination of Vera Cruz when attacked by privateers on the *White Lion* and the *Treasurer* in the Gulf of Mexico. England's Virginia, a colony of only twelve years, along with Bermuda, were known landing sites of early seventeenth-century British pirates who regularly attacked Spanish cargo ships. When the *White Lion* docked at Point Comfort, it carried about twenty Angolans whom the buccaneers sold for supplies.[3] The *Treasurer* arrived a short time later and traded some of their captives, including the woman, Angela. They sold the remaining people across the Spanish and British colonies, trading twenty-four boys in Jamaica. Others went to Vera Cruz and beyond.[4] Several months later, Virginia's

"Slaves harvesting tobacco in Virginia," c. 1670. Unknown artist, public domain, via Wikimedia Commons.

first census documented thirty-two Africans in residence—fifteen women and seventeen men. All are believed to have arrived as part of those pirated cargoes.⁵

These Africans found themselves in a foreign land inhabited by peoples of at least two distinct and hostile societies. They were strangers among strangers in a contested space thousands of miles away from their homes. Beyond Jamestown and the other fledgling colonial British settlements in North America were towns inhabited by large numbers of Indigenous peoples in the Powhatan Confederacy.⁶ The Powhatans, some fifteen thousand of them, dominated—spatially, militarily, and in actual numbers—the lands that bordered Virginia's rivers and the great Chesapeake Bay.⁷ They were an organized people who had societal norms they deemed worthy of protection. So, too, did the British and the Africans, who had come from developed societies of their own. Neither group was poised to abandon their ways of life, including their ideas, ideals, and practices of family. Indeed, Africans had no intention of giving up the experience of family, even as a racial hierarchy set in over the next several decades that meant English enslavement of both Blacks and Indigenous people.

All had to make adjustments. Some took place quickly, others more slowly. White immigrants mostly were males who faced, for decades, a lack of adult Christian females necessary to create heterosexual marital relations. Even when they did marry, high death rates wreaked havoc on these relationships and families. Africans lacked both substantial numbers of persons and, increasingly by the end of the seventeenth century, many marriageable females. Both Europeans and Africans married among their "own," but also extended their social contacts, sexual relations, and marriages across racial, ethnic, and class lines. Miraculously, Isabel and Antonio, who arrived in 1619, married (or were already married when they arrived) and managed to gain their freedom from the man who claimed them, Captain William Tucker. They had and baptized their son in Jamestown.[8] Some of their descendants still live in Hampton today, the site of their arrival from Africa.[9]

Others found themselves scattered across early colonial landscapes with distances between work sites beyond the walking, or swimming, abilities of most—at least in the few leisure hours slaveholders permitted. Some Africans longed for years for the wives, husbands, children, parents, siblings, and other kin and communities that enslavers forced them to leave. Language and other significant cultural differences, such as religion, influenced their choices of new family ties. Fully one-third of African captives were Islamic in faith, others had been introduced to Catholicism, and some quickly converted to Protestant practices since doing so might permit freedom (at least until 1667) or even more family protections.[10] The majority, however, adhered to other religious beliefs. These were linked to different attitudes about family structure and identity, composition and governance: some that captors and culturally distinct captives would understand or allow, others that might have proven to be irreconcilable and unsanctioned.

Health concerns also had serious impact on one's ambitions to create a family in the Americas. Arriving from Middle Passage probably ill,[11] all captives suffered high rates of morbidity, mortality, and the typical threat of Indigenous retaliation and dangers of frontier life that resulted in their shortened life spans. Historians T. H. Breen and Stephen Innes noted, for example, that "before 1680 the life expectancy in the Chesapeake colonies for a migrant was only about forty years." Most marriages among those who were fortunate enough to have a partner did not last even ten years because of the death of one of the spouses. The chance of a couple nurturing to adulthood any children was just as bleak—50 percent of children born of these marriages died before they reached age twenty.[12]

The social modifications these gruesome conditions caused, however, did not mean loss of the central importance of family to an African captive's identity or of the bondsperson's perception of family as foundational to their community's development and survival. North American captives maintained the idea of family as essential, as evidenced in their attempts to create and sustain kin relations in settler colonies—as they already had done on their forced march to the African coast, in the dungeons of the slave castles, and in the holds and decks of ships during Middle Passage. Documentation from court records, legal statutes, slave sales and lists, family wills and inventories, fugitive advertisements, and church and census records indicate that, from the first years of enslavement onward, Africans in North America created family in various configurations. Having survived the horrors of capture and violent transport to the Americas, why would they relinquish family just as they settled into what must have seemed like a more stable—albeit brutal—lifestyle than what they had been forced to endure since their taking? These familial manifestations were very diverse, including nuclear, matrifocal, and extended households; residential and abroad living arrangements; blood, marital, and fictive kin networks; and marriage practices that included monogamy, serial monogamy, and polygamy.

The very first Africans to Virginia were small in number but almost equally male and female. Their gender parity, shared languages and cultures, and claim by a small number of elite men who continued to increase their captive labor force allowed for localized communities to develop. These conditions, along with English Virginia's delay in passing laws that firmly relegated the African captive as "slave," encouraged within these communities some marriages and the beginning of foundational kin networks.

The 1619 shipments were mostly comprised of the Ambundu, who had been kidnapped during a series of violent raids that Portuguese forces mounted in present-day Angola between 1618 and 1620. They likely were from matrilineal societies in the "royal district" of the Kingdom of Ndongo. Fifteen of those kidnapped Kimbundu speakers went to live and work for Britain's most powerful and wealthy resident in the colony, Governor George Yeardley, at his one-thousand-acre frontier estate known as Flowerdew Hundred (present-day Prince George County). Angela became the property of another elite member of this colonial community, William Pierce of Jamestown.[13] The rural nature of Virginia at the time, with its very thin population, would have been a definitive change for these captives. Flowerdew Hundred had only sixty residents in 1624. The Ambundu mostly were an urban people, living in and around a group of cities, some as large as twenty to thirty thousand residents.[14] They had an ethnic identity based in part on their shared language, culture (including family practices and ideals), political affiliations, and perceptions of themselves as "people of the court."

Angela's home society had a variety of classes and occupations, including farmers, skilled metalworkers, potters, cloth makers, royal servants, and royal persons. Unless of a particularly high class, most would have known a great deal about the kind of agricultural work they were made to perform in Virginia. Even Ndongo urban dwellers used hoes to work the land, removed weeds, and practiced crop rotation when they cultivated grains like millet and sorghum. They raised cattle, goats, chickens, sheep, pigs, and other livestock.[15] Some probably had been introduced to Catholicism and would not have found the religious beliefs and practices of Anglican English colonists very unfamiliar. As the expert John Thornton noted, "By 1619, a

Woman Hoeing, c. 1687. João António Cavazzi de Montecúccolo, *Descrição Histórica dos Três Reinos do Congo, Matamba e Angola* (Lisbon: Junta de Investigações do Utramar, 1965), 39.

Kimbundu-speaking Christian community existed in Angola" which "quite possibly" included those who arrived in Virginia in 1619.[16]

African captives did not automatically abandon these long-standing customs once they reached the colonies in order to completely assimilate the kinship relations and obligations they observed when they came into contact with Indigenous peoples and Europeans. They creatively maintained essential ideas and ideals of family life, some drawn from the rich and diverse kinship traditions of western and western central Africa, surveyed earlier. Among those most visible and lingering traits were the reverence of ancestors and elders; the recognition of extended kin, whether derived from singular or multiple spouses; and certain gender prescriptions. Gendered roles for females included premarital female purity and postmarriage sexual loyalty, the significance of the mother/child bond, and a wife's responsibilities as housekeeper, farmer, and provider of income and goods earned in local markets. Fathers and senior male family members held leadership, disciplinarian, and protective roles. Of course, colonial Blacks' familial experiences also came about in part as responses and resistance to their social, material, economic, cultural, medical, religious, and legal deprivations as enslaved people. Records of their "kin-work"—that is, bondspeoples' earnest efforts to form and maintain family—creates a window into this aspect of enslaved Black life in colonial America.

An African captive named Mary who reached Virginia in 1622 came to marry Anthony (known as Antonio a Negro), who arrived the year before.[17]

By 1625, Mary (who had married by then) was the only woman residing on the plantation where she worked, indicating the difficulty captives had finding a spouse with whom they could live on a full-time basis. Mary and Anthony, who have the surname Johnson in court records, eventually had four children (two daughters and two sons), all of whom lived to be adults. Their remarkable relationship is a marker of rare marital success. The two not only remained husband and wife for more than forty years but managed to gain permanent freedom and even to acquire 250 acres of land. Like their British neighbors, this family farmed, raised livestock, and even acquired Black bondspeople whom they claimed as their own. Their grandson, John Jr., named his farm at Somerset, Maryland, for his kin's ancestral homeland: Angola.[18] There is little doubt that their lasting cultural affiliation with Angola was in part due to the arrival of other captive cargoes from their place of birth. Six years after Mary arrived, the sailors on the English ship *Fortune* pirated one hundred Africans from Angola and brought them to Jamestown, where they were sold for tobacco.[19]

Mary and Anthony were not the only Black bonded workers who created family ties. But not all kin relations were like theirs: structured as nuclear or even extended ties based on marriage. Living among them was an African man named John Graweere, who paid for the "freedom" of his child by an African woman. There is no further documentation that he married or even had a lasting relationship with the mother of his child. He kept the child himself and, along with the child's godfather, raised him or her to be a Christian.[20] Angela, on the other hand, did not have a documented family in Virginia. There is no indication in census, baptismal, or her enslaver's family notes or correspondence that she ever married or had a surviving child.[21] The enslaved family's invisibility in the archive, however, does not document its absence. Angela could have been married, had a female partner, and/or had a stable sociosexual relationship that remained unrecorded. It certainly is possible that she had friends in the local African community as well as among the indentured White workers with whom she worked.[22]

ENSLAVED BLACK COLONIAL POPULATIONS IN NORTH AMERICA

Across the decades of the colonial era, Virginia remained a ground zero of sorts for slave society in North America. It imported the largest numbers of Africans and maintained the largest population, Black and White, during the colonial era.[23] By 1650, there were three hundred Black residents. While most were bought to live and work on farms and in households that included only one or a few Black captives, others resided on expansive estates like that of

Captain Samuel Matthews, who claimed forty Africans.[24] Twenty years later, the Black population, most of it enslaved, had swollen to two thousand, and many, except those who had arrived just recently, had created families.[25] Virginia was the center of North American slavery, but certainly not the only site of it. Along the Chesapeake Bay and southward through the Carolinas, Black slavery took hold in the British colonies. The institution already was in place by the time they acquired former Dutch colonies that included New York and New Jersey. By the end of the seventeenth century, as well, Massachusetts slave traders were selling African men, women, and children to Virginia and the other British colonies all along the mainland's coast, including locally. Massachusetts claimed only 170 enslaved Africans in 1680, but that number rose to 1,250 in 1720 and 4,100 in 1750.[26]

The British, and the Africans forced to work for them, therefore, were not the first White or Black peoples to settle on the continent. The French, Spanish, and Dutch set up colonies, too, as part of their New World empires, some before and others while the British were doing so. They likewise bought and brought with them kidnapped Africans and Indigenous peoples whom they forced to work for them, although the British imported more. None of their plans for those they enslaved prioritized family life over labor demands.

As early as the mid-1550s, the French initiated temporary colonies near present-day Charleston, South Carolina, and Jacksonville, Florida. They also constructed a series of small fortifications in what would become Tennessee and North Carolina.[27] As part of their enormous claim of land that extended from the Hudson Bay southward, the French settled in the Gulf of Mexico during the late 1600s, establishing mercantile and agricultural settlements in and around the lower Mississippi River. Their first shipment of Africans there purportedly came in the second decade of the eighteenth century. Historian Ronald Davis noted that "the first evidence of African-Americans in Natchez dates from around 1720, when black slaves were brought into the area by the French."[28] The Natchez District of West Florida included present-day Mobile and Biloxi, as well as smaller Mississippi River villages between Point Coupee and Baton Rouge. John Law, with the Company of the West, was to develop the area with enslaved Black labor expected to produce exportable tobacco and indigo, to build forts, and to work in the fur trade.[29] The French exploited and traded just as readily Indigenous peoples extensively in other parts of their New France territories.[30]

Historian Tiya Miles indicated that the first African to arrive on the St. Lawrence River Valley was a boy, perhaps from Guinea or Madagascar, purchased by a French trader from an English corsair in about 1628. It would be a century before the French brought other Africans to this land. Imagine the terror and great yearning for kinship that this single African boy endured through the loss of his family of origin, his pirated Middle Passage

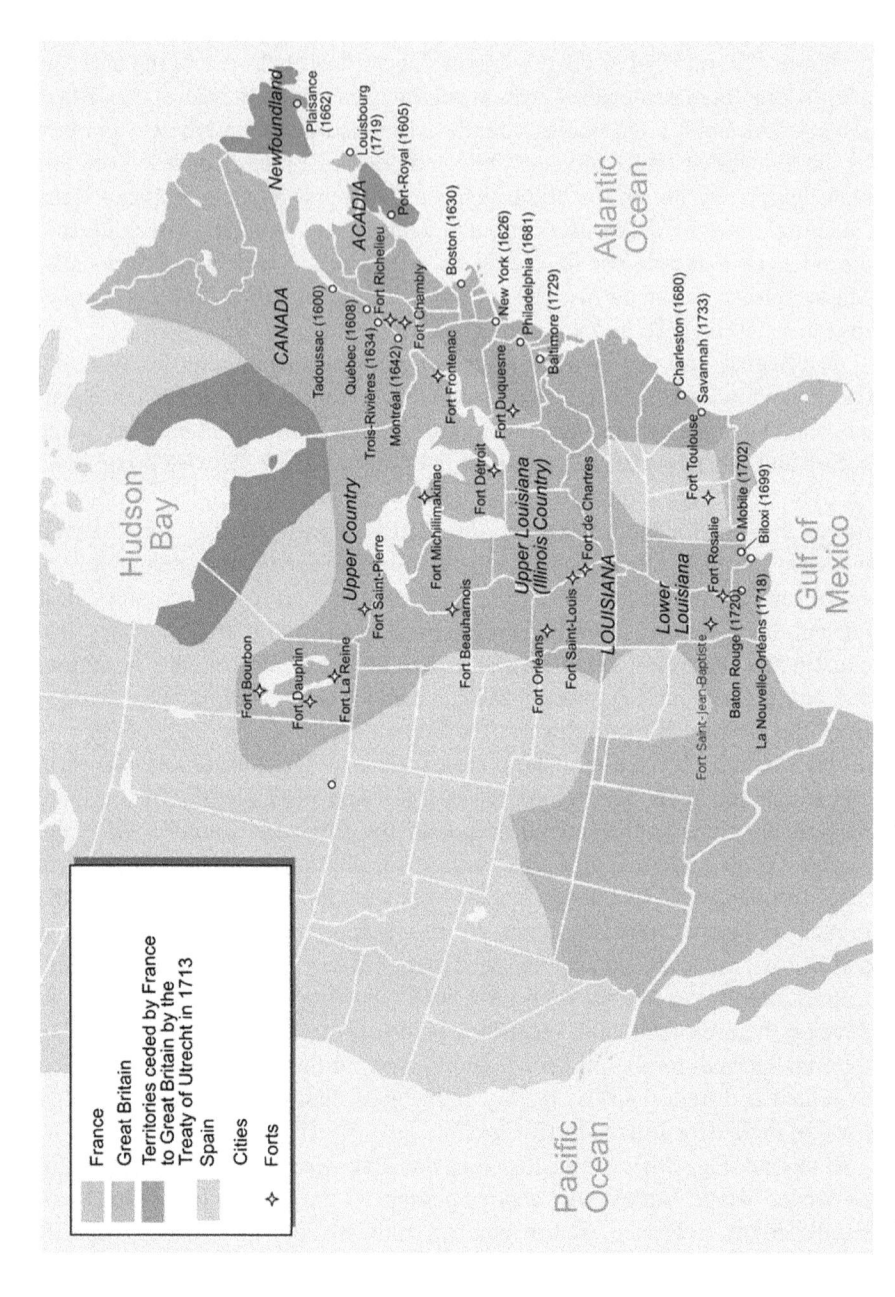

North America, 1650-1750. Pinpin, CC BY-SA 3.0 <https://creativecommons.org/licenses/by-sa/3.0>, via Wikimedia Commons.

experience, and his forced settlement in a foreign land that held no possibility of him ever seeing another person of like culture, or even appearance, for the remainder of his life.[31] One can only hope that, as happened with other extremely isolated Africans in North America, he was able to create family relations among the Indigenous or French traders and settlers he encountered. Over the next two hundred years, fewer than fifteen hundred Black bondspeople appear to have resided in this French territory—some undoubtedly traded from the French Gulf and Caribbean.[32]

Even before France, Spain started to settle parts of North America during the first decades of the 1500s. Contact with Africans and their exploitation on the Iberian Peninsula as laborers, bonded and free, began during the eighth century. Africans had a substantial presence in southern Spanish cities by the thirteenth century.[33] They socialized across racial lines, created family relations through common law and legal marriages, and converted to Catholicism or maintained their Islamic faith (until 1492 at least) and other Indigenous cultural practices. Free Africans in Spain also paid taxes, worked as merchants and craftsmen, owned property, and even had administrative oversight of their communities as *mayorales*. Spain's African residents established confraternities (charitable organizations), and the Catholic Church even created two Black parishes.[34] Urban captives could live away from their slaveholders and often had an unusual amount of autonomy. This "history" of Africans in Spain, Jane Landers explained, had some influence on the status of African captives in the Spanish American colonies. They certainly used Africans in their "discovery" voyages to the Americas. The Portuguese, unlike the Dutch, British, and French, had similar experiences with Africans as the Spanish, especially in Lisbon and other locales, before colonizing the Americas.[35]

Juan Ponce de Léon claimed Florida for Spain in 1513, with at least two African explorers in his company: Juan Garrido (Angolan) and Juan Gonzalez.[36] Beginning in 1540, explorer and conquistador Hernando de Soto traveled through what would become the Lower South, bringing numerous captive (and some free) Africans with him and enslaving the Indigenous people he encountered. One descendant of two such bondspeople was Bob Samuels of Arkansas. According to Samuels's oral history that had passed down to him through his maternal ancestors, his forebearers traveled from Spain to Cuba and then throughout Florida, the Lower South, and parts of the southwest with de Soto.[37] Likewise, Admiral Pedro Menéndez de Aviles created a Spanish fort at St. Augustine in 1565 as well as other settlements in what would become North and South Carolina and Tennessee. Spanish immigrants, Catholic priests, Blacks, and some Indigenous people came to build and live in St. Augustine and neighboring Fort Mosé, towns they maintained for more than two hundred years.[38]

Lisbon c. 1570. Berardo Collection Museum, Public domain, via Wikimedia Commons.

Indeed, Gracia Real de Santa Teresa de Mosé, otherwise known as Fort Mosé, an agricultural community with a military component in northeast Spanish Florida, became an early permanent settlement of free people of color and their families in what would become the United States. The Spanish supported the fort's settlement because its Black and multiracial inhabitants provided labor and military protection to St. Augustine against the British, French, and Indigenous neighbors, all opposed to Spain's expansive land claims.[39] The fort's Black residents benefited from a 1693 decree by King Charles II of Spain that offered religious sanctuary, via conversion to Catholicism, and freedom to escaped male and female captives, many of them Africans, from British colonies. Legal sanctuary for these freedom-seeking people was possible until 1790.[40] Spanish men and women still could import Black captives for their own use. Indeed, Spain did not abolish the African slave trade to the colonies until ten years after the British.[41]

Regardless of Spain's own political and military agendas, many of the enslaved people who managed to escape to Florida were able to find freedom and family in this contested Spanish colonial sanctuary. Roderick McIver and John Forbes of South Carolina believed this was the plan of their four bondsmen—Whan, Jack, Isaac, and Christopher—who escaped in 1763. Advertising in the *Georgia Gazette*, they noted that "they are all supposed to be gone toward Georgia and St. Augustine."[42] Fort Mosé's residents, like those in other Spanish American colonies, created families—there were thirty-eight kin units in 1739—and a solid, multiracial community that included Africans, Spaniards, Indigenous peoples, other Europeans, and creole Blacks.[43] The Indigenous among them could not be formally enslaved, as a result of a Spanish decree of 1524.[44] The combination of their free status and the lack of Black women among the runaways who safely made it to Fort Mosé meant that "males of that group were forced to look to the local possibilities for marriage partners—either Indian women . . . or free and slave woman from St. Augustine."[45] Indeed, Kathleen Deagan argued that "native women were the primary agents of change in Spanish colonial society," because the biracial children born to them technically were free.[46] Their extended families were comprised of mixed-race people with mixed legal status. Juan, the son of Carolina refugees to Fort Mosé named Juan Jacinto Rodriguez and Ana Maria Menendez, for example, married a Mandingo enslaved woman known as Cecilia. Cecilia's sister-in-law, Maria Francisca, married a free Black man originally from Cartagena, Colombia. When he died, Maria Francisca married the former Congo bondsman Thomas Christomo. They were close friends to Pedro Graxales, another Congo captive, and his wife, Maria de la Concepcion Hita, a Caravali (Igbo) bondswoman.[47] Little by little, families and kinship networks evolved to create close-knit communities in Spanish Florida as in British Virginia.

In 1528, Estevanico (also known as Esteban the Moor), an enslaved man originally from Morocco, arrived with his Spanish "master" near present-day Galveston. Sold in 1513 as a child by Portuguese traders without parents or any kin, Estevanico was enslaved in Spanish-claimed lands that became not only Texas, but Florida, Mexico City, New Mexico, and the Baja California.[48] As many as three hundred other Africans traveled up the Pacific Coast in the 1530s as part of an expedition ordered by Cortes. There also is evidence of other African-descended people in California (provocatively named for the mythical Black Amazonian queen fictionalized in the sixteenth-century novel *Las sergas de Esplandia*)[49] as part of Spanish exploratory envoys in the late 1600s. Those who remained worked as domestics, mule drivers, cattle and livestock handlers, miners, and soldiers. Two-thirds of the "Spanish" colonial families, mostly couples and parents with children who founded Los Angeles in 1781, were racially mixed (indio, mulatto, mestizo, Spanish, and African/Negro). Some undoubtedly had ancestors who had been enslaved in Mexico.[50] Likewise, those parts of Spain's North America that became eastern and central Texas, as well as El Paso del Norte Ciudad Juarez (across the Rio Grande from El Paso, Texas today), were sites of Black slavery and Black enslaved families created first under Spanish and then Mexican control.[51] In 1692, for example, Francisco Javier held the mulatto Maria Madrid and her four children on lands north of El Paso del Norte.[52]

As part of the Spanish empire, Texas was the site of slavery largely centered in and around the towns of San Antonio, Nacogdoches, and Goliad (Bahia).[53] There, Black bondage was relatively marginal—in terms of economic impact and the numbers enslaved—when compared to the African presence and influence in other parts of the Spanish empire, particularly Hispaniola (later Santo Domingo), Venezuela, Peru, Puerto Rico, Cuba and even when compared to other areas of New Spain such as Mexico City, Veracruz, Guerrero, Oaxaca, Morelos, Michoacan, and the Yucatan.[54] Historian L. B. Rout Jr. calculated that overall, 1.5 million Africans arrived during the entire Spanish colonial era (1500–1810);[55] while Herman Bennett estimated that almost 680,000 Blacks (enslaved and free) resided in all of Mexico in 1796.[56] In 1790, however, only thirty-seven Black captives lived in what today is Texas, building families among themselves and with Indigenous peoples, Spaniards, and others.[57] In New Mexico, African families along with those of mixed-race peoples—some enslaved and some free—were visible in legal and ecclesiastical papers from the sixteenth century onward. Don Juan de Oñate established his New Mexico settlement 1598 with several enslaved Africans whom he brought with him from Zacatecas in central Mexico.[58] Black and mixed-race captives had a variety of roles in the colonial economies of New Spain—working in gold and silver mines, on agricultural estates and livestock ranches, in Catholic missions, as pearl divers, in textile factories, as domestics of all sorts, and as skilled artisans, sex laborers, teamsters, and even members of the local militias.[59]

Under the early seventeenth-century Dutch occupation known as New Netherland, captive and free Blacks created visible families and communities. New Amsterdam (like St. Augustine) is credited with having one of the first free Black communities in North America, this one located in and around what is today Greenwich Village. Historian Leslie Harris argues that the Dutch actually "promoted family life among its slaves," noting that in 1628 the Dutch West India Company brought three female captives for "the comfort of the company's Negro men" and, undoubtedly, to encourage the birth of enslaved children.[60] Dutch Reformed Church annals recorded thirteen marriages of Black New Amsterdam couples between 1639 and 1652.[61] Twice as many couples had married by the next decade.[62] Others married, too, and had families, but outside the sanction of the church.[63]

As the image *Nieu Amsterdam* (c. 1642–1643) depicts, Africans in the colony were common at varied work sites and in the public imagination by the mid-seventeenth century as workers, entrepreneurs, and sources of European settler wealth. What other records note is that some Black people found it particularly difficult to protect their loved ones or to gain the protection of kin and community, even if one was a child. Among the early court cases concerning enslaved persons in New Netherland, for example, is the 1646 trial of Jan

Nieu Amsterdam, c. 1642-1643. *Nieu Amsterdam*, engraving, c. 1624-1699, I.N. Phelps Stokes Collection of American Historical Prints, P.1642-43, B-10, The Miriam and Ira D. Wallach Division of Art, Prints and Photographs: Print Collection, The New York Public Library.

Creoly (an enslaved man) convicted of sodomizing "by force and violence" ten-year-old Manuel Congo (an enslaved boy). Jan was found guilty and executed—strangled and then burned.[64] Manuel also was brutally punished, since "any participant in sodomy, even an unwilling one, could be put to death."[65] In another case, from 1641, the bondsman Jan Premero was killed by nine other enslaved men "in the woods near their houses." The group's confession indicates that they were part of a community that had excluded, in the most violent manner, Premero, for an unspecified reason. They had all participated in the death of Premero but decided that one among them would take the blame. Unfortunately for Gerrit de Reus, he drew the short straw and had to stand as the murderer of Premero.[66]

After the British took over New York in the mid-1660s, enslaved people's family life may have been more difficult to sustain, at least initially. Their new captors seemed less eager to support Black marriage and natural increase. They preferred to import adolescents or adults who would be full-time workers instead of spouses or parents. Some actually sold enslaved women who proved to be fertile.[67]

AFRICAN ETHNIC ORIGINS AND FAMILY FORMATION IN NORTH AMERICA

Who were those captive Africans who arrived, married, had children, and began to create kinship networks across the British, French, Dutch, and Spanish colonies of North America?[68] The differences in their actual numbers, sex ratios, and cultural markers could have had substantial bearing on marital rates and the ways in which they recovered and reinvented family in slavery sites.[69]

When considering the impact of the large African male population on the cultural formation of smaller communities of enslaved African females during the first generations in the colonies, one also must understand that African men had particular notions of, and social and cultural investment in, the gendered identities and practices of the women who would become their wives, mothers of their children, and members of their families and communities. That is, even if enslaved African males and females represented different ethnic groups, the presence of large numbers of men from a specific cultural group in a localized area might indicate that these men would be able to impose their knowledge of their memories of female culture from their indigenous societies on the smaller numbers of African women present. On the other hand, the sociosexual power that women traditionally have had and exercised when their availability is limited may have allowed "minority group" African women to exert pressure on "majority group" African men to recognize and allow their indigenous cultural expression and even to adhere to these women's ideas about gendered cultural expression and behavior.

While there is evidence of much linguistic and cultural compatibility among western/western central captives, some differences would have been quite important, perhaps socially insurmountable. One can reasonably expect that enslaved men and women from cultures with diverse gender power dynamics, roles and rituals, belief systems, and rules of family inclusion and descent might resist adopting cultural attributes that challenged, or even undermined, their sense of individual, gender, and communal identity. It certainly mattered, for example, whether one was raised in a matrilineal society—such as those who were Kongo, Wolof, or Akan peoples—as opposed to a patrilineal society, including the Igbo, Yoruba, Bamana or Mende. Allan Kulikoff's notation that in the Chesapeake "immigrant [African] women often waited two or three years before marrying" and "some African women may have been so alienated that they refused to have children," for example, suggests that some African women resisted marriage and childbearing with men from ethnic groups other than their own or those that were fundamentally similar vis-à-vis prescribed gender roles.[70] Others refused to relinquish the ties they had with partners, children, and kin from whom they had been taken or were too emotionally devastated by the violence and loss of capture, enslavement, and exile. Sylvia King remembered until her death that she had a family in Morocco, even though her enslaver forced her to marry a man that he owned. "I know I was borned in Morocco, in Africa, and was married and had three chillen befo' I was stoled from my husband," she recounted decades later.[71]

Those who had the opportunity to create family and friendship ties with those from similar cultural groups often chose to do so. These Africans seemed to have shared a common language and perhaps important cultural traits that must have provided some semblance of normalcy. Charley Barber recalled that his married grandparents had been born in Africa, could speak to one another in the same language, and had other similar cultural traits. They found it difficult to communicate with or culturally connect with others.[72]

When such cultural compatibility was not available, some still chose lovers, spouses, and co-parents from culturally distinct groups and even across racial lines. As Dedra McDonald noted regarding African captives in the colonial southwest, "Despite the relatively small African population in colonial New Mexico, the Spanish system of racial stratification and coerced labor placed Africans and Indians in a context of deep intercultural contact" that led to sociosexual relations, marriage, and kinship.[73]

Peoples from the Bight of Biafra, particularly the umbrella group associated with the ethnic title Igbo, eventually dominated the African peoples of the Chesapeake.[74] Indeed, during the 1700s, 40 percent of Igbo imports to the British southern colonies came to the Chesapeake.[75] Females proved to be a large minority among Igbo captives, representing about 45 percent.[76] The second largest group of enslaved Black people arrived from western central Africa.[77] Most were Kongolese, but there also were Nsundi, Yombe, Mbala, and Yaka peoples.[78] Unlike the Igbo, the groups from the Congo-Angola area had fewer women among them, only about 35 percent. Senegambians, principally Bamana and Wolof, accounted for only about 7 percent of captives overall, most arriving at the turn of the eighteenth century.[79] The numbers of Senegambian women varied greatly among their diverse ethnicities. Among the Bamana, one of the major Senegambian ethnic groups in the Chesapeake, men were a whopping 93 percent. Wolof women, however, were quite significant in number, about 40 percent of Wolof bondspeople there. The Mende, Temme, and Kissi from Sierra Leone and other parts of the Windward Coast were about 7 percent of Chesapeake imports, but their numbers swelled during certain years. Fewer women generally came from that region, only about one for every two men. Bondspersons from the Gold Coast, a collective of Akan and Ga peoples often referred to as Coromantees, were just slightly more numerous overall, even if they arrived less consistently across the decades. The Gold Coast peoples had a high gender ratio compared to those from the Bight of Biafra (Igbo) or central Africa (Kongo or Angolan), and it is believed that few women were among those enslaved in colonial Virginia and Maryland. By the time of the American Revolution, peoples from Senegambia, the Gold Coast, and Angola were arriving in large numbers to the Chesapeake. That region, like other colonial sites of enslavement, also received captives from transshipments. While the Royal African Company held a monopoly of traded captives to the British colonies from 1672 to 1698, enslaved persons in substantial numbers were bought from other British colonies, particularly Barbados. Others came from New York, which was the northeastern center of the slave trade.[80]

While the Igbo were the majority of those enslaved in the eighteenth-century Chesapeake,[81] Congo/Angolans dominated those African captives whom traders sold to the South Carolina/Georgia low country. Forty percent of peoples from western central Africa in North America were bound in South Carolina, and before 1739, 70 percent of South Carolina's enslaved Africans were from there.[82] The colony imported much fewer Igbo[83] but growing numbers from Sierra Leone and Senegambia.[84]

Along the Gulf Coast, the Africans sold to French Louisiana in the eighteenth century were from Senegambia, Ivory Coast, the Bight of Benin, and Angola.[85] In the early years of that century, Senegambians dominated. "Two-thirds of the slaves brought to Louisiana by the French slave trade," Gwendolyn Midlo Hall concluded, "came from Senegambia."[86] Once the Spanish gained control of the colony in 1763,[87] they began a vigorous slave trade that brought in Africans from Senegambia and other places, especially the Bights of Benin and Biafra, and central Africa. The Whitney Plantation along the lower Mississippi, for example, had enslaved people described as from Congo, Guinee, and representing Mina, Soso, Igbo, Bambara, and Mandingo ethnicities.[88] Fon-Ewe-Yoruba peoples from the Bight of Benin were an estimated 26 percent of arrivals during the latter half of the eighteenth century, clearly distinguishing the ethnic makeup of Louisiana's enslaved population from that of those in the Chesapeake and the low country. The gender ratio of the Yoruba remained high, and only small numbers of females ever arrived. The ratio of the Fon-Ewe fluctuated, however, and females remained a comparatively vital sector of that import population.[89]

Midlo Hall reasonably maintained that the large number of Africans present during the French period already had created strong cultural, communal, and, presumably, familial ties that were not so easily undermined by other groups of arrivals during the Spanish era.[90] She noted as well that while there is some evidence that enslaved Africans waited to be able to unite with others of their same ethnicities, exceptions were not rare when numbers were scarce. Documents indicate that eighteenth-century enslaved Bamana men in Louisiana, for instance, married Wolof, Igbo, and creole women (who were perhaps the offspring of Bamana) when they could, presumably because so few Bamana women were available.[91] Given the low sex ratio for the Wolof, it is not surprising that they typically married each other. Igbo were, in Midlo Hall's words, "the least endogamous among African peoples" and the "least likely to remain as a separate enclave culture among Africans in the Americas."[92] One also might surmise, then, that Igbo culture was much more likely to be influential, not only because of their large numbers in the Chesapeake overall,[93] but also because they were less endogamous than some. Enslaved Igbo women, with their relatively large numbers, could pick and choose their husbands to their benefit. It is likely that they chose marriage partners who would allow them to continue the cultural traits they desired to retain.[94] Many enslaved men competed fiercely for women, despite their cultural origins. Historian Allan Kulikoff recalled the story of George, an enslaved African on Edmond Jennings's plantation in King William County, Virginia, who believed his fellow countrymen poisoned him "for his wife."[95] Jane Landers, as noted earlier, documented some marriages across African ethnic and racial lines in Spanish Florida. Fugitive captive advertisements from other colonies denoted some cross-cultural marriages as well. The Angolan born "Roger," for example, escaped with the Virginia-born "Moll," his wife who was "very big with Child" in October 1739.[96] In the end, the desire to marry and to have a family often proved to be more important incentives than cultural concerns.[97]

The Spanish in other parts of colonial North America imported Africans who mostly came from Senegambia and Guinea in the sixteenth century. In the seventeenth century, their captives were brought from Angola and the Kingdom of Kongo and, to a lesser extent, the Gold Coast, Senegambia, and the Bights of Benin and Biafra. Approximately two thousand arrived annually to their American empire during those decades, including the southwest.[98] In the 1700s, particularly mid-century, captives were from more diverse locations. Those from Kongo were still largest in number, followed by *criollos* (born in other Spanish colonial territories), Mandingos, Efik (Carabali), and various Akan groups. Still, traders also imported Igbo, Susu, Wolof, Bambara, and others.[99]

After the British gained control of Florida between 1763 and 1783, most of the Spanish, along with their bondspeople and many Blacks who lived in Fort Mosé moved to Cuba. The new British occupants, who wanted to build a plantation economy similar to those settler colonies of South Carolina and Georgia, went on to purchase thousands of Africans from Sierra Leone, Ivory Coast (Senufo and Guro peoples, for example), Akan regions, Bight of Biafra, Gambia, and Angola.[100] At the end of the America Revolution, when England ceded Florida back to Spain, further legal slave trading from Africa continued until the Spanish relinquished control of Florida to the United States in 1821. The illegal African slave trade operation then moved from St. Augustine to Fernandina on Amelia Island off Florida's northeast coast.

While evidence of specific ethnicities of these captives is small, some have been identified as being from Guinea, the Bight of Biafra, and Zanzibar in the Indian Ocean.[101]

The Dutch West India Company started to import Africans in 1626. Soon thereafter, the company began to grant large landed estates in their northeastern colony of New Amsterdam that also came to be worked by African captives from Congo, Angola, and the Gold Coast and transshipments from other Dutch colonies such as Curaçao.[102] Company officials guaranteed estate holders a minimum of twelve male and female captives, later extending that quota to "as many as possible."[103]

Under British control, the African slave trade to New York was a cornerstone of the colonies' mercantile wealth.[104] English merchants in that colony imported enslaved people directly from Africa and through transshipments with South Carolina, Rhode Island, Jamaica, St. Kitts, Barbados, and Antigua.[105] New York traders then sold Africans locally, to other British colonies, to New France, and to Swedish settlers in what became Delaware.[106] Few arrived in the seventeenth century.[107] More captives were brought the next century, but the records are vague regarding provenance except for transshipments. There are some indicators of persons originating from the Gold Coast and the Senegambia region.[108] African baptismal papers from Philadelphia indicate comparable patterns of importation—Senegambians, Akan and others taken on the Gold Coast, Igbo, and Angolans.[109] Ships' manifests of slavers to Massachusetts also document similar origins. For example, an enslaved woman, Hagar, testified before a Massachusetts court in 1699 that she had been kidnapped away from her husband and her infant child three years earlier in Angola.[110]

COLONIAL LAWS' IMPACT ON ENSLAVED MARRIAGE AND FAMILY

The bare details of Hagar's life in Angola and Massachusetts are available because she appeared in court records. Indeed, legal statutes regarding bonded families constituted a generous portion of the laws that defined the institution of slavery, the bondsperson's lack of rights, and the kinds of state-guaranteed power over these people and their kin relations that their "owners" could claim. Elite colonial men and women demanded these binding rules and regulations in order to maintain as much control of the enslaved as possible and to maintain the institution of chattel slavery as a financially beneficial enterprise. The courts and governing bodies therefore began to codify Black family life soon after captives began to arrive.

One must be careful when relying on laws as an accurate measure of enslaved family life since, as with all laws, there were many mitigating circumstances, but none more influential than the praxis and intensity of enforcement. These laws nonetheless remained a legal baseline for some behaviors and practices. The Spanish drew their slave codes in large part from the thirteenth-century *Las Siete Partidas* (an edition from 1555 was popular during the era of colonization); the French utilized Louis XVI's 1685 *Code Noir*.[111] Both were influenced by their home countries' state religion, Catholicism.[112] *Las Siete Partidas*[113] and the *Code Noir* both demanded that enslaved people be converted to Catholicism.[114] They also forbade captives being forced to work on Sundays and holy days and required that they adhere to the holy sacraments. Significantly, three of these sacraments—baptism, marriage, and burial—were important familial cultural markers, providing documentation of Black family life within enslaved community and within the larger society.

Enslaved people deeply desired the right to have some legally recognized bond to their children *and* to marry someone whom they chose. Slaveholders still had some say as to whom their captives could marry, but according to Spanish law, they could be required by authorities to prove that interference was only to prevent harm to their "interests." Baptism not only certified a child's parentage and inclusion in the "brotherhood of the church" but also was supposed to provide the child with an extended family. The child's godparents, as "compadres," were expected to make available support, protection, and opportunity to their charge as well as to his or her parents.[115] Within the broad religious and legal context of New Spain (and in resistance with it), enslaved and free Africans and their descendants created marriages and family networks within and across racial, ethnic, and class lines, and sometimes competing colonial empires.

One of the earliest families in Spain's Fort Mosé–St. Augustine region included Francisco Garzia and his Indigenous spouse, Ana, both escaped captives from Britain's South Carolina. Their Catholic marriage in Spanish territory and the children born to them, as well as descending generations of marriage, childbirth, and godparenthood within their family, demonstrate essential and widespread kin networks based on blood, marriage, church, and fictive ties. Their multiracial children—Francisca, Xaviera, and Calisto—were born and baptized in the 1730s, both sacraments witnessed by their free mulatto godfather/patron, Francisco Rexidor. In 1759, Ana, by then a widow, remarried—this time to an enslaved African. Her daughter, Francisca, eventually married a free Black man from South Carolina, and the couple had two free children.[116]

There were examples of growing and diverse family networks in other Spanish North American colonial settlements. In Albuquerque, records from 1730 to 1752 include the baptisms of twenty-one mulattoes and, within a similar twenty-five-year period, marriage certificates for ten couples with at least one Afrohispana/o spouse.[117] There were examples of Black-descended and mixed nuclear families, both enslaved and free, with extended and fictive kin networks created through orphan adoptions. In 1750, for example, Juana Carillo and her husband, Bartholomé Lobato, had not only their two daughters by birth living with them but also five other children residing in their home, including an Indigenous girl and an orphan.[118] Other families included stepchildren born of concubinage relationships. As historian Dedra McDonald noted, the trend that "many negroes have Indian females as *mancebas* [concubines]" was documented in legal records. A 1572 law mandated that these biracial children, though legally free through their mothers, "pay tribute 'like the rest of the Indians.'"[119]

The *Code Noir* designated that priests, with enslavers' consent, preside over captive marriages. Catholic officials recorded these marriages and the births of the children who resulted. The *Code* nonetheless did not encourage enslaved people belonging to different captors to meet socially, considerably limiting their sociosexual lives and marriage pools. Of great importance, French slaveholders were forbidden from separating enslaved families (at least while the children were preadolescent), starving their captives, and exploiting them sexually. The *Code* also restricted owners of extremely labor-intensive businesses, in particular sugar and indigo plantations, from selling elderly people except for the prices set by those to be sold (in a nod to assisting these people to buy themselves or their aged loved ones).[120]

The *Code Noir*, as with other slave codes enforced across North America, could be particularly punishing to bonded mothers because it dictated that their offspring take the mother's legal status regardless of the status of the father. It also mandated that the children born of sexual relations (forced or not) between enslaved women and their slaveholders be separated from their mothers as well as from fathers who were denied this "property." Instead, in Louisiana, the children were given to local hospitals. The *Code Noir* likewise kept masters from preventing enslaved persons from earning money (outside of the labor they owed their masters) with which they could purchase their freedom or that of others. The Louisiana French Slave Code of 1724 largely drew on the *Code Noir* but did provide several stipulations regarding an enslaved person's petition for freedom that the *Code* did not.[121]

Historians studying the Louisiana Code to determine whether French colonial slaveholders complied with this body of laws noted a variety of responses. For example, Carl Brasseaux documented that "forty percent of the French-period entries in the baptismal and marriage registers at St. Francis Catholic Church (Natchitoches) . . . pertain to black slaves."[122] Likewise, attorneys general seemed to have sometimes enforced the stipulation regarding not separating enslaved husbands and wives or preadolescent children from their families if they had the same captors. Information from public auctions of plantation estates and Jesuit property substantiate that "nuclear" families were maintained. Still, Brasseaux added, these same French colonial attorneys general were very lax about demanding that slaveholders baptize or instruct their bondspeople as Catholics.[123] Failure to do so would have denied enslaved people some of the protections that the law prescribed. Other laws that were not well enforced were those that banned "interracial cohabitation" between French males and Black and Indigenous women,[124] along with those that restricted the gatherings of enslaved people for weddings and other social events without White supervision and surveillance.[125]

When the Spanish gained control of Louisiana from the French in 1763 (and West Feliciana Parish from the British in 1780), they implemented stricter regulations regarding manumission, biracial relationships, and biracial children as included in the slave codes and customs they implemented elsewhere in the Spanish empire.

The slave codes the British imposed in North America, as well as in their Caribbean colonies and West Florida when they had control, were similar in some respects to those of the French and Spanish, but if the letter of the law were followed, the British codes would have had a more restrictive impact on Black captive domesticity. Minimally, they were written with a more guarded tone and broader reach than those of the Spanish and French. Among the British North American colonies themselves, all of which legalized slavery,[126] there were many similarities, particularly in the statutes that created and shaped the institution. Once the status of "slave" was determined legally, the negative impact on bondspeople and their family lives was settled. As historian Peter Wood eloquently noted: "The laws of the land they [Africans] had entered viewed them not as humans with rights but as property to be controlled by others. Specific statutes prohibited enslaved Blacks from earning wages, moving about freely, congregating in groups, seeking education, marrying Whites or Indigenous peoples, carrying firearms, resisting punishment, or testifying in court."[127]

During British occupation of West Florida, their laws impeded enslaved family life in numerous ways. Black captives could not own livestock (cows, pigs, or chickens), a necessary form of protein for families' diets; could not earn their own income, which would have enhanced material well-being; and could not travel more than two miles away from their place of work without a pass—a burden to the large numbers of abroad marriages. These laws also restricted the right of enslavers to emancipate their bonded people.[128]

Colonial New England's slavery legislation was somewhat more lenient. Unlike the courts in the British colonial south and colonial New York, for example, those in New England allowed enslaved people to testify in court against, and to sue, Whites. They also could own certain forms of property.[129]

More importantly, enslaved people, with the permission of their enslavers, could marry in a civil service and could wed free Blacks as well as Indigenous people.[130]

New England captive marriages probably did not acquire the same legal and customary weight as those of free people, but they certainly were more socially and civically respected than those of enslaved people in other British colonies. New England customs, for instance, mandated that enslaved men and women, like nonbonded people, have their intentions to marry, or "banns," published or announced locally. As such, the banns of "Semit Negro and Jane Negro" appeared on November 16, 1700; those of "Charles Negro and Peggee Negro" on August 3, 1710; and those of "Lewise Negro and Martha Negro" on January 18, 1710. All were published in Boston, allowing a public face to marital relations usually invisible to White society.[131]

The property element of slave status in British North America (with some exceptions, as noted above) tended to erase, legally and customarily, any claim that any enslaved man, woman, or child had to their body—its intimacies, its labor, its reproductive capacities, its nourishment or medical treatment, its rest or leisure, the space it occupied, its movement, or its placement in the colonial landscape, while in utero, alive, or dead. Being someone's property meant that regardless of family ties, you could be bred, aborted, beaten, killed, branded, raped, dismembered, burned, cut, broken, starved, sold, swapped, inherited, experimented on, or abandoned by the side of any road once you were deemed no longer of any value. This was the reality that most bondspersons endured, a reality made even more devastating when imposed on one's kin.

To be an enslaved mother in the British colonies meant that your children, too, would be bound because, as Virginia, for example, noted in its 1662 law, "all children borne in this country shall be held bond or free only according to the condition of the mother." This law was a break with "Old World" paternity statutes in which children derived status from their fathers. Most British colonies—beginning with Virginia in 1691—also outlawed biracial relationships.[132] Still, enslaved women (and their children) remained in jeopardy as a result of the monetary incentive their captors had to impregnate these women, to say nothing of their vulnerability to rape and sexual abuse without legal protections. Given the inferior legal status of these women since the 1661 Barbadian "Act for the better ordering and governing of Negroes" that stipulated "brutish" captives had no right to a trial by jury "of twelve men of their peers," these women (as well as men) could not testify against Whites or have a customary trial. Likewise, most British colonies recognized the right of slaveholders to chastise their bondspeople to the point of murder without fear of penalty.[133] Colonial law that established a Black child's status as linked to that of the mother also meant a further distancing of this child from the father, who could not claim formal recognition of paternity. To be an enslaved father in the British colonies, therefore, typically meant that your children belonged to their mother's captor. You could not have sanctioned contact with them without consent of both your and their mother's enslavers. This consent was further complicated by laws that forbade enslaved persons with different slaveholders from meeting or congregating together, even for ritualized communal and familial events.[134] And while the French and Spanish allowed some very qualified benefit to those bondspeople who were baptized in the Catholic tradition, the Protestant British, by the end of the seventeenth century, did not. Virginia's law of 1667, for example, declared that "the conferring of baptisme doth not alter the condition of the person as to his bondage or freedome." Similarly, British law in its southern holdings, unlike those of the French and Spanish or New England, did not recognize captive marriages, did not protect the sale of young children from their mothers, and did not allow enslaved persons who gained their freedom to physically stay with their enslaved family members.[135] If emancipated men were determined to stay with their enslaved wives, they also faced the additional burden of her taxation, unlike those men married to White or Indigenous women. The Virginia law of 1643, after all, created a tax status for support of the local Anglican church that relegated Black women as uniquely different from other colonial women—African women, and their daughters, were tithable.[136] Against this growing body of debilitating antifamily slave legislation, enslaved adults nonetheless formed kin relations, married, and had children. The first true obstacle to the enslaved's family formation, after all, was not the legal strictures; rather, it was accumulating enough adults in the captive population to allow couples to form.

Black population statistics from colonial North America generally indicate the growth of communities and the people who comprised them. Some families developed very early, like that of Anthony and Mary Johnson who met in the 1620s, married, and had four children. The same phenomenon, in diverse measures, took place in Dutch New Netherland,[137] British New England,[138] Spanish Florida, and the southwest as well as French Louisiana. It was among these small, far-flung North American communities of competing European colonial empires that Africans began to create marital bonds, have children, and establish extended and fictive kin ties.[139] Important conditions that contextualized these processes included population density; emotional, cultural, and physical necessities; captives' health; and the desire to create collaborative resistance strategies.

North American settler communities, regardless of what European empire claimed them, were overwhelmingly rural. What urban centers there were typically were along strategically located seacoasts and rivers where markets met mariners. Because most enslaved persons were positioned in the rural countryside where they were forced to work in agricultural endeavors, few urban households held many bondspeople. Still, much of the labor in urban areas also was performed by Blacks, even if in overall smaller numbers. Eighteenth-century captives of Captain John Perkins of Norwich, Connecticut, therefore, probably were better able to develop a localized Black community and marry among each other, given they numbered fifteen on that estate. Most others in that colony were "held in very small parcels," and would have had greater difficulty doing so.[140] Rhode Island was like Connecticut, except the towns of Newport and South Kingstown. In the latter, Blacks were approximately one-third the number of Whites, a statistic that likened this area to slaveholding patterns in parts of the Chesapeake. British Pennsylvania and Delaware had a limited number of slaveholding households, most with small numbers of enslaved Africans. Tobacco farms in the latter and ironworks in the former, however, were the sites of larger numbers of captives. These populations provided the possibility of moderate family and community development, particularly in the tobacco region. Still, labor in the ironworks meant that the mostly male workers had female spouses and children who resided away from them.[141]

British New York had the largest number of Black enslaved men, women, and children in the colonial Northeast; and New York City had the largest urban slave population in the mainland colonies. A few slaveholders claimed more than ten captive workers. Lewis Morris, a large landholder and judge, had twenty-nine. Wealthy Peter DeLancy, a member of the New York's colonial legislature, owned twelve. Five others held ten captives each. It certainly was possible for Black families to form among these slaveholdings, and one historian surmised that "the typical slaveholding family had a single small family of slaves in its service."[142] There also was the probability of interhousehold families based on abroad marriages and extended kin, particularly in the city of Manhattan, where more than 40 percent of households included enslaved Blacks.[143]

Comparatively few Africans worked in the Spanish colonial territory of southwestern North America. New Mexico was believed to have only a 2.5 percent Black population in 1750.[144] Still, there was enough slave ownership for the practice to be well recognized, particularly in Albuquerque.[145] Many Black people intermarried with Indigenous peoples, a practice enhanced both by the availability of Indigenous women and the 1542 Spanish law that forbade their formal enslavement. Children born to these women, even those with enslaved Black fathers, could not be formally committed to slavery, unlike the children of bound Black females.[146]

By 1680, many British colonies had a least one hundred Black people, and some, such as Virginia and Maryland, had well over one thousand, indicating the bases for widespread community growth.[147] Twenty years later, their population, and the potential for community and family growth, had extended impressively. Indeed, many colonies had more than quadrupled their numbers. By 1700, the Black enslaved population in British North America was close to thirty thousand, more than half enslaved in Virginia.[148] The rapid increase in their numbers was linked both to natural increase and growth in the African slave trade to the continent. Slave trade demographers David Eltis and David Richardson documented that while the British northern colonial region imported only thirteen hundred Africans between 1700 and 1725, twelve thousand more arrived over the following twenty-five years, and eleven thousand more from 1750 to 1775. This trend held for the remaining British regions.[149]

The Gulf Coast, whether under French or Spanish control, had the same importation pattern, although the lesser European population meant a different sociocultural context for the captives and their families. Indeed, Africans were a majority of the French Louisiana colonial population in the early 1730s.[150] Mississippi River planters bought seven thousand captives between 1719 and 1730,[151] and smaller, but still substantial numbers over the next several decades.[152] These large groups of imports, and a growing numerical equality between the sexes due to natural increases, meant there were more and more adults available to form communities, increasing the possibility of potential family ties, if not with persons who resided together in the same quarters, then with persons located nearby. In most colonies by the 1730s, and even earlier in many places, there were examples of various forms of enslaved Black families—nuclear, extended, stem, and even dual or multi-generational—based on love, blood, marital and fictive relations—residing within and between nearby slaveholdings.[153]

Some colonial slaveholders encouraged childbirth among captives. When the British, for example, gained control of Spanish Florida in 1763 as part of the Treaty of Paris,[154] many settlers hoped to purchase bondspeople to enhance plantation development. Some wanted to import good "breeding" women who would have children by their husbands or be forced to do so with others. One investor noted that "a few likely young Wenches must be in the parcell, & should their Husbands fail in their duty, I dare say . . . other publick Spirited Young Men, will be ready to render such an essential service to the Province as to give them some help."[155]

The larger the residential quarters of the enslaved, the more likely that couples and spouses lived together with their children and perhaps with additional blood, marital, and fictive kin. In the British colonial South, early large tobacco plantations in the Chesapeake were the most significant sites of enslaved community and family development of several iterations. The average tobacco-growing Virginia or Maryland slaveholder had between eight and thirteen enslaved workers, with large holders dividing their human property on various work "quarters" of approximately the same size.[156] There were, of course, those who owned much larger numbers of bondspeople. By the end of the seventeenth century, for example, Elizabeth Digges owned 108 Black captives, Ralph Wormely had 91, and John Carter held 106.[157] Natural increase of enslaved peoples in Virginia began to be significant by 1710, indicating the development of both blood and some marital kin ties.[158] Historian Russell Menard indicated that in Maryland the enslaved were reproducing themselves in the 1720s.[159] By the 1730s, they were having enough children to "replace adults of the previous generation."[160]

Until the end of the first quarter of the eighteenth century, the pattern of large Chesapeake slave ownership was mostly concentrated along tidewater riverways such as the York, James, Elizabeth, and later the Rappahannock and Potomac. Virginia tobacco planter, merchant, and politician Robert "King" Carter claimed approximately 750 captives housed in forty-eight quarters across his land holdings of 300,000 acres in nine separate but largely contiguous counties.[161] The average size of the enslaved population on Carter's individual quarters was fifteen. Sizeable slaveholdings also eventually developed in Virginia's piedmont. The presence of substantial numbers of enslaved people (they comprised 24 percent of the general population in 1715 and 41 percent by 1756)[162] still did not mean that couples and families lived together, for many resided on diverse quarters spread across large tracts of tobacco lands belonging to their enslavers, even though family formation regularly occurred.[163]

George Washington, with his wife Martha, held one of largest slaveholdings in the region. These Black men, women, and children worked and lived on the five farms of the Washington Mount Vernon estate, and couples had no guarantee that they could reside together, even after they had children. Residence was determined by work assignment, not family relations. As a result, there were an especially large numbers of abroad marriages, single-female-parent homes, and single adults who typically lived in sex-segregated buildings.[164]

South Carolina had fewer enslaved people than Virginia, but fewer Whites as well. As early as 1708, there were forty-one hundred enslaved Blacks, as compared to thirty-five hundred Whites and fourteen hundred enslaved Indigenous peoples.[165] By 1730, two-thirds of the South Carolina population was Black.[166] Significant as well for the low country was the development of rice plantations requiring large labor forces. Rice planters in South Carolina and Georgia usually acquired a minimum of thirty captives to work their properties and typically held between thirty-three and seventy-two Black workers

The Washington Family, c. 1787-1796, Edward Savage, *The Washington Family, 1789-1796*, oil on canvas, Andrew W. Mellon Collection, National Gallery of Art, Washington.

on each of their multiple scattered quarters along the Atlantic coast or on the Sea Islands.[167] These, as such, provided close physical proximity of tens of enslaved people.[168]

Documents indicate that the very elite rice planters tended to buy large quantities of captives together, allowing for those who had met and gotten to know each other during their Middle Passage (some of whom may have come from the same villages or certainly the same cultures) to often be housed together once purchased in South Carolina.[169] Retaining their indigenous patterns of marital and familial structures, some men even managed to have multiple wives, insisting that polygamous marriage was valid. The Reverend Francis Le Jau complained in his journal in 1709 regarding his proselytizing efforts in South Carolina that "one of the most Scandalous and common Crimes of our Slaves is their perpetual Changing of Wives and husbands, which occasions great disorders." Le Jau insisted that those he baptized understand that the "Christian Religion does not allow plurality of Wives, nor any changing of them: You promise truly to keep to the Wife you now have till Death dos part you."[170]

Still, enslaved family formation and practice in this region was undoubtedly impacted by high rates of absentee ownership due to fear of malaria and the dislike of hot summer temperatures and high humidity. The presence of an owner suggests better physical care and sometimes encouragement of slave family development. Likewise, slaveholders tended to believe that they would have a more content and therefore more easily worked male labor force if they provided them with wives, or at least female sex partners. Historian Daniel Littlefield noted that South Carolina planter, slave trader, and politician Henry Laurens wrote to his overseer in 1765 that "'I send up a stout young Woman to be a Wife to whome she shall like best amongst the single men. The rest of the Gentlemen shall be served as I have opertunity. Tell them that I do not forget their request.'"[171] In East Florida, another planter explained that he wanted to purchase African women to "'render the Negroes I now have happy and contented, wch I know they cannot be without having each a Wife. This will greatly tend to keep them at home and to make them Regular.'" The women, this slaveholder added, will not work as hard as the men, "yet amends will be sufficiently made in a very few years by the Great Encrease of Children.'"[172] Overseers who worked for absentee captors, however, typically prioritized large harvests, not enslaved people's social or family life. The absence of an enslaver, on the other hand, also gave enslaved people an opportunity to express their traditional cultures more openly, including family and marital rituals and behaviors, naming, religion, housing, language, dress, trading, music, and dance customs.

In colonial French Louisiana along the lower Mississippi River, where most of the enslaved resided in the early part of the eighteenth century, there were some large holdings (more than ten persons) that also would have supported the development of families on single holdings and certainly families based on abroad marriages or extended and fictive kin networks. The 1727 census from this area documents that 78 percent of all slaveholdings between New Orleans and Point Coupee had fewer than twenty captives and 28 percent of lower Mississippi River slaveholders had fewer than five Blacks whom they could count as their property.[173] As the enslaved population became more urbanized by the middle of the century, enslaved family life changed accordingly.[174]

The swells and dips in African imports also caused some disruptions in family, community, and cultural formation and practice over the 220-year period of legal trade to North America. African imports always tended to be skewed toward young men, thereby limiting the possibility for the development of heterosexual marriages. Natural increase, then, slowed with the influx of large numbers of new Africans.[175] Expansive numbers of imports to a particular region also could cause culturally derived social friction between different ethnic groups—particularly if one or two groups already residing in a certain locale were faced with a large influx of another group. Similarly, cultural disruptions could occur when a community of largely creolized people received a large quantity of Africans over a relatively short period of time, such as in the decades in the middle of the eighteenth century that witnessed the largest importations. When illegally trafficked African captives arrived in the antebellum period, they likewise could expect some cultural rejection. Benin captives Kossola and his wife, Abila, for example, gave their children both African names "because we not furgit our home; den another name for de Americky soil so it won't be too crooked to call." Still, creole slaves "picks at dem." Cudjo recalled with pain that "dey callee my chillun ig'nant savage and make out dey kin to monkey. . . . Me and dey mama doan lak to hear our chillun call savage. . . . We Afficans try raise our chillun right. . . . I love my chillun so much!"[176]

British colonial communities included White indentured servants of English, Scots, Irish, and German descent, convict laborers, political exiles, and Indigenous bondspeople, all of whom worked, lived, and socialized with Africans, even though sex and marriage were legally forbidden.[177] These various unions were documented in laws and court cases as well as fugitive slave advertisements that described multiracial persons who escaped and groups of diverse peoples who went away together. As early as 1640, Captain Peirce (the claimer of Angela, who arrived in 1619) complained that six of his White servants and one of his neighbor's Africans had escaped in an attempt to reach New Netherland. They stole ammunition and a boat, but were captured.[178] That same year, a Black woman was "whipt at the whipping post" for bearing a biracial child. Ten years earlier, Virginia had whipped a White man for "defiling his body in lying with a negro."[179] White indentured servant Christopher Mason of Massachusetts was found guilty of impregnating a Black servant named Bess in 1672.[180] In 1688, the "Negro Servant" Toney of Milford, Connecticut, confessed to consensual sexual relations with the White servant "Sarah," who concurred.[181] Historian Wendy Warren's wise pronouncement that the northern British colonies' antifornication codes "failed spectacularly to legislate sexual behavior among enslaved people," and between persons of different races easily could be generalized across North America and the rest of the "New World."[182]

There certainly were significant sexual, social, and familial ties between Indigenous peoples, Africans, the French, and later the Spanish in Louisiana. "Matings between Africans and Indians," Gwendolyn Midlo Hall noted, "took place on and off the estates throughout the eighteenth century," and the two groups "continued to run away together."[183] Indeed, there were "formal alliances" between African and native leaders in the colony at least until the 1730s as the two peoples, both subject to French enslavement, combined efforts to rid themselves of their French captors. This joint liberation project strengthened social, cultural, and familial bonds between them.[184] Indeed, French, and Spanish North American colonies witnessed different racialized social realities, at least in the public eye and in law, than those found in British North America. The southern British colonies, unlike Britain itself at the time, all outlawed sexual contact and marriage across racial lines.[185] Miscegenation was openly widespread among the colonial Spanish and French.[186] The *casta* system in the Spanish American empire, for example, publicly recognized mixed racial (*mestizaje*) families, creating an elaborate labeling and pictorial account of the various races and mixed-raced persons who had sexual contact, bore children, and sometimes married.[187]

In the British colonies, mixed-race categories were "typically" labelled as mulatto, quadroon, octoroon, and zambo (African descent/Native American descent).[188] *Castas*, however, included not only the Spanish terms for these groups, but several more, approximately sixteen altogether. "Coyote," meant one whose ancestry was both Native American and mestizo (Native American and European). A "morisca" had parents who were mulatto and Spanish (European), and an Albarazado was descended from one Native American parent and one parent of mixed Native American and African heritage.

By the early to mid-eighteenth century, many African-descended people held by the British, Spanish, French, native peoples, or American creoles across North America had managed to maintain the significance of kinship to the African identity and actually acquire the roles of spouses, parents, siblings, and other kin. Some had been born into them. Not a few searched decades before they were able to marry and establish their own families. Some enslaved children trained as domestics, eventually bonded with other Black workers or White servants in their masters' homes. Some even gained their freedom because of intimate relations between themselves and their slaveholders. But life as a free Black person in a slave society was never easy, even when one did have a family of one's own creation. Those who succeeded, personally and familially, had tremendous fortitude, unusual good fortune, often exceptional talents and/or opportunities, familial/community aid, and sometimes assistance from Whites. Consider the evolving family histories of three Africans from the colonial era introduced in the last chapter—Phillis Wheatley, Chloe Spear, and Olaudah Equiano—who gained freedom and eventually family.

Phillis Wheatley was bound in the Boston home of John and Susanna Wheatley. Her slaveholders had twins, Mary and Nathaniel, who were eighteen years old when she arrived. Wheatley's wife and daughter trained young Phillis to household service and in the family business of sewing. A gifted child who became a favorite of Mary and other household members, Phillis soon learned English and how to read and write. With no family of her own with her, the child soon became their "pet" as well as the Wheatleys' cultural

De India y Zambaigo, Albarazado. *De India y Zambaigo, Albarazado, late 1700s,* Southwest Museum of the American Indian Collection, Autry Museum, Los Angeles, 457.G.58.

and academic experiment. Obviously precocious, Phillis's intellect amazed her enslavers.[189] Indeed, her brilliance brought a certain status to the family, as they wasted little time exploiting her accomplishments for public consumption and their own prestige.

It is not certain if there were other Black female captives in the Wheatley household or in their vicinity whom Phillis could, or did, consider to be a fictive mother. The decade she arrived, the colony's number of Blacks increased by about 600 persons, to 4,750.[190] According to the census, there were 647 bonded males and 342 females over the age of sixteen in Boston at that time.[191] While Black men outnumbered Black women by almost two to one, there were enough local adults to have encouraged the formation of families and even kinship and communal networks that eventually included Phillis. Phillis also came to recognize Mrs. Wheatley as someone who was, at least in the bondsgirl's retrospective discourse on their relationship, akin to an endearing female relation. Her letter to her best friend, Obour Tanner, spoke to her exceptional feelings of loss when Mrs. Wheatley died:

110 *Chapter 2*

Phillis Wheatley. *Phillis Wheatley*, illustration, 1834-1842, Revue des Colonies Collection, Manuscripts, Archives and Rare Books Division, Schomburg Center for Research in Black Culture, Manuscripts, Archives, and Rare Books Division, Sc Rare 325. 344-R.

> I have lately met with a great trial in the death of my mistress; let us imagine the loss of a Parent, Sister or Brother the tenderness of all these were united in her.—I was a poor little outcast & a stranger when she took me in: not only into her house but I presently became a sharer in her most tender affections. I was treated by her more like her child than her Servant; no opportunity was left unimprov'd, of giving me the best of advice, but in terms how tender! how engaging! This I hope ever to keep in remembrance.[192]

Phillis's extraordinary scholarly aptitude and serious commitment to Christianity—two essential assimilationist claims to civilization for the Wheatleys—no doubt convinced them that Phillis was one African worthy of inclusion in their close domestic circle. She learned Latin and English, geography, classical and English literature, Christian scripture, and, of course, to compose sophisticated elegies and secular poetry.[193] Many of her poems centered on themes of familial loss, echoing the pangs of emotional and physical turmoil that Phillis, despite her attachment to the Wheatley mistress, probably continued to have after she was stolen from her family and that she witnessed among Boston friends and acquaintances trying to cope with the losses of their children, husbands, wives, and others. Reading through Phillis's poems, one comes to fundamentally understand the depth of her desire for family.[194]

Phillis, remarkably, even traveled to England with a member of the Wheatley family. There, her book of poetry, *Poems on Various Subjects, Religious and Moral*, was published in 1773, when she was about twenty years old. Her fame led to meetings with Benjamin Franklin and Granville Sharpe and gained her an invitation—which she was unable to accept—to the court of George III. The next year, Phillis gained her freedom.

By any stretch of the imagination, Phillis Wheatley was an exceptional person with rare accomplishments for any woman (or man) in the eighteenth-century Americas. Her exceptionalism no doubt framed her social relations, as both an enslaved and free woman.[195] The kinship relations she was able to forge, unfortunately, proved to be fraught. The problems resulted, in part, because of the restrictions racism imposed on her while enslaved and due to the gripping financial limitations free Black people (including herself and eventual husband) had to endure, again because of racial discrimination.

After gaining her freedom, Phillis did marry. Her spouse, John Peters, was a proud, literate, free Black entrepreneur, described as "a man of very handsome person and manners," who "wore a wig, carried a cane, and quite acted out 'the gentleman.'"[196] Peters, unfortunately, did not succeed in his many financial ambitions, at least not consistently when he was married to Phillis. It was not because he did not try, as many court records document. Neither Phillis nor John received any compensation for their years of labor while enslaved. And despite her rare experiences as an enslaved woman recognized for her intellectual merit and literary talents, as well as her eventual freedom, marriage to a man with extended kin, and even motherhood, Phillis suffered greatly. Most importantly, there were the pangs of maternal loss—none of her three children lived beyond infancy. There also was the experience of marital discord and material want. John Peters had a reputation for not treating Phillis well. Both of these problems were compounded by her frail health. One contemporary of Phillis noted, "She was herself suffering for want of attention, for many comforts, and that greatest of all comforts in sickness—cleanliness.

She was reduced to a condition too loathsome to describe.... In a filthy apartment, in an obscure part of the metropolis.... The woman who had stood honored and respected in the presence of the wise and good... was numbering the last hours of life in a state of the most abject misery, surrounded by all the emblems of a squalid poverty!"[197] Although still a poet, Phillis could not get a planned second book of poetry published. Eleven years after gaining her freedom, Phillis Wheatley Peters died, her remaining belongings sold to pay her debts.[198]

Also residing in Boston, Chloe Spear was a domestic and childcare provider for Captain Gamaliel Bradford. Although, like Phillis, she worked within the intimate space of her slaveholder's family, her relationship with Bradford family members was much more typical than that of young Phillis. In Chole's workspace, none of the Bradfords initially took any particular interest in the young captive's religious conversion, literacy, or emotional needs. Chloe did attend church on Sundays, sitting away from the Bradfords and with other captives. Her segregation gave the sociable child the opportunity, as she took during her Middle Passage, to nurture friendships and perhaps even some fictive kin relationships among the enslaved. Church life for Chloe continued to be a source of rich family and community ties. Her memoir notes that as a child "the seat assigned to herself and her associates was remote from the view of the congregation; and she confessed that as they did not understand the preaching, they took no interest in it, and spent the time in playing, eating nuts, &c."[199]

Not only were the Bradfords disinterested in Chloe's Christian conversion, but her captor also was vehemently opposed to her intellectual development. However, she was determined to gain literacy. One of Chloe's tasks was to walk the Bradford children to and from school. She secretly bargained with their instructor to teach her. Chloe had to acquire her own book and pay the teacher out of her "small presents of money from visitors at the house of her master," and she could only study secretly. Eventually her captor caught her with the book (a small Christian text) and forbade her from learning because he feared it would make her "saucy." Bradford threatened that if he caught Chloe reading again, he would have her "suspended by her two thumbs, and severely whipped."[200]

The Bradfords relocated to Andover—some twenty miles from Boston—during the latter half of the American Revolution, taking Chloe with them. Their move certainly would have severed some of the communal and fictive ties Chloe had made for herself in Boston. But it also gave her a chance to meet new people, expanding her community. The move also furthered Chloe's opportunity for Christian conversion and literacy. The Bradford household lived with a devout friend who taught Chloe about his faith and how to read scripture. When they returned to Boston, Chloe's apparent

Christian devotion persuaded Mr. Bradford to have her baptized and even consider freeing her.[201]

Fellowship in Boston's Christian community expanded Chloe's social world even more. General emancipation arrived in Massachusetts in 1783, allowing the then thirty-four-year-old African woman to work for wages.[202] Chloe, who attended the Second Baptist Meeting House, was part of the expanding Boston Black community tied to its seafaring economy. Her freedom was soon followed by marriage, children, and business interests. At all of these efforts, she was much more fortunate than Phillis Wheatley.

Chloe married Caesar Spear, and the two established a boarding house business that catered to seaman. The couple eventually had seven children. She saved earnings and purchased other property in Boston.[203] Chloe also remained close to the Bradfords and other Whites with whom she had business and communal ties, her home serving as an integrated place of familial, social, and religious gatherings. At her death in 1815, Chloe Spear was buried in the Bradford family crypt.[204] A literate woman who understood the importance of documenting one's property and concerns, she composed a will that indicated both family and communal ties. Chloe had amassed some wealth and distributed it to family and friends, particularly those she worshipped with at Second Baptist. According to her will, Chloe left $500 (a handsome sum) to her grandson, who resided in Salem. She gave gifts of money (between $20 and $50) and her clothing and linens to six of her female friends, identified primarily as other free Black women who worshipped at her church. Chloe also bequeathed $50 each to two men, one named for her late husband Caesar, and another who also attended Second Baptist.[205]

Olaudah Equiano never found a family during his short stay as a child captive in Virginia. He eventually did, however, find close friends and communities—Black, White, and mixed race—with whom he felt comfortable. Once Olaudah reached Virginia, his social world from his Middle Passage evaporated. Language, as with many others, was a stiff barrier. He did not speak English, and did not know the languages of his fellow captives on the plantation where he was taken. Put first in the field to weed and remove stones, Olaudah was lonely, frightened, and socially alienated. Since he was taken from Africa, he had been forced to answer to two different English names—Michael on the slave ship, and Jacob with his new Virginia captor. "I was now exceedingly miserable, and thought myself worse off than the rest of my companions," he noted, "for they could talk to each other, but I had no person to speak to that I could understand. In this state I was constantly grieving and pining, and wishing for death rather than any thing else."[206]

Olaudah's desolation increased even more when he was moved from the fields into his enslaver's home, where White surveillance and cultural difference were much more pronounced. There, Olaudah's great curiosity was aroused by British technology, but he mostly felt fear because of his captor's awful treatment of an enslaved woman whom he forced to wear an "iron muzzle" that kept her from speaking, eating, spitting, or drinking.[207]

Olaudah was relieved when he was bought by an English captain. He went off to sea for the next twelve years as a bondsperson, but did enjoy the companionship of some of his fellow workers and the African diasporic communities that he regularly visited on the trading vessel.[208] At sea, Olaudah became literate and learned math and naval tactics, including sea military strategies. Sold again to a merchant, he was able to use his skill and ambition as a petty trader to accumulate a savings. Olaudah successfully purchased his freedom in 1766, when he was about twenty years old. Afterward, he continued to work across the Atlantic world and eventually settled in England. He still did not marry until twenty-five years later, but had close friends within Black and White abolitionist circles. Like Phillis Wheatley, he published. Olaudah's autobiography was a financial and political success, helping to increase his financial stability and the number of important Britons who opposed the African slave trade. England, unlike her mainland colonies, did not legally forbid marriages across racial lines. Olaudah married Susan Cullen, a White woman, and the couple had daughters Anna Maria and Johanna. Already older at the time of his marriage, Olaudah died five years later, soon after his wife. Their daughter Anna Maria passed shortly thereafter. Olaudah, like Chloe Spear, left a relatively substantial estate, which his daughter Johanna inherited when she became twenty-one. Her maternal grandmother, Anne Cullen, raised Johanna after her parents died.[209]

Phillis, Chloe, and Olaudah lived mostly in cities. Most colonial-era Blacks, whether enslaved or free, did not. Documentation of family life on farms and plantations indicate the creation, over the colonial decades, of layered, often geospatially wide kinship networks descended from a central elder family member. For example, most of the family members in the Abigail-Bridget clan (see appendix A) were owned by Matthew Godfrey or some of his tidewater kin. Godfey's earliest colonial ancestor, John Godfey, arrived in Jamestown in 1635 at the age of twenty-one. By the end of the next decade, he had married and was a tobacco "planter," who had acquired more than one thousand acres of land, mostly by transporting White indentured servants to the colony. He began to purchase Africans sometime later. John Godfey's own Virginia family grew rapidly, with he and his wife, Sarah, having eight children, including a son named Matthew in 1652, probably the grandfather of Abigail and Bridget's captor.

The latter Matthew Godfrey came to own his Black bondspeople mostly through inheritance, from his father and his Aunt Kezia. Indeed, he inherited both Abigail and her children from Kezia Godfrey.[210] Matthew's first tithable list (White male, Black and Indigenous male and female workers sixteen years or older)[211] appeared in the records in 1752 and only included the enslaved woman, Bridget. Two years later, he added Abigail (Rose). China (Chany), perhaps the daughter of Bridget or Abigail, was part of his 1757 list. By 1766, Matthew claimed six enslaved females old enough to be counted as workers—Bridget, her daughters Jenny and Kate, Abigail, China, and Peggy. Matthew Godfrey listed Ned (Edward), Abigail's son, the following year. Then came Sam, another child of Bridget who had been moved into the labor force in 1772. Pleasant Godfrey, perhaps the daughter of Abigail, began to appear on Godfrey's tithable list in 1773. The husbands of Abigail and Bridget presumably were abroad, perhaps owned by a local planter who was either friend or kin to Matthew. He also owned the man Acky and the male descendants of Abigail and Bridget. Five years later in 1788, Matthew Godfrey's tithable list included all the persons mentioned above with the additions of Afraca, who may have been recently purchased and was named Valentine, inherited from his aunt in 1775, Bridget's son James (Ely), and James's wife, Hannah.[212]

The Black Godfreys in the mid-to-late-eighteenth century demonstrate the various forms enslaved families took. Their blood, marital, and fictive relations collectively amassed a sprawling kinship group across rural and urban spaces, land, water, colonies, and even continents. Within this group were nuclear structured families (such as Elizabeth; her husband, Edward; and their children, Jeffrey and Betsy), abroad marriages with matrifocal households (such as Pleasant, the twenty-six-year-old mother of an eleven-year-old daughter named Lettius and with a six-year-old son, Ned), single women and men, and multigenerational quarters. Men and women acquired spouses in their quarters, but just as typically at neighboring quarters or on the farms and plantations, and in the households of White neighbors who were co-holders of captives, business associates, fellow church members, and long-term friends who were related through blood and marriage to Matthew Godfrey. Godfrey's community of fellow slaveholders provided his bondspeople with the opportunity to have social relationships off his property. This was more than evident when a significant number of enslaved escaped from the region, not just from Godfrey's plantation but from those of his neighbors and relatives. A detailed chart of Godfrey's captives and their familial relations documents that his enslaved men and women were married to persons, or had children, who belonged to their enslaver's neighbors, relatives, or co-holders who absconded. Local slavers George Ramsey and Stephen Shakespeare were co-holders of China's husband, Cato. Likewise, Robert Bartee owned Kate's husband, Lewis. Dr. Simmons, related through marriage to Matthew

Godfrey, was Peggy's husband's enslaver. Francis Rice, also nearby, claimed as his property Sam's wife, Sucky. Willis Wilkinson and his partner, Captain John Gilchrist, owned Acky's parents and siblings. Mr. Quimby was enslaver of Acky's wife, Clara; and Captain Hullett of South Carolina shared in the "ownership" of Kitty, who would become Pleasant's daughter-in-law.[213] Collectively, these enslaved men, women, and children were a large network of kin and friends whose tight-knit social bonds helped them to survive enslavement together and contributed the support and strategies to escape.

The famed Black abolitionist Frederick Douglass, who was born in 1818, represented the sixth generation of an enslaved family located within the Skinner family (and their descendants) in Talbot County on Maryland's Eastern Shore. Douglass's family, or clan, traced its early "founder" to the mid-eighteenth-century enslaved man Baly, who had been born in 1701. Baly more than likely was the father to the children borne by one, but possibly by both, of the bound women Skinner owned—Selah and Sarah. Baly's name, as well as that of Selah, along with others—both male and female—followed their descendants in Douglass's kin group across the generations.[214] As historian Dickson Preston emphasized, "identity with the kin group was important to eighteenth century Talbot County blacks."[215]

Enslaved men, women, and children in Spanish Florida generally created similar family types. Historian Jane Landers explained that "slaves lived in fairly durable families and developed extensive and long-term networks of kin, shipmates, and friends across plantations and in the city."[216] Francis Phelipe Fito had a 10,000-acre plantation named Nueva Suiza, west of St. Augustine, where he housed eighty-six Black captives and four free Black workers, mostly in family groups, in twenty-seven cabins.[217] Some of these families were three-generational. Old Tom, who was sixty-nine in 1801, for instance, lived with his wife, Artemesia, four of their children (Rose, Sarah, Lawrence, and John), as well as Rose's children (Primus, Peter, and Cuffee). Like other plantations in the South at the time, Fito divided his property into working farms, some of them outlying, where captives, like Simon and his wife, Susy, had to reside.[218] Don Francisco Xavier Sanchez owned nine plantations and hundreds of enslaved people. He determined their residences—in the countryside of Florida, St. Augustine, Havana, and the Bahamas—by his labor needs, not their family ties.[219] Don Juan McQueen moved from Georgia to Florida with seventy-seven bondspeople (thirty-three males, twenty-one females, and twenty-three children) onto a huge estate of more than 20,000 acres that he had his captives convert to cotton, rice, and indigo fields. Most were able to live in family residences over the short weekend, many with nuclear structures. Still, their labor routines determined their location during the workweek. The large size of McQueen's holdings and relatively equal adult sex ratios over time also provided conditions for multigenerational families who represented marriages across his widespread quarters, creating extensive kin networks.[220]

LABOR AND FAMILY

The lives of most African captives and their families across the generations were ordered in large measure by the labor relationships they had with their enslavers and other work supervisors.[221] Living arrangements likewise depended on perceived labor needs. The intersection of these two conditions was especially significant. Many who had the same "owner" on small farms in the middle and northern colonies, in North American households, on the tobacco and grain farms of the Chesapeake and southern piedmont, and in the indigo and rice plantations of the low country and gulf often lived and worked together with at least some family members, but not necessarily all their kin, including parents and siblings. Still, those who could do so created among themselves a work culture of familial and communal training, support, correction, and protection. Slaveholders with substantial agricultural units, for example, often divided their laborers into "gangs" who had specific tasks completed communally. Others, particularly on the rice estates on the coasts of South Carolina, Georgia, and the East Florida colony, insisted that their bondspeople be placed on the "task" system, with each individual responsible for a certain amount of labor.[222] Families also were able to manipulate their work routines to help one another. Supervision could be less intense, and family took the opportunity to socialize when possible and come to each other's aid when needed. If workers completed their tasks early, they might spend their remaining workday growing their own crops for consumption or trade, or they could assist other kin. Historian Joyce Chaplin documented that travelers through the colonial low country often commented on the initiative enslaved men and women took to complete their tasks early so they could benefit from their "free time." One such person, she indicated, wrote that a "field negro frequently completes his task of a days work by 12. . . . [He then could use] the remainder of the day at work in his own corn field."[223] Enslaved persons also sometimes spent their Sundays at work in assigned garden plots where they grew cash crops such as tobacco or corn, other vegetables, rice, and tubers.[224]

Skilled men and women often worked independent of kin, with other artisans, or were hired out. Domestics, even children, often lived in their captors' homes, away from other family. Those enslaved artisans living off their captors' property who did not reside with their wives might have had opportunity to visit them more frequently than other abroad husbands. An eighteenth-century waterman named Ned, for example, hired himself out and lived away from his slaveholder for several years. Ned was known to refer to himself as a "free man" and to frequently visit his wife, who lived across the Chesapeake Bay from him, when he was not at work.[225] Elderly workers had tasks that brought them together with kin of other generations since they often took care of the young. Adolescents sent to work and reside far from their families formed fictive kinships with others in the same pitiable situation. These close bonds were indicated, in part, by their decisions to escape together as did Isaac, Caesar, Lester, and Mingo of New York, who ranged in age from fifteen to forty.[226]

HOUSING OF COLONIAL ENSLAVED FAMILIES

Housing in colonial North America, even for bondspeople, was found in an array of styles, sizes, and materials. Enslavers usually insisted that captive housing guarantee their close surveillance and control. As archeologist Teresa Singleton noted, "Nearly every aspect of plantation space from the location and arrangement of slave quarters to the details of slave-house construction resulted from conscious decision making on the part of planters to maximize profits, exercise surveillance and reinforce the subordinate status of enslaved people."[227] Control and profit mattered, not an enslaved family's comfort or cultural tastes.

Among the early British colonies, many of the enslaved, along with White indentured servants, lived in the attics, basements, and back rooms of slaveholders' homes. On small holdings with only one or a few captives, some slept in barn lofts, storage areas, kitchens, laundries, or other outside structures.[228] This pattern changed somewhat after African imports began to equal or outnumber White servants. Then, most Africans and their descendants began to live in independent nearby structures.[229]

Single families who worked together away from the manor home typically lived in one-room wooden cabins. Some also stayed in "duplex" cabins that accommodated two families or several single workers.[230] On some plantations with outlying quarters, one's housing changed when the location of one's work assignment shifted. One's physical home, like that of one's family members, was not stable. Similarly, on those estates—particularly in the Chesapeake, where soil fertility was likely to decline greatly after several years—older captive quarters were abandoned when their adjacent fields were no longer planted.[231]

Being quartered near one's enslaver often meant interference of one sort or another that had implications for Black family life. William Byrd described in his diary in June 1710 his breaking up a love triangle among the enslaved at

Westover. "In the afternoon," he recorded, "I caused L-s-n to be whipped for beating his wife and Jenny was whipped for being his whore."[232]

Colonial captive houses on the home estates of the very elite were made from stone or even brick. George Washington had a large building of brick, known as the "House For Families," that collectively housed many of the children and their parents who resided at his home estate.[233] Because these captives lived close to the Washington family, and because of their elevated status as skilled and domestic captives, their family quarters were constructed substantially better than the quarters of those who lived on Mount Vernon's four outlying farms. Resembling a large dormitory with rows of beds, these quarters no doubt promoted community ties, even if they prevented marital and familial privacy. Of course, privacy was at a premium no matter where an enslaved person resided or the styles of their structures, since captors took it as their right to search sites where the enslaved lived whenever they felt the need or desire to do so.

To avoid prying eyes, many enslaved people constructed their cabins with additional space in cellars or lofts. Some of these cabins, such as those found at eighteenth-century Kingsmill Plantation outside of Williamsburg and later throughout the South, had porches as well. Porches on more than one side of the structure provided additional family space and a place for social activities, both private and public.[234] Historical archeologist James Deetz considered these cellars and porches to be a West African contribution.[235] Sometimes called "hidey holes" by captors, lofts were especially popular and unique.[236] The enslaved constructed them, often against orders, for storage and also to hide food, clothing, medicines, tools, musical instruments, seeds, tobacco for their pipes, weapons, stolen goods, and other items they felt necessary for themselves and their families, regardless of their enslavers' disapproval.

Africans and their descendants who typically had to construct their own living spaces, both in the Caribbean and Central and North America, drew on other memories of western/western central African architecture to provide housing for their families and communities. Many, but not all—depending on the cultural origins of the builder—had curved, dried-mud walls and floors, along with cylindrical thatched grass roofs.[237] Some captive Africans also arranged their houses in "a tightly clustered, asymmetrical village compound" style, as they had done in their home countries.[238]

Remnants of such housing from 1740 have been found in South Carolina. "Excavations at the sites of Curriboo and Yaughan, two former indigo plantations in Berkeley County, South Carolina," one scholar noted, "have revealed the earliest archaeological evidence of African-styled slave housing identified on a southern plantation. These slave quarters made of mud walls and presumably covered with thatched palmetto leaves are like the thatch-roof houses found in many parts of Africa."[239] Each of these buildings housed an average of three or four persons. Tahro of Kuluwaka in Congo, who arrived on one of the last slave ships smuggled into the United States, did build a home very reminiscent of those in his village, made of tightly bound reed walls and a thatched roof.[240] *Redondos* (round houses) have been found to have existed among Spanish owned African captives and their descendants.[241] Others under Spanish control resided in timber-framed small dwellings with clay walls, thatched roofs, and earthen or wood-plank floors.[242]

Still, some slaveholders resisted the desire of Africans to replicate western/western central African architectural styles on their properties. On St. Simon's Islands in low country South Carolina, one enslaved man named Okra built an African-style house, but, his friend recalled, "Massa make 'im pull it down. He say he ain' want no African hut on he place.'"[243]

By 1790, most African-style housing was being replaced by wood frame structures, some to accommodate the few; others, to provide domestic space for many.[244] Somerset plantation near Edenton, North Carolina, had five two-story buildings, each with four rooms that measured twenty by twenty feet, used as sleeping space for 115 enslaved workers. The houses had windows and fireplaces on both floors. Families, sometimes multigenerational ones, occupied the same rooms.[245] Urban captive housing ranged from rooms in the back and basement of slaveholders' homes and garrets above kitchens in rooming houses to captive quarter structures built in alleys in the rear of White-owned shops and housing.[246]

The largest slaveholders in colonial Massachusetts, the Royall family, housed some of their enslaved peoples in a two-story brick building facing an enclosed courtyard at the back of their Medford mansion. Others stayed in nearby workshops, kitchens, and other outhouses.[247] Some urban "industrial" workmen (sometimes ten to fifty of them) lived together in "multistoried wood or brick" buildings.[248] High, thick walls that permitted White surveillance and control enclosed many urban quarters.[249] Other urban captives—the lucky ones—in North American colonies controlled by the British as well as the Spanish, Dutch, and French—had to provide their own housing. This "choice" guaranteed greater privacy, agency, and the ability to form communities with other enslaved and free persons.

It was in these small, often congested spaces that enslaved people witnessed and were part of the defining moments of family life—birth, coupling, death, and illness—ritualized in ways that mostly are lost to us now, given the veil of secrecy they pulled closed in order to avoid, and survive, their captors' gaze and interference. Still, archeology from southern sites, visitors' accounts, and folklore recall some of what occurred in those homes and what material culture helped to frame enslaved Black domesticity during the colonial era and beyond.

Enslaved people's housing in the colonial era typically had fireplaces and chimneys to heat the space, support cooking, and dry clothes. Black captives, such as those at Thomas Jefferson's Monticello, sometimes constructed chimneys that leaned slightly away from the house, so they could be detached quickly if a fire burned out of control. There also is evidence found by archeologist Leland Ferguson that captive housing in South Carolina sometimes did not have fireplaces, which meant that enslaved families might have prepared most of their cooked food outdoors or lived on sites where food preparation was centralized through the labor of designated cooks.[250]

Bondspeople were given little material compensation for the labor that slaveholders demanded. They made do with what they found locally, manufacturing

Traditional Housing Construction by Congo Male Enslaved in South Carolina (front) "The House that Romeo built - front view." Plate XLII in Charles Montgomery, "Survivors from the Cargo of the Negro Slave Yacht Wanderer," *American Anthropologist* (Oct.-Dec. 1908). Courtesy of the American Antiquarian Society Catalog Record 20462.

Quarters Interior, Mount Vernon Home Estate c. 1700s. Photo taken at George Washington's Mount Vernon Historic Site, Mount Vernon, Virginia. *Source*: Outlying quarter log cabin (recreated). Author photograph, December 26, 2016.

some objects for themselves or repurposing found or discarded objects. Up and down the southeastern coast as well as in the Caribbean, archeologists have found in enslaved quarter sites spoons and spoon bowls with decorative geometric markings made by the enslaved.[251] African-influenced pottery, named colonoware, document African artistic, religious, recreational/relaxation, and culinary attributes that were a part of enslaved family life. Not surprisingly, given their consistently large import numbers, some pottery designs resembled those from the Congo-Angolan region.[252] Archeologists uncovered some fifty-eight thousand pieces of colonoware at the Dean Hall Plantation in Beaufort, South Carolina, at the site where a large captive housing unit—as many as nineteen cabins at one point—had existed across generations.[253] Colonoware pottery, according to expert Teresa Singleton, "suggests that enslaved African-Americans prepared food to suit their own tastes, perhaps incorporating aspects of traditional African cuisines," particularly meat and vegetable stews.[254] Patterns on seventeenth-century clay pipes found in the Chesapeake—a staple tool of relaxation for men and women—resembled ritual object designs found in Senegal, Mali, Ghana, and Nigeria.[255]

Archeologists also have found, represented in drawings and paintings and described in accounts from the era, glass beads worn by the enslaved—especially blue ones found in their graves—along with animal horn, bone, and wooden rings that they used for personal adornment. They have located charms and ritual objects of specific, polished shapes and colors purposed by religious practitioners. These ephemera document the many and diverse influences of western/western central Africa on the internal and intimate lives of enslaved families.[256] Likewise, there is much evidence of traditional African basketry used to carry, store, and hide a family's possessions.[257]

COLONIAL BLACK RECREATION

Families came to be spread across farms, cities, and other sites within colonial empires. So, too, did the social and cultural communities that they created.

Slave pipes, Cat Island, SC, 18th-19th century. Sharon Moses, Archaeologist/ Primary Investigator of the Hume Plantation Slave Street Project, *Pipes found under slave cabins*, 2015, Items were recovered from the Hume Plantation Site, Tom Yawkey Wildlife Center, Georgetown, SC.

Weekends meant not only an opportunity for enslaved men and women to farm, hunt, fish, and sometimes hire themselves out for their own benefit, but also a time for family reunification, recreation, worship, courtship, physical care, and emotional healing.

Recreational events held at Christmas, Easter, and Whitsuntide (Pentecost), along with harvest and corn shucking season, promoted familial, fictive kin, and communal activities. Pinkster celebrations in some parts of New York and New Jersey, introduced by the Dutch as part of their recognition of Pentecost and the beginning of the spring season, became important sites of ritualized play and politics, communal unification, and cultural socialization for enslaved and free Blacks. Some allowed their captives three to five days of revelry, including permission to visit family and friends. From large gatherings in Brooklyn, New York City, and Albany to smaller ones at other locales, Black women sang and prepared (and sold) special foods and drinks while drummers and other musicians played the banjo, bones, rattles, and hand claps to accompany dancing and pageantry. Men constructed temporary shelters and a "throne" where an "African King" (purportedly an enslaved man of royal lineage from the Kongo people) was crowned and sat as "ruler" for the remainder of the festivities, collecting coin tribute from all in attendance. Refusal to cooperate sometimes meant the threat of damage to a captor's property.[258] After the "coronation," the real party began, with music and a "Guinea dance" known as Toto. Historian Shane White shared the following description from a local newspaper of events as they unfolded. Although filled with the culturally insensitive and racist judgments of the colonial era, the article nonetheless reveals the presence of African cultural and even political influences. There are depictions of African music, instruments, dance, religion, masquerade, language, and social stratification, alongside and intertwined with ritual attributes of the colonial Dutch.

> The apparent highlight of the festival, was Toto, or the Guinea dance. This took place in the amphitheater in front of the royal arbor. There sat the "chief musician dressed in a horrid manner–rolling his eyes and tossing his head with an air of savage wildness; grunting and mumbling out certain inarticulate but hideous sounds" as he beat upon a Guinea drum. On either side of this character were two imps, "decorated with feathers and cow tails," performing similar "uncouth and terrifying grimaces" while playing on smaller drums and imitating "his sounds of frightful dissonance." Meanwhile, males and females danced but, as "there is no regular air in the music, so neither are there any regular movements in this dance." In fact, the dancers placed their bodies "in the most disgusting attitudes" and performed the "most lewd and indecent gesticulation, at the crisis of which the parties meet and embrace in a kind of amorous Indian hug, terminating in a sort of masquerade capture, which must cover even a harlot with blushes to describe."[259]

Pinkster festivals in the middle colonies were similar to John Canoe masquerades in Virginia, North Carolina, Florida, and still practiced in the Caribbean, as well as Negro Election Day celebrations in Connecticut, Rhode Island, Massachusetts, and New Hampshire. They not only combined African dance, masquerade, and recreation, but also sometimes included suggestions of racialized political upheaval—all while allowing families and communities to share precious time bonding and reasserting a cultural ethos derived, in part at least, from western and western central Africa. So, too, did the carnival masquerades, where African male drumming and rhythmic hand clapping, female singing, and group performances of the calinda, bamboula, jarocho, and other dances by captives and their descendants took place in the Spanish and French colonies of North America.[260]

Holidays and special events, of course, were not the only times during the long colonial era and beyond that enslaved people gathered to enjoy themselves, to worship, and to express their ancestral cultures in music, dance, song, cloth/statuary making, and storytelling—especially animal tales used to pass on moral lessons, communal principles, and resistance strategies—to all listeners, particularly their children.[261] Some even divided into their specific ethnic groups and performed something of a pageant or competition, keeping alive the rich traditions of their homelands, each group waving "flags" made

Winslow Homer, "Dressing for Carnival" Winslow Homer, Dressing for the Carnival, oil on canvas, c. 1877, Amelia B. Lazarus Fund, 1922 (22.220). © The Metropolitan Museum of Art. Imagesource: Art Resource, NY

to represent their ethnicity.[262] Music, song, and dance—sacred, secular, and romantic—filled the quarters on Saturday evenings and throughout Sunday. The enslaved man Dick noted, for example, that before the American Revolution, he spent some of his time romancing a young woman through African song, explaining, "by moonlight I used to play my *banger* [drum] under her window and sing a *Guinea* Love-song my mother taught me."[263]

Christian observers often complained about these African-derived familial/communal affairs. In 1665, Reverend Morgan Godwin of York County, Virginia, grumbled about the enslaved people he encountered, remarking that "nothing is more barbarous, and contrary to Christianity, than their *Idolatrous Dances,* and *Rebels;* in which they usually spend the *Sunday* . . . they use their Dances as *means to procure Rain.*" From South Carolina, Anglican missionary Francis Le Jau noted in 1709 of the enslaved that it was "customary among them to have their feasts, dances, and merry Meetings upon the Lord's day." A few years late, Reverend John Sharpe wrote from New York that Black captives were performing rituals with dance and music over the graves of their dead. Likewise, Reverend George Whitefield accused slaveholders in both the Chesapeake and the low country of taking no interest in converting their enslaved to Christianity as was obvious in letting them use their Sundays for "dancing, piping, and such like."[264]

CONCLUSION

"From the first of our acquaintance, to this moment, I have loved you with unabated fervor, unceasing tenderness; and the purest attachment: and even at this so truly awful and solemn moment, all that seems terrible in death is the parting from you."[265]—Abraham Johnstone, Woodbury Jail, July 8, 1797

Sitting in a hot jail in July in late eighteenth-century Woodbury, New Jersey, Abraham Johnstone consoled himself by writing to his wife, Sarah. He had been found guilty of murdering his former friend, a "Guinea negro" named Thomas Read, and would be hanged the next day. The condemned blacksmith's letter seemed to have had multiple purposes and details at least one Black man's ideas about marriage, family, and spousal relations and responsibilities as the colonial era drew to a close.

Abraham, originally called Benjamin, wanted an opportunity to personally plead his innocence to Sally—his special name for her. He went to his death declaring that he had not killed Read, explaining that his guilty verdict was based on perjury. Equally importantly, he wanted to declare his deep and abiding love and affection for his wife. It was only the thought of leaving her behind once he was executed, Abraham lamented, that made his impending death "appear unfriendly or unwelcome."[266] He needed, as a last act as her husband, to put in order the state of their marriage. He asked Sally to forgive him for his infidelity. Abraham also took the opportunity to challenge Sally's commitment to him given that she had refused to visit him in jail, even though he had asked the sheriff to guarantee her safety. Hoping to extend some counsel to, and perhaps control over, her after his death, Abraham offered some instruction for her future well-being. It is in his poignant declarations and questions to Sally just before his death that Abraham, who had been born enslaved, became a fugitive, and later argued that he was a free man (a fact that was not clearly established by legal documents) outlined many of the foundational designs of his marital relationship as he believed them to be.

What did it mean to be in a marriage at the end of the eighteenth century for Black people whose lives were anything but stable? Abraham married Sally, a freeborn woman, while he was still enslaved. As a couple, the two had lived both together and abroad. Abraham's itinerant lifestyle—a result of being hired out, being sold five times, and his fleeing of "Georgia traders"— probably contributed to his wandering eye and infidelity. He had, at the time of his death, a thirteen-year-old son born free of another woman. He "went astray and lusted after other women" and "transgressed" their marriage bed, he acknowledged to Sally.[267]

Abraham's confessions and advice to Sally indicate a strong sense of gendered responsibilities, including patriarchal and wifely obligations, that he believed should be upheld in a marriage. Both spouses should love each other deeply and passionately, as he did Sally. Even though he had been sexually unfaithful, "yet still my dear Sally," he wrote, "my true and fond heart rested with you, and love for you always brought your wanderer back."[268] It was this deep abiding love, Abraham went on to profess, that moved him to want to see her one last time. Hoping that she, too, had loved him as much, he chided: "Indeed my dear Sally had it been your case as it was mine: no earthly consideration should or would have kept me from seeing. Even was certain death to be the consequence."[269] Her absence felt like a "dagger" thrust into his already "rankled wound."[270] Although Sally had failed what Abraham contended was a true test of her love, he still detested not being able to continue to serve as her husband—to be her protector, her supporter, and a comfort to her. "Leaving you behind in the world without a husband to protect you, or friend to sooth, console, or alleviate your distresses, miseries or wants, or support, and enable you to bear up under," was a painful thought.[271]

Abraham's notions of a husband's duty also extended to financial support. He left his wife the bulk of his small estate, including an undisclosed sum of money and a special hat of his that he knew she particularly liked.[272] Another reason that he wanted to see Sally was to give her "consel. . . with respect to your future conduct." Once he was gone, she should as any Christian woman would, he implied, strive to follow the teachings of their faith and resist being drawn into a life of "frolicking" or participating in "lewdness, excesses, debaucheries, licentiousness, obscenity, [and] profanity."[273] He also cautioned Sally to avoid busybodies and gossips. Perhaps most importantly, Abraham wanted her to choose a new husband, reminding her that she "certainly will need one" who will "love and protect you." This man should be one whom she could respect and not fear, who would be a true husband rather than a "pretty baby" who might harbor a bad character—that is, be violent or unfaithful.[274] With his final instructions and bequeaths, Abraham kissed his letter as a farewell gesture to their Black marital bonds of love, marriage, and family in early America.[275]

Chapter 3

Traditions of Resistance and Family from the Colonial Era Forward

The Revolutionary War was drawing to a close, and the enslaved African known as Ben Maul, who was brought to Maryland in about 1730, was growing old[1]—so old, in fact, that his captor had reduced Ben's workload dramatically and allowed him to live away from his closely watched and controlled prime workers. Ben had been a captive in Maryland for some fifty years, and even though he had been sold at least once, he had managed to marry and have at least one child and several grandchildren. His family had become culturally African American, but he was still the African who held himself aloof from creolized Blacks, continued to practice the religion of his ancestors, and faithfully passed on many stories of his African life and culture to his American-born descendants. Ben's determination to maintain his indigenous African subjectivity was a legacy of resistance that lived on in his multigenerational family, fueling both his son's and his grandson's freedom dreams. The American Revolution had been an important event in their lives, but their pursuit of freedom had been internalized long before the war between Britain and the thirteen mainland colonies that rebelled against it came to be and would continue long after the new United States of America was formed.

Family was essential to a bondsperson's life, and resistance was crucial to their familial endeavors. Family not only meant love, support, procreation, socialization, protection, and reverence; its humanizing impulse also meant resistance. Resistance—to dehumanization, ill treatment, emasculation and defeminization, infantilization, suppression of one's culture, destruction of one's family, and the undermining of family roles—was a fundamental ethos located not only within the individual but also within enslaved families and communities.

Slave Hunt: Dismal Swamp, Virginia, c. 1862. Thomas Moran (American, 1837-1926). *Slave Hunt, Dismal Swamp, Virginia*, 1861-62. Oil on canvas, 34 x 44". Philbrook Museum of Art, Tulsa, Oklahoma. Gift of Laura A. Clubb, 1947.8.44.

Enslaved parents ignored the notion of "illegal" behavior imposed by their captors as they socialized their children through example, oral tales, and instruction to resist oppression. The lessons began when youth witnessed their parents, older siblings, other kin, and members of their quarters find effective ways to avoid material deprivation and physical, sexual, and psychological abuse, while keeping as much of their interior lives and cultural expressions beyond the gaze of enslavers, supervisors, and patrols. Enslaved children learned to walk a fine line to maintain their humanity and agency while not annoying, angering, frightening, or openly disrespecting White authority figures—or at least not being caught doing so.

One of their first resistance lessons was to "mask"—that is, to hide as much as possible about themselves and others close to them. This "invisibility" was essential to their survival. As captive children grew into adolescents and adults, they learned how to recognize and factor in the consequences of rebellious or compliant behavior on themselves and their kin. Family ties often were at the root of an individual's defiance. It also forced submission. Slaveholders understood that families were one of their most potent weapons they could use to "control" a bondsperson. Disobedience often led to brutal punishment and also threats to the well-being of one's children, spouse, siblings, or parents.

Enslaved adults realized that resistance occurred on a continuum that extended from the smallest act of personal rebellion to full-scale, community-wide revolt. So, too, did White authority understand that a Black refugee[2] could become part of a maroon society, and how maroons might plot and sponsor rebellion and revolution. As early as 1691, the colonial legislature in Virginia passed "An Act for suppressing outlying Slaves" that noted the "many times negroes, mulattoes, and other slaves unlawfully absent themselves from their masters and mistresses service, and lie hid and lurk in obscure places," creating a life for themselves and their families that their enslavers could neither control nor extract benefit from.[3] Slaveholders and their state-sponsored advocates were prepared to eliminate all these threats with both legal and extralegal actions, including violent destruction of the individual, marriages, and families.

CUSTOMARY WHITE-ON-BLACK VIOLENCE

Children/I've been 'buked and I've been scorned.[4]

Black captives and their kin endured incredible amounts of material, physical, psychological, and sexual violence from captors, overseers and their wives, drivers, patrollers, slave merchants, sheriffs, and other "policing" forces. Most of these perpetrators received little or no punishment for their acts as indicated from the following examples.

"Ann Smith, Spinster" of Maryland was convicted and later "reprieved" for killing someone's son—"a Negro boy"—in 1696.[5] Thomas Sorrell of Westmoreland County, Virginia, was placed on trial in April 1786 for murdering a child—one whom Sorrell had hired. The jury found him not guilty, but there was enough information for at least one among them to challenge traditional White privilege and declare that the verdict was "directly contrary to evidence."[6] In French Natchez in September 1727, court testimony was heard regarding an overseer who had bound an enslaved man's hands for five hours and "inflicted" "600 rawhide lashes." His Black family—perhaps even a wife, parent, or child—endured the pain of knowing their kinsman had suffered such physical agony and gangrene that led to the loss of two fingers from his right hand and two fingertips from his left "in sequel to strangulation by tight cords." A Louisiana mother, Junon, threatened to kill herself if her female captor continued to mistreat her child.[7] A Black father and husband suffered the loss of his wife and children. She died as a result of violence while being confiscated, along with their four children, as payment for their

Flogging a Slave Fastened to the Ground. Walter George Mason, Flogging of a Slave Fastened to the Ground, Five Hundred Thousand Strokes for Freedom: A Series of Anti-Slavery Tracts, of which Half a Million are Now Issued by the Friends of the Negro Collection, Sc Rare 326.4-A, Manuscripts, Archives and Rare Books Division, Schomburg Center for Research in Black Culture, Manuscripts, Archives and Rare Books Division, The New York Public Library.

slaveholder's debt.[8] In the spring of 1791, Defendant Gee of South Carolina was pronounced guilty for shooting and killing someone's son, "a negro boy, named Sawney," and sentenced to seven years' hard labor. The prosecution had asked for the death penalty, arguing that "the frequency of the offence" of captive murder was due, in part, to the light sentences imposed on those found guilty. The motion was denied.[9] In that same state in 1804, a sheriff was found guilty and fined for "killing a negro by undue correction."[10] Records also document the trial of a Georgia master who shot and killed his bondsman (someone's son, father, husband, or brother) Ezekiel in 1822.[11] A South Carolina enslaver admitted in 1807 to abusing and then refusing to provide medical care for someone's kinswoman. A local physician had found her on the road "in a miserable condition, almost naked, shockingly beaten, and having an iron on her leg of fifteen pounds weight." The enslaver threatened to have the doctor, who had given the desperate woman medical attention, prosecuted for "harboring his slave."[12] And in an account of one of the most grisly treatments of someone's son, Pierre Viaud, who experienced a shipwreck on the way to French New Orleans in 1766, wrote that he killed and ate his enslaved man to avoid starvation and that of his White female companion.[13] "What wrong shall I be guilty of?" Viaud asked. "This animal is my entire property; I have bought him for my sole use, and what greater service can his whole life amount to than relieving the miseries which now oppress me."[14]

Enslaved people routinely confronted sexual violence.[15] Sexual abuse of women and children was taken for granted by those who had power over Black captives. Even White men who were not their slaveholders demanded sexual access and control. Magdalena testified that in 1778 she was "seated on the steps of her master's house" in French Louisiana when the carpenter Titon tried to convince her to "concede him favors." When she repeatedly refused to do so and Magdalena's captor threatened to have him arrested, Titon broke into her room. When he found her with another man, he attacked her and the man with a sharp object like a "sword or knife."[16] Enslavers and labor supervisors also used sexual and physical assault of females to punish their male kin. The "steward" Jacques Charpentier was tried in Louisiana in January 1730 "on charges of cruelty to slaves, and the suspicious death of one or more of them." The court noted in particular his "causing frequent abortions among the women by corporeal punishment in pregnancy." There was the "insinuation" in the testimony that he had tortured these women because they had refused his sexual advances—"his lust in the open field." Evidence also indicated that Charpentier had sought revenge on one of the males, Brunet, by viciously beating his wife "on the head and breast with closed fists." Charpentier eventually killed Brunet.[17]

Families constantly faced the threat of separation through sale, exchange, or inheritance. Intra- and intercolonial sales were regular occurrences in colonial North America and the newly formed United States, with the enslaved sold and distributed across empires. The enslaved woman Daffney was sold from Jamaica to South Carolina two years before she managed to escape. Likewise, Sylvia from Bermuda was suspected to have tried to return there after she escaped from a new captor in the Carolinas.[18] The advertiser for her return explained that he believed Sylvia might "endeavor to get off to the West Indies," where she undoubtedly hoped members of her family still resided. Even those claimed by clergy found little sympathy to family connection when their status as property was at stake.[19]

Typical advertisements were like one found in the 1723 *American Weekly Mercury* of Philadelphia concerning the sale of "three very likely Negro girls, being about 16 years of age and a Negro boy being about 14."[20] Elkanah Watson also noted of a 1778 auction in Wilmington, North Carolina, in which a family was separated, "A poor wench clung to a little daughter, and implored, with the most agonizing supplication, that they must not be separated. But, alas, either the master or circumstances were inexorable—they were sold to different purchasers. The husband and the residue of the family were knocked off to the highest bidder."[21] Several years earlier, Sambo had been convicted and castrated for unsuccessfully trying to prevent the sale of his daughter to a woman who had the reputation for being a mean mistress. An herbal doctor known locally for his medicinal practice, Sambo, with the assistance of another enslaved man, tried to administer to the White woman a mind-altering drug known among enslaved people as "touck."[22]

These separations came particularly at the birth, marriage, financial crisis, or, especially, the death of a slaveholder. Some did try to protect families. In the case of the human property of Mrs. Hannah Beale Bull (widow of an acting governor) whose Ashley Hall Plantation was located in low country South Carolina, executors compiled in December 1797 a list of her ninety captives and the prices both of persons to be sold as individuals and the values of enslaved families if they were to be sold intact.[23] Since the Bulls had no children, their Black captives in South Carolina and the proceeds from the labor of those in Jamaica were distributed to their nieces and nephews.[24] George Brown of North Carolina determined that his daughters, Mary and Peg, were to receive the enslaved females Lucy and Chloe when they married or reached the age of twenty-one. Others were distributed at the time of his death.[25] Robert Raper of Charleston stipulated that his enslaved people should choose their new "masters" among his heirs or be sold by private sale ("not by public"). Remarkably, he also freed parts of two bonded families. Raper's "old Negro woman Judy" was to receive 150 pounds sterling and her freedom, while Betsy was bequeathed 150 pounds and the emancipation of her children, Jack and Betsy.[26]

More seventeenth- and eighteenth-century enslavers were like Benjamin Sherrod of North Carolina, who wrote in his 1759 will that his two sons should each receive a "negroe of his choice." Sherrod's widow and daughter were bequeathed the right to hire the remaining out. He made no stipulation for the retention of family groups. Mr. Mullington, also of North Carolina, made certain the destruction of families when he noted in his 1800 will that "the children which . . . may be born of the . . . negro wench Moll, [be] bequeathed to my granddaughter Lucy Lewis."[27] Notations on the captive lists of the Gatewood family in Virginia indicate that they gave away more than a third of all their enslaved youth born between 1773 and 1793, and more than a fifth of those born in the next generation. There also were losses to families divided when the younger Gatewood moved some 200 miles westward, taking many of his father's bondspeople with him.[28] Even when stipulated that a Black family should be sold together, they had no control over the actions of whomever purchased them. For example, when Mr. Smelie "offered for an entire family" in South Carolina in January 1802, their new slaveholder sold one because he believed them to be "worthless and diseased."[29]

Adolescence in the colonial period, as in the nineteenth century, typically was marked by the first-time enslaved family members were forced to leave their kin (if not first separated as a result of the division of an estate). A few examples underscore a common occurrence.

Isabella Baumfree, better known as Sojourner Truth, born in 1797 in New York, was sold the first of three times at age twelve or thirteen.[30] Many colonial family members never saw each other after these separations; some were more fortunate. One female recalled that after her master died, her family was divided between heirs. Her mother had already died, and, like many extended families, another kinswoman was raising her. "My grandmother had begged hard to be reckoned with me," but the two had been given to different family members. They came to reside with the same heir several years later.[31] Others, who lived close to their loved ones but were forbade to have contact with them, resisted this deep cruelty. One South Carolina master who owned "several small children" but whose mother was claimed by a neighbor refused to either sell the children to their mother's enslaver or to let the children see her. Nonetheless, the children would run away to her, and she would "harbor" them in the kitchen where she worked. The children's captor was so determined to control the access of the children to their mother that he sued the mother's enslaver on the grounds that he was "harboring his negroes." When he lost the suit, he went on to petition the state's attorney general and then the state legislature. They failed to appease him.[32] The family, however, remained separated. Captive hire across or between colonial empires could mean devastating losses for families as well. Monsieur Maurin of New Orleans, for one, hired out some of his slaves to Cuba and Hispaniola.[33]

RELIGION AND RESISTANCE

Slaveholders routinely regarded the resistance efforts of enslaved peoples as indicative of their moral shortcomings rather than as a rational response to slaveholder mistreatment and immorality. However, many bondspeople invested in belief systems that created a spiritual and cultural distance between themselves and their "masters" and provided psychological support and resistance for them and their families, as will be noted here and in subsequent chapters.[34]

The "religions" of the enslaved during the colonial eras varied greatly, with aspects of indigenous African beliefs and rituals blended with Islamic, Protestant, and Catholic texts and practices. Examples of syncretic religious practices were flush in the Black Atlantic, including North America. Hoodoo and voodoo drew on Yoruba rituals and beliefs. Beliefs and activities linked to the Mende's Poro and Sande societies, the Kongo, and Muslims were evidenced in South Carolina, along with Igbo practices that were well documented on Sapelo and other low country Sea Islands. Moreover, as religious historian Albert Raboteau noted, conjure was not just a way to explain "evil" but also a way for "root" doctors to invoke harm as well as to remove it. This sentiment certainly was appealing to people who otherwise had very limited control of the good and bad in their lives and those of their loved ones.[35]

Parents and family elders passed on these practices through their own actions and oral traditions in the form of auto/biographical tales, recitations of conjure ingredients, ghost and animal stories, dream interpretations, and song. Consider, for example, some of the evidence of the practice of Islam or some syncretic religious forms. One low country woman whom historian Sylvianne Diouf identified as "Old Lizzy Gray" explained of her religious beliefs that "Christ built the first church in Mecca and he grave was da."[36] Belali Mohomet and his wife, Phoebe, according to their children and grandchildren, made certain to pray with the sunrise and sunset, bowing to the sun three times and then kneeling on mats to pray with their string of beads. Phoebe also wore a white veil from her head to her shoulders. So, too, did another Muslim woman named Daphne.[37] Others remembered the African they called Old Israel, who wrapped his head in a white cloth and kept a hidden "book," presumably a copy of the Koran, that he brought out while kneeling on a mat and praying, also with the rising and setting of the sun.[38] There also was Omar Ibn Said, enslaved in North and South Carolina, a learned man of Islam from Futa Toro in Senegal who could still quote, and write in Arabic, long passages of the Koran years after his capture and sale in 1807. He eventually came to know and practice Christianity, but never forgot his family, their faith and teachings, or the sheiks in his homeland.[39] Recording his autobiography in the 1830s, he recalled that before his capture at the age of thirty-seven, he studied Islam for several years, made several pilgrimages to Mecca, routinely fought "infidels," prayed five times daily, and gave alms in gold, silver, seeds, cattle, sheep, goats, rice, wheat, and barley.[40]

The importance of religion was part of long family traditions derived from their African pasts and sustained through their enslavement.[41] Bondspeople embraced religious beliefs, practices, and public demonstrations as central to their identities and kin relations. As a fundamental cultural marker that could be experienced visually and orally, religious beliefs and practice styles were some of the most portable, and therefore enduring, of cultural attributes—and potentially revolutionary ideology—for enslaved people across the generations. African women and men could, and did, transfer the ideal that religion was a central component of one's identity with them from western/western central Africa to the mainland colonies during the era of the African slave trade and then again along the roadways from the Upper to the Lower South and southwest as part of the domestic trade in humans.[42] Others renewed these beliefs when they arrived as part of the illegal African trade in the decades before the Civil War.

Charles Ball recalled that his grandfather, the Ben Maul whose story opened this chapter, continued to practice his traditional religion and took great pains to explain it to Charles. He prayed daily, sometimes multiple times when his workload allowed him to do so. Rejecting Christianity as "altogether false," Ben recalled a "holy man" who had received his religious tenets from the "true God" in heaven, preached it on Earth and recorded it in a book, a copy of which was kept in every family. Rules of one's moral and social behaviors, especially in the treatment of family and community, were strict and uncompromising. All adherents had to express a deep "love of country, charity and social affection," avoid being

Photo of Omar Ibn Said, c. 1850. Photographer unknown, *Half Length Formal Portrait of "Uncle Moreau" [Omar Ibn Said]*, c. 1850, Randolph Linsly Simpson African-American Collection. James Weldon Johnson Memorial Collection in the Yale Collection of American Literature, Beinecke Rare Book and Manuscript Library.

cruel, remain sober, and be truthful. Ben's grandfather's faith also required "tenderness to wives and children."[43] The many children of Hannah and Calina, both Igbos in the low country, likewise learned much about their parents' indigenous cultural lives from them, including religious rituals.[44] "Dey talk lot of funny talk tuh each udduh," a past acquaintance noted, "an dey is mighty puhticuluh bout prayin. Dey pray on duh bead"—that is, they used beads for divination purposes. Others recalled participation in African-influenced harvest rituals that included praying, singing all night, and, with the sunrise, "we go out an dance" to "big beatin uh drums." One noted that they shouted and danced in a circle not only to drums but also to rattles made from dried gourds with seeds in them and to the beating of tin plates. "Hahves festival, dey call it."[45] Families and fictive kin took part in this annual communal religious practice, similar in description to Igbo yam festivals.[46]

Christian missionaries and ministers of various denominations continued to have potent competition from deeply embedded African religious traditions that were sources of Black diasporic pride, belonging, and knowledge that enslavers could not manipulate for their own purposes. Many complained of the "heathenist rites," "superstition" and "idolatry" that bondspeople clung to despite efforts to rid them of this resource.[47]

Certainly, by the time of the American Revolution, some enslaved people in North America had become Christian converts—at least outwardly, or in conjunction with the retention of their traditional African and Islamic religious practices.[48] Colonial missions like that of the French Huguenot Francis Le Jau in South Carolina included catechism, rituals, and religious counsel for free and enslaved peoples. The reverend centered much of his counsel on trying to get enslaved people to be monogamous and not to dance, feast, and have "merry Meetings" on Sundays.[49] In all the British colonies, being a Christian also could mean "benefit of clergy" that could spare one a death penalty if found guilty for a first criminal offense. Similarly, Catholic conversion in Maryland, as among the Spanish and French, allowed for some marital and familial protections. So, too, for those in the Dutch colonies who married in the Dutch Reformed Church.[50]

These "privileges," and the tenet that all were equal before God, associated with Christian conversion are precisely why many British colonial and early republic slaveholders would not allow their bondspeople to be a part of an organized church or religious society.[51] The Great Awakenings of the 1740s and later decades, however, still helped to swell the numbers of Black converts in the Northeast, middle colonies, and southern locales. Thousands attended revivals and camp meetings. The Methodists recorded more than 12,000 Black members by the turn of the century, with the Baptists claiming closer to 18,000 Black converts.[52] Nonetheless, many slaveholders still resented Black Christian conversion and those who sponsored it.

Christian adults, like those who adhered to their indigenous belief systems, passed on the benefits of their faith to their children and other kin. The formerly enslaved woman Elizabeth, for example, who was born in 1766 in Maryland, spoke of the lifelong imprint of her parents' religious faith and teachings. Both were Methodists, and her father "read in the Bible aloud to his children every Sabbath morning." Elizabeth felt deeply God's presence in her life from the age of five. Once separated from her parents, her mother comforted her by reminding her that God always cared for her. Her parents' teachings of Christianity helped Elizabeth to reject her utter sense of hopelessness. "I betook myself to prayer," she explained, "and in every lonely place I found an altar."[53]

STRIKING BACK

"Maybe it just sags like a heavy load. *Or does it explode?*[54]

Murder, Rape, Arson

Laws were of little help to many enslaved people, providing little means to defend themselves, assuage their rage, or answer their needs for revenge. Legal statutes typically forbade bondspersons from holding weapons, and enslaved people could not physically assault Whites, even in their own defense. Those with judicial or legislative power usually were unwilling to forgive an enslaved person for even shielding their spouse, children, or other kin from a slaveholder's abuse. Racial privilege and property ownership held supreme. Still, some men and women—out of necessity, despair, rage, or even a sense of fair play—were willing to risk torture, exile, and even death to protect themselves and their kin. Harry, whom his French Louisiana captor regarded "ungovernable," resisted a whipping and fought until the slaveholder shot and killed him.[55]

As colonial judicial records indicate, poison proved a ready remedy and one that many Africans had knowledge of from their traditional cultures. In Orange County, Virginia, Turk, Pompey, and a woman named Dido, who may have been Turk's wife, were found guilty in 1732 of poisoning Ambrose Madison, the paternal grandfather of James Madison.[56] "Negro Bess" of Maryland "was convicted for feloniously attempting to murder with poison . . . her Master in 1738."[57] Tida was hanged for a similar offense in 1757.[58] Sue of North Carolina was found to have tried to poison her captor and "several of his family" with arsenic.[59] "Negro David" in 1766 was indicted for attempting to "Poison and Murder his Master, and found Guilty."[60] Bett and Poll, North Carolina domestics, poisoned their slaveholder with "white arsenic."[61]

Sometimes couples, families, or even neighbors were involved in the plot. Bondspeople Pompey and Indey of Maryland were executed for trying to poison the overseer, clerk, and gardener on their captor's estate in 1739.[62] Likewise, "Negro Anthony and Negro Jenny" were sentenced to death several years later for "Consulting, Conspiring and advising to Poison their late Master Jeremiah Chase."[63] Toe, Sambo, and Betty attempted to poison both their male and female slaveholders in 1764.[64] Seven enslaved persons—Seymore, Ceasar, Charles, Ben, Cooper, Mol, and Marlborough—were sentenced to be executed in 1742 for the murder of their captor, Jeremiah Pattison.[65] In South Carolina, the enslaved man Manuel stood trial for "administering poison."[66] So, too, did Bernardo, Cipion, Carlos, and Francisco of Mrs. Trepanier, and Mr. de Bellile of Louisiana "for having wished to poison [de Bellile] and his overseer" in 1773.[67]

Poison was hardly the only manner of murder that bound people employed. Jacob stabbed his captor, Mary Utye of Baltimore, twice in the arm in 1645, causing her to bleed to death.[68] A French Louisiana captive was believed to have stabbed both his enslaver and the enslaver's son-in-law in 1763.[69] Peter killed his "master," his "mistress," and their child in 1761, in a manner described by the court as "barbarous and cruel." It was ordered that he "be hanged in Chains on the main Road as near the Place where the Fact was committed as possible," no doubt to discourage others from harming their captors.[70] A late-eighteenth-century North Carolina enslaved man killed his enslaver the day before he was to be sold.[71] The captured refugee Temba, with several accomplices, murdered his Louisiana slaveholder in June 1771. Temba was angry because he could not visit his wife, Mariana, who was held at a neighboring plantation. Others of his co-conspirators, including the blacksmith Mirliton, resented their captors for refusing to give them time off to be with kin and other activities. He and Temba were both placed on the rack and tortured to death publicly before Temba's hands were cut off to display. Mariana received one hundred lashes and had her earlobes removed. A comrade, the Guinea-born Carlos, was tarred and feathered.[72]

Not only did enslaved people fight and kill their slaveholders, but some were accused and convicted of sexually assaulting their female captors or other White women. If these accusations were true, these violent, misogynistic attacks struck at the heart of gendered, racialized privileges and protections. Arthur, an inveterate escapee, alcoholic, thief, and adulterer from Massachusetts, reputedly raped a widow, Deborah Metcalf, and was hanged for his crimes in 1768.[73] "Negro Robin" of Maryland was found guilty of theft and rape, resulting in his hanging.[74] In 1769, David was condemned to death for rape, as was a mulatto bondsman called Jack.[75] The following year, Abraham faced charges of theft and attempted rape. He "confessed" to both—"extorted from him upon a Whipping inflicted on him by his said Master." The colony of Maryland transported him within ten days of his conviction.[76] More than a decade earlier, however, plaintiffs had not been able to provide enough evidence to convict Harry of "ravishing . . . a Widow Woman." The court concluded that, with "not sufficient" evidence and since the community had known Harry to always have been "an orderly Fellow," he was to be pardoned of the crimes that he had been accused of committing."[77]

Others resorted to arson and work animal abuse—destroying the means and results of their bound labor. A Black captive woman was executed for burning up a "rolling house" and the tobacco inside of it in Virginia in 1731.[78] In Maryland, two women, "Negro Jenny and Negro Grace the slaves of . . . Galloway," were ordered executed in 1751 after "willfully burning a Tobacco House belonging to the Said Galloway."[79] "Negro Cesar" set fire to his captor's barn in 1765.[80] "Negro Abraham" was pardoned for burning the kitchen.[81] In another case of arson, a pardon was not forthcoming for the enslaved woman Beck. She had drunk some cider and accidentally left the tap open, resulting in most of it spilling out in the barn. One of her captors, Mrs. Smith, discovered the fiasco and threatened Beck, who did not have permission to drink the cider, that she would tell what had happened. Fearing the beating that Mr. Smith would give her, Beck begged Mrs. Smith not to tell him. The woman refused. Beck, desperate to cover up her act, burned down the barn. Mrs. Smith later appealed to the court to pardon Beck, noting that she would feel guilty if Beck was executed. The court refused to spare Beck's life.[82] Similarly, a New York court found an enslaved man guilty of "fir[ing] his master's barn and outbuildings, and thus destroyed much grain, together with live-stock."[83] He was burned at the stake for his crimes.

Economies of the Enslaved

Theft was another popular form of resistance. Many, as responsible family members, actively participated in an underground economy that provided them, and their kin, with necessary food, clothing, and other material resources. Colonial court records confirm that theft was a common crime. The typical sentence was death. Captives, uncompensated for their labor, stole what they could use, sell, or barter, or that they simply wanted. Pompey, Sambo, and Jack were found guilty in 1754 for stealing "fifty Pounds of Bacon and Ten Gallons of Rum," both popular items for consumption and trade. The court eventually pardoned Sambo, the son of Pompey, because they believed he had been "influenced by the Authority of Father." Pompey suffered the death penalty. So, too, did Jack, but only after he was convicted a second time for stealing bacon and attempting to kill his captor.[84] Other common items stolen were horses, money, weapons, and ammunition. Mulatto Charles, Tom, Nace, Ned, Jack, and James—along with many others—were convicted of such crimes. Stephen received the death penalty in 1764 for stealing gunpowder from his captor.[85] Mulatto Jack and Negro Ishmael tried to steal horses in the 1740s and were convicted but pardoned.[86] Testimony in October 1713 implicated Jenny, who intended to exchange two "sticks of whalebone" with a local White woman, Mary Guthrie, for two "fould or Dunghill Cockes." Jenny, no doubt, would use the chickens to produce both eggs and chicks that would provide necessary protein to her family and provide a means to acquire additional items she could use to trade for other necessities.[87]

In French Louisiana in 1723, the court examined "Negro Songot" on a "charge of robbery," and "negro Petit Jean" of theft, along with an Englishman named Langolis."[88] Five years later, a Louisiana court heard the case of two Bambara males, Pierot and Sabany, and Changereau, a Mande male, and one known as Francois for either stealing or receiving "heifers for fresh meat." Pierot admitted to stealing corn but denied the charge of pilfering heifers. Francois confessed that he had stolen some bacon that he exchanged with another captive for tobacco. Changereau explained to the court that he had run away and eaten the stolen meat because he was "underfed."[89]

The following decade, enslaved Louisiana people were charged with stealing, among other items, rice,[90] weapons, gold, turkeys, blankets and other linens,[91] fine clothes,[92] money,[93] indigo, potatoes, fruit, and pigs.[94] The couple Cesario and Marguerita, along with Marguerita's sister, Rozeta, were all found guilty in 1777 of theft and conspiracy. Marguerita, who was hired out, explained that her husband Cesario sometimes helped her to pay her rent—presumably from the money he stole, and she and Rosa helped him to hide.[95] Far to the North in Detroit, the enslaved woman Ann Wyley was arrested as part of a suspected group who committed arson and robbery. Wyley, whose family connections are unknown, was found in the possession of a stolen purse, money, and women's clothing.[96] In Savannah, the court heard testimony in 1772 that suspicious meetings were being held in those houses that bondspeople rented, where not only "Spirits and other liquors" were sold, but also "Stolen goods often Concealed."[97] The prior year, Georgia justices sentenced a "Slave Man" to death for "breaking a Shop and Stealing Sundry goods."[98] In 1797, "Negro Peter" was found guilty of stealing a "game cock of the value of fifty pounds of tobacco." He received as punishment "ten stripes" on his back and a five-minute stay in the pillory.[99] Meanwhile in South Carolina, a pregnant woman named Chloe miscarried after being violently beaten by a neighboring slaveholder who accused her of stealing his chicken. According to witnesses, the man "assaulted Chloe violently with his fists, knocked her down, gave her four or five blows about the head, kicked her twice in the back, and swore he would have her ears." Court testimony revealed that it was Chloe's husband, and not her, who had stolen the fowl. The defendant had to pay $500 to Chloe's captor for harming her and killing her unborn child—his property.[100]

Self-Emancipators

> Freedom, Freedom where are you? . . . I'ma keepa running 'cause a winner don't quit on themselves.[101]

No other form of documentation provides more insight regarding enslaved family resistance than enslaved escape notices and recapture advertisements published in the British, Spanish, Dutch, and French colonies in North America. The same phenomenon existed in the newly formed United States during and after the Revolution. The thousands of recovery advertisements found in colonial and later newspapers, as well as the budding number of maroon societies in the swamps, mountains, and other physically isolated areas, document this very family-centered mode of resistance. Many colonial-era refugees were Africans recently separated from their homelands and families. A court in Louisiana ordered that a "Bambara" captive man who had just arrived on the ship *L'Aurore* be whipped "by the public executioner" because he repeatedly escaped and, when captured, had "seized his master's gun."[102] Surveys of enslaved people on the run in South Carolina from 1732 to 1782 indicate that about two-thirds were Africans. A similar account of refugees from Georgia for the period 1763 to 1775 document three-quarters were African born.[103] Some of the accounts from the era also indicate that when Africans escaped in groups, they often did so with persons of the same ethnicity—most probably their first fictive kin relations in the colonies. "TWO LUSTY NEW EBO NEGRO FELLOWS" in Georgia, for example, escaped together from Joseph Gibbons in 1767.[104] Two "Mandinga" men and one from "Guinea" managed to get away from James Laurens of Charleston in 1774.[105] Some who had managed to marry and have children in the colonies escaped with them. In 1777, three African male/female couples—five individuals designated as being from the "Guiney country" and one male from the "Kishee" (Kisi) country—escaped together from Lachlan McGillivray in Georgia."[106]

Enslaved men and women usually absconded in attempts to reunite with family from whom they had been separated or to seek freedom as couples, families, and fictive kin groups. Refugees left on their own or with children, siblings, or spouses; a few others from their quarters; and sometimes in larger groups. Barbery in South Carolina ran away with her young child who was not yet walking.[107] Frances supposedly went to her husband, whom her captor believed was "harboring" her.[108] In Louisiana, Temba routinely escaped to "sleep with a negress called Mariana."[109] Silvia was believed to have escaped to her mother, who recently had been sold.[110] John Jones estimated that two of his fugitive men—twenty-year-old "country born" Joe and eighteen-year-old "African born" Tom, who had "his Country Marks in his Cheeks"—returned after six months to get 10-year-old James."[111] Some, like Tom. who had parents on George Washington's plantation and was still in that vicinity one year after his escape, lingered even longer near loved ones to try to take them to freedom or to seek their protection from catchers.[112] Abraham and his disabled wife, Hagar (she had a wooden leg), escaped with their three-year-old son, Jacob.[113] Four other refugees—a Guinea man named Moses; his creole wife, Lettice; a Guinea woman called Juno; and a creole man named Jack, perhaps the husband of Juno—escaped together.[114] Isaac and Isabel ran away with their child once they arrived from New York in Charleston, where they were to be sold.[115] A group of ten refugees—including a mother, Affy, and her eight-year-old son Peter—escaped from a captive ship in the Charleston harbor that was carrying them from Baltimore to the Spanish Caribbean.[116] Nine bondspersons left the Georgia plantation of James Deveau in 1770—three men, three women, and three children.[117] Sancho, Warwick, Bella, and Phebe, all from the same "quarters" in Virginia, and no doubt either friends, family, or both, escaped together in April 1738. They were not alone when they did so. The others who accompanied them included brothers Dollar (age twenty-one) and Greenock (age twenty-three), the mulatto couple James and Tabitha, and a mother with her adolescent son. Three slaveholders claimed these ten refugees, who all lived close to one another in the same expansive Black community comprised of fictive kin and communal ties across numerous miles. Equally important, their group exodus, followed by their armed burglary of several houses and the theft of a canoe, suggests that these relatively young men and women (aged seventeen to thirty-five) might have planned to form a maroon society once they reached the nearby Dismal Swamp.[118] The *New York Gazette* of June 24, 1734, carried an advertisement regarding the escape in Monmouth County, New Jersey, of an Indigenous man, Stoffels, with a man of half Indigenous/half Black descent and a mulatto. The multiracial refugee group had stolen a canoe, and it was believed that they were trying to reach Rhode Island or Connecticut.[119]

Not only did refugee couples and family units abscond together, some imagined "coupling" within the context of their escape plans. Billy, a South Carolina bondsman, tried unsuccessfully to "induce" a Black woman living on a nearby farm "to go off with him." When she refused, he managed to convince another woman from those quarters, Hannah, to do so, promising to bring a horse to help with their departure. "Hannah went out, and has never been since seen or heard of by her owner." Billy was later caught, but Hannah was not. He was executed for aiding her escape.[120] More than a few enslavers, realizing that men desired wives, purchased women as potential spouses for their bondsmen, hoping that so doing would prevent their prime male workers from leaving. James Sterling of Detroit purchased two Black women in 1764 in order to keep his "two big Negroes" from absconding.[121]

While there are many examples of male refugees escaping with their wives or love interests, sometimes freedom proved to be the more important aspiration. When four men and a woman in Georgia left in a "small paddling canoe," it did not take the men long to decide that there was not enough room in the canoe for everyone. Under examination, the bondswoman noted that "they intended to go to look for their own country, and that the boat was not big enough to carry her with them." They left her on shore, where she was later captured.[122] Likewise, the Louisiana refugee woman Marianna, "who was continually running away," was shot in the leg by another fugitive in May 1771 and subsequently recaptured.[123]

Others went alone, leaving everyone and everything behind. Virginia Burns escaped into the woods from the farm of a family she was hired out to in North Carolina. According to her daughter, the Frizelles beat Virginia, "give her scraps lak a dog an' make her wuck lak a man." They even forced her to clean out deep wells, a task that frightened the woman. When she was old enough to stand up for herself, Virginia decided to escape. Her story contained some of the difficult details of those on the run. Like many, Virginia determined to claim her freedom only when she knew that she just could not take the abuse any longer. "Dey wus a-fixin' ter chain her up an' beat her lak dey usually done when she 'cides ter go away. She has ter go den or take de whuppin' an' she ain't got time ter make no plans," her daughter recounted. The female refugee put on a pair of her captor's shoes and perhaps grabbed some of his other clothes for her life on the run. Virginia hid that first night in one of the farm's chicken houses while dogs and patrollers searched for her in the woods. She left for the woods once she realized they had called off the search until the next morning. It was in the North Carolina forests, however, that Virginia faced other threats. Always afraid that she would be caught, she was continuously haunted by the sounds of wildlife. She bit her tongue to keep from screaming when she heard hoot owls and other creatures. Virginia slowly moved away from where she had been bound, sleeping in empty caves and hollow logs, always wary of the snakes she encountered. Starved and weak from hunger, she stole food along the way, trekking about ninety-five miles before she met a White ally who took her to live, and hide, among a free Black community. There, at a dance—a luxury she never had experienced before—Virginia met her future husband, Jake. Freedom and family were within her grasp at last.[124]

Enslavers were forced to recognize family ties in their efforts to reclaim their "property." Advertisement after advertisement published in local and regional newspapers included details of the missing person's familial relationships with the assumption that these escapees would try to seek refuge or to reunite with the persons they were bound to through blood and marriage. Spouses, siblings, and parents were the relations that captors most recognized, although certainly other extended kin were included in the general term "relations." Even when they were not certain of the details of the refugee's kin, slaveholders calculated that they would try to reach the place from where they had been purchased, with the implicit assumption that they had someone there (kin, fictive or otherwise) who they wanted to see or who they could expect assistance with their escape. It is not surprising, for example, that Daffney's enslaver wrote in his recapture advertisement in the Charleston *City Gazette* that she probably "will endeavor to get off to the West Indies," where she must have hoped that some of her family was still residing.[125] In 1747, the *Virginia Gazette* carried an advertisement for thirty-five-year-old Harry noting, "It is supps'd he is gone to Richmond County, where he has a wife."[126]

Advertisement, Virginia Gazette, c. 1769. Runaway Advertisement for Sandy placed by Thomas Jefferson, *Virginia Gazette*, published by Purdie & Dixon, September 14, 1769, page 4. Courtesy of the John D. Rockefeller Jr. Digital Library, The Colonial Williamsburg Foundation.

Fleeing and fugitivity were such popular solutions to the curse of enslavement that captors concluded that flight was a unique disease that infected their human property: drapetomania.[127] Although the name was coined by southern physician Samuel Cartwright in the late antebellum era, slaveholders associated running away with black "madness" as early as the colonial period. As such, a Louisiana businessman who purchased a bondswoman proclaimed in court in 1725 that the "slave went mad, and subsequently ran off to the bush, never to come home again."[128] But many years later, the refugee Nash was clear when he spoke in another Louisiana court regarding why he had left, noting that "he had ran away from the plaintiffs [who had promised him his freedom], and did not like to return to them, on account of a wife and children he had in New Orleans."[129]

"I'm George Floyd/I'm George Floyd/I'm George Floyd.... My heart hurt to see how it all would end."[130]

Failure at self-emancipation could result in physical and psychological torture or even death. Some died by suicide rather than face re-enslavement.

Emmanuel was burned in the face with an "R" and received "30 stripes" when he escaped, along with five White indentured servants, from his Virginia captor in July 1640.[131] A Maryland court heard the trial in 1658 of a Mr. Overzee, who beat to death Tom, who, according to witnesses, "commonly did runne away, and absent himselfe from his Mr. Overzee's service." Not only was Tom tied to a ladder and "whip'd upon his bare back," his slaveholder then poured hot grease on him before beating him again, refusing to release Tom even after an observer noted that the man appeared to be dying. Tom did die four hours later. The court acquitted Overzee of the murder charge.[132] Landon Carter not only had his Virginia runaways whipped, but, fearing they might escape again while at work, he "was obliged to make them work in Chains."[133] His father, Robert "King" Carter dismembered some of his runaways, including chopping off the toes of Bambara Harry and Dinah in 1707 and those of two others, Will and Bailey, in 1725. He asked, and received, court permission to do so, explaining that he had "cured many a negro of running away by this means."[134]

In Louisiana, a captured refugee who had badly assaulted a soldier was to be "flogged" every Sunday, have his right ear cut off, and wear a six-pound chain on his foot for the rest of his life.[135] In Tennessee in 1804, Andrew Jackson's advertisement for an escaped man captured his violent intentions—in addition to the fifty-dollar reward and expenses for the return of the thirty-year-old mulatto male, Jackson promised to pay extra for "every hundred lashes any person will give him, to the amount of three hundred."[136] A patroller who tied an escapee's arms behind his back above his elbows with a stick across was charged with excessively abusing an enslaved man who was not his. The lack of water, food, and mobility caused the refugee to fall repeatedly. The

"The Hanging of the Slave Paul" c. 1838. "Drawing made of an enslaved man's demise described in Charles Ball's autobiography in the *American Anti-Slavery Almanac* 1838. Courtesy of the American Antiquarian Society. Mass A600 1838a. Castlog Record 223407.

patroller, Walker, believed the man was feigning difficulty and began to beat him. After cutting him across his face with a gum tree switch when he was on the ground, repeatedly kicking him in his head, and grinding his foot into his neck, Walker then wrapped a rope around the refugee's neck and tied him to a horse. After witnesses reported that the enslaved man appeared not to be breathing, Walker responded that "the scoundrel is holding his breath." The captive was dead. Taken to court by the bondsman's "owner," Walker was found guilty of murder. However, the state's governor, William Miller, a plantation owner himself, pardoned the convicted murderer.[137] A South Carolina court in 1823 heard the case of a captor who deliberately shot a recovered refugee, stating as he did so, "Damn you, you shall never kill any more hogs." The enslaved man eventually died from his wound.[138]

Marronage

Some couples, families, and kinship groups managed to escape the bonds of slavery for the remainder of their lifetimes. If they "passed" into the ranks of free people of color, they remained hunted and marginalized, for certainly by the time of the American Revolution to be a Black person on the continent was to be viewed as a "slave." Anyone without that status invited suspicion and overt surveillance. Moreover, "freedom" for African-descended people in North America did not come with the rights of citizenship, but rather with an increasing number of restrictions regarding education, cultural expression, movement, employment political agency, and social endeavors. Black freedom certainly did not translate to equal protection under the law or access to an equal judicial process. At best, it was a limited and unstable, sometimes fleeting, and largely resented freedom.

Instead of establishing a different identity or disappearing in plain sight, many refugees preferred marronage. The vast territories that surrounded but were not part of the European settler colonies of the seventeenth and eighteenth centuries provided somewhat safe spaces for enslaved Black individuals, families, and parts of communities who sought freedom. Mountain ranges, swamps, caves, thick forests, and small islands that had to be reached by boat were the sites of numerous Black maroon societies in North America. The most significant were those of the Great Dismal Swamp (two thousand square miles, or the size of Delaware) that extended from southeastern Virginia to the northern tidewater of North Carolina; slightly inhabited islands off the coasts of Virginia, the Carolinas, and Georgia; swamps and marshes in South Carolina and Louisiana; the Florida everglades and cays; and in the southwest territories of New Spain where communities of *cimarrones* (refugee captives) resided sometimes in alliance with native groups who lived nearby and occasionally with native peoples who also resisted enslavement or exploitation.[139]

As early as 1672, Virginia's General Assembly passed "An act for the apprehension and suppression of runawayes, negroes and slaves" and thirty years later "An Act for Ye More Effectually Apprehending an Out Lying Negroe, whoe hath committed divers Robberies and Offences" to capture notorious refugees and marooners.[140]

Archeologist Daniel Sayres noted that the first inhabitants of the Great Dismal Swamp were Indigenous peoples of the Virginia and North Carolina tidewater, who continued to reside in the swamp because it was their homeland and hunting grounds but also to avoid enslavement by encroaching British colonials. Native people inhabitants later were joined by disaffected White indentured servants trying to flee the terms of their contracted labor, abuse, or even the threat of imprisonment if they had been accused of a crime. By 1680, self-emancipating Africans, too, had begun to take refuge there in greater numbers. Historian Herbert Aptheker believed approximately 2,000 Black men, women, and children lived in the Great Dismal Swamp. The total number who escaped and came to reside there over the decades from the seventeenth century forward was no doubt substantially larger.[141] "After 1700 or so, African and African American maroons were the majority of newcomers. This remained the case until circa 1800," Sayers explains. There, they "formed permanent or long-term communities."[142] J. D. Smyth wrote in 1784 of the swamp's Black residents: "Run-aways have resided in these places for twelve, twenty, or thirty years and upwards, subsisting themselves in the swamp upon corn, hogs, and fowls that they raised on some of the spots not perpetually under water, nor subject to be flooded, as forty-nine parts out of fifty are; and on such spots they have erected habitations, and cleared small fields around them."[143]

As the eighteenth century passed, the Great Dismal Swamp remained a reasonable site for self-emancipating captives to seek refuge with families, even though much of it was below sea level and was filled with snakes, jaguars, bobcats, and bears. The swamp had numerous large, dry islands, reachable only by boat, that provided promising settlement sites. Archeological excavations from one of the islands found the "footprints" of five seventeenth- and eighteenth-century cabins, some with traditional West African walls made with wattle, and in close enough proximity to indicate a small community or family compound.[144] Another location on that same island had evidence of six other structures.[145]

Throughout the swamp, families lived off crops that they cultivated, livestock they raised, and the wide variety of fish and game the wetlands provided. They made furnishings, stone tools, and items they used for food service (such as hand-thrown pottery) or leisure (clay pipes) with natural resources or repurposed abandoned items found within the swamp. What some could not grow, make, or repurpose, they traded for with other residents across various maroon sites in the swamp or with allied workers in the area. They also stole from outlying farms and unsuspecting travelers. While these refugees created their communities with an eye to becoming self-sufficient, they did not hesitate to raid local farms, plantations, and towns to acquire food, clothing, weapons, liquor, and other items.[146] Some were even believed to have raided nearby areas for enslaved women to have as their wives.[147] Local militias, residents, and sometimes Indigenous peoples, such as the Catabaw in South Carolina or the Coweta in Florida, who were promised Black Seminoles as "war booty," hunted them relentlessly.[148] Not surprisingly, archeologists have found numerous examples of weapons at maroon sites, especially bullets and knives. Refugees, of course, often tried to take weapons with them when they ran away, in anticipation of having to defend themselves against bounty hunters, hunting dogs, and the animals and reptiles of the swamp.

Even after the turn of the nineteenth century, enslaved Africans and their families sought refuge in the heavily forested swamplands, but, with a growing timber industry and attempts to construct canals, they were hardly the only Black families on site. This was true even in the earlier era when pioneering canal companies hired enslaved Blacks to work in the swamp. In 1764, for example, George Washington sent fifty-four bondspeople (forty-three men, nine women, and two children), provided by the investors of the Dismal Swamp Canal Company, to the "Dismal Plantation." The adults among them were to build a canal, but also to "build houses, grow corn, and tend livestock for their own support."[149] These workers sometimes created trading and social ties with Black maroons, providing the refugees with necessary goods and essential news of the encroaching slave society they had fled. There also is evidence that some who worked for lumber companies in the swamp even "subcontracted" out to refugees and free Blacks, since most of this work was done with little White supervision.[150] One former Dismal Swamp maroon, who eventually escaped to Canada, explained that he made wooden shingles for a man who paid him $2 per month. Of maroon family life in the swamp, he added, "Dar is families growed up in dat ar Dismal Swamp dat never seed a white man, an' would be skeered most to def to see one. Some runaways went dere wid dar wives, an' dar childers are raised dar."[151]

This site was not the only one in Virginia where maroons flourished. In 1729, the lieutenant governor wrote "of some runaway Negroes beginning a settlement in the mountains," who had been recaptured.[152] Further south and to the west, marronage was just as significant.

In 1711, the governor of South Carolina noted that White colonists were being harassed by groups of escaped refugees.[153] Three decades later, his predecessor asked for "the assistance of some Notchee Indians in order to apprehend some runaway Negroes, who had sheltered themselves in the Woods, and being armed, had committed disorders."[154] Large numbers of maroons, described as "a numerous collection of outcast mulattoes, mustees and free negroes," in the colony led to fears of a large slave revolt in 1765.[155] The governor of the neighboring colony of Georgia also complained of maroons where "a great number of fugitive Negroes had Committed many Robberies and insults between this town [Savannah] and Ebenezer and that their Numbers [which] were now Considerable might be expected to increase daily."[156]

The swamps that were a part of the Savannah River complex, which formed a border between South Carolina and Georgia, as well as the swamps near the Congaree, Stono, Ashepoo, Edisto, and the Santee rivers in South Carolina were known locations of maroon communities comprised of Black refugee families. In December 1765, for example, militia forces from Georgia came upon a maroon town on the Savannah River. Their description of four houses, each "seventeen feet long and fourteen feet wide," "boiling kettles" that had rice cooking in them, blankets, pots, shoes, axes, a scaffold (with colored flags attached), and drums indicate that the escaped persons had formed a functional community comprised of family housing and with means to support their material needs.[157] One local South Carolina newspaper described three maroon communities that had been discovered near Georgetown on the Gullah Coast. According to the article, they had snug little habitations, and could have accommodated twenty. . . . At each of them there was a well. At one they had left chaff and straw enough to show that they must lately have pounded out at least fifty bushels of rice; at another place, there was a good stack yard and threshing place. The relics of ducks, turkeys, vegetables, and beef, which were found, proved that they had been abundantly provided with delicacies as well as necessities.[158]

Another camp in the same vicinity was comprised of a "large Savanna in which there were many Negroe men, some Women & Children."[159] A Georgia court heard testimony in July 1772 "that a Number of fugitive Slaves have Assembled . . . on or near the borders of the River Savannah and are frequently committing Depredations . . . with Impunity."[160] When the governor of Georgia lost six captives, it was assumed that they had "got with a parcel" of his enslaved people "who have been run away some time."[161]

The trial records of those maroons who were captured also document the presence of families—those who escaped together and those formed once in the maroon. Such a trial that took place in May 1787, for example, indicated that males—Captain Cudjoe (he had been called Sharper when enslaved, but took the name reminiscent of the famed Jamaica maroon leader Cudjoe) and Captain Lewis—were in leadership positions in the Savannah River maroon society at Martin's Swamp, responsible for providing armed protection and stealing livestock and rice that was shared communally. The remaining "plunder" was split between the leaders. The woman Juliet reported that she escaped with her husband, Pope; and Peggy, with her husband, Little Coke.[162] Family structure in the maroons varied. Some were heterosexual couples with children, forming a nuclear kinship group. Other families were comprised of siblings or a collective of persons related through blood and/or marriage. Many became fictive kin over the course of forming their communities. Some men had more than one wife. One of the most legendary of the South Carolina maroon leaders, "Joe," for example, had at least two wives.[163]

Some low country maroons began as groups of refugees who were trying to find freedom in Florida but were unable to reach the Spanish colony or arrived after sanctuary was no longer available. The "notorious" Titus, for example, successfully led twelve refugees seeking freedom from Georgia to Florida. Once they were there, they discovered that they had to be sent back to their captors in the United States. Rather than return, Titus and some of the others escaped again, this time going north to the Savannah River. According to government reports, "There Titus formed a party with some other outlaying negroes who became very troublesome to the people by plunder and as a receptacle for runaways."[164] There also is evidence that those who wanted to return to enslavement, or Whites who were found near or in the camps, were silenced through death because they could not be trusted with the secret location of others and their families.

The Gulf Coast had its own traditions of marronage. Escaped bondspeople who resided with the Natchez during the early decades of eighteenth century helped them attack local French settlements.[165] In 1727, the court heard testimony from a captured refugee woman of the Oquelonex who had "enticed a slave 'savagess' . . . to rob her mistress and runaway." The two had escaped with a group claimed by a local man named Tisserant. This group, led by one of Mr. Tisserant's bondspeople, in turn "joined a party of fugitives, beyond the lake."[166] Likewise, the "Negro Guela" was found guilty of "frequent marooning" in 1737. Guela answered that he escaped because of his frequent beatings and "little food." The court ruled that both his ears should be cut and his shoulder branded.[167] Pierrot, an Igbo captive, also was found guilty of marooning. He testified that he had run away because he was falsely accused of stealing. He and the other refugee with him had lived on "wild cats and rats" in the woods.[168] By the 1770s, there also was a large collective of maroons in Bas du Fleuve, with passageways leading from the major plantations on the multiple waterways located in the cypress swamps and bayous between New Orleans, the mouth of the Mississippi, and Lake Borgne.

Maroons, both in the gulf and other locales, were notably diverse—most were fleeing Black refugees, others were indigenous, and there also were pirates and other criminals of various racial identities. A contingent of Filipino sailors who had escaped from their impressment as workers on Spanish galleons trading between Manilla and Acapulco also settled in the marshlands in the 1760s.[169] Under the direction of a refugee known as "Juan Saint Malo,"[170] many Black bondspeople escaped to these maroons or moved back and forth from captivity to freedom, often related to familial issues such as visiting wives or returning very temporarily to get spouses and their children.[171] Saint Malo's wife, Cecilia Canuet, was known to be his "inseparable companion in all his exploits."[172] There also were nine other women attached to his inner circle, some who were undoubtedly wives or kin to Malo's compatriots.[173] Another maroon, Juan Pedro, also kept his wife, Maria, and son, Joli Coeur, with him.[174]

Family connections found among the refugees, free creoles, and those persons still enslaved also meant maroon societies often had the material support of their kin, many who readily helped to hide them and deceive authorities about their locations, numbers, and sources of food and ammunition. Wives and children, for example, sometimes remained on the plantations to avoid the possibility of being killed by those hunting the escapees, while husbands and fathers lived as maroons. These men made themselves available, under cover of night, to help their enslaved kin with their work and to spend time in their domestic circle. They reunited in the cabins they had built in the swamps and forests, those essential liminal spaces just at the edge of the plantation, that afforded an illusory Black freedom. Maroons also created familial and communal ties as they bargained with plantation bondspersons for food, arms, information, and secrecy—the maroons often trading their own labor for these precious commodities.[175] A captured maroon from Louisiana reported that he "kept in the woods and the negroes gave him corn when he came at night to their cabins."[176] So, too, did Marianna, who had been missing from New Orleans for eight months when she was discovered. While hiding, she met another refugee, Louis, who "took her to the woods" where she resided with another woman, Charlot.[177] Within their own maroon campus, they shared housing, fields, livestock, and ammunition.

French colonial military and municipal authorities repeatedly campaigned to discover and destroy these extended family and communal units in southern Louisiana. They killed Juan Saint Malo in 1784 after successfully capturing sixty within his group—forty men and twenty women—some of whom were couples and family units.[178] However, their success was limited. As long as there were swamps, forests, mountains, and barely navigable waterways, marronage persisted. In New Orleans, for example, a female returned to her slaveholder after sixteen years reported that she had been living in a maroon community of about sixty persons north of the city.[179]

Black escapees in Spanish and British Florida also formed maroon societies in nearby swamps and forests and took refuge within the Seminole nation.[180] One of the most important of these was "Negro Fort," located on the Apalachicola River near an abandoned British fort.[181] They planted small fields in the rich soil of the riverbanks for about fifty miles on both sides. Altogether there were about 300 Black and Seminole residents, comprised of about 100 men and 200 women and children. According to historian Patrick Riordan, family life and freedom were integral parts of the maroon society that they created. By 1816, when the US Navy destroyed the fort, he noted, "The maroons' population had grown; they were living in family groups, and their children were growing up in a richer, freer life than their parents had known."[182] Afterward, they re-created in more fractured forms or re/connected with other maroon communities on the Suwanee and Manatee riverbanks (there was one long-standing maroon named "Angola" on the Manatee, for example,) and adjacent forested wetlands.[183]

Other Black Seminoles moved into the Florida Keys and, in the early 1820s, facing even more hostility as a result of the US annexation of Florida, risked canoeing some seventy miles eastward to create communities and villages on isolated locales of Andros Island in the Bahamas. Some of them subsequently married previously settled Black loyalists or those who had left with the British after the War of 1812. A letter by a British official in 1828 noted that they were living on the island "peacefully and quietly and have supported themselves upon Indian corn, plantains, yams, potatoes, and peas which they have raised."[184] Remarkably, it was not until 1968 that the communities, accessible only by boat or footpaths through dense forested land, were forced into regular contact with "outsiders."[185]

Early North American Slave Revolts

Like escapes and marronage, armed revolts were family affairs. Wives, siblings, children, and fictive kin took part, either as active rebels and/or in the planning stages, recruitment of participants, provision of essential surveillance data to make certain that conditions were optimal for the strike, and contribution of resources such as meeting places, food, clothing, weapons, divination, and prayers. One of the most important necessities for a successful revolt was secrecy. All members of the families of those who were active participants had to adhere to this mandate. They also had to help hide and materially support participants being hunted by colonial responders. Evidence from the events provide some glimpses into familial participation. One also needs to understand the implications of a successful or failed revolt on a family. Seeking freedom always was an extremely difficult task fraught with many dangers. Even if they succeeded, life continued to be hemmed in by fear of detection. Family leaders thought long and hard before committing their loved ones to the enormous long shot that slave revolt always was. Even though the triumph of the Haitian Revolution during the 1790s spread hope throughout the Atlantic world, and particularly in those areas of North America such as New Orleans, Charleston, Baltimore, and Norfolk, where many Saint Domingue refugee slaveholders, their captives, and free people of color moved, most bondspeople were aware of the many failed attempts of revolt that resulted in widespread persecution, terror, and death.

One of the most successful colonial slave revolts took place in 1680 in the northern region of the Spanish empire that today is New Mexico. The Pueblo Revolt included not only Indigenous peoples from the many groups collectively called Pueblo as well as Apache and Hopi, but also the Black and mixed-race enslaved men and women who lived among them, worked beside them, and had intimate and marital relations with them as signified in their *casta* designations. Eyewitness accounts from the revolt, which resulted in a twelve-year ouster of Spanish rule, documented the important leadership role of José Naranjo—described as a tall "el negro" with yellow eyes—but also the roles of other men and women who were at least partially African descended who supported the revolt and benefitted from the outcome. As historian Dedra McDonald noted:

Native Americans and castas shared a marginal status in Spanish New Mexican society, in which pretensions to power required at least the illusion of limpieza de sangre [purity of blood]. Both groups stood to gain from rebellion against Spanish authority. By joining Pueblo rebels, New Mexico castas constructed a group identity as "not-Spanish," which meant they would no longer acquiesce, at least for the revolt years, to Spanish domination over Puebloans and castas alike.[186]

Once freed from Spanish juridical and religious control, many returned to marital styles and family life resonant with their native ancestral beliefs (and perhaps African), ignoring the laws and customs imposed by Catholic Spanish slaveholders.

In the largest of the colonial slave societies in North America, slave revolts began in the seventeenth century. Records of attempted revolts, both Black and mixed race, are found for 1687, 1688, 1709, 1710, 1722, 1730, and more. These plans often included large locales, indicating the early creation of widespread communication and community networks that enslaved people could use to gain freedom for themselves and their families.[187] Captives organized under the cover of their leisure day of Sunday or at funerals and other public events, prompting laws and customs that prevented such gatherings, such as the ban on funerals in the Northern Neck region of Virginia after the 1687 attempt there, and increased surveillance of enslaved "spaces," communications, and communal gatherings.

On April 1, 1712, Black (particularly Akan/Coromantee) and some indigenous residents of New York City put into action their joint plan for freedom. Approximately twenty-five people gathered with weapons, broke into a barn, set fire to it, and attacked those Whites who tried to extinguish the blaze, killing ten. Their attempt failed when English colonists overcame them militarily. Some of those who were not captured escaped to the countryside, where they consented to group suicide before they could be taken. Colony officials arrested seventy, eventually convicting twenty-one and executing eighteen. Those who died for their freedom acts were beheaded, some burned at the stake, all left for the public to view as rotting reminders of the cost of seeking emancipation.[188] Women as well as men participated, and some were related through marriage. When one married couple was threatened with capture, the husband "shot his wife and then himself" rather than have either taken alive.[189]

Three decades later, in 1741, it was believed that enslaved men and women attempted another revolt in New York that was to include burning down the city and killing its residents. Historians disagree as to whether or not such a revolt (which included enslaved Blacks and Whites with whom they had social connection) actually was planned, but the consequences are not contested. One can easily understand that even the rumor of a revolt had dire consequences for individuals and, of course, their family members who might have been implicated or who lost a loved one to brutal abuse, death, or exile. Included in those accused, for example, was the bondsman Caesar and his White consort, Peggy, who had borne their biracial child the previous year.[190] Peggy offered herself as a witness against others to help distract investigators away from herself and Caesar.[191] Some testified that they participated in the revolt because their captors had denied them access to family members. Quack complained that he was not allowed to see his wife, Cuba. Another testified that she participated because her child had been sold away from her. Authorities imprisoned 150 Blacks, hanged 20 (including 4 Whites), burned to death 13, and exiled more than 70 to the Caribbean.[192]

In neighboring New Jersey, authorities accused enslaved people of plotting revolts in 1734, resulting in hundreds arrested. Most were flogged, but two were hanged. Forty years prior, two enslaved persons were hanged and one burned to death for "conspiracy."[193]

In the southern colonial hamlet of Stono, South Carolina, some twenty miles from Charleston, bondspeople also rebelled with the hope of gaining freedom for themselves and their families. On September 9, 1739, an assemblage of approximately twenty people killed two storeowners, stole weapons, and murdered a local White family before marching "in a warlike manner" with beating drums, calls for freedom, and flags flying, toward the Edisto River.[194] There, they hoped to find passage to St. Augustine in Spanish Florida and claim their freedom. As the Black insurgents moved toward the river, others joined in, building the force to approximately eighty to one hundred persons, particularly persons who were of the local Kongo-influenced enslaved communities. They attracted others not only through their drumming and flag flying, but also by dancing and singing."[195] The flags and banners may have been made by wives or other female kin, and the dancing performed by family and community associates. The rebels killed approximately thirty additional Whites and burned approximately seven houses as they marched forward.[196] When finally stopped, those taken (about fifty) were tortured, killed, and decapitated—colonial authorities placing their bloody heads on poles for all to see, including their horrified kin.[197]

British North American colonies certainly were not the only ones that experienced Black revolts during the eighteenth century. Enslaved Africans cooperated with the Natchez when they attacked France's Fort Rosalie in 1729, hoping a Natchez victory would end their enslavement.[198] In Spanish-controlled Louisiana, a plot instigated by Mandinga and Bambara men and women in 1795 at Point Coupee, north of New Orleans, also included family groups. Evidence indicates that the entire family of one mulatto captive,

Antoine Sarzain, participated in the plot, but all managed to escape except Antoine. Likewise, one male plotter employed his wife to relay messages about the event.[199] One female also was found with a musket, powder, and shot in her cabin.[200] The revolt was exposed before it really came to fruition, and White authorities tortured, hanged, and beheaded twenty-six. Some were drawn and quartered. Others faced long sentences of hard labor at the Spanish prison in Cuba.[201]

Sixteen years later, perhaps the largest known Black slave revolt in North America took place in Louisiana. It occurred in the most densely populated of slave regions in the colony. Indeed, historian Robert Pauette has noted that the area in which the revolt began "had about twenty large sugar plantations that ran like an almost unbroken village of plantations along the east bank."[202] The quarters for enslaved families on these plantations, situated as they were away from the riverfront, were closer together than one might imagine. This clustering encouraged abroad marriages and extended families across these properties and supported communal revolt.[203] On January 8, 1811, forty miles up the east side of Mississippi River (also known as the German Coast, after its early settlers) in St. John the Baptist Parish, the captives of sugar planter Manuel Andry broke into his house and attacked him. Andry managed to alert his neighbors and rally help but did lose one of his sons in the attack. Self-freed men and women, no doubt married couples and other family members included, moved on with the rebellion, marching south toward New Orleans through St. Charles and St. James parishes. More and more bondspeople joined the ranks as they moved forward, increasing into hundreds, some on horseback and some on foot, flying colored flags, beating drums, and carrying guns and cane knives, marching from plantation to plantation with the motto "On to New Orleans." As word of the insurrection spread, local sugar planters rushed their families into New Orleans, while the governor called on local militias and military units from the US Army, Navy, and Marines in the area to protect them and to destroy the rebel forces.[204]

Ten days after the revolt began, an inventory of those captured indicated the widespread nature of the freedom venture: Sixty-six of the rebels represented sixteen different plantations. Twenty-four had died, either during the actual fighting or after their capture. Those taken alive were tortured, dismembered, beheaded, or burned to death. Again, local authorities placed rebel heads on poles throughout the area to dissuade others from resorting to revolt. There were a documented seventeen other rebels who had not been captured, and others were imprisoned.[205] Many believed that those who escaped fled to the swamps with kin to join or form maroons.

In 1800, in the new United States, bondsman Gabriel—a literate husband, father, skilled Virginia blacksmith often hired out by his captor, Tom

Prosser—plotted a widespread revolt with family members and an expansive network of friends. Born in 1776, Gabriel had been able to remain emotionally and physically close to his brothers, Martin and Solomon, and the others who lived on and near the Brookfield plantation.[206] Indeed, Prosser's captive community was a large one in itself, with forty-nine bondspeople in 1783, some of whom would go on to help Gabriel to plot his rebellion.

The success of Gabriel's plan, nonetheless, hinged on him being able to gain the support of a wide swath of other working people, including free Blacks and White artisans. Believed by some historians to have been influenced by the late-eighteenth-century revolutionary tide that swept Saint Domingue, France, and the British colonies, resulting in "free" nations, Gabriel's plan embraced persons who resided in Richmond and several towns and tidewater and piedmont counties in Virginia and North Carolina.[207]

The rebels were to march toward Richmond on August 30, 1800, where they would gather weapons and kidnap Governor James Monroe. A heavy rain that evening led to their postponement and the plot's revelation by two enslaved men who were freed and paid for their treachery. The courts found twenty-six persons guilty and ordered them to be hanged, including Gabriel and his brothers. Gabriel's siblings—Martin, a preacher, and Solomon, a blacksmith—had worked to recruit rebels and provide weapons.[208]

"ON TO ORLEANS": THE NEGRO INSURRECTION.

"On to Orleans": The Negro Insurrection. "On to New Orleans": The Negro Insurrection, illustration, 1888, The Story of Louisiana Collection, ITP, Irma and Paul Milstein Division of United States History, Local History and Genealogy, The New York Public Library.

Several other persons involved in the plot also had called for kin assistance. Sam Byrd Jr. relied on his local family, both enslaved and free, to take part in it and to help recruit "hundreds" of others.[209] One of his comrades was George Smith, who enlisted his family members and friends to the cause. Wives, like Gabriel's Nancy, provided food and clothing, gave valuable information about the whereabouts and activities of enslavers, helped to enroll the sons and husbands of their female friends and relations, served as credible excuses for rebel movements that obscured plotting the revolt, and hid conspirators once the scheme was spoiled. Not all family members, as one might imagine, were supportive given the possible negative ramifications. Isham's wife was opposed to his attending organizational meetings and perhaps participating at all. Her concern was well-intended, given that Isham already had been promised future freedom. Instead, he became one of the rebels hanged for his intended role.[210]

Still, one's family's encouragement, acceptance, and participation in insurrectionary actions overwhelmingly mattered. Some kin socialized youth from an early age to not only resist, but rebel. A cursory glance at the youth of perhaps the most "notorious" of enslaved rebels—Nat Turner—demonstrates the impact his family had on his later actions. Turner's account of how he came to organize and lead the slave revolt of August 1831 in Southampton County, Virginia, is full of references to his socialization by his parents, his grandmother, and local Blacks, who convinced him that he was intellectually and psychically gifted. "Having soon discovered to be great," Turner noted of his local acclaim, he believed that he "must appear so, and therefore studiously avoided mixing in society, and wrapped myself in mystery, devoting my time to fasting and prayer."[211] This path, and his family's sustained insistence that he was an exceptional man capable of rare accomplishments, allowed Turner to eventually become convinced that God had chosen him to lead the revolt. "My father and mother strengthened me in this my first impression," he noted, "saying in my presence, I was intended for some great purpose."[212]

THE AMERICAN REVOLUTION AND THE BLACK FAMILIAL FIGHT FOR FREEDOM

The disarray that the Revolutionary War brought to the physical landscape and the everyday activities of people residing throughout the thirteen British colonies of North America provided a rare opportunity for enslaved women and men with their children, extended kin, and community friends to escape. It was an opportunity that many took. Others, like Crispus Attucks—the first to be killed by British soldiers, with two shots to his chest at the Boston Massacre of March 5, 1770—were refugees who hoped the patriots' call for freedom would include their petitions for that status. Crispus was of both African and Indigenous descent. Historians believe he was reared in Framingham, Massachusetts, and sold by Joseph Buckminster away from his family of birth to William Brown in 1747. Brown's 1750 advertisement for Crispus indicates that he escaped to Boston, some twenty-two miles away. In the bustling seacoast trading center, Crispus could "disappear" among those who lived and worked there, as well as maintain a clandestine relationship with family.[213] Since the majority of those enslaved lived in the southern colonies, most who joined the revolution, or were able to escape as a result of it, were from that region.[214]

John Murray, 4th Earl of Dunmore (Lord Dunmore), the last colonial governor of Virginia, had much to do with these mass escapes. But Africans and their descendants, with an eye to gaining freedom for themselves and their families, initiated the process. In early 1775, enslaved Blacks in southeastern Virginia petitioned Lord Dunmore, offering to fight on behalf of the British crown if he would guarantee their freedom. Dunmore outright refused to consider their request, threatening corporal punishment if they continued to pursue this avenue. A few months later, the unpopular governor was reconsidering. Surrounded and outnumbered by armed patriots, Dunmore fled his

"**Boston Massacre.** *Boston Massacre*, after the well-known lithograph of that title by Paul Revere, c. 1856, Courtesy of the National Archives, photo no. 69-N-4877-C

Williamsburg palace, exiling himself on a British ship in the Norfolk harbor. On November 7, he circulated his "infamous" proclamation, which stated in part: "I do . . . hearby declare free all indentured servants, Negroes or others . . . that are able and willing to bear arms, they joining the Majesty's troops."[215] Within a month, he had approximately eight hundred recruits.[216] He also had the family members of these recruits. As historian Alan Taylor noted, "An equal number of women and children, flocked to Dunmore's encampments and ships. If Dunmore wanted men as soldiers, he also had to receive their families, although feeding and sheltering them all strained his resources."[217] Over the next few years, hundreds, perhaps thousands, of enslaved men, women, and children made the leap for liberty, walking, swimming, and sailing boats in their unprecedented attempt to reach the British. When the escaped captives got to them, they worked for their freedom. They were Black loyalists, most loyal to their families and their determination to be free.[218]

Black matrons Abigail and Bridget Godfrey, whose sprawling, multigenerational extended family was introduced in the previous chapter, grew up and reared their children and grandchildren on the properties owned by the Godfrey family on the south side of Tanner's Creek, a branch of the Elizabeth River near Portsmouth, Virginia. Both women were born in the colonies, and by the end of the eighteenth century, they and many of their family members were among the Black loyalists who successfully claimed their freedom and secured their families behind British lines. They did not leave with Dunmore's first recruits, but rather in small family groups over the next three years when they believed it most safe to do so. Abigail arrived behind British lines in 1779 and may have been part of the five hundred to one thousand refugees taken up by the British after the burning of Portsmouth, and its important harbor, that year. Bridget, her children, and her grandchildren escaped in 1778.[219]

Their enslaver, Matthew Godfrey, reported in 1779 that he had lost eleven captives: the two multigenerational families that included Abigail; her son Ned, his wife, Elizabeth, and their son, Jeffrey; Abigail or Bridget's daughter China, and her children, Nelly and Betsey; Bridget; Bridget's daughter Kate and her children, Port and Lucy; Bridget's son Sam and Bridget's daughter Jenny.[220] Most members of both families came to reside in Nova Scotia, Canada, but some later traveled back to Africa as founding colonists of Britain's Sierra Leone experiment. Abigail, also known as Rose, and Bridget bore, nurtured, socialized, and helped their children and their grandchildren, along with several other members of their families and sprawling tidewater Virginia community, to acquire a fragile freedom.

Matthew Godfrey obviously sustained heavy losses, but not unusual ones. Many captors, particularly those in the captive-rich southern colonies, had similar experiences. All eighty-seven bondspeople of John Willoughby, Godfrey's wealthy neighbor, escaped.[221] George Washington himself lost twenty-six to the British, including some of his most valuable tradesmen, such as his Black driver, forty-five-year-old Frederick, and his groom, Harry Washington, a young man from the Gambia River area of West Africa who had been captured and enslaved in the early 1760s.[222] Thomas Jefferson estimated that Virginia slaveholders lost more than 30,000 Black captives to flight in 1778 alone—the year Bridget Godfrey escaped. Jefferson lost thirty himself.

Historians have suggested that 25,000 to 30,000 people escaped from South Carolina and that the colony, along with Georgia, collectively witnessed the eventual escape of more bonded people than Virginia during the Revolutionary War years.[223] This is not surprising given the British control of the low country's eastern coast by the beginning of the 1780s. For example, three families were among the many who escaped from South Carolina in 1780, including the African Sam; country born Tom and Jemmy with African-born Phebe and her five children, one "at her breast"; and fifteen-year-old Priscilla.[224] A three-generational family and others related by blood, marriage, or fictive ties also left that same year. The travelers included Old Rose, fifty-six, an "Ebo"; her husband, Cato; and their children Celia, Country Sue, and Dick, along with Celia's daughter Elsey, who was six years old. Their refugee group also included Kate from Angola, Scipio, Town Sue, and Will, the waiting boy.[225] Planters on Edisto Island witnessed particularly large groups who escaped together. In June 1779, twenty-one persons—fourteen men, five women, and two children—left. A month later, Benjamin Edings advertised for the return of thirty-seven bondspeople who had been on his Edisto plantations—twenty-three men and fourteen women.[226]

In Georgia, slaveholder after slaveholder reported the loss of enslaved men, women, children, and families in the 1770s and 1780s. Many were trying to reach freedom in Spanish Florida rather than to join British forces. The war was the distraction and disruptor that allowed them to abscond. Notices in the *Georgia Gazette* in 1774 included the escape of London and "his wife" June and, from the governor's plantation, the loss of four men and two women.[227] The following year, James and Isaac escaped with two women—probably their wives—Fanny and Sall. Fanny took her four-year-old daughter with them, and Sall was "big with child."[228] Sarah Gibbons advertised in the same Georgia newspaper in 1779 for the capture of seventeen people—seven men and four women, including Chloe and Cretia, who carried their children with them. A few months earlier, the cooper Jack escaped with "a little Boy named Mingo."[229]

The escapes never were easy, and freedom, though promised, was not guaranteed. The first major crisis many Black refugees faced was a medical one—smallpox. The disease ravaged Black military recruits and their families killing, by some estimates, 70 percent of those among Dunmore's Black ranks. Indeed, more persons died from the smallpox than from the war itself. Fewer than twenty of John Willoughby's eighty-seven escapees from Norfolk survived the first wave of the epidemic.[230] Those who did live quickly formed into fictive kinship groups. When they reached New York, for example, Mary was accompanied by her daughter, Patience, and three other children whom Mary had adopted after they lost their parents.[231]

Boston King, one enslaved man among thousands who escaped from his captor's plantation in South Carolina, managed to stay alive.[232] Having been separated from his family of birth through rentals to different persons after he became an adolescent, King was unable to leave with them or be reunited. He did, however, marry a fellow refugee in 1780: sixteen-year-old Violet, who was among those fugitives attached to the British Army in Charleston.[233]

The story of King's labor during the Revolutionary War is indicative of the multiple jobs and difficult services that Black refugees performed for the British military in their pursuit of liberty. While gender roles were somewhat predictable—men typically fought, spied, served White officers in numerous capacities, and handled livestock; wives and other female family members cooked, washed, ironed, sewed, and nursed ailing troops—labor shortages were filled by those available, regardless of sex. Making oneself "useful" in some way, after all, increased the possibility of a permanent freedom. Over the course of his fugitive state, King did whatever he was asked to do, serving as a hospital nurse at times and a private servant to an imperial army officer at other times. He also worked as a spy and messenger behind patriot lines. King traveled with the British from Charleston to New York, where he still faced possible re-enslavement and starvation. Women and children, who were less able to escape or find labor that might have afforded them some protection, were more subject to loss of the freedom they claimed.[234]

The war ended with patriot forces marching into New York and catching former captives to return to bondage. As King noted in his autobiographical accounts, "Many of the slaves had very cruel masters, so that the thoughts of returning home with them embittered life to us. For some days, we lost our appetite for food, and sleep departed from our eyes."[235] King was acutely aware of the threat of re-enslavement for he and his wife, writing, "They carried me to Brunswick [New Jersey] and used me well. Notwithstanding which, my mind was sorely distressed at the thought again of being reduced to slavery and separated again from my wife and family."[236]

Fewer than one-half of those who supported the loyalist cause gained freedom at the end of the war. Although 10,000 purportedly fought for the

Crown, only 3,000 were able to leave with those defeated forces as nominally free. Hunted by their slaveholders and allied to an ambivalent British military, they fled to Canada, where they led difficult lives. The fortunate "free" were with family and worked vigorously to establish homesteads. King noted of his arrival at Birchtown, Nova Scotia, in August 1783 that he and others "exerted all of our strength in order to build comfortable huts before the cold weather set in."[237] Nevertheless, most came to reside in poor, racially segregated settlements in the British Maritimes, particularly Nova Scotia. About one-half lived in Birchtown. The British government eventually assigned families small parcels of land with which to create farms, but the soil there was of very poor quality. Likewise, unemployment rates for those who did not farm were high and wages very low—about one-quarter of what Whites earned. Many could only afford to support their families by entering into indentured servitude for local Whites, as domestics, chimney sweeps, sailors, and artisans, including shoemakers, seamstresses, barbers, weavers, and bakers. They labored in these positions, often beside and treated similarly to enslaved Blacks who were compelled to perform similar work.[238]

Others became bonded again, both with and without family members. A significant number of enslaved men, women, and children were forced to accompany their loyalist captors who escaped to other British colonial territories. Those who were claimed by Mr. Knox of Georgia, a loyalist, were at first confiscated by patriot forces and sold. When the British took Georgia, Knox regained them, and at the end of the war, he re-enslaved his bondspeople in Jamaica. He eventually resold them to persons in South Carolina.[239] Timothy Ruggles of Massachusetts, a slaveholder and loyalist brigadier general, took his Black bondspeople with him when he resettled in Nova Scotia and established a plantation there. Among those he claimed in Canada were seven-year-old Hester and six-year-old Jeffrey.[240]

Post–Revolutionary War race relations in British Canada generally were hostile, even extremely so at times. Black refugees traveled with 27,000 White loyalists, including slaveholders who insisted on retaining their property—some 2,500 bondspeople—once they arrived.[241] While some areas of Canada began to pass gradual emancipation legislation in the last decade of the eighteenth century, Black slavery did not legally end in all regions until 1834, subjecting "free Blacks" to the constant physical and emotional threat of the all-too-familiar American racial hierarchy. The first known race "riot" concerning Blacks and Whites in North America actually occurred in Nova Scotia in Shelbourne's "Black Town" during the summer of 1784. There, White loyalist soldiers, angry about the labor competition the formerly enslaved posed, attacked and chased many families from their homes. Benjamin Marston, a local White resident, recorded the events as a "great riot," writing, "Riot continues [a second day]. The soldiers forced the free negroes to quit the Town—pulled down about 20 of their houses."[242]

It is little wonder that some refugees regarded Nova Scotia as only one of the places they stopped to settle before picking up and moving their families elsewhere. Some even left for England, which had abolished slavery in the homeland in 1772. Even there, Black refugees hardly were welcome. They soon found that many of their race who already resided there did so in poverty and on the very margins of English society.[243] Many of the most adamant eighteenth-century White British abolitionists believed that Blacks should not live among Whites but be relocated to the African continent. They created the colony of Sierra Leone on the coast of West Africa for this purpose.

By 1792, Blacks from the Maritimes joined others in the move to Sierra Leone. Their desire to leave Canada was actually far beyond the expectations of the new colony's organizers. At least 1,190 sailed on January 15, 1792. Among them was Boston King, who had become an important minister among his fellow Black loyalists in Canada. He and his wife, Violet, went as missionaries with the desire to convert Sierra Leone's indigenous peoples to Christianity. Violet died two years after they arrived, but King eventually gained theological training in England and opened a church and school in the colony.[244]

Enslaved Blacks who fought on the side of the patriots also certainly did so with an eye to gaining freedom for themselves and family members. Given George Washington's reluctance to trade Black military service for freedom, it was an uncertain path. By 1777, however, some patriot colonies were allowing enslaved men (occasionally) and free Blacks to be used as substitutes for Whites. New Jersey did so that year, as did New Hampshire and Connecticut. In 1780, Maryland permitted Black captives to enlist if their enslavers agreed. New York did the same in 1781. Still, neither state guaranteed that these men would gain freedom if they survived their service in the war. Rhode Island was the first to offer such a reward, beginning to recruit enslaved men in 1781 with the promise that they would be granted their freedom if they served.[245] Virginia eventually armed and freed five hundred men to fight.[246]

Those patriot slaveholders who were not compelled to emancipate or enhance the rights of Black fighting men had few reservations about using local free Blacks and enslaved males as their soldier substitutes and servants. James Roberts, of the Eastern Shore of Maryland, fought in George Washington's army during the revolution, enduring several battles in Virginia and Maryland.[247] He also served with his slaveholder, Francis de Shields, during the Seven Years' War. James did not earn freedom for either sacrifice. Instead, he was "separated" from his spouse and children, "taken to New

Orleans, and sold at auction" for $1,500 to a brutal Louisiana planter. He noted that he received this treatment "for all of my fighting and suffering in the Revolutionary War for the liberty of this ungrateful, illiberal country."[248] His new "owner" had James "broken in" by ordering his overseer to give him ninety-nine lashes. He even refused to let the Black veteran retain some of the clothing that he had worn in the war, clothing James hoped to "keep as memorials of revolutionary times." Instead, he was given a "bare breechcloth" and sent "into the field to work." James was somewhat hopeful when his new captor later purchased one of his cousins who also had been sent to New Orleans for sale. His hope, however, soon turned into a living nightmare of familial abuse. The cousin responded to his "initiation" whipping by running away. When caught, he was whipped again and then set on fire. His untreated burns became infested with vermin. According to James, his cousin then "lived till Thursday evening in great agony, and died, having been on the place just one week."[249]

Instead of promising Black captives emancipation or expanded rights for free people of color, patriot leaders lured White men to pick up arms and fight in the revolution by promising them "slave bonuses."[250] In 1780, Virginia recruited White soldiers with an offer of three hundred acres of land and a male slave or £60—their choice. The following year, South Carolina began to give Black captives to those White men who enlisted.[251] These kinds of "incentives" for White male participation in the war effort, of course, destroyed enslaved families. Their "bonuses" were captive fathers, sons, uncles, and brothers who certainly could not take family members with them when they were given to White soldiers, many of whom would claim land in the emerging western frontier and take their enslaved "bounty" with them—without their loved ones. Seymour Burr of Connecticut escaped with several other friends and kin. Although captured, Burr was able to extract a promise from his slaveholder that if he fought for the patriots and gave him his bounty money, he could claim his freedom after the war ended.[252] Others, like the enslaved man of General John Sullivan of New Hampshire, bargained for their freedom when first volunteering to fight.[253]

Petit Jean, an enslaved cattle ranger in Mobile with an English captor, was among those in overlapping colonial terrains that comprised the British, French, and Spanish gulf who were able to earn greater freedom by participating in the Revolutionary War on competing sides. After the Spanish attacked the British loyalist outpost of Mobile, for example, enslaved people found an opportunity to align themselves with the Spanish in the hope that they could gain freedom for themselves and their family members. Petit Jean served as a messenger and spy for the Spanish forces, while others supplied food, labor, and military support.[254] His abroad wife, for one, provided goods and services. At the end of the war, Spanish authorities arranged for both their manumissions, paying outright for Petit Jean's freedom and helping him to purchase his wife with money the two had managed to save.[255]

Likewise, Congress asked Lower South states to enlist Black captive men when the patriots lost Savannah in 1778, guaranteeing compensation to their "owners" and freedom to those enslaved men in military units. The British, under General Henry Clinton, extended the same emancipatory promise to those who fought for them.[256] Still, many military officials treated the enslaved men, women, and children whom they encountered and captured as war contraband that they could, and did, sell in New Orleans and other slave markets, recklessly destroying families through their commercial acts.[257]

The American Revolution proved to be a tumultuous, if opportunistic, time in the lives of enslaved men and women, and it had a great, and lingering, impact on the institution of slavery in the former British mainland colonies. Efforts of African Americans practically ended slavery in the Northeast and northern plains, destabilizing the institution in the Upper South well into the nineteenth century. These efforts also were foundational to the moral debate about slavery that only legally ended in 1865 with the ratification of the Thirteenth Amendment to the US Constitution.

The first formal antislavery societies in North America formed during the years of the Revolution. The Pennsylvania Society for Promoting the Abolition of Slavery was founded in 1775; the New York Manumission Society, in 1785; and the Providence (Rhode Island) Abolition Society, in 1790. In the Upper South and middle states, the ideals of the revolution, dwindling profits from captive grown tobacco and other crops, a naturally increasing captive population that threatened profits even more, and the impact of relatively larger numbers of Quakers, Mennonites, and Moravians, who began to insist that their members not be slaveholders, undergirded lenient manumission laws and a growing number of organizations dedicated to gradual emancipation.[258] The African slave trade to the states also began to legally end between 1774 and 1798.[259]

These efforts, however, did not mean the end to Black slavery or the international African slave trade. South Carolina even reopened its African slave trade in late 1803, importing more than 39,000 Africans between 1804 and 1808 alone. Moreover, while the federal government banned this trade from 1808 forward, its success in doing so was spotty. Slave traders continued to import Africans through many southern ports, including Norfolk, Charleston, Mobile, Pensacola, Galveston, and New Orleans.[260] What lacked in the international trade was more than made up for in the growing domestic traffic, causing tremendous harm to Black family life. Indeed, merchants in the domestic slave trade moved almost one-half of the captive population of the Upper South to the Lower South and southwest between 1820 and 1860, disrupting marriages, generations-old extended families, and parent-child relations.

Revolutionary-era Blacks, whether enslaved or free, did not simply relinquish the legal fight to end the African trade or the institution of slavery to allied Whites. The intended consequences were too important to their domestic lives for them not to be at the forefront of these movements. During the first years of the 1770s, Africans and African-descended people began to petition colonial legislatures, individually and in small groups, and sue in court for their freedom. Most of their efforts relied on philosophical (Enlightenment), religious, and legal arguments that aligned with the ideals of the American Revolution. The decline of economic incentives to slaveholders in many of the northern, middle, and Upper South states contributed to these complementary exertions. Success, even if partial, had life-changing consequences for many. Measures of immediate and gradual emancipation became law in the states north of Maryland and in the Northwest Territory.[261] Vermont was the first state to end slavery, doing so in 1777 through its state constitution.[262] Three years later, the Massachusetts 1780 state constitution pronounced that "all men are born free and equal, and have . . . the right of enjoying and defending their lives and liberty."[263] Testing the implications of these "universal rights," Elizabeth "Mum Bett" Freeman, who resided with her sister, Lizzie, and daughter, Betsey, and was the enslaved woman claimed by John Ashley of Sheffield, sued for her freedom in 1781 and won. That same year, the Akan-descended slave Quock Walker sued Nathaniel Jennison, in court for his freedom and back wages as reparation. The Massachusetts court agreed that, like Freeman, Walker's enslavement violated the terms of the state's 1780 constitution.[264] New Hampshire's 1784 state constitution also included the declaration that "the enjoying and defending life and liberty" were "natural, essential and inherent rights" held by all men.[265] Many states went on to pass gradual emancipation laws in the last two decades of the eighteenth century: Pennsylvania in 1780, Connecticut in 1784 and 1797, Rhode Island in 1784, New York in 1799, and New Jersey in 1804.[266]

While the next several decades witnessed the actual growth of the numbers of those enslaved, relaxed manumission laws also increased the numbers of freed people and free Black families, particularly in the Upper South. Virginia, which had the largest Black captive population in the eighteenth century, never really became close to general emancipation, but its legislature did pass in 1782 "An Act to Authorize the Manumission of Slaves" that allowed slaveholders to free enslaved people in their last will and testament and other witnessed statements, such as deeds.[267] Prior to that time, a petition for freedom had to be approved by the colonial legislature. A similar action was taken varying from 1816 to 1830 in the North Carolina legislature.[268]

Owners typically freed captives as a reward for long-term service and loyalty. Some manumitted their biracial children or elderly people who could no longer work. Religious conversion convinced others to do so. Within a decade after the passage of this new law in Virginia, slaveholders had freed 10,000 captives.[269] As Philip Davis of Southampton County, and others of his contemporary Virginia slaveholders, noted in the emancipation deeds of their enslaved men and women, there was in the region some sense that their ideal that "freedom is the natural right of all mankind and that it is my duty to do unto others as I would desire by in the situation" that compelled them to release their human property. Davis chose to manumit the twenty-year-old "negro" woman Sier in 1784.[270] While the manumission deed for Sier did not indicate any of her family ties or their future status as enslaved or free, her emancipation certainly meant that any future children she bore could not be claimed by Davis. Other slaveholders released entire families, but they often retained some control over minor children until they reached adulthood (as was common for indentured servants, not free people), thereby retaining significant control over these families for some time. In the case of Benjamin Spratley of Surry County, Virginia, for example, who signed a legal deed on November 28, 1783, releasing his eleven captives who appear to have comprised two nuclear families that included parents Will (thirty-four years old), Natt (twenty-seven), Lucy (thirty-seven), and Betty (twenty-six). Spratley's decision, however, to retain control over their children—Simon (fifteen years old), Jane (eleven), Mary (eight), Sally (five), Cuffee (six), Anarcy (three); and Judah (six months)—until the girls reached the age of eighteen and the boys twenty-one—certainly hindered parental guardianship, familial mobility, and labor options. Neither Judah nor her family would be fully released from Spratley's control until 1801![271]

No example of private slave manumission was more infamous than that of Robert Carter III of Nomini Hall in Westmoreland County, one the richest men in North America. To the chagrin of his Virginia neighbors and his heirs, Carter produced in 1791 a "Deed of Gift" which gradually emancipated his 450-plus captives—more than any other private slaveholder "would *ever* free."[272] Carter did so for reasons about which historians continue to argue, but most agree that it partly was his practice of fierce independent thought and his deep religious beliefs. Like Davis and Spratley, Carter wrote that "I have for some time past ben convinced that to retain them in Slavery is contrary to the true Principles of Religion and Justice, and that therefore it was my Duty to manumit them."[273] He also wanted to avoid harming his White neighbors, who feared living among free Black people whom they believed would either seek revenge or tempt other captives to seek their own freedom. "I have with great Care and Attention," Carter explained, "endeavoured to discover that Mode of Manumission from Slavery which can be effected consonant to Law and with the Least possible Disadvantage to my fellow Citizens."[274] What was important to his enslaved men and women, who were spread across twenty-two quarters in several counties, however, was that they were free. It was equally important that they remain with their families. Recognizing the importance of kinship ties to his bondspeople, Carter tried to organize the timing of the emancipations to maintain family stability. After freeing Prince Johnston and Samuel Harrison, for example, Carter allowed them to rent farms from him and to have their "still enslaved" wives and children to work on them. He also made certain that they had food and housing and employed them for part of the year so that they could afford to pay their rent.[275]

Still, Carter's reluctance to free everyone at the same time did leave families vulnerable to physical separation and, after his death in 1804, to the devious attempts of some of Carter's heirs to keep those enslaved who had not yet been freed. One son, John Tasker Carter, "declared that the Negroes who became his property would be sold and taken to a place where they would never hear talk of freedom again." Three sisters later ran away, afraid that they, too, would be sold before their emancipation dates, as another sister had.[276] Some undoubtedly never were freed, while others were still waiting for their emancipation in 1852.[277]

Robert Carter was the revolutionary-era patriot who privately emancipated the most enslaved people, but George Washington was the most famous of those to manumit his bondspeople property. During the war years, Washington was still selling enslaved persons, regardless of family status, and diligently searching for those of his captives who managed to escape. As he moved into a very public political life, however, Washington changed his last will and testament to emancipate, upon the death of his wife Martha, all his enslaved men, women, and children. The Washingtons jointly owned 317 bonded persons in 1799 when the first president of the United States died. One year later, his wife completed the legal process to free Washington's 123 captives on January 1, 1801, retaining in slavery those 194 individuals she owned outright.[278] While Washington had decided to free his captives and worried openly about the impact his manumission efforts would have on bonded families that included people bound to him and his wife, Martha initially refused to emancipate her human "property" either in her lifetime or upon her death. Despite his spouse's determination to retain her own enslaved people, Washington framed the terms of the emancipation of his bondspeople to render some support for bonded family members. He stipulated, for example, the care of elderly enslaved men and women, to be paid for with his estate funds. He also requested that orphaned captive children be bound out to learn a trade as well as the bare rudiments of literacy—reading and writing. They were to gain their freedom at twenty-five years of age.[279]

Some bonded men and women, believing they had been illegally denied their free status, sought redress in court. Many were the biracial descendants of White women who had been indentured at birth as a punishment for their mothers' sexual attachment to Black men. Still, they were supposed to be freed when they reached adulthood. As such, Howell, the grandson of a White woman who had borne a mulatto woman (Howell's mother) by a "negro man," sued for his freedom in a Virginia court in 1770. The court found in his favor, noting—in some distinction from previous like cases—that the law had been put into place to "deter and punish women from that confusion of species, which the legislature seemed to have considered an evil, and not to oppress their innocent offspring."[280]

Enslaved men who fought or who served as seamen for the patriot cause also sued for their freedom after the war ended, with mixed success. James Armistead of New Kent County, Virginia, was as a spy for the Marquis de Lafayette. Posing as an escaped slave who wanted to gain his freedom by fighting for the British, Armistead infiltrated Benedict Arnold's camp in Portsmouth, and later that of General Charles Cornwallis, in order to provide valuable intelligence to patriot military officers. He eventually gained his freedom in 1786, after petitioning the Virginia legislature with a supportive letter from Lafayette. Armistead also received a pension for his service. In recognition of the aid Lafayette had rendered him in his quest for freedom, Armistead took Lafayette as his surname.[281] Others were not nearly as successful. When Robin Brandum sued for his freedom on the basis of having fought in the Revolutionary War, his captor murdered him.[282] Even those who gained their freedom via cooperation with, and service to, the patriot cause could not take their family members into this new legal status with them. Wives and children remained enslaved unless those emancipated could raise the money to purchase them.

These trends did not just occur during the Revolutionary War period in North America, and not just in the United States. Similar events occurred in French and Spanish North America. The "Negro Diocou" in French Louisiana, for example, earned his freedom in 1737 from his "toils in the Natchez war." As a freed man, Diocou worked for Councillor D'Auseville on his St. Julien estate, earning at least 450 francs by the time he appeared in court to sue for his wages. He wanted to have the money due him "deducted from the price of his wife," whom he was buying in increments. Diocou not only had to ask the court to retrieve his earnings, but also to make certain that D'Auseville did not sell his spouse away from that area but instead hire her out locally until he could buy her outright. The court allowed Diocou his earnings and his right to finish purchasing his spouse.[283] Joseph Casenave, a free mulatto, successfully petitioned a court in 1779 that he be able to purchase and emancipate the enslaved woman Magdalena and their son.[284]

Black women in colonial French and Spanish North America also sued in court to be allowed to purchase their freedom and that of their children. The mulatto Catalina went to court in June 1773 to solidify the opportunity to buy herself and her youngest child, Felicite, a five-year-old daughter, from the estate of her deceased captor. Catalina presented evidence that he had promised to let her do so. As a well-known washerwoman and seamstress, she no doubt had saved the money from her additional work. Unfortunately, she still had to leave her older children, Carlota and Manon, who were fifteen and eleven years old, respectively, in bondage.[285] Rose and Maria Isabel both sued for their freedom and that of their small children in 1776. When the case did not go their way, they asked that it be referred to the Spanish tribunal in Havana. They eventually received their freedom under slightly different terms than their slaveholder had mandated. The court ruled that they would have to work to earn their value and that of their children and pay it to their deceased captor's estate before they could "enjoy the full use of their freedom."[286] Angelina "begged an alms from various charitable people" and was able to purchase her four-year-old granddaughter, Maria Antonia, for whom she bore "great love."[287] And the mulatto Adelle was successful in obtaining her freedom from a Louisiana court in 1810. Her "patron," Monsieur Beauregard, had purchased Adelle in the Caribbean and after putting her in a New York boarding school, "sent for her to New Orleans, where she resided a few months with him." Later, Adelle left Beauregard and sued for her freedom and back wages. The court granted her emancipation but thought her "services" were the "return of gratitude" for Beauregard's having educated her and refused to grant her payment.[288] Sometimes, however, these emancipations—even when family members were involved—did not endure.

Freed people faced particular difficulty in Louisiana when the United States gained control of the colony, which previously was ruled by more lenient emancipation laws and customs as French and Spanish colonial possessions. In May 1820, the slaveholder Bazzi, for example, was able to challenge the emancipation of Rose and her baptized children in a court in Louisiana after he had freed Rose's mother (a Congolese woman) and the teenage Rose several years earlier in Cuba. The court indeed did have Rose and her children re-enslaved because in Louisiana, it explained, "the law requires certain formalities for the acquisition of freedom" and these "formalities" had not been fulfilled. It also was not certain that Bazzi had fulfilled even his required legal obligations in Cuba.[289]

It was challenging to maintain family with any peace of mind even after one was emancipated. Nonetheless, freedom remained the best alternative for Black family survival and well-being. The population of free Blacks and free people of color grew immensely during the era of the American Revolution, allowing Blacks to marry and rear their children without the constant dread of being separated. While there is no direct census of free Black families, the numbers of those freed during their lifetimes and those born as free people of color because they were descended from free mothers began to be recorded with the first federal census of 1790. At that time, the young United States had a free Black population of close to 60,000 persons. Ten years later, they numbered more than 100,000.[290] Virginia had the largest number of free Blacks in 1790, with more than 12,000, followed by Maryland, Pennsylvania, North Carolina, and New York.[291]

After 1800, the national free Black population remained approximately one-tenth of the number of enslaved. This continual growth primarily was due to positive birth rates, since "slave" states began to legally, and customarily, dissuade private manumissions just before the legal end to the African slave trade in 1808. Profit from the growing domestic slave trade and the fear of free Blacks supporting or inspiring captive resistance and revolt discouraged emancipation and the practice of allowing those who had been freed to remain in slave societies in the South and southwest. Some of those forced to leave or face the risk of re-enslavement went without their spouses, children, and other loved ones who had not been emancipated. Others remained clandestinely nearby or skirted the law by leaving for six months out of the year and returning for the remainder.[292]

As free Black families emerged out of the Revolutionary era, many found themselves living within majority Black households, even though some family members remained enslaved because of gradual emancipation stipulations. New York had a relatively large free Black population, but its 1799 emancipation law kept adult captives as indentured servants. Their children remained the legal "property" of their mothers' slaveholders until they were adults—-males at age twenty-eight and females at age twenty-five. Any children born of these females before that age also would be held in servitude until age twenty-five.[293] This stipulation crippled the heart of Black family life—the care and control of children born to these families. Moreover, slaveholders like those of Sojourner Truth still could (and did) transfer or sell these indentureships, thereby dividing families, even over long distances. New Jersey's gradualist law of 1804 had similar results.[294]

Many free Blacks who had captive family members worked to purchase them. They again placed great thought into devising successful strategies. Husbands and fathers attempted to free their wives and young children first, in order to keep the young with both parents, to make certain that any other children born of the marital bed would be born free, and to provide physical and sexual protection of their spouses. Likewise, males with lucrative skills (such as blacksmiths, carpenters, painters, etc.) and other females of childbearing age had to be a priority in order to avoid the likely sale of prime artisans and "breeders." Families also needed skilled members freed so they could earn money to help purchase others.[295]

Enslaved persons not only made extraordinary sacrifices to liberate persons related to them through blood and marriage, but in rare cases, they did so for fictive kin as well. South Carolina court records, for example, include the case of "a negro wench slave" who, by working out in town with permission of her slaveholder, had acquired through her industry a considerable sum of money over and above what she had stipulated to pay her enslaver. She used the money, and other funds she had been accumulating for years, in order to buy a "negro girl named Sally" for whom she had great "affection."[296] Typically, no plan of self- or familial emancipation through the courts could move forward without the consent of the slaveholder. This South Carolina case, however, proved to be an exception. When the girl's captor, Beaty, refused to release Sally from bondage, arguing ostensibly that the "property" of his "property" belonged to him, the enslaved woman arranged for an attorney to represent her case in court. He argued before the jury that since Beaty had received the amount of payment owed him for Sally's purchase from her fictive mother working on her own, "all that" this enslaved woman earned in this manner "ought to be at her own disposal." Furthermore, the lawyer noted, "if the wench chose to appropriate the savings of her extra labour to the purchase of this slave girl [Sally], in order afterwards to set her free, would a jury of the country say no? He trusted not." "Why not?" he asked rhetorically. "They were too humane and upright, he hoped, to do such manifest violence to so singular and extraordinary an act of benevolence." The jury concurred and Sally "was set at liberty."[297] A similar case involved a free "Guinea" woman in Louisiana who, as a seamstress, had acquired a modest estate she hoped to use, in part, to purchase and then liberate twenty-five-year-old Joseph and twenty-year-old Juana because "of the great love she bears for them having raised them as her own children."[298]

Another War/Another Chance for Freedom

Perhaps even more than the American Revolution, the War of 1812 provided an opportunity for captive men and women to escape, gaining freedom for themselves and their families. Many who fled worked for the British military, mostly as part of the Colonial Marines or Royal Navy, as spies and as guides. Some, no doubt, either remembered or were told of the escapes during the earlier war eras. Others may have even had family members or ancestors who had fled during the Revolutionary War. Enslaved people were not the only ones who remembered. The British military also seemed to do so, perhaps recalling especially the lure of freedom for Black families. As such, the 1814 proclamation of commander and chief of Britain's North American Station—Vice Admiral Alexander Cochrane—offered even more than Lord Dunmore's proclamation. Cochrane's actually encouraged the escape and emigration of not just able-bodied enslaved men but also their families—women, children, and the elderly. Imagine the excitement in the quarters and their environs when captives heard even a hint of Cochrane's proclamation: "All those who may be disposed to emigrate from the United States will, with their Families, be received on board His Majesty's Ships or Vessels of War, or at the Military Posts that may be established . . . when they will have the choice of either entering into His Majesty's Sea or Land Forces, or of being sent as FREE Settlers to the British possessions in North America or the West Indies, where they will meet with all due encouragement."[299] This "encouragement," in part, included land to establish their own family farms. Moreover, the promise of freedom did not openly hinge on military service, or service of any kind. Certainly, the British wanted and needed Black military assistance, but they relied on the desire of the escaping men to "guarantee" their families' safe removal to freedom to persuade them to contribute to the British military cause.

All in all, about 5,000 were able to take advantage of this avenue to freedom, and the Colonial Marines, as those who enlisted were called, proved to be worthy military forces.[300] Repeated British raids in heavily enslaved populated areas—the Chesapeake Bay beginning in 1813; in Baltimore, Washington, and lands adjacent to the Potomac and Rappahannock rivers in 1814; and in the Sea Islands of Georgia and Spanish East Florida in early 1815—ushered in this pathway to freedom for enslaved families.[301] According to historian Alan Taylor, "The British incursion enabled many Tidewater slaves to reconstitute families that had been divided by sale, inheritance, and rental."[302] There was even one documented same-sex couple who managed to escape and leave their story in the archival record. The enslaved woman "Unity," from Calvert County, Maryland, had been married briefly to a male captive. She then became intimate with a woman, Philis Caden, and the two women seemed to have established an abroad marriage. They acknowledged a "sisterhood" in the Methodist Church, and Unity took the name of Minty Caden. The couple later escaped to the British.[303] Charles Ball recalled in his autobiographical account the escape of more than one hundred Maryland bondspeople—several family and fictive kin groups—from the plantation of a Mrs. Wilson to the British naval forces. One enslaved man on the plantation refused to go because he refused to leave behind his wife and children, who lived on an adjacent farm. The rest purportedly were taken, as free people, to Trinidad. It was during that same war, Ball added, that "several thousand Black people deserted from their masters and mistresses and escaped to the British fleet. None of these people were ever regained by their captors, as the British naval officers treated them as free people."[304]

On the Georgia Sea Island plantation of Pierce Butler, 138 members of enslaved families managed to escape to the British.[305] Butler's overseer understood emphatically the desire of the enslaved to gain their freedom and that this freedom meant familial unity and protection. In response to his failed efforts to keep them from running away to the British forces, he ranted to his employer, "How will it please me to have the pleasure to git your Negroes back and pick out one husband, one wife, one fellow, one wench and sell them—leaving their children or parents behind, as it may happen, to reflect on their wanton, impudent folly."[306]

At the war's end in February 1815, many of those who had been freed—about 4,100—sailed with their families to the British colonies of Bermuda, Trinidad, and the Maritimes, undoubtedly ending physical ties with those who had not managed to escape, but providing some hope of rebuilding and expanding families as free people in the remaining British settlements in the Americas.[307] Some 1,663 refugees (892 men, 583 adult women, and 188 youth, including Gabriel Hall) arrived in Halifax, Nova Scotia, with at least 30 percent married and with many families among them.[308]

More than four hundred others, however, chose to stay in a "maroon fort" constructed with British soldiers in the Gulf of Mexico. The fortification not only protected their own freedom and those of their families, but also provided some sanctuary for the enslaved who continued to try to reach them. Unfortunately, American forces destroyed the fort in August 1815.[309] The Merikians, as the escapees called themselves in Trinidad, moved onto government provided plots of land, about sixteen acres each. They developed them into farms and villages and were led by those who had been "sergeants" in the Black Colonial Marines.[310] Records collected by historian John Weiss provided ample evidence of the couples and relations that reconstituted family life on this British Caribbean Island.[311]

ONE ENDING

When the enslaved man Fortune and his wife, Aminta, decided to flee the bustling market hamlet of Petersburg, Virginia, for freedom, they could not have anticipated the course of events that would punctuate their lives as fugitives in Philadelphia, in service to the loyalist cause only a few years later, and eventual "freedom" in the northern British province of Halifax, Nova Scotia. Aminta and Fortune prepared for a free future, even though they knew that the odds were, as ever, stacked incredibly against them. Having recently been "brought" from Rhode Island, they had not put down any kin roots in Virginia. As a couple who would soon be parents themselves—perhaps the reason they decided that they had no time to waste—they took to the open road, or water, as clandestine, hunted fugitives. Aminta and Fortune dressed as would be expected of free people, not enslaved. Indeed, the quality and quantity of the clothing they had at their disposal indicates that even as bondspeople, they had been valued, perhaps skilled "property." William Bradley, their new captor, seemed well aware of their unusually rich

"Photograph of Gabriel Hall," c. 1890. "Photograph of Gabriel Hall," c. 1890, Courtesy of Novia Scotia Archives.

bundle of "belongings," which he described in detail for the fugitive slave advertisement.[312]

The forty-year-old Fortune had buckskin pants that were "almost new," two heavy coats, a sailor's jacket (suggesting he had been a seaman, with unusual mobility, geospatial knowledge, and perhaps a seaman's network of associates and friends), a large-brimmed hat that he wore (perhaps as a gesture of masculine pride) "cocked to the side," a cap for warmth, and maybe even a silk one. Regardless of his escape route, Fortune would not have appeared as a frightened enslaved man out of place with free people; he would have looked confident and competent, on his way to some place where he was expected. Aminta, a thirty-year-old mixed-race woman with the "look of an Indian" and descended in part from an Indigenous person who had been brought from a Spanish colony, wore her "long black hair" on her neck and also carried with her the costumes of an elite domestic or freed woman. She had numerous items for dress—a red flannel petticoat, three dresses, a black bonnet, and "several other things"—as well as a black quilt that undoubtedly was used to keep the couple warm during the cool spring nights. The two

PETERSBURG, *April* 21, 1773.

RUN away, laſt Night, from the Subſcriber, two Slaves, namely: A Negro Fellow named FORTUNE, about ſix Feet high, flim made, has a thin Noſe for one ſo black as he is, and appears to be about forty Years of Age; he took with him ſundry Wearing Apparel, particularly a Pair of Buckſkin Breeches almoſt new, a Thickſet Coat, a brown Sailor's Jacket, a red great Coat, a fine Hat, pretty much worn, with a large Brim, and commonly has it cocked up, wears a red Worſted Cap in common, and ſometimes a Silk one. Alſo a Wench named A M I N T A, appears to be about thirty Years of Age, ſhort and well made, has much the Look of an *Indian*, and is ſo, her Mother having been brought from the *Spaniſh* Main to *Rhode Iſland*, has long black Hair, which ſhe wears in her Neck, and took with her a black Quilt, a red Flannel Petticoat, a dark Ground Calico Gown, a blue and white one, and an old light coloured Stuff ditto, a red Cardinal, a black Bonnet, and ſeveral other Things. I lately had them of Captain *John Atkinſon*, and as they were brought from *Rhode Iſland*, it is probable they will endeavour to get there again, as they pretend to Freedom. I requeſt it as a Favour of all Maſters of Veſſels not to harbour or entertain them, as it will probably be attended with bad Conſequences. I will give a Reward of THREE POUNDS if they are taken fifty Miles from home and ſecured ſo that I may get them again, and THIRTY SHILLINGS if within that Diſtance. WILLIAM BRADLEY.

Run Away notice, April 29, 1773. Runaway Advertisement for Fortune and Aminta placed by William Bradley, *Virginia Gazette*, published by Purdie & Dixon, April 29, 1773, page 3. Courtesy of the John D. Rockefeller Jr. Digital Library, The Colonial Williamsburg Foundation.

had claimed to be "free," a distinct possibility given the practice of kidnapping free people from various colonial empires and selling them to another as unfree, but the author of the advertisement was having none of it. Bradley was willing to pay three pounds for their return.[313] He would be disappointed.

Fortune and Aminta made it to freedom. Their daughter, Rose, born in 1774 in Philadelphia, traveled with them and other refugees to British Nova Scotia. Despite the many difficulties that loyalist free Blacks suffered, Rose Fortune (her father's "slave" name became his family's surname in freedom) grew up, married, and had children—at least three—and a business. She began a baggage carriage business that gained her public recognition and some respect. Rose also became an unofficial policewoman, helping to keep Halifax safe for her community. And she did have a community. In fact, the Fortune family came to be close to another group who had dared to

An anonymous sketch of Rose Fortune. Unknown, Rose Fortune, watercolor, c. 1830s, Courtesy of Nova Scotia Archives.

leave Virginia with the British for freedom, also eventually settling in Nova Scotia. In the 1830s, two of Rose's children, Jane and John, married siblings Isaac and Hester Godfrey, part of the Godfrey clan that had stolen away from southern Virginia.[314] The Fortune family extended even more to include the connections that took place when Rose's daughter Margaret married a man named John Francis. These three married couples gave Rose Fortune at least eight grandchildren and a host of future descendants who, today, live in both Canada and the United States. The family that Fortune and Aminta could only have dreamed of when they escaped came to be and to thrive. Indeed, one of their descendants, Daurene Lewis, became the first Black woman mayor in Canada.[315] Enslaved family resistance not only mattered, but it also sometimes succeeded spectacularly.

THE ANTEBELLUM FAMILIAL EXPERIENCE

Chapter 4

Antebellum Courtship and Marital Rituals

INTRODUCTION: THE DENIED PROMISE OF ONE ANTEBELLUM MARRIAGE

If you wait for me/Then I'll come for you.[1]

Henry Walton Bibb believed he would not marry and begin his own family until he had gained his freedom. It was not that family was insignificant to him. Kinship lay at the crux of his social identity. Still, as much as a spouse, children, and other kin could offer in the way of comfort and support in the bleakest moments of enslavement, Henry knew from the time he was a child in Catalonia, Kentucky, that family could be a heavy cross to bear if you were unfree.

Born in 1815, Henry grew up in a matrifocal family, deeply loving his mother, Mildred Jackson, and having an abiding affection for his six younger brothers. His love and commitment, and their reciprocity, however, did not eliminate the inevitability of pain, loss, mystery, anger, and frustration that was integral to the enslaved kinship reality. Henry knew, as did most Black captives, that the notion that a "paternalistic" slaveholder would recognize or protect a captive's family ties was a cruel lie. What White man, Henry wondered, was his father? Who were the White fathers of his siblings? His mother had told Henry that his father was a local planter by the name of James Bibb, but the boy still grew up with "no personal knowledge of him."[2] His brothers, also the children of local White men, had no known connection—legal, emotional, or material—with their paternal kin. While not entirely true, Henry lamented, "it is almost impossible for slaves to give a correct account of their male parentage."[3] Certainly true, though, was that bondspersons who were conceived as the result of coerced sexual encounters and breeding schemes, or

Celebration of Slave Wedding in "Kitchen Ball," c. 1838 Christian Friedrich Mayer, *Kitchen Ball at White Sulphur Springs, Virginia*, 1838, oil on canvas, 14 x 29 1/2 in. (61 x 74.9 cm). North Carolina Museum of Art Raleigh. Purchased with funds from the State of North Carolina 52.9.23.

lost their fathers through sale or death before they could form a clear sense of them, found that contemplating their paternal ancestry resulted in an unyielding mystery and sometimes outright deception, bitterness, and shame. Henry decided early in life that he did not want to become a "lost" husband or one of those fathers hustled away from his children at the drop of an auctioneer's gavel. He wanted more for himself and for those he loved.

There were, of course, several other good reasons to resist becoming an enslaved husband, father, wife, or mother. While some aspects of enslaved family life changed over time, many of the menacing conditions always threatening to pull the rug out from under family in the seventeenth and eighteenth centuries persisted and even became more exaggerated during the antebellum years. An enslaved child's early loss of kin as a result of rental, sale, inheritance, or death was an experience Henry understood only too well. "The first time I was separated from my mother," he wrote on the very first page of his autobiographical account, "I was young and small." His captor's practice of hiring him out lasted for the next "eight or ten years in succession."[4] This division, he went on to explain, was a fundamental condition of his enslavement: "It was then my sorrows and sufferings commenced. It was then I first commenced seeing and feeling that I was a wretched slave."[5] One can well imagine the feelings that Henry's mother had at the early loss of her son and her inability to continue to protect and nurture him, or the anxiety, upset, and loss his younger brothers, or even boyhood friends, suffered when he was rented out away from them.

The litany of common abuses—including physical and sexual brutality, grinding poverty, and a routine lack of adequate food, clothing, housing, furnishings, and medical attention—laid the foundation for a Black captive's lifelong traumas, physical disabilities, rage, depression, and anxiety. Even as a child, Henry explained, he was "compelled to work under the lash without wages and often, clothes enough to hide my nakedness. I often worked without half enough to eat. . . . I have often laid my wearied limbs down at night upon a dirt floor, or a bench, without any covering." Without attentive kin to intercede, material and working conditions were even more harrowing. Henry labored "through all kinds of weather, hot or cold, wet or dry" without any shoes until winter. He recalled of his solitary suffering and frustration: "No arm to protect me from tyrants aggression;/No parents to cheer me when laden with grief."[6]

Henry Bibb's devised remedy was to escape, and he did not believe he could do so with a wife and children in tow. He began a career of fugitivity when he was just ten years old, at that time trying to evade an abusive female captor who daily scolded, flogged, and pulled his ears.[7] He continued his short-term escapes for the next several years, each attempt deepening his determination and skills necessary to gain permanent freedom. Only then, Henry believed, could he have a family of his own design.[8]

As an adolescent, Henry's romantic interests and sexual arousal proved to be fierce competition to his determination to find freedom before marrying. After some failed attempts to win the affections of enslaved women he found physically attractive, Henry met Malinda. His notations about their courtship and early marriage provide an intimate view to the social and romantic experiences as well as to the family lives, concerns, and commitments of young enslaved men and women during Henry's generation and beyond.

"The circumstances of my courtship and marriage," Henry explained, "I consider to be among the most remarkable events of my life while a slave"—remarkable, he was quick to add, because "the fascinating charms of a female" had caused him to temporarily focus on something other than freedom.[9] He recalled that "the first two or three visits that I paid this dear girl, I had no intention of courting or marrying her, for I was aware that such a step would greatly obstruct my way to the land of liberty."[10] But he soon found himself recklessly, "deeply in love" and came to understand that Malinda, who resided on a plantation some four miles away from where he worked, felt similarly about him. Love—indeed, romantic love, Henry soon discovered once he began to court Malinda—was a kind of miraculous emotional respite from some of the hardships of his enslaved life, even if slavery always would be a clear threat to this love. Nothing seemed to be able to curb his growing affection for the beautiful Malinda.

Henry perceived Malinda's love for him through her "warm reception," "affectionate shake of the hand," "gentle smile," and even her willingness to defy her mother's wish that she marry someone else.[11] Henry insisted that Malinda consent to two promises before they married: that she would not interfere with his commitment to be a faithful Christian and that they would escape to Canada together as soon as possible. "I never will give my heart nor hand to any girl in marriage," Henry insisted, "until I first know her sentiments upon all important subjects of Religion and Liberty."[12] To his delight, Malinda not only agreed but readily confessed that she felt likewise. Both promised to live "pious" lives while they courted another year before marriage.[13]

Their proposed marriage drew the opposition of Henry's captor as well as the couple's close kin relations. These are important revelations because they open a window into the emotional struggles enslaved families and communities underwent when their young people fell in love. Henry's mother believed that, at only nineteen, her son was too young to marry and that assuming such a commitment would bring him greater difficulty than he already was experiencing. Malinda's mother, who had gained her freedom from her daughter's White father, wanted Malinda to marry someone who lived closer to her. She had hoped Malinda would marry the biracial son of a wealthy planter who might also someday gain his freedom from his father. This proposed son-in-law, she reasoned, could do more to help her daughter than a man like Henry, who had no such possible options. Henry's enslaver, Albert Sibly, disapproved of the couple's intentions because he did not want his captive involved in an abroad marriage, fearing the groom's new marital responsibilities would tempt him to "steal" to help support his wife. Malinda's captor, William Gatewood, approved of the marriage. He would, after all, benefit from his claim of any children Malinda birthed. A stable marriage, even an abroad one as Henry and Malinda's would have been, would reap new "property" for him over the next several years.[14]

Despite the swirl of doubts, objections, and lingering fears, Henry and Malinda did marry in 1833. Their Christmastime nuptials signified a typical marriage date for enslaved men and women because the holiday schedule of released work time and additional leniency to travel locally to connect with friends and family meant the couple could begin their married lives more leisurely and with communal support. Henry recalled that their wedding celebration was a happy occasion: "We had quite a festival given us. All appeared to be wide awake, and we had quite a jolly time at my wedding party."[15] Perhaps their celebration was similar to that captured in 1838 by

Christian Mayer in his painting *Kitchen Ball*, which opens this chapter. Henry described it as a time of "sweet remembrance and pleasure."[16] He believed that his marriage, albeit without legality, was sanctioned by God and that his marital bed was "undefiled."[17]

Henry complimented his wife on her living up to his (and other husbands') expectations. Their first months were a happy time. "She was with me in sorrow, and joy," Henry remembered, "in fasting and feasting, in trial and persecution, in sickness and health, in sunshine and in shade."[18] However, they still were enslaved. It did not take Henry long to regret that he and Malinda had spent precious time enjoying each other and their community after their marriage, rather than immediately escaping to Canada.

The pain and insecurity of enslaved people's marriages soon imposed themselves on Henry and Malinda. Henry's master decided to move his slaveholding operation further west, to Missouri, threatening the couple's abroad marriage with a permanent separation. After what must have been several weeks of grave anxiety, Sibly sold Henry to a relative who resided about seven miles from Malinda. Like other abroad husbands, Henry could only visit his wife once a week, from Saturday evening until the beginning of work on Monday morning. Henry's new slaveholder, however, then sold him to Malinda's captor for $850, fearing that if he did not do so, Henry would escape. Henry's closer proximity to his wife, however, created new frustrations and sadness—the pain of watching her being "shamefully scourged and abused" without any recourse. His emotional struggle (and certainly Malinda's) deepened after the birth of their daughter, Mary Frances.[19]

Mary Frances's enslavement caused her parents tremendous psychological trauma. Malinda's work largely was confined to the fields, and there was no person left to care for their child. Mary Frances spent her days in the home of their captor's wife, a woman who did not hesitate to hit the child whenever it pleased her. Henry noted that he had known Mrs. Gatewood to "slap with her hand the face of little Frances, for crying after her mother, until her little face was left black and blue."[20] Once Mrs. Gatewood's handprint was visible on the very light-skinned child's face for more than a week after she had beaten the child. "Who can imagine," Henry wrote for the generations of enslaved parents who came before and after him, "what could be the feelings of a father and mother, when looking upon their infant child whipped and tortured with impunity, and they placed in a situation where they could afford it no protection."[21]

Henry was determined to free himself and his family, even though he realized the risk of being caught meant permanent separation by being sold further away from them. He tried multiple times. Sometimes people helped him; other times, they betrayed him for money. Henry reached the "free states" more than once and even got as far as Canada, but he was never able to do so with Malinda and Mary Frances. He repeatedly attempted to retrieve them, but failed each time. His successful escapes were interspersed with captures that, although painful, temporarily reunited Henry with his wife and child. Eventually, Gatewood sold all three. Henry's mother, with other kin and friends, came to the Louisville slave market to bid a tearful goodbye.[22]

Madison Garrison, a long-distance slave trader, bought Henry, Malinda, and little Mary Frances as part of a "parcel" he was gathering to sell in New Orleans. The three suffered terribly waiting in prison. Garrison separated the spouses, and the prison conditions were horrific—a veritable "hell" of chained, ragged, dirty, sometimes violent, nearly starved captives. Even more alarming, Garrison had decided to use Malinda as his concubine until he sold her. Her refusal to oblige him meant daily whippings and the threat that he would sell Mary Frances away from both parents. Henry was aware of Garrison's actions, but chained within the prison, he was unable to help either his wife or his daughter.[23] His autobiographical account leaves his readers to conclude what Garrison "did" with Malinda when he removed her from their prison for three weeks before she, Mary Frances, and Henry were reunited in the coffle headed south.

In New Orleans, Francis Whitfield, a cotton planter from Claiborne Parish on the Red River, bought the Bibb family for $2,200. When Henry first met Whitfield, a purported deacon in the Baptist Church, he believed that he would not be such a difficult slaveholder. He was terribly mistaken. Life for the Bibb family, although they now lived together, still was very difficult. Whitfield soon proved to be a brute. He punished any resistance with a harsh whipping. Henry witnessed as Whitfield demanded that a young female become his son's concubine, whipped her until she complied, and publicly gave two hundred lashings to another enslaved female who had displeased the manor's mistress. All of his captives had to work long and hard hours, received only minimal food and clothing, and had to give complete obedience, even to his sexual demands, or face back lashings followed by saltwater washings.

Henry and Matilda worked primarily as domestics, but Henry took particular note of how badly Whitfield treated field workers and their families. Mothers had to leave their small children under trees or in the weeds while they worked, since Whitfield would not let them return to the quarters to nurse their babies. These infants and toddlers were always in danger of being bitten by snakes, eaten by alligators, burned by the scorching sun, or ravaged by mosquitoes or other insects.[24] Mothers, fathers, their children, and other kin suffered from fatigue, malnutrition, and ineffective medical treatments. Malinda and their second child both were the victims of untreated illnesses. The baby died, and Henry buried it "without even a box to put it in."[25]

Throughout, Henry remained a devout Christian and undoubtedly Malinda did as well. But even their faith was a source of distress, since Whitfield would not allow them to attend religious meetings. Facing a staked lashing for doing that or an expansive number of other "offenses," he and Malinda debated the merits of Henry escaping. She feared that if he ran away and was caught, he would be sold away, and she had no other kin nearby from whom to seek aid or solace. "This was truly heart-rending to my poor wife," Henry explained, "the thought of our being torn apart in a strange land after having been sold away from all her friends and relations, was more than she could bear."[26] Still, he persisted.

Henry initially escaped on one of his captor's mules to avoid tracking by bloodhounds. But he could not bear leaving his wife and child behind. The following day, he returned and decided to take Malinda and Mary Frances with him, believing that if they escaped together and were caught, that Whitfield (who had bought them as a family) might sell them as a family, too. The three escaped to an uninhabited island on the Red River. Some days later, they were violently captured by slave hunters with bloodhounds. Their greatest fear was realized: Henry survived his brutal whipping but was sold away from Malinda and Mary Frances.[27]

The couple begged Whitfield to keep them together, but his only response was a whipping in their terrified child's presence.[28] He then sold Henry to gamblers who agreed to try to unite the family, but Whitfield refused to sell Malinda and Mary Frances. Henry eventually was sold to a Cherokee but managed to escape when this slaveholder died.[29] Sometime after reaching freedom in Detroit, Henry learned that Whitfield had sold Malinda and Mary Frances to another man, who had taken Malinda as his concubine. She was, Henry admitted bitterly, living "in a state of adultery."[30]

In 1847, Henry married again. This time, he betrothed Mary Elizabeth Miles, an abolitionist and Massachusetts State Normal School–trained teacher who was the daughter of free Black Quakers. Comparing his new marital state with his former, the self-emancipated Henry reiterated the problems incumbent in marriage for enslaved people and, from his perspective as a husband, in having an enslaved wife. Mary, his free spouse, Henry elaborated, "is a bosom friend, a help-meet, a loving companion in all the social, moral and religious relations of life. She is to me what a poor slave's wife can never be; for she can not be true to her husband contrary to the will of her master. She can neither be pure nor virtuous."[31] Mary moved to Windsor, Ontario, with Henry to avoid his being re-enslaved. There, the two were actively involved in the Underground Railroad and published a newspaper, the first by African Americans in Canada. It was appropriately titled the *Voice of the Fugitive*.[32]

Unfortunately, Malinda Bibb's tragic story remains spoken only through Henry's words. We can be certain, however, that Malinda, too, was forever horrified by the devastating losses of her husband, birth relations, and extended family—and of her dreams of freedom for herself and her daughter.

"*My heart is almost broken.*"

Illustration of Henry, Malinda, and Mary Frances Bibb "My heart is almost broken," illustration in Bibb, *Narrative of the Life and Adventures of Henry Bibb* **(New York: Author, 1849) 81.** Courtesy of Documenting the American South, Libraries of the University of North Carolina, Chapel Hill.

We must remember that it was Malinda, after all, who lessened her chances for gaining freedom and remaining close to her kin of birth when she married Henry. She must have deeply regretted, perhaps even fiercely resented, the marriage, given Henry's inability to keep his promise to her, and undoubtedly her family, that he would help her and their children to gain liberation. It was Malinda who had to live with the painful consequences of humiliation, shame, and desperation of being forced out of a marriage to a man whom she loved and into sexual slavery with another. What became of the Bibbs's daughter is uncertain, but Malinda also likely had to witness Mary Frances's traumas for years to come.

The family life Henry Bibb had with Malinda resonates with much of what has been expressed in this book regarding kinship ideals, heteronormative marriage and familial relations, and the difficulties of Africans and African-descended peoples enslaved in the Americas from the early colonial period forward. But heterosexuality was not their only reality. Single-sex

Henry Bibb. Henry Bibb, c. 1850, HS5230, P.H. Reason, engraver, Life and Adventures of Henry Bibb, Courtesy of Bentley Historical Library, University of Michigan.

relationships, both romantic and fictive kin inclusive, certainly existed, even if they remained hidden or practically invisible given legal and customary hostility centered on homoerotic practices. The evidence, however, emerges bit by bit. For example, it was recently uncovered that Pierce Lafayette, the "property" of Confederate vice president Alexander Stephens, was known to have a "Negro mistress," another enslaved man named Felix Hall. After the Civil War, Lafayette became part of a fictive kinship of "queens" in Washington, DC. Many had been born in slavery. As freed people, they routinely met, danced, dressed extravagantly as women, and loved each other romantically, sexually, and familially, strongly indicating the same-sex love lives they had always pursued, even while enslaved.[33]

Henry and Malinda Bibb's domestic life, like that of Pierce Lafayette and Felix Hall, played out during the antebellum era, a period when the nation's demographic, economic, political, and cultural forces affected Black family life with somewhat different emphases than in earlier generations. This chapter describes the marriage rituals and experiences during the last four decades before the Civil War, roughly during the lifespan of Henry Bibb, who was born in 1815 and died in 1853.

The early to mid-nineteenth century was a time of great expansion in the United States and its slave society. Black bondage was coming to a gradual close in other places—Mexico and Central America, Bolivia, Ecuador, Peru, and the British, Danish, and French colonies in the Caribbean all legally ended slavery before the United States did. More importantly, the number of enslaved Black people in the nation was not diminishing, but rather increased an astonishing 265 percent to nearly four million during this era, making the United States the largest slave society in the Americas. The US territory and the places where slavery was legal, likewise, grew incredibly at the same time. With the Louisiana Purchase of 1803, the nation's acquisition of Spanish Florida and the Pacific Northwest in 1821, Mexico's loss of Texas in 1836 and its annexation to the United States nine years later, along with the forced "removal" of most of the remaining Indigenous peoples from their lands in the South in the 1830s and the expulsion of Mexico from other territories north of the Rio Grande in 1848 and 1854, the country's mid-nineteenth-century physical boundaries expanded from the Atlantic to the Pacific. Slave territory expanded with it.[34]

Why did Black slavery increase in the United States in the early nineteenth century? Simply put, the bodies, labor, and skills of enslaved Black people fueled the agrarian, industrial, and commercial economies that financed the nation's domestic growth and its increasing importance on the world stage. The invention of the cotton gin in the late eighteenth century, along with cotton textile manufacture investments and advancements in the Northeast and Britain, meant unprecedented attention turned to the planting, growing, and harvesting of short-staple cotton, the nation's most important export. The national production of cotton increased 921 percent between 1819 and 1855, while a new slavery frontier in Arkansas, Alabama, Mississippi, Louisiana, and Texas formed.[35] It was a frontier created and transformed into a national gold mine by the arrival of more than a million slaves via the domestic slave trade to and across this broad region. This forced migration, with a social impact on bondspersons' lives akin to the Atlantic slave trade at its height in the eighteenth century, meant a 34 percent increase in the enslaved population laboring in the Lower South from 1850 to 1860 alone, and a significant inflation in the number of householders who held bondspersons in the Lower South and southwest. By 1860, 49 percent of White household heads in Mississippi were slaveholders. Percentages in South Carolina, Georgia, Alabama, Florida, Louisiana, and Texas were not far behind. (See tables 2.1 and 2.2 in Appendix B.)

Winslow Homer, "The Cotton Pickers. Winslow Homer (1836-1910), *The Cotton Pickers,* 1876, oil on canvas, 24 1/16 x 38 1/8 in. (61.12 x 96.84 cm), Digital Image © Museum Associates / LACMA. Licensed by Art Resource, NY. Acquisition made possible through Museum Trustees: Robert O. Anderson, R. Stanton Avery, B. Gerald Cantor, Edward W. Carter, Justin Dart, Charles E. Ducommun, Camilla Chandler Frost, Julian Ganz, Jr., Dr. Armand Hammer, Harry Lenart, Dr. Franklin D. Murphy, Mrs. Joan Palevsky, Richard E. Sherwood, Maynard J. Toll, and Hal B. Wallis (M.77.68).

These forty years of the antebellum period witnessed a vast "natural" increase in the enslaved population. This increase, however, did not mean that couples like Henry and Malinda could marry and live together happily. Many married, but long-term cohabitation, or even the possibility of long-term abroad marriage, often eluded even those most determined to remain together. Shifts in the Spanish, French, British, and Mexican colonial empires in North America vis-à-vis US expansion also meant layered consequences for Black domestic life.

Black slavery was maintained among some Indigenous peoples, who were tremendously affected by colonial settler and US national policies. During the early to mid-nineteenth century, four of the so-called Five Civilized Tribes of the Lower South—the Choctaw, Chickasaw, Creek, and Cherokee—held Black bondspeople. Undoubtedly, many enslaved family members were lost, along with those of the Indigenous, on the Trail of Tears during the late 1830s.[36] Likewise, the multiple military expeditions (1817–1818, 1838–1842, late 1855–1858) the United States mounted against the Seminoles also displaced and destroyed some of the Black families among them.[37]

Changing legal structures had their own social consequences. One important alteration for those persons who had been enslaved for generations in the

"The Indians and Negroes Massacreing the Whites in Florida" Saunders & Van Welt, Public domain, via Wikimedia Commons.

Lower South and southwest (when these areas were comprised of Spanish and French colonial settlements) was that new US control meant less tolerance of bondspeople's marital and familial relations. As chapters 2 and 3 detailed, the influence of Catholicism on France's *Code Noir* and Spain's *Las Siete Partidas*, at least technically, offered some familial protections that neither British colonial law nor the state governments of the newly formed United States proffered.

Another custom/law restricted the dismissal of older, perhaps less productive kin.[38] Captives now living in these areas could not expect to benefit in any manner from such "leniencies" as part of the United States. Certainly, those several hundred thousand bondspeople who arrived with or were sold to "Americans" acquired few such familial "protections."

MATRIMONY AND MATING

More slaveholders permitted marriage and encouraged sexual relations among enslaved people during the antebellum era than earlier periods because of their desire to increase their "slave property" through sustained procreation. In the Upper South, where the agrarian economy had shifted somewhat from tobacco production to much less labor-intensive grain farming, slave traders and slaveholders found the domestic slave trade to be a lucrative business from which they could benefit through selling "breeders" and enslaved people not needed to work on their grain estates. "Dey would have two or three women on de plantation dat was good breeders en dey would have chillun pretty regular fore freedom come here," Josephine Bacchus of South Carolina explained.[39]

The assumed fecundity of a given female or male enhanced their monetary value, particularly the female's antebellum market price.[40] As Peter Brown of Mississippi noted regarding his mother's relatively good treatment, "They prized fast breeders. They would come to see her and bring her things then. She had ten children, three pairs of twins."[41] Willie McCullough of Marion, South Carolina, described the way enslaved females were valued: "Some of the slave women were looked upon by the slave owners as a stock raiser looks upon his brood sows. . . . If a slave woman had children fast she was considered very valuable."[42] John Adams's mother was seventeen when she married his father, then eighteen, in Frederick County, Virginia. Their owners undoubtedly were pleased with the couple's fertility. They had twenty-three children, including four sets of twins.[43] Alice Sewell of Alabama recalled that her grandmother's captor "swapped" her because she did not "bear children like dey wanted her to," a decision he came to regret more and more—she bore thirteen children at her new residence.[44] Not surprisingly, enslavers, along with some members of the enslaved community, looked on a woman who did or could not bear children as unworthy of marriage. As former captive Pierce Cody pointed out about couples in his vicinity, "All marriage unions were permanent and a barren wife was considered the only real cause for separation."[45] Berry Clay confirmed that it was his experience that captors were eager for their captives to marry as soon as they "manifest interest in the opposite sex." Slaveholders only rarely took their captives' wishes into consideration, demanding that they "be fruitful." "A barren woman," Clay continued, "was separated from her husband and usually sold away."[46]

Some slaveholders promoted high birth rates among their slave property through marriage, even if they refused to view Black marriage as a legally binding contract or to guarantee that a woman, or man, could choose their own spouse, or keep and raise the children they bore. Lulu Wilson from Kentucky was clear about her female enslaver's intentions regarding her fertility and how she manipulated the young teen to comply to her breeding scheme, first by offering Lulu a beautiful wedding that would be otherwise unobtainable: "Missus told me I had ought to marry" and promised a white dress and a wedding dinner when she did so. Lulu married a man held by her captor's nephew. Then came the pressure for her to bear children. The local physician was complicit, boldly lying to Lulu about the medical consequences of not having children. "I know it warn't long after that when Missus Hodges got a doctor to me," Lulu explained. "The doctor told me less'n I had a baby, old as I was and married, I'd start in on spasms. So it warn't long till I had a baby."[47] A generation earlier, the Hodges family also had pressured Lulu's mother to marry and bear children. After Lulu was born, her mother did not have any additional children. Her captor decided that it was the fault of her husband. "They say my paw am too old and wore out for breedin'," Lulu testified, "and wants her to take [up] with this here young buck." They purportedly "ran Lulu's father away," and her mother had many additional children with the new man they chose for her. The white folks, Lulu concluded, wanted enslaved people "to breed like livestock."[48]

The Hodges were not exceptional in their demands. Enslavers often forced Black males and females to marry and mate with persons whom they did not desire. An enslaved man known as Robert wanted to marry Isabella Baumfree (Sojourner Truth) when she was still a captive in New York, but his slaveholder did not want him to do so because he would not be able to claim Robert's children as his property; they would instead belong to Isabella's captor. Robert still clandestinely visited her, but once caught (he had gone to visit her because she was ill), his enslavers beat him bloody. Robert no longer came to visit her and was forced to marry a woman held by his enslaver. Isabella eventually married another bondsman, Thomas, whose two prior wives had been sold from him.[49] Adeline Taylor of Tennessee spoke of her mother's marriage while captured, noting that "she had been made to marry by her master. . . . She was only thirteen years old. . . . She was fine and stout and her husband was fine and stout, and they wanted more from that stock." The couple split with emancipation, and Adeline's mother married again.[50]

The 1850 image on page 199 demonstrates quite clearly that female captors, as indicated by Lulu and Adeline, could be as insistent as their husbands on these "arranged marriages." The drawing depicts an enslaved woman being forced—on pain of a whipping—to marry the man her captor has chosen for her. None of the witnesses, Black or White, dared to interfere.

Those captors who did not approve of a marriage simply forbade it. Harriet Jacobs knew that her female enslaver would never allow her to marry the man she loved, a local free man of color. "My mistress, like many others," Harriet wrote, "seemed to think that slaves had no right to family ties of their own; that they were created merely to wait upon the family of the mistress."[51] Some appeared to be more obliging. Arnold Gragston of Kentucky remarked that his captor "let us go a-courtin' on the other plantations near anytime we liked, if we were good." If they found someone whom they wanted to marry on a plantation that belonged to their captor's kin or friend, "he would swap a slave so that the husband and wife could be together." When this could not be arranged, he allowed the husband to spend his nights with his wife. Those arrangements, Gragston made clear, were unusual and resented by the other local slaveholders.[52]

Antebellum enslavers used "racial science" to pair females and males not only according to the physical traits they desired in captive offspring, but also according to what they believed were the natural "intellectual" or

"Jumping the Broom" (Virginia), c. 1850. Emily Clemens Pearson or unknown, Public domain, via Wikimedia Commons.

"skilled" capacities of their bound workers. They readily imposed their sense of an internal racial hierarchy on bondspeople's social lives. Rosa Starke from Winnsboro, South Carolina, noted this attitude as she explained how female enslavers sometimes became involved in the "matchmaking" that went on among couples and insisted that the various "classes" of bondspeople marry within their "class." According to Rosa, these classes consisted of butlers, maids, chambermaids, cooks, and nurses who were the most privileged, followed by carriage drivers, gardeners, carpenters, barbers, and the stable hands. Other skilled workers with elevated status included wheelwrights, waggoners, blacksmiths, and slave drivers. Knowledge of animal husbandry also could raise one's status. Skilled agricultural workers, such as "cradlers of de wheat, de threshers and de millers of de corn and de wheat, and de feeder of de cotton gin," Rosa added, were next. "De lowest class" were the field workers. A man who worked in the house would not likely marry a field hand's "good lookin" daughter, although occasionally one might do so "for pure love of her." Still, Rosa knew of no "house gal" who would "lower herself" to marry a field man. "Dat offended de white folks," who thought it their right to interfere with the courtship and marital choices of domestics.[53]

Willie McCullough expanded on Starke's delineation of "classes," noting the importance of color, particularly in the valuation of women and their accessibility—not to Black males who might want to marry them, but to White men. "There were classes of slavery," he shared. "Some of the half-white and beautiful young women who were used by the marster and his men friends or who was the sweetheart of the marster only, were given special privileges."[54] Those who refused were brutally punished. Frederick Douglass explained that the first time he witnessed the trauma of a blood-curling whipping, it was that of his Aunt Hester. Her "offense" was her forbidden courtship with the enslaved man Ned. "Now you d——d b——h," the abuser screamed at the young woman whom he stripped, bound, and beat until blood ran from her, "I'll learn you how to disobey my order!"[55]

Men and women were angered by the lack of control they could exercise in choosing a spouse. According of Charles Grandy of Virginia, if a man desired a wife, his slaveholder would buy one from a trader passing by, regardless of the man's (or woman's) preferences. The "bride" just had to be cheap and bear the physical markings of fertility.[56] Sarah Ford of Texas recalled that "de white folks don't let de slaves what works in def field marry none, dey jus' puts a man and bredin' woman together like mules. Iffen the women don't like the man, it don't make no difference, she better go or dey gives her a hidin.'"[57] Willie McCullough's grandmother and mother assured him that neither was allowed to choose her husband; both women were treated callously as breeders. "Mother tole me that when she became a woman at the age of sixteen years her marster [Billy Cannon] went to a slave owner near by and got a six-foot nigger man, almost an entire stranger to her, and told her she must marry him. Her marster read a paper to them, told them they were man and wife and told this negro he could take her to a certain cabin and go to bed." Neither man asked her for her consent. Willie added that his grandmother, who was enslaved on an adjoining plantation, "said that several different men were put to her just about the same as if she had been a cow or sow."[58] Jacob Manson of North Carolina testified regarding the slave breeding schemes he witnessed. According to him, "A lot of de slave owners had certain strong healthy slave men to serve de slave women. Ginerally dey give one man four women an' dat man better not have nuthin' to do wid de udder women an' de women better not have nuthin to do wid udder men."[59] Hillard Yellerday, also from North Carolina, concurred. He explained that when a girl became a woman—that is, of the earliest childbearing age—she was required to "marry" and begin to have children. Captors, he noted, obliged even girls as young as twelve years old to do so. "Master would sometimes go and get a large hale hearty Negro man from some other plantation to go to his Negro woman. He would ask the other master to let this man come over to his place to go to his slave girls. . . . Negro men six feet tall went to some of these children."[60]

Some slaveholders violated close kin marriage taboos that enslaved people believed important to maintain. "My husband told me that in slavery if your Master told you to live with your brother, you had to live with him," Francis

Bridges of Texas recalled. "My father's mother and dad was first cousins."[61] Others refused to let husbands and wives be sexually exclusive to one another. Male and female enslavers involved in slave breeding sometimes forced married men to have sexual relations with women other than their wives. Elige Davidson from Richmond explained that he was married, but his slaveholder forced him to have sex with other women as a male breeder: "Massa, he bring some more women to see me. He wouldn't let me have just one woman. I . . . [had] about fifteen and I don't know how many chillen."[62] Julia Moore of Lockhart, Texas, stated that her father was "made de husbands of lots of women on de place, 'cause he de big man."[63]

Some men also had more than one wife, or at least had the appearance of multiple spouses, either because of their forced physical isolation from wives or because, for some, it was a cultural preference, even in the antebellum decades. Although the practice of polygamy was more common during the eighteenth century, when the largest numbers of enslaved Africans arrived in North America and brought marital practices directly from their original cultures, polygamy was not extinct by the antebellum era. At Pierce Butler's Georgia plantations, for example, Frances Kemble recalled meeting Judy, who had two children by Joe. The same Joe "had another wife, called Mary, at the Rice Island."[64] An overseer on another low country plantation explained to Basil Hall, a captain in the British Navy and traveler scouring the area, what he believed were enslaved marital traditions noting, probably with some exaggeration, that polygamy was "their own keeping. . . . The men may have, for instance, as many wives as they please, so long as they do not quarrel about such matters."[65]

Abroad marriages were frowned upon not only because of the additional "freedom" they gave men who requested passes to visit their wives and families who lived elsewhere, but also because these husbands' children, like the man Robert who wanted to marry Isabella Baumfree, would belong to their wives' captors. Some enslavers of females also denied permission for these women to marry men abroad because the likelihood of consistent childbirth was reduced if husbands did not reside with wives and could visit only occasionally.

An antebellum slaveholder's determination that an enslaved female should bear as many children as possible also meant that once her husband died or was sold away, she only had a short window of opportunity to marry another man of her choosing, or her enslaver might threaten to sell her or provide another husband for her without regard to the widow's feelings. Sylvia King's captor knew that she had been married in her "old country," but nonetheless married her to another man. Women's fecundity often was measured by their girth—big women were assumed to be fertile. Sylvia's captor bought her because of her size. King noted that "when Marse Jones seed me on de block, he say, 'Dat's a whale of a woman.'" He married her to Bob, who was in charge of the oxen teams.[66]

There also are a few known examples of other kinds of sexual depravity enslavers conflated with marital ritual. Sam and Louisa Everett were from Virginia. "Big Jim" McClain was vicious and voyeuristic, a rapist and breeder who forced his bondspeople to have "orgies" as a kind of sex show. McClain invited his friends to participate, "choosing for themselves the prettiest of the young women" and "sometimes" forcing "the unhappy husbands and lovers of their victims to look on." When McClain decided that Louisa and Sam should marry, he

> ordered Sam to pull off his shirt—that was all the McClain niggers wore—and he said to me: "Nor [the name Louisa's owner preferred for her], do you think you can stand this big nigger?" He had that old bullwhip flung across his shoulder, and Lawd, that man could hit so hard! So I jes said "yassur, I guess so," and tried to hide my face so I couldn't see Sam's nakedness, but he made me look at him anyhow. Well, he told us what we must git busy and do in his presence, and we had to do it. After that we were considered man and wife. Me and Sam was a healthy pair and had fine, big babies, so I never had another man forced on me, thank God. Sam was kind to me and I learnt to love him.[67]

The only marital ritual McClain allowed Louisa and Sam was the sexual act—held in public for him and the others of his community to watch.[68] Both Sam and Louisa were humiliated. Years later, Sam would not even speak of it. Enslavers combined this type of sexual exploitation with more blatant and often violent acts of White male sexual aggression toward female (and male) captives and their children, creating multiple levels of intra- and interracial and gender conflict that had negative consequences for both enslaved and enslaver families. William Wells Brown's mother, Elizabeth, had seven children but, he explained, "no two of us were children of the same father." His father was a "white man, a relative of my master, and connected with some of the first families in Kentucky." Brown's "master" took great interest in the accumulation of the enslaved infants "he claimed to be born his property."[69]

COURTSHIP

> Love is a itchin' round the heart you can't get at to scratch.—Former bondswoman Sally Neal[70]

Despite these abuses, teen and adult males and females sought romance. One former antebellum bondswoman named Arrie Binns remarked that when she was fifteen or sixteen years old, she "wuz big enough to be lookin' at boys an' dey lookin' at me."[71]

Their best opportunities to find someone to share their emotional and sexual desires occurred on their time off—particularly in Saturday night, Sunday, and, of course, during the longer work breaks during the Christmas holidays. Dances, "frolics," communal quilting bees, storytelling times, corn shuckings, and even prayer meetings were the backdrop (or cover) to courtship. Lizzie Farmer of Texas mentioned some activities she enjoyed, even remembering a song that they sang: "We would have dances and play parties.... We had 'ring plays' centered on romance had, lost and began again— a cycle that many enslaved people (and others as well) experienced. We'd all catch hands and march round, den we'd drop all hands 'cept our pardners and we'd swing round and sing:

You steal my pardner, and I steal yours, Miss Mary Jane.
My true love's gone away, Miss Mary Jane!
Steal all round and don't slight none, Miss Mary Jane.
He's lost out but I'se got one, Miss Mary Jane."[72]

Wade Owens of Opelika, Alabama, likewise recalled fun times in the quarters or the nearby woods: "When dey had dem Saddy night frolics an' dance all night long an' nearly day when hit was goin.... My daddy pick de banjo. At de cornshuckings dey'd sing 'All 'Roun' de Corn Pile Sally,' an' dey had whiskey an' gin."[73] Sara Colquitt reminisced that on Saturday nights "us sho' had it, cutting monkeyshines and dancing all night long sometimes."[74] Nellie Lloyd of South Carolina spoke of the popular "flat foot" dance when a person would "slam his foot flat down on de floor. De wooden bottom shoes sho would make a loud noise."[75]

Males often brought small gifts of candy, the spoils of their hunts, nuts, fruit, scarves, or ribbons to their sweethearts. Arrie remembered with great "sentiment" that Franklin Binns would ride miles to see her when they were courting and "brought her candy and nice things to eat," even though she refused to tell him that she would marry him until her parents agreed.[76] There also was plenty of alcohol on hand at courting parties. "On Sadday nights us would frolic an' dance all night long iffen you wanted to, buckdance, sixteen-hand reel and cake walk. Dey would blow reed quills an' have all the licker dey wanted.... Oh, dem cornshuckings! Shuk corn, drink an' holler all night long," Frank Menefee recalled.[77] The next day, Sunday church meetings also gave young couples the opportunity to meet and spend time with each other in the company of their friends and families, and sometimes alone. So, too, did revivals. Religion and recreation went hand in hand, especially at baptism time at the "swimming hole." "Everybody fetched a big basket of grub and, sakes alive!" Sydney noted, "sech another dinner you never see, all spread out on de grassy grove by de ole graveyard."[78]

Beauty mattered in the courtship game. Girls dressed and adorned themselves prettily, while men wore their best when they expected, or hoped for, romance. Martin Richardson of Kentucky was so taken by a young woman's beauty that he eventually agreed to help her to escape. At first, Martin refused the request, "but then I saw the girl, and she was such a pretty little thing, brown skinned and kinda rosy, and looking as scared as I was feelin', so it wasn't long" before he decided to help her.[79] Neal Upson of Georgia recalled Abraham, a domestic who was so determined to appeal that he even stole his captor's shoes to wear to a party. The shoes were too tight, and his master found him out, but Abraham was the highlight of the party, attracting most of the young women who attended. It seemed to Neal that no one wanted to dance with the other men there who did not sport such a sartorial luxury.[80] Lucindy Jordon of Alabama explained that she and her friends picked hickory nuts, strung them together into necklaces, and "smile at our fellers" when they were courting.[81] Molly Dawson of Texas remembered the "charm strings" that females wore that was "supposed ter bring good luck ter de owner of it." They would collect buttons and beads from "deir friends and kinfolks" to place on their strings, some as long as five feet. Molly believed that the necklaces were "some of the prettiest I ever seed in my life," much more beautiful than store-bought ones.[82]

Females had to wear dresses or skirts, even when they performed the most arduous and dirty work. Enslavers insisted that they do so, typically imposing a firm gender binary in most things except labor quotas, punishment, and property status. Victoria Adams, a formerly enslaved woman from South Carolina, recalled that her female captor whipped her "pretty bad" when she wore a pair of her brother's pants to scrub the floor. "She say it's in de Bible dat: 'A man shall not put on a woman's clothes, nor a woman put on a man's clothes.' I ain't never see that in de Bible though, but from then 'til now, I ain't put on no more pants," Victoria added.[83]

Skilled spinners, weavers, designers, seamstresses, dyers, quilters, embroiderers, crocheters, quilt makers, and knitters obliged by helping to dress and adorn the females of their families, especially when they wanted to enhance their femininity, whether at work, courtship, or weddings. "Ma made our clothes and we had pretty dresses too," Arrie Binns of Georgia explained. "She dyed some blue and brown striped. We grew the indigo she used for the blue, right there on the plantation, and she used bark and leaves to make the tan and brown colors."[84] Dan Bogie from Kentucky recalled that his mother made his sister's clothing all different colors, using dyes that she made from berries and mustard seeds.[85] Nancy Williams of Virginia made most of her own clothing that she wore to dances and while courting. She exclaimed of her exquisite and exclusive style ("no, dem other gals did' dress lak me"),

> Lawd, I kin 'member dat Junybug [turquoise or green] silk dress. Dis dress had three ruffles. Den I had slippers wid tassels on em. Mm! De wais' o' dat dress all puffed up all 'roun. Den dere was dem Junybug morrocan slippers. Had dress all colors. 'How I get 'em?' Jes' change dey colors. Took my white dress out to de polk berry bush an' jes' a-dyed it red, den dyed my shoes red. Took ole barn paint an' paint some mo shoes yaller to match my yaller dress.[86]

Courtship not only meant singing and dancing on Saturday nights, during the holidays, and at corn shucking time or church dinners. It often also included physical and sexual intimacy. Some families and/or communities pressured females (not males) to remain virginal until marriage. "Iffen a gal went wrong," Frank Menefee of Alabama noted of the extremes taken in his enslaved community, "dey beat her nearly to death."[87] Minnie Folkes's mother in Virginia warned her not to let anyone "bother yo principle" and she was determined, at fourteen, to abide by her female parent's instructions, even after she married. The exasperated groom appealed to his mother-in-law to give Minnie permission to have sexual relations with him. Her instruction to Minnie, as a married woman, spoke to her sexual duties as a wife: "tellin' me to please my husband, an' 'twas my duty as a wife, dat he had married a pu'fect lady."[88] Minnie still lived with her mother (three of her siblings had been sold south) during her adolescence, and her mother's presence, no doubt, held Minnie's sociosexual experiences and vulnerabilities in check. Her early marriage also might have secured some additional protection. Others, who abided by less strict guidelines, were left to their own sexual designs once removed from their families and communities if they were not forced into premarital sexual relations.

Despite the testimonies of Frank and Minnie, the absence of a "virgin" status for whatever reason, however, did not seem to deter most antebellum enslaved men or women when they choose their spouses. What little evidence does exist regarding biological anomalies, however, indicates that women who did not have distinctly "female" sexual organs, but who identified as female, faced the rejection of male suitors. Josie Martin of Arkansas, for one, explained that "she wasn't popular with men" because she was intersex.[89] Little information also has been found regarding genital surgeries that might have inhibited sexual contact or pleasure. Female genital surgeries and clitorectomies certainly were a part of a female's ritual initiation into womanhood in several of the cultural groups from which enslaved captives were taken.[90]

At fourteen, Minnie Folkes readily deferred to familial authority (specifically her mother), but others were not shy about making their feelings known to potential suitors or husbands. When one rice worker along the coast of South Carolina came to Elizabeth Botume to have her write letters to her boyfriend who was away in the army during the Civil War, she directed Botume to describe her feelings for him coyly—"You mus' talk stiff, but kinda' a easy too." He was not yet her husband, and she did not want him to think he had the upper hand in their relationship before they had wed. He should just know that she only "'members him sometimes."[91] Another woman was more forthcoming. She wanted Botume to assure her love interest that he was still the center of her attention. "Tell him 'I can't forgit him, an' I 'specs him ain't forgit me. I stan' jes' where he lef' me, an' I shall stan' there 'till he gits back; an' ef he never comes back, I shall stan' there still as long as I live.'"[92] One woman wanted her lover to know that she "would give" her eyes to see him again.[93] Someone else requested the teacher write of her passion for her love interest: "I eat you and I drink you."[94] Asking that another woman in their presence leave before she made her request to the letter writer, Susannah asked Botume to set one of her suitors straight—she did not want him. The letter, she instructed, should begin with the greeting "Sir," because Susannah wanted him to understand that she did not even consider him a friend. She also needed him to know that he had erred when he had not appropriately acknowledged her self-worth and that she had no intention of lowering herself to his estimation. She was, Susannah assured him, an apple "high up on de top branch ob de tree," out of his reach. He could not reach her, she reiterated, even if he "jump an' jump till he jump his head off."[95]

Indeed, not every man was able to secure the woman he wanted to marry, not only because of enslaver interference, but also because of the woman's refusal. Lunsford Lane of North Carolina was so disappointed when his first great love was not available that it was another two to three years before he changed his resolve that he "never would marry."[96] Porter Scales, also of North Carolina, had been trying to court "Betsy Ann, house girl slave of Mrs. Nancy Watkins Webster but was 'cut out' by another man."[97] And before Henry Bibb met his future wife Malinda, he tried to gain the romantic attention of two other females by seeking the advice of conjurers who guaranteed their methods would be successful. One instructed Henry to touch his intended lover with the dried bone of a bullfrog. Another conjurer insisted that he had to wear the lock of a girl's hair in his shoe for a certain amount of time. Neither ploy worked. Instead, both young women responded with anger, not surprising responses given that Henry carried out both escapades without their permission. The second young woman was especially angry after he forcefully pulled a lock of hair from her head![98]

Courtship signified the exchange of affection and getting to know one another as well as coming to terms with each other's families, communities, social worlds, and perceived obligations. Culturally prescribed gender roles largely determined expectations of sexual and emotional loyalties, prospects of dedicated time and attention, and anticipation of good behavior after nuptials. Isaac Lane of Tennessee boasted that his chosen bride was "a young woman of eighteen years, who had attracted considerable attention because of her industry, modesty, neatness in dress, and ladylike bearing."[99] Gifts as indicators of a growing affection also were welcomed. Females hoped their male companions would donate material and monetary support when they could do so. One frustrated male suitor responded to his lover's demand for money that he already had sent her two dollars even though he "has no money for myself. . . . I has [however,] money for you when ebber you axes." She, in turn, reminded him that her expectation of financial support was not all she required. Respect was requisite. He was quick to respond: "You treat me as a gentleman, I will treat you as a lady."[100]

Molly Dawson recalled some of the questions that were asked by one slaveholder to couples who required his permission to wed. His queries indicated he expected, within the boundaries of slave system etiquette, "traditional" gendered behavior of married couples—the male as patriarch/provider and the female as obedient, loving wife and mother. After finding out the man's preference for the woman by asking, "You laks Nancy and wants ter marry her?" he then inquired of Mose, "Will you work fer her and bring food ter her?" If the man answered affirmatively, he would then ask the woman "if she will obey Mose and love him and raise his chiluns."[101]

Many enslavers may not have been interested in spouses behaving as "lady" and "gentleman" toward each other, but they strongly opposed marriage between couples whose behavior might prove disruptive in the quarters or to their work routines. Lunsford Lane, who initially had an abroad wife, explained that when he asked her captor's approval of their marriage, he had only two conditions: that Lunsford "behave" himself and "make her behave herself." Lunsford "assented" to both, knowing full well that this delegated power over his wife did not breach the control that their enslavers had over their "married property."[102] One formerly enslaved man from Kentucky bitterly recalled a driver who had been compelled by his captor to "severely" whip his wife for stealing food. Her wounds from his beating contributed to her death.[103]

MARRIAGE RITUALS

"[L]ive right and be honest and kind to each other."—Harriet McFarland's Recollection of Enslaver's Instruction to Arkansas Bondspeople He Married[104]

Antebellum bondspeople's marital rituals—some simple, some elaborate, some seemingly ridiculous to outsiders—reiterated the control that captors were determined to maintain, even in the face of steadfast resistance. Charles Grandy's memories are instructive: His enslaver's creation of a wedding vow for him and his "bride" was just as insulting to Grandy's sense of what a marriage ritual should be as his captor's casual choice of a wife for him. According to Grandy, the woman purchased from the trader "would git off de wagon an' he would lead you bof to yo' cab'n an' stan you on de po'ch. He wouldn't go in. . . . He say somepin f'om de Bible an' finish up wid dis: Dat you wife/Dat yo' huban'/Ise yo' Marser/She yo Missus/You're married."[105] Lizzie Jones of Texas recalled that the slaveholder allowed enslaved men and women to romance one another, but they could not marry until they were twenty years old. He would then give his permission, but there was no ceremony. "Slaves warn't married by no Good Book or the law, neither," Lizzie explained. "They'd jes' take up with each other and go up to the Big House and ask massa to let them marry. If they was ole enough, he'd say to the boy, 'Take her and go on home.'"[106] Alabama domestic Matilda Pugh Daniel, however, was clearly proud of the wedding she and her betrothed, Joe, had in the parlor, officiated by General Hunter, an elder in her captor's family. Elizabeth Keckley's Missouri wedding "was a great event in the family. . . . The ceremony took place in the parlor, in the presence of the family and a number of guests. . . . The day was a happy one."[107]

While Elizabeth's nuptials were officiated by "Bishop Hawks," who had married her captor's children, the use of the broom as a ritual object that signified marriage between enslaved women and men was perhaps the most prevalent form of antebellum marriage ceremony—or, at least, the most remembered.[108] "Me and Julie jus' jumped over de broom in front of Marster and us was married. Dat was all dere was to it," Robert Shepherd from Georgia noted. "Dat was de way most of de slave folks got married dem days."[109] "De marriage ceremony was simple," Elmo Steele added. "Dey used branches from bushes for brooms, an' one ob dese brooms wuz laid across de floor, an' de boy an' gal run an' jumped over it an' dey wuz married."[110] "My aunt married up at de big house an' dey give her a big dance. Dey had de fiddle and had a great big time. Dey jes' jumped over de broom to marry," Jim Gilliard of Alabama confirmed.[111] Not everyone jumped the broom in the same manner, and even those who did ritualize this common household object ascribed different meanings to it.

James Bolton remembered that when bondspeople married "the couple jined hands and jumped back-uds over the broomstick."[112] Paul Smith, who came from the same county in Georgia as Bolton, noted that "him and de gal come up to de big house to jump de broomstick 'fore deir white folkses. De gal jumped one way and de man de other."[113] Georgianna Gibbs of Virginia recalled that the people in her quarters had to jump three times over the broom before they were considered married.[114] Mary Reynolds from Louisiana explained that on her plantation in Concordia Parish, her captors stood inside the door of the cabin holding a broom crosswise. As she and her groom stepped from the outside into the interior of the cabin, her female enslaver placed a flower wreath on Mary's head and her male captor pronounced the couple married.[115] Likewise, Julia White, from Little Rock, Arkansas, stated that at their "broomstick weddings," their "mistress and master" each held one end of the broom while the couple jumped over it.[116] At other places, enslavers mostly were witnesses, not active participants. "When us . . . ma'ied, dey didn't have no preacher. We jes' jumped over de broom, an' went on an' lived together," a former enslaved man from Alabama explained.[117] Betty Foreman Chessier of North Carolina also explained that she married by jumping the broom: "To git unmarried, all you had to do was to jump backwards over the same broomstick."[118] Josephine Anderson of Florida noted that no one held the broom at their weddings. She then went on to describe why the broom was so ritually important to those in her community: "Mos folks dem days got married by layin' a broom on de floor an jumpin' over it. Dat seals de marriage, an at de same time brings em good luck. Ya see brooms keeps hants away."[119] On Caroline Harris's farm in Virginia, the broom could bring bad luck if, while stepping over it, you touched it. "Ant Sue," she added, "used to say which every one teched de stick was gonna die fust."[120]

The ritual of jumping the broom has not been found in African traditions, but rather among Anglo-Saxon and western European pre-Christian marriage and divorce rituals; later in the nineteenth century it was used to indicate a sexual union not recognized as marriage, such as the caricature of the "broomstick" wedding from 1822 England.[121]

Interpretations of the ritualistic meaning of the "broom" have been multiple, even lending itself to sexual analysis—the broomstick as a phallic symbol and "jumping over" by a female, code for sexual intercourse.[122] Tempie Herndon was born and raised in Chatham County, North Carolina, enslaved by George and Elizabeth Herndon, who owned a moderate sized plantation of tobacco, wheat, cotton and corn production and, in 1860, twenty-seven captives.[123] Tempie's description of her wedding suggests that the broom was used in her marriage ceremony to Exeter to create a site of public, gendered competition, ridicule, and even minstrelsy, where the ruler of the newly established marital household supposedly was determined. The act was imposed by George Herndon. Tempie recalled that her captor insisted: "Come on, Exeter, you and Tempie got to jump over de broomstick backwards. You got to do dat to see which one gwine be boss of your household." Exeter, who was by then intoxicated, fell when trying to jump. Tempie "sailed right over dat broomstick same as a cricket." To Herndon's great amusement, he pronounced that Exeter "gwine be bossed 'twell he scared to speak lessen [Tempie] told him to speak."[124] The bitter ruse, of course, was that Tempie and Exeter's enslavers would be the true "bosses" of their marital home.[125]

Not only did Exeter and Tempie jump the broom, they also were the recipients of an exceptional wedding and reception—a clear indication of Tempie's favored status in her captors' home. As the bride described it, she was dressed all in white—dress, shoes, long gloves, and a veil Mrs. Herndon made out of a window curtain. Someone even played the wedding march on the Herndon's family piano to accompany the couple as they walked down the aisle. Tempie and Exeter then kneeled before an altar that Mrs. Herndon had decorated herself with candles and roses, while Uncle Edmond Kirby, the plantation's Black preacher, performed the ceremony. Afterward, there was a reception of barbequed shoat, iced white wedding cake, liquor, and dancing.[126]

"Marrying over the Broomstick," c. 1822. James Catnach, Public domain, via Wikimedia Commons.

While this kind of elaborate wedding celebration was rare, some of the more privileged female domestics did experience similar festivities. Eliza Evans's grandmother, who had arrived in Alabama from a slave ship as a child, passed down her recollection of her extravagant wedding. Not only did John Mixon support Gigi's nuptials because "they thought so much of her"; more importantly, Mixon promised that "he'd never sell none of her chillum." To her delight, it was a promise that he kept: "He never did sell any of her grandchildren either. He thought it was wrong to separate famblys."[127]

One Edgefield, South Carolina, resident even commemorated the ritual of bondspeople's marriages in artistic form as a scene on a stoneware water jug, capturing the ornate marriage event and costumes. The bride's clothing is distinguished by a necklace, while the groom is wearing a suit and has a top hat. The artist captures a couple toasting one another. The jug also has symbols of the couple's future domestic life in the form of an image of a pig and the jug itself. The back of the stoneware piece includes a large-leafed wreath image, another symbol of blissful homelife.[128]

Former bondsman James Bolton of Georgia spoke openly of different kinds of wedding ceremonies, documenting further an imposed class system on large plantations comprised of Black field laborers, domestics/artisans, and slaveholding Whites as well as the marital rituals that marked this hierarchy. Location, dress, audience, the time spent on and at the event, and the ceremonial elements at play were essential variables. He explained that field workers jumped the broom in the quarters with other bondspersons acting as principal witnesses. Domestics and artisans, he added, jumped the broom, too, but sometimes also had some religious reading from the Bible, typically were married on their captor's back porch or in the yard, and had family and friends as well as their enslavers in attendance.[129]

A few, usually domestics, sometimes received secondhand dresses or other accessories for the event. Matilda Pugh Daniel wore one of her mistress' "party" dresses. According to her, "It sho' was purty; made outen white tarleton wid a pink bow in de front." She adorned her hair with pink ribbon, and Joe, she emphasized, "look proud of me."[130] Ellen Betts of Louisiana remembered that her new female captor, Cornelia, handed down her wedding dress to her mother. Many in the enslaved community wore that purple and green silk dress when they married, including fellow workers Sarah and Hannah as well as Ellen's sister Sidney.[131] Ida Henry of Texas likewise recalled that she wore a "blue serge" dress, one that two others had worn previously as their wedding costumes. She added that wedding dresses were not worn by the same person after she married because their "mistress" had told them that it would bring bad luck to do so. "Therefore, 'twas handed down from one generation to the other one."[132] The famed designer and seamstress Elizabeth Keckley no doubt wore a beautiful gown of her own making when

Figure 4.8 Water Cooler, c. 1840. Thomas Chandler, Water Cooler, c. 1840, alkaline-glazed, slip-decorated stoneware, acc.1996.132. Photo by Michael McKelvey / courtesy of High Museum of Art, Atlanta.

she married.[133] Hannah Jones of Alabama explained of her nuptials: "When I was ma'ied, de ceremony tuk place at my Mammy's house an' I wo' a pretty white dress."[134]

As part of the distinction they created between themselves and the people they claimed as their property, wealthy enslavers typically exchanged elaborate religious marital vows in their parlor with the White community and family serving as witnesses inside, while bondspersons stood outside and looked through the window or doorways. While they compelled bondspersons' nuptials to take place on their days off, slaveholders' wedding rituals could last several days, filled with elaborate dinners and gifts. As Ida Rigeley of Arkansas explained, the wedding rituals and customs of elite White persons could persist across an entire week. The brides, she noted, "had a second day dress and a third day dress and had suppers and dinner receptions about among the kinfolks." Their trousseaus consisted of "big chests full of quilts and coverlets and counterpanes they been packing back." The pleasantries also included "big dances." Such a wedding, Ida concluded, "would last a week, night and day."[135]

Still, weddings of the enslaved mattered very much to them, and many tried to make theirs special. Females strove to be beautiful and wear lovely clothing when they married not just to impress their spouses-to-be, but also to set aside their enslavers' imposed masculine image of them and to place their femininity on display. At the same time, newlywed or prospective husbands took on the gendered ideal of the male provider and protector, often building cabins and making furniture for the new families they hoped they were creating. Matilda Poe, who had been enslaved in Indian Territory, remembered that all her family's furniture was homemade from local trees such as oak and hackberry. She was proud to tell her interviewer in the 1930s that she still had a chair that had belonged to her mother.[136] Amanda Ross of Alabama documented that her father made their family's beds and table.[137] Some grooms also wanted to doff their plain, sparse work wardrobe for their weddings, scraping up bits of money to buy special clothing for themselves or their brides.

Nevertheless, the racial hierarchy that these comparative locations, vows, timing, clothing, preparations, food, and audience indicate was, and remained, real for enslaved people throughout most of North America. Even the marriages of domestics were considered outside the bounds of legitimacy and importance that the "master's parlor" and days away from work represented. As Ida Rigeley's description demonstrates, the differences between enslaved and enslaver familial status also were sealed by the exchange of property as wedding "gifts." Some newly married bondspeople, like Tempie and Exeter, for example, received a cabin to live in and the broom they jumped as presents. Others were given space in the provision grounds and seed. These were the kinds of "gifts," however, that benefited slaveholders as much as their Black captives, and that captors could reclaim whenever they pleased.

Conversely, slaveholders made certain that their family members not only had land and appropriate household goods to begin their married lives, but also Black labor to provide comfort, status, and income. Planter weddings wreaked havoc on slave marriages and families because many enslavers did not hesitate to divide their Black "property," married or not, and distribute them as wedding gifts to their own offspring. Bill Homer of Louisiana and Texas explained what happened when his enslaver's daughter married—both the father of the bride and the groom's father gave the couple fifty enslaved people each, with no concern to these captives' marital status or familial loss.[138] As an elderly man, Ben Johnson of North Carolina could recall only one of his family members, a brother named Jim, whom he lost when their slaveholder decided to sell Jim "ter dress young missus fer her weddin'." The tree under which he sat watching the only blood relation he could claim being sold was still standing decades later. "I set dar an' I cry an' cry, 'specially when dey puts de chains on him an' carries him off, an' I ain't neber felt so lonesome in my whole life. I ain't neber hyar from Jim since," Ben confessed.[139]

No matter how determined enslavers were to control the work and private lives of their enslaved men and women, antebellum married couples within the intimacies of their relationships with each other had their own ideas and ideals that they pursued. Enslaved men, for example, like those who were free people of color and White, often acted out of a sense of patriarchal responsibility, authority, and "ownership." Elizabeth Botume clearly was taken aback by what she witnessed in the lowcountry. Speaking of one woman's husband, she noted, "He spoke of her as if she were his slave. A manner most of the colored men had."[140] There is evidence that some husbands expressed their masculine "power" in verbal and physical ill treatment of their spouses. George Taylor of Alabama noted that there was absolutely one thing that "us warn't lowed to do, an' dat was to abuse or cuss our wives, an' you betta not strike 'em, ca'se hit would be jes too bad."[141] Why? Slaveholders feared disruption of workers' routines if domestic disputes became serious and wanted to make certain that harm did not come to potential "breeders." Aunt Rachel was a favorite of her captor because she had proven to be fertile and to have healthy children. No bondsperson in her community dare to harm her, not even her husband, Jim, without facing the ire of their enslaver. When Rachel's husband hit her with a poker, causing a noticeable bump on her forehead, she protected Jim by telling their inquiring slaveholder "that she done bump de head" or "Marse sho' beat him."[142]

Many marriages among the enslaved were not happy ones for long periods of time. The pressures and brutalities of their lives, even when spouses "chose" each other and lived together, were immense and took a debilitating toll. Incompatibility also led to deep divisions. Elizabeth Keckley's husband lied before they were married, telling her that he was a free man. She had arranged to purchase herself and her son from their captor and thought that once she had done so, their family would all be free. His deceit and alcoholism led to her profound unhappiness.[143] Often, some of those forced to be together were just miserable, indeed, as unhappy as those who loved one another, but were forced to live apart.

Infamous among historians of enslaved women is the story of Rose Williams, forced by her enslaver, Mr. Hawkins, to marry and breed with Rufus, a man she despised outright. Hawkins had bought Rose's family, an act for which she was extremely grateful, and for which he expected her full cooperation. At first, he threatened to beat her if she did not bed down with Rufus. "Dere am one thing Massa Hawkins does to me what I can't shunt from my mind," she explained decades later. "I knows he don't do it for meanness, but I allus holds it 'gainst him... he force me to live with... Rufus, 'gainst my wants." Rufus, according to Rose, was a big bully who expected everyone in the enslaved community to do "what him say" because of his commanding size. Rose did not realize that when she was ordered to fix a cabin and supper for Rufus, it meant her captor had made her Rufus's wife. Rose refused to sleep with Rufus twice, fighting him off with a poker. After Hawkins threatened her with a whipping at the stake, Rose "yield[ed]." She gave no indication that Rufus ever amended his boorish ways. When the Civil War ended, the marriage was over. Rose was determined to have "no truck with any man" again.[144] Rose and Rufus were hardly the only couple who separated when they could. Molly Dawson remembered how quickly her parents left one another after emancipation. "Mah mother and father never did love each other lak dey ought to," she explained.[145]

Some voluntarily split up and sought out new partners even before general emancipation. Others stayed together, but unhappily. One former bondswoman recalled that her mother found relief from her captor and her husband, both of whom she described as typically "cross," when she was rented to others. "She had pleasure hired out," the daughter emphasized.[146] Charles Ball remembered in some detail the married life of Lydia, whose husband did little to assuage Lydia's physical or psychological miseries. He refused to trap and hunt animals or work in their assigned garden patch to provide additional food. Lydia's spouse was African who, in his homeland, had been a privileged priest with several wives. "The husband," Ball noted, with no little cultural affront, "maintained the same kind of lazy dignity, that he had enjoyed at home." Ball could not appreciate the status and polygamous privilege of the man's not-too-distant past. As far as Ball understood, Lydia's husband was a "morose, sullen man" who "thought himself badly off here, in having but one woman to do any thing for him."[147] He often "beat and maltreated his wife, on the slightest provocation."[148]

As in all communities, past and present, domestic abuse was a reality of enslaved couples and other romantic or sexual relationships. Green Cumby of Texas described the hunt for an enslaved man who killed his wife by stabbing her in the heart.[149] Court records from across the centuries and North America included not a few records of spousal discord and even murder. A small selection of cases from Louisiana, for example, included that of the death penalty sentence for a bondsman who had killed his wife, the escape of another man whose spouse had been found dying from his "blow of an axe on her head," and the escape of one Pierrot of the "Biefada" nation who had absconded purportedly because he was "discontented with his wife."[150] An overseer explained to the traveling observer Frederick Law Olmsted that he believed that the context of most of enslaved couples' domestic upset derived from suspected adultery. "They get jealous and quarrel among themselves sometimes about it," the manager explained, "or come to the overseer and complain, and he has them punished."[151]

The suspicions that spouses had of one another were not only related to adultery. Sometimes they feared that their husband (or wife) was "two-headed"—that is, had unnatural and exaggerated abilities to control them. It was this suspicion, derived from traditional African belief systems, about which distraught spouses sought to uncover the truth and to destroy if found legitimate. George Conrad of Kentucky believed that a neighboring husband was "two-headed.[152] Amanda Sykes of Georgia knew of two women whose husbands believed that they were witches. Both men purportedly cut off an appendage of their spouses while they were in the form of cats to prove, one way or the other, that they were married to witches who could shape shift and take on the appearance of felines. According to Sykes, both wives were proven to be "two-headed" when one was found the next day missing a finger, and the other, a leg.[153]

Others believed that the problems they had within their families, including husband/wife disagreements, were the result of supernatural harm from Black community members external to their households. Potential victims sought the aid of local conjurers to protect them. Moslie Thompson explained that in her house "thar am always de p'otection mixture" made from equal measures of salt and black and red pepper. She advised using it if someone came to your house determined to cause problems by "flirt wid de wife or de husband, or tries to do somethin' dat will cause separation." To provide protection from "flirty women," she explained, "when de husband begins to care fo' a tudder woman, if de wife puts a pinch of de p'otection mixture under de bed befoah gwine to bed, dat will cause de man to fo'get de tudder woman."[154] Some turned to these measures to win the affections of a woman or man already betrothed to another. "When my paw, 'Obie' wuz a courtin,'" one former bondsman recalled, someone "put a spell on him kaise he was a wantin' my maw too." The assailant "got a conjure bag and drapped it in de spring what my paw drunk water from. He wuz laid up on a bed o' rheumatiz fer six weeks."[155]

Nevertheless, countless enslaved couples loved each other dearly. A fugitive who had managed to escape, then helped his wife and children escape to a forested Louisiana maroon they created, was not shy about his feelings for his spouse and their offspring when he unexpectedly met and befriended the naturalist and artist John James Audubon in the swampy woods: "My wife, though black, is as beautiful to me as the President's wife to him; she is my queen, and I look on our young ones as so many princes."[156] According to Freedmen's Bureau records, many managed to stay married past the slavery era despite episodes of internal and external turmoil. When Daniel and Mary "legally" married in 1865, they had been husband and wife for thirty years and had thirteen children.[157] Lucy and Green Coleman had been married for several years and had five children at the end of the Civil War.[158] Thomas and Jane Harris had lived as man and wife for fifteen years and shared nine offspring by 1865.[159] At ages sixty-four and fifty-four, respectively, in 1866, Thomas and Julia Henderson married at their district Freedmen's Bureau. The longtime couple had eleven children.[160] Former Georgia captive Charlie King noted that his parents had been married by the "broom stick wedding." They remained united for more than fifty years and, according to their son, "allus treated each other right."[161]

Chapter 5

Antebellum Family Life

By the time that Edward Williams Clay finished his romanticized image of bondspeople's lives, the institution of slavery, and enslaved Black families, had existed in the Americas for more than three hundred years. Unable or unwilling to depict the critical perspective of African-descended subjects, Clay dedicated much of his body of drawings and cartoons to opposing abolition. He did so by denigrating the attempts of freed urban Blacks to live as equals even as they faced the toxic threat of racist White America *and* by popularizing images of the "good" of enslaved life. For example, the illustration on page 220 creates a scene of happy Black social relations, with multigenerational families, dancing and courting couples, well-fed and well-dressed children, and the paternalistic presence of an attentive slaveholder carefully surveying his "family, Black and White." Clay's proslavery fantasy of the utopian slave society hardly was the reality enslaved people experienced, especially with regard to family concerns and connections. During the 1840s, when Clay displayed "America," literally tens of thousands of enslaved spouses, parents, children, siblings, and other cherished kin were ripped away from family members as part of the lucrative domestic slave trade. Clay's pictorial fantasy of enslaved family bliss, unity, and leisure was, in reality, the antebellum Black captive's all too real nightmare.

Juxtapose, if you will, the sheer acts of desperation of some who hoped to save their families from slavery's horrors. None is more striking than that of Margaret Garner, enslaved on Maplewood Farm in Kentucky. She and her husband, Robert, managed to escape in 1856 with their four children—Tom, Sam, Mary, and Priscilla—along with Robert's parents and nine others. The group was headed for Canada but separated once they reached Ohio. There, Margaret and her family sought the aid of her free kinsman—her Uncle Joe Kite. He went out to get them help, and while he was away, the refugees were

Edward Clay, America (c.1841). Edward Williams Clay, *America*, c. 1841, lithograph, Courtesy of Library of Congress, LC-DIG-pga-05677.

caught. Determined not to return to slavery with her family, Margaret killed her daughter Mary and attempted to end her own life and that of her other children. Robert, Margaret, and their three remaining children were captured. Priscilla later drowned, and Margaret died of typhoid fever two years later. Robert was sold to Mississippi and fought in the Civil War until he had the opportunity to escape. He later located his sons, Tom and Sam, and took them back to Ohio, finally as free people.[1]

Antebellum African American families, communities, and cultures in bondage existed and persisted under the most arduous of material, psychological, legal, and physical circumstances. Despite the persistence of familial ideals and kinship of varying patterns, the dramatic shift in slave concentrations from the Upper South to the Lower South and southwest during these decades before the Civil War did mean devastating consequences in the enslaved's domestic life, as hundreds of thousands lost husbands, wives, sons, and daughters, other kin, and friends to the inter- and intrastate trades. "If'n you wants to know what unhappiness means," said Uncle John Rudd, "jess'n you stand on the Slave Block and hear the Auctioneer's voice selling you away from the folks you love."[2] "The plantation owners just sold and traded Negroes in dem days, like de horse and cattle traders do now," lamented Calvin Moye, who had been enslaved in Georgia and Texas. "A Negro did not know any more about where his mama was den a calf does, now."[3]

As more blood, marital, and fictive relatives were disappeared, childcare, spousal relations, youth socialization, and family life in general were disrupted, destroyed, and begun again in unprecedented ways. John and Elizabeth of southern Delaware escaped when John found out that Elizabeth would be sold.[4] Elizabeth Keckley remembered the soul shattering she and her mother experienced when her father was forced to leave them in Virginia when he was moved to Tennessee with his captor. The scene played out vividly in her memory—"how my father cried out against the cruel separation; his last kiss; his wild straining of my mother to his bosom; the solemn prayer to Heaven; the tears and sobs." Elizabeth also readily recalled the callous, even cruel, disregard of her "mistress" in scolding her heartbroken mother: "Stop your nonsense; there is no necessity for you putting on airs. Your husband is not the only slave that has been sold from his family.... [I]f you want a husband so badly, stop your crying and go and find another."[5] Sarah, an enslaved woman in South Carolina's low country, complained that "no slave mother could have her children after they were old enough to be of use; they were sold or hired out."[6] Ann Maria of Maryland convinced her husband to run away when their son Nathan was about to be sold.[7]

As the trade grew in size and profitability, more and more women were forced into it and made to leave their families. Like the enslaved Africans during the Middle Passage across the Atlantic, those sold domestically carried their broken dreams of family and fate along with whatever few material items they could that reminded them of a stolen past. Tillie Watts had a pair of white gloves that her grandmother knitted for her, the only family heirloom she was able to take with her when sold away from her Virginia family of birth. Decades later in Tennessee, Tillie's daughter buried her with these precious gloves that she miraculously had managed to keep.[8]

"I seen chillun sold off and de mammy not sold, and, sometimes de mammy sold and a little baby kept on de place and give to another woman to raise. Dem white folks didn't care nothing 'bout how de slaves grieved when dey tore up a family," recalled Katie Rowe of Oklahoma, whose own mother was saved from the trade only because she belonged to the "mistress" rather than the "master" who tried to sell her to cover his debt.[9] Sojourner Truth begged her father to find a new slaveholder for her after she was purchased by an extremely abusive couple. He worked tirelessly to do so and eventually prevailed.[10] The elderly, many of whom were leaders in their families and communities, were deeply missed when captors sold or removed them. Jane Lee was the subject of much grief when her enslaver moved to Texas, taking her along. "We all cried when she left us," one of her friends recalled. "We felt lost, because we had nobody to lead us in our little [religious] meetings. They all promised to meet her again in heaven. Aunt Jane cried and we cried too."[11]

Many slaveholding migrants to the cotton empire of the Lower South and southwest carried their able-bodied workers with them, including large sections of families. Those moving further west did, too. This was the case when Mormon convert Robert Marion Smith made enslaved midwife Biddy Mason and Hannah Embers walk 1,700 miles overland, first to Utah and then on to San Bernardino, California. The children of both accompanied them. The Smiths had purchased Hannah and her offspring but had refused to buy Hannah's husband, Frank, who remained in South Carolina.[12]

Some slave traders even forced mothers from their infants if they believed the child might impede their sale or migration to far-off locations. A woman named Nellie, who was being walked from the Upper to the Lower South, had a baby while in transit. "The speculator gave the child to a white woman nearby where they camped that night. The speculator said they could not take care of the child on the road."[13] The bottom line was the bottom line—enslavers and traders' priorities were strictly to satisfy their labor, financial, and security needs.

The records of Charles Ayer, a physician who owned more than 4,000 acres and in excess of seventy Black captives in the Barnwell District of South Carolina, for example, indicated that he purchased a woman Rachel; her husband, Tony; and their three children, Phillis, Nan, and James, for $1,252 in the mid-1820s. During that same decade he also sold independently and bought at various sheriff's sales individual captives and parts of families rather than entire units.[14] So, too, did William Garrett of Texas. Receipts from his estate indicate that in 1851, he purchased two fragments of families—forty-year-old Fanny and her infant son, as well as an eighteen-year-old mother and her baby. He bought other captives that year as individuals with no apparent family members accompanying them—twenty-two-year-old Sally, sixteen-year-old Harriet, twelve-year-old Hagar, and ten-year-old Massey—and even younger children—Daniel, Queen, and Marinda. A decade earlier, he had procured Polly and her young twins along with a single child, eight-year-old Madison.[15]

Mandatory migration affected most enslaved people, regardless of gender, age, or work history. You either had to go or you lost others who were forced to do so. It was not unusual for entire families to be dispersed to separate locations. Adolescence, typically when one became responsible for a full day's work, was, not surprisingly, usually the age at which individuals were first separated or removed from their family of birth. Modern psychological studies of youth traumatically separated from family offer clues to some of the physical and emotional consequences enslaved teens and children undoubtedly suffered from such losses: post-traumatic stress disorder, panic attacks, social and separation anxiety, depression, bipolar disorder, a propensity for alcoholism, and obsessive-compulsive disorder.[16]

The last generations of those born in bondage spent the remainder of their lives wondering and worrying about what happened to their kin. Who survived? Where, and how? Did they have new family members they would never meet? Could they have come across them in their later lives and not known? Who might be able to answer any of these questions? The search for these tens of thousands of families, ripped apart at the seams and blown to the far corners of slave territory, still persists today, reignited in the last few decades by the fruition of generations of careful genealogical work, passed-along oral histories, new technologies such as DNA, and promising computer search engines. Answers and stubborn silences play both joyfully and painfully in the imaginations of those who need to know their family.

Men and women who were permanently separated and lived away from other kin sometimes started families again—and some were forced to do so. One can imagine that at other times, they wanted to do so, even if they did not (and could not) forget those no longer with them. Freedmen's Bureau records from the 1860s record the marriages of persons just gaining their freedom. Bureau records from Tennessee, for example, document that a significant number of those seeking marriage licenses had previous spouses with whom they had had children but from whom they had been separated. When thirty-seven-year-old Eliza married Simon Adams in Memphis in 1865, the officiant recorded that Eliza, from Mississippi, had lost her first husband, with whom she had two children, as a result of his sale.[17] Likewise, Elizabeth, who married Caleb, had been married for twelve years to a previous husband before they were separated by "the owner."[18] Christina had two children with her first spouse before their enslaver separated them and she came to marry James Anderson.[19] These records repeat the same tragic divisions over and over again.

Family reconstitution, if even possible after the withering trauma of such losses, was not easy for anyone. Andrew Moss of Georgia knew that his father had been sold three times and had two wives and several children by those women.[20] Jacob Thomas recounted the story of how his mother, Isobel, had been sold away from his father in North Carolina and taken to Georgia. His mother had told him that she was put on the block, sold, and "carried off, chained 'hind a wagin." Her husband had been inconsolable. "She turn' roun' an' looks back at her husban' who cries an' de oberseer's lash cuts his back, 'case dey ain't 'lowed ter cry at a sale." Jacob was born in Georgia. He never knew his father.[21] Elizabeth Botume met an elderly enslaved woman in Georgia who had been sold decades earlier from Virginia. When she found out that Botume had been in Virginia, "she came to me to know if I had ever seen her 'little gal.' With tears streaming down her face, she told me what a 'store she set by that little child . . . such a pretty little gal.'"[22] Another enslaved mother Botume knew was, as she described, "the saddest person." She always kept to herself after being sold to pay for her captor's gambling debt and forced to leave her small child behind. "I cannot sleep nights," she told Botume. "Every time I shut my eyes I hear my baby cry, 'Take me wid you, mammy; take me wid you!'" The distressed woman explained that she just could not stop hearing her child begging. "I put my fingers in my ears," she added, "but all the time I hear him just the same, crying, 'Take me wid you, mammy; take me wid you!'"[23] Susan Boggs remembered an enslaved mother who used to cook and sell food on the wharves of Norfolk. She "went crazy because her two sons were sold and sent to the trader's jail. She went up and down the streets, crying like an animal."[24] Benjamin and Harriet Ross of Maryland decided to escape their capture after many years of abuse and the sale of some of their children to the Deep South.[25] Caleb Craig and his siblings lost their mother when they were gifted to their enslaver's daughter. Caleb longed for his mother during the remainder of his long life. Interviewed during the 1930s, he explained that she "was a mighty pretty colored woman and I has visions and dreams of her, in my sleep, sometime yet."[26] Charlie Arons noted that when he was about ten years old, he was sold from Petersburg, Virginia. Charlie left with a speculator on his way to Mobile, Alabama, without his parents and siblings, whom he never saw again.[27] John Sella Martin's mother ran away three times (and was whipped harshly as a result each time) trying to locate him after he was sold. When child and parent finally found each other, they spent the first few hours, Martin recalled, in conversation "as sweet as ever mother and child indulged in, as it concerned the blessedness of reunion and the buoyancy of the hope for freedom; and as bitter as was ever realized when it touched on the sufferings of a mother, torn from her children."[28] Bitterness, rage, and shame accompanied the anxiety, sorrow, and loss of both those taken and those left behind.

"I was born in Chester, South Carolina, but I was mos'ly raised in Alabama," Mingo White said. "When I was 'bout fo' or five years old, I was loaded in a wagon wid a lot mo' people in 'hit. Whar I was boun' I don' know. Whatever become of my mammy an' pappy I don' know for a long time." Mingo remembered the instructions that the slaveholder gave to all the bondspeople being sold that day: to tell anyone who asked that they were healthy. "Us had to tell 'em all sorts of lies for our Marsa or else take a beatin'."[29] Mingo lamented that he "was jes' a li'l thang; tooked away from my mammy an' pappy, jes' when I needed 'em mos'." The only person who initially took care of him after he was sold was a fiddler named John White, who had been his father's friend. Mingo's concerned father had asked John to take care of his son. Once they reached their new destination, the boy lived in the rough cabin of his father's friend. Mingo told of how materially poor their domestic space was: no stove, cornhusk mattresses, barely any cover, only a few furnishings. "To live lack us did was 'nouf to make anybody soon as be dead," he added indignantly. "De white folks tol' us dat us born to work for 'em an' dat us was doin' fine at dat."[30]

Mingo tried to take some comfort in the tiniest reminders of what his life had been before the sale away from his family. He had a pet sheepdog named Trailer that successfully followed him on the trek to Alabama. Mingo recalled proudly how Trailer followed them even across a deep stream. "I was watchin' him clost so if he gived out I was goin' to try to git him," the former bondsman recounted. "He didn't giv' out, he didn't even hab to swim. He jes' walked 'long an' lapped de water lack a dog will."[31]

After several years, the boy came to believe that his mother was Selina White, the woman on his new plantation whom everyone referred to as "mammy." Selina undoubtedly offered some of the comforts of a mother to many of the orphaned children, teens, and young adults living there. Against all odds, however, Mingo's mother did manage to find him.[32]

One day, Selina told Mingo that his mother was coming to see him. "I thought dat you was my mammy," Mingo replied. "No," Selina answered. "I ain't your mammy, yer mammy is 'way way from here." Mingo found it very hard to believe that he had "a nudder mammy" and soon dismissed the idea. Several days later, a wagon approached. "When de wagon got to de house," he stated, "my mammy got out an' broke and run to me an' th'owed her arms 'roun' my neck an' hug an' kiss me. I never even put my arms 'roun' her or nothin' of de sort. I jes' stood dar lookin' at her." Disappointed at his response, his mother asked, "Son ain't you glad to see your mammy?" Not knowing what to feel, Mingo walked away. Mammy Selina told him that he had hurt her feelings and that the woman was indeed his mother. Mingo tried to recall a life that seemed so distant in his memory. Finally, he began to remember the painful loss, a loss Selina told him had taken place when he was "jes' a li'l chile." Mingo apologized to his mother for his cold response. "After I had talked wid my real mammy," he explained further, "she told me of how de family had been broke up an' dat she hadn't seed my pappy sence he was sold. My mammy never would of seen me no mo' if de Lawd hadn' a been in de plan."[33] His mother's captor died, and as she was the personal maid to his wife, she returned to that woman's home—close to where her son had been sold. The domestic circumstances of their enslavers' families, once the source of Mingo's orphaning, were now the reason for his mother's opportunity to re-create family ties with him.[34]

It was Moses Roper's mother who did not recognize her quadroon son ten years after he had been sold from her when he was only six. His mother had since had several other children by her enslaved husband, a blacksmith, before Moses (whose father was White) was able to escape and find her. Once she did come to know that he was her stolen son, the two embraced tenderly "amidst the ardent interchange of caresses and tears of joy." Moses and his family's desire to spend some time together before he took off again in his quest for freedom led to his eventual capture. He never saw any of them again.[35]

Some were lucky, but not many. Wade and Hannah were sold together from Virginia to Alabama, where they remained as a married couple, eventually having several children there.[36] Molly Parker also was born in Virginia and was sold to Opelika, Alabama, with her family, including both her parents and three siblings—Edna, Sam, and Albert.[37] As the antebellum decades passed, being disappeared from one's family, or even families, seemed almost inevitable. Still, Black family life continued in myriad forms, with episodic fulfillment, frustrations, and failings.

PARENTHOOD

Bound children depended on their parents to care for them and to act in their best interests despite the interference of male and female captors. Parents, too, were affirmed in their humanity, masculinity, and femininity through their children's presence, the sacrifices they made, and their deep love for them. They hoped, against all odds, that their offspring would be able to care for them as they aged. One "contraband" woman offered her pitiable account for many when she noted that her last child had died—the eight others had been sold away. Of the one who passed she sighed, "She was amazing helpful. She could sew and knit. She could spin and weave, and mind the chickens, and tend the children. Oh, I should go wild, if I had not any children to look upon."[38] To be without children meant to be vulnerable to a miserable old age without love or support. Two other women in Charleston, aged 95 and 103, complained that they had "plenty of children in the World—some whar! If they only knew whar[,] they'd take good care of de mudders."[39]

Motherhood played a precious, even if precarious, role in enslaved women's sense of themselves as women, as people, and as part of a family and a community. The countless efforts they made to help their sons and daughters materially, spiritually, medicinally, emotionally, and with their labor routines

Enslaved Family. Unknown photographer, *Uncle Tom and his family*, nineteenth century, stereograph photo, Graphics Collection, PR 065-760-0013, New-York Historical Society.

document the reverence enslaved women (like their western/western central African female ancestors) placed on having children and raising them. Not surprisingly, many adhered to their own ritualistic and practical knowledge to address the needs of their young. For example, some waited for several weeks before naming their children because they considered it "bad luck" to do so earlier.[40] As one White female visitor to the South noted, "We sometimes hear that the slave mothers lacked natural affection. On the contrary, I have thought the maternal feeling was intensified in them. Children were all they had in the world that they could ever call their own. Whether with them or separated, they could say, 'My child, him is mine.'"[41]

Mothers spent their precious little time when not compelled to work, and even while working, trying to care for their young. Fanny Berry was one of many who recalled her mother's heroic efforts. When she was about eight years old, Fanny's slaveholder sent her to bring him a jug of liquor from his father-in-law's plantation, a relatively long distance for a child on foot—barefoot at that. Although a dramatic, thundering squall had started before she began the journey back, she was forced to return anyway. Fanny's cotton shift became so soaked with rain that she took it off and ran naked most of the way, through a landscape turned terrifying and unfamiliar by swollen creeks, sharp lightning flashes, and booming thunder. Pliny, Fanny's mother, had taught her not to move beneath trees when there was an electric storm. Between trying to avoid the windblown, dripping trees, lightning strikes, and malevolent spirits she believed haunted the woods, little Fanny was at her wit's end. She was certain that a spirit was about to confront her as it moved quickly in her direction. That "spirit" was Pliny, come out in that horrific storm to find Fanny, wrap her child's naked body in a blanket, and lead her home safely. Once there, Fanny's mother dried her, carefully rubbing the child's entire body with heated grease, before putting her to bed.[42] Harrison Beckett of Texas also complimented his mother's commitment. She worked long hours—only coming "in from de field at nine or ten o'clock at night," and often "she be all wore out and too tired to cook lots of times." Still, she prepared dinner for the family and then "she's so tired she go to bed without eatin' nothin' herself."[43]

Still, there were many instances when enslaved mothers could not give their young ones the attention they, or their children, would have liked or needed. Very heavy workloads, physical and mental illness, and temporary and permanent separation all but guaranteed a parent's unintended lapses in care. Charlotte, a former bondswoman in Louisiana, confirmed that all of her children had died while very young. "They died from want of attention," she explained. "I used to leave them alone half of the time." Her captor "sometimes" had someone to look after them until they could walk, but not once they were on their feet. "I was glad the Lord took them," she admitted, "for I knowed they were better off with my blessed Jesus than with me."[44]

Nat Love confided in his autobiography that sometimes neither his mother nor her surrogate—Love's older sister—had the opportunity to care for him, given the work demanded by their enslaver "Mother presided over the kitchen at the big house and my Master's table, and among her other duties were to milk the cows and run the loom, weaving clothing for the other bondspeople. This left her scant time to look after me," he explained. "My sister Sally was supposed to look after me when my mother was otherwise occupied; but between my sister's duties of helping mother and chasing the flies from Master's table, I received very little looking after from any of the family."[45]

James Abbott of Missouri recalled of his parent: "Muthuh, she shore did have a hard time. Dey warn't never nuthin' for her but work hard all de time, she neveh came in fum de fiel' 'til dark, den had to feed wid a lantern."[46]

Mother Ran the Loom

Nat Love's Depiction of His Mother's Consuming Work Nat Love, *The Life and Adventures of Nat Love, Better Known in the Cattle Country as Deadwood Dick, by Himself,* Los Angeles: Nat Love, 1907, as found on Documenting the American South, 7-9. Courtesy of Documenting the American South, Libraries of the University of North Carolina, Chapel Hill.

Frederick Douglass complained bitterly about the absence of his mother during his early life. Their captor hired Harriet Bailey out some twelve miles from Frederick, her other children, and her parents. "My mother and I were separated when I was but an infant—before I knew her as my mother," Douglass recounted. As an adult, he could not remember seeing her but a few times, and "each of these times was very short in duration, and at night." Harriet died when her son was about seven.[47] In her travels in the low country, Mary Ames came across an enslaved woman, Affey, who had taken in a little girl named Pleasant Riddle to care for since the child seemed to be without a mother or father. "I couldn't lef' him [her]," Affey explained, "so, an I take him [her] wid me."[48]

Aged grandmothers, as powerful anchors of extended, multigenerational families, continued to provide material, spiritual, and emotional support to younger members of their families across decades. Harriet Jacobs's grandmother, for one, remained her strength and foundation through years of abuse and fugitivity, hiding Harriet in a small, secret space in her home for years, while also caring for her granddaughter's children.[49] One South Carolina witness noted that when a mother died leaving a young baby behind, "the old grandmother . . . sat all the time, day and night, on a blanket on the floor watching and tending the baby."[50] Nellie Smith of Georgia explained that her mother died when she was a small child and her grandmother raised her afterward.[51] Elias Dawkins explained that his mother died when he was young and he, along with the other small children, was cared for during the day by his grandmother, Kissy, and four other older women, including Aunt Peggy and Aunt Cilla.[52]

Grandmothers, elderly women, aunts, and female fictive kin and sometimes elderly or disabled men stepped in, either out of their own desire or as part of their workload, to take care of the children in their families, and those of others, when mothers were unable to do so. Elderly women in particular, whether related by blood, marriage, or through fictive ties, often had the task of caring for the young children of field, house, and skilled women while they worked during the day. Harriet McFarland of Arkansas remembered Aunt Mandy, "an old mammy" who "nursed and fed" her and the other "little chillun" because she was "too old to go to the field." Typically, Harriet added, "we wouldn't see our mammy and daddy from early in the morning till night when their work was done."[53] John James of Louisiana recalled that his mother "lef' me in de nursery with all de other cullud babies when she go work in de field. De old nurse, Jane, tooks care of us."[54] Most slaveholders did not allow suckling mothers to take their children with them to the fields or even if they worked in captors' homes, forcing mothers typically to return to their infants at least twice a day to suckle them.[55]

Enslaved women on the Abbott farm in Virginia helped Fanny Berry's mother to rear her. Maternal Aunt Ella probably also pitched in, particularly once she was bought from a neighboring plantation. Even Mrs. Abbott occasionally offered attention. Her limited acts of kindness prompted Fanny to conclude of her character—"Miss Sarah Ann was uh fine woman, even ef she was uh slave owner."[56] A Georgia woman also recalled that her female captor took care of the babies and new mothers.[57] Clayton Holbert of Tennessee remembered similarly that when his mother, who was plantation cook, was working, his "mistress" "would nurse both me and her baby, who was four weeks older than me." His mother likewise nursed her mistress' son. Sharing the task of raising other people's children, he added, was common in bondspeople's communities. "When the old people died, and they left small orphan children, the slaves would raise the children," he explained.[58]

Nevertheless, some feared evil intent among fellow bondspeople toward their children, especially if childcare providers were known to be conjurers or something awful and unexpected happened to those in their care. George

Conrad of Kentucky believed that an elderly woman who was the plantation nanny resented their captor's affection for his twin baby brothers. According to George, Aunt Sarah "killed both of the babies" through conjure. "When they cut one of the babies open they took out two frogs." The belief that the child had frogs internally was a common trope of conjure malevolence.[59]

Some female captors who helped to take care of children whose mothers worked away from them also were known to cross the line, taking infants and toddlers from their Black families and claiming them as their own. Charles Lester, born in 1815 in New Jersey, described how his captor excluded his mother, Dinah, from his life when he was an infant. Charles's enslaver had a son at about the same time that he was born, but her child died. She took Charles and nursed him—certainly a painful intrusion and separation for Dinah. She came to take her son back after he was weaned, but their slaveholder refused to relinquish the child. "No Dinah, I mean to bring him up myself," she answered the horrified mother. "And so she kept me, and called me Peter Wheeler, for that was my father's name, and so I lived in master's family almost jist like his own children."[60]

Slaveholders greatly restricted the time that parents, especially fathers, could spend with their children and interfered with *every* aspect of enslaved youngsters' lives, regardless of what their parents desired. Mothers, however, did have much more contact than fathers. Beyond the blistering reality that enslavers were much more likely to sell male captives and that these bondsmen would be sold multiple times, regardless of their marital or parental status, captors believed that mothers, not fathers, should be children's daily caretakers. Abroad husbands saw their children only on the rare evening, Sundays, and holidays. Some enslavers allowed hired-out mothers to take their youngest children with them, but not so the males. And like mothers, fathers' work quotas kept them away from their young ones most of the waking day.

Fathers who were on site, or nearby, took some responsibility for their children's physical, material, and emotional needs. They especially helped with providing food through gardening in assigned plots, raising chickens, hunting, fishing, and trapping. Enslaved men on Shirley Plantation in Virginia, for example, earned small amounts of cash for rearing (along with their family members) chickens and ducks. In 1850, one bondsman named Peter provided the Carters with nineteen chickens, for which he was paid $8.50.[61] Fathers also were known to make cabin furnishings, help socialize their young, and give them psychological comfort.[62] Thomas Wentworth Higginson was happy to report from his time in South Carolina that while investigating the unusual sound of baby talk coming from the stables, he discovered the heartwarming image of a "happy father frolicking with his child, while his mother stood quietly by."[63] "My father was a carpenter . . . and he made his own furniture out of dressed lumber, and made a box to put clothes in," Carey Davenport of Texas remembered.[64] Skilled fathers like Carey's often passed their knowledge and artistry onto their sons. Campbell Davis proudly recalled his father's ability as a carpenter, wheelwright, and plow, loom, and spinning wheel maker: "He was a very valuable man."[65] Lunsford Lane detailed the important ways that his father, who lived abroad, repeatedly helped him to earn money so that Lunsford could support himself and his family. The two comprised a brilliant father/son inventor team. The senior taught his son a unique way to cure smoking tobacco. Lunsford himself crafted a new type of pipe that enhanced the smoker's experience. He sold both items in Raleigh.[66]

Some fathers contributed to their children's socialization by teaching them their family history and essential survival tactics. Chaney Mack of Georgia repeated the oral history of his father's and his uncle's theft in Africa (near Liberia) and sale to Georgia, stories his father passed on to him. "Dere wuz a boat load of 'em, all stolen. Dey sold my daddy and uncle Peter, to Mr. Holland. Dey wuz put on a block and Mr. Holland buyed 'em. Dat wuz in Dalton, Georgy."[67] Fathers were also disciplinarians. As Mary Ames noted in her diary while in South Carolina, "We have found out that the boys are afraid of their fathers, who are 'Great on licking.'"[68] Discipline, after all, often meant an enslaved person's survival. It was an essential skill children had to learn. Abram Sells recalled how his "great-grandaddy" was tasked with caring for the White and Black children on the plantation. "Us sho' have to mind him," Abram explained, "'cause iffen we didn't us sho' have bad luck. He allus have the pocket full of things to conjure with." The elderly man kept his young charges in line with fear that he could manipulate a "rabbit foot" and dried "fish scales" to punish them, physically and psychologically, if they disobeyed.[69]

Fathers, grandfathers, and other male kin, however, were not the only parental source of discipline.[70] Mothers, Elizabeth Botume recorded, believed that some corporal punishment was fine, but not castigations they thought would humiliate their children. "I punished a boy by placing him in a corner with his face to the wall," Botume noted. When his mother heard of it, she was highly offended, because it "hurt the feelings of her boy. She . . . said I 'could lick him, for licks is a very good thing for a chile, but she didn't want his feelings hurt.'"[71]

Parenting became even more difficult once slaveholders, overseers, and drivers assigned children tasks. Some bondspeople began working as young as four years old and were hirelings by the time they reached preadolescence. According to Adeline Marshall of Texas, "It didn't make any difference to captain how little you were, you went out to the field almost as soon as you could walk."[72] Wes Brady, also of Texas, recalled his first jobs: dropping seed corn, herding sheep, tending the cow pen, and shelling corn at night.

He missed his mother, who worked on a different schedule, terribly. "Many times I have walked through the quarters when I was a little chap," he recalled, "crying for my mother. Us children were in bed when the folks went to the field and come back. We mostly only saw her on Sunday."[73]

Some Black children had to serve as the companions of White children. Consequences still could be devastating. Olivia Morgan of Arkansas lost her sister when she was working as a "play mate" to her captor's child. While participating in a game of hide and seek, "just as she come running to the base from round the house, young master hit her on the forehead with a rock. It killed her."[74] Although not killed, another family's child returned from the place where she had been hired out severely traumatized, and she never recovered. "Mah po' little girl," Betty Brown lamented. The child would yell out "'Heah dey's comin' afth me," seemingly responding to a threat that others around her could not see. "I nevuh knowed whut wuz de mattuh with her. De priest wouldn't tell me, de doctuh wouldn't tell me" what had happened that destroyed her daughter.[75]

Like adult artisans and domestics, those children in training or already bound out to learn skills were compelled to literally live in their workspaces, even if that meant staying on a distant property owned by those who rented them. Lulu Wilson angrily recalled the unrealistic work routine and suffering as a bound child: "Now, when I was li'l they was the hardes' times," she began her narrative. "They'd nearly beat us to death. They taken me from my mammy, out the li'l house built onto they house and I had to sleep in a bed by Missus Hodges. I cried for my maw but I had to work and wash and iron and clean and milk cows when I was most too li'l to do it."[76] Ike Simpson recalled, "Nights, I allus slept by Missus' bed. Daytimes, my bed was push' up under her'n. Dis was called a trundle bed." Separated from his mother, Ike became his captor's "pet." "She kept me right wid her most ob de time, an' when mealtime come she put me under de table an' I ate out ob her hand. She'd put a piece ob meat into a biscuit an' hand it down to me."[77] Edgar Bendy of Texas recounted that he rarely spent time with his mother or father, since he was hired out as a nurse in town while they worked on his enslaver's cotton and sugar plantation.[78] Cheyney Cross of Alabama, who worked as a nanny when she was just a child herself, explained that she stayed with her White charges and "slep' on de little trundler bed what pushed up under de big bed.... I watched over dem chillun day an' night. I washed 'em an' fed 'em an' played wid 'em."[79] Lou Smith of Oklahoma also was a baby nurse when he was a child and recalled that he "took keer of them from daylight to dark," regardless of his parents' concerns or their need for him to perform chores in their home.[80]

James Pennington of Maryland reminisced passionately about what he recognized, even as a child, were the "evils" of slavery. His foremost pain derived from the absence of parental care because of his father's temporary work-driven absences and his parents' outrageous workloads even when they resided together. As a result, he "suffered much from *hunger* and other similar causes." Pennington likewise felt agony as the "companion" to his captor's children and because of the "tyranny and the abuse" of the overseers. The former was a kind of psychological pain; the latter, more physical. "My master," he explained, "had two sons about the ages and sizes of my older brother and myself." The enslaved boys had to "recognize these young sirs" as their "masters" and their "young masters . . . felt themselves to be such; and, in consequence . . . , they sought to treat us with the same air of authority that their father did the older slaves." As mortifying as this was to young Pennington, the overseers' cruelty was even more galling. "These men," he noted, "look[ed] with an evil eye upon children." They "seem[ed] to take pleasure in torturing the children of slaves, long before they are large enough to be put at the hoe, and consequently under the whip." By the age of nine, James and his brother both had been hired out, away from the daily care and support of their close kin.[81]

Moses Grandy of North Carolina experienced many difficulties without the protection of his parents once he became a field worker and was hired out. One renter, he noted, became angry with him because he did not "hill" the corn as instructed. He stripped the young Moses and whipped him so savagely that the sapling broke off and pierced the boy's stomach. "I was not aware of it until on going to work again it hurt my side very much," Moses explained and "when on looking down I saw it sticking out of my body. I pulled it out and the blood spouted after it. The wound festered, and discharged very much at the time, and hurt me for years after." Subsequently, Moses was rented out to a ferryman who refused to clothe or feed him properly, leading to near frostbite and starvation.[82]

Lunsford Lane of Raleigh echoed some of the same ugly pangs of childhood and adolescence. His greatest fear, from the time that he began to work, was of sale and permanent separation. "My friends were not numerous but . . . were dear and the thought that I might be separated from them forever, was like that of having the heart torn from its socket; while the idea of being conveyed to the far South, seemed infinitely worse than the terrors of death."[83] Depressingly, Lane also came to realize that even as a valuable worker, he could not exercise his free will. "Deep was this feeling," he later wrote, "and it preyed upon my heart like a never-dying worm."[84]

Parents suffered gravely from observing the abuse of their children and their inability to mediate or end it. Mary Younger lamented the hard work her children had to endure, even being forced to carry heavy buckets of water on their heads to the field. "Many a time I have looked out in the moonlight, and seen my little children, just able to walk to the fields, carrying buckets of water to the hands, she explained. "They would wear off the hair, and I used to make pads to protect the sore places where they carried the buckets."[85]

Female enslavers were as demanding as males and overseers. Mary Estes of Missouri knew from her own mother that her female parent had been tortured when she was a child. Burdening the girl with too much work to be completed in the time allotted, she "beat my mother down to the ground, and then took one of the skillets and bust her over the head with it."[86] One of America Morgan's elderly captors in Kentucky was so abusive that she feared even getting physically close to her. America's job was to fan the flies off the sick woman. When her enslaver finally died, America still was haunted by her presence, believing she "could hear her knocking on the wall with her cane" or climbing the stairs. She could not turn to her own kin to help her. Her male captor whipped America's mother to death when the child was five. He then sent America off to work for his daughter, separating the girl from her father and five siblings.[87] One woman named Sarah in low country South Carolina prayed for the death of her eldest daughter because she was consistently ill-treated. According to her, the girl was young, physically weak, and unable to care for the baby assigned to her watch. "At last God heard her prayer, and her child died. No one could tell how thankful she was."[88]

Enslaved people took particular care of those kin we would today designate as "disabled." They were "innocents" whom their kin and friends tried to protect, even if slaveholders and overseers abused them, when they could not complete their tasks.[89] The desire to watch over those who could not care for themselves, while not an ideal honored by everyone, was valued among many families, who realized the need and power of being able to call on kin and friends to provide nurture and protection when circumstances did not allow them to do so for themselves.

Children likewise experienced psychological distress when they witnessed captors and overseers treating their parents, siblings, and other kin inhumanely. Moses Grandy recalled painfully the sale of his two brothers and, as an immediate result, his mother's whipping: her shrieks and fainting when she could not prevent the sales. She previously had taken her family to hide in the woods in order to prevent her children from being sold away. One brother Moses never saw again. The other sibling, who lived nearby, soon died from harsh treatment—whipping, starvation, and lack of appropriate clothing. He was found dead in a nearby forest, his eyes plucked out by turkey buzzards.[90] Campbell Davis of Texas remembered witnessing his sister being whipped because she had not completed her spinning quota. "They pulled her clothes down to her waist and laid her down on the stomach and lashed her with the rawhide quirt."[91] Elizabeth Keckley learned from her mother that her maternal uncle had died by suicide rather than face another whipping from their enslaver.[92] "My poor mama," Jacob Branch complained. Her female captor would beat her every wash day because the flies would damage the wet wash. "'Renee, I'm going to teach you how to wash . . . ,' Old Lady Liza" would say as she pulled out her cowhide. "Looked like she would cut my mama in two." Jacob tried to "take some of the licks" by standing close to her.[93] William Wells Brown explained, after experiencing the horror of his mother screaming from an overseer's lashing, that "nothing can be more heart-rendering than for one to see a dear and beloved mother or sister tortured, and hear their cries, and not be able to render their assistance."[94] He himself felt chills and could not stop himself from weeping aloud on that Missouri morning at his feelings of impotency.

Children also felt particularly troubled when other kin were tasked to administer these harsh punishments. Campbell Davis saw his Uncle Lewis beaten for not picking enough cotton. The driver, another one of his uncles, administered the punishment. "He wasn't tied down," Campbell noted. "He said he was too scared to move."[95] Enslaved children, too, were ordered to assist in abusive acts against members of their families and Black community. Henry Gerald of South Carolina never recovered from the revulsion of not only watching his White father/captor strip and whip his mother, but being ordered to pour salt brine on her cut and bloodied back when his father had finished.[96] After having his back slashed from being whipped, Christopher Nichols explained that his captor "made a boy take spirits of turpentine and rub on my back."[97]

As children became adolescents and moved into their "prime" as laborers, their painful work-related conditions only increased. They suffered whippings that lacerated the skin and soul, dehumanizing scolding, teasing and violent threats, along with unsafe and unrealistic work mandates that resulted in burns, wounds, broken bones, amputations, dehydration, heat strokes, exhaustion, and frostbite. Despair and depression could not be avoided in children or their kin who stood as witnesses to the grim lifestyle captors and their designated labor supervisors commanded. A fifteen-year-old in 1850s Louisiana who had an argument with his child "master" reaped the ultimate punishment—murder by his young captor.[98]

Delia Garlic's life growing up as an enslaved family member in the antebellum South was not atypical. Born in 1837 in Powhatan County, Virginia, Delia and her mother were sold to the local sheriff when she was a child. Her captor, she explained, was not mean, but his daughter and wife were very cruel. While Delia was nursing a baby boy one day, he hurt his hand. The baby's mother blamed the Black child and retaliated by running a hot iron up and down Delia's arm and hand, taking "off de flesh." Another incident left the young girl beaten almost unconscious. Shortly thereafter, Delia was sold, this time without her mother, to Georgia and then to a man in Louisiana. There she was a "regular fiel' han', plowin' an' hoein' an' choppin' cotton."

Delia's hard, unrewarded labor, her multiple sales that severed her family ties, and the brutal punishments she underwent embittered and threatened to dehumanize her. She felt, profoundly, her enslavement. "It's bad to belong to folks dat own you sol an' body," she admitted decades later. "Dat can tie you up . . . wid yo' face to de tree an' yo' arms fastened tight aroun' it; who take a long curlin' whip an' cut de blood [with] ever' lick."[99]

For those parents and kin with teenage girls, sexual abuse was a particular evil they had to battle. Most females, and probably more males than frequently thought, suffered sexual abuse. Their families suffered with them. "When my sister was 16 years old," Lewis Clark of Madison County, Kentucky, explained, "her master sent for her." It was a meeting that changed the girl's life, and that of her family, forever. According to Clark, his sister was "pretty" and near White. "She was whiter than I am, for she took after her father," he explained. "When he sent for her again, she cried, and didn't want to go." Finally, she confided her troubles to their mother who, as an adolescent, had lived through the same peril. Unfortunately, their mother could offer little in the way of comfort. She told the girl to try to "be decent, and hold up her head above such things, if she could." Their captor, William Campbell, enraged by both Lewis's sister's public exposure of his desire for her and her rejection of him, "sold her right off to Louisiana."[100]

"I was regarded as fair-looking for one of my race, and for four years a white man . . . had base designs on me," Elizabeth Keckley said of her adolescence. "I do not care to dwell upon this subject, for it is one that is fraught with pain. Suffice it to say, that he persecuted me for four years, and I—I became a mother." Thinking of the shame that her son's status might have brought on him, she was quick to add that "he could not blame his mother, for God knows that she did not wish to give him life."[101] Forced sex; humiliation for the girl, her family, and children; and being sold away as part of the "fancy girl" or sex market were the fate many females endured, their families ripped apart and lives destroyed. It was especially demoralizing for the victims, but also for the children borne as a result of sexual aggression. They faced taunts by other children because of their biracial appearance, hostility and physical abuse by jealous White half siblings and offended captors' wives, and even sometimes the rejection of mothers traumatized by the physical reminders of their sexual assaults.[102]

Former slave James Pennington explained in his autobiography the commonality of the experience:

> It is under the mildest form of slavery, as it exists in Maryland, Virginia and Kentucky, that the finest specimens of coloured females are reared . . . for the express purpose of supplying the market [to] a class of economical Louisiana and Mississippi gentlemen, who do not wish to incur the expense of rearing

Elizabeth Keckley, c. 1860. Unknown, Elizabeth (Lizzy) Hobbs Keckley, photograph, c. 1861. Courtesy of Moorland Spingarn Research Center, Howard University.

legitimate families, they are, nevertheless, on account of their attractions, exposed to the most shameful degradation.[103]

James illustrated his claims by presenting the case of Mary Jane and Emily Catherine Edmondson, enslaved girls aged fourteen and sixteen, priced together at $2,250. Their captors charged such an exorbitant fee, Pennington asserted, because they intended to sell Mary Jane and Emily as sex captives

Figure 5.5 "Virginian Luxuries,"c. 1825. Unknown artist, Virginian Luxuries, ca. 1825, oil on canvas, acc. 1993.100.1, image T1994-121. Courtesy of The Colonial Williamsburg Foundation, Museum Purchase.

in the Deep South.[104] Louisa Picquet fetched a price of $1,500. Louisa's mother, Elizabeth Ramsey, sold for $900. Her captor had asked for $1,000 for the aging quadroon domestic, explaining, "It's true she is getting old but she carries her age well, and look as young as she did twenty years ago."[105]

Nancy Grathan from Virginia and Alabama explained that she sought to escape slavery to avoid the violent lust of her enslaver. "The very day before I escaped," she explained, "I was required to go to his bed-chamber to keep the flies off of him as he laye, or pretended to be so." Once Nancy arrived, her captor made his sexual intentions known: "He said that he was coming to my pallet that night, and with an oath he declared if I made a noise he would cut my throat." She hid from him and "was beaten awfully" the next morning as a result. Later, Nancy successfully escaped by concealing her gender, "dressing herself in male attire."[106]

Most could not escape. Annie Young, enslaved in Tennessee, recalled how her aunt hid in the woods to avoid her captor's sexual advances. His bloodhounds hunted her down. He then hit her in the head with a heavy stick, took her back, and raped her. When the abused woman asked her female captor for assistance, she told Annie that she should comply or he would kill her. Her enslaver forced Annie into sexual slavery that resulted in her birthing children that were nearly White. Her captors, Annie's aunt, and Annie's biracial children "all worked in de fields side by side."[107] When Nellie Johnson, who was enslaved in Louisiana, tried to escape, the "almost white woman" with "pretty, long, straight hair" was punished in part by defeminizing and shaming her: "They made her wear men's pants for one year. They made her work in the field that way . . . they put deer horns on her head . . . with bells on them."[108]

Enslaved girls and women on antebellum college campuses and their surroundings, too, often were the victims of sexual abuse. At the University of Virginia, evidence indicates that in 1850 "a small negro girl, a slave about 12 years old" was raped by three students: George H. Hardy, Armistead C. Eliason, and James E. Montandon. The university expelled the students, but none of the men were held legally accountable.[109]

Wherever their assigned labor took place, bonded girls and women often suffered sexual assault, especially by young captors, overseers, and drivers. Rose Maddox, an enslaved woman raised in Mississippi and Louisiana, emphasized that "a white man laid a nigger gal whenever he wanted her. Seems like some of them had a plumb craving for the other color. Leastways they wanted to start themselves out on the nigger women."[110] Rose's suggestion that slaveholding adolescents demanded sexual favors from enslaved females was quite true. Teenage boys seeking sexual pleasure, experience, and domination forced captive girls and women to comply.

Former bondsman Jacob Manson recalled that many of the slaveholding men in his neighborhood required sex from their bondswomen. "Marster had no chilluns by white women," he noted. "He had his sweethearts among his slave women. I ain't no man for tellin' false stories. I tells de truth, an' dat is de truth." Manson stated that his captor, Colonel Bun Eden, was so sexually proprietary of his enslaved women that he refused to hire White overseers but used Black drivers instead: "He liked some of de nigger women too good to have any uder white man playin' arou' wid 'em." At that time, Manson added, "it wus a hard job to find a marster dat didn't have women 'mong his slaves. Dat wus a ginerel thing 'mong de slave owners."[111]

The sexual double standard in slaveholding families that rewarded patriarchs and their male heirs with the right to demand sexual favors of bonded girls, teens, and women was a tradition passed down from one generation of enslavers to the next.[112] Judge Maddox grew up with his mulatto half-sister working in his home. After he was married and settled on his own plantation in Marion County, Georgia, he bought a "pretty mulatto . . . seamstress" for himself.[113]

Sally Hemings was made the concubine of Thomas Jefferson while living in his household in Paris in the early republic period. Her mother, Elizabeth, had been the domestic of John Wayles during the colonial era and had served as maid to his two wives before Wayles made her his concubine and mother to six of his children. Elizabeth's African mother, too, was the concubine of an English sea captain named Hemings.[114] Both Louisa Picquet and her mother were sex captives. When Louisa reached puberty, the father of four of her mother's children also tried to rape her.[115] Incest, of course, was the most extreme and perverse example of how physical intimacy lent itself to serial concubinage and sexual predation. Jacob Bryan of Duval County, Florida, repeatedly raped his quadroon daughter, Celia, in the late 1840s. She ultimately murdered him and was hanged for it.[116]

Since the children born to sex captives like Celia Bryan, Louisa Picquet, and Sally Hemings and her mother often were doomed to be forced into sexual relations with White men, their chances of having a functional family, by birth or through marriage, were minimal at best. Harriet Jacobs's grandmother, who angrily called Harriet a "disgrace" and temporarily banished her from her home when she found out that Harriet was pregnant, directly queried the elite White man with whom Harriet had sexual relations why he had taken her innocence, why "he could not have left her one ewe lamb."[117] Law, custom, selfishness, perversity, and racialized power were the answers he undoubtedly did not offer.

John Sella Martin, who was the child of a concubine born in 1832, angrily retold his mother's story and how his family's sale and dispersal were fueled by his father's family's rejection of their mixed-race kin. "Like too many girls," he began, "my mother had been a victim of the selfish designs of her mistress in securing an eligible match in marriage for the heir of her property." John's father was not wealthy, but his family had arranged for him to marry someone of substantial means. His betrothed, however, was several years younger, and it would be at least a decade before she was ready to marry. In order to persuade her nephew to wait to marry the heiress, his aunt created for him a concubinage relationship with Winnifred, John Martin's mother. Accordingly, "Mrs. Henderson, by methods known only to the system of slavery, encouraged, and finally secured a relationship between Mr. Martin and my mother, of which my sister Caroline and myself were the fruits."[118] Mrs. Henderson arranged for Winnifred, who was a "griff" (one-quarter White) to have a separate cabin, "nominal" housekeeping duties for her, and food from the "big house." In exchange, Winnifred was assigned as Mr. Martin's sex captive for the next ten years. According to John, his father had grown attached to his biracial family and refused to marry at the allotted time. Mrs. Henderson would hear nothing of this. She sent her nephew away on family business to Virginia and sold Winnifred and her two children to Georgia while he was gone.[119]

We will never know if Mr. Martin sought to recover this "family." John did not see his father again, and his family soon became scattered to the winds through sale and resale. John's suggestion that his father was tricked into losing them may have been truthful, or it may have been a story concocted to spare his feelings. It was through his own efforts that John eventually freed himself, his sister, and her two children—whom she bore after being forced into a sexual relationship with one of her new enslavers. Winnifred died before her son could emancipate her.[120]

Most concubines and their children could expect no long-term protections or privileges. There were a relative few, however, who fared otherwise. James C. James of South Carolina explained that his White father was very wealthy and treated him well, giving him money and "allowing" him and his "beautiful" mixed-race mother to live in the domestic captive quarters located at the back of their enslaver's expansive home. His White half siblings were kind as well, until they realized that they were related to him.[121] "Master John was bad after slave women," Solomon Oliver of Mississippi explained of his "grandfather's" behavior. His enslaver's biracial children "always got special privileges because . . . he didn't want his children whipped like the rest of the slaves." The overseer, however, took out his "jealousy" of Solomon's mother on him. "He would whip me just for the fun of it," the former bondsman noted. "It was fun for him but not for me."[122]

Samuel Adams "cohabitated" with the enslaved woman, Rebecca Kelly, for several years before eventually emancipating her. Upon his death, he bequeathed to Rebecca "two slaves and an annuity of 60 pounds for 10 years." He also left her his cattle, household furnishings, his land, and eleven other enslaved people. When his bequest was challenged in court, one of Adams's friends, a Mr. Squib, testified concerning the great service that Rebecca had given to Adams and the income she had supplied him through her hand-manufacture of mattresses. According to Squib, "he would have gone to pieces without her."[123] A vice president of the United States, Richard Mentor Johnson, notoriously was "married" to a biracial woman for many years before his political career placed him as number two in command of the nation. Although the couple could not legally marry, Johnson and Julia Chinn still exchanged vows in a local church and enjoyed a celebration at his plantation in Kentucky. The couple shared two daughters, Imogene and Abilene, whom Johnson publicly acknowledged, educated, enriched, and married off to White men.[124] Francis Jelineau, who escaped the Haitian Revolution and moved to South Carolina, brought with him not only his White wife but also his enslaved concubine and their child. According to the divorce/alimony petition Madame Jelineau filed, her husband continued to "cohabitate" with his concubine after their marriage and "lavished his affection" on their child. She added that her husband routinely humiliated her by allowing her to eat only after he and his Black paramour had dined. Jelineau defended his actions, telling the court that in Saint Domingue such relations were not "disgraceful" and that his wife knew, prior to their marriage, that he had a Black lover and that she "had promised to treat the[ir biracial] child well."[125]

A Virginia Slave Child in 1863. [First name absent] Van Dorn, A Virginia Slave Child in 1863, photograph, c. 1863, Library of Congress, Prints and Photographs Division, Library of Congress, LC-DIG-ppmsca-11248. The child is thought to be Fannie Virginia Casseopia Lawrence, a "redeemed slave child," from Virginia.

Madame Jelineau was correct in suggesting that the public acknowledgment of a racially mixed relationship was considered by most people in the United States, exclusive of those in places that had been parts of the French and Spanish empires, an assault on the White family's honor. Black people felt similarly regarding the honor of their females. Indeed, White persons often sued and won libel cases when such accusations came to light. A Mr. Neese, for example, was found guilty of defamation in a Maryland court in 1818 when he nailed on a tree along a public road a "Notice to all Persons" that he had witnessed Betsy, a White neighbor's daughter, engaged in sex with a "Negro Boy."[126]

Still, privileged White men dispersed their property and protection as they pleased, and local institutions, such as the courts, often allowed them to do so. Eliza Bremar found this out when she sued her deceased husband's Black paramour, Tabitha Singleton, for the property that he bequeathed to her. The court case revealed that Tabitha had been F. Bremar's concubine both prior to and after his marriage. Bremar freed Tabitha, continued his sexual relationship with her, and paid for her household expenses, including a house, a lot of land, and her daily living expenses as well as those of her mother and sisters. Upon his death, he left Tabitha the house, lot, and "two negroes, Sally and Polly" (perhaps Tabitha's sisters). The court allowed Bremar's will to stand and ordered that his wife, who had seized the house and lot, to return to Tabitha the $2,000 from its illegal sale. Witnesses even testified that Bremar "had been [Tabitha's] guardian and that she had a "virtuous character"—certainly not the typical description of a Black woman in antebellum South Carolina.[127]

As historian Jane Landers has documented regarding the practice of concubinage in Spanish Florida,[128] concubines and their families were more likely to receive somewhat better treatment in Louisiana given its history as part of the Spanish and French colonial empires. New Orleans was known for its "quadroon balls" that often led to long-term sexual and familial relations between wealthy White men and the most beautiful of mixed-race women: some enslaved, others free. Some of these women came to have, at least for a time, relatively fine homes, clothing and food, horses and carriages, education for their children, and perhaps even enslaved domestics to control. Many of these relationships ended when the man married and had legal, White heirs. Others did not.[129]

Numerous legal cases from Louisiana reveal concubines who prevailed in court to win the freedom and property promised to them or their children by wealthy men with whom they had long-term sexual and domestic relations. Such was the case of Venus, the biracial "bastard child" of C. Beard and the "negro woman Nancy." Venus was to receive "six negroes, men and women that is three of each, to be delivered when she arrives at the age of eighteen"; along with a "proper" education that included being taught to read and write and trained to be a seamstress.[130] Beard's propertied acknowledgement of his "colored" family undoubtedly harmed the families of those enslaved people bequeathed to Venus.

There also were some women who took pride in their intimate connections with White men and their White ancestry. Ary from southern Virginia was a quadroon who felt more akin to Whites than the dark-skinned men and women enslaved with her. When she "boasted of her white blood," the enslaved people who heard her became "enraged." When Ary responded to their anger by pointing out the near whiteness of her child, someone challenged her directly concerning her own claims to whiteness: "Just tell me how many folks it takes to make a white person?" Ary was obliged to answer, "One white man and one white woman."[131] That seems to have ended the dispute.

White men sexually and emotionally attached to Black women destroyed their White families when they, like Francis Jelineau, exercised the privilege of having an "honorable" legal marriage alongside a Black or biracial mistress. Others did not marry at all. As Andrew Moss of Tennessee noted of his enslaver who remained "single": "Marster Hopper had five children by my grandmother. She was his house woman, dat's what he call 'er. An' when he died he willed her and all dem chilluns a house, some land, and a little money."[132]

While slaveholding women's responses ran the gamut from divorce to violent outrage to quiet, perhaps tortured, compliance, they also were known to enable their husbands' demands that enslaved women provide sexual favors. "One of de slave girls on a plantation near us went to her missus and tole her 'bout her marster forcing her to let him have something' to do wid her," one former North Carolina bondsperson related, "and her missus tole her, 'Well, go on. You belong to him.'"[133] "In them times white men went with colored gals and women bold," another bondsman recounted. "Any time they saw one and wanted her, she had to go with him, and his wife didn't say nothin' 'bout it."[134]

These were slaveholding women's public responses. A strong sense of propriety, especially in the face of a captive female's humiliating accusation of such damnable acts, was probably their best public defense against total loss of face. Some women were afraid to confront their husbands, a fear that did not escape the knowing eyes of Blacks: "Before my old marster died, he had a pretty gal he was goin' with and he wouldn't let her work nowhere but in the house, and his wife nor nobody else didn't say nothin' 'bout it; they knowed better. She had three chillun for him."[135]

When wives actually caught their husbands "in the act," they were much less likely to mask their outrage and pain well. "Another marster named Jimmie Shaw," one person recalled, "owned a purty slave gal, nearly white, a' he kept her. His wife caught 'im in a cabin bed wid her. His wife said somethin' to him 'bout it, an' he cussed his wife." Her reaction was deadly. "She went back to de greathouse an' got a gun," the captive continued. "When de marster come in de greathouse, she tole 'im he must let de slave girls alone, dat he belonged to her. He cussed her agin an' said she would have to tend to her own damn business an' he would tend to his." After more heated words, "She grabbed de gun an' let him have it. She shot 'im dead in de hall."[136]

Outraged slaveholders' wives were much more likely to violently attack bonded females and their children than their errant husbands, demanding they be sold away. When the men refused to do so, some acted quickly to deprive them of their concubines' pleasures. For example, one day Jack Maddox's enslaver brought home "a pretty mulatto gal. She was real bright and she had long black hair and was dressed neat and good." His wife was immediately suspicious. "What you bring that thing here for," she snapped. Judge Maddox's reply that the woman would do all of his wife's "fine needle work" was less than convincing. "Fine needlework, your hind leg," she retorted. As soon as the judge left the plantation, his wife cut off the woman's hair "to her skull."[137] Others attacked biracial offspring. "One white lady that lived near us at McBean," a former bondsman from Georgia remembered, "slipped in a colored gal's room and cut her baby's head clean off 'cause it belonged to her husband. He beat her 'bout it and started to kill her, but she begged so I reckon he got to feelin' sorry for her. But he kept goin' with the colored gal and they had more chillun."[138]

GEOGRAPHIES OF KIN RESIDENCE AND RESISTANCE

The size and composition of antebellum enslaved families and households, like their sundry housing options, varied tremendously. Indeed, variability was the only certainty. Family membership and family members' distance from one another expanded, contracted, and disappeared, not only with the singular acts of birth and death of the enslaved and their captors, but repeatedly with the desires and financial priorities of their enslavers. Marriage hardly guaranteed living under the same roof or in a nuclear family, even if spouses had the same captor—and definitely not if they did not. Slaveholders typically did not give passes to women, and they could refuse to grant them to men whenever they pleased. Any hint of resistance, refusal to comply with labor quotas, or plans to use one's pass to escape meant a loss of these "privileges," at least for several weeks.

Spouses' physical separation always was a source of emotional pain and marital conflict in antebellum families. "A man dat had a wife off de place, see little peace or happiness," a former captive from South Carolina complained. "He could see de wife once a week, on a pass, and jealousy kep' him 'stracted de balance of de week, if he love her very much."[139] More opportunities for visits existed, as in earlier eras, for couples who resided at different sites of the same slaveholder's business venture(s). These couples could not live with each other on a daily basis but had more contact than abroad spouses. Those who stayed in the same quarters usually shared domestic quarters, but they did not necessarily have privacy. Many still were housed with other adult kin, orphaned children, the elderly, or unmarried prime workers—either temporarily or on a long-term basis.

The small cabins typically associated with bondspeople's residences are not a myth. Most rural antebellum living spaces for bondspeople were made from wood, with hardened dirt floors, single doorways, and sometimes windows. Northern visitors commented that many dwellings were "dark and dingy."[140] Some were constructed like barracks, housing multiple families and nonattached adults. Others, but certainly not the majority, were made from brick or stone. Husbands, with the help of other men in their community, constructed housing at the time of their marriage, although wealthy slaveholders occasionally employed carpenters to build them. Some older quarter spaces also had flowers and trees. One visitor to coastal South Carolina plantations described the space where field workers lived as "a nice little street of huts which have recently been whitewashed, shaded by a row of the 'Pride of China' trees. These trees are just in bloom and have very large clusters of purple flowers." There also were fig trees and a vegetable garden.[141]

Although generally small and uncomfortable, particularly by southern gentry standards, bondspeople's housing nonetheless provided some respite from long laboring hours, weather extremes, and the constant hostile gaze of White authority. Harriet McFarland of Arkansas and Texas reminisced about life in the quarters that she grew up in, noting that

> all their houses were in a row, all one-room cabins. Everything happened in that one room,—birth, sickness, death and everything, but in them days . . . [they] kept their houses clean and their door yards too. . . . I used to love to walk down by that row of houses. It looked like a town and late of an evening as you'd go by the doors you could smell meat a frying, coffee making and good things cooking.[142]

While many nineteenth-century bondspeople, as those in the eighteenth century had, expanded their living spaces and privacy by constructing upstairs lofts and root cellars, countless domestics continued to be housed in uncomfortable makeshift spots in their captors' homes, while craftspeople resided in their workshops. A large domestic staff sometimes had some social and cultural distance from their captors if they were provided special quarters. Those in personal service, however, usually had to sleep near those they were expected to take care of day and night.

If members of the same family did different types of work, they sometimes were housed in different sites. Betty Foreman of North Carolina explained that as a domestic, she could not stay with her mother in the field workers' quarters. She "slept under the dining room table with three other darkies. The flo' was well carpeted."[143] Betty and her mother saw each other only when both had completed their assigned duties and captors gave them permission.

Housing at Stagville Plantation, North Carolina. Photo taken at Historic Stagville State Historic Site, Department of Natural and Cultural Resources, NC. Source: Author, Slave quarters building, Stagville Plantation Complex, photograph, c. 1850, Durham County, NC. Author's photograph archive.

Those like Betty, who served as private maids and valets, often found it difficult to carve out time for their own families, since they were at the beck and call of their captors' families even when skilled and field workers were at rest. Any special event, additional house guests, or illness within the enslaver's family meant additional work for domestics and less time for their own kin. Of course, many still resisted these restrictions and took the opportunity to visit and even spend nights with kin, risking punishment if caught.

Antebellum quarters sometimes included the group houses popular among the colonial gentry, but only on the largest estates. The sugar- and cotton-producing bondspeople living at Duparc/Locoul plantation in Louisiana—190 persons in 1850—stayed with their families in small wooden structures, some built as double houses. In North Carolina, the 592 enslaved people on the Bennehan-Cameron Stagville plantations lived in fifteen separate structures. Some occupied two-story buildings with two living spaces on the bottom floor and two directly above, accommodating either four family groups or a combination of families and non-kin-related workers. When Paul Cameron decided to extend his family's agricultural operation from the Upper to the Deep South in the 1840s, he divided some family groups, fracturing the expansive enslaved community that had been growing since the Revolutionary era. He relocated 100 of his bondspeople to Alabama, where he established a cotton plantation. Later, these same persons faced further separation when Cameron moved some to Mississippi. Slave census records from 1860 indicate that Cameron housed 116 enslaved men, women, and children in twenty-five cabins at his Alabama work site and 83 in sixteen huts on his Mississippi plantation.[144]

Not all living spaces were clustered into "quarters." A former Georgia bondsman explained that most of the cabins he lived in were not constructed as a communal space, but instead "were more or less scattered over the plantation."[145] The lack of a designated communal space marked by designated housing occurred on small farms or work sites where only a few bondspersons worked. It also was usual on new holdings that captors were expanding rapidly without much forethought given to eventual housing needs, security, or community.

Family residential geographies in the antebellum decades, as earlier, were not just a part of rural landscapes. Southern towns and cities housed large enslaved populations. One-third of the residents in Charleston, Richmond, and Savannah in 1860 were bondspeople, and their presence had been even greater in the 1820s and 1830s. Most urban captives were female domestics, but men also were present, working in a variety of skilled, construction, and industrial occupations. Charleston, Norfolk, Baltimore, Raleigh, New Orleans, Savannah, Richmond, and Washington, DC, all shared this gendered

Slave Quarters building, Duparc/Locoul Plantation Complex, c. 1850, Vacherie, Louisiana. Author, Slave quarters building, photo taken at Laura: Louisiana's Creole Heritage Site, photograph, Vacherie, Louisiana, Author's photograph collection.

trend. Many enslaved mothers who were assigned to work in the town residences of their enslavers took their young children with them. This rarely was the case for those women who were rented out for a set period of time and money. Exceptions included some hired Black seamstresses, who provided income from their labor to their captors but could live on their own under strict surveillance. The presence of large numbers of urbanized Black people, captive and not, meant that southern cities were the site of vibrant African American social, familial, and communal ties and activities.[146]

Urban bondspeople's housing consisted of wooden huts behind slaveholders' houses and along the nearby alleyways. Others slept in makeshift spaces in workshops as well as in the inconspicuous storage spaces of captors' dwellings.[147] Black housing in Norfolk, for example, was described as crowded "dilapidated buildings, lofts, basements, sheds, and hotels" as well as barber shops, kitchens, wharves, and cellars."[148] Lunsford Lane recalled his childhood dwelling in Raleigh, North Carolina, as "an apartment" in the "kitchen situated some fifteen or twenty rods from the 'great house.' Here the house servants lodged and lived, and here the meals were prepared for the people in the mansion."[149] He slept on his captor's dining room floor.[150] Charleston's urban bondspeople lived in "backlots,"[151] as did many in the deeper South. William Johnson, the famed free Black barber and diarist from Natchez, housed his enslaved people in backyard rooms.[152]

As ever, there were the exceptions. In Wilmington, the Black residence located in the "yard" of the Bellamy Mansion was a two-story brick building with three rooms per floor. It had front and side windows and was built in the style (Greek revival mantels and relatively spacious rooms) and substance (brick, pine, and glass) of the mansion house.

Enslaved laborers built both the Bellamy Mansion and their own living quarters.

Family and community life clearly did not just occur on the inside of small, cramped cabins in the rural countryside or in the crowded, dingy spaces most urban families occupied. Much of enslaved domesticity took place in outdoor communal spaces afforded by circular and linearly arranged rural housing, in city alleyways, and in the forested spaces, everywhere, of the encroaching countryside. These alternate geographies of enslaved social life were the sites of combined pleasure seeking, utilitarian labor, spiritual outreach, resistance, and even crime—all with some impact on family. Kinfolk witnessed or participated in all manner of human and communal behavior, including carousing and courtship, drinking, joking, cooking, gardening, quilting parties, candy pulling, storytelling, singing and praising God, clothes making and cleaning, hair adornment, hunting, fishing, weddings, burials, fights, gambling, stealing, trading, and other forms of underground economies at work.

Urban Slave Quarters, Lexington, Kentucky, Unknown, Buckner House (Rose Hill), Slave Quarters, Designed or Constructed in 1820, photograph, c. 1935-1936, National Parks Service, Historic American Buildings Survey: Kentucky Photographic Collection, University of Kentucky Libraries Special Collections Research Center.

Bellamy Mansion Slave Housing. "Urban Slave Quarters," Bellamy Mansion, Wilmington, NC. Image courtesy of Bellamy Mansion Museum of History and Design Arts.

Outdoor spaces in the quarters, one former Georgia bondman recalled, were where "young folkses frolicked, sung songs, and visited from cabin to cabin."[153] Lunsford Lane recounted his childhood days spent with "children playing in the same yard."[154] Wade Hampton of Alabama not only remembered that his father provided the quarters with banjo music, but also that "when dey had dem Saddy night frolics an' dance all night long an' nearly day when hit was goin,' dey would turn de pot upside down in de floor to hold de soun' in."[155] Hamp Kennedy from Mississippi fondly recalled the candy pulling, noting that they met and "tol' ghost stories, sung plantation songs, an' danced de clog while de candy was cookin.'"[156] Julia Frazier of Virginia noted of the Sunday activities among the "long row" of housing where the bondspeople would gather to "sing an' have a big time." On holidays, it was the site of ring games, rope jumping, and dancing.[157]

Relaxed restrictions on mobility and public entertainment venues that enslaved people found in the cities of the early nineteenth century allowed some to visit nearby friends and family. They took in the sights of the day—traveling fairs, carnivals, horse races, cock fights and boxing matches. Some patronized local grog shops, where they drank, caroused across the color line, and gambled. Still, one's time was not one's own, even after dark and even where one slept. This was especially so after the 1830s, the decade of Nat Turner's Rebellion, when those who resided in cities faced extreme surveillance and increasing restrictions on mobility, recreation, sacred activities, and work choices.

On the farms and plantations, it was not unusual to labor after sunset, particularly during harvest season, evaporating much of one's "family time." For some, late evening and night work was more rule than exception. One former Virginia bondswoman made certain that her interviewer knew that her mother's duty as the laundress kept her working sometimes until midnight. In order to wash her own family's clothes, she had to do so even later in the night or on her day off.[158] These women were too burdened to enjoy the few social outlets that were a possibility for others. "Some o' de womans worked in de fiel' an' when dey comes in dey has tuh set down an' peel apples an' peaches fo' fryin' an' put 'em on big racks out in de sun an' when dey's dry, put 'em in bags, an' hang 'em up fo' wintuh," Mollie Sides of Missouri elaborated.[159] In the evenings, it was a place where "mens rested" and "womans cyard de cotton and wool," Marriah Hines explained. A bondsperson's domestic space had to be used for nighttime work, especially for the complex production of cloth assigned to girls and women. In the evenings, Hines added, nighttime chores and recreation often blended together—work exhaustion ameliorated somewhat by the company of other females, some kin, and friends. Collectively, they would spin, quilt, make clothes, talk, and tell jokes, and a few had learned to "weave a little bit from Missus."[160] Others gossiped and told ghost stories while they worked. Children lingered nearby, playing marbles, ring games, and chase. "We played mumble-peg an' hop-scotch when I wus a child, we played jumpin' de rope a lot," Chana Littlejohn of North Carolina explained.[161]

Women and men, as well as their children, also derived great pride in accomplishments as skilled, even brilliant, workers, artisans, and artists, particularly when their skills and talents could be purposed for the comfort of their own families. This esteem was shared among kin. The clothing, covers, and quilts were potent and lasting reminders of a family members' care and love. "Weaving was a thing the women prided in doing—being a fast weaver or a fine hand at weaving," Charles Anderson of Kentucky explained. "They wove pretty coverlets for the beds."[162] Maggie Black spoke of the pride she felt: "I c'n see my ole mammy how she look workin' dat spinning wheel.... She set dere at dat ole spinnin wheel en take one shettle en t'row it one way en den annuder de udder way en pull dat t'ing en make it tighter en tighter. Sumptin say sum, sum, sum, en den yuh hadder work you feet dere too."[163] Tempie Herndon spoke with awe when she recalled the weavers, spinners, and dyers who lived with and near her. "Mammy Rachel stayed in de dyein' room," she explained. "Dey wuzn' nothin' she didn' know' bout dyein'." Tempie added that, as if almost with magical powers, Rachel made cloth turn "every color of de rainbow."[164] Children and teens watching the adult women work longed to have their knowledge and artistry. Josephine Bristow of South Carolina recalled that "I would stand dere en want to spin so bad, I never know what to do. Won' long fore I got to whe' I could use de shuttle en weave, too. I had a grandmother en when she would get to dat wheel, she sho know what she been doin."[165]

Among outdoor spaces of familial importance, forests were essential alternative geographies for contact, care, and communion. They were places where kin offered clandestine support and protection of loved ones harmed, hunted, and haunted by abusive enslavers and other enemies. Celestine Avery, formerly enslaved in Georgia, retold the stories she heard of the importance the forest came to play in her grandparents' lives. At one time, their captor, Peter Heard, tied and stripped Celestine's pregnant grandmother, Sylvia, and beat the skin off her back because she refused to give up praying. When night fell, Sylvia's husband cut her down, and she crawled to the woods to hide. Her spouse followed, bringing with him grease to apply to her "raw" body. There she, with his help, was able to elude recapture for two weeks. During that time, Sylvia gave birth to her twins while alone. Sylvia was a midwife and "always carried a small pin knife which she used to cut the navel cord of the babies." After the birthing, the exhausted mother tore a part of her clothing into two pieces, wrapping each of her newborns.[166] Some of Fanny Berry's earliest and most dramatic memories also were focused on the times that she spent in the Virginia forests: where she played with her young slaveholder; where she "disappeared" her captor's dog, who routinely terrorized her little brother; the paths through which she ran errands; and the places where she feared she would meet departed souls, desperate refugees, or mean-spirited patrollers.[167]

SETTING SPIRITS FREE

Forested areas adjacent to quarters, brush harbors, and caves also were popular locales for religious gatherings. Examples of syncretic religious practices remained flush in the nineteenth-century Black Atlantic.

Congregants invested spiritually, artistically, and intellectually in their religious practices for several reasons, not the least of which was that doing so promoted familial memory, unity, protection, and liberation—physical, emotional, and spiritual. "In slavery days Sundays was one day we glad to see come," Alice Marshall of Virginia explained. "Yes, we went to church. Had to walk four or five miles, but we went. We took our shoes in our hands an' walked barefooted. When we got near de church door, den we put on our shoes."[168] "On Sunday's you should o' seen us in our Sunday bes' gon' ter church 'hind be missus coach," Henrietta McCullers of North Carolina added. "We can't read de hymns ebben iffen we had a book 'cause we ain't 'lowed ter have no books, but we sung jist the same."[169] A woman who had been enslaved in Alabama noted that they all "love to go to church an' sing." John, who had been bound in Georgia, remembered that when his wife Nancy "got religion," it was a joyous occasion for everyone around her. "Nancy cried out in church when she was converted and said, 'Glory be to God and the Lamb forever! I am washed clean by the blood of Jesus,' Nancy shouted, and was so happy we could hardly get her home that evening. She shouted all along the road as we walked. We all got happy on our way back that night."[170]

Enslaved people who were religious overwhelmingly appreciated those in their families and fictive kin networks who were devout and committed to the spiritual experience, who provided moral guidance, and whose personal control was an example to others. Annie Williams told the story of "Aunt Rebecca," an elderly enslaved woman who not only attended their mandatory daily prayer meetings, but actively participated.[171] According to Annie, Rebecca often gave lengthy, passionate prayers garnering the attention and respect of other congregates. Williams was struck by this phenomenon for two reasons: Aunt Rebecca was a woman, and she was enslaved. "Aunt Rebecca used to git up an' pray regular," Annie explained. "Didn't let women do much prayin' in dem days."[172] This was especially so for enslaved women.[173] "[B]ut Marsa never sot Aunt Rebecca down. Pray sometimes fo' half-hour an' white folks would sit there jus' as 'spectful as if she was de white preacher."[174] Rebecca's gender typically would have limited her accessibility to public power.[175] Her advanced age, her knowledge of religious text, and perhaps the "memory" of female "leaders" in traditional African religions, however, allowed her to create social space for religious leadership.[176] Aunt Rebecca certainly was not the only enslaved woman revered for her holy demeanor.

Antebellum religious gatherings, whether at church or at some private or clandestine place, were not just time to learn about and publicly revere God (or gods). Bonded people also used them to create opportunities to strengthen familial and communal spiritual bonds. Isaiah Jeffries passionately recalled his mother's conversion experience and the impact it had on her, their family, and the community. These kinds of events bound the living with ancestors of similar faith and were the site of the creation of dynamic rituals and cultural expressions. "She shouted and sung fer three days," Jeffries explained of her ecstatic expressions, "going all over de plantation and de neighboring one, inviting her friends to come to see her baptized and shouting and praying fer dem. She went around to all de people dat she had done wrong and beg ed dere forgiveness. She sent fer dem dat had wronged her, and told dem dat she was born again and a new woman, and dat she would forgive dem. She wanted everybody dat was not saved to go up wid her."[177]

The extended families and communities that enslaved people were bound to through their religious beliefs and rituals reached across long distances. They were especially important as the domestic trade increased in volume. Charlotte was sold from Virginia to Louisiana when she was a young teen. She often thought longingly of her life in the Upper South, where she had lived with her mother and other family members. An essential part of her familial and communal life in Richmond was her expression of faith, attending church regularly, and the religious text and hymns that she had learned and shared with her kin. Charlotte was not just a Black Christian; she identified as a Protestant. She detested the Catholicism of her new captor in Louisiana. "My mother used to take her children to church every Sunday," she recalled. "But when I came to Louisiana I did not go to church any more. Everybody was Catholic where I lived, and I never had seen that sort of religion that has people praying on beads. That was all strange to me. The older I got the more I thought of my mother's Virginia religion. Sometimes when I was away off in the cane-field at work it seemed I could hear my mother singing the 'Old Ship of Zion.' I could never hear any of the old Virginia hymns sung here." One day, Charlotte learned that another enslaved woman from Virginia had arrived at a nearby plantation. When Charlotte finally got to meet Aunt Jane Lee, she was disappointed to find that she was not any of her kin, but glad to know that Jane also spoke English (as opposed to French) and was a Protestant (instead of Catholic) who was able to read biblical text, lead their Protestant religious meetings, and convert those who were so inclined. Charlotte soon came to view Aunt Jane as a surrogate mother and the others who worshipped with them as her new community.[178]

Together, members of these religious communities studied and worshipped, exhorted and shouted, sang, hummed songs, praised, and prayed. While doing so, they centered much of their energy on enjoying, improving, and defending their lives and those of their loved ones. God (or gods), they believed, could do for them and their kin what they could not do. God (or gods) was the family that could not be made powerless or separated from them.

One former bondswoman from Tennessee explained that she first sought God as a means of protection from her brutal captor: "I was a slave and started to pray when I was nine years old." Trained as a domestic when quite young, she had constant contact with her ailing enslaver, rendering her a life without her family and one that was barely tolerable. "My mistress was mean to me and one day she said, 'I am going to kill you. Go and eat and come back to me, for I am going to kill you,'" she remembered. The girl started to the kitchen as she was directed, but stopped to pray, asking God to spare her life. "I went back in the house, and she didn't touch me." "From then on I prayed more and more."[179] For the next several years, through her adolescence and early adulthood, she used the power derived from her belief in God to survive her captor's daily doses of physical and verbal abuse. A Louisiana enslaved girl named Hattie, the victim of sexual and physical abuse, ran away to avoid a beating and then suffered terribly from the cold and want of food and medical attention. When a fellow bondsperson asked her how she had managed to survive and give birth to a child in the woods all alone, she answered, "All I can tell, God took care of me in these woods."[180] Even when some bondspeople became so desperate that they took their own lives, it was so they finally could be with God. Aunt Nellie told her friend before she died by suicide, "I don' had my las' whippin'. I'm gwine to God."[181]

Some antebellum captors encouraged Christian conversion, particularly of their domestics, in order to "civilize" and make them culturally akin to themselves. Victor Duchon of Louisiana recalled that he went to Catholic Mass presided over by a priest who baptized children and married couples.[182] Georgia Smith attended the segregated church services of her captors and had the benefit of prayer meetings in the quarters twice a week.[183] Many slaveholders also believed they could manipulate Christian teachings to enhance obedience in their converted bondspeople.

Parents, particularly mothers in abroad marriages and within matrifocal households, socialized their children to rely on their faith for survival and for a reality of their purpose beyond what their male and female enslavers tried to impose. Fannie Moore was proud to relay the story of how her mother's conversion helped her to withstand the awful whippings that she and her children had to endure on a South Carolina plantation. Her mother was a powerful example of the strength and resolve religious conversion provided the enslaved to resist the dehumanizing features of enslavement, an example that Fannie could emulate in her own life. "One day she [her mother] [was] plowin' in de cotton fiel'. All sudden like she let out a big yell," Fannie explained. "Den she start singin' an' a shoutin' an' a whoppin' an' a hollerin'. Den it seem she plow all de harder." When Fannie's mother returned to her captor's house that evening, a member of his family asked her why she had been making so much noise and accused her of using her religious outburst as an excuse not to work. "My mammy jes grin all over her Black wrinkled face," Fannie continued, "and say: 'I's saved. De Lawd done tell me I'se save. Now I know de Lawd will show me de way.'" The slaveholding woman to whom she was speaking immediately became angry and began to whip her, "but mammy nebber yell," Fannie added. "She jes go back to the fiel a singin.'"[184] Another former bondswoman recalled her mother's expression of faith and the influence that her parent's example had had on her own religious conversion. Watching her mother, who was a Baptist, singing and shouting attracted her to a tradition that seemingly could produce feelings of happiness and freedom even in the face of her oppression. "I went to church and tried to get religion," she explained, "because I wanted to shout like Mama."[185]

Still another woman revealed, in a lengthy explication of her own conversion experience, how her mother's and her aunt's examples of religious womanhood had influenced her. "My mother was a good old time Christian woman," she began.[186] She was impressed by their example and desired to imitate them, but she also was drawn to the notion of a spiritual experience that produced the kind of obvious comfort and joy her mother and aunt derived from their faith. "Me and my sister used to lay in bed at night and listen to her and my aunt talk about what God had done for them," she noted. "From this I began to feel like I could be a Christian."[187] This woman progressed through her conversion ordeal, again relying on her mother's guidance through the psychologically wrenching experience. "I got so I felt heavy and burdened down," she added. "My mother noticed it and asked me what was the matter. I told her I had heard a voice, and that I had been trying to pray. She clapped her hands and said 'Pray on daughter, for if the Master has started working, he will not stop until he has freed your soul.'"[188] A formerly enslaved woman from Tennessee also recounted how her mother had reassured her of the authenticity of her conversion visions, convincing her that God actually had spoken to her.[189]

Bethany Veney's female captor warned her, after she had caught the children taking apples off of a tree, that "every little child that told a lie would be cast into a lake of fire and brimstone, and would burn there for ever and ever."[190] Bethany was, in her own words, "dreadfully frightened" and decided to take her concerns to her mother, who, despite the young captor's claim to authority, still was the singular authority figure in Bethany's life, at least when it came to matters of religion and morality. Bethany's mother explained to her that sinners would be punished, but "those who told the truth and were good always would always have everything they should want." This promise resonated deeply within Bethany, helping to provide her with a spiritual and psychological wall against the hardships she faced while enslaved. Her mother's words of faith, she noted, "made a very strong impression upon me. . . . I believed every word she said, and from that day to this I have never doubted its truth."[191] Their belief communities also assured enslaved people that not only would God support them, but that their God also would punish those who harmed them. As Charles Crawley explained, "God is punishin' some of dem ole suckers an' dey chillum right now fer de way dey use to treat us po' cullud folks."[192] Fanny Berry concurred: "Do you know, God done whipped some of dem mean devils an' given 'em some dey own medicine?"[193]

The religion and religious communities embraced by enslaved people also were the source of happiness, identity, and a sense of worth and purpose beyond their propertied values assigned by the institution of slavery. "De most fun we had was at our meetin's," Clara Young shared. "De preacher I lakked de bes' was name Matthew Ewing. . . . [H]e sho' knowed his Bible, an' wud hole his han out an' mek lak he wuz readin', an' preach de purt'est preaching's you ever heard. De meetin's last from early in de mawnin' till late at night."[194] Emily Dixon felt similarly about the religious gatherings she attended but asserted in particular the importance of culturally bound worship traditions that attracted her to racially segregated meetings rather than integrated services. "On Sundays," she noted, "us would git together in de woods an' have worship. Us could go to de white folks' church, but us wanted to go where us could sing all de way through, an' hum 'long, an' shout—yo all know, jist turn loose lak."[195]

As Clara Young's memories suggest, enslaved Africans and African Americans who met separately from Whites often did not have Bibles to read; if they had them, they could not read them, and if they could read them, they chose different texts to emphasize. The songs they created also substituted for biblical text and a minister's sermon. "They say us can carry de song better than white folks," Dinah Cunningham explained. "Well, maybe us does love de Lord just a little bit better, and what in our mouth is in our hearts."[196] Minerva Grubb concurred. While reminiscing about how her plantation community combined religious worship with fieldwork, Grubb emphasized the permeable walls between the spheres of secular and sacred activity that characterized their worship style and belief systems. She also stressed important cultural, intellectual, and stylistic differences in Black and White worship modes: "[We] would git to singin', prayin', an' a shoutin'. When de overseer hear 'em, he always go make 'em be quiet. . . . You see de white folks don't git in de spirit. Dey don't shout, pray, hum, an' sing all through de services, lak us do."[197] She explained that their religion was centered not just on Christianity. "Dey [Whites] don't believe in a heap o' things us . . . knows 'bout. Dey tells us dey ain't no ghos', but us knows better'n dat."[198]

The creation of these religious communities with their own belief systems and styles of worship, by virtue of their existence and expression outside of the guise and control of enslavers, was a profound act of resistance that gave its members, both female and male, a sense of personal, familial, and communal value and control.[199] It also offered them hope for a future characterized by other kinds of empowerment and freedom. The newly converted mother of Fannie Moore shocked one of her South Carolina slaveholders when she told her that one day she would escape her abuse. "No matter how much yo' all done beat me an' my chillun de Lawd will show me de way," she asserted. "An' some day we nevah be slaves."[200]

The belief of eventual freedom was one routinely held. The connection between heavenly and earthly freedom was so important that many bondspeople rejected ministers and churches that were opposed to such aspirations. It certainly was the reason Loredo rejected her Louisiana Catholic Church. "I made my first communion when I was fifteen years old in the Catholic Church," she recalled, "and I was Catholic for a long time. I tell you, I used to think no other religion was good like mine. . . . I'd tell the priest everything I did wicked. But . . . one time I had a cousin that told the priest he wanted to get free, and asked him to pray to God to set him free, and . . . the priest was about to have my cousin hung. . . . [F]rom that day on I could not follow my Catholic religion like I had."[201]

Similarly, some White Islamic believers refused to abandon their faith for Christianity because white Christians appeared to them to be hypocrites. Abdul Rahman Ibrahima ibn, enslaved in Natchez, was clear when asked why he had not become a Christian. "The [New] Testament very good law; you [Christians]," he purportedly added, "no follow it; you no pray often enough; you greedy after money. [Y]ou good man, you join the religion. [Y]ou want more land, more neegurs; you make neegur work hard make more cotton. Where you find dat in you law."[202] Ibrahima, however, was married to a practicing Baptist.

Not a few slaveholders understood the power religion played in the spiritual imaginations of enslaved people to render their enslavers' authority as inferior to that of God's. "Down in Georgia," Andrew Moss explained, "us colored folks had prayer grounds. My Mammy's was a ole twisted thick-rooted muscadine bush. She'd go in dar and pray for deliverance of de slaves. Some colored folks cleaned out knee-spots in de cane breaks." According to

Andrew, they prayed in the cane breaks in order to avoid White interference in their sacred lives. If his enslaver found a bondsperson praying, he would ask him why he was doing so. If the enslaved replied that they were preparing for the afterlife, the enslaver would respond, "Youse my negro. I git ye to Heaven. Git up off'n your knees."[203]

Enslaved Black families rejected messages of captor dominance delivered as if they were biblical text. For them, these pronouncements lacked substance, spirit, and authority. "Dat ole white preachin' wasn't nothin'," Nancy Williams retorted. "Ole white preacher used to talk wid dey tongues widdout saying' nothin'[;] but Jesus told us slaves to talk wid our hearts."[204] Charlotte Brooks's assessment of her captor's religious practices in relation to her own was clear: "Mistress' religion did not make her happy like my religion did. I was a poor slave, and every body knowed I had religion, for it was Jesus with me everywhere I went. I could never hear her talk about that heavenly journey."[205] Matilda Perry and her kin went even further in delineating the differences between Black and White religiosity. For Perry, the two races did not even worship the same God. "White folks can't pray right to de black man's God," she explained. "Cain't nobody do it for you. You got to call on God yourself when de spirit tell you to and let God know dat you bin washed free from sin."[206]

One of their most constant indictments was the manner in which slaveholders distorted Christian text and rituals to benefit themselves. Alice Sewell of Alabama explained that her captors allowed their bondspeople to attend church, but she rejected their minister's message: "He never did tell us nothing but be good servants, pick up old marse and old misses' things about de place, and don't steal no chickens or pigs and don't lie 'bout nothing."[207] Sarah Douglass rendered a typical complaint when she explained the process by which Black worshippers at her church became members. After telling their "determination" to join the church and stating that they believed God had forgiven their sins, the minister would ask their enslavers of their "judgment" in the matter. "They would git up and say, 'I notice she don't steal, and I notice she don't lie as much, and I notice she works better.' Then they let us join. We served our mistress and master in slavery time, not God," she added angrily.[208] Sister Robinson complained that those enslaved on her plantation were not allowed to go to the "regulah" Sunday school, but they had to memorize a "catechism" just the same: "Be nice to massa an' missus, don't tell lies, don't be mean, be obedient, an' wuk hard."[209] A former bondswoman from Maryland who escaped to live free in Canada noted in her 1863 interview, "The ministers used to preach—'Obey your masters and mistresses and be good servants.' I never heard anything else. I didn't hear anything about obeying our Maker." Moreover, she emphasized, "those who were Christians & held slaves were the hardest masters. A card-player and drunkard wouldn't flog you half to dath."[210] Nineteenth-century female writers who had been enslaved detailed the hypocrisy of White "holy" men who would not heed their calls for help. Elizabeth Keckley famously wrote openly of her enslaver, a Presbyterian minister, who had a member of his congregation whip her barebacked and then, upon her questioning him as to why he had her beaten, struck her to the floor with a chair. He later beat her with the handle of an oak broom. Elizabeth fought back but was physically subdued. After this last whipping, she was unable to work for five days.[211]

Slaveholders refused to let enslaved folk worship if they could not control the message they received. Whites realized that the promise of "freedom" was an important tenet of most Black religion. Some rightly feared that enslaved people would try to use their religious beliefs and ideals to gain greater freedoms for themselves and family members. This was reiterated as their worst nightmare when religious leaders like Nat Turner were inspired to execute revolt. Additional surveillance ensured more control. Following the Turner rebellion, many captors did not allow their captives to hold religious services without a White person present who could prevent revolutionary discourse. Those enslaved on her plantation could go to church separately from Whites, Marrinda Jane Singleton asserted, but a "white preacher would be the overseer."[212] Many captors did not allow separate meetings at all, insisting that bondspeople worship with them, if they worshipped at all. "When Mammy was converted she jined the white folks church and was baptized by a white preacher 'cuse in dem days slaves all went to de same churches wid deir marster's famblies," Alice Green of Georgia noted.[213] Some enslaved African Americans, on the other hand, were not opposed to worshipping with Whites. Mary Frances Brown, who was a domestic in South Carolina, remembered the religious instructions of her captor fondly. "My missis was good to me," she noted, "teach me ebbery ting, and take the Bible and learn me Christianified manners, charity and behavior and good respect, and it with me still."[214]

Conversely, some antebellum slaveholders allowed their bondspeople religious privileges only rarely; others, not at all. "Church was something we seldom went to," former bondswoman Caroline Hunter explained. "We could sing an' shout 'round de house as much as we chose, but massa always said if we went to church we wouldn' keep our min's on our wuk durin' de week an' he would have to beat us. When we did go to church it was in de basement of de church dat massa an' missus went to."[215] "I did not know anything about the Bible and God. . . . I was almost grown before I had ever heard the bible read and the word of God explained," another explained. "When a slave I didn't know nothing but my earthly marster and mistress. We had to call them mars' and missey as soon as they were born, so I hadn't learnt anything about a heavenly Father and Marster of all."[216] When the local patrollers heard Blacks worshipping in their secret meetings, they would "horse whip ev'ry las' one o' dem, jes' 'cause de poor souls was prayin' to God to free 'm f'om dat awful bondage," Minnie Folkes recounted. "All dis was done to keep you f'om servin' God an' do you know some o' dem devils was mean an' sinful 'nough to say, 'Ef I ketch you heah agin servin' God, I'll beat you. You havn't time to serve God. We bought you to serve us.'"[217]

One of the most profound characteristics of African American religious life among enslaved families and communities, noted briefly in a prior chapter, was the syncretic terrain derived from a variety of West African and European religious mores. The religion of many enslaved Africans and African Americans was neither distinctly "Christian" or "African/Islamic"; but it operated between the complex array descriptive of these multifaceted traditions, often sharing similar forms, beliefs, practices, cosmologies, and even perceptions of who could, or who could not, be prominent within a community of devotees. All was passed down to, and shaped further by, younger kin and descendants. Being an enslaved Christian, for example, did not mean that one did not believe in some form of voodoo/hoodoo.[218]

Many couples turned to their non-Christian religious beliefs in their efforts to remain together or protect their children. "Doc Quinn" told of one remedy practiced to keep married couples together: "wrap a rabbit's forefoot, a piece of loadstone, and 9 hairs from the top of the head in red flannel, and bury it under the front door steps."[219] "[M]y mammy, Junny, wuz a queen in Africa," and a "witch," asserted a formerly enslaved woman born in 1835 in Wake County, North Carolina. "She tol' dem not ter tell hit an' dey doan tell, but when dey is out of sight of de white folkses dey bows down ter her an' does what she says." Junny probably exhibited an array of powers to her devotees, but they especially appreciated her ability to predict the future through an interpretation of signs. "A few days 'fore de surrender," Junny's daughter added, "mammy . . . says ter dem dat she sees hit in de coffee grounds dat dey am gwine ter be free so all' o' us packs up an' gits out."[220] Laura Towne wrote of Maum Katie "an old African woman, who remember[ed] worshipping her own gods in Africa." According to Towne, Maum Katie was more than one hundred years old and was a "spiritual mother, . . . fortune teller or, . . . prophetess, . . . a woman of tremendous influence over her spiritual children."[221] On one of the plantations belonging to the husband of the English actress and author Frances Kemble, Sinda was another bound woman, perhaps an African, who also exerted much religious power over those who believed she could predict the future.[222]

Not surprisingly, most captors did not support religious practices or rituals linked to their bondspeople's ancestral pasts. Even the most "sympathetic" of White Christian observers and "allies" easily dismissed them as "savage." Towne penned a typical response when she witnessed her first of such ritual displays: "To-night I have been to a 'shout,' which seems to me certainly the remains of some old idol worship," she began her description: "The negroes sing a kind of chorus,—three standing apart to lead and clap,—and then all the others go shuffling round in a circle following one another with not much regularity, turning round occasionally and bending the knees, and stamping so that the whole floor swings. I never saw anything so savage. They call it a religious ceremony, but it seems more like a regular frolic."[223]

FAMILY, FOOD, AND MEDICAL CARE

Individual, familial, and communal religious beliefs and practices addressed emotional and spiritual needs. Food and medical attention provided for physical wants. Outdoor and indoor food preparation was a necessary part of enslaved family life and culture. Slaveholders provided some of the staples that bondspeople consumed—mostly rationed cornmeal, coffee, and pork—although some also gave mush (milk and cornbread mixed together) to small children. For those close to a fish-bearing body of water, as many in the tidewater, low country, and gulf regions were, fish were sometimes added to rations. Silas Jackson of Ashbie's Gap in Virginia remembered that "our food was cooked by our mothers or sisters and for those who were not married by the old women and men assigned for that work." Enslaved people he knew also fished and hunted, grew vegetables, raised poultry on allotted plots, and received rations of cornmeal, flour, blackstrap molasses, and pork fatback.[224]

Wealthy enslavers had cooks to prepare midday meals. Some served food in the quarters and occasionally at the captors' houses. Carrie Davis of Georgia recalled that her parents and siblings, and others in the quarters, ate their supper at their slaveholder's home. "Us et at de big house. 'Course de food was cooked on de fireplace, but us had meat and greens but not much biscuits. Us had collards an' cabbage, too."[225] Female captors with few bondspeople under their command also sometimes prepared meals or portions of them.

Some remembered the food that enslavers provided with more delight than others. Millie Barber recalled that her mother's captor allotted "peas, hog meat, corn bread, 'lasses, and buttermilk on Sunday," but mostly vegetables during the week. The children ate at the "kitchen out-house."[226] While the food the enslavers supplied often was poor in nutritional value, monotonous in flavor, and minimal in amount, bondsmen and bondswomen took the opportunity to supplement their diets in order to increase the variety, taste, and nutritional value of meals—in the process, conveying their love and concern for their kin, especially their children.

All family members, regardless of gender or age, contributed to the family plate by working the little patches of garden space that captors sometimes allowed and drawing on the natural resources of the local forests and waterways. Adolescent and adult male kinfolk chopped wood; hunted; fished; netted clams, crabs, and other shellfish; and dug garden spaces. Along with female kin, they sold or traded excess food and other crops if allowed to do so (and if not, some did so clandestinely). Ria Sorrell of North Carolina said that her captor allowed them to have patches and gave them time off to work their gardens and "all dey made on it."[227] Annie Parks of Louisiana explained that her "father could have an extra patch and make a bale of cotton or whatever he wanted to on it. That was so that he could make a little money to buy things for hisself and his family."[228] Lunsford Lane felt it his responsibility to provide adequate food and clothing for his family. When they changed hands and their new enslaver reduced support, he used the money he had been saving to purchase their freedom to take suitable care of their material needs.[229] Carrie Davis of Georgia knew that even though her kin ate at their captor's house, both married and single men provided supplements that added variety. "Sometimes us would have wild game, 'case de men hunted lots an' kotched rabbits, 'possums and coons. Dey also kotched a lot of fish."[230] Others caught and devoured birds, deer, wild turkey, and boars.[231]

Women and older girls gardened, hunted, and fished, too, especially those mothers without local husbands or male kin who could help. Females commonly planted and grew vegetables, including corn, rice, sugar cane, a variety of peas, collards, and cabbage. They caught and cleaned fish, raised fowl, hunted small animals, and usually cooked family meals. Emily Burke, a northern teacher, wrote to her friends of the hard work enslaved people dedicated to their garden plots, even working well into the night. "In this way," Burke explained, "they often raise considerable crops of corn, tobacco and potatoes, besides various kinds of garden vegetables." They consumed their harvest and traded parts of it for staples that enslavers did not provide, such as tea, coffee, sugar, and flour, as well as additional clothing.[232] Amanda Ross of Arkansas remembered that they "et what was raised" and kept their food in boxes and gourds her parents made: "My mammy had a lot of 'em and they were nice and clean too."[233] According to a former captive from Kentucky, his mother did most of her cooking over a "bed of coals" in a yard oven. They ate "baked possum and ground hog, . . . stewed rabbits, fried fish and fried bacon," along with vegetables, cornbread, and molasses. Adults drank coffee and children had milk.[234] Meals sometimes included eggs, chickens, and other fowl, when captors allowed bondspeople to raise them (or when they, under cover of night, stole and cooked them anyway). Mothers, of course, also nursed their infants and toddlers, usually for about two years, providing them with much-needed comfort, intimacy, food, and immunity. Older children contributed to the familial table by collecting kindling, discarded cotton, and flint rocks to start fires; washing dishes; tending to family garden spaces; picking wild berries, fruit, and wild greens; and sometimes trapping small animals and birds.[235]

Antebellum Black food culture created in the quarters, ritualized in special recipes on specific occasions or times of the year, linked enslaved families to their western/western central African past, but also extended these traditions to incorporate animals, plants, spices, and recipes available in the Americas. The recipes and tastes passed, along with their historical context, from one family generation to the next. Charley Barber of South Carolina recalled that his parents, who both were brought from Africa, continued to long for their birth cuisine. They "want deir collards, turnips, and deir 'tators, raw" and loved "sweet milk."[236] When child domestic Cheyney Cross of Alabama did get to visit her grandmother in the quarters, it was a cherished treat to learn how to prepare and eat the elder's food. "My gran'ma," she stated, "hung dat pot up on dem pot hooks over de fire an' washed de meat an' drap it in. Time she done pick an' overlook de greens an' den wrinched 'em in spring water, de meat was bilin'. Den she take a great big mess of dem fresh turnip greens an' squash 'em down in dat pot. Dey jes' melt down an' go to seasonin'."[237]

Corn shucking, logrolling, and Christmas were special times of ritualized food, replete with delicious and rarely accessible cuisine items. Frank Gill loved the food that enslaved women cooked communally and served at logrolling. "De women would help wid de cookin'," he noted, "an' you may be shore dey had something to cook. Dey would kill a cow, or three or four hogs, and den hab peas, cabbage, an' everything lack grows on de farm."[238]

Enslaved people took some of the most coveted food from their owners. Lewis Clark of Kentucky told how Aunt Peggy, who cooked for her family, him, and another single man named George, took pigs for them to eat when their captor deprived them of the food they needed or wanted. "It was a kind of first principle, too, in her code of morals," he explained, "that they that *worked* had a right to eat."[239] It was a lesson Aunt Peggy passed on to an impressionable Lewis and to her children. They each kept watch for one another. When Lewis's attempt at getting a pig failed, he luckily "escaped detection" and being brutally whipped as a punishment, but he still had to "suffer" the "ridicule of old Peggy and young George."[240] Uncle Griffin recalled with absolute glee the hogs eaten at secret barbeques on Saturday nights. We had "de mos'es fun at a barbecue dat dare is to be had" he noted, until they were caught and punished for "stealing."[241] Charley Barber's African parents pilfered the milk that was such an important part of their traditional diet.[242]

Growing vegetables and picking fruit and herbs went hand in hand with medicinal care of one's kin. The forest yielded much of what they gathered, dried, ground, stored, and mixed to produce medicines from available "roots, herbs and flowers."[243] Both men and women performed as doctors and nurses in their families, and the Black community held their scientific knowledge in high esteem.[244] Mammy Mary certainly had the confidence of those she helped. So, too, did the midwife or granny on Rebecca Hooks's plantation in Georgia who "doctored" all the enslaved and free women. Her arsenal of medicines included horehound and pine top teas, lightwood drippings on sugar to help with colds, a tea made of pomegranate seed and crushed mint for fevers, catnip and sheep shandy teas for whooping cough, and garlic as one remedy for "spasms."[245] According to Georgia Baker, Mammy Mary's expertise also lent itself to her making different "teas " (or liquid medications from boiled leaves and roots) to address certain "ailments . . . boneset tea was for colds . . . for sore throat . . . tea made of red oak bark wid alum. Scurvy grass tea cleant us out in the springtime, and . . . [we] wear little sacks of assfiddy [asafetida] 'round our necks to keep off lots of sorts of miseries."[246] It also was popular to wear little necklaces of pawpaw seeds to ward off illness.[247] Many relied on Jerusalem brush-reed and chinaberry tea to treat parasitic infections, which were rampant in the shoeless South, and "life-everlasting tea" for fevers.[248] A bondsman from Alabama also knew of the use of "bone-set" tea to "sweat" out colds and fever, but also "bleeding" for other sickness.[249] Another Alabama resident recalled that her grandmother took care of the family's medical needs. The older woman was, according to her unofficial biographer, "a great doctor" and a "midwife" who would administer homemade "teas" for illnesses and "turpentine and castor oil" to rid children of worms (roundworm, tapeworm, hookworm) which were a common and sometimes life-threatening illness for enslaved children.[250] In South Carolina, some healers prescribed the water of boiled branch elder twigs and dogwood berries to end chills.[251] A female doctor, also from South Carolina, added teas made from cherry bark and peach leaves to the list of remedies.[252] Others gave black snakeroot and Sampson snakeroot added to whiskey and sometimes sugar to increase appetites and settle upset stomachs.[253]

Black doctors often combined natural medicines and medical experiences with conjure to treat the ill. Indeed some, White southerners among them, considered conjurers to be skilled medical experts. Tishey Taylor of Missouri recalled that when they were sick, "mos' de time 'Old Uncle Nee John' and 'Uncle Jake' would conjure us; they was called 'Voo-Doo's.'"[254] Patsy Moses remembered how her "conjure doctor, old Dr. Jones . . . walk 'bout in de Black coat like a preacher, and wear sideburns, and use roots and sich for he medicine." According to Patsy, his "old granny" taught Dr. Jones what plants and roots to cure various illnesses. "He didn't cast spell like de voodoo doctor," she added, "but used roots" and combinations of natural elements to treat common illnesses including smallpox, mumps, whooping cough, and snakebite.[255]

Adults gave particular medical attention to children. Enslaved youth up to the age of ten were prone to serious illness and early death, given the limited attention, nutrition, and other material resources that captors afforded them. For example, between 1823 and 1863, only six of forty-five children on the Whitney sugar plantation near New Orleans lived past the age of four.[256] Among the thirty enslaved persons who died from cholera on Hill Carter's Shirley Plantation in Virginia in 1849, thirteen were ten years or younger. Mothers, their closest caretakers, also suffered early deaths. Records indicate that among the Shirley dead were Fanny and her son Fielding; Judy and her one-year-old; and Mary Ann and her two children, Smith and Nelly.[257]

The poor health and loss of enslaved children began even before they were born. Sexual violence, forced reproductive labor, and whether or not Black bound women had knowledge of abortifacients—and, if so, how frequently they used them—affected their childbearing success and the frequency of stillbirths and miscarriages. So, too, did their work routines and punishments; lack of nutritional, familial, and medicinal resources; overall health; breastfeeding customs; and proximity to husbands, lovers, or even breeding men. Josephine Bacchus of South Carolina replied to a query about her pregnancy experience: "I ain't never had a nine months child. . . . Being dat I never had no mother to care for me en give me a good attention like, I caught so much of cold dat I ain' never been safe in de family way."[258] A former Mississippi bondsman graphically recalled that his mother died in miscarriage brought on by a cruel whipping. "When the women slaves were in an advanced stage of pregnancy," he explained, "they were made to lie face down in a specially dug depression in the ground and were whipped."[259] Odee Jackson of Louisiana remembered the same kind of punishment for a pregnant bondswoman, explaining, "They didn't want her child to get hurted. It worth money. Then they would bat her 'til her back was a mass of blood. After that they'd rub salt into it, or throw a bucket of salt and water over her."[260,]

Frances Kemble recorded some of the most painful oral histories of the treatment of mothers and their children on her husband's Georgia Sea Island plantations. There was the bondswoman Die, who had sixteen children, fourteen of whom had not lived to maturity. Four of her pregnancies had ended in miscarriage. The bereaved mother noted that "one had been caused by falling down with a very heavy burthen on her head, and one from having her arms strained up [while partially nude and tied to a tree post] to be lashed" with a "rawhide."[261] Die, and all of the other mothers on the Butler plantations, had little chance to care for their infants, since they had to return to the fields three weeks after giving birth. When they complained about the lack of time that they had to clean and care for their children, overseers whipped them.[262] Another woman who appealed to Kemble for help had witnessed nine of her fifteen children die.[263] One of their overseers had even threatened to whip the enslaved woman Caroline, who said she could not work because of a fever and a chill. Caroline had been sick since she "had been delivered of a dead child about six weeks before." In the overseer's opinion, she was feigning illness to avoid work—"the laziest woman on the estate."[264] While most enslaved pregnant women had the assistance of a midwife among the Black community, Malindy Maxwell recalled that a White midwife and her female captor attended her risky breech birth.[265] A few enslavers also hired physicians to assist with enslaved womens' birthing and other reproductive issues.[266]

Not surprisingly, mothers and other family members often looked for signs of sickness, even supernatural ones, and routinely calling on local conjurers to keep their children safe and well. A dog sliding on his stomach convinced one former enslaved woman that her child's death was imminent. Some feared that dreaming about a new baby could predict death of another baby or person.[267] Easter Wells of Texas feared that a mule or dog behaving strangely would signify the coming demise of one's child.[268] When they named their babies, it often was with the purpose of extending memories of their familial past and connecting their children to their ancestors.

Some relied on traditional western/western central African naming practices for their children—that is, if their captors allowed them to do so openly. Some named their offspring after ancestral kin, as the Kongo peoples did. Others gave their children names of places where they had lived before being sold, a kind of mapping of their kin/communal geographies. Some had "day names," a tradition of the Akan-Twi and Igbo. Others had "basket names," or those known only by kin and close friends.[269] Enslaved people also had second and third names, which were titles that extended family used to identify blood relations. These practices helped to seal familial and cultural intimacies that outsiders misunderstood or missed altogether. Among the Gullah, for example, Elizabeth Botume had to confess that she was "forced to believe that all belonged to one immense family," since they called each other not only by first names but generally "bubber" for brother, "titty" for sister, "nanna" for mother, "mother" for grandmother, and "father for all leaders in the church and society."[270]

Most took the medical care of family members very seriously, but some did not welcome all sorts. They feared and resented enslavers, members of their communities, and even kin, whom they believed imposed their knowledge, privilege, and power for malevolent purposes against them. Tom Wylie Neal of Georgia noted that "witches took on other forms and went out to do meanness," and that a bondsperson would kill them once they discovered them.[271] Likewise, not all captors approved all medical interventions for their captives. One, Drew Norwood of Virginia, even whipped his own pregnant wife when she tried to dress the wounds of an enslaved woman named Luzanne, whom Norwood had beaten because she purportedly burned his biscuits. The story passed down to Dave Lawson was that a pregnant Mrs. Cary Norwood gave Luzanne some salve to treat the cuts on her back. Her husband angrily responded by whipping his wife because "when he want his niggers doctored he . . . gwine doctor dem hese'f." According to Lawson, "Mis' Cary got so skeered dat de baby come dat night befo' 'twuz time. De baby wuz bawn dead an' Mis' Cary went on to glory wid it."[272]

There were many instances when female captors, such as Fanny Berry's Miss Sarah Ann and Mrs. Norwood, provided medical care for infirm workers. In contrast to Norwood's objections, many enslavers expected their wives to treat their ill "property" as part of their routine domestic duties. "Old Mistress Emily was a doctor woman," Mary Scott DeValls Biscoe of Arkansas testified. When a young enslaver hit Mary with a heavy stick, causing a permanent injury, it was the older enslaver who cleaned the maggot-ridden wound and helped it to heal, at least temporarily. "Mistress Emily kept me a month with her and doctored my head every day. I slept on a pallet and on a little bed she had in the room," the former bondswoman recalled.[273] Mary's mother was not available to help the child because she had died in childbirth a short time before Mary's assault.

Male captors, too, sometimes could be found assisting with the medical care of their "property."[274] One enslaved man recalled that if the "boneset" tea did not cure the illness, they went to their enslaver, who always paid for doctors when valuable captives were "powerful sick."[275] Another former captive explained that the slaveholder gave everyone a glass of whiskey at dinner and a glass of tar water in the morning to keep them healthy.[276] Those slaveholders, male and female, who did not provide adequate medical attention risked being sued if they tried to pass off a sick bondsperson as a healthy one during a sale. Asthma,[277] epilepsy,[278] extreme rheumatism, damaged or irregularly formed bones or musculature, and infertility, along with stubborn cases of venereal diseases, were conditions considered serious enough to cancel or revoke a purchase or even a rental agreement. One slaveholder in South Carolina sued in 1822 because he bought a woman suffering from venereal disease whom he also claimed had "communicated the disease to others of his negroes, by which he had incurred great losses and expenses." Her former captor countered that he had paid for her medical attention and that she seemed cured after a "course of medicine."[279] These types of lawsuits were not limited to physical illness, but also mental disorders,[280] which were covered in the contractual guarantee of a "sound" bondsperson.[281] Among the extensive papers of the Carter family at Shirley Plantation in Virginia are several receipts for the care of Hill Carter's enslaved woman, Celia, in the Eastern Lunatic Asylum in Williamsburg.[282] Slaveholders also sued, and won, in court when they believed that physicians had neglected to treat competently ailing captives.[283]

ELDERLY FAMILY MEMBERS

Older men and women had diverse—and essential—roles in enslaved families. Not only did their mere survival underscore the necessity of perseverance in the face of awful odds against Black life, but their narratives of what and how they survived and how they resisted and even found moments of joy and fulfillment helped their descendants and larger communities to navigate the violence, evil, and dehumanization of chattel slavery. Their crucial socialization included passing on lucrative skills to the younger generations. Calvin Moye's enslaver ordered his elderly blacksmith, Uncle Zeke, to train the adolescent. Uncle Zeke did the job patiently and efficiently. "Uncle Zeke was watchin' and tellin' me all de time," Calvin noted, "and befo' we got through he said I was about as good as he was."[284]

More than a few enslaved people had no recollection of their recent ancestors, since they had either died before they were born or were sold away. Calvin, who so appreciated the role Uncle Zeke played in his life, still had cause to complain that he did not have the opportunity to know, love, and learn from his elderly blood relations. "I never did know anything about my grandmamas and grandpapas. There wasn't many slaves dat could tells you about dem, either, and plenty of dem didn't knows anything about der mothers and fathers. The plantation owners just sold and traded Negroes . . . like de horses and cattle," he noted.[285]

Many older bondspeople continued to work until the day they died, but their job descriptions typically shifted to more domestic and "scrap" work or selling market wares rather than full days in the fields planting, weeding, and harvesting. On any site where there were a few or more enslaved children, elderly enslaved men or women might be assigned to care for them, and for White children as well. As Ed McCree of Georgia noted, those who were too small and weak to do field work carried water to field hands and "waited on de old' omas what was too old to wuk. . . . Den old' 'omans looked atter de babies and piddled 'round de yards."[286] Another formerly enslaved survivor recalled his maternal grandmother, Grandma Cindy. As an elderly woman, "Marster let her do odd jobs 'round de big house. De most I seed her doin' was settin' 'rond smokin' her old corncob pipe."[287] Grandpa Stafford, William McWhorter recalled, was from Virginia. "He was a old man what slept on a trundle bed in de kitchen, and all he done was to set by the fire all day wid a switch in his hand and tend de chillun."[288] Those who treated older people well left a lasting good impression on Black family members, particularly formerly enslaved elders living through the deprivation of the Great Depression as context for their recollections. "I had a good master," Bill Simmons of Missouri claimed. "When a slave got too old to work they would give him a small cabin on the plantation and have the other slaves wait on him. They would furnish him with victuals, and clothes until he died."[289]

Many, however, did not witness laudable treatment of old and infirm family members. Earlier in the nineteenth century, Sojourner Truth witnessed her elderly parents being "freed" once they were past productivity. Their children, sold elsewhere, were unable to assist. Her mother, Mum Bett, was much younger than the father, Bomefree, and was able to care for him for a short time. When Mum Bett died unexpectedly, Bomefree had to rotate between past captors' establishments, the care given by another elderly freed couple, Betty and Caesar, and self-care, which he could hardly manage. After Betty and Caesar died, Bomefree was left alone, "blind" and close to "helpless," unable even to clean himself. He died, "chilled and starved, with none to speak a kindly word, or do a kindly deed for him, in that last dread of hour of need!"[290]

Formerly enslaved people were not the only ones who exposed the ill treatment of bondspeople past their "prime." Frances Kemble wrote of the "old and infirm-looking" women who had never had proper medical treatment and, when elderly, suffered from pain and material want. Kemble quoted Nancy, who spoke for her enslaved community when she declared, with tears of pain from an ulcerated leg, "I have worked every day through dew and damp, and sand and heat, and done good work; but oh, missis, me old and broken now, no tongue can tell how much I suffer."[291]

Chapter 6

Death and Resurrection

> Won't you help to sing
> These songs of freedom?
> 'Cause all I ever have
> Redemption songs[1]

"Death," Charles Ball recalled sadly of his friend Lydia's attitude about her impending demise, "was to her a welcome messenger who came to remove her from toil that she could not support, and from misery that she could not sustain." The young woman died from "consumption of the lungs" and a life of hardship and grief. Her death could not have arrived quickly enough for the woman after the loss of her infant son just three months earlier. The mother's grief was marked, like many aspects of enslaved life, with multiple, even conflicting responses. How heartbreakingly sad it was that Lydia's beautiful son was gone, but her despondency was haunted by her relief that he was "out of a world in which slavery and wretchedness must have been its only portion."[2] Ball helped to bury Lydia beside her son in the appointed graveyard. Speaking her name and telling her story in his autobiographical account have had to suffice as her eulogy and redemption song.

For others, their physical remains also form a type of eulogy. The small number of substantial archeological digs of plantations and other work sites of the enslaved have brought to light the circumstances of some of their lives and deaths. For example, Palmetto Grove Plantation near Charleston had a cemetery where thirty-six skeletons of persons who had been enslaved during the antebellum years were found. Analyses of their remains documented the harsh work and lifestyle as well as the material deprivation that, collectively, hurried Black bondspeople to the grave. Men and women died young on the low country plantation, with lifespans of thirty-five years for the former

A NEGRO FUNERAL.

Funeral on a Rice Plantation, c. 1859. "Funeral on a Rice Plantation,"1859, *Harper's New Monthly Magazine* 19. Courtesy of the American Antiquarian Society. Catalog Record 17781.

and forty for the latter. Indications of poor diet were particularly strong for children after they were weaned, with many suffering from anemia. Most had also been exposed to high levels of lead. Among adults, there was skeletal evidence of extreme stress on the shoulders and hips due to hard labor.[3] Likewise, the skeleton of an enslaved man in colonial Delaware indicated a blow to his upper face so hard that it chipped a piece of skull bone close to his eyebrow. The thirty-five-year-old's spine showed the effects of the hard labor he had been forced to perform.[4] The collarbones of a young enslaved Ashanti woman in Maryland, whose re-created face is seen in the illustration on page 275, document as well her hard agricultural labor.[5]

While no remains have been identified as those of the people Charles Ball described, he noted in detail one child's burial—the son of his friend Lydia. The boy's father, a man who had been a highly respected priest in his African homeland, had made certain to bury their child traditionally, ritually designating their son's resurrection to be in the land of, and among, his ancestors. His careful priestly preparations—finding or constructing,

Her Recreated Likeness. "The Young Woman from Harleigh Knoll," National Museum of Natural History, The Smithsonian Institution. Photo by Chip Clark, Smithsonian Institution. Sculpted bust by StudioEIS.

painting, inscribing, and assembling the necessary burial items—were a moving testament to the man's deep love for the boy, his religious knowledge, and identity with his African kin as well as his insistence that his son would live again, free in his ancestral homeland with family. The doting father buried the child with "a small bow, and several arrows; a little bag of parched meal; a miniature canoe about a foot long and a little paddle, with which he said he [his son] would cross the ocean to his own country." The priest also included a stick to which he attached a flag marked with red and blue figures he had painted on that would allow his "countrymen" to know that this was his son—their family—and welcome him among them. Lastly, the grieving father placed hair from his head in the child's grave, then sealed the burial place with the dream that they both would be resurrected and reunited in their homeland.[6] Physical death promised a resurrection of one's unfettered spiritual essence, reunion with ancestors, and a revered presence among one's earthbound clan. As Charles wrote of the enslaved Africans he encountered: "They are universally of opinion, and this opinion is founded in their religion, that after death they shall return to their own country, and rejoin their former companions and friends, in some happy region, in which they will be provided with plenty of food, and beautiful women, from the lovely daughters of their own native land."[7]

For many people, including the majority of enslaved Africans and African Americans who believed in an active spirit world of ancestors, death was an ending, but also a beginning and a continuation. Resurrection was a part of bondsperson's worldview, regardless of if one's faith was Christian, Muslim, of indigenous African sacred practice, or a syncretic blend.[8] Countless generations, from the colonial era up through the Civil War, experienced the institution of slavery itself as a kind of near-death experience—at least when viewed through the lens of lack of control over one's body, kinship ties, and familial obligations—that only freedom or one's physical end could terminate. As William Johnson, a self-emancipated man from Virginia, noted from the safety of freedom in Canada, "I look upon slavery as I do upon a deadly poison. . . . I would rather have died on the way than to go back."[9] "We would not even shed a tear," a former bondswoman explained of her community's expression at a funeral, "because he was gone where there would not be any more slaves. That was all the slaves thought about then: not being a slave."[10] In many cases across the generations, as earlier chapters have documented, to be enslaved meant facing the possibility of death at any moment. M. Valsin Mermillion in antebellum Louisiana, for example, gained the reputation as the "crudest" slaveholder for nailing a captive in a tightly fitted coffin. Another time he commanded a disobedient adolescent to dig his own grave before shooting him over it.[11] Is it no wonder that death was often welcome because the threat of it was so palpable?

Slavery was not only a kind of loss of life but also a living "hell."[12] For those who claimed Christianity as their religious faith, heaven, the antithesis of hell, was their eventual destination and a meeting place of family and friends. One woman named Mary had managed to free herself and two daughters and was working to purchase her son, but she died before she was able to do so. He explained that one of his sisters had let him know that their mother "hoped to meet me in heaven, if she was not permitted to see me on earth again."[13] Resurrection for her was the fantastical, restorative promise of a reunited family in heaven.

Regardless of what the otherworldly future held, bonded life in real time was filled with deprivation and the death of a loved one—a husband or wife, child, parent, friend, or lover—still was painful to bear. Sarah Fitzpatrick of Alabama lamented "deaf' jes' comes on 'yer lacka thief in de night an' steals 'yer love' uns way."[14] Susan Brooks of Norfolk recalled that she was so hurt by her husband's death that she experienced "alarming fits" on "two or three occasions."[15] Harriet Jacobs of North Carolina sadly remembered how devastated she was at the loss of her maternal aunt. Likewise, the death of her grandmother's last daughter left the elderly woman inconsolable.[16] One woman was so certain that her husband would not be able to carry on without a wife after she died that she chose a new one for him when she was on her deathbed. "I can't lef' poor Billy here all alone," she told a witness to her wishes. "He can't fend fur hisself no how, an' he can't live alone. So I axes sister Hagar to come here and tuck my place, an' min' Billy, a' the house ... I gives Billy to she."[17]

Across time and their communities, funerals, burials, and remembrance rituals took different forms due to competing forces, including captors' input, locations, work schedules, and the cultural beliefs and practices of those honoring the lives and wishes of the dead. Captors typically determined whether there was a public funeral, when one was buried, and where. Not surprisingly, family members often resented the irreverent ways in which enslavers treated their loved ones at death, as they had done in life. When we die, Alice Sewell of Missouri explained, "dey bury us next day and you is just like any of de other cattle dying on de place. Dat's all 'tis to it and all 'tis of you."[18] "Us never had no big fun'als," Dora Franks of Mississippi complained. "All de cullud folks was buried on what dey called Platnum Hill. Dey didn' have no markers nor nothin' at de graves. Dey was jus' sunk in places. My brother Frank showed me once where my mammy was buried."[19] Like Dora, Mary Gaffney of Texas remembered only the barest of funerary ceremonies: "When a slave died, we just dug a hole in the ground, built a fence around it, and piled him in. No singing, no preaching or praying, ever took place during slavery time."[20] John Sella Martin lamented that his mother was "buried in unconsecrated ground, outside the graveyard for the whites, and her grave was walked over every day by the beasts of the field."[21] Others noted that, as in life, imposed work schedules determined much about the events that transpired after a loved one died. Lewis Jones stated that "a short time before I come away my aunt died, all the kin I had, and they wouldn't let me go to the funeral. They said, 'the time couldn't be spared.'"[22] Georgia Baker said that she never went to "no baptisms nor no funerals neither, den she 'members very well when Aunt Sally and Aunt Catherine died," they were just placed in a "box" and buried.[23] James Smith told of one incident concerning an enslaved woman whose baby had died. When her family and friends requested permission to have a funeral and bury the baby on that Sunday, her captor replied that they could bury the baby but "without funeral services."

They interred the child, but that night about fifty to seventy enslaved people nonetheless met secretly at a cabin in a remote location to hold the services.[24]

Smith's example documents a reality: despite adverse barriers, death was too significant an event in one's life and the life of one's family and community to go unmarked by those who could manage, even clandestinely, to do so. Burials often took place on the first day or two after the passing, both for hygienic reasons and so that workers could return to their scheduled tasks as soon as possible. This would have been especially so during planting and harvest seasons, when captors fiercely protected their production demands.

Family and community members had special duties of burial and remembrance, typically determined by gender, expertise, age, and relationship to the deceased. Everyone had a role, even if it was only as mournful attendant or observer who could relate the event in the family's oral history. Women washed, cared for, and dressed female bodies, while men usually helped dress the males, and then wrapped them in a cloth. Some were dressed in all of their clothing, because there was a belief that to wear a dead person's clothing would cause one to "die hisself real soon."[25] One former bondswoman from Missouri recalled that all of the dead in her vicinity were handled by an elderly woman on their plantation, perhaps because of her role as medicine woman, caretaker of the infirm, keeper of community rituals, and respected leader due to her advanced age, which aligned her closely with ancestors. She "said de funeral sayings by herself. She knew it by heart."[26] Others reported that several other members of the community had tasks attendant to burial and remembrance.

When communities required that the dead be kept in their home until buried, the "sitting up" or "wake" was an essential ritual. As Hemp Kennedy noted, "Dey neber lef a dead . . . 'lone in de house, but all de neighbors was dere an' helped. Dey turned de mirrors to de wall" so that the person's spirit would not remain. At the wake, "we clapped our hands an' kept time wid our feet—Walking Egypt, dey call hit—an we chant an hum all night" until the funeral.[27]

Enslaved carpenters made the coffins, an important service for families and communities. Some, however, were interned in the earth without the benefit of a coffin. West Turner in Virginia reported that the overseer would tie the dead to a wooden board from the local sawmill that was shaped to have a "point" at the head and foot, then have the body placed in a grave.[28] Still, other evidence suggests that many indeed were buried in coffins. For example, 86 percent of the graves that archeologists could excavate at the African Burial Ground in New York City (1630s–1795) contained remains buried in coffins, a strong indication of the prevalence of coffin burials at least in urban colonial America.[29]

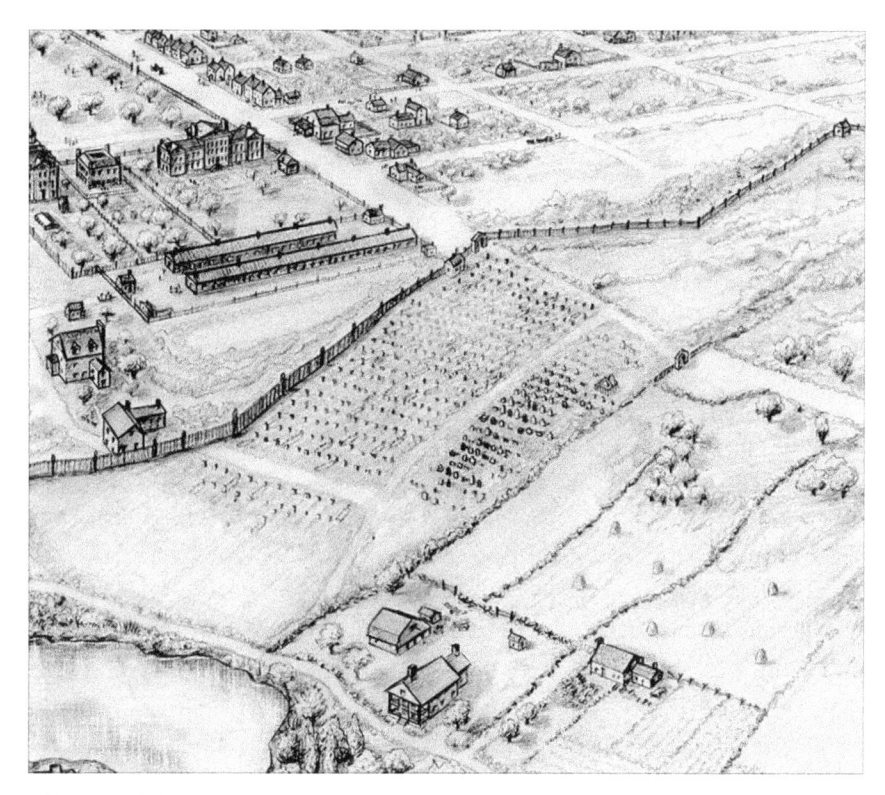

African Burial Ground, New York City, c. late 1700s. Unknown author, Public domain, via Wikimedia Commons.

Calvin Moye and Uncle Zeke made the coffins on their plantation in Texas. "De coffins was made out of pine or some other soft lumber," Calvin recalled, "and we lined dem wid black cloth dat was made and dyed on de plantation. We had to make de planks and plan dem smooth wid de tools we had in de shop."[30] Female community members no doubt made the cloth and colored it, but the cotton came from the efforts of all the field people. Some women also helped to design burial cloth with special details. When Rody Hodell's mother died "her coffin was made right out on de work bench." She was wrapped in a "winding sheet scalloped nicely and a shroud for de body."[31] Isaam Morgan remembered that the men "make de coffins right on de place dar."[32] Bonded blacksmiths produced the nails.[33] Neal Upson testified that enslaved carpenters measured the bodies and made the coffins accordingly. As with deceased White peoples' coffins, they lined those for bondspeople with black calico and painted the exterior black or covered it with the same calico.[34] Some enslaved people also were buried with beaded jewelry and other keepsakes reminiscent of their lives or that might be useful to them in

John Antrobus, *A Plantation Burial*, c. 1860. John Antrobus, *A Plantation Burial*, c.1860, oil on canvas, The Historical New Orleans Collection, The L. Kemper and Leila Moore WIlliams Founders Collection, 1960.46

their afterlives.[35] Grave toppings, too, included items symbolic of one's life, family, and sacred allegiances. Archeologists and other scholars have compiled lists of these items, documenting that the most frequently found include bottles, pottery, seashells, and reflective glass.[36]

The community expected every available family member and friend who could do so to attend the funeral in the quarters or at the designated burial plot, usually located in a distant field. Austin Steward, who was enslaved in Virginia, described a funeral of several enslaved men killed by patrollers. The attendants marched in the following order: At the front of the procession was a local enslaved minister who prayed, repeated scripture, preached, and sang hymns. Next came the "remains of the dead," followed by "weeping relatives," along with captors and plantation community members paying their "qualified" respects. Last in the queue were "friends and strangers, black and white," lengthening the mourning space, all eventually arriving at the place of burial.[37]

Gravesites could be a place of collective burials of the enslaved; singular, isolated spots; or large designated areas that included both deceased captives and their captors. One formerly enslaved man described their burial place as a plantation "pasture over in one corner" that was fenced in and kept tidy by the men.[38] Another noted that deceased bondspeople were buried on their plantation with rocks "put up fer tombstones."[39] The cemetery at Rachel Cruze's farm was "on the hill."[40] Malindy Maxwell's grandfather was taken back to his original captor's plantation to be interred. It was his former enslaver's "request [that] all his slaves be brought back and buried on his land." Surprisingly, all of his family were able to attend. "We all got to go—all who wanted to go," Malindy noted. "It was John Saunders let us go mean as he was."[41]

Community musicians were very important to death and remembrance rituals. Even today, music remains a central cultural marker for life stage transitions in the Black community. The "jazz funerals" in New Orleans are among the most well-known of these events and are directly related to African ancestral rites of passage. Singing at funerals of the enslaved was of the utmost importance. Vinnie Bruson of Texas noted that singing signaled family joy during celebrations and provided comfort when they were sad. Regardless of the occasion, attendees clapped their hands and patted their feet "to keep time" and express the tone of their emotions. At funerals, "dey sung slow and moanful."[42] Vocalists, and sometimes drummers, walked behind the coffin bearers or the wagon carrying the coffin "all the way" to the burial grounds, regaling the deceased and their loved ones with songs and sometimes rhythmic steps. "We're travelin' to the grave, We're travelin' to the grave, We're travelin' to the grave, To lay this pore body down," one young woman sang as she walked behind the coffin.[43] Children, who also attended family funerals, contributed through song, movement, and assistance in covering the deceased's body or coffin with soil. "Everybody," Harriet Robinson of Texas added, "chillun and all picked up a clod of dirt and throwed in on top the coffin to help fill up the grave."[44]

Two men who had been enslaved in the Georgia low country explained how drumming and moving in a circle (also known as "ring shout") while praying and singing at the gravesite were important in the ritualization of their dead. "Use tub alluz beat duh drums at fewnuls," he noted. They did so to announce the death and to notify the community of the funeral. They drummed on the way to the burial place, while those attending "marched along" in a "long processional." Once at the gravesite, "dey dance roun in a ring an dey motion wid duh hans. Dey sing duh body tuh duh grabe and den dey let it down an den dey succle roun in duh dance.... Ebrybody shout roun duh grabe in a succle, singin an prayin."[45]

Many funerals took place on Sundays or at night, sometimes weeks after the actual burial, to allow the largest number of mourners to attend while accommodating their work details. Additional time between burial and actual funeral rites also provided an opportunity for a preacher or holy person to officiate. Northern-born journalist Frederick Law Olmsted recorded that one of the enslaved men he encountered in Mississippi was a preacher and "a favourite" in the Black community. "He sometimes went to plantations twenty miles away," or even further, Olmstead estimated, to "preach a funeral sermon." Afterward, the attendants passed the collection hat in recognition of their appreciation for his service.[46] Catholic priests often presided at the funerals of enslaved converts in Maryland, Louisiana, California, Texas, and elsewhere. "We were taught the rituals of the Catholic church and when anyone died," Charles Coles of Maryland explained, "the funeral was conducted by a priest," and the body buried in his enslaver's graveyard, marked with "plain" stones.[47] Most would have considered these stones a luxury or indication of a slaveholder's favored captive. Some burial spaces had small crosses or a wooden marker, but most did not.

Enslaved people in urban areas sometimes had more elaborate funeral rituals than those in rural locales, particularly if they had kin or friends who were freed people of financial means. Harriet Jacobs's uncle, a free man, paid for his enslaved sister's burial, which was presided over by a local minister. Her captor had thought to bury this "favored" bondswoman in the White graveyard, but the deceased woman's mother wanted her placed in the Black cemetery so that she would lie close to kin.[48] Olmsted recalled that while traveling in Richmond, a city with a large free Black and enslaved population, he again witnessed a large gathering of Black people. These free and enslaved folk were participating in the funeral procession of a child. Some were on horses, a few in coaches, and twenty to thirty persons were walking. The Sunday procession of about fifty men and women left the city and ended at the Black cemetery in the nearby countryside. Mourners, some crying passionately, dug the grave while singing and chanting a sacred song (described by Olmsted as "wild and barbarous") in call-and-response fashion. A Black preacher, "neatly dressed" and "very good looking," presided over the service with prayer and a sermon. Another man of similar description, the designated song leader, also had a prominent role. The event concluded with the lowering and covering of the dead child's "neatly made" coffin of "stained pine." The mourners marked the grave with two small branches, one at the head of the coffin and the other opposite it. A White witness, as legally mandated at gatherings of Black people for "religious exercises," was present.[49] Charleston also was the site of large Black antebellum funerals. They usually occurred at night and were so well attended, one White resident complained, that "it appeared to be a jubilee for every slave in the city," estimating the "crowd" of free people of color and the enslaved to be "three or four hundred," making it impossible for carriages to "safely be driven."[50]

RESURRECTION, FINALLY

> She pressed eagerly forward to greet me, and we seemed to each other as one risen from the dead.[51]

In 1860, on the brink of the Civil War, enslaved Blacks numbered close to four million and comprised tens of thousands of family units.[52] When freedom finally did arrive five years later, Black family members had undergone myriad experiences as witnesses and sometimes actors, victims, and victors in the profound unsettling that the war, and its economic, political, cultural, legal, and social consequences, had engendered. Slaveholders, their sons, or substitutes, had marched off to war, leaving their farms, plantations, and businesses to others, not the least of whom were "trusted" bondsmen, women, and children.[53] Many enslavers did not return, and many who did were physically, psychologically, and financially disabled. Death was all around: in soldiers' bodies stacked up and strewn across destroyed fields, the surrender of the Confederacy, and the assassination of President Abraham Lincoln.[54]

The South, as known to enslaved husbands, wives, grandparents, and other Black family members in 1860 was by 1865, profoundly changed, having itself sustained something of a death. By the time the Thirteenth Amendment to the US Constitution was ratified on December 6, 1865, most Black southerners were vividly aware that they were now "free."[55] Freedom was defined in federal and state laws in what might have seemed like bold terms, but the experiences of those who became free made up thousands of shades, none more poignant, or insisted upon, than the beginning, solidification,

Sgt. Samuel Smith of 119th USC, wife Mollie and Daughters, c. 1865. Unknown, Sgt. Samuel Smith and Family, photograph c. 1865, Prints and Photographs Division, Library of Congress, LC-DIG-ppmsca-36454. The Ebony Bridal, c. 1871 The Ebony Bridal – Wedding Ceremony in the Cabin, engraving, c. 1871, original published in Frank Leslie's Illustrated Newspaper, August 19, 1871. Courtesy of the Library of Virginia.

or re-creation of family ties. Resurrection finally had come. Black people embraced it mightily. The words and actions of the "freed" described below indicate something of the very large swath of responses centered on family resurrected in body, law, and spirit.

James Smith was among the many desperate ones who sought to reconnect with family. He sorrowfully left them in Virginia to gain freedom. When the moment finally came that he was able to lay eyes on his siblings, it was a joyful resurrection for the three:

> We got hold of each other and put our arms around each other's neck without speaking for some minutes; the silence was broken, and I exclaimed: "Dear brother, is it possible that we are standing on Virginia's free soil, and we are free?" My brother replied, "yes, dear brother, and you too have been living in the 'land of the free and the home of the brave.'" We wept and rejoiced, and praised God for his goodness in bringing us together once more on free soil. For a short time all was excitement and confusion. When it had subsided we started for the house, where I met my eldest sister. She pressed eagerly forward to greet me, and we seemed to each other as one risen from the dead. We, too, fell on each other's neck and clasped each other and wept. My joy and excitement rose to such a height, that I scarcely knew whether I was in the body or out.[56]

C. W. B. Gordon was instrumental in his mother's reunion with her mother. His grandmother, Rosette, had been sold away from her North Carolina family and friends to Louisiana. A few years after the war ended, Gordon's mother received hopeful news: "Some friend of my mother's wrote her that they had seen granny working on a sugar and cotton farm in New Orleans." Gordon continued to search for Rosette until she was found and reunited with her family, then living in Virginia. The elderly freedwoman lived with her daughter and grandson until she died at the age of 105.[57]

Tempie Herndon was certain why she was glad when the Civil War ended—it was the moment of her familial resurrection. She and her husband, Exeter, could now live together all the time instead of the abroad arrangement they had endured for years. "I was glad when de War stopped," she declared, "cause den me and Exeter could be together all de time 'stead of Saturday and Sunday." To Tempie's delight, Exeter moved to where she was located, and the couple—along with their nine children (two more were born after Exeter arrived)—lived under one roof as a family. Exeter's new role as the patriarchal head of the family, or at least as Tempie's equal, also meant providing financial stability. Without the ability to buy their own land, the two sharecropped for several years and saved their money. Eventually, they accumulated $300 and bought a farm. They would not have been able to do so if their children had not contributed to the work. Tempie was clear that "freedom" meant a united family under one roof, but it also meant that she and Exeter had control over their children and their children's labor.[58]

"When de war was over," recalled Dora Franks of Mississippi, "my brother [Frank] slipped in de house where I was still a-stayin'. He told me us was free and for me to come out wid de rest."[59] Dora was glad to oblige Frank, even though her work status quickly changed from that of a privileged domestic to a field worker in a sharecropping arrangement at a neighboring farm. She suffered mightily from the physical strain of her labor in the hot sun, noting that "I'd faint away most every day about eleven o'clock. It was de heat. Some of 'em would have to tote me to de house. I'd soon come to. Den I had to go back to the field."[60] Still, she did not return to her former captors once she was reunited with her family.

It was not just that Dora wanted to be close to her brother; it was also that she now could have a family of her own, on her own terms. When she lived with her former enslavers, Dora observed how Black life, and Black family life in particular, were sacrificed for the financial well-being of slaveholding Whites and their families. In Dora's estimation, rituals—or rather, the lack of them—marked the casual manner with which enslavers regarded enslaved families. This casualness, in turn, meant that their families were under constant threat of disruption or destruction.[61] Dora vividly recalled that men would have to "slip off" to see their lovers, wives, and children and try to get back before it was time to go to the fields. Even her Uncle Alfred—"Alf," as she called him—"one of de biggest . . . on de place and a powerful fas worker," received "one hundred lashes wid de cat-o' nine tails," because he "run off to 'jump de broom'" and did not return by daylight. Alf's whipped back, Dora added, "was somethin' awful" with blood "a-runnin." After that day's work, Alf left again, choosing to hide in a nearby swamp cave until after the Civil War ended. Uncle Alfred's actions deepened the powerful image in Dora's imagination of the absolute importance of family—he was willing to be beaten and exiled for it. Two years after general emancipation, Dora formally married Pete Franks, something her mother, who was a concubine, was never allowed to do.[62] Dora marked her marriage and renewed family life with an elaborate wedding and a "big supper."[63]

The federal government implemented policies, primarily through military officials and especially the Freedmen's Bureau, that were supposed to regularize the marriage status of the newly freed in accordance with the ideas, if not necessarily the ideals, of Christian citizens. Freedmen's Bureau officials, along with freedmen aid and missionary societies who came to the South as early as 1861 to assist in the transition from enslavement to freedom, wanted Blacks to establish the marital constructs to create patriarchal nuclear families. They exhorted the former bondsmen and bondswomen to remain with the spouses and children they had at the time of their freedom;

The Ebony Bridal, c. 1871. Wedding Ceremony in the Cabin, c. 1871, original published in Frank Leslie's Illustrated Newspaper, August 19, 1871. Courtesy of the Library of Virginia.

to abandon multiple liaisons; to seek written documentation, in the form of marriage licenses and certificates, of their marital state; and to live peaceably as husband and wife under one roof, all working for the support and success of family members. Postbellum southern state legislators, via their constitutional conventions, also weighed in, creating rules and regulations to validate Black marriages.

Among this confusing, complicated, and sometimes conflicting patchwork of "instructions," most newly freed couples sought a legal resurrection, social legitimacy, and equality for their relationships and the children that had been, and would be, born of them. It was a moment of resurrected kinship that they savored. Some continued to "jump the broom" even after freedom,[64] others were told by officials that their "marriage would stand long as ever he lived,"[65] and some took part in mass marriages held at military camps, churches, the homes of clergy, Freedmen's Bureau offices, and district courthouses.[66] Mary Biddy of Florida noted that soon after emancipation: "A big supper was given, it was early, about twenty-five slave couples attended. There was gaiety and laughter. A barrel of lemonade was served. A big time was had by all, then those couples who desired to remain together were joined in wedlock according to civil custom. The party broke up in the early hours of the morning."[67] While teaching among the freedmen on St. Helena Island, South Carolina, under the auspices of the Port Royal Relief Association, the free Black woman Charlotte Forten noted in her diary on November 23, 1863, "Six couples were married to-day. Some of the dresses were unique. Am sure one must have worn a cast-off dress of her mistresses. It looks like white silk covered with lace. The lace sleeves, and other trimmings were in rather a decayed state and the white cotton gloves were well ventilated. But the bride looked none the less happy for that."[68]

The recently freed spoke right to the point of why they, or their parents, chose to marry and "remarry." "My mammy and daddy got married after freedom, 'cause they didn't git de time for a weddin' befo.' They called deirselves man and wife a long time befo' they was really married," Charles Davis of South Carolina explained.[69] Willis Dukes wanted to be clear about the legitimacy of his postbellum marriage, noting, "We didn't jump over no broom neither. We was married like white folks wid flowers and cake and everything."[70] As far as Willis was concerned, since he and his bride shared the same marital rituals as Whites, their union now had to be legitimate. Former bondsman Gus Clark, who had lived both in Virginia and Mississippi, also was clear: "I'se had three wives. I didn't have no weddin's, but I mar'ied 'em 'cordin to law. I woan stay with one no other way. My fust two wives is dead."[71] Mildred Graves of Fredericksburg, Virginia, recalled that as a captive, her female slaveholder had given her a cast-off dress and she "stepped over de broomstick," but "arter de war we had a real sho' nuff weddin' wid a preacher. Dat cost a dollar."[72] Texan Mary Reynolds, who also had been married by stepping across the broom, noted, "After freedom I git married and have it put in the book by the Preacher."[73]

Those who decided, or had the ability, to marry with elaborate rituals and celebrations brought serious thought and planning to the manifestations of their "freedom" marital bonds. Clothing, food, location, audience, vows, the license, the celebrant, and the dance celebration were all important items to consider, since each was an indication—a declaration—of one's newly won free status and a reclaiming and resurrection of family.

Both men and women believed the clothing they wore when they married were important indicators of their emancipation and, as such, their right to commit themselves to a legally binding and/or God-ordained union. Very few, after all, could expect to have special clothing when enslaved, since law, custom, and expense typically forbade it. And a wedding afforded women the opportunity of a lifetime to show off to their family and community their femininity through their physical beauty and wearing attractive, even glamorous or extravagant, clothing that they designed and created.

Not surprisingly, even decades after their weddings, freedwomen spoke lovingly of their bridal dresses. Some dresses were long and white; and many brides wore white veils as well—symbols of moral and sexual purity that flew in the face of racialized, gendered stereotypes of Black women, both enslaved and free. Beneath their veils, some women had powdered faces, but, according to Eliza Washington of Arkansas, "no paint."[74] Molly Horn, also from Arkansas, recounted that "Mama bought me a pure white veil. I was dressed all in white."[75] So, too, was Mandy Hadnot of Texas, who explained that she "had purty long, black hair and a veil with a ribbon 'round de fron.'"[76] Nellie Smith, a successful cake baker in Athens, Georgia, was delighted to give the details of her first wedding, especially her attire: "I wore a white dress made with a tight-fittin' waist and a long, full skirt that was jus' covered with ruffles. My sleeves was tight at the wrists but puffed at the shoulders, and my long veil of white net was fastened to my head with pretty flowers. I was a mighty dressed up bride." Nellie wore a "very pretty, plain, white dress" when she married the second time.[77] Liza Jones of Texas wore a "white Tarleton dress with de white Tarleton wig." The white dress and wig, Liza explained, were signs "you ain't never done no wrong sin and gwinter keep bein' good."[78]

Other colors and styles for bridal wear also prevailed and suggested that freedwomen's bridal fashion tastes were determined by their age, generation, previous marital status, locale, religious beliefs, and financial standing. Harriet Jones of North Carolina and Texas accessorized a used dress from her former captor with "red stockin's and a pair of brand-new shoes and a wide brim hat," when she married Bill Jones the year after emancipation.[79] Less elaborate bridal clothing, no doubt, indicated operative class distinctions. Most, for example, certainly could not afford Liza's elaborate "Tarleton" look. Still, the relative "finery" of a woman's wedding ensemble allowed her to resurrect a feminine and moral identity not possible when enslaved. Josephine Anderson of Florida recalled that her wedding dress was blue: "blue for true," she explained. "I thought it was the prettiest dress I ever see."[80]

"I ain't never seed nothin' lak dat pretty flowerdy weddin' dress dat I wore and I had de prettiest hat and things dat I ever seed," Julia Cole of Georgia recounted.[81] Minerva Edwards of Texas wore a "blue serge suit."[82] "The dress I married in was red silk," Susan MacIntosh of Georgia recalled.[83] Julia Larken and Will Sheets's bride, whose financial resources no doubt probably were more typical of most freedwomen, both wore a "new calico dress."[84] Nettie McCree of Georgia wore a "black silk dress . . . [that] had a overskirt of blue that was scalloped 'round de bottom." Her husband, Ed, added with pride: "I never will forgit how you looked dat day." Nettie also wore white silk gloves.[85] William McWhorter could not remember precisely what his wife wore, but still boasted: "I'se tellin' you she looked pretty and sweet to me."[86] Few men could have hoped to have their brides beautifully adorned when enslaved, not only because captors tightly controlled clothing allocations, design, and quality,[87] but also because they typically retained the most "beautiful" women for concubinage.[88]

Wedding attire was so important that freedwomen and their daughters bartered and sold eggs, chickens, other livestock, and their labor to acquire it. They also rarely refused assistance in acquiring the various items needed for their proud day of beauty, romance, and marital commitment, reaching out to friends, local seamstresses, teachers and missionaries, former enslavers, current employers, kin, and their grooms for help. Some men were pleased to be able to display their patriarchal capabilities by providing financial support for their bride's or daughter's costume.[89]

In the assemblage process of clothing and adornment for body and hair that they wore on this most special day, postbellum brides represented those who were operative members of their communities and kinship networks as freed people. The necessity to beg, borrow, and, in some instances, steal[90] wedding clothing also suggested the precarious economic status of freedwomen, many of whom could not afford, on their own, this elaborate and costly clothing. Some of this pre-wedding activity also indicated functional economic relations between working southern White and Black women at the time when fledgling local economies were a burden for both. The resurrection of systems of exchange and barter between marginalized Whites and Blacks was no surprise, given that they had existed, within the context of the operative racial etiquette, from the colonial through the antebellum eras. Susan MacIntosh bought her clothing secondhand from a local White woman, Mrs. Ed Bond.[91] The white silk gloves that Nettie McCree wore at her wedding were given to her by a local White seamstress whom Nettie patronized.[92]

Like their brides, grooms placed great importance on their wedding attire. Dressing for their wedding afforded them the chance to doff their plain work clothes and take on the look of men of leisure, even sophisticated gentlemen, in striking contrast to nineteenth-century racist stereotypes of freedmen that held they were beastlike in manners, intelligence, appearance, and appetite.[93] Ike Derricotte of Athens, Georgia, sported a Prince Albert coat he was so proud of that he intended to will it to his children.[94] Sam Bond of Arkansas wore a tie, white vest, watch, and gold chain, all borrowed from a local attorney.[95] Nellie Smith's bridegroom stood at the altar in a "real dark-colored cutaway coat with a white vest."[96] Anderson Edwards also wore a Prince Albert cutaway suit,[97] as did Ed McCree, who completed his ensemble with a pair of brown pants, white shirt, and a vest.[98] Julia Larken's private wedding afforded her groom the opportunity to dress much less formally. Given the expense of formal wear, and the inability to acquire it in the rural countryside, Matthew's dress probably was more typical. According to his bride, he "wore some new blue jeans breeches."[99]

Private ceremonies, like that of Julia and Matthew Larken, usually included the couple, kinfolk, a few close friends, and sometimes employers, who gathered at the courthouse, at a preacher's home, the bride's residence, or that of an employer or even former captors who might now be employers. Josephine Anderson was married at a local courthouse in Florida.[100] Laura Thornton recalled that she had a marriage license and was married by the local justice of the peace. "I was married right at home where me and my old man stayed. Wasn't nobody there but me and him and another man named Dr. Bryant," she explained.[101] Betty Curlett had a minister marry her in her home.[102] Sylvia Durant of Marion, South Carolina, was wed by a minister in the local Bethel Methodist Episcopal church.[103] Ministers could be Black or White, depending on the religious affiliations of the couple. Julia Larken was married by "Reverend Hargrove, de white folks preacher."[104] Molly Horn recalled that she had a "colored preacher" marry her.[105]

Fanny Berry also was married by a local Black preacher, Elder Williams, in Appomattox County, Virginia. Still, her wedding hardly was a "private affair." It gave Fanny the perfect opportunity to boldly pronounce her free status and protected family relations to the entire community, Black and White. She held her wedding at night at her White employer's house and was waited on by two White friends who accompanied her down the aisle with lighted lanterns. Most of those in attendance were Black, although Fanny credited her White employers with providing the food and the space for the ceremony and the party that followed. "After marriage de white folks give me a 'ception,'" Fanny explained delightedly. "An', honey, talkin' 'bout a table—hit wuz stretched clean 'cross de dinin' room. We had everythin' to eat you could call for. No, you didn't have no common eats. We could sing in dar, an' dance ol' squar' dance all us choosed, ha! ha! ha! Lord! Lord! I can see dem gals now on dat flo'; jes skippin' an' a trottin'. An' honey, dar wuz no white folks to set down an' eat 'fo yo.'"[106]

Harriet Jones of Texas also told of her large, elaborate wedding and the vows that she and her husband took before a biracial crowd under a large elm tree after emancipation. Her marriage was officiated by a local minister. Two flower girls held her gown's train. The rituals she described from that day drew both on Christian and African marital rituals:

> De [Christian] preacher say, "Bill, does you take dis woman to be you lawful wife?" and Bill say he will. Den he say, "Harriet, will you take dis nigger to be you lawful boss and do jes' what he say?" Den we signs de book and de preacher say, "I quotes from de scripture: 'Dark and stormy may come de weather, I jines dis man and woman together. Let none but Him what make de thunder, Put dis man and woman asunder.'"[107]

Freed Slave Wedding Dance, c. 1870s. Via Alamy.

Bill gave Harriet a gold ring, a ritualistic luxury item, ripe with multiple public declarations of the couple's unending circle of love, of Bill's ability to support his wife and future family, and of the great value Harriet was to her husband. At the end of their ceremony, the happy couple was regaled with a beautifully set table covered by a white cloth and decorated with red berries, provided by Harriet's former enslaver. Harriet's wedding guests feasted on "barbecue pig and roast sweet 'taters and dumplin's and pies and cake."[108]

It was at the reception that Harriet's mother presented the bride her wedding present that symbolized their African past: a rabbit's toe for good luck. According to Harriet, her mother recited as she handed over the animal appendage: "Here take dis lil gift, and place it near you heart; It keep away dat li'l riff what causes folks to part." Harriet's mother offered the bride a gentle reminder of her family's cultural past, one on which they had relied on for generations for survival and marital bliss. Bill and Harriet might now be "free," with the ability to marry in the same manner and, hopefully, with the same benefits as Whites, her mother acknowledged, but they should not abandon their traditional ways of ritualizing and protecting marriage bonds. This rabbit's toe, Harriet's mother went on to explain, was so lucky that it was worth much more than the ritualized items typically valued at free people's marriages, such as monetary gifts and wedding rings. This rabbit's toe, she told her daughter, was worth "a million dimes or more. More'n all de weddin' rings."[109] After dinner, the wedding party, led by the bride and groom, paraded to "Marse Watson's [her former slaveholder] saddle shop to dance and dance all night."[110] The dances they performed that night were no doubt also reminiscent of their ancestral past.

Ceremonies and receptions were integral parts of freed persons' wedding rituals. Being able to have a legitimate marriage and the rights it signified were more than ample reasons to celebrate. Special food, décor, music, and dance were the icing on the cake. Night weddings, like Fanny Berry's, were somewhat popular given that few could get off from work during weekdays. Molly Horn also married at night. She "borrowed lamps and had em settin' about." Like Fanny, Molly had a sumptuous wedding meal—"roast pork, goose and all sorter pies," along with several cakes.[111] Others served beef, pork, turkey, and antelope.[112] Former bondswoman Harriet Gresham grandly married a member of Company I, 35th Regiment, at a military camp in South Carolina. Decades later, she recalled delightedly when she "waltz onder citadel green and march down aile [aisle] o' soldiers in blue, in der arms o me husban, and over me haid de bay'nets shined."[113] Martha Colquitt, who had a "big weddin" at her sister's house, had two "fine dinners" in Georgia, one given by her family and the other by her husband's family, with the help of his former employers.[114] Warren McKinney and his wife had several waiters and an elaborate reception in South Carolina provided by both families.[115] Alex Pope of Georgia recalled that he "had a awful big weddin' de fust time. . . . Us drunk and et and danced and cut de buc most all night long." These types of wedding, with layered meanings of freedom and resurrection, impressed all who viewed them. Even Alex's White neighbor was impressed, commenting that "he never seed sich a weddin' in his life."[116]

Most receptions, however, were much more modest and, like those significantly less elaborate wedding clothes and venues already noted, suggested the class differences found among freed people and their families derived from diverse levels of economic well-being. Sylvia Durant of South Carolina[117] explained that after her marriage ceremony, she, like Susan MacIntosh in Georgia, had "nothing but pound cake en wine."[118]

Wedding cakes, which reminded attendees of the sweetness of love and commitment between the couple, were particularly important ritualized food items and usual fare for most. The cakes could be very elaborately decorated. A favorite was a yellow cake with white icing that had the engagement ring baked inside.[119] Nellie Smith bragged of her special dessert, "I think my weddin' cake was 'bout the biggest one I ever saw baked in one of them old ovens in the open fireplace. They iced it in white and decorated it with grapes."[120] Bunny Bond's employer donated her wedding cake.[121] Employers, some of whom were former captors, had good reason to lend a helping hand. Given the difficulty of retaining Black workers after emancipation, many were anxious to impress with tokens of generosity and supposed familial support, even if it meant treating them to a wedding that pronounced that Blacks had acquired status with emancipation. This type of help also could be a burden.

It suggested how involved former enslavers remained in the family lives of their Black workforce and how they ensured Black economic dependency. This aid barely disguised the continued financial exploitation Whites imposed on Black laborers, leaving them little financial ability to finance their own weddings or to create new, separate households.

Being able to survive financially was very difficult for those who wanted to create or resurrect a family after freedom. Labor statistics and personal narratives document this certainty. Arthur Green, who had been enslaved in Virginia, spoke for many when he recalled his family's financial struggles. The year the war ended, he, his siblings, and his parents stayed on the plantation as sharecroppers. They were promised one-fourth "of the crop" but received nothing after "de marster took out his part for yo' board. Dat left you wid nothin' an' God knows de 'jority of us had nothin'. Dis was done all through the country." His family moved to another sharecropping situation, and the same thing occurred. Finally, the Greens decided to live off what animals they trapped, eating the meat and selling the skins. They also performed what day work they could find. Arthur Green's family was together, but deeply impoverished: "No we never could git 'nough money together to buy a home. A few years after den my mother an' father died."[122]

Delia Garlic, an enslaved women who told a story of brutal family separations, torturous whippings, and near starvation, tried hard to create a family for herself both before and after freedom. Having been sold from her family of birth as a child and enduring three additional sales before she ended up on a cotton plantation in Louisiana, far from her birthplace in Virginia, Delia's desire to have a family of some sort never was worked, beaten, or starved out of her. She had feelings of loss of and desire for a family that she was not going to deny before, during, and certainly not after the Civil War.[123]

Delia first married a man on a nearby plantation, but he left during the war, and whether death or determination for some type of freedom took him away, she never saw him again. She then wed Miles, who lived on her plantation. By the end of the war, they had had a child. With few economic options but to stay and work for her former captor, she reluctantly did so while Miles traveled to Alabama to find work. After their second child was born, Delia decided it was time to reunite her family. "My secon' baby soon come, an' raght den I made up my min' to go to Wetumpka where Miles was workin' for de railroad," she explained. "I went on down dere an' us settled down."[124]

Like that of most freedwomen, Delia's labor was essential to her family's survival. She continued to work while raising their children, especially after Miles died. In 1910, the census indicated she was a cook. When she was physically unable to earn a living for herself, she moved to Montgomery to live with other family members. By 1930, and again in 1940, Delia was living with her daughter Mary, who was also a cook; her granddaughter Georgie, a seamstress; and Georgie's husband, Charles Brown, a waiter. Freedom and family had extended to three generations that she had lived and worked to see.[125] "I'se eatin' white bread now an' havin de best time of my life," she told a WPA interviewer in the 1930s. Life had finally turned sweet, but Delia could not forget or let go of the bitterness derived from abuse and familial absence. She noted that she had never forgiven the Whites who had treated her so badly as a worker and who ultimately had been responsible for the loss of her family. "Massa Garlic had two boys in de war," she explained. "When dey went off de Massa an' missis cried, but it made us glad to see dem cry. Dey made us cry so much."[126] Black resurrection did not bring White absolution.

Many people chose to marry the spouse they had at the time of general emancipation and remain with "that" family, sometimes with the children from previously separated relationships becoming a part of these "blended" households. Others did not remain with these later families. Harrison Beckett's father, for one, left once the war ended. It is not clear whether Harrison knew that his father had another family before his, but he soon found out once his father had the opportunity to "resurrect" his past kin connections. His father, who initially had been sold away from a family in Florida, returned to them, leaving Harrison, his Texas wife, and their other children behind. Harrison's mother, who was from Georgia, remained in Texas, making the difficult decision not to claim her former kin.[127]

Choice, as Harrison Beckett's father made painfully clear, was part and parcel—and a privilege—of Black freedom. No element of choice was more important than choosing the family or spouse you wanted, regardless of what others thought of that choice. A soldier of Colonel Thomas Wentworth Higginson, commander of the all-Black First South Carolina, for example, refused to take the advice that Higginson and another White officer offered him regarding his choice for a bride. Higginson confided in his diary that the bride was "a most unattractive woman, jet black with an old pink muslin dress, torn white gloves, and a very flowery bonnet, that must have descended through generations of tawdry mistresses." Not only did Higginson find her unattractive, he also disliked that she was the mother of seven children. The groom, however, would not be deterred. He insisted that the officers could not "lub [love]" for him. "I mus lub for myself and I lub [s]he," he declared flatly.[128]

Others chose not to marry at all. That decision, however, did not mean they did not have, or cling to, a cherished family. Neither Susan nor her mother, Venus, married at the end of the war. Family was the two of them: an African woman, captured and smuggled into the South after the end of the legal international trade, and her mixed-race daughter. They lived as enslaved, and then as free, in Alabama and Mississippi. Susan and Venus left their captor's

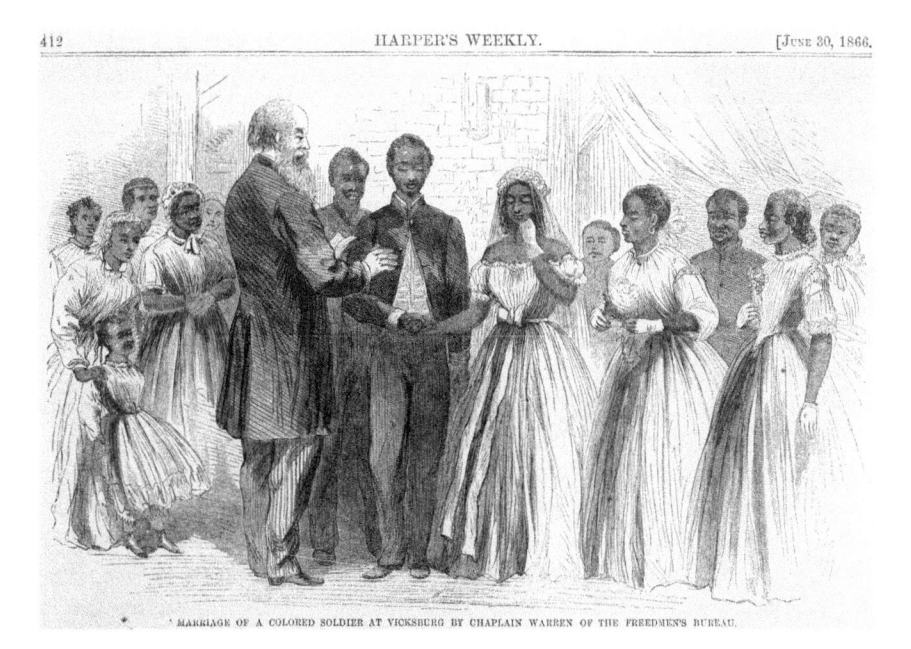

Marriage of a Soldier at Vicksburg, c. 1866. Unknown, Marriage of Colored Soldier at Vicksburg by Chaplain Warren of the Freedmen's Bureau, original published in Harper's Weekly June 30, 1866, as found on Library of Congress, Prints and Photographs Division, Library of Congress, LC-USZ62-138383.

farm in 1865, immediately after learning of their freedom. It is doubtful that the two took anything with them except pieces of clothing and perhaps a few household items—textiles, pipes, and crockery—accumulated over the years. African Venus had not managed, or perhaps had not wanted, to create close relations with anyone except her daughter.[129]

"My ma was de first to leave de plantation after de surrender," Susan recalled. "All de other [captives] . . . had a contract to stay, but she didn't. She went to Newton County and hired out. She never wanted to stay in one place, no how."[130] Venus felt no ties to the land where she had been held. Perhaps memory of her homeland was still too profound. Maybe the loss of three home sites (at least one in Africa and two in the United States prior to gaining freedom) had left Venus with the stark reality that, for her, home and family were embodied in her daughter and her fading memories of a place and people in Africa whom she would never see again. Some family resurrections, after all, were not meant to be—at least while one was still alive.

Many of those who continued to arrive from Africa well into the nineteenth century had continued to hope to be reconnected with kin whom they were forced to leave when captured. Some managed to make their way back to Africa as part of a colonization program or as part of the effort to return those shipped illegally after 1808. Most did not. It was a pain that was not easily soothed. Elizabeth Burke, who taught in Georgia in the 1830s and 1840s, wrote home about an elderly African woman she had met on a plantation who "always looked cast down and sorrowful, and never appeared to take any interest in what caused the joy and mirth of those around her." According to Burke, this woman was still mourning for her family and "playmates." She recalled that she had been gathering shells on the shore when captured. The woman had hoped that one day she would again see some of those whom she still held so dearly, but now, she said, "I begin to despair of ever seeing those faces which are still fresh in my memory, for now I am an old woman." Asked to sing songs of her homeland, she would do so, but "tears would trickle down" her face before she finished.[131] This woman seemingly had not married or had children while enslaved.

Venus and Susan's family unit remained just the two of them for several years. Venus had no intention of trying to find Susan's father. When asked, she told her daughter that her father was so "mean" that she had been glad to leave him behind when they were sold. Venus also made it clear to Susan that she would never marry, even though she was now free.[132] Susan knew very little else about her father, who was so light in color that she, his offspring, was described as "mulatto." The few details her mother allowed her suggest that Venus wanted to conceal from Susan that her father was a White man and that she was the product of rape. Susan's very light skin color, her mother's characterization of her father as a brute, and their sale soon after Susan's birth strongly suggest that Venus had been bound to a sexually abusive White man, whom she absolutely detested but whose daughter she loved and considered her only family. No one else mattered. As with many other families, the pangs of slavery followed Venus into freedom.

Susan's narrative makes it clear that, for her African mother, freedom meant access to Susan (the child who physically had be removed from her care and put to domestic work before freedom came), mobility, and control over her labor and body. Venus did not suffer fools, or captors, and when she found herself in the company of either, she did not hesitate to fight or leave. "If she had a crop half made and somebody made her mad," Susan explained, "she'd up and leave it and go somewheres else."[133] Venus sought a freedom that sometimes took her beyond the physical confines of daily contact with Susan, but she never moved very far away from her child. Venus was approximately thirty-five and Susan about sixteen years old when they were emancipated, and for the remainder of their lives, mother and daughter resided within the geographic boundaries of five contiguous Black Belt counties[134] tucked away in the upper southeast corner of Mississippi. Despite their desire to experience their freedom and family away from where they had been enslaved, practicality dictated that they, as most other freed people, still would live where they could find employment.

An experienced child nurse, Susan had more postwar work opportunities than her mother. Initially, the two began working together as sharecroppers. By 1870, Susan had begun to work as a domestic for the farmer Jackson Craven.[135] Venus continued to sharecrop in neighboring county. Sometime during that decade, the two reunited and moved together again, this time to the hamlet of Enterprise.[136] Recalling the racially turbulent, often violent 1870s and 1880s, Susan explained how difficult it was for Blacks to succeed. One can imagine that the mother and daughter had an especially challenging time.

"De Kloo Kluxes was out nights," Susan explained. "I heard tell about 'em whippin' people."[137] She also learned, probably from those in contact with the Freedmen's Bureau, that freed Blacks were supposed to receive some kind of formal assistance. In the end, however, Susan and her mother "never got nothin' to my knowledge, 'cept de government let 'em homestead land."[138]

Sometime before 1880, mother and daughter relocated to Meridian, the county seat.[139] By then, Meridian was becoming something of a boomtown, teeming with Black and White rural migrants seeking economic relief. General William Tecumseh Sherman torched Meridian during the Civil War, but the city's location at the juncture of two major railroad lines made it a keen spot for New South industrial development. It was a place where Susan could at least find steady work as a child nurse and domestic so that she could support her aging mother.[140]

Despite the economic opportunities Meridian might have offered, however, it still was a dangerous place for freed people and their families. In 1871, Meridian was the site of a deadly race massacre in which at least thirty Blacks were killed and numerous Black women raped and violently brutalized. The White-on-Black violence had several sources, but was principally related to White opposition to local Republican (White and Black) political leadership and black land ownership. The Ku Klux Klan and other local domestic terrorists, as well as a contingent of like-minded men from neighboring counties across the state line in Alabama, led the assault. Before it was over, they had killed three Black lawmakers, a Black policeman, and a White Republican judge. One freedwoman named Ellen Parton recalled that during the riot "companies" of men raided her home three nights in a row; on the third night, they raped her.[141]

While Venus and Susan may not have been living in Meridian at the time of the massacre, they certainly had heard the stories of the racialized and gendered violence that took place, devastating Black families, businesses, homesteads, and political opportunity for personal, familial, and communal protection. Mother and daughter had to have hedged their bets carefully. Should they remain in the countryside, where they could barely make a living and could be killed or raped without any hint of justice to be had? Or should they move to Meridian and at least have a chance at gainful employment and greater familial stability? They chose Meridian.

In 1880, Venus and Susan were not living only with each other. Census records indicate that there was another female named Katie in their household. The girl was eleven years old, "at school," a mulatto with an Irish father.[142] Later census records reveal that Katie was Susan's daughter.[143] Venus's family now incorporated three generations. Katie's father might have been Craven, for whom Susan worked as a "housekeeper" during the time she and Venus had temporarily parted ways. Certainly by the time they moved to Meridian, Susan was known to live by her own social rules. Freedom also meant having a good time, even if your mother disapproved.

By her own admission, Susan "cut loose" in Meridian. "I'se a woman, but I'se prodigal," she noted of her rowdy behavior. She frequented juke joints and other night spots, often getting drunk, disorderly, and arrested. Venus did not (perhaps could not) come to her aid. Her employers did. "My white folks kept tellin' me if I got locked up one more time dey wouldn't pay my fine. But dey done it again and again," she confessed.[144] Further evidence of Susan's maternity was her work in Meridian, where she had at least one job as a wet nurse.[145] Domestic service, of course, brought Susan in constant contact with, and vulnerable to, sexually aggressive White, male employers. She also could have entered a concubinage relationship. After all, without husbands, brothers, or fathers, Susan and Venus had fewer options for financial security or chances of avoiding physical or sexual abuse than those freedwomen who had spousal or paternal male protection.[146] Venus died sometime between 1880 and 1900,[147] but Susan continued to tell the stories of her African mother and the life they had together even after she had her own child and grandchildren.[148]

Despite the common lack of opportunity Susan and Venus faced when they left the Snow plantation in 1865, they both were able to find some familial stability and survive economically within the limited work opportunities the Deep South offered freedwomen. Theirs was not the nuclear family that Dora Franks and Tempie Herndon had dreamed of and accomplished, but rather a matrifocal family that Venus had decided she preferred. Like her mother, Susan never married. While these two generations of Snow women remained "single," the third generation, Katie, seemed to have married, as did her daughter, Daisy. Daisy Allen and her husband, both literate, also managed to own a house, and Mr. Allen's work and their boarders provided enough household income to remove Daisy from the vulnerable position of working outside the home that Venus and Susan could not escape in the first decades of working and constituting family after "freedom."[149]

Many freed people and their descendants obviously enjoyed their wedding rituals, legal marriages, and many other aspects of their resurrected family life. Their difficulties due to the Reconstruction and post-Reconstruction eras' legal, economic, political, and social inequalities and marginalization, however, were ever present. The Black family nevertheless survived generations of slavery and grew more stable because of freedom. Men and women brought their commitment to kin relations with proven and ever-evolving coping strategies for familial resurrection, survival, and even success into the post–Civil War decades.

Conclusion
Bob Samuels's American Family

This book speaks to the truth that the Black family has been the central and essential site of virtually every aspect of Black life, culture, and history. Regardless of what political and intellectual critics have said across the years about Black family dysfunction in the past and the present, the importance of family to the individual and the community remains, as it has been, a reality and protected resource. Likewise, the Black family is the American family, enduring every painful legacy and helping to create every triumphant moment that has come to define the nation and the national narrative. The story of the Black family within and outside of slavery in the lands and empires that have become the United States is, then, an American story that is worth telling, knowing, and claiming. It is an essential knowledge, an "American reckoning."[1] The last of these stories told here begins now.

In late April 1936, elderly Robert Grigsby Samuels had an incredible family story to tell.[2] It was one that he had spoken repeatedly over the years to his wife, his children, his grandchildren, neighbors, friends, and strangers. Bob was proud of his family's lineage; of his ancestors from Spain, Africa, and Cuba; of the lands they had traversed and the problems they had solved, resolved, or survived. He had lived to tell their truths and pass them on to other kin. It was Bob's grandmother who had bestowed this gift of family lore to Bob's mother, Mary, and then his mother to him. As his life pushed forward, he still busied himself repeating and remembering so that he, too, could pass on the precious narrative bonds of his family's claim to being and belonging. No doubt many people had listened incredulously as the blind octogenarian with a "tall and straight" physique and a "short, clean grey beard" insisted on speaking up about his ancestry. No one was surprised when he told his family's chronicle at least once more, this time to Hazel Horn, the

WPA interviewer from Little Rock who, that Depression-era day, arrived at Bob's multigenerational home in Washington, Arkansas, to hear him speak.[3]

According to federal census records, Robert Samuels was born in October 1851, the son of Richard and Mary Samuels, all enslaved before general emancipation in 1865. Mary, her spouse, and their children, including Bob, were held as the property of David and Almadene Block in Hempstead County, Arkansas.[4] The antebellum county, in the southwest corner of the state bordering on the shifting settler-colonized/nationalized landscapes of Texas, Oklahoma, and Louisiana, was a burgeoning slave society with increasing numbers of bonded people, slaveholding households, and cotton plantations. By 1840, Hempstead was close to 40 percent Black. It became increasingly more so before the Civil War.[5] Bob would have been born into a community of Black people "native" to Arkansas, but who had been also sold and brought from the Upper and Lower South (like his father, from Kentucky) and who were still being smuggled in from Africa via Cuba and Texas. They all brought with them rich cultural traditions and family memories.

Bob's maternal lineage and its connection to the land on which they were enslaved began long before he, or even his mother, was born. His grandmother Amarilla and his mother were Spanish, "mixed with Negro blood." Amarilla probably was free when she arrived in Gaines Landing, Arkansas, with her son Edmin and her husband in the early decades of the nineteenth century.[6] Bob believed his grandmother had been well educated. His story also strongly suggests that these three kinspeople came in search of gold. Three hundred years after Hernando de Soto and his fellow invaders set eyes on the Mississippi River looking for a mythologized gold supply to rival that which the Spanish had uncovered in Mexico and Peru, Amarilla, her husband, and their son were still in that quest.

Amarilla had kept a trunk of maps and other papers that she passed onto her daughter Mary. Bob believed these documents had originated with de Soto's sixteenth-century explorations and would lead them to a gold mine.[7] Where would Amarilla have acquired such documents? According to her, one of their female ancestors had traveled from Madrid, Spain, with de Soto when he returned to the Americas in the late 1530s as part of his 600-plus-strong expeditionary force. Some women were a part of this effort, accompanying their husbands or other male kin and even dressing as men for the journey.[8] Among this group were multiracial "Atlantic" creoles from Portugal and Spain, perhaps including Amarilla's ancestors. Each contingent had an essential role to play, and the vast majority hoped to become rich from their efforts. De Soto had been made governor of Cuba, but it was his great ambition to find gold sources and riches, as he had done years earlier as a part of Francisco Pizzaro's plundering forces in Peru. Amarilla repeatedly told Bob's mother, who then relayed to Bob, the story of their ancestors and the paths taken with de Soto.

Amarilla used her maps and other documents to point out the route and oral details to animate the locales. Mary shared the contents of the box with Bob when he was a child. The maps and ephemera were lost before Bob's adulthood, but his mother's and grandmother's oral accounts of their early "American" family roots were the source of Bob's family narrative.

Bob was told that his ancestors traveled from Madrid to Havana and then to Tampa in 1539 with de Soto through what was then a relatively small part of Spain's American empire in what is modern-day Alabama, Arkansas,[9] Louisiana, Oklahoma, and Texas. Amarilla reported that de Soto had been killed—others believed that he died of a "fever"[10]—after gold was found near the "Boiling Springs."[11] The group then scattered, with Bob's ancestors eventually making their way back to Spain.[12]

This part of Bob Samuel's family story might seem far-fetched, but the Black presence among early European travelers, explorers, and wealth seekers in the Americas has been well documented.[13] Bob also offered as evidence detailed knowledge of parts of the routes his ancestors had taken. While it is still not completely clear where the various bands of de Soto's forces journeyed, or even precisely where in the lower Mississippi River de Soto died and was buried, Bob's description of his ancestors' travels does fit within the general geographies of scholars who have tried to retrace de Soto's steps.[14] According to Bob,[15] once his ancestors arrived in Florida, they moved eastward, then

> came to some point in Alabama. From this place she came to the Mississippi river and the East Bank and crossed where it is called Gaines Landing.[16] After they crossed the river they went ten kilometers from there, traveled north from there to where Arkansas County is close to the mouth of the Arkansas River.[17] Here they camped awhile. When they broke camp there they traveled northeast to Boiling Springs.[18] Making their way from here they crossed the Ouachita River[19] on the other side of Arkadelphia. They traveled on, crossing Little Missouri River[20] below Wallaceburg.[21] Here they found some Indian mounds.[22]

Imagine how difficult it must have been for the eighty-five-year-old to have retained such details (real, imagined, or both) during his childhood in slavery and his adolescence and young adulthood during Reconstruction, to say nothing of while he farmed, married, and raised children in the Jim Crow era, embedded in a southern society bent on stripping away his, and his family's, rights as American citizens. Consider what a burden it had been for Amarilla, Mary, and the numerous generations of their ancestors before them to pass down this information as oral text and written documents (the trunk of maps, etc.). The importance of family—his American family—to Bob no doubt fueled his determination, against all odds, to keep their history alive in his oral account.

Bob's oral account to Hazel Horn did not end with the search for gold but continued with his remembrance of family members and events of the nineteenth century that had been told to him or that he had witnessed. Undoubtedly, his maternal and paternal kin both experienced various shades of unfreedom and freedom as they traversed, or were forced across, the expanse of the Atlantic world. It was not long after his grandmother Amarilla reached what was then Arkansas that she was enslaved.

Amarilla, her husband, and her son traveled from Cuba to the United States. The family crossed the Mississippi River and came to what they believed had been one of de Soto's campsites. Probably hoping to move more efficiently through the area, they hired Nick Trammel and John Morrow as guides.[23] It is not certain if the family knew these men were slave traders before they joined company with them, but if not, they soon recognized their error. Slave traders were known to always be on the lookout for free people whom they could kidnap and sell. Spanish people of mixed blood were no exception to these victimizations. After all, enslaved people from Africa via Cuba were being sold in the Gulf of Mexico, even after the end of the legal slave trade. Language barriers would have worked in Trammel and Morrow's favor if Amarilla could not find an interpreter. Frontier slave societies like Arkansas and Texas also were rife with persons willing to buy people with unclear legal status. Purportedly leading them further down de Soto's trail, Trammel and Morrow instead took the family to Waco, Texas, where they killed Amarilla's husband, enslaved her, and then forced her to marry "either a half-breed Mexican, an Indian or a Negro."[24] They took her son, Edmin, back to Arkansas. He might have been indentured, given that he returned to briefly visit his mother when he was about the age of seventeen, and eventually may have moved on to Mexico. Amarilla, it seems, was told he was in Mexico, but she believed that Edmin, like his father, had been killed so that he could not expose Trammel and Morrow's treachery.[25]

Amarilla and her new spouse became the parents of Bob's mother, Mary. Robert Trammel kept Mary and Amarilla in Bowie County, Texas, on the border with Arkansas, Louisiana, and Oklahoma. Mary was a spinner and weaver, as was, perhaps, her mother. David Block later acquired Mary as settlement of a debt from Trammel. The latter moved, taking Amarilla to another location on the Guadalupe River. It is not certain when, or if, Mary saw her mother again.[26]

As a bondswoman for Block, Mary, who was bilingual and described as "tall and fair with straight black hair," worked as head domestic at his plantation.[27] She no doubt was very busy in the growing Block household. By 1860, thirty-eight-year-old Dave Block, who was a Methodist minister, merchant, and farmer, was married to twenty-five-year-old Almadene, and the couple had five children ranging in age from one to eleven. Theirs was a wealthy family—Block owned $60,000 in real estate and $100,000 in personal property that year.[28] The slave census also indicated that Block claimed seventeen enslaved people—including several mulattoes—who could have included nine-year-old Bob and his kin, all designated as multiracial in later census records.[29]

Mary, too, was married and had children by the late antebellum period. Bob's father was the enslaved blacksmith Richard Samuels, whose parents had been born in Kentucky and Texas. Mary's domestic role, along with Richard's skilled work, probably deemed them a "privileged" couple among their community. Privileged and skilled, however, hardly meant that Richard and Mary could have turned most of their attention to their own family, in which there were at least three children (Bob had a sister and a brother).[30]

Like so many other freed couples who had managed to remain married during their enslavement, Bob's parents remarried during Reconstruction, securing a coveted legal foundation for their relationship as man and wife and for their family.[31] As freed parents, Richard and Mary had ambitious goals that they hoped would secure all their futures. These plans included education for their offspring, land ownership for the family, and political prominence for Richard.[32]

Bob's father succeeded politically and economically after the Civil War—much better than most freedmen. Although illiterate himself, Dick, as Richard was called, became involved in the state's powerful Republican Party and, through it, was chosen to serve in the Arkansas State Constitutional Convention. Just months later, he was elected to represent Hempstead County in the Arkansas State House of Representatives, one of just five Black elected members in 1868.[33] Dick's political importance no doubt elevated the status of, and opportunities for, the entire Samuels family. Bob, and probably his siblings, secured a formal education through at least the sixth grade.[34] Dick believed he had an opportunity to elevate not just his family but also his race through his efforts in the Arkansas legislature. Along with other members of the state's Republican Party, Black and White, he supported several key measures meant to oppose racial segregation, to provide freed people security against White terrorism, to support Black equality, and to fund Black public education—including a female academy and college.[35]

Bob and the family lived in Little Rock while his father was a legislator, giving them the advantages of urban amenities, educational resources, and a powerful Black elite at work—at least half of the city council was Black and there were multiple examples of successful Black entrepreneurship.[36] In 1872, county voters elected Dick Samuels again, this time to serve as county clerk for Hempstead.[37] Bob's father also managed to acquire eighty acres of homesteading land, a place of their own where the Samuels clan could live and work and that would be passed on to further generations.[38]

A freed Bob spent his adolescence in the city and countryside of Arkansas, living with his parents and siblings, and later, a stepmother named Fannie. By the early 1870s, he was settling into adult life and domesticity. In March 1871, at the age of twenty, Bob married a mulatto woman named Sarah J. Paxton Howard, who was from Louisiana.[39] The young farming couple quickly began to have children of their own. Bob and Sarah honored family members in the names they gave their children. Two carried the names of Bob's parents, Richard, and Mary.[40] One daughter was named for Bob—young Bobbie. Their others—Isadora, Emanuel, Lillian, John, Lela, and Lucy—were perhaps named for Sarah's kin or for other Samuels relations for whom there is no remaining record.[41]

Bob was a farmer, and certainly his children all helped with the work, as was the custom of family farms. Still, he and Sarah made certain their offspring were educated. Their daughters, in particular, all finished high school and probably attended one of the normal schools and colleges located in the state by the 1880s.[42] They all became teachers in the segregated local public schools, considered a marker of female success, service, and respectability. The family was a large one, and as Bob and Sarah's children grew up—all except Emmanuel, who died at age eight[43]—most remained close to their parents. The Samuels homeplace was a bustling site at the turn of the twentieth century, comprised of family across multiple generations.[44]

The extended family of Mary and Richard, including that of their son Bob and his wife Sarah, fared unusually well in Reconstruction and post-Reconstruction southwest Arkansas. Still, they were not exempt from the typical racial discrimination, even horrors, that Black families experienced during that time. White domestic terrorists in the state purportedly lynched 24 Blacks in one county alone in 1866, and at least 244 other persons in the state between 1882 and 1927.[45] Hempstead County was 49 percent Black and largely segregated in 1880, but with a significant percentage of Black landholders, including the Samuels clan.[46] As such, their county was something of a haven for black families, even though Black landownership, like Black male political power, proved to be a persistent source of racialized conflict. In July 1883, such a struggle broke out in western Hempstead County concerning a contested property line between two White farmers and two Black farmers, who were brothers. Black neighbors also accused one of the White men, Thomas Wyatt, of attempting to rape the daughter of one of the Black farmers, James Marshall. A confrontation between Whites and Blacks led to the death of Wyatt and four Black males, including a teen, along with weeks of open suspicion and discord between Black and White residents.[47] Although there is no direct evidence that Bob, his father, or any of his kin were involved, certainly they felt the threat of White vigilantism as well as the need to support Black neighbors who had become embroiled in conflict because of an assault on a female relation and attempted threat of loss of their hard-won landed property.

In due course, Bob and Sarah's children married and had families of their own. Richard was the first to move away. A farmer like his parents, he settled hundreds of miles away in the small hamlet of Lamar, Texas, on the Gulf Coast. There, he wed Nannie Richman in 1898.[48] Records indicate that Richard remained a farmer, renting land. He and Nannie had three children. Several years later, Isadora married Ben Benson, a local sawmill worker.[49] Lela wed Green Samuels, who may have been a distant relation, at about the same time.[50] Their youngest sister, Lucy, married James Hamilton in 1916.[51] Hamilton soon was drafted to fight in World War I. He left his family to serve in France as a wagoner in a supply company that was a part of a field artillery unit.[52] Lucy, pregnant with their first child, moved back to her parents' home in her husband's absence.

It must have been a difficult year for Bob's family. Not only was Lucy's husband far away in the war, but Lillian, who had married some years earlier, died in childbirth.[53] They named her surviving baby boy for her—J. Lillian. Bob and Sarah took in Lillian's young sons, Robert and Irving, along with the baby. With four adult daughters still at home, there were plenty of people to care for Lillian's children. Those old enough to work who were not otherwise employed or in school worked on the family farm, sharing the labor and its proceeds.[54] Daughter Leila married in 1922,[55] and Bobbie wed in 1930.[56] Mary and her four teenage children also shared the home.[57] Their son John, also a cotton farmer, lived next door in a house he rented with his wife, Mary, and their daughters, Sarah, age fourteen and Johnnie, age twelve.[58]

Sarah Samuels, Bob's longtime spouse and the maternal center of the Samuels's sprawling family, died of a heart attack on March 11, 1933, at the age of seventy-four.[59] The family no doubt rallied around their aging father. Those living with and near Bob made certain that he was well provided for, as indicated by the manner in which his WPA interviewer described him three years later. Along with Lillian's children and Mary and her children, Bobbie also lived with him, having moved back to her father's home after divorcing in 1939.[60] She had grown up suffering from sickle cell anemia and may have needed additional care and support from family members.[61] Another daughter and granddaughter, Lucy and Vivian Jefferson, helped to fill Bob's house to the brim in 1940. But their paternal head and the family's historian extraordinaire was not to live much longer. Bob Samuels died on February 3, 1941, having succumbed to gangrene after a two-month battle.[62]

Bob Samuels's children lived on through the twentieth century: working, raising their children, and carrying forward the proud legacy of a family with a deep connection to American history that their father, and earlier family members, had made certain that they knew. By the 1980s, Lucy was the last living child of Bob and Sarah Samuels. She and her daughter Vivian, like millions of other Black southerners in the twentieth century, had migrated from the South, where their families had been so long rooted. As with their storied ancestors from the sixteenth century, they sought prosperity away from their place of birth. Vivian married US Army Staff Sargent Henry Hardin of Mississippi and moved to Detroit, probably taking her aging mother with her.[63] Lucy died in Detroit in 1986.[64]

Bob Samuels's Black American family, regardless of its varied structures and household members' legal identities, marriage statuses, and care experiences over the generations, was just that: an American family in all its struggles, survivance, and hopes for a better future. Regardless of "what sorrows labour in [their] parent's breast,"[65] family remained.

Appendix A
Godfrey Family Units[1]

Table 1.1 Godfrey Family Unit A

Name	Description[1]	Relations
Abigail Godfrey	75, nearly worn out	Mother of Ned Godfrey Mother-in-law of Elizabeth Grandmother of Jeffery Godfrey and Betsey Godfrey
Ned (Edward) Godfrey	42, a thin fellow	Son of Abigail Godfrey Husband of Elizabeth Godfrey Father of Jeffery Godfrey, Betsey Godfrey, and Ned Godfrey, Jnr.
Elizabeth Godfrey	30, short and stout	Daughter-in-law of Abigail Wife of Ned Godfrey Guardian of Jeffery Godfrey[2] Mother of Betsey Godfrey and Ned Godfrey, Jnr.
Jeffery Godfrey	17, a likely boy	Grandson of Abigail Godfrey Son of Ned Godfrey Ward of Elizabeth Godfrey[3] Brother of Betsey Godfrey and Ned Godfrey, Jnr.
Betsey Godfrey	1.5	Granddaughter of Abigail Godfrey Daughter of Ned and Elizabeth Godfrey Sister of Jeffery Godfrey and Ned Godfrey, Jnr.

(continued)

Table 1.1 (Continued)

Name	Description[1]	Relations
Ned Godfrey, Jnr.	5 weeks	Grandson of Abigail Godfrey Son of Ned and Elizabeth Godfrey Brother of Jeffery Godfrey and Betsey Godfrey

[1]Descriptions are also taken from the Black Loyalist site and reflect how individuals were described in the *Book of Negroes* at the time of the Evacuation of New York in 1783. [2]Evidence suggests that Jeffery might be Ned Godfey's child from a previous relationship.

Table 1.2 Godfrey Family Unity B

Name	Description	Relations
Bridget Godfrey[1]	55, stout wench	Mother of Jenny Kelley, Kate Godfrey, and Sam Godfrey Mother-in-law of Moses Kelley, Lewis Church, and Sucky Godfrey Grandmother of Port Godfrey, Lucy Godfrey, Salley Godfrey, Sally Godfrey, James Godfrey, Robert Godfrey, and William Godfrey[1]
Jenny Kelley	32, stout wench	Daughter of Bridget Godfrey Wife of Moses Kelley Sister of Kate Godfrey and Sam Godfrey Sister-in-law of Lewis Church and Sucky Godfrey[2] Aunt of Port Godfrey, Lucy Godfrey, Salley Godfrey, Sally Godfrey, James Godfrey, Robert Godfrey, and William Godfrey,
Moses Kelley	37, stout fellow	Son-in-law of Bridget Godfrey Husband of Jenny Kelley Brother-in-law of Kate Godfrey, Lewis Church, Sam Godfrey, and Sucky Godfrey[3] Uncle of Port Godfrey, Lucy Godfrey, Salley Godfrey, Sally Godfrey, James Godfrey, Robert Godfrey, and William Godfrey
Kate [Katty] Godfrey	30, ordinary wench	Daughter of Bridget Godfrey Partner of Lewis Church[4] Mother of Port Godfrey, Lucy Godfrey, and Salley Godfrey Sister of Jenny Kelley and Sam Godfrey Sister-in-law of Moses Kelley and Sucky Godfrey Aunt of Sally Godfrey, James Godfrey, Robert Godfrey, and William Godfrey
Lewis [Lymas] Church	27, stout fellow	Son-in-law of Bridget Godfrey[5] Son of Rose [Bartree] Partner of Kate Godfrey[6]

(continued)

Table 1.2 (Continued)

Name	Description	Relations
		Guardian of Port Godfrey, Lucy Godfrey, and Salley Godfrey
		Brother-in-law of Jenny Kelley, Moses Kelley, Sam Godfrey, and Sucky Godfrey[7]
		Uncle of Sally Godfrey, James Godfrey, Robert Godfrey, and William Godfrey
Port Godfrey	12, a likely boy	Grandson of Bridget Godfrey
		Son of Kate Godfrey
		Ward of Lewis Church[8]
		Brother of Lucy Godfrey and Salley Godfrey
		Nephew of Jenny Kelley, Moses Kelley, Sam Godfrey, and Sucky Godfrey
		Cousin of Sally Godfrey, James Godfrey, Robert Godfrey, and William Godfrey
Lucy Godfrey	7, ordinary child	Granddaughter of Bridget Godfrey
		Daughter of Kate Godfrey
		Ward of Lewis Church[9]
		Sister of Port Godfrey and Salley Godfrey
		Niece of Jenny Kelley, Moses Kelley, Sam Godfrey, and Sucky Godfrey
		Cousin of Sally Godfrey, James Godfrey, Robert Godfrey, and William Godfrey
Salley [Sarah] Godfrey	1.5	Granddaughter of Bridget Godfrey
		Daughter of Kate Godfrey
		Ward of Lewis Church[10]
		Sister of Port Godfrey and Lucy Godfrey
		Niece of Jenny Kelley, Moses Kelley, Sam Godfrey, and Sucky Godfrey
		Cousin of Sally Godfrey, James Godfrey, Robert Godfrey, and William Godfrey
Rose [Bartree]		Mother of Lewis Church
Sam Godfrey	26, stout fellow	Son of Bridget Godfrey
		Husband of Sucky Godfrey
		Father of Sally Godfrey, James Godfrey, Robert Godfrey, and William Godfrey
		Brother of Jenny Kelley and Kate Godfrey
		Brother-in-law of Moses Kelley and Lewis Church[11]
		Uncle of Port Godfrey, Lucy Godfrey, and Salley Godfrey

(continued)

Table 1.2 **(Continued)**

Name	Description	Relations
Sucky Godfrey	22, stout wench	Daughter-in-law of Bridget Godfrey Wife of Sam Godfrey Mother of Sally Godfrey, James Godfrey, Robert Godfrey, and William Godfrey Sister-in-law of Jenny Kelley, Moses Kelley, Kate Godfrey, and Lewis Church Aunt of Port Godfrey, Lucy Godfrey, and Salley Godfrey
Sally	6, ordinary child	Granddaughter of Bridget Godfrey Daughter of Sam and Sucky Godfrey Sister of James Godfrey, Robert Godfrey, and William Godfrey Niece of Jenny Kelley, Moses Kelley, Kate Godfrey, and Lewis Church Cousin of Port Godfrey, Lucy Godfrey, and Salley Godfrey
James		Grandson of Bridget Godfrey Son of Sam and Sucky Godfrey Brother of Sally Godfrey, Robert Godfrey, and William Godfrey Nephew of Jenny Kelley, Moses Kelley, Kate Godfrey, and Lewis Church Cousin of Port Godfrey, Lucy Godfrey, and Salley Godfrey
Robert	2	Grandson of Bridget Godfrey Son of Sam and Sucky Godfrey Brother of Sally Godfrey, James Godfrey, and William Godfrey Nephew of Jenny Kelley, Moses Kelley, Kate Godfrey, and Lewis Church Cousin of Port Godfrey, Lucy Godfrey, and Salley Godfrey
William Godfrey	Infant	Grandson of Bridget Godfrey Son of Sam and Sucky Godfrey Brother of Sally Godfrey, James Godfrey, and Robert Godfrey Nephew of Jenny Kelley, Moses Kelley, Kate Godfrey, and Lewis Church Cousin of Port Godfrey, Lucy Godfrey, and Salley Godfrey

(continued)

Table 1.2 (Continued)

Name	Description	Relations
Henry Givin	33, stout fellow	Son of Bridget Godfrey[12] Brother of Jenny Kelley, Kate Godfrey, and Sam Godfrey Brother-in-law of Moses Kelley, Lewis Church, and Sucky Godfrey Uncle of Port Godfrey, Lucy Godfrey, Salley Godfrey, Sally Godfrey, James Godfrey, Robert Godfrey, William Godfrey

[1]Some records suggest that Petter Godfrey (son of Ely and Hannah Godfrey) might also be Bridget's grandchild, but the relationship remains unclear. [2]Records are unclear if Kate and Lewis were ever married. I have listed him here as a brother-in-law for clarity. [3]Records are unclear if Kate and Lewis were ever married. I have listed him here as a brother-in-law for clarity. [4]Records are unclear if Kate and Lewis were ever married. [5]Records are unclear if Kate and Lewis were ever married. I have listed him here as a son-in-law for clarity. [6]Records are unclear if Kate and Lewis were ever married. [7]Records are unclear if Kate and Lewis were ever married. I have listed him here as a brother-in-law for clarity. [8]Evidence suggests that Port, Lucy, and Salley Godfrey were not Lewis Church's children. [9]Evidence suggests that Port, Lucy, and Salley Godfrey were not Lewis Church's children. [10]Evidence suggests that Port, Lucy, and Salley Godfrey were not Lewis Church's children. [11]Records are unclear if Kate and Lewis were ever married. I have listed him here as a brother-in-law for clarity. [12]Henry is listed as Bridget's son once in the records, but no references to siblings or other relatives are present.

Table 1.3 Godfrey Family Unit C

Name	Description	Relations
Pleasant [Godfrey]	26, ordinary wench	Mother of Lettius and Ned
Lettius [Godfrey]	11, likely child	Daughter of Pleasant [Godfrey] Sister of Ned [Godfrey]
Ned [Godfrey]	6, likely boy	Son of Pleasant [Godfrey] Brother of Lettius [Godfrey]

Table 1.4 Godfrey Family Unity D

Name	Description	Relations
Sally Godfrey	36, sickly wench	Mother of John Godfrey, Kate Godfrey, and Jacob Godfrey
Kate Godfrey [Simmons]	15, a likely girl	Daughter of Sally Godfrey
		Sister of John Godfrey and Jacob Godfrey
John Godfrey[1]	13, a sick boy	Son of Sally Godfrey
		Brother of Kate Godfrey and Jacob Godfrey
Jacob Godfrey	10, stout boy	Son of Sally Godfrey
		Brother of Kate Godfrey and John Godfrey

[1] Maybe the John Godfrey described as wounded cripple in list of Nova Scotia loyalists who wanted to travel to Sierra Leone, listed as twenty-five years old and who has a wife. "List of Those Wishing to Go to Sierra Leone," Black Loyalist, http://www.blackloyalist.info/assets/SierraLeoneList/SL-List-5.JPG.

Table 1.5 Godfrey Family Unit E

Name	Description	Relations
Ely Godfrey[1]		Husband of Hannah Godfrey
		Father of Petter Godfrey, John [Godfrey], [Unknown] [Godfrey], and Polly [Godfrey][2]
Hannah Godfrey		Wife of Ely Godfrey
		Mother of Petter [Godfrey], John [Godfrey], [Unknown] [Godfrey], and Polly [Godfrey][3]
Petter [Godfrey]	6, fine boy	Son of Ely and Hannah Godfrey
		Brother of John [Godfrey], [Unknown] [Godfrey], and Polly [Godfrey][4]
John [Godfrey]	Infant	Son of Ely and Hannah Godfrey
		Brother of Petter [Godfrey], [Unknown] [Godfrey], and Polly [Godfrey][5]
Polly [Godfrey]	Infant	Daughter of Ely and Hannah Godfrey
		Sister of Petter [Godfrey], John [Godfrey], and [Unknown] [Godfrey][6]
[Unknown] [Godfrey]		Child of Ely and Hannah Godfrey
		Sibling of Petter [Godfrey], John [Godfrey], and Polly [Godfrey][7]

[1] Because Petter is listed as Bridget's grandson in several records, it is possible that Ely is Bridget's son. If so, this family may be part of Bridget's larger familial unit. Unlike Bridget's other children, however, Ely is not listed as such in the collections. [2] The records are unclear if [Unknown] [Godfrey] is Ely and Hannah's child together or a child under their care. [3] The records are unclear if [Unknown] [Godfrey] is Ely and Hannah's child together or a child under their care. [4] The records are unclear if [Unknown] [Godfrey] is a biological sibling. [5] The records are unclear if [Unknown] [Godfrey] is a biological sibling. [6] The records are unclear if [Unknown] [Godfrey] is a biological sibling. [7] The records are unclear if [Unknown] [Godfrey] is a biological sibling.

Table 1.6 Godfrey Family Unity F

Name	Description	Relations
Bristol Godfrey	20, stout fellow	Likely the husband of Kitty Godfrey Likely the relative of Edward Godfrey and Valentine Godfrey
Hannah Godfrey	22, likely wench	Likely the wife of Bristol Godfrey Likely the relative of Edward Godfrey and Valentine Godfrey
Valentine Godfrey	22, likely lad	Likely the relative of Bristol Godfrey, Kitty Godfrey, and Edward Godfrey
Edward Godfrey	17, likely lad	Likely the relative of Bristol Godfrey, Kitty Godfrey, and Valentine Godfrey

Table 1.7 Godfrey Family Unity G

Name	Description	Relations
Cato Ramsey	45, slim fellow	Husband of China Ramsey Father of James Ramsey, Betsey Ramsey, and Nelly Ramsey
China [Jane] Ramsey [Godfrey]	35, ordinary wench	Wife of Cato Ramsey Mother of James Ramsey, Betsey Ramsey, and Nelly Ramsey
James Ramsey	20, stout lad	Son of Cato and China Ramsey Brother of Betsey Ramsey and Nelly Ramsey
Nelly Ramsey	15, fine girl	Daughter of Cato and China Ramsey Sister of James Ramsey and Betsey Ramsey
Betsey [Betty] Ramsey[1]		Daughter of Cato and China Ramsey Sister of James Ramsey and Nelly Ramsey

[1] Nelly Ramsey's records suggest that Betsey is the younger of the two sisters.

Table 1.8 Godfrey Family Unit H

Name	Description	Relations
John Brown [Simmons]	45, ordinary fellow	Husband of Peggy Brown Father of Jenny Brown, James Brown, and Nancy Brown
Peggy Brown	30, stout wench	Wife of John Brown Mother of Jenny Brown, James Brown, and Nancy Brown
Jenny Brown	5, ordinary child	Daughter of John and Peggy Brown Sister of James Brown and Nancy Brown
James Brown	2	Son of John and Peggy Brown Brother of James Brown and Nancy Brown
Nancy Brown	1.5	Daughter of John and Peggy Brown Sister of Jenny Brown and James Brown

Appendix B

Percentage of Households Per State with Enslaved People, 1860

Table 2.1 Percentages of Households Per State with Enslaved People, 1860[1]

Slave Holding State 1860	Households with Enslaved African Americans
Mississippi	49%
South Carolina	46%
Georgia	37%
Alabama	35%
Florida	34%
Louisiana	29%
Texas	28%
North Carolina	28%
Virginia	26%
Tennessee	25%
Kentucky	23%
Arkansas	20%
Missouri	13%
Maryland	12%
Delaware	3%

[1] Table compiled from Table 4.2, Brenda E. Stevenson, *What Is Slavery?* (London: Polity Press, 2015), Kindle Edition, Kindle Location 3550–61.

Appendix B

Table 2.2 Enslaved Men and Women Per State in the United States, 1820–1860[1]

US States	Gender	1820 Totals	1820 %	1830 Totals	1830 %	1840 Totals	1840 %	1850 Totals	1850 %	1860 Totals	1860 %
Alabama		41,879		117,549		253,532		342,844		435,080	
	Male	21,780	52.0%	59,170	50.3%	127,360	50.2%	171,804	50.1%	217,766	50.0%
	Female	20,099	47.9%	58,379	49.6%	126,172	49.7%	171,040	49.8%	217,314	49.9%
Arkansas				4,576		19,935		47,100		111,115	
	Male			2,293	50.1%	10,119	50.7%	23,658	50.2%	56,174	50.5%
	Female			2,283	49.8%	9,816	49.2%	23,442	49.7%	54,941	49.4%
Florida						25,717		39,310		61,745	
	Male					13,038	50.7%	19,804	50.3%	31,348	50.77%
	Female					12,679	49.3%	19,506	49.6%	30,397	49.23%
Georgia		149,656		217,531		280,944		381,682		462,198	
	Male	75,916	50.7%	108,817	50.0%	139,335	49.6%	188,857	49.4%	229,193	49.5%
	Female	73,740	49.2%	108,714	49.9%	141,609	50.4%	192,825	50.5%	233,005	50.4%
Kentucky		126,732		165,213		182,258		210,981		225,483	
	Male	63,914	50.4%	82,309	49.8%	91,004	49.9%	105,063	49.8%	113,009	50.1%
	Female	62,818	49.5%	82,904	50.1%	91,254	50.0%	105,918	50.2%	112,474	49.8%
Louisiana		69,064		109,588		168,452		244,809		331,726	
	Male	36,566	52.9%	57,911	52.8%	86,529	51.3%	125,874	51.4%	171,977	51.8%
	Female	32,498	47.0%	51,677	47.1%	81,923	48.6%	118,935	48.5%	159,749	48.1%
Maryland		107,398		102,994		89,737		90,368		87,189	
	Male	56,373	52.4%	53,442	51.8%	46,068	51.3%	45,944	50.8%	44,313	50.8%
	Female	51,025	47.5%	49,552	48.1%	43,669	48.6%	44,424	49.1%	42,876	49.1%
Mississippi		32,814		65,659		195,211		309,878		436,631	
	Male	16,850	51.3%	33,099	50.4%	98,003	50.2%	154,963	50.0%	219,301	50.2%
	Female	15,964	48.6%	32,560	49.5%	97,208	49.8%	154,915	49.9%	217,330	49.7%
Missouri				25,091		58,240		87,422		114,931	
	Male			12,439	49.5%	28,742	49.3%	43,484	49.7%	57,360	49.9%
	Female			12,652	50.4%	29,498	50.6%	43,938	50.2%	57,571	50.0%

North Carolina	Male	205,017 106,551	51.9%	245,601 124,313	50.6%	245,817 123,546	50.2%	288,548 144,581	50.1%	331,059 166,469	50.2%
	Female	98,466	48.0%	121,288	49.3%	122,271	49.7%	143,967	49.8%	164,590	49.7%
South Carolina	Male	258,475 130,472	50.4%	315,401 155,469	49.2%	327,038 158,678	48.5%	384,984 187,756	48.7%	402,406 196,571	48.8%
	Female	128,003	49.5%	159,932	50.7%	168,360	51.4%	197,228	51.2%	205,835	51.1%
Tennessee	Male	80,107 39,747	49.6%	141,603 70,216	49.5%	183,059 91,477	49.9%	239,459 118,780	49.6%	275,719 136,370	49.4%
	Female	40,360	50.3%	71,387	50.4%	91,582	50.0%	120,679	50.4%	139,349	50.5%
Texas	Male							58,161 28,700	49.3%	182,566 91,189	49.9%
	Female							29,461	50.6%	91,377	50.0%
Virginia	Male	425,153 218,274	51.3%	469,757 239,077	50.8%	449,087 228,661	50.9%	472,528 240,562	50.9%	490,865 249,483	50.8%
	Female	206,879	48.6%	230,680	49.1%	220,426	49.0%	231,966	49.0%	241,382	49.1%

¹Table compiled from Table 4.1, Stevenson, *What Is Slavery?* Kindle Edition, Kindle Location 3552.

Notes

INTRODUCTION

1. Michelle Obama, "Michelle Obama's Speech at the 2016 Democratic National Convention," National Public Radio, July 26, 2021, http://www.npr.org/2016/07/26/487431756/michelle-obamas-prepared-remarks-for-democratic-national-convention.

2. Ibid.

3. Julie Bosman, "Obama Sharply Assails Absent Black Fathers," *New York Times*, June 16, 2008, http://www.nytimes.com/2008/06/16/us/politics/15cnd-obama.html; see also William Darity Jr., "How Barack Obama Failed Black Americans," *Atlantic*, December 22, 2016, https://www.theatlantic.com/politics/archive/2016/12/how-barack-obama-failed-black-americans/511358/.

4. Tanasia Kenney, "Another Racist White Woman Fired for Disgusting Comments on First Lady Michelle Obama," *Atlanta Black Star*, July 27, 2016, http://atlantablackstar.com/2016/07/27/another-racist-white-woman-fired-for-disgusting-comment-on-first-lady-michelle-obama/; Nina Golgowski, "Doctor Calls Michelle Obama 'Monkey Face,' but Says She's Not Racist," *HuffPost*, December 1, 2016, updated December 5, 2016, https://www.huffingtonpost.com/entry/doctor-michelle-obama-monkey-face_us_584069a7e4b017f37fe35241.

5. Patrice Peck, "Michelle Obama Pictured as Nude Slave in Spanish Magazine Fuera de Serie: Is it Offensive?" *HuffPost*, August 28, 2012, updated December 5, 2016, https://www.huffingtonpost.com/2012/08/28/michelle-obama-pictured-a_n_1836570.html.

6. See, for example, some coverage of this vilification as documented in Gary Younge, "Michelle Obama, Reluctant Presidential Consort," *Guardian*, January 13, 2012, https://www.theguardian.com/commentisfree/cifamerica/2012/jan/13/michelle-obama-reluctant-first-lady.

7. Maureen Dowd, "She's Not Buttering Him Up," *New York Times*, April 25, 2007, https://www.nytimes.com/2007/04/25/opinion/25dowd.html?hp.

8. Josh Levin, "The Welfare Queen," *Slate*, December 19, 2013, http://www.slate.com/articles/news_and_politics/history/2013/12/linda_taylor_welfare_queen_ronald_reagan_made_her_a_notorious_american_villain.html.

9. Ibid.

10. "Can the Children Be Saved? One Block's Battle against Drugs and Despair," *Newsweek*, September 11, 1989, cover page.

11. Douglas Besharov, "Crack Babies: The Worst Threat Is Mom Herself," *Washington Post*, August 6, 1989, https://www.washingtonpost.com/archive/opinions/1989/08/06/crack-babies-the-worst-threat-is-mom-herself/d984f0b2-7598-4dc1-9846-3418df3a5895/?utm_term=.dcae8fb0c671.

12. Ellen Hopkins, "Childhood's End: What Life Is Like for Crack Babies," *Rolling Stone*, October 18, 1990, https://www.rollingstone.com/culture/culture-news/childhoods-end-what-life-is-like-for-crack-babies-188557/.

13. "A Woman's Rights: Part Four: Slandering the Unborn, Opinion," *New York Times*, December 28, 2018, https://www.nytimes.com/interactive/2018/12/28/opinion/crack-babies-racism.html.

14. Judith Cummings, "Breakup of Black Families Imperils Gains of Decades," *New York Times*, November 20, 1983, http://www.nytimes.com/1983/11/20/us/breakup-of-black-family-imperils-gains-of-decades.html?pagewanted=all.

15. Stephina Zwane, dir. *Baby Mamas*, Netflix, 2017, https://www.netflix.com/title/81244451.

16. Bill Cosby, "Dr. Bill Cosby Speaks at the 50th Anniversary Commemoration of the Brown v. Topeka Board of Education Supreme Court Decision, May 22, 2004," *Black Scholar* 34, no. 4 (winter 2004): 2–5, http://www.jstor.org/stable/41069098.

17. Ibid., 2–3.

18. "California Deposes Its 'Welfare Queen," *New York Times*, July 23, 2016, https://www.nytimes.com/2016/07/24/opinion/sunday/california-deposes-its-welfare-queen.html?_r=0.

19. Regarding the sterilization of Black women in the South, the Midwest, the West, and other locales, see Kevin Begos, "The American Eugenics Movement after WW II (part 3 of 3), *Indy Week*, June 1, 2011, https://indyweek.com/news/american-eugenics-movement-world-war-ii-part-3-3/.

20. Annie Waldman, "Michael Brown's 'No Angel' Controversy," BBC News, August 25, 2014, http://www.bbc.com/news/blogs-echochambers-28929087.

21. See, for example, the assessment of the "cultural deprivation" argument regarding its impact on K–12 education in Donna Tileston and Sandra Darling, *Why Culture Counts: Teaching Children of Poverty* (Bloomington, IN: Solution Tree Press, 2008).

22. Robert Staples, "Towards a Sociology of the Black Family: A Theoretical and Methodological Assessment" *Journal of Marriage and Family* 33, no. 1 (1971): 120, https://doi.org/10.2307/350160.

23. M. Belinda Tucker and Claudia Mitchell-Kernan, "Trends in African American Family Formation: A Theoretical and Statistical Overview," in *The Decline in Marriage Among African Americans: Causes, Consequences, and Policy*

Implications, ed. M. Belinda Tucker and Claudia Mitchell-Kernan (New York: Russell Sage Foundation, 1995), 6. The authors were referring to the ideological perspectives that sociologist Walter Allen identified as dominating twentieth-century social science literature regarding the Black family: cultural equivalence, cultural deviance and cultural variance. See, for example, Walter Allen, "Black Family Research in the United States: A Review, Assessment and Extension," *Journal of Comparative Family Studies* 9, no.2 (summer 1978): 167–68, http://www.jstor.org/stable/41601045.

24. Allen, "Black Family Research in the United States," 170–71. Black Americans were not the only racialized groups stereotyped with family dysfunction and pressured to take up the middle-class model of patriarchy, nuclear structure, and heteronormative marital relations. Native Americans, along with Latinx, Irish, Asian, southern and eastern European immigrants—all considered at some point in the nation's history, like Black Americans, as racial "others"—endured condemnation for some perceived gender role variance and family deviance. European American society demanded that everyone take on the "White" (western European–descended) middle-class, Protestant, patriarchal, heterosexual norm they claimed as the ideal, or face marginalization, vilification, and even criminalization. See, for example, Ryan Seelau, "Regaining Control over the Children: Reversing the Legacy of Assimilative Policies in Education, Child Welfare, and Juvenile Justice That Targeted Native American Youth," *American Indian Law Review* 37, no. 1 (2012–2013): 63–108, http://www.jstor.org/stable/41940641; Kathy Fejes-Mendoza, Darcy Miller, and Robert Eppler, "Portraits of Dysfunction: Criminal, Educational, and Family Profiles of Juvenile Female Offenders," *Education and Treatment of Children* 18, no. 3 (August 1995): 309–21, http://www.jstor.org/stable/42899416; D. Russell Crane, So Wa Ngai, Jeffrey H. Larson, and McArthur Hafen Jr. "The Influence of Family Functioning and Parent-Adolescent Acculturation on North American Chinese Adolescent Outcomes," *Family Relations* 54, no. 3 (July 2005): 400–10, http://www.jstor.org/stable/40005293; Jillian M. Duquaine-Watson, "The Politics of Single Motherhood in the United States," in *Mothering by Degrees: Single Mothers and the Pursuit of Postsecondary Education* (New Brunswick, NJ: Rutgers University Press, 2017), 13–42; Ronald E. Hall, Jonathan N. Livingston, Valerie V. Henderson, Glenn O. Fisher, and Rebekah Hines, "Post-modern Perspective on the Economics of African American Fatherhood," *Journal of African American Studies* 10 (June 2007): 112–23, https://doi.org/10.1007/s12111-007-9004-7; Z. Lois Bryant and Marilyn Coleman, "The Black Family as Portrayed in Introductory Marriage and Family Textbooks," *Family Relations* 37, no. 3 (July 1988): 255–59, https://doi.org/10.2307/584558; Sarah Deer, "Federal Indian Law and Violent Crime: Native Women and Children at the Mercy of the State," *Social Justice* 31, no. 4 (2004): 17–30; Paul R. Smokowski, Roderick Rose, and Martica L. Bacallao, "Acculturation and Latino Family Processes: How Cultural Involvement, Biculturalism, and Acculturation Gaps Influence Family Dynamics," *Family Relations* 57, no. 3 (July 2008): 295–308, doi/10.1111/j.1741-3729.2008.00501.

25. Although Senator Daniel Patrick Moynihan's *The Negro Family: The Case for National Action* was published more than fifty years ago and largely excluded a discussion of Black middle-class domesticity, this document has done much to

essentially shape the mythology of Black familial dysfunction in the popular imagination and to affect the design and implementation of public policy aimed at the Black community since 1965. Moynihan, who had training as a sociologist, was an assistant for policy planning and research in the Department of Labor when he penned the report. It was published at a time when African Americans and other activists were forcing the nation to recognize, and attempt to remedy, its racially based social, political, and economic inequalities. See Daniel P. Moynihan, *The Negro Family: The Case for National Action* (Washington, DC: US Department of Labor, Office of Policy Planning and Research, 1965).

26. Ibid., 1.

27. Ta Nehisi Coates, "The Black Family in the Age of Mass Incarceration," *Atlantic*, October 2015, http://www.theatlantic.com/magazine/archive/2015/10/the-black-family-in-the-age-of-mass-incarceration/403246/.

28. Ulrich B. Phillips, *American Negro Slavery: A Survey of the Supply, Employment and Control of Negro Labor as Determined by the Plantation Regime* (New York: Appleton, 1969), 306.

29. Ibid., 291.

30. Ibid., 309.

31. John David Smith, "Ulrich Bonnell Phillips (1877–1934)," *New Georgia Encyclopedia*, April 1, 2003, updated July 9, 2021, http://www.georgiaencyclopedia.org/articles/history-archaeology/ulrich-bonnell-phillips-1877-1934; Richard Hofstader, "U.B. Phillips and the Plantation Legend," *Journal of Negro History* 29, no. 2 (April 1944): 109–24, https://doi.org/10.2307/2715306.

32. See the report references and his conclusions in Frank Tannenbaum, *Slave and Citizen* (New York: Alfred Knopf, 1946); Moynihan, *The Negro Family*, 15.

33. Tannenbaum, *Slave and Citizen*, 77. Tannenbaum is equally critical of slavery in the British Caribbean.

34. Gilberto Freyre, *The Masters and the Slaves: A Study in the Development of Brazilian Civilization* (New York: Knopf, 1964); Roger Bastide, *The African Religions of Brazil: Towards a Sociology of the Interpretations of Civilizations* (Baltimore, MD: Johns Hopkins University Press, 1978); Emilia Viotti, daCosta, Robert Selenes, "Black Homes, White Homilies: Perceptions of the Slave Family and Slave Women in Nineteenth Century Brazil," in *More Than Chattel: Black Women and Slavery in the Americas*, ed. David Barry Gaspar and Darlene Clark Hine (Bloomington, IN: Indiana University Press, 1996), 126–27.

35. Brenda E. Stevenson, "What's Love Got to Do with It: Concubinage and Enslaved Black Women and Girls in the Antebellum South," *Journal of African American History* 98, no. 1 (winter 2013): 99–125, https://doi.org/10.5323/jafriamerhist.98.1.0099.

36. Kenneth Stampp, *The Peculiar Institution: Slavery in the Ante-Bellum South* (New York: Knopf, 1956), 198.

37. Ibid., 198.

38. Ibid., 29.

39. Stanley M. Elkins, *Slavery: A Problem in American Institutional and Intellectual Life* 2nd ed. (Chicago: University of Chicago Press, 1968), 55.

40. W. E. B. Du Bois, *The Philadelphia Negro* (Philadelphia: University of Pennsylvania Press, 1899).

41. W. E. B. Du Bois, ed. *The Negro American Family* (Cambridge, MA: MIT Press, 1970), 127–48; see also Frank Furstenberg, "The Making of the Black Family: Race and Class in Qualitative Studies in the Twentieth Century," *Annual Review of Sociology* 33 (2007): 433, http://www.jstor.org/stable/29737770.

42. Du Bois, *Negro American Family*, 129–30.

43. William B. Thomas, "Black Intellectuals' Critique of Early Mental Testing: A Little-Known Saga of the 1920s," *American Journal of Education* 90, no. 3 (May 1982), 264–65.

44. Frederick Hoffman, *Race Traits and Tendencies of the American Negro* (New York: American Economic Association/Macmillan, 1896), 207–208.

45. Du Bois, *Negro American Family*, 132–34.

46. Ibid., 134.

47. E. Franklin Frazier, *The Negro Family in the United States* (Chicago: University of Chicago Press, 1966).

48. Nathan Glazer and Daniel P. Moynihan, *Beyond the Melting Pot: The Negroes, Puerto Ricans, Jews, Italians and Irish of New York City* (Cambridge, MA: MIT Press, 1963).

49. Ibid., 26.

50. Ibid., 23.

51. Ibid., 50.

52. Ibid., 50–51.

53. Ibid., 52.

54. Frazier, *Negro Family in the United States*, xii–xiii.

55. W. E. B. Du Bois, *Black Folk Then and Now: An Essay in the History and Sociology of the Negro Race* (New York: Holt, 1939).

56. Carter G. Woodson, *The African Background Outlined: Or, Handbook for the Study of the Negro* (Washington, DC: Association for the Study of Negro Life and History, 1936).

57. Frazier, *Negro Family in the United States*, 6.

58. Ibid., 8.

59. Ibid., xi.

60. Ibid., 92–101, 107, 112.

61. Ibid., 249, 255.

62. See, for example, Bruce Western and Christopher Wildeman, "The Black Family and Mass Incarceration," *Annals of the American Academy of Political and Social Science* 621 (January 2009): 221–42, http://www.jstor.org/stable/40375840; and Bruce Western and Sara McLanahan, "Fathers behind Bars: The Impact of Incarceration on Family Formation," *Center for Research on Child Wellbeing*, Working Paper #00-08 (June 2000), http://citeseerx.ist.psu.edu/viewdoc/download?doi=10.1.1.25.3289&rep=rep1&type=pdf.

63. The reality that Black females were more than likely thanks to their male peers to be better educated up to the point of acquisition of a college degree was not recognized or evaluated in the discourse on family stability. See, for example, Anne

McDaniel, Thomas A. DiPrete, Claudia Buchmann, and Uri Shwed, "The Black Gender Gap in Educational Attainment: Historical Trends and Racial Comparisons," *Demography* 48, no. 3 (August 2011): 889–914, https://www.jstor.org/stable/41237816.

64. Melville J. Herskovits, *Myth of the Negro Past* (Boston: Beacon Press, 1990), 3–6.

65. Ibid., 145.

66. Ibid., 139.

67. Ibid., 139–40.

68. Gunnar Myrdal, *An American Dilemma: The Negro Problem in Modern Democracy* (New York: Harper and Brothers, 1944), 928.

69. Ibid., 928–29.

70. Ibid., 929.

71. Ibid., 931.

72. Ibid.

73. Ibid., 930–31.

74. Charles S. Johnson, *Shadow of the Plantation* (Chicago: University of Chicago Press, 1934).

75. Myrdal, *American Dilemma*, 935.

76. Ibid.

77. See, for example, St. Clair Drake and Horace R. Cayton, *Black Metropolis: A Study of Negro Life in a Northern City* (Chicago: University of Chicago Press, 2015), Kindle version, Kindle location 10558–10673.

78. Ibid., 11037.

79. Ibid., 11028–11076.

80. Ibid., 10059.

81. Ibid., 12532.

82. Ibid., 11053.

83. Hortense Powdermaker, *After Freedom: A Cultural Study in the Deep South* (New York: Viking, 1939).

84. Oscar Lewis, *Five Families: Mexican Case Studies in the Culture of Poverty* (New York: Basic Books, 1959).

85. Oscar Lewis, "Culture of Poverty," in *Poor Americans: How the White Poor Live*, ed. Marc Pilisuk and Phyllis Pilisuk (Chicago: Aldine, 1971), 21.

86. Oscar Lewis, "Culture of Poverty," *Society* 35, no. 2 (January 1998), 7, 9, https://doi.org/10.1007/BF02838122.

87. Quoted in Eleanor Burke Leacock, "Introduction," in *The Culture of Poverty: A Critique* (New York: Simon and Schuster, 1971), 11.

88. Ibid.

89. Elkins, *Slavery*, 271.

90. Lyndon B. Johnson, "Commencement Address at Howard University: 'To Fulfill These Rights,' June 4, 1965," https://teachingamericanhistory.org/document/commencement-address-at-howard-university-to-fulfill-these-rights/. Most of the speech, however, was written by Johnson's veteran speechwriter Richard Goodwin.

91. Steve Bogira, "Fifty Years after LBJ Challenged the Nation, the Rights of African-Americans Remain Unfulfilled," *Chicago Reader*, June 3, 2015, http://www

.chicagoreader.com/Bleader/archives/2015/06/03/fifty-years-after-lbj-challenged-the-nation-the-rights-of-african-americans-remain-unfulfilled.

92. Quoted in ibid.

93. Johnson, "Commencement Address at Howard University".

94. See, for example, Dudley Randall, "Review of *Marriage and Family among Negroes*," *Negro Digest* (July 1967): 83–84; Jesse Bernard, *Marriage and Family among Negroes* (Englewood Cliffs, NJ: Prentice-Hall, 1966); Andrew Billingsley, *Black Families in White America* (Englewood Cliffs, NJ: Prentice-Hall, 1968); Staples, "Towards a Sociology of the Black Family"; Joyce A. Ladner, *Tomorrow's Tomorrow: The Black Woman* (Garden City, NY: Doubleday, 1971); Carol B. Stack, *All Our Kin: Strategies for Survival in a Black Community* (New York: Harper and Row, 1974).

95. John W. Blassingame, *The Slave Community: Plantation Life in the Antebellum South* (New York: Oxford University Press, 1972).

96. Eugene Genovese, *Roll, Jordan, Roll: The World the Slaves Made* (New York: Pantheon, 1974).

97. Herbert Gutman, *The Black Family in Slavery and Freedom, 1750–1925* (New York: Pantheon, 1976).

98. John B. Cade, "Out of the Mouths of Ex-Slaves," *Journal of Negro History* 20, no. 3 (July 1935): 294–337, https://doi.org/10.2307/2714721.

99. John W. Blassingame, *The Slave Community: Plantation Life in the Antebellum South*, revised and enlarged (New York: Oxford University Press, 1979), 149.

100. Ibid., 151.

101. Genovese, *Roll, Jordan, Roll*, 485.

102. Ibid., 486–87.

103. Ibid., 491.

104. Ibid., 491–92.

105. Gutman, *The Black Family in Slavery and Freedom*, xvii.

106. Ibid., 9.

107. Angela Y. Davis, *Women, Race and Class* (New York: Random House, 1981), see especially chapter 1, "The Legacy of Slavery: Standards for a New Womanhood," 3–29.

108. Jacqueline Jones, *Labor of Love, Labor of Sorrow: Black Women, Work and the Family from Slavery to the Present* (New York: Basic Books, 1985).

109. Deborah G. White, *Ar'n't I a Woman? Female Slaves in the Plantation South* (New York: Norton Press, 1985); see also Deborah G. White "Female Slaves: Sex Roles and Status in the Antebellum Plantation South," *Journal of Family History* 3, no. 8 (fall 1983): 248–61, https://doi.org/10.1177/036319908300800303.

110. Elizabeth Fox-Genovese, *Within the Plantation Household: Black and White Women of the Old South* (Chapel Hill: University of North Carolina Press, 1988).

111. In so doing, she also underscored some of the limitations of the theses of Blassingame, Eugene Genovese, and, to a lesser extent, Gutman concerning familial stability and marital monogamy. A decade earlier than White's analyses, their embrace of a Black "semi-patriarchy" had inadvertently pushed aside some of the prominence of enslaved women in their households.

112. Deborah G. White provided the best reckoning of this denunciation of the enslaved woman and her descendants in her lucid discourse on prevalent stereotypes

of the lascivious Jezebel who "emasculates men by annulling their ability to resist her temptations"; Mammy, "devoid of maternal compassion and understanding" for her own Black family; and Sapphire, the "domineering female who consumes men and usurps their role. White, *Ar'n't I a Woman?* 27–61, 176.

113. Indeed, racists made it clear that First Lady Obama not only espoused all of these stereotypes, but also fit another one that emerged initially with Europeans' first contact with sub-Saharan Africa—"an ape in heels"—as she was repeatedly described. See also the insults lobbed at Michelle Obama documented in Mikki Kendall, "22 Times Michelle Obama Endured Rude, Racist, Sexist or Plain Ridiculous Attacks," *Washington Post* November 16, 2016, https://www.washingtonpost.com/posteverything/wp/2016/11/16/22-times-michelle-obama-endured-rude-racist-sexist-or-plain-dumb-attacks/?utm_term=.a19e0e17c627.

114. For example, Ann Patton Malone, in her 1992 monograph of captive kinship and household in antebellum Louisiana, documented that enslaved people resided in a variety of households and contributed to numerous kinds of kin-based relationships. Both households and familial relationships, she wrote, could (and did) change greatly overtime. Still, many of Malone's significant conclusions were those of the early revisionists. She asserted that "all recent historians of slavery, including myself, agree that the two-parent nuclear family was the societal ideal; that the dominant household type was the simple family; and that within the simple family category, the two-parent nuclear family usually prevailed." Ann Patton Malone, *Sweet Chariot: The Slave Family and Household Structure in Nineteenth-Century Louisiana* (Chapel Hill: University of North Carolina Press, 1992), 258.

115. Allen Kulikoff documented a substantial amount of diversity in household and family membership of the Black enslaved people during the eighteenth century. He discovered that on large plantations, for example, slightly less than half of enslaved people resided in nuclear households, and that on smaller farm units, less than 20 percent did. Allen Kulikoff, *Tobacco and Slaves: The Development of Southern Cultures in the Chesapeake* (Chapel Hill: University of North Carolina Press, 1986), 317, 370–72.

116. JoAnn Manfra and Robert Dykstra, "Serial Marriage and the Origins of the Black Stepfamily: The Rowanty Evidence," *Journal of American History* 72, no. 172 (June 1985): 18–44, https://doi.org/10.2307/1903735.

117. Brenda Stevenson, "Distress and Discord in Virginia Slave Families, 1830–1860," in *Joy and In Sorrow: Women, Family and Marriage in the Victorian South*, ed. Carol Bleser (New York: Oxford University Press, 1991): 103–24, 293–99; Brenda E. Stevenson, *Life in Black and White: Family and Community in the Slave South* (New York: Oxford University Press, 1996), 226–57.

118. *Life in Black and White* also is a study of family among regional free Blacks and Whites, both yeoman and planter. Like other studies of the White southern families, the findings in this work also indicate that there also were a variety of family styles among Whites and free Blacks, not just the enslaved. Indeed, White and Black families were similar, but not because of a nuclear structure. They were similar because of the importance of extended family relations, shared resources and governance. Extended families, after all, were a characteristic of rural life for most,

regardless of race and class. They also were important among the southern gentry and yeomen because of their desire to consolidate and maintain property holdings, to marry within one's class and faith, and the need to pool familial resources at a time of crisis. These extended White families, like enslaved Black families to a certain extent, shared economic resource and social events and conferred closely on important life issues. Stevenson, *Life in Black and White*, 37–156, 226–319.

119. B. W. Higman, "African and Creole Slave Family Patterns in Trinidad," *Journal of Family History* 3, no. 2 (June 1978): 164, https://doi.org/10.1177 /036319907800300205.

120. Higman found that smaller holdings meant more female-headed households than larger. Still, his data indicated that while there were some notable variabilities between African and creole populations, those who resided in urban arenas and those in rural as well as those with significantly different sized holdings, the majority of family units were matrifocal. Ibid., tables 2, 3, 170–71.

121. Ibid., 171.

122. Marietta Morrissey, *Slave Women in the New World: Gender Stratification in the New Caribbean* (Lawrence: University of Kansas Press, 1989), 92.

123. Barbara Bush, *Slave Women in Caribbean Society, 1650–1838* (Bloomington: Indiana University Press, 1990).

124. Ira Berlin, *Many Thousands Gone: The First Two Centuries of Slavery in North America* (Cambridge, MA: Harvard University Press, 1998), 130–32.

125. Ibid., 163.

126. Ibid., 272, 345.

127. Philip D. Morgan, *Slave Counterpoint: Black Culture in the Eighteenth-Century Chesapeake and Lowcountry* (Chapel Hill, NC: University of North Carolina Press, 1998).

128. Ibid., 501.

129. Ibid., 502.

130. Ibid., 510.

131. Richard Dunn, A *Tale of Two Plantations: Slave Life and Labor in Jamaica and Virginia* (Cambridge, MA: Harvard University Press, 2014).

132. Darlene Clark Hine and Rosalyn Terborg Penn, *Encyclopedia of Black Women in America* (New York: Carlson, 1993).

133. Daina Ramey Berry and Deleso Alford, eds., *Enslaved Women in America* (Westport, CT: Greenwood Press, 2012).

134. Darlene Clark Hine and Kathleen Thompson, *A Shining Thread of Hope: The History of Black Women in* America (New York: Broadway Press, 1998).

135. Daina Ramey Berry and Kali Gross, *A Black Women's History of the United States* (Boston: Beacon Press, 2020).

136. Wilma King, *Stolen Childhood: Slave Youth in Nineteenth-Century America* (Bloomington: Indiana University Press, 1998).

137. Margaret Washington, *Sojouner Truth's America* (Urbana: University of Illinois Press, 2011).

138. Jessica Millward, *Finding Charity's Folk: Enslaved and Free Black Women in Maryland* (Athens: University of Georgia Press, 2015).

139. Jane Landers, *Black Society in Spanish Florida* (Urbana: University of Illinois Press, 1999); Tiya Miles, *The Dawn of Freedom: A Chronicle of Slavery and Freedom in the City of the Straits* (New York: New Press, 2018).

140. Erica Nelson Dunbar, *Never Caught: The Washingtons' Relentless Pursuit of Their Runaway Slave, Ona Judge* (New York: 37 Ink, 2018).

141. Annette Gordon Reed, *The Hemings of Monticello: An American Family* (New York: Norton, 2009); Lucia Stanton, *"Those Who Labor for My Happiness": Slavery at Thomas Jefferson's Monticello* (Charlottesville: University of Virginia Press, 2012). See also Lucia Stanton, *Free Some Day: The African American Families of Monticello* (Chapel Hill: University of North Carolina Press, 2002).

142. Elizabeth Dowling Taylor, *A Slave in the White House: Paul Jennings and the Madisons* (New York: St. Martin Press, 2012); Paul Jennings, *A Colored Man's Reminiscences of James Madison (*Brooklyn: George C. Beadle, 1965), https://docsouth.unc.edu/neh/jennings/jennings.html.

143. Marissa Fuentes, *Dispossessed Lives: Enslaved Women, Violence, and the Archive* (Philadelphia: University of Pennsylvania Press, 2018); William Thomas, *A Question of Freedom: The Families Who Challenged Slavery from the Founding of the Nation to the Civil War* (New Haven, CT: Yale University Press, 2020); Jessica Marie Johnson, *Wicked Flesh: Black Women, Intimacy and Freedom in the Atlantic World* (Philadelphia: University of Pennsylvania Press, 2020); Vanessa Holden, *Surviving Southampton: African American Women and Resistance in Nat Turner's Community* (Urbana: University of Illinois Press, 2021); and Camilla Cowling, *Conceiving Freedom: Women of Color, Gender and the Abolition of Slavery in Havana and Rio de Janeiro* (Chapel Hill: University of North Carolina Press, 2013).

144. Heather Williams, *Help Me to Find My People: The African American Search for Family Lost in Slavery* (Chapel Hill: University of North Carolina Press, 2016); Tera Hunter, *Bound in Wedlock: Slave and Free Black Marriage in the 19th Century* (Cambridge, MA: Harvard University Press, 2019); Daina Ramey Berry, *The Price for Their Pound of Flesh: The Value of the Enslaved from Womb to Grave, in the Building of a Nation* (Boston: Beacon Press, 2017).

145. Regarding the work of early archivists and scholars who created a tradition of archival building and interrogation, see Brenda E. Stevenson, "'Out of the Mouths of Ex-Slaves': Carter G. Woodson's *Journal of Negro History* 'Invents' the Study of Slavery," *Journal of African American History* 100, no. 4 (fall 2015): 698–720; and "Creating History (and an archive) at the Intersection of Gender, Jim Crow and Remembrance:" Susie Byrd's Life and Lessons," Inaugural Address, Hilary Rodham Clinton Chair in Women's History, St. John's College, University of Oxford, October 25, https://www.youtube.com/watch?v=K5LUCg56ZjU&t=3s2021.

146. Nell Irwin Painter, *Soul Murder and Slavery* (Waco, TX: Baylor University Press, 1993).

147. Saidiya Hartman, "Venus in Two Acts," *Small Axe: A Journal of Criticism* 12, no. 2 (July 2008): 1–14; and *Scenes of Subjection: Terror, Slavery, and Self-Making in Nineteenth Century America* (New York: Oxford University Press, 1997).

148. Bethany Veney, *The Narrative of Bethany Veney, A Slave Woman*, 14, electronic edition, https://docsouth.unc.edu/fpn/veney/veney.html.3

149. Ibid., 10–32, passim.
150. Ibid., 33–44, passim.
151. Terry Alford, *Prince among Slaves: The True Story of An African Prince Sold into Slavery in the American South* (New York: Oxford University Press, 1977), 4–40.
152. Ibid., 54–55.
153. Ibid., 97–187, passim.

CHAPTER 1

1. "Notices Of Sales, 1759–1762," in *Documents Illustrative of the History of the Slave Trade to America: Volume III: New England and the Middle Colonies*, ed. Elizabeth Donnan (Washington, DC: Carnegie Institution of Washington, 1932), 67–68.

2. Gwendolyn Midlo Hall noted that Wheatley was from "Gambia," and most likely a Mandingo. Others, such as Henry Louis Gates Jr., believe she may have been Wolof. See Gwendolyn Midlo Hall, *Slavery and African Ethnicities in the Americas: Restoring Links* (Chapel Hill: University of North Carolina Press, 2005), Kindle edition, 9; Henry Louis Gates Jr., *The Trials of Phillis Wheatley: America's First Black Poet and Her Encounters with the Founding Fathers* (New York: Basic Books, 2003), 17.

3. Babacar M'Baye, *The Trickster Comes West: Pan African Influence in Early Black Diasporan Narratives* (Jackson: University of Mississippi Press, 2009), 23–24.

4. Other ethnicities include the Serer, Fula, and Mandinka. David Geggus, "Sex Ratio, Age and Ethnicity in the Atlantic Slave Trade: Data from French Shipping and Plantation Records," *Journal of African History* 30, no. 1 (1989): 35, n. 48, http://www.jstor.org/stable/182693.

5. Ebou Momar Taal, "Senegambian Ethnic Groups: Common Origins and Cultural Affinities Factors and Forces of National Unity, Peace and Stability," *Point*, April 22, 2010, http://thepoint.gm/africa/gambia/article/senegambian-ethnic-groups-common-origins-and-cultural-affinities-factors-and-forces-of-national-unit.

6. See, for example, Joaneth Spicer, ed., *Revealing the African Presence in Renaissance Europe* (Baltimore, MD: Walters Art Museum, 2012).

7. The first arrived, Midlo Hall explained, at about 1502 in Santo Domingo, but soon made up the exports to Mexico (New Spain). Midlo Hall, *Slavery and African Ethnicities in the America*, 82.

8. Ibid., 83–85.
9. Ibid., 83.
10. Ibid.,89.
11. Ibid., 142.
12. Timothy Insoll, "East Africa," *The Historical Encyclopedia of World Slavery*, vol. 1, ed. Junius P. Rodriguez (Santa Barbara, CA: ABC-CLIO, 1997), 239.
13. James Walvin, *Atlas of Slavery* (Harlow, UK: Pearson Longman, 2006), 23.
14. Midlo Hall, *Slavery and African Ethnicities in the Americas*, 2.

15. Timothy Insoll, "Timbuktu," in *The Historical Encyclopedia of World Slavery*, vol. 2, ed. Junius P. Rodriguez (Santa Barbara, CA: ABC-CLIO, 1997), 636.

16. Linda Heywood, "Slavery and Its Transformation in the Kingdom of Kongo, 1491–1800," *Journal of African History* 50, no. 1 (2009): 3, https://www.jstor.org/stable/40206695.

17. John N. Oriji, "Igboland, Slavery, and the Drums of War and Heroism," in *Fighting the Slave Trade: West African Strategies*, ed. Sylviane A. Diouf (Athens: Ohio University Press, 2003), 121–31; Charles T. Montgomery, "Survivors from the Cargo of the Negro Slave Yacht *Wanderer*," *American Anthropologist* 10, no. 4 (October–December, 1908), 615, https://doi.org/10.1525/aa.1908.10.4.02a00110.

18. John Warner Barber, *A History of the Amistad Captives: Being a Circumstantial Account of the Capture of the Spanish Schooner Amistad, by the Africans on Board; Their Voyage and Capture Near Long Island, New York* (New Haven, CT: E. L. and J. W. Barber, 1840), 15.

19. James Albert Ukawsaw Gronniosaw, *A Narrative of the Most Remarkable Particulars in the Life of James Albert Ukawsaw Gronniosaw, an African Prince, as Related by Himself* (Bath, UK: W. Gye, 1770), electronic edition, as found on Documenting the American South, 7–8, http://docsouth.unc.edu/neh/gronniosaw/gronnios.html.

20. Heidi J. Nast, "Islam, Gender, and Slavery in West Africa Circa 1500: A Spatial Archaeology of the Kano Palace, Northern Nigeria," *Annals of the Association of American Geographers* 86, no. 1 (March 1996): 44–77, https://www.jstor.org/stable/2563946.

21. Catherine Coquery-Vidrovitch, "Women, Marriage, and Slavery in Sub-Saharan Africa in the Nineteenth Century," in *Women and Slavery*, vol. 1, *Africa, the Indian Ocean World and the Medieval North Atlantic*, ed. Gwyn Campbell, Suzanne Miers, and Joseph C. Miller (Athens: Ohio University Press, 2007), 50.

22. Olaudah Equiano, *The Interesting Narrative of the Life of Olaudah Equiano, or Gustavus Vassa, the African, Written by Himself* (London: Author, 1789), electronic edition, as found on Documenting the American South, 63, https://docsouth.unc.edu/neh/equiano1/equiano1.html.

23. Ibid., 7.

24. Ibid., 19.

25. Ibid., 64–65.

26. Ibid., 51–58.

27. Paul E. Lovejoy, *Transformations in Slavery: A History of Slavery in Africa*, third edition (New York: Cambridge University Press, 2012), Kindle edition, Kindle location chap. 1, 967; David Eltis, *The Rise of African Slavery in the Americas* (Cambridge: Cambridge University Press, 2000), 244–50.

28. Ronald F. Davis, *1720–1880 Natchez: Special History Study* (Denver: United States Department of the Interior, National Park Service, 1993), 1.

29. Walvin, *Atlas of Slavery*, 31–36; Kate Lowe, "The Lives of African Slaves and People of African Descent in Renaissance Europe," in *Revealing the African Presence in Renaissance Europe*, ed. Joaneath Spicer (Baltimore, MD: Walters Art Museum, 2012), 19; Allison Blakeley, "Problems in Studying the Roles of Blacks in Europe," *Perspectives on History*, May 1997, http://www.historians.org/publications

-and-directories/perspectives-on-history/may-1997/problems-in-studying-the-role-of-blacks-in-europe.

30. Lisa A. Lindsay, *Captives as Commodities: The Transatlantic Slave Trade* (Upper Saddle River, NJ: Pearson Prentice Hall, 2008), 34–35; Vincent Carretta, *Phillis Wheatley: Biography of a Genius in Bondage* (Athens: University of Georgia Press, 2011), Kindle edition, 2.

31. See, for example, table 5 in David Galenson, "The Atlantic Slave Trade and the Barbados Market, 1673–1723, *Journal of Economic History* 42, no. 3 (September 1982): 505, https://www.jstor.org/stable/2120603.

32. "Timothy Fitch to Peter Gwin, Boston, 8 November 1760," Slave Trade Letters, Medford Historical Society, http://www.medfordhistorical.org/collections/slave-trade-letters/voyage-timothy-fitch-peter-gwinn.

33. Venture Smith, *A Narrative of the Life and Adventures of Venture, a Native of Africa: But Resident above Sixty Years in the United States of America. Related by Himself* (New London, CT: C. Holt, 1798), electronic edition, as found on Documenting the American South, 13, http://docsouth.unc.edu/neh/venture/venture.html.

34. Equiano, *The Interesting Narrative of the Life of Olaudah Equiano*, 6.

35. "Invoice of Sundry Merchandize Shipt, Boston 8th November 1760," Slave Trade Letters, Medford Historical Society and Museum, http://www.medfordhistorical.org/collections/slave-trade-letters/invoice-sundry-merchandize-shipt.

36. Reverend T. H. Galludet, *A Statement with Regard to the Moorish Prince, Abduhl Rahhahman* (New York: Daniel Fannshaw, 1828), electronic edition, as found on Documenting the American South, 3–4, http://docsouth.unc.edu/neh/gallaudet/summary.html.

37. United States Works Projects Administration, Slave Narratives: A Folk History of Slavery in the United States from Interviews with Former Slaves, Arkansas Narratives, Part 6 (New York: Firework Press), Kindle edition, Kindle location 1170–1184.

38. Paul Lovejoy, *Transformations in Slavery: A History of Slavery in Africa*, 7th ed. (Cambridge: Cambridge University Press, 1998), 44–50.

39. Equiano, *The Interesting Narrative of Life of Olaudah Equiano*, 66–67.

40. Ibid.

41. Ibid., 67.

42. John S. Mbiti, *African Religions and Philosophy*, 2nd ed. (Oxford: Heninmann, 1989), 130.

43. See, for example, the discussion of fertility in sub-Saharan Africa in John C. Caldwell and Pat Caldwell, "The Cultural Context of High Fertility in Sub-Saharan Africa," *Population and Development Review* 13, no. 3 (September 1987): 409–37, https://doi.org/10.2307/1973133.

44. Mbiti, *African Religions and Philosophy*, 130.

45. Ibid., 131.

46. The term also denotes one's familial identity. Clans are larger than lineages. The term can be applied to persons in both matrilineal and patrilineal societies. The distinction between a clan and lineage, anthropologist A. R. Radcliffe-Brown noted is that "in a lineage group each member can actually, or at least theoretically, trace his

genealogical connexion with any other member by descent from a known ancestor, whereas in a clan, which is usually a larger body, this is not possible. . . . The term should be used only for a group having unilineal descent." A.R. Radcliffe-Brown, "Introduction," in *African Systems of Kinship and Marriage*, ed. A. R. Radcliffe-Brown and Daryll Forde (London: Oxford University Press, 1958), 39–40.

47. Daryll Forde, "Double Descent among the Yako," in *African Systems of Kinship and Marriage*, ed. A. R. Radcliffe-Brown and Daryll Forde (London: Oxford University Press, 1958), 285–86.

48. Radcliffe-Brown, "Introduction," 76.

49. Smith, *A Narrative of the Life and Adventures of Venture*, 5.

50. Regarding polygamy in Africa, see, for example, James Fenske, "African Polygamy: Past and Present," Conference Keynote, London School of Economics Research Online, 1–53. http://eprints.lse.ac.uk/39246/1/African_polygamy_past_and_present_%28lsero%29.pdf.

51. D. W. Ames, "The Selection of Mates, Courtship and Marriage among the Wolof," *Bulletin de L'Institut Francais D'Afrique Noire* 18, no.1–2 (January–April 1956): 157–58.

52. Ibid., 160.

53. Ibid.

54. Ibid., 156.

55. Ibid., 160.

56. Ibid., 156–57.

57. Thomas Bluett, *Some Memoirs of the Life of Job, the Son of Solomon, the High Priest of Boonda in Africa; Who Was a Slave About Two Years in Maryland; and Afterwards Being Brought to England, Was Set Free, and Sent to His Native Land in the Year 1734*, electronic edition, as found on Documenting the American South, 40–42, http://docsouth.unc.edu/neh/bluett/bluett.html.

58. Radcliffe-Brown, "Introduction," 49.

59. Bluett, *Some Memoirs of the Life of Job, the Son of Solomon*, 40–42.

60. Radcliffe-Brown, "Introduction," 51.

61. Bluett, *Some Memoirs of the Life of Job*, 40–42; Yvla Hernlund, "Cutting without Ritual and Ritual without Cutting: Female 'Circumcision' and the Reritualization of Initiation in Gambia" in *Female "Circumcision" in Africa: Culture, Controversy and Change*, ed. Bettina Shell-Duncan and Yvla Hernlund (Boulder, CO: Lynne Reiner, 2001), 237.

62. Sahr J. Yambasu, "Order and Disorder: The Mende and Missionary Case," *Paideuma* 39 (1993): 114, http://www.jstor.org/stable/40341658; Anthony J. Gittins, *Mende Religion: Aspects of Belief and Thought in Sierra Leone*, Studia Instituti Anthropos 41 (Nettetal, Federal Republic of Germany: Steyler Verlag–Wort und Werk, 1987), 55.

63. Ruth Phillips, Henrietta Consentino, and Rebecca Busselle, "Women's Art and Initiation in Mendeland," Art and Life in Africa, University of Iowa Museum of Art, https://africa.uima.uiowa.edu/topic-essays/show/33, 1.

64. Yambasu, "Order and Disorder," 114; Babatunde Lawal, *The Gelede Spectacle: Art, Gender and Social Harmony in an African Culture* (Seattle: University of

Washington Press, 1966), 8–9; Sylvia A. Boone, *Radiance from the Waters: Ideals of Feminine Beauty in Mende Art* (New Haven, CT: Yale University Press, 1986), 157.

65. K. L. Little, "The Role of the Secret Society in Cultural Specialization," *American Anthropologist* 51, no. 2 (1949): 201, http://www.jstor.org/stable/664104.

66. Frederick Lamp, "Cosmos, Cosmetics, and the Spirit of Bondo," *African Arts* 18, no. 3 (1985): 28, https://doi.org/10.2307/3336353.

67. Ruth B. Phillips, "Masking in Mende Sande Society Initiation Rituals," *Africa: Journal of the International African Institute* 48, no. 3 (1978): 265–67, https://doi.org/10.2307/1158468.

68. Barber, *A History of the Amistad Captives*, 25–26.

69. Ibid., 26.

70. Phillips, "Masking in Mende Sande Society Initiation Rituals," 271.

71. Barber, *A History of the Amistad Captives,* 12.

72. Little, "The Role of the Secret Society in Cultural Specialization," 202.

73. Ibid., 203.

74. Ibid., 204.

75. Meyer Fortes, "Kinship and Marriage among the Ashanti," in *African Systems of Kinship and Marriage*, ed. A. R. Radcliffe-Brown and Daryll Forde (London: Oxford University Press, 1958), 254.

76. Ibid., 256.

77. Ibid., 261.

78. Ibid., 256–57.

79. Tarikhu Farrar, "The Queenmother, Matriarchy, and the Question of Female Political Authority in Precolonial West African Monarchy," *Journal of Black Studies* 27, no. 5 (May 1997): 588, http://www.jstor.org/stable/2784870.

80. Ibid., 588.

81. Ibid., 582–88, 590.

82. Fortes, "Kinship and Marriage among the Ashanti," 262.

83. Ibid., 262–63.

84. Ibid., 264.

85. Ibid., 266.

86. Ibid., 268.

87. Ibid., 262.

88. W. E. B. Du Bois, *The Negro American Family* (Atlanta: Atlanta University Press, 1908)*,* 10–11.

89. Fortes, "Kinship and Marriage among the Ashanti," 262.

90. Equiano, *The Interesting Narrative of the Life of Olaudah Equiano*, 8–9.

91. Radcliffe-Brown, "Introduction," 590; Andrew Apter, *Oduduwa's Chain: Locations of Culture in the Yoruba-Atlantic* (Chicago: University of Chicago Press, 2018), Kindle edition, 101.

92. K. H. Crosby, "Polygamy in Mende Country," *Africa: Journal of the International African Institute of African Languages and Cultures* 10, no. 3 (July 1937): 251, https://doi.org/10.2307/1155294.

93. Equiano, *The Interesting Narrative of the Life of Olaudah Equiano*, 8–9.

94. Ibid., 7–8.
95. Ibid., 32.
96. Ibid., 15–17.
97. Ibid., 20–26.
98. Ibid., 28–29.
99. Gronniosaw, *A Narrative of the Most Remarkable Particulars in the Life of James Albert Ukawsaw Gronniosaw*, 1–6.
100. Oluwaseun Foluso Phillips, "Peacemaking and Proverbs in Urhobo and Yoruba Marital Conflicts: Part 2," *African Conflict and Peacebuilding Review* 1, no. 2 (fall 2011): 138, https://doi.org/10.2979/africonfpeacrevi.1.2.136.
101. Ibid., 141.
102. Ibid.
103. Ibid., 139.
104. Emma Langdon Roche, *Historic Sketches of the South* (New York: Knickerbocker Press, 1914), Kindle edition, Kindle location 829.
105. Zora Neale Hurston, *Barracoon: The Story of the Last "Black Cargo"* (New York: Amistad Press, 2018), 6.
106. Female kings were found in Ondo Yoruba kingdoms. Farrar, "The Queenmother, Matriarchy, and the Question of Female Political Authority in Precolonial West African Monarchy," 590.
107. Lawal, *The Gelede Spectacle*, xiii.
108. Henry J. Drewal, "Yoruba Gelede Masquerade," Art and Life in Africa, University of Iowa Museum of Art, https://africa.uima.uiowa.edu/topic-essays/show/13?start=1, 2.
109. Phillips, "Peacemaking and Proverbs," 140.
110. Ibid., 140–41.
111. William Russell Bascom, *The Yoruba of Southwestern Nigeria* (Prospect Hills, IL: Waveland Press, 1984), 60.
112. Phillips, "Peacemaking and Proverbs," 140.
113. William Bascom, *The Yoruba of Southwestern Nigeria* (New York: Holt, Rinehart and Winston, 1969), 59–62.
114. Ibid., 62.
115. Ibid.
116. W. E. B. Du Bois, *The Negro American Family*, 12–13.
117. Bascom, *The Yoruba of Southwestern Nigeria*, 61.
118. Exceptions to groups that were matrilineal include the Luba, Songhe and Nkundo. A. I. Richards, "Some Types of Family Structure among the Central Bantu," in *African Systems of Kinship and Marriage*, ed. A. R. Radcliffe-Brown and Daryll Forde (London: Oxford University Press, 1958), Kindle edition, 207.
119. Anne Hilton, "Family and Kinship among the Kongo South of the Zaïre River from the Sixteenth to the Nineteenth Centuries," *Journal of African History* 24, no. 2 (1983): 189, http://www.jstor.org/stable/181640.
120. Ibid. 190.
121. Ibid., 191, 197–200.
122. Ibid., 204–206.

123. Ibid., 191, 197; Wyatt MacGaffey, "Lineage Structure, Marriage and the Family amongst the Central Bantu," *Journal of African History* 24, no. 2 (1983): 180, http://www.jstor.org/stable/181639.

124. MacGaffey, "Lineage Structure, Marriage and the Family amongst the Central Bantu," 180.

125. Richards, "Some Types of Family Structure among the Central Bantu," 211.

126. Hilton, "Family and Kinship among the Kongo," 192.

127. Chloe Spear and Rebecca Warren Brown, *Memoir of Mrs. Chloe Spear, a Native of Africa, Who was Enslaved in Childhood, and Died in Boston, January 3, 1815 . . . Aged 65 Years* (Boxton: James Loring, 1832), electronic edition, as found on Documenting the American South, 10–11 https://docsouth.unc.edu/neh/brownrw/brownrw.html.

128. Barber, *A History of the Amistad Captives*, 9–15.

129. Smith, *A Narrative of the Life and Adventure of Venture*, 9–11.

130. Benjamin F. Prentiss and Boyrereau Brinch, *The Blind African Slave, or Memories of Boyrereau Brinch, Nick-named Jeffrey Brace. Containing an Account of the kingdom of Bow-Woo, in the Interior of Africa; with the Climate and Natural Productions, Laws, and Customs Peculiar to That Place. With an Account of His Captivity, Sufferings, Sales, Travels, Emancipation, Conversion to the Christian Religion, Knowledge of the Scriptures, &c. Interspersed with Strictures on Slavery, Speculative Observations on the Qualities of Human Nature, with Quotation from Scripture* (St. Albans, VT: Harry Whitney, 1810), electronic edition, as found on Documenting the American South, 14, https://docsouth.unc.edu/neh/brinch/brinch.html.

131. Ibid., 71.

132. United States Works Progress Administration, *Slave Narratives: A Folk History of Slavery in the United States from Interviews with Former Slaves Oklahoma Narratives* (2011), Kindle edition, Kindle location 1214–1221.

133. Prentiss and Brinch, *The Blind African Slave*, 71, 80–85.

134. Ibid.

135. Ibid., 93–94, 96.

136. Ibid., 96–100.

137. Ibid., 98–100.

138. As quoted in Hurston, *Barracoon: The Story of the Last "Black Cargo"*, 6–7.

139. Ottobah Cugoano, *Narrative of the Enslavement of Ottobah Cugoano, a Native of Africa; Published by Himself, in the Year 1787* (London: Hatchard and J. and A. Arch, 1825), electronic edition, as found on Documenting the American South,123–24, http://docsouth.unc.edu/neh/cugoano/cugoano.html.

140. Ibid., 124.

141. Ibid.

142. Ibid., 12.

143. Equiano, *The Interesting Narrative of Life of Olaudah Equiano*, 45.

144. Ibid., 216.

145. *Memoir of Mrs. Chloe Spear*, 11–12.

146. Ibid., 12–13.

147. Hurston, *Barracoon: The Story of the Last "Black Cargo"*, 7.

148. Ibid.

149. *Sections of a Slave Ship*, found in Robert Walsh, *Notices of Brazil in 1828 and 1829*, vol. II (London: Frederick Westley and A. H. Davis, 1830). Public domain and digitally retouched image: Mschlindwein, *Cross-section of Slave Ship used in the Atlantic Slave Trade*, 1830, as found in "São José Paquete Africa," *Wikipedia*, https://en.wikipedia.org/wiki/S%C3%A3o_Jos%C3%A9_Paquete_Africa#/media/File:NavioNegreiro.gif

150. Carretta, *Phillis Wheatley*, 7.

151. Hurston, *Barracoon: The Story of the Last "Black Cargo"*, 8–9.

152. Equiano, *The Interesting Narrative of the Life of Olaudah Equiano*, 70–71.

153. Ibid., 71–73.

154. Ibid., 73.

155. Ibid., 73–74.

156. Alexander Falconbridge, *An Account of Slave Trade on the Coast of Africa* (London: J. Phillips, 1788), 29.

157. Equiano, *The Interesting Narrative of the Life of Olaudah Equiano*, 81.

158. Prentiss and Brinch, *The Blind African Slave*, 92–94.

159. See, for example, Roche, *Historic Sketches of the South*, 87–88.

160. United States Works Progress Administration, *Slave Narratives: A Folk History of Slavery in the United States From Interviews with Former Slaves, Texas Narratives, Part 2* (2011), Kindle edition, Kindle location 3268–3275.

161. Falconbridge, *An Account of Slave Trade on the Coast of Africa*, 32.

162. Ibid.

163. Colin Palmer, "The Middle Passage," in *Captive Passage: The Transatlantic Slave Trade and the Making of the Americas* (Washington, DC: Smithsonian Institution Press and the Mariners' Museum, 2002), 70.

164. Falconbridge, *Account of Slave Trade on the Coast of Africa*, 33.

165. Cugoano, *Narrative of the Enslavement of Ottobah Cugoano*, 124.

166. Prentiss and Brinch, *The Blind African Slave*, 89–90.

167. Sowande Mustakeem, *Slavery at Sea: Terror, Sex, and Sickness in the Middle Passage* (Champaign: University of Illinois Press, 2019), Kindle edition, Kindle location 2612; Palmer, "The Middle Passage," 70; Brendan Wolfe, "Slave Ships and the Middle Passage," *Encyclopedia Virginia*, http://www.encyclopediavirginia.org/Slave_Ships_and_the_Middle_Passage#start_entry.

168. Palmer's estimate is drawn from RAC records of 1680–1688. Palmer, "The Middle Passage," 69.

169. The *Antelope*, with crew and owners from the United States, for example, arrived illegally in Savannah in 1825 with 280 captives—one-third had died during the Middle Passage. Helen Tunnicliff Catterall, ed., *Judicial Cases concerning American Slavery and the Negro*, vol. 3: *Cases from the Courts of Georgia, Florida, Alabama, Mississippi, and Louisiana* (New York: Negro Universities Press, 1968), 9.

170. Helen Tunnicliff Catterall, ed., *Judicial Cases concerning American Slavery and the Negro*, vol. 2: *Cases from the Courts of North Carolina, South Carolina, and Tennessee* (New York: Negro Universities Press, 1968), 288.

171. Quoted in Dena T. Epstein, "African Music in British and French America," *Musical Quarterly* 59, no. 1 (1973): 66, http://www.jstor.org/stable/741460.

172. "Timothy Fitch to Capt. Peter Gwin, 12 January 1760," Slave Trade Letters, Medford Historical Society, https://www.medfordhistorical.org/collections/slave-trade-letters/peter-gwinns-first-voyage-record-behalf-timothy-fitch/.

173. Ibid.

174. "Affidavit of Singweh, an AMISTAD African, October 7, 1839, State of Connecticut, County of New Haven," Library of Congress Manuscript, Lewis Tappan Papers, as found on African American Odyssey, Slavery—The Peculiar Institution, The Amistad Mutiny, Library of Congress, https://memory.loc.gov/ammem/aaohtml/aopart1b.html.

175. Cugoano, *Narrative of the Enslavement of Ottobah Cugoano*, 123.

176. Ibid., 124–25.

177. *Memoir of Mrs. Chloe Spear*, 16–17.

178. Ibid.

179. Equiano, *The Interesting Narrative of the Life of Olaudah Equiano*, 74–75, 87–90.

180. Hurston, *Barracoon: The Story of the Last "Black Cargo"*, 9.

181. Boyrereau, *The Blind African Slave*, 97–108.

182. Equiano, *The Interesting Narrative of the Life of Olaudah Equiano*, 51, 59.

183. Helen Tunnicliff Catterall, ed., *Judicial Cases concerning American Slavery and the Negro*, vol. 4: *Cases from the Courts New England, the Middle States, and the District of Columbia* (New York: Negro Universities Press, 1968), 28.

184. Bluett, *Some Memoirs of the Life of Job*, 16–31.

185. Randy J. Sparks, *The Two Princes of Calabar: An Eighteenth-Century Atlantic Odyssey* (Cambridge, MA: Harvard University Press, 2009), Kindle edition, Kindle location 741–745.

186. Ibid.

187. Ibid., 758–766.

188. Ibid., 767–69.

189. Ibid., 789.

190. Ibid., 789–850.

CHAPTER 2

1. Charlie Smalls, lyrics to "Home" from *The Wiz*, as found in Josiah Smalls, "'The Wiz' (Original Cast Album) (1975)," Library of Congress, https://www.loc.gov/static/programs/national-recording-preservation-board/documents/TheWiz.pdf.

2. According to John K. Thornton, the *São João Bautista* was one of thirty-six documented slave ships that left Luanada for the New World in 1619. Thornton argued admirably that the vast majority of these slaves were Kimbundu speakers, but also suggested that a few may have been Kikongo speakers from the Nsundi region of Kongo. Engel Sluiter, "New Light on the '20. and Odd Negroes' Arriving in Virginia, August 1619," *William and Mary Quarterly* 54, no. 2 (April 1997): 396–98, https://doi.org/10.2307/2953279; John K. Thornton, "Notes and Documents: The African Experience of the '20. and Odd Negroes' Arriving in Virginia in 1619," *William and Mary Quarterly* 55, no. 3 (July 1998): 421–34, https://doi.org/10.2307/2674531;

William Thorndale, "The Virginia Census of 1619," *Magazine of Virginia Genealogy* 33, no. 3 (August 1995): 155–70.

3. Thornton, "The African Experience of the '20. and Odd Negroes,'" 432–34; John K. Thornton, "African Dimension of the Stono Rebellion," *American Historical Review* 96, no. 4 (October 1991): 1101–13, https://doi.org/10.2307/2164997; Anne Hilton, *The Kingdom of Kongo* (Oxford: Clarendon Press, 1985), 90–103; Annette Laing, "'Heathens and Infidels'? African Christianization and Anglicanism in the South Carolina Low Country, 1700–1750," *Religion and American Culture: A Journal of Interpretation* 12, no. 2 (summer 2002): 199–200, 206–209, 211–12, https://doi.org/10.1525/rac.2002.12.2.197; Peter Wood, *Strange New Land: Africans in Colonial America* (New York: Oxford University Press, 1993, 2003), Kindle edition, Kindle location 60.

4. Sluiter, "New Light on the '20. and Odd Negroes,'" 395–98.

5. Lorena Walsh, "Assessment of Contemporary Literature," in *A Study of the Africans and African Americans on Jamestown Island and at Green Springs, 1619–1803*, ed. Martha W. McCartney (Williamsburg, VA: Colonial Williamsburg Foundation, 2003), 8.

6. Regarding population statistics in North American north of the Rio Grande, see Jeffrey Ostler, "Genocide and American Indian History," *Oxford Research Encyclopedias: American History*, March 2, 2015, https://doi.org/10.1093/acrefore/9780199329175.013.3.

7. Regarding the Powhatan Confederacy, see, for example, Frederick W. Gleach, *Powhatan's World and Colonial Virginia: A Conflict of Cultures* (Lincoln: University of Nebraska Press, 1997); April Lee Hatfield, "Spanish Colonization Literature, Powhatan Geographies, and English Perceptions of Tsenacommacah/Virginia," *Journal of Southern History* 69, no. 2 (May 2003): 245–82, https://doi.org/10.2307/30039922; Helen C. Rountree, *The Powhatan Indians of Virginia: Their Traditional Culture* (Norman: University of Oklahoma Press, 1989); Helen C. Rountree, *Pocahontas's People: The Powhatan Indians of Virginia through Four Centuries* (Norman: University of Oklahoma Press, 1990); Helen C. Rountree, ed. *Powhatan Foreign Relations, 1500–1722* (Charlottesville: University Press of Virginia, 1993); Kristalyn Marie Shefveland, *Anglo-Native Virginia: Trade, Conversion, and Indian Slavery in the Old Dominion, 1646–1722* (Athens: University of Georgia Press, 2016); Margaret Homes Williamson, *Powhatan Lords of Life and Death: Command and Consent in Seventeenth-Century Virginia* (Lincoln: University of Nebraska Press, 2003).

8. James Horn, *1619: Jamestown and the Forging of American Democracy* (New York: Basic Books, 2018), 98–99.

9. Janet Roach, "'20 and Odd Africans' Arrival in 1619," 13 News Now, January 31, 2019, updated August 21, 2019, https://www.13newsnow.com/article/news/20-and-odd-africans-arrival-in-1619/291-fbc6da88-586e-41f9-a7ee-8ab9f94c6657.

10. S. Mintz and S. McNeil, "Virginia Slave Laws," *Digital History*, 2019, http://www.digitalhistory.uh.edu/disp_textbook.cfm?smtID=3&psid=71.

11. Charles J. Montgomery, "Survivors from the Cargo of the Negro Slave Yacht Wanderer," *American Anthropologist* 10, no. 4 (October–December 1908), 620, https://www.jstor.org/stable/659691.

12. Both quotes found in T. H. Breen and Stephen Innes, *"Myne Owne Ground": Race and Freedom on Virginia's Eastern Shore, 1640–1676* (New York: Oxford University Press, 1980), 45.

13. "William Peirce of Mulberry Island," Geni.com, September 29, 2021, https://www.geni.com/people/William-Pierce-of-Mulberry-Island/6000000076911754004.

14. Thornton, "The African Experience of the '20. and Odd Negroes,'" 431–34; James Deetz, *Flowerdew Hundred: The Archaeology of a Virginia Plantation, 1619–1864* (Charlottesville: University Press of Virginia, 1993), 20–22.

15. Thornton, "The African Experience of '20. and Odd Negroes,'" 431–34; Deetz, *Flowerdew Hundred*, 20–22; Breen and Innes, *"Myne Owne Ground"*, 71.

16. Thornton, "The African Experience of '20. and Odd Negroes,'" 431–34; Deetz, *Flowerdew Hundred*, 20–22.

17. Thornton, "The African Experience of '20. and Odd Negroes,'" 431–34; Breen and Innes, *"Myne Owne Ground"*, 8.

18. Thornton, "The African Experience of '20. and Odd Negroes,'" 431–34; Writers Program of the Works Progress Administration in the State of Virginia, *The Negro in Virginia* (New York: Arno Press, 1969), 10; Breen and Innes, *"Myne Owne Ground"*, 9–10.

19. Martha W. McCartney, ed. *A Study of the Africans and African Americans on Jamestown Island and at Green Springs* (Williamsburg, VA: Colonial Williamsburg Foundation, 2003), 37.

20. "The Case of John Graweere, March 31, 1641," *Encyclopedia Virginia*, https://www.encyclopediavirginia.org/The_Case_of_John_Graweere_March_31_1641; S. Mintz and S. McNeil, "Virginia Slave Laws."

21. For more on Angela, see Brenda E. Stevenson, "They Called Her Angela," *Journal of African American History* 105, no. 4 (fall 2020): 673–93, https://doi.org/10.1086/710998.

22. Ibid., 673–93.

23. McCartney, *A Study of the Africans and African Americans*, 45–46.

24. Ibid., 56.

25. Writers Program, *The Negro in Virginia*, 8.

26. Brenda E. Stevenson, *What Is Slavery?* (London: Polity Press, 2015); George Henry Moore, *Notes on the History of Slavery in Massachusetts* (New York: Appleton, 1866), 51.

27. Paul E. Hoffman, "Legend, Religious Idealism, and Colonies: The Point of Santa Elena in History, 1552–1566," *South Carolina Historical Magazine* 84, no. 2 (April 1983): 59–71, https://www.jstor.org/stable/27563624. Spain and Portugal were united between 1580 and 1640.

28. Ronald L. F. Davis, *The Black Experience in Natchez, 1720–1880* (Fort Washington, PA: Eastern National, 1999), 1.

29. Davis, *The Black Experience in Natchez*, 1.

30. See, for example, Tiya Miles, *The Dawn of Detroit: A Chronicle of Slavery and Freedom in the City of the Straits* (New York: New Press, 2017), Kindle edition.

31. Ibid., 39.

32. Ibid., 40–41. The area where they resided included the northern midwest of what became the United States.

33. Jane Landers, *Black Society in Spanish Florida* (Urbana: University of Illinois Press, 1999), 7.

34. Ibid., 7–9.

35. Ibid.

36. Ibid., 11–12.

37. United States Works Progress Administration, *Slave Narratives: A Folk History of Slavery in the United States From Interviews with Former Slaves, Arkansas Narratives, Part 6* (New York: Firework Press, 2015), Kindle edition, Kindle location 1170–1184. Spanish Jesuit priests also founded what became temporary missions in Virginia in the 1560s and 1570s; "The Spanish in Virginia before Jamestown," Spanish Exploration and Settlement in the South East, Virginia Places, http://www.virginiaplaces.org/settleland/spanish.html. See also Clifford M. Lewis and Albert J. Loomie, *The Spanish Jesuit Mission in Virginia* (Chapel Hill: University of North Carolina Press, 1953).

38. Ronald Wayne Childers, "The Presidio System in Spanish Florida 1565–1763," *Historical Archaeology* 38, no. 3, Presidios of the North American Spanish Borderlands (2004): 26–28, http://www.jstor.org/stable/25617178.

39. Jane Landers, "Gracia Real de Santa Teresa de Mosé: A Free Black Town in Spanish Colonial Florida," *American Historical Review* 95, no. 1 (February 1990): 9–10, https://doi.org/10.2307/2162952.

40. Ibid., 11.

41. Dedra S. McDonald, "To Be Black and Female in the Spanish Southwest: Toward a History of African Women on New Spain's Far Northern Frontier," in *African American Women Confront the West, 1600–2000*, ed. Quintard Taylor and Shirley Ann Wilson Moore (Norman: University of Oklahoma Press, 2003), 36.

42. "Runaway," *Georgia Gazette*, August 25, 1763, in *Runaway Slave Advertisements: A Documentary History from the 1730s to 1790, Volume 4: Georgia*, ed. Lathan A. Windley (Westport, CT: Greenwood Press, 1983), 3.

43. Jane Landers, "Black Frontier Settlements in Spanish Colonial Florida," *OAH Magazine of History* 3, no. 2 (spring 1988): 28–29, http://www.jstor.org/stable/25162596.

44. McDonald, "To Be Black and Female in the Spanish Southwest," 33.

45. Landers, "Gracia Real de Santa Teresa de Mosé," 23.

46. Bonnie G. McEwan, "Columbus' Foundation of Hispanic America: Review Article," *Antiquity: A Quarterly Review of Archeology* 77, no. 295 (March 2003): 194, https://doi.org/10.1017/S0003598X00061512.

47. Genealogies found in Landers, "Gracia Real de Santa Teresa de Mosé," 24.

48. Randolph B. Campbell, *An Empire for Slavery: The Peculiar Institution in Texas, 1821–1865* (Baton Rouge: Louisiana State University Press, 1989), 10.

49. Novel by Garcí Rodríguez de Montalvo, published in 1508. See Garci Rodriguez de Montalvo, *Sergas de Esplandián*, trans. Salvador Bernabéu Albert (Madrid: Doce Calles, 1998); Marne L. Campbell, "African American Women, Wealth Accumulation, and Social Welfare Activism in 19th Century Los Angeles," *Journal*

of African American History 94, no.4 (fall 2012): 376–77, https://doi.org/10.5323/jafriamerhist.97.4.0376.

50. Jack D. Forbes, "The Early African Heritage of California," in *Seeking El Dorado: African Americas in California*, ed. Lawrence B. De Graff, Kevin Mulroy, and Quintard Taylor (Seattle: University of Washington Press, 2001), 77–82, 91–95.

51. It is not certain if there were enslaved Blacks who participated in Rene Robert Cavelier, sieur de La Salle's failed attempt to establish a French colony in what is today Inez, Texas from 1685 to 1688. See, for example, volume 2 of *The Journeys of Rene Robert Cavelier, sieur de La Salle published in 2 volumes*, ed. Isaac Cox (New York: Allerton, 1905), https://hdl.handle.net/2027/uc2.ark:/13960/t35145656.

52. McDonald, "To Be Black and Female in the Spanish Southwest," 38.

53. Campbell, *An Empire for Slavery*, 11.

54. Herman L. Bennett, *Africans in Colonial Mexico: Absolutism, Christianity and Afro-Creole Consciousness, 1570–1640* (Bloomington: Indiana University Press, 2003), 27. These Africans mostly came from Senegambia and Guinea in the sixteenth century but largely were born in Angola and the Kingdom of Kongo and to a lesser extent the Gold Coast, Senegambia, and the Bights of Benin and Biafra in the seventeenth century, when approximately two thousand arrived annually. M. Malowist, "The Struggle for International Trade and Its Implications for Africa," in *General History of Africa*, vol. 5: *Africa from the Sixteenth to the Eighteenth Century*, ed. B. A. Ogot (Berkeley: University of California Press, 1992), 8–9; J. E. Inikori, "Africa in World History: The Export Slave Trade from Africa and the Emergence of the Atlantic Economic Order," in *General History of Africa*, vol. 5: *Africa from the Sixteenth to the Eighteenth Century*, 106; Douglas W. Richmond, "Africa's Initial Encounter with Texas: The Significance of Afro-Tejanos in Colonial Tejas, 1528–1821," *Bulletin of Latin American Research* 26, no. 2 (April 2007): 4–6. http://www.jstor.org/stable/27733919; Lorena Madrigal, "The African Slave Trade and the Caribbean," in *Human Biology of the Afro-Caribbean Populations* (Cambridge: Cambridge University Press, 2006).

55. Inikori, "Africa in World History," 81.

56. Bennett estimates that 151,018 lived in New Spain fifty years earlier, in 1646. Bennett, *Africans in Colonial Mexico*, 19; Inikori, "African in World History," 96, 103–104.

57. Campbell, *An Empire for Slavery*, 11.

58. McDonald, "To Be Black and Female in the Spanish Southwest," 37.

59. Bennett, *Africans in Colonial Mexico*, 17–19; Matthew Restall, "Manuel's Worlds: Black Yucatan and the Colonial Caribbean," in *Slaves, Subjects, and Subversives: Blacks in Colonial Latin America*, ed. Jane Landers and Barry M. Robinson (Albuquerque: University of New Mexico Press, 2006), 147–74, passim.

60. They were able to marry in the church because of their Christian conversion. Leslie Harris, *In the Shadow of Slavery: African Americans in New York City, 1626–1863* (Chicago: University of Chicago Press, 2003), 21.

61. Wood, *Strange New Land*, 233.

62. Harris, *In the Shadow of Slavery*, 21.

63. Ibid., 21.

64. *New York Historical Manuscripts: Dutch*, published under the direction of the Holland Society of New York, trans. Arnold J. F. Van Laer (Baltimore, MD: Genealogical Publishing, 1974), 326–27.

65. Peter R. Christoph, "The Freedman of New Amsterdam," in *A Beautiful and Fruitful Place: Selected Rensselaerswijck Seminar Papers*, ed. Nancy McClure Zeller (New York: New Netherland Project, 1991), 157, https://www.newnetherlandinstitute.org/files/7313/5067/3659/6.2.pdf.

66. Ibid., 158; *New York Historical Manuscripts: Dutch*, 98–100.

67. Harris, *In the Shadow of Slavery*, 33.

68. The data from this section is derived from several sources, but primarily from David Eltis, David Geggus, Michael Gomez, Allan Kulikoff, Gwendolyn Midlo Hall, and Douglas Chambers, among others. All of these scholars were responding in one way or another to Curtin's critical 1968 text, *The Atlantic Slave Trade: A Census*. Kulikoff and Chambers made good use of Elizabeth Donnan's *Documents Illustrative of the Slave Trade to the Americas*. Eltis and Geggus compiled their statistics from a massive collection of slave trade documents, much of it now available on the *Slave Voyages Database*, https://www.slavevoyages.org/. Gomez drew statistics from Donald Wax and David Richardson, Geggus, Manning, and Donnan as well as from Midlo Hall. He also used qualitative evidence from Margaret Washington to substantiate his findings. Thus, while these findings have been sanctioned by many and are used by most, the evidence still presents significant problems. Records of ethnic distinctions, for example, are available for only between 40 and 50 percent of African imports. The distinctions that are available are "rough" in the sense that they primarily record the origin as a large region, not as an actual ethnic group. Moreover, some Africans had no real "ethnic" distinction at the time. Midlo Hall provided the most recent breakthrough in her 2005 text. There she incorporated a new body of evidence suggestive of ethnic identity—the testimony of the enslaved people themselves in various scenarios, such as trials, where they must self-identify their ethnicities. This approach eliminated one problem presented by slave trade statistics—it is not the sea captains or slaveholders who have to identify ethnic origins (their estimates have proven to be "rough")—and it provided another base of creditable evidence of ethnic origin to bolster what other scholars have drawn from slave trade information. Gwendolyn Midlo Hall, *Slavery and African Ethnicities in the Americas: Restoring the Links* (Chapel Hill: University of North Carolina Press, 2005). See also Gwendolyn Midlo Hall, *Africans in Colonial Louisiana: The Development of Afro-Creole Culture in the Eighteenth Century* (Baton Rouge: Louisiana State University Press, 1992); David Richardson, "Slave Exports from West and West-Central Africa, 1700–1810: New Estimates of Volume and Distribution," *Journal of African History* 30, no. 1 (1989): 1–22, http://www.jstor.org/stable/182692; James A. Rawley, *The Transatlantic Slave Trade: A History* (New York: Norton, 1981); Joseph E. Inikori, "Measuring the Atlantic Slave Trade: An Assessment of Curtin and Anstey," *Journal of African History* 17, no. 2 (1976): 197–223, http://www.jstor.org/stable/180398; Roger Anstey, "The British Slave Trade, 1751–1807: A Comment," *Journal of African History* 17, no. 4 (1976): 606–607, http://www.jstor.org/stable/180742; David Geggus, "Sex Ratio, Age and Ethnicity in the Atlantic Slave

Trade: Data from French Shipping and Plantation Records," *Journal of African History* 30, no. 1 (1989): 23–44, http://www.jstor.org/stable/182693; Philip Curtin, *The Atlantic Slave Trade: A Census* (Madison: University of Wisconsin Press, 1969).

Some of most recent studies of the ethnic backgrounds of captive Africans in the Americas include additional topics of consideration, including DNA analysis and nuanced discussions of the relevance of "ethnicity" as a category of analysis both ideally and "on the ground." See, for example, Rebecca Shumway, "Naming Our African Ancestors: Pushing, and Respecting, the Limits," *Journal of the Early Republic* 40, no. 2 (summer 2020): 195–200, https://doi.org/10.1353/jer.2020.0030; Sarah Abel and Hannes Schroeder, "From Country Marks to DNA Markers: The Genomic Turn in the Reconstruction of African Identities," *Current Anthropology* 61, no. 22 (October 2020): 198–209, https://doi.org/10.1086/709550; and Joan Marie Johnson, "Markup Bodies: Black [Life] Studies and Slavery [Death] Studies at the Digital Crossroads," *Social Texts 137* 36, no. 4 (December 2018): 57–79, https://doi.org/10.1215/01642472-7145658.

69. For more detail on these topics see Brenda E. Stevenson, "The Question of the Slave Female Community and Culture in the American South: Methodological and Ideological Approaches," *Journal of African American History* 92, no. 1 (winter 2007): 74–95, http://www.jstor.org/stable/20064155.

70. Allan Kulikoff, *Tobacco and Slaves: The Development of Southern Cultures in the Chesapeake, 1680–1800* (Chapel Hill: University of North Carolina Press, 1986), 357.

71. United States Works Progress Administration, *Slave Narratives: A Folk History of Slavery in the United States From Interviews with Former Slaves, Part 2, Texas Narratives*, Kindle edition, Kindle location 3268–3275.

72. George P. Rawick, *The American Slave: A Composite Autobiography, vol. 1, South Carolina Parts 1 and 2* (Santa Barbara, CA: Greenwood Publishing, 1972), 498–50.

73. Dedra S. McDonald, "Intimacy and Empire: Indian-African Interaction in Spanish Colonial New Mexico, 1500–1800," in *African American History in New Mexico: Portraits from Five Hundred Years*, ed. Bruce A. Glasrud (Albuquerque: University of New Mexico Press, 2013), Kindle edition, Kindle location 559–560.

74. Regarding the Igbo in the Chesapeake and in other sites of "American" enslavement, see Douglas B. Chambers "'My Own Nation': Igbo Exiles in the Diaspora," *Slavery and Abolition* 18, no. 1 (1997): 72–97, https://doi.org/10.1080/01440399708575204.

75. Midlo Hall discusses the debate regarding the contention that the majority of the enslaved people leaving the Bight of Biafra for the New World, and clustered in the Chesapeake, Guadeloupe, Haiti, Louisiana, etc. were Igbo. Her conclusion is that they were indeed Igbo, as indicated through self-identification records as well as those of slaveholders and traders. Other groups from the Bight of Biafra represented in the trade include Ibibio, Moko, Ekoi, Esan/Edoid, Bioko and Calabar. Midlo Hall, *Slavery and African Ethnicities in the Americas*, 127–31. See especially 131, table 6.1.

76. Midlo Hall indicates that the actual percentage of women among the Igbo was, in some clusters, larger than 45. In her data regarding Igbo in Guadeloupe, for

example, Igbo women were 53 percent of that enslaved group; in St. Domingue/Haiti, they were 50.8 percent. Midlo Hall, *Slavery and African Ethnicities in the Americas*, 131, table 6.1.

77. These persons were taken from the modern-day African countries of Angola, Congo, Gabon, Zaire, and the Democratic Republic of Congo.

78. Kulikoff, *Tobacco and Slaves*, 322; Chambers, "'My Own Nation,'"465; Geggus, "Sex Ratio, Age and Ethnicity in the Atlantic Slave Trade," 36, n. 52.

79. Midlo Hall, *Slavery and African Ethnicities in the Americas*, 94–95.

80. While Coromantees were less than 4 percent among arrivals from 1730 to 1745, they were fully one-third of African imports to the Chesapeake fifteen years later. Morgan, 64. Philip D. Morgan, *Slave Counterpoint: Black Culture in the Eighteenth-Century Chesapeake & Lowcountry* (Chapel Hill: University of North Carolina Press, 1998), 63–64 Table 11 (Marissa, check that this statistic comes from this source).

81. Chambers, "'My Own Nation,'" 84–90.

82. Sierra Leonean Africans, combined with enslaved people from Senegambia, comprised about 12 percent disembarking in South Carolina in the 1730s, 54 percent in the middle decades, and 64 percent by the time of the American Revolution. David Eltis, *The Rise of African Slavery in the Americas* (Cambridge: Cambridge University Press, 2000), 105, table 4-4. His sample included 4 percent girl children and 9.4 percent boy children, suggesting a sexual imbalance for the near future as well. Eltis's sample is drawn from an early period, 1663–1713. Geggus suggested a lower sexual ratio for Congo-Angola slaves, 132 per 100 women for all British imports.

83. Ibid.

84. Low Country Digital History Initiative, "Africans in Carolina," African Passages, Lowcountry Adaptations, Lowcountry Digital History Initiative, https://ldhi.library.cofc.edu/exhibits/show/africanpassageslowcountryadapt/sectionii_introduction/africans_in_carolina.

85. Midlo Hall, *Africans in Colonial Louisiana,* 29, 61; Peter Caron, "'Of a Nation the Others Do Not Understand': Bambara Slaves and African Ethnicity in Colonial Louisiana, 1718–60," *Slavery and Abolition*, 18, no. 1 (April 1997): 98–121, doi.org/10.1080/01440399708575205.

86. Midlo Hall, *Africans in Colonial Louisiana*, 29.

87. Spain controlled all of French Louisiana except New Orleans, the land surrounding it and Lake Ponchatrain and adjacent lands until 1800. Stevenson, *What Is Slavery?*

88. Whitney Plantation Estate Inventories, Enslaved Workers at Whitney Plantation, Whitney Plantation, https://www.whitneyplantation.org/history/slavery-in-louisiana/enslaved-workers-at-whitney/. See also for greater detail, particularly regarding African ethnicities, Table 8: African Nations and Afro-Indians Listed on Habitation Haydel (1819–1860) in Ibrahima Seck, *Bouki Fait Gombo: A History of the Slave Community of Habitation Haydel (Whitney Plantation) Louisiana, 1750–1860* (New Orleans: University of New Orleans Press, 2014), Kindle edition, 1146, Table 8.

89. Enslaved peoples from Sierra Leone comprised 5 percent of the African population in Louisiana, those from the Gold Coast only about 1 percent, and the Igbo

approximately 9 percent. Among Yoruba, sex ratios were an average of 178 men per 100 women, while that of the Fon-Ewe fluctuated from a high of 183 men per 100 women to 126 men. Sex ratio is expressed here as a relationship to the number of men compared to every 100 women in the enslaved population. Geggus, "Sex Ratio, Age, and Ethnicity in the Atlantic Slave Trade," 35, table 4; Gomez, *Exchanging Our Country Marks*, 151; Midlo Hall, *Slavery and American Ethnicities in the Americas*, 125, 131.

90. Midlo Hall, *Africans in Colonial Louisiana*, 284–86; see also in the Kindle version of Midlo Hall's book, 2797–2814.

91. Midlo Hall, *Africans in Colonial Louisiana*, 115.

92. This assessment might have been something of an exaggeration, however, since there is little information from the Chesapeake, which is a great center of Igbo clustering, on this marital pattern. Midlo Hall, *Slavery and African Ethnicities in the Americas* (Chapel Hill: University of North Carolina Press, 2005), 127–29.

93. Ibid., 131, table 6.1.

94. Ibid., 294–301.

95. Kulikoff, *Tobacco and Slaves*, 334.

96. Lathan A. Windley, ed., *Runaway Slave Advertisements: A Documentary History from the 1730s to 1790*, vol. 1: *Virginia and North Carolina* (Westport, CT: Greenwood Press, 1983), 10–11.

97. While the African slave trade to the young United States legally ended in 1808, some merchants still imported Africans, at least fifty thousand over the next five decades. Many originated from western central Africa. This criminal activity was especially intense along the Gulf Coast to sites in West Florida; Mobile, Alabama; Galveston, Texas; and New Orleans, Louisiana. These nineteenth-century African captives would have had some social and cultural impact on the places where they were bound, if only to strengthen the creolized cultures that had been derived from earlier shipments. Those who found themselves at sites with only American-born bondspeople whose African ancestors had arrived several decades earlier struggled to connect.

98. Bennett, *Africans in Colonial Mexico*, 27; Malowist, "The Struggle for International Trade and Its Implications for Africa," 8–9; Inikori, "Africa in World History," 106; Richmond, "Africa's Initial Encounter with Texas," 4–6; Lorena Madrigal, "The African Slave Trade and the Caribbean," 3.

99. Jane Landers, "Slavery in the Spanish Caribbean and the Failure of Abolition," *Review (Fernand Braudel Center)* 31, no. 3 (2008), 349, http://www.jstor.org/stable/40241723. Other groups Landers included were: Coromante, Susu, Pul, Gangâ, Bara, Besi, Dudrian, Mondongo, Limba, Moyo, and Pati, which she indicated were only a few of the many communities who had been identified.

100. Ibid., 351–52.

101. Ibid., 357–59.

102. Oscar Williams, *African Americans and Colonial Legislation in the Middle Colonies* (New York: Garland, 1998), 4–5; Wood, *Strange New Land*, Kindle edition, Kindle location 239.

103. As quoted in Williams, *African Americans and Colonial Legislation in the Middle Colonies*, 6.

104. James G. Lydon, "New York and the Slave Trade, 1700 to 1774," *William and Mary Quarterly* 35, no. 2 (April 1978): 375, https://doi.org/10.2307/1921840.

105. Elizabeth Donnan, ed., *Documents Illustrative of the Slave Trade to America*, vol. 3: *New England and the Middle Colonies* (Buffalo, NY: William S. Hein, 2002), 444. These documents do not specify the location or ethnicity of those imported slaves directly from the coast of Africa.

106. Regarding New York supply slaves to New France see, for example, Miles, *The Dawn of Detroit*, 26.

107. Lydon, "New York and the Slave Trade," 376.

108. Donnan, *Documents Illustrative of the Slave Trade to America*, 3: 453.

109. Ibid., 456.

110. Wendy Warren, *New England Bound: Slavery and Colonization in Early America* (New York: Norton, 2016), 154.

111. *Le Code Noir ou recueil des reglements rendus jusqu'a present* (Paris: Prault, 1767), https://s3.wp.wsu.edu/uploads/sites/1205/2016/02/code-noir.pdf; Jennifer M. Spear, "Colonial Intimacies: Legislating Sex in French Louisiana," *The William and Mary Quarterly*, 60, no. 1(Jan., 2003), 91–92; "La Siete Partidas Excerpts," trans. Samuel Scott Parsons (Chicago: Com- parative Law Bureau of the American Bar Association, 1931), http://www.rogerlouismartinez.com/wp-content/uploads/2015/01/Las-Siete-Partidas.pdf.

112. Willian Renwick Riddell, "Le Code Noir," *Journal of Negro History* 10, no. 3 (July 1925): 321–29, https://doi.org/10.2307/2714119.

113. Luis Martinez-Fernandez, "Marriage between Slaves: Analyzing Legal Documents from Spain and the United States," *Social Education* 82, no. 3 (2018): 138–42; https://doi.org/10.2307/2714119; Jessica Marie Johnson, *Wicked Flesh: Black Women, Intimacy, and Freedom in the Atlantic World* (Philadelphia: University of Pennsylvania Press, 2020), 131–133.

114. We will never be certain how well these bodies of laws ever were enforced in the colonies—and some scholars have insisted that the "leniency" indicated in the written word of these codes barely existed in the Americas. See, for example, David M. Davidson, "Negro Slave Control and Resistance in Colonial Mexico, 1519–1650," *Hispanic American Historical Review* 46, no. 3 (August 1966): 235–53, https://doi.org/10.2307/2510626.

115. Jane G. Landers, *Atlantic Creoles in the Age of Revolutions* (Cambridge, MA: Harvard University Press, 2010), Kindle edition, Kindle location 400.

116. This genealogy is recounted in Landers, "Gracia Real de Santa Teresa de Mosé," 23–24.

117. McDonald, "To Be Black and Female in the Spanish Southwest," 42.

118. Ibid., 39.

119. McDonald, "Intimacy and Empire," 608–611.

120. Riddell, "Le Code Noir," 325.

121. The Louisiana Slave Code of 1724 further stipulated, for example, that the governor general and intendant had to approve the petition; those manumitting the slave had to be at least twenty-five years old and they could not receive financial or material help from Whites. Liliana Obregon, "Black Codes in Latin America,"

Africana: Encyclopedia of the African and African American Experience (New York: Oxford University Press, 2005), https://www.academia.edu/273291/Black_Codes_In _Latin_America.

122. Carl A. Brasseaux, "The Administration of Slave Regulations in French Louisiana, 1724–1766," *Louisiana History: The Journal of the Louisiana Historical Association* 21, no. 2 (spring 1980), 148, http://www.jstor.org/stable/4231984.

123. Ibid.,147–48.

124. Ibid., 148–49.

125. Ibid., 146.

126. Slavery was codified in Massachusetts (and by extension Vermont, Maine, and New Hampshire) in 1641; Connecticut in 1650; Rhode Island in 1652; Virginia in 1661; Maryland, New York, and New Jersey in 1663; North and South Carolina around 1670; Pennsylvania in 1700; and Georgia in 1735.

127. Wood, *Strange New Land*, 396–98.

128. Kathleen DuVal, *Independence Lost: Lives on the Edge of the American Revolution* (New York: Random House, 2015), Kindle edition, Kindle location 1025.

129. Lorenzo Johnston Greene, *The Negro in Colonial New England* (New York: Atheneum, 1969), 177–79, 182.

130. Ibid., 198–99.

131. Ibid., 193–97.

132. Wood, *Strange New Land*, 407.

133. Edward Barlett Rugemer, "Making Slavery English: Comprehensive Slave Codes in the Greater Caribbean During the Seventeenth Century," 1–4, 9–14, https://docplayer.net/21782144-Rugemer-1-34-making-slavery-english-comprehensive-slave-codes-in-the-greater-caribbean-during-the-seventeenth-century.html.

134. These laws purportedly were to keep enslaved persons from plotting insurrections. See, for example, Virginia statue of 1680, the New York's 1702 "Act for Regulating of Slaves," and the South Carolina Slave Code of 1740. For Virginia, see General Assembly, "'An act for preventing Negroes Insurrections' (1680)," *Encyclopedia Virginia*, Virginia Humanities, September 7, 2021, https://encyclopediavirginia.org/entries/an-act-for-preventing-negroes-insurrections-1680/; for New York, see New York State Historical Society, "Laws Affecting Blacks in Manhattan," Slavery in New York, New York State Historical Society, http://www.slaveryinnewyork.org/PDFs/Laws_Affecting_Blacks_in_Manhattan.pdf; John Belton O'Neall, ed., *The Negro Law of South Carolina* (Columbia, SC: John G. Bowman, 1848), https://archive.org/details/negrolawsouthca00goog/page/n4/mode/2up.

135. Wood, *Strange New Land*, 408–409.

136. Brenda E. Stevenson, "1639–1644: Black Women's Labor," in *Four Hundred Souls: A Community History of African America, 1619–2019,* ed. Ibram X. Kendi and Keisha N. Blain (New York: One World, 2021), 18–21.

137. Wood, *Strange New Land*, 233.

138. Greene, *The Negro in Colonial New England*, 195.

139. Littlefield notes, as did Peter Wood, that equal numbers of adult and females did not necessarily indicate a surge in heterosexual marriage because the ratio was specific to a region, colony, or locale, not to an individual slaveholding. Daniel C.

Littlefield, *Rice and Slaves: Ethnicity and the Slave Trade in Colonial South Carolina* (Urbana: University of Illinois Press, 1981), 59.

140. Ulrich Bonnell Phillips, *American Negro Slavery: A Survey of the Supply, Employment, and Control of Negro Labor as Determined by the Plantation Regime* (Baton Rouge: Louisiana State University Press, 1966), Kindle edition, Kindle location 1275–1281.

141. Ibid., 1720–1723; William Johnston, *Slavery in Rhode Island, 1755–1776* (Providence: Rhode Island Historical Society, 1894), 19.

142. Phillips, *American Negro Slavery*, 1673–1679.

143. Leslie M. Harris, *In the Shadow of Slavery: African Americans in New York City, 1626–1863* (Chicago: The University of Chicago Press, 2003, Kindle. Kindle Location 470.]

144. McDonald, "Intimacy and Empire," 556.

145. Ibid., 39.

146. Ibid., 603.

147. Massachusetts (170); Rhode Island (175); New York (1,200); New Jersey (200); Maryland (1,611); Virginia (3,000) and the Carolinas (410). See Brenda E. Stevenson, *What Is Slavery?*, table 3.

148. Massachusetts (800); Rhode Island (300); Connecticut (450); New York (2,256); New Jersey (840); Pennsylvania (430); Delaware (135); Maryland (3,227); Virginia (16,390); North Carolina (1,000); and South Carolina (3,000). See Brenda E. Stevenson, *What Is Slavery?*, table 3.

149. The Chesapeake area received more than 30,000 captives in the first quarter of the century: 54,000 in the second; and 31,000 in the third. The Carolinas and Georgia took 5,500 between 1701 and 1725; 36,000 over the next twenty-five years, and then another 76,000. This Lower South area continued to import large numbers of Africans even after other sections had ceased to do so. The Carolinas (particularly South Carolina) and Georgia secured an additional 27,000 African slave imports during the last quarter of the eighteenth century and a whopping 67,000 as the legal African slave trade came to a close during the first decade of the nineteenth century. See David Eltis and David Richardson, *Atlas of the Transatlantic Slave Trade* (New Haven, CT: Yale University Press, 2010), 200, table 6.

150. Michael T. Pasquier, "French Colonial Louisiana," *64 Parishes*, August 4, 2011, https://64parishes.org/entry/french-colonial-louisiana.

151. Arrivals counted 4,700 over the next two and a half decades, 1,600 in the quarter before the American Revolution, 2,900 between 1776 and 1800, and 10,000 over the next twenty-five years, when under US control. DuVal, *Independence Lost*, 1179.

152. Eltis and Richardson, *Atlas of the Transatlantic Slave Trade*, 200, table 6.

153. Regarding the impact of thinly populated frontier societies, see Kulikoff, *Tobacco and Slaves*, 357.

154. The 1763 Treaty of Paris, which concluded the Seven Years' War, instituted substantial colonial land changes between European nations. France withdrew claims of colonial territory in North America. The impact on slave life included Spain's receipt of French Louisiana and Britain's receipt of Spanish Florida. "Treaty of Paris, 1763," Milestones: 1750–1775, Office of the Historian, US Department of State, https://history.state.gov/milestones/1750-1775/treaty-of-paris.

155. As quoted in Littlefield, *Rice and Slaves*, 64.

156. Phillips, *American Negro Slavery*, 1275–1281.

157. Herbert Klein, *Slavery in the Americas: A Comparative Study of Virginia and Cuba* (Chicago: University of Chicago Press, 1967), 174.

158. Philip Morgan's compilation of slave inventories in British South Carolina, for example, documented that slightly more than half the captives had recognizable family ties by the 1730s, and 80 percent in the 1790s. Philip D. Morgan, *Slave Counterpoint: Black Culture in the Eighteenth-Century Chesapeake and Lowcountry* (Chapel Hill: University of North Carolina Press, 1998), tables 30 and 31, 504–506.

159. Russell R. Menard, "The Maryland Slave Population, 1658 to 1730: A Demographic Profile of Blacks in Four Counties," *William and Mary Quarterly* 32, no. 1 (January 1975): 29–54, https://doi.org/10.2307/1922593.

160. Morgan, *Slave Counterpoint*, 81. The same was true for French Louisiana by 1740 and South Carolina by 1750. Ira Berlin, *Generations of Captivity: A History of African-American Slaves* (Cambridge, MA: Harvard University Press, 2003), 89; Joyce E. Chaplin, *An Anxious Pursuit: Agricultural Innovation and Modernity in the Lower South, 1730–1815* (Chapel Hill: University of North Carolina Press, 1993), 54.

161. Edmund Berkeley Jr., "Alphabetical List of Robert Carter's Slaves Compiled from the 1733 Inventory of His Estate," *The Diary, Correspondence and Papers of Robert "King" Carter of Virginia, 1701–1732*, http://jti.lib.virginia.edu/users/berkeley/; Morgan, *Slave Counterpoint*, 503.

162. Klein, *Slavery in the Americas*, 177.

163. Morgan, *Slave Counterpoint*, 501.

164. The "home" plantation, for example, had the largest number of residential captives—90. There resided six "nuclear" families. But this familial structure hardly characterized the majority. Indeed, only 27 percent fell into this category. Eighty-one percent of the married men lived away from their wives, sometimes as far as seventeen miles away and across the Potomac, and one-third of all the men were not married, or at least not married to women on the Washington estate. These men lived instead with extended family members, fictive kin, friends, and other workers, sometimes in gender-distinct housing or even in the quarters of Washington's business associates in neighboring counties. Brenda E. Stevenson, *Life in Black and White: Family and Community in the Slave South* (New York: Oxford University Press, 1996), Kindle edition, 206–208.

165. Phillips, *American Negro Slavery*, 1319–1321.

166. Charles Joyner, *Down By the Riverside: A South Carolina Slave Community* (Urbana: University of Illinois Press, 1984), 15.

167. Phillips, *American Negro Slavery*, 1350–1354.

168. Ibid., 1352.

169. Morgan, *Slave Counterpoint*, 77.

170. Francis Le Jau, "The Carolina Chronicle," in *A Documentary History of Slavery in North America,* ed. Willie Lee Rose (Athens: University of Georgia Press, 1999), 29.

171. Littlefield, *Rice and Slaves*, 61.

172. As quoted in ibid., 64–65.

173. Carl A. Brasseaux, "The Administration of Slave Regulations in French Louisiana, 1724–1766," *Louisiana History: The Journal of the Louisiana Historical Association* 21, no. 2 (1980): 148, http://www.jstor.org/stable/4231984.

174. Berlin, *Generations of Captivity*, 89.
175. Morgan, *Slave Counterpoint*, 80–84.
176. Zora Neale Hurston, *Barracoon: The Story of the Last "Black Cargo"* (New York: Amistad Press, 2018), as quoted in "The Last Slave," *Vulture*, http://www.vulture.com/2018/04/zora-neale-hurston-barracoon-excerpt.html.
177. Aaron S. Fogleman, "From Slaves, Conflicts and Servants to Free Passengers: The Transformation of Immigration in the Era of the American Revolution," *Journal of American History* 85, no. 1 (June 1998): 51–59. https://doi.org/10.2307/2568431.
178. McCartney, *A Study of the Africans and African Americans*, 44.
179. McCartney, 42.
180. Warren, *New England Bound*, 162.
181. Ibid., 163.
182. Ibid., 166.
183. Midlo Hall, *Africans in Colonial Louisiana*, 115.
184. Ibid.
185. Kenneth James Lay, "Sexual Racism: A Legacy of Slavery," *National Black Law Journal* 13, no. 1 (1993), 165, https://escholarship.org/uc/item/3qd7s83r.
186. Campbell, *Making Black Los Angeles*, 16.
187. Ilona Katzew, "Painters and Painting: A Visual Tradition and Its Historiography," in *Casta Painting: Images of Race in Eighteenth-Century Mexico* (New Haven, CT: Yale University Press, 2004), 5.
188. They were: mulatto (50 percent African descent/50 percent European descent), quadroon (25 percent African descent/75 percent European descent), octoroon (12 percent African descent/88 percent European) and zambo (50 percent African descent/50 percent Native American descent).
189. Vincent Carretta, *Phillis Wheatley: Biography of a Genius in Bondage* (Athens: University of Georgia Press, 2011), Kindle edition, 14–15.
190. Stevenson, *What Is Slavery?*, table 3.3. Moore, *Notes on the History of Slavery in Massachusetts*, 51.
191. "1754 Massachusetts Slave Census," *Primary History: Local History Closer to Home*, 2022, http://primaryresearch.org/slave-census/?town=Boston&county=Suffolk.
192. Carretta, *Phillis Wheatley*, 143.
193. Phillis Wheatley and Vincent Carretta, *Complete Writings: Phillis Wheatley* (New York: Penguin Books, 2001), 1–2.
194. Phillis Wheatley, *Poems on Various Subjects, Religious and Moral* (Albany: Thomas Spencer, 1793).
195. John C. Shields, "Phillis Wheatley's Use of Classicism," *American Literature* 52, no. 1 (March 1980): 97, https://doi.org/10.2307/2925190.
196. Merle A. Richmond, as quoted in Sondra O'Neal, "Phillis Wheatley, 1753–1784," Poetry Foundation, 2022, https://www.poetryfoundation.org/poets/phillis-wheatley.
197. Margaretta Matilda Odell, as quoted in O'Neal, "Phillis Wheatley, 1753–1784," https://www.poetryfoundation.org/poets/phillis-wheatley.
198. "Phillis Wheatley," African Americans and the End of Slavery in Massachusetts, Massachusetts Historical Society, https://www.masshist.org/endofslavery/index.php?id=57.
199. Chloe Spear and Rebecca Warren Brown, *Memoir of Mrs. Chloe Spear, a Native of Africa, Who was Enslaved in Childhood, and Died in Boston, January 3, 1815 . . .*

Aged 65 Years (Boston: James Loring, 1832), electronic edition, as found on Documenting the American South, 21, https://docsouth.unc.edu/neh/brownrw/brownrw.html.

200. Ibid., 23–26.

201. Chloe Spear's biography was summarized by Jenn Williamson for Documenting the American South's electronic edition of *Memoir of Mrs. Chloe Spear*. See Jenn Williamson, "Summary," Documenting the American South, https://docsouth.unc.edu/neh/brownrw/summary.html.

202. Spear, *Memoir of Mrs. Chloe Spear*, 35–42.

203. Ibid.

204. Ibid., 62–75.

205. Margot Minardi, "Chloe Spear, Leaving a Legacy, Listing a Life," Royall House and Slave Quarters, 2022, http://royallhouse.org/chloe-spear-by-margot-minardi/.

206. Olaudah Equiano, *The Interesting Narrative of the Life of Olaudah Equiano, or Gustavus Vassa, the African, Written by Himself* (London: Author, 1789), electronic edition, as found on Documenting the American South 90–91, https://docsouth.unc.edu/neh/equiano1/equiano1.html.

207. Ibid., 91–92.

208. Ibid., 92–96.

209. Lay, "Sexual Racism," 165; "The Plaisters and the Abolition of Slavery," The Worshipful Company of Plaisters, July 17, 2020, https://plaistererslivery.co.uk/news/public/plaisterers-and-abolition-of-slavery/.

210. Cassandra Pybus, Kit Candlin, and Robin Petterd, "Matthew Godfrey," *Black Loyalist*, 2022, http://www.blackloyalist.info/person/display/502/; "Re: John and Sarah Godfrey of Norfolk, Co. Va.," Genealogy.com, March 20, 2002, http://www.genealogy.com/forum/surnames/topics/godfrey/1748/; "Matthew Godfrey (1652–1717)," WikiTree, September 21, 2021, https://www.wikitree.com/wiki/Godfrey-292.

211. "Tithables," Library of Virginia, 2019, http://www.lva.virginia.gov/public/guides/tithables_vanote.htm.

212. Pybus, Candlin, and Petterd, "Matthew Godfrey."

213. Ibid.

214. Dickson J. Preston, *The Young Frederick Douglass: The Maryland Years* (Baltimore, MD: Johns Hopkins University Press, 1980), 4–6.

215. Ibid.

Richard Skinner Slave Inventory, 1746

Name	Age
Baly	45
Sue	25
Selah	Adult
Stepney	
Jacob	9
Baly	6
Jem	5
Phil	2
Harry	18 months
Jenny	6 months
Dol	5 months

216. Landers, *Black Society in Spanish Florida*, 163.
217. Ibid.
218. Ibid.
219. Ibid., 164.
220. Ibid., 164–65.
221. Staple crop development in both the upper and the lower colonial South required very intense work routines linked to a decline in natural increase in the early eighteenth century. Littlefield, *Rice and Slaves*, 57-8.
222. Judith Carney, "Landscapes of Technology Transfer: Rice Cultivation and African Continuities," *Technology and Culture* 37, no. 1 (1996): 31–22, https://doi.org/10.2307/3107200.
223. As quoted in Chaplin, *An Anxious Pursuit*, 86.
224. Ibid., 86.
225. Windley, *Runaway Slave Advertisements*, 1:35.
226. William Bull, "Advertisement for Viz, et. al," *New York Gazette*, October 27, 1763, as found on Runaway New England, http://18.219.57.234/items/show/6217.
227. Theresa A. Singleton, "Slavery and Spatial Dialectics on Cuban Coffee Plantations," *World Archaeology* 33, no. 1 (June 2001): 105, http://www.jstor.org/stable/827891.
228. Gwendolyn Wright, *Building the Dream: A Social History of Housing in America* (Cambridge, MA: MIT Press, 1981), 41.
229. James Deetz, *In Small Things Forgotten: An Archaeology of Early American Life*, rev. ed. (New York: Anchor, 1996), Kindle edition, Kindle location 2959.
230. "Slave Quarters," George Washington's Mount Vernon Digital Encyclopedia, 2022, http://www.mountvernon.org/digital-encyclopedia/article/slave-quarters/.
231. Wright, *Building the Dream,* 41.
232. Thomas A. Foster, *Documenting Intimate Matters: Primary Sources for a History of Sexuality in America* (Chicago: University of Chicago Press, 2012), Kindle edition, 19.
233. Teresa A. Singleton, "The Archeology of Slave Life," in *Images of the Recent Past: Readings in Historical Archaeology*, ed. Charles E. Orser Jr. (Walnut Creek, CA: AltaMira Press, 1996), Kindle edition, Kindle location 2959.
234. Deetz, *In Small Things Forgotten*, 2449.
235. Ibid., 2547–2548.
236. Ibid., 2452.
237. Stevenson, *Life in Black and White*, 65, 166.
238. Wright, *Building the Dream*, 41.
239. Singleton, "The Archeology of Slave Life," 2950.
240. Montgomery, "Survivors from the Cargo of the Negro Slave Yacht Wanderer," 614, 515, plates XLII, XLIII.
241. Debra D. Green, "African Mexicans in Spanish Slave Societies in America: A Critical Location of Sources," *Journal of Black Studies*, 40 no. 4 (March 2010), 691, http://www.jstor.org/stable/40648535.
242. Singleton, "Slavery and Spatial Dialectics on Cuban Coffee Plantations," 102.
243. As quoted in Wright, *Building the Dream*, 46.
244. Singleton, "The Archeology of Slave Life," 2870.

245. Margaret Supplee Smith and Emily Herring Wilson, *North Carolina Women: Making History* (Chapel Hill: University of North Carolina Press, 1999), 68.

246. "Hudson Valley Architecture," Hudson River Valley Institute, http://www.hudsonrivervalley.org/themes/colonialera.html; Bernard L. Herman, "Slave and Servant Housing in Charleston, 1770–1820," *Historical Archeology* 33, no. 3 (1999): 88, http://www.jstor.org/stable/25616727.

247. Anne Grady, "The Slave Quarters," The Royall House and Slave Quarters Museum, 2022, https://royallhouse.org/what-youll-see/the-slave-quarters/.

248. Wright, *Building the Dream*, 55.

249. Ibid.

250. Deetz, *In Small Things Forgotten*, 2457.

251. Eric Klingelhofer, "Aspects of Early Afro-American Material Culture: Artifacts from the Slave Quarters at Garrison, Plantation, Maryland," *Historical Archeology* 21, no. 2 (1987): 21, http://www.jstor.org/stable/25615636.

252. Singleton, "Archeology of Slave Life," 2838.

253. Ibid., 2811; "Thousands of Pieces of Slave Pottery Found in South Carolina," *Augusta Chronicle*, May 25, 2010, https://www.augustachronicle.com/article/20100525/NEWS/305259932.

254. Singleton, "Archeology of Slave Life," 2860–2861.

255. Ibid., 2811.

256. Ibid., 2899.

257. Deetz, *In Small Things Forgotten*, 2517.

258. Shane White, "Pinkster: Afro-Dutch Syncretization in New York City and the Hudson Valley," *Journal of American Folklore* 102, no. 403 (January—March 1989): 68, https://doi.org/10.2307/540082.

259. Quoted in ibid., 68–69.

260. Katrina Hazzard-Gordon, "Dancing under the Lash: Sociocultural Disruption, Continuity, and Synthesis," in *African Dance: An Artistic, Historical, Philosophical Inquiry*, ed. Karimu Welsh-Asante (Trenton, NJ: Africa World Press, 1996), 116–19; Green, "African Mexicans in Spanish Slave Societies," 692; Dena J. Epstein, "African Music in British and French America," *Musical Quarterly* 59, no. 1 (1973): 73, 78–80, 86–87, http://www.jstor.org/stable/741460.

261. John Blassingame, *The Slave Community: Plantation Life in the Antebellum South* (New York: Oxford University Press, 1979), 31–32.

262. Epstein, "African Music in British and French America," 87.

263. As quoted in ibid., 81.

264. All quoted in ibid., 79–81.

265. Abraham Johnstone, *The Address of Abraham Johnstone, A Black Man, Who Was Hanged at Woodbury, in the County of Glocester, and State of New Jersey, on Saturday the 8th Day of July Last; to the People of Colour. To Which is Added His Dying Confession or Declaration, Also, A Copy of a Letter to His Wife, Written the Day Previous to His Execution* (Philadelphia: Printed for the Purchasers, 1797), electronic edition, as found on Documenting the American South, http://docsouth.unc.edu/neh/johnstone/johnstone.html.

266. Ibid., 42.

267. Ibid., 32–34.

268. Ibid., 43.
269. Ibid.
270. Ibid., 43–44.
271. Ibid., 42–43.
272. Ibid., 46.
273. Ibid., 45.
274. Ibid., 43-46.
275. Ibid., 46.

CHAPTER 3

1. Charles Ball, *Slavery in the United States. A Narrative of the Life and Adventures of Charles Ball, a Black Man, Who Lived Forty Years in Maryland, South Carolina and Georgia, as a Slave Under Various Masters, and was One Year in the Navy with Commodore Barney, During the Late War* (New York: John S. Taylor, 1837), 16–19.

2. "Refugee" is used in this text to indicate an enslaved person who is actively seeking freedom through escape and fugitivity.

3. "Slavery Becomes a Legal Fact in Virginia: [1691] An Act for Suppressing Outlying Slaves," in *A Documentary History of Slavery in North America*, ed. Willie Lee Rose (Athens: University of Georgia Press, 1999), 20–21.

4. "I've been 'buked and I've been scorned," as found on negrospirituals.com, https://www.negrospirituals.com/songs/i_ve_been_buked_and_i-ve_been_scorned.htm.

5. Helen Tunnicliff Catterall, ed., *Judicial Cases concerning American Slavery and the Negro*, vol. 4: *Cases from the Courts of New England, the Middle States, and the District of Columbia* (Washington, DC: Carnegie Institution, 1936), 31.

6. Helen Tunnicliff Catterall, ed., *Judicial Cases concerning American Slavery and the Negro*, vol. 1: *Cases from the Courts of England, Virginia, West Virginia, and Kentucky* (Washington, DC: Carnegie Institution, 1926), 94.

7. Helen Tunnicliff Catterall, ed., *Judicial Cases concerning American Slavery and the Negro*, vol. 3: *Cases from the Courts of Georgia, Florida, Alabama, Mississippi, and Louisiana* (Washington, DC: Carnegie Institution, 1936), 419.

8. Catterall, *Judicial Cases concerning American Slavery and the Negro*, 3:451.

9. Helen Tunnicliff Catterall, ed., *Judicial Cases concerning American Slavery and the Negro*, vol. 2: *Cases from the Courts of North Carolina, South Carolina, and Tennessee* (Washington, DC: Carnegie Institution, 1927), 273.

10. Ibid., 286.

11. Catterall, *Judicial Cases concerning American Slavery and the Negro*, 3:9.

12. Catterall, *Judicial Cases concerning American Slavery and the Negro*, 2:288–89.

13. William Coker et al., "Spanish Colonial St. Augustine," in *Florida: From the Beginning to 1992* (Houston, TX: Pioneer Publications, 1991), as found on University of Florida, George A. Smathers Library, Digital Collections, 2, https://ufdc.ufl.edu/UF00025122/00008/3j.

14. Pierre Viaud, *Shipwreck and Adventure of Monsieur Pierre Viaud: A Native of Bourdeaux, and Captain of a Ship*, trans. Mrs. Griffith (London: T. Davis, 1771), as found on Library of Congress, 167–77, https://www.loc.gov/item/16020220/.

15. Catterall, *Judicial Cases concerning American Slavery and the Negro*, 3:402.

16. Ibid., 439.

17. Ibid., 405.

18. Thomas Brown and Leah Sims, eds., *Fugitive Slave Advertisements in the* City Gazette: *Charleston, South Carolina, 1787–1797* (Lanham, MD: Lexington Books, 2015), Kindle edition, Kindle location 739–745, 937–942.

19. Otto Lohrenz, "Clergyman and Revolutionary Committeeman: Thomas Lundie of St. Andrews Parish, Brunswick County, Virginia," *Kentucky Review*, vol. 15, no. 1 (2000): 12, http://uknowledge.uky.edu/cgi/viewcontent.cgi?article=1001&context=kentucky-review.

20. "Eighteenth Century Slaves as Advertised by their Masters," *Journal of Negro History*, vol. 1, no. 2 (April 1916): 164, https://doi.org/10.2307/3035637.

21. As quoted in Marvin L. Michael Kay and Lorin Lee Cary, eds., *Slavery in North Carolina: 1748–1775* (Chapel Hill: University of North Carolina Press, 1995), 154.

22. Ibid., 154, 186–87.

23. Slave List of Hannah Beale Bull, December 13, 1797, in Kenneth M. Stampp, *Records of Antebellum Southern Plantations from the Revolution Through the Civil War*, Selections from the South Carolinian Library, University of South Carolina, Series A, Part 2, Miscellaneous Collections, 55–56, 63–67.

24. Slave List of Hannah Beale Bull; "Bull, William II (1710–1791)," in *The South Carolina Encyclopedia Guide to the American Revolution in South Carolina*, ed. Walter Edgar (Columbia: University of South Carolina Press, 2012), https://www.scencyclopedia.org/sce/entries/bull-william-ii/.

25. Sonya Brown, ed., "Will of George Brown of Bladen County, North Carolina, 20 March, 1782," Records of Wills, Bladen County 1762–1892, vol. 1, Bladen County Public Library, Brown Family File, May 6, 2000, http://freepages.rootsweb.com/~brownandmeares/genealogy/georgebrownwill.htm.

26. "Robert Raper of Charles Town in South Carolina. Will 24 November 1774; proved 1 October 1789," in Lothrop Withington and H. F. Waters, "South Carolina Gleanings in England (Continued)," *South Carolina Historical and Genealogical Magazine* 7, no. 3 (1906): 150–51, http://www.jstor.org/stable/27575136.

27. "Richard Mullington's Ex'rs vs. James Shipman," in *North Carolina Reports, Embracing Cases Determined in the Superior Courts of the Law and Equity of the State of North Carolina . . . also Reports of the Cases Ruled and Determined by the Court of Conference of North Carolina*, ed. William H. Battle (Raleigh: Turner and Hughes, 1844), 243–44; Catterall, *Judicial Cases concerning American Slavery and the Negro*, 2:16.

28. Slave Ledger of William and Samuel Vance Gatewood, 1773–1813, Virginia State Library Archive, Richmond, Virginia.

29. Catterall, *Judicial Cases concerning American Slavery and the Negro*, 2:281.

30. Margaret Washington, *Sojourner Truth's America* (Urbana: Chicago University Press, 2011) Kindle edition, Kindle location 921.

31. Bethany Veney, *The Narrative of Bethany Veney, A Slave Woman* (Worcester, MA: N.p., 1889), electronic edition, as found on Documenting the American South, 10, http://docsouth.unc.edu/fpn/veney/veney.html.

32. Catterall, *Judicial Cases concerning American Slavery and the Negro*, 2:287.

33. Catterall, *Judicial Cases concerning American Slavery and the Negro*, 3:448.

34. Regarding the religious practices of enslaved people see Albert J. Raboteau, *Slave Religion: The "Invisible Institution" in the Antebellum South* (New York: Oxford University Press, 2004), Kindle edition.

35. Ibid., 276.

36. Sylviane A. Diouf, *Servants of Allah: African Muslims Enslaved in the Americas*, 15th Anniversary Edition (New York: New York University Press, 2013), Kindle edition, 83.

37. Georgia Writers' Project, *Drums and Shadows: Survival Studies amongst the Coastal Georgia Negroes* (Athens: University of Georgia Press), Kindle edition, Kindle location 3526, 3599, 3848.

38. Ibid., 3846.

39. Omar ibn Said, "Autobiography of Omar ibn Said, Slave in North Carolina, 1831," ed. John Franklin Jameson, *American Historical Review* 30, no. 4. (July 1925): 787–95, electronic edition as found on Documenting the American South, https://docsouth.unc.edu/nc/omarsaid/omarsaid.html#n3.

40. Ibid., 793–94.

41. For a discussion of Islam among slaves in the US South, see Michael A. Gomez, *Exchanging Our Country Marks: The Transformation of African identities in the Colonial and Antebellum South* (Chapel Hill: University of North Carolina Press, 1998), 59–87; Raboteau, *Slave Religion*, 5–6; Charles Joyner, "'Believer I Know': The Emergence of African American Christianity" in *Religion and American Culture*, ed. David G. Hackett (New York: Routledge, 2003), 188–89; Gayraud S. Wilmore, *Black Religion and Black Radicalism: An Interpretation of the Religious History of African Americans*, 3rd ed. (Maryknoll, NY: Orbis Books, 1998), 13–17; Aminah Beverly McCloud, *African American Islam* (New York: Routledge, 1995), 9–40, passim, but this discussion centers on the postbellum period.

42. "Africans," Mbiti writes, "are notoriously religious, and each people has its own religious system with a set of beliefs and practices. Religion permeates into all the departments of life so fully that it is not easy or possible always to isolate it." Raboteau notes, "One of the most durable and adaptable constituents of the slave's culture, linking African past with American present, was his religion." John S. Mbiti, *African Religions and Philosophy*, 2nd ed. (Portsmouth, NH: Heinemann, 1990), 1 and passim; Raboteau, *Slave Religion*, 4 and passim. See also John W. Blassingame, *The Slave Community: Plantation Life in the Antebellum South* (New York: Oxford University Press, 1979), 130–47; Eugene D. Genovese, *Roll, Jordan, Roll: The World the Slaves Made* (New York: Pantheon, 1974), 161–284; Wilmore, *Black Religion and Black Radicalism*, 22–50, passim; Mechal Sobel, *Trabelin' On: The Slave Journey to an Afro-Baptist Faith* (Princeton, NJ: Princeton University Press, 1988), 22–57, 108–35; Gomez, *Exchanging Our Country Marks*, 59–87, 244–90; Sterling Stuckey, *Slave Culture: Nationalist Theory and the Foundations of Black America* (New York: Oxford University Press, 1987), 7–11; Margaret Creel, *"A Peculiar People": Slave Religion*

and Community-Culture among the Gullahs (New York: New York University Press, 1988), 259–328; and John Thornton, *Africa and Africans in the Making of the Atlantic World, 1400–1800* (Cambridge: Cambridge University Press, 1992), 235–71.

43. Ball, *Slavery in the United States,* 22–24.

44. Georgia Writers' Project, *Drums and Shadows,* 3579.

45. Ibid., 3478.

46. Ibid., 3584.

47. Raboteau, *Slave Religion,* 66.

48. A Christian baptism in Virginia until 1667 meant that an African, and his or her baptized children, could be treated as indentured servants rather than as perpetual slaves. See "An Act Declaring the Baptisme of Slaves Doth Not Exempt Them from Bondage," in *A Documentary History of Slavery in North America,* ed. Willie Lee Rose (Athens: University of Georgia Press, 1999), 19.

49. Francis Le Jau, "The Carolina Chronicle," *A Documentary History of Slavery in North America,* ed. Willie Lee Rose (Athens: University of Georgia Press, 1999), 29.

50. William E. Nelson, "Law and the Structure of Power in Colonial Virginia," *Valparaiso University Law Review* 48, no. 3 (spring 2014): 789–91, https://scholar.valpo.edu/cgi/viewcontent.cgi?article=2343&context=vulr.

51. Raboteau, *Slave Religion,* 66.

52. Ibid., 128–31.

53. Elizabeth, *Memoir of Old Elizabeth, A Coloured Woman* (1863) in Six Women's Slave Narratives, ed. William L. Andrews (New York: Oxford University Press, 1988), 3–4.

54. Langston Hughes, "Harlem," as found on Poetry Foundation, 2022, https://www.poetryfoundation.org/poems/46548/harlem.

55. Catterall, *Judicial Cases concerning American Slavery and the Negro,* 3:466.

56. Douglas B. Chambers, *Murder at Montpelier: Igbo Africans in Virginia* (Jackson: University Press of Mississippi, 2005), 6–10.

57. Catterall, *Judicial Cases concerning American Slavery and the Negro,* 2:34.

58. Catterall, *Judicial Cases concerning American Slavery and the Negro,* 4:40.

59. Catterall, *Judicial Cases concerning American Slavery and the Negro,* 2:15.

60. Ibid., 46.

61. Ibid., 42.

62. Catterall, ed., *Judicial Cases concerning American Slavery and the Negro,* 4:34.

63. Ibid., 3, 39.

64. Ibid., 43.

65. Ibid., 35.

66. Catterall, *Judicial Cases concerning American Slavery and the Negro,* 3:315.

67. Ibid., 427.

68. Catterall, *Judicial Cases concerning American Slavery and the Negro,* 2:19–20.

69. Catterall, *Judicial Cases concerning American Slavery and the Negro,* 3:408.

70. Catterall, *Judicial Cases concerning American Slavery and the Negro,* 2:42.

71. Ibid., 13.

72. Catterall, *Judicial Cases concerning American Slavery and the Negro*, 3:424–25.

73. Arthur, *The Life, and Dying Speech of Arthur, a Negro Man; Who Was Executed at Worcester, October 20, 1768. For a Rape Committed on the Body of One Deborah Metcalfe* (Boston: Printed and Sold in Milk-Street, 1768), 1.

74. Catterall, *Judicial Cases concerning American Slavery and the Negro*, 4:34–35.

75. Ibid., 47.

76. Ibid., 48.

77. Ibid., 38–39.

78. Catterall, *Judicial Cases concerning American Slavery and the Negro*, 1:84.

79. Catterall, *Judicial Cases concerning American Slavery and the Negro*, 2:38.

80. Ibid., 44.

81. Catterall, *Judicial Cases concerning American Slavery and the Negro*, 4:43

82. Catterall, *Judicial Cases concerning American Slavery and the Negro*, 2:45.

83. William J. Allinson, *Memoir of Quamino Buccau, A Pious Methodist* (London: Charles Gilpin, 1851), 5.

84. Catterall, *Judicial Cases concerning American Slavery and the Negro*, 4:39.

85. Ibid., 44.

86. Ibid., 35.

87. Catterall, *Judicial Cases concerning American Slavery and the Negro*, 2:8.

88. Catterall, *Judicial Cases concerning American Slavery and the Negro*, 3:398.

89. Ibid., 403–404.

90. Ibid., 408.

91. Ibid., 410.

92. Ibid., 417.

93. Ibid., 437.

94. Ibid., 438.

95. Ibid., 437.

96. Tiya Miles, *The Dawn of Detroit: A Chronicle of Slavery and Freedom in the City of the Straits* (New York: New Press, 2017), Kindle edition, 67.

97. Catterall, *Judicial Cases concerning American Slavery and the Negro*, 3:6.

98. Ibid.

99. Catterall, *Judicial Cases concerning American Slavery and the Negro*, 4:53.

100. Catterall, *Judicial Cases concerning American Slavery and the Negro*, 3:315.

101. Lyrics from Beyoncé Knowles, "Freedom," *Lemonad*e, Parkwood Entertainment and Columbia Records, 2016, https://www.youtube.com/watch?v=7FWF9375hUA.

102. Catterall, *Judicial Cases concerning American Slavery and the Negro*, 3:403.

103. Patrick Riordan, "Finding Freedom in Florida: Native Peoples, African Americans, and Colonists, 1670–1816," *Florida Historical Quarterly* 75, no. 1 (summer 1996): 25, http://www.jstor.org/stable/30142151. Fugitive slave advertisements from neighboring colonies and states (such as Georgia and South Carolina), often included escape information from these adjacent places.

104. Lathan A. Windley, ed., *Runaway Slave Advertisements: A Documentary History from the 1730s to 1790*, vol. 4: *Georgia* (Westport, CT: Greenwood Press, 1983), 21.

105. Ibid., 46.
106. Ibid., 41.
107. Brown and Sims, *Fugitive Slave Advertisements in the* City Gazette, 746–750.
108. Ibid., 609–614.
109. Catterall, *Judicial Cases concerning American Slavery and the Negro*, 3:424.
110. Brown and Sims, *Fugitive Slave Advertisements in the* City Gazette, 1632–1637.
111. "*Virginia Gazette,* December 12, 1777," as found in Lathan A. Windley, ed., *Runaway Slave Advertisements: A Documentary History from the 1730s to 1790*, vol. 1: *Virginia and North Carolina* (Westport, CT: Greenwood Press, 1983), 189.
112. "*Virginia Gazette*, February 12, 1779," as found in Windley, *Runaway Slave Advertisements*, 1:198.
113. Brown and Sims, *Fugitive Slave Advertisements in the* City Gazette, 595–599.
114. Ibid., 582–588.
115. Ibid., 371–375.
116. Ibid., 1916–1932.
117. Windley, *Runaway Slave Advertisements*, 4:43.
118. "*Virginia Gazette,* May 24, 1751," as found in Windley, *Runaway Slave Advertisements*, 1:21–22.
119. "*The New York Gazette* # 452, June 24, 1734" as found in Graham Russell Hodges and Alan Edward Brown, eds., *"Pretends to be Free": Runaway Slave Advertisements from Colonial and Revolutionary New York and New Jersey* (New York: Fordham University Press, 2019), 10.
120. Catterall, *Judicial Cases concerning American Slavery and the Negro*, 3:313.
121. Story recounted in Miles, *The Dawn of Detroit*, 58.
122. Windley, *Runaway Slave Advertisements*, 4:60–61.
123. Catterall, *Judicial Cases concerning American Slavery and the Negro*, 3:423.
124. United States Works Progress Administration, *Slave Narratives: A Folk History of Slavery in the United States from Interviews with Former Slaves*, Part 2, North Carolina Narratives, Kindle edition, Kindle locations 2298–2301.
125. Brown and Sims, *Fugitive Slave Advertisements in the* City Gazette, 739–745.
126. "*Virginia Gazette*, March 20 to March 27, 1746," as found in Windley, *Runaway Slave Advertisements*, 1:16.
127. Regarding drapetomania, see Bob Eberly Myers II, "'Drapetomania': Rebellion, Defiance and Free Black Insanity in the Antebellum United States" (PhD diss., University of California, Los Angeles, 2014), https://www.proquest.com/dissertations-theses/drapetomania-rebellion-defiance-free-black/docview/1648436283/se-2?accountid=14512.
128. Catterall, *Judicial Cases concerning American Slavery and the Negro*, 3:399–400.
129. Ibid., 453.
130. Lil B, "I'm George Floyd," 2020, https://www.youtube.com/watch?v=clcfknHQ66k.
131. Catterall, *Judicial Cases concerning American Slavery and the Negro*, 1:77.
132. Catterall, *Judicial Cases concerning American Slavery and the Negro*, 2:11–13.

133. Landon Carter, *The Diary of Colonel Landon Carter of Sabine Hall*, ed. Jack P. Greene (Richmond: Virginia Historical Society, 1987), 149.

134. Tom Costa, "Runaway Slaves and Servants in Colonial Virginia," *Encyclopedia Virginia*, Virginia Foundation, January 12, 2021, https://www.encyclopediavirginia.org/Runaway_Slaves_and_Servants_in_Colonial_Virginia#start_entry.

135. Catterall, *Judicial Cases concerning American Slavery and the Negro*, 3:415–416.

136. "*Tennessee Gazette*, October 3, 1804," as found in Cynthia Cumfer, *Separate Peoples, One Land: The Minds of Cherokees, Blacks, and Whites on the Tennessee Frontier* (Chapel Hill: University of North Carolina Press, 2007), 140.

137. Catterall, *Judicial Cases concerning American Slavery and the Negro*, 4:32–34.

138. Catterall, *Judicial Cases concerning American Slavery and the Negro*, 2:323.

139. Daniel O. Sayers, *A Desolate Place for a Defiant People: The Archeology of Maroons, Indigenous Americans, and Enslaved Laborers in the Great Dismal Swamp* (Gainesville: University Press of Florida, 2014); Dedra McDonald, "Intimacy and Empire: Indian-African Interaction in Spanish Colonial New Mexico, 1500–1800," in *African American History in New Mexico: Portraits from Five Hundred Years*, ed. Bruce A. Glasrud (Albuquerque: University of New Mexico Press, 2013), Kindle edition, Kindle locations 633–648.

140. Herbert Aptheker, "Maroons within the Present Limits of the United States," *Journal of Negro History* 24, no. 2 (1939):168, https://doi.org/10.2307/2714447; H. R. McIlwaine, *Legislative Journals of the Council of Colonial Virginia*, 2nd ed. (Richmond: Virginia State Library, 1979), 306.

141. Aptheker, "Maroons within the Present Limits of the United States," 168.

142. Sayers, *A Desolate Place for a Defiant People*, 3–4.

143. Ibid., 89.

144. Sayers, *A Desolate Place for a Defiant People*, 120–27.

145. Ibid., 131.

146. Timothy James Lockley, *Maroon Communities in South Carolina: A Documentary Record* (Columbia: University of South Carolina, 2009), 37.

147. Ibid., 108.

148. Aptheker, "Maroons within the Present Limits of the United States," 168–83; Rosalyn Howard, "The 'Wild Indians' of Andros Island: Black Seminole Legacy in the Bahamas," *Journal of Black Studies* 37, no. 2 (November 2006): 279, http://www.jstor.org/stable/40034414.

149. Sayers, *A Desolate Place for a Defiant People*, 92.

150. Ibid., 100–103.

151. Ibid., 102–103.

152. Aptheker, "Maroons within the Present Limits of the United States," 169.

153. Lockley, *Maroon Communities in South Carolina*, 8–9.

154. Aptheker, "Maroons within the Present Limits of the United States," 169.

155. Ibid.

156. Ibid.

157. Lockley, *Maroon Communities in South Carolina*, 20–21.

158. Ibid., 120–21.

159. Ibid., 20–21.
160. Catterall, *Judicial Cases concerning American Slavery and the Negro*, 3:6.
161. Windley, *Runaway Slave Advertisements*, 4:58–59.
162. Lockley, *Maroon Communities in South Carolina*, 62–64.
163. Ibid., 113.
164. Jane Landers, *Black Society in Spanish Florida* (Urbana: University of Illinois Press, 1999), 79–80.
165. Ronald L. F. Davis, *The Black Experience in Natchez, 1720–1880* (Fort Washington, PA: Eastern National, 1999), 6.
166. Catterall, *Judicial Cases concerning American Slavery and the Negro*, 3:401.
167. Ibid., 410.
168. Ibid., 414.
169. "Pacific Worlds in the South," in *The New Encyclopedia of Southern Culture*, vol. 24: *Race*, ed. Charles Regan Wilson, Thomas Holt, and Laurie Green (Chapel Hill: University of North Carolina Press, 2013), 121.
170. Gwendolyn Midlo Hall, *Africans in Colonial Louisiana: The Development of Afro-Creole Culture in the Eighteenth-Century* (Baton Rouge: Louisiana State University Press, 1992), Kindle edition, Kindle location 3772.
171. Ibid., 3888.
172. Ibid., 4149.
173. Ibid., 3987–4006.
174. Ibid., 4143.
175. Ibid., 3932.
176. Catterall, *Judicial Cases concerning American Slavery and the Negro*, 3:415.
177. Ibid., 425.
178. Midlo Hall, *Africans in Colonial Louisiana*, 4095–4102.
179. Aptheker, "Maroons within the Present Limits of the United States," 177–78.
180. Landers, *Black Society in Spanish Florida*, 163.
181. Nathaniel Millett, "Defining Freedom in the Atlantic Borderlands of the Revolutionary Southeast," *Early American Studies* 5, no. 2 (fall 2007): 367–94, http://www.jstor.org/stable/23546613.
182. Riordan, "Finding Freedom in Florida," 41–42.
183. Riordan, "Finding Freedom in Florida," 42–43; Uzi Baram, "A Haven from Slavery on Florida's Gulf Coast: Looking for Evidence of Angola on the Manatee River," *African Diaspora Archaeology Network Newsletter.* 11, no. 2 (June 2008): 3, https://scholarworks.umass.edu/cgi/viewcontent.cgi?referer=https://www.google.com/&httpsredir=1&article=1784&context=adan.
184. As quoted in Howard, "The 'Wild Indians' of Andros Island," 281–82.
185. Ibid., 282–83.
186. McDonald, "Intimacy and Empire," 707–710.
187. Mary Miley Theobald, "Slave Conspiracies in Colonial Virginia," *Colonial Williamsburg Journal* (winter 2005–2006), http://www.history.org/foundation/journal/winter05-06/conspiracy.cfm.
188. Thelma W. Foote, *Black and White Manhattan: The History of Racial Formation in Colonial New York City, 1624–1783* (New York: Oxford University Press, 2004), 132–34; Walter Rucker, "Conjure, Magic, and Power: The Influence

of Afro-Atlantic Religious Practices on Slave Resistance and Rebellion," *Journal of Black Studies* 32, no. 1 (September 2001): 86, http://www.jstor.org/stable/2668016.

189. Herbert Aptheker, "American Negro Slave Revolts," *Science and Society* 1, no. 4 (summer 1937): 515, http://www.jstor.org/stable/40399115.

190. Daniel Horsmanden, *The New York Conspiracy*, ed. Thomas J. Davis (Boston: Beacon Press, 1971), 41–45.

191. Ibid., 54–55.

192. Ferenc M. Szasz, "The New York Slave Revolt of 1741: A Re-Examination," *New York History* 48, no. 3 (July 1967): 215, http://www.jstor.org/stable/23162951; Horsmanden, *The New York Conspiracy*, vii.

193. Giles R. Wright, *Afro-Americans in New Jersey: A Short History* (Trenton, NJ: New Jersey Historical Commission, 1988), 20–21.

194. Walter C. Rucker, *The River Flows On: Black Resistance, Culture, and Identity Formation in Early America* (Baton Rouge: Louisiana State University Press, 2006), 100–102.

195. Ibid.

196. Aptheker, "American Negro Slave Revolts," 516–17; Rucker, *The River Flows On*, 100–101.

197. Rucker, *The River Flows On*, 101.

198. Davis, *The Black Experience in Natchez*, 6.

199. Jack D. L. Holmes, "The Abortive Slave Revolt at Point Coupée, Louisiana, 1795," *Louisiana History* 11, no. 4 (autumn 1970): 346, n. 16, http://www.jstor.org/stable/4231151.

200. Ibid., 348.

201. Ibid., 353–54.

202. Robert L. Paquette, "'A Horde of Brigands?' The Great Louisiana Slave Revolt of 1811 Reconsidered," *Historical Reflections* 35, no. 1 (spring 2009): 80, http://www.jstor.org/stable/41403653.

203. Ibid., 80.

204. Ibid., 73–78.

205. Ibid., 77–78.

206. Philip J. Schwartz, "Introduction," in *Gabriel's Conspiracy: A Documentary History* (Charlottesville: University of Virginia Press, 2012), 1.

207. Douglas Egerton, *Gabriel's Rebellion: The Virginia Slave Conspiracies of 1800 and 1802* (Chapel Hill: University of North Carolina Press, 1993), x.

208. Michael L. Nicholls, *Whispers of Rebellion: Narrating Gabriel's Conspiracy* (Charlottesville: University of Virginia Press, 2012), Kindle edition, Kindle location 933, 1137.

209. Ibid., 502.

210. Ibid., 933.

211. Nat Turner, "The confessions of Nat Turner; leader of the late insurrection in Southampton, Va. As fully and voluntarily made to Thos. R. Gray, in the prison where he was confined, and acknowledged by him to be such, when read before the court of Southampton, convened at Jerusalem, November 5, 1831, for his trial" in *The Confessions of Nat Turner and Related Documents*, ed. Kenneth S. Greenberg (Boston: Bedford St. Martins, 2016), 44–45.

212. Thomas Gray and Nat Turner, *The Confessions of Nat Turner* (Baltimore: Lucas and Deaver, 1831) as found on Digital Commons at University of Nebraska–Lincoln, 7, https://digitalcommons.unl.edu/cgi/viewcontent.cgi?article=1014&context=etas.

213. Jerome Palliser, "The Hidden Life of Crispus Attucks," *Journal of the American Revolution* (March 5, 2014), https://allthingsliberty.com/2014/03/the-hidden-life-of-crispus-attucks/.

214. William Cooper Nell, *Services of Colored Americans, in the Wars of 1776 and 1812* (Boston: Robert F. Wallcut, 1852) Kindle edition, Kindle location 90; Mitch Kachun, "From Forgotten Founder to Indispensable Icon: Crispus Attucks, Black Citizenship, and Collective Memory, 1770–1865," *Journal of the Early Republic* 29, no. 2 (summer 2009): 249–86, http://www.jstor.org/stable/40208199.

215. John Murray, Earl of Dunmore, "Lord Dunmore's Proclamation, November 7, 1775," *Pennsylvania Weekly Advertiser*, December 6, 1775, as found on The Gilder Lehrman Institute of American History, https://www.gilderlehrman.org/history-resources/spotlight-primary-source/lord-dunmores-proclamation-1775.

216. "Lord Dunmore's Proclamation," *Black Loyalists: Our History, Our People*, Canada's Digital Collections, http://blackloyalist.com/cdc/story/revolution/dunmore.htm.

217. Alan Taylor, *The Internal Enemy: Slavery and War in Virginia, 1772–1832* (New York: Norton, 2013), Kindle edition, Kindle locations, 393–394.

218. Esther Pavao, "Skirmish at Kemp's Landing," Revolutionary-War.net, http:///www.revolutionary-war.net/skirmist-at-kemps-landing.html; Dunmore, "Lord Dunmore's Proclamation."

219. "Abigail Godfrey," Black Loyalist, 2022, http://www.blackloyalist.info/person/display/213.

220. "Matthew Godfrey," Black Loyalist, 2022, http://www.blackloyalist.info/person/display/502 .

221. "At a Court of Enquiry Held, May 6, 1776," *Virginia Magazine of History and Biography* 15, no. 4 (April 1908): 411–12; "John Willoughby, II Petition," *Journal of the House of Delegates of the Commonwealth of Virginia* (Richmond: Thomas W. White, 1827), 55, as found on Black Loyalist, http://www.blackloyalist.info/john-willoughby/.

222. "Washington's Runaway Slaves," Black Loyalist, 2022, http://www.blackloyalist.info/washington-s-runaway-slaves.

223. Sylvia R. Frey, "Between Slavery and Freedom: Virginia Blacks in the American Revolution," *Journal of Southern History* 49, no. 3 (August 1983): 376, https://doi.org/10.2307/2208101.

224. Windley, *Runaway Slave Advertisements*, 4:81.

225. Ibid., 81–82.

226. Ibid., 84–85.

227. Ibid., 58–59.

228. Ibid., 74.

229. Ibid., 75.

230. Alan Gilbert, *Black Patriots and Loyalists: Fighting for Emancipation in the War for Independence* (Chicago: University of Chicago Press, 2012), 30–34; "Smallpox Outbreak," Black Loyalist, 2022, http://www.blackloyalist.info/event/display/146.

231. Cassandra Pybus, *Epic Journeys of Freedom: Runaway Slaves of the American Revolution and Their Global Quest for Liberty* (Boston: Beacon Press, 2006), Kindle edition, 20.

232. Boston King, "Memoirs of the Life of Boston King: A Black Preacher," *Methodist* (March–June 1798), 105.

233. Ibid., 109.

234. Gilbert, *Black Patriots and Loyalists*, 188.

235. As quoted in ibid., 189.

236. It is not certain if Boston and Violet King had children at this time. He may have been speaking of fictive kin, children had by her in a former relationship, or some of his family of birth who also had managed to get behind British lines at Charleston and travel north with the troops. King, "Memoirs of the Life of Boston King," 109.

237. Ibid., 157.

238. Debra Hill, "Black Loyalists in Nova Scotia," November 1, 2019, Library and Archives Canada, https://www.bac-lac.gc.ca/eng/discover/immigration/history-ethnic-cultural/under-northern-star/Pages/black-loyalists.aspx.

239. Harvey Amani Whitfield, "The American Background of Loyalists Slaves," *Left History* 14, no. 1 (2009): 58–87, https://doi.org/10.25071/1913-9632.24905; Catterall, *Judicial Cases concerning American Slavery and the Negro*, 2:280.

240. Catherine Cottreau-Robins, "A Loyalist Plantation in Nova Scotia, 1784–1800," (PhD diss., Dalhouse University, 2012), 46.

241. Catherine Cottreau-Robins, "Searching for the Enslaved in Nova Scotia's Loyalist Landscape," *Acadiensis* 43, no. 1 (2014): 125–36, http://www.jstor.org/stable/24329580.

242. "Shelburne Riot," *Black Loyalists: Our History, Our People*, Canada's Digital Collections, http://blackloyalist.com/cdc/story/prejudice/riot.htm.

243. Laura Neilson Bonikowsky, "The Arrival of Black Loyalists in Nova Scotia," *Canadian Encyclopedia*, Historica Canada, December 5, 2019, https://www.thecanadianencyclopedia.ca/en/article/black-loyalists-feature.

244. Boston King, "Memoirs of Boston King," as found on *Black Loyalists: Our History, Our People,* Canada's Digital Collection, https://blackloyalist.com/cdc/documents/diaries/king-memoirs.htm.

245. Robert A. Selig, "The Revolution's Black Soldiers," AmericanRevolution.org, 2020, http://www.americanrevolution.org/blk.php.

246. Taylor, *The Internal Enemy*, 4755.

247. James Roberts, *The Narrative of James Roberts, a Soldier under Gen. Washington in the Revolutionary War, and under Gen. Jackson at the Battle of New Orleans, in the War of 1812: "A Battle Which Cost me a Limb, Some Blood, and Almost My Life"* (Chicago: James Roberts, 1858), electronic edition, as found on Documenting the American South, 9–10, https://docsouth.unc.edu/neh/roberts/roberts.html.

248. Ibid., 9–10.

249. Ibid., 10–11.

250. Gilbert, *Black Patriots and Loyalists*, 168–69.

251. Selig, "The Revolution's Black Soldiers."

252. Nell, *Services of Colored Americans*, 174–180.
253. Ibid., 317.
254. Kathleen DuVal, *Independence Lost: Lives on the Edge of the American Revolution* (New York: Random House, 2015), Kindle edition, Kindle location 3017.
255. Ibid., 4818–4721.
256. Ibid., 1853.
257. Ibid., 1871.
258. These organizations include the Maryland Society for Promoting the Abolition of Slavery and for Relief of Poor Negroes and Others Unlawfully Held in Bondage, founded in 1789; the Virginia Abolition Society, founded in 1790; the New Jersey Society for Promoting the Abolition of Slavery, founded in 1793; the Dover and Wilmington, Delaware, abolition societies, founded in 1788 and 1789, respectively; and many other local societies as well as the first national "umbrella" organization, the American Convention for Promoting the Abolition of Slavery, founded in 1794. Douglas Harper, "Emancipation in New York," Slavery in the North, 2003, http://slavenorth.com/nyemancip.htm.
259. The African slave trade was made illegal in Rhode Island and Connecticut in 1774, Delaware in 1776, Virginia in 1778, Maryland in 1783, New York in 1785, and New Jersey the following year. South Carolina legally ended the importation of slaves in 1793, North Carolina in 1794, and Georgia in 1798. Douglas Harper, "Slavery in the North," Slavery in the North, 2003, http://slavenorth.com/slavenorth.htm; "The Slave Trade and the Revolution," *The Abolition of the Slave Trade*, The Schomburg Center for Research in Black Culture, http://abolition.nypl.org/essays/us constitutions/2/; Steven Deyle, *Carry Me Back: the Domestic Slave Trade in American Life* (New York: Oxford University Press, 2005), Kindle edition, Kindle location chap. 2, 293.
260. Jed Handelsman Shugerman, "The Louisiana Purchase and South Carolina's Reopening of the Slave Trade in 1803," *Journal of the Early Republic* 22, no. 2 (summer 2002): 264, https://doi.org/10.2307/3125182.
261. Brenda E. Stevenson, *What Is Slavery?* (London: Polity Press, 2015), Kindle edition, Kindle location 2431.
262. Commonwealth of Massachusetts, Mass. Const. art. I, https://malegislature.gov/Laws/Constitution.
263. "Natural and Inalienable Right to Freedom': Slaves' Petition for Freedom to the Massachusetts Legislature, 1777," in *Collections of the Massachusetts Historical Society* 3 (Boston, 1877), 436–37, as found on History Matters, George Mason University, http://historymatters.gmu.edu/d/6237.
264. Stevenson, *What Is Slavery?*, 2431.
265. State of New Hampshire, N.H. Const. art. I, as found in Nathaniel Bouton, ed., *Town Papers: Documents and Records Relating to Towns in New Hampshire* (Concord, NH: Charles C. Pearson, 1875), 896.
266. Harper, "Slavery in the North"; Catherine Adams and Elizabeth H. Pleck, *Love of Freedom: Black Women in Colonial and Revolutionary New England* (New York: Oxford University Press, 2010), 128.
267. "Act XXI: An Act to Authorize the Manumission of Slaves," in *The Statutes at Large: A Collection of All the Laws of Virginia*, vol. 2, ed. William Waller Hening

(Richmond: Samuel Pleasants, 1809), as found on The Geography of Slavery in Virginia, Tom Costa and the Rector and Visitors of the University of Virginia, 2005, http://www2.vcdh.virginia.edu/xslt/servlet/XSLTServlet?xsl=/xml_docs/slavery/documents/display_laws2.xsl&xml=/xml_docs/slavery/documents/laws.xml&lawid=1782-05-02.

268. John Hope Franklin, *The Free Negro in North Carolina* (New York: Norton, 1971), 10–25.

269. Andrew Levy, *The First Emancipator: Slavery, Religion, and the Quiet Revolution of Robert Carter* (New York: Random House, 2005), 138.

270. "Deed of Manumission, 1784, issued by Philip Davis of Southampton, County, VA, to an African American Slave, Sier," Digital Collections of the Library of Virginia, Virginia Historical Society, http://digitool1.lva.lib.va.us:8881/R/M9G7VBI524SL9LFI161I664LS7P4VVY3GX2NHH9K8I6T6BRAPM-02495?func=search-advanced-go&LOCAL_BASE=2694&ADJACENT=N&find_code1=WRD&request1=Sier&find_operator=AND&find_code2=WTY&request2=Deed+of+Emancipation&find_operator2=AND&find_code3=&request3=&pds_handle=GUEST.

271. "Deed of Manumission, 1783, issued by Benjamin Spratley of Surry County, VA, for the Emancipation of several African American Slaves," Digital Collections of the Library of Virginia, Virginia Historical Society, http://digitool1.lva.lib.va.us:8881/R/RR38XREDM9D5NPRNXP42I167SR658BLBJ44FCUALKI3HC47IRV-03527?func=results-jump-full&set_entry=000002&set_number=319088&base=GEN01-LVA01.

272. Levy, *The First Emancipator*, xi.

273. Ibid., 144.

274. Ibid.

275. Ibid., 147.

276. Brenda E. Stevenson, *Life in Black and White: Family and Community in the Slave South* (New York: Oxford University Press, 1996), 265–66.

277. Levy, *The First Emancipator*, 168–70.

278. "Washington's Will: A Decision to Free His Slaves," George Washington's Mount Vernon, 2022, http://www.mountvernon.org/george-washington/slavery/washingtons-1799-will/.

279. Ibid.

280. Catterall, *Judicial Cases concerning American Slavery and the Negro*, 1:90–91.

281. Gilbert, *Black Patriots and Loyalists*, 169.

282. Ibid., 171.

283. Catterall, *Judicial Cases concerning American Slavery and the Negro*, 3:410.

284. Ibid., 441.

285. Ibid., 427–28.

286. Ibid., 433–34.

287. Ibid., 441.

288. Ibid., 447.

289. Ibid., 463.

290. Campbell Gibson and Kay Jung, *Historical Census Statistics on Population Totals by Race, 1790 to 1990, and by Hispanic Origin, 1970 to 1990, for the United States, Regions, Divisions, and States*, Population Division Working Paper no. 56

(Washington, DC: US Census Bureau, 2002), 19, https://www.census.gov/content/dam/Census/library/working-papers/2002/demo/POP-twps0056.pdf.

291. The number in Virginia grew to almost twenty thousand by 1800, followed closely by those in Maryland, Pennsylvania, and New York. Stevenson, *What Is Slavery?*, 106, table 3.4.

292. Marvin L. Michael Kay and Lorin Lee Cary, *Slavery in North Carolina, 1748–1775* (Chapel Hill: University of North Carolina Press, 1995), 67.

293. Leslie M. Harris, *In the Shadow of Slavery: African Americans in New York City, 1626–1863* (Chicago: University of Chicago Press, 2003), 70–71.

294. Wright, *Afro-Americans in New Jersey*, 24–27.

295. Stevenson, *Life in Black and White*, 260–64.

296. Catterall, *Judicial Cases concerning American Slavery and the Negro*, 2:275.

297. Ibid., 275–76

298. Catterall, *Judicial Cases concerning American Slavery and the Negro*, 3:434–35.

299. John McNish Weiss, *The Merikens: Free Black American Settlers in Trinidad, 1815–16* (London: McNish and Weiss, 1995), 9.

300. Taylor, *The Internal Enemy*, Kindle edition 6542; Harvey Amani Whitfield, *Blacks on the Border: The Black Refugees in British North America, 1815–1860* (Burlington: University of Vermont Press, 2006), 32–37.

301. Frank A. Cassell, "Slaves of the Chesapeake Bay Area and the War of 1812," *Journal of Negro History* 57 no. 2 (April 1972): 144–52, https://doi.org/10.2307/2717218; Taylor, *The Internal Enemy*, Kindle edition 4810–4837.

302. Taylor, *The Internal Enemy*, Kindle edition 3657–3723.

303. Ibid., Kindle edition 3749.

304. Ball, *Slavery in the United States*, 469–70.

305. Taylor, *The Internal Enemy*, Kindle edition 4844.

306. As quoted in ibid., Kindle edition 4858.

307. Ibid., Kindle edition 4987, 5015, 6542.

308. Whitfield, *Blacks on the Border*, 37; Harvey Armani Whitfield, "'We Can Do As We Like Here': An Analysis of Self Assertion and Agency Among Black Refugees in Halifax, Nova Scotia, 1813–1821" *Acadiensis* 32, no. 1 (2002): 38, http://www.jstor.org/stable/41427106.

309. Taylor, *The Internal Enemy*, Kindle edition 5022.

310. "Saturday, April 4, 1814: The Merkins Community Is Established," *Journal of the African American Registry*, https://aaregistry.org/story/the-merikins-community-established/.

311. John McNish Weiss, (London: by author, 2002), *revised edition of Free Black American Settlers in Trinidad 1815-16: A handlist (London: by author 1995)*.

312. Runaway notice regarding Fortune and Aminta, *Virginia Gazette*, April 29, 1773, https://www.newspapers.com/clip/47222327/run-away-last-night-from-the/.

313. Ibid.

314. "Rose Fortune, a 'Privileged Character,'" Annapolis Heritage Society, https://annapolisheritagesociety.com/community-history/notable-personalities-past/rose-fortune-privileged-character/.

315. Daurene Lewis became mayor of Annapolis Royal in the 1980s. Ibid.

CHAPTER 4

1. Lyrics from Tracy Chapman, "The Promise," *New Beginning* (Elektra Entertainment, 1995), https://www.youtube.com/watch?v=XcfswBZpSBU.

2. Some suggest that Henry Bibb was related to George Mortimer Bibb, a senator from Kentucky who became secretary of the US Treasury. See, for example, Maria-Louisa Castillo, "Henry Walton Bibb (1815–1854), *Ottawa Citizen*, September 29, 2007. https://web.archive.org/web/20070929121310/http://www.canada.com/ottawacitizen/features/freedom/story.html?id=6ea0a628-070c-4221-a011-e8bc51166c6e&k=36861.

3. Henry Bibb, *Narrative of the Life and Adventures of Henry Bibb, An American Slave Written By Himself* (New York: Author, 1849), electronic edition, as found on Documenting the American South, 14, https://docsouth.unc.edu/neh/bibb/bibb.html.

4. Ibid., 13.
5. Ibid., 13–15.
6. Ibid., 14–15.
7. Ibid., 16.
8. As quoted in ibid., 18.
9. Ibid., 33.
10. Ibid., 34.
11. Ibid., 34–35.
12. Ibid., 36–37.
13. Ibid., 37.
14. Ibid., 39–41.
15. Ibid., 40.
16. Ibid., 41.
17. Ibid.
18. Ibid.
19. Ibid., 42–43.
20. Ibid., 43.
21. Ibid.
22. Ibid., 87–89.
23. Ibid., 98–99.
24. Ibid., 116.
25. Ibid., 117–18.
26. Ibid., 120–22.
27. Ibid., 148–49.
28. Ibid.
29. Ibid., 143–50.
30. Ibid., 188–90.
31. Ibid., 191–92.
32. Afua Cooper, "Black Women and Work in Nineteenth-Century Canada West: Black Woman Teacher Mary Bibb," in *"We're Rooted Here and They Can't Pull Us Up": Essays in African Canadian Women's History*, ed. Peggy Bristow, Dionne

Brand, Linda Carty, Afua P. Cooper, Sylvia Hamilton, and Adrienne Shadd (Toronto: University of Toronto Press, 1994), 143–70.

33. Channing Gerard Joseph, "The First Drag Queen Was a Former Slave," *Atlantic*, January 31, 2020, https://www.thenation.com/article/society/drag-queen-slave-ball/.

34. Brenda E. Stevenson, *What Is Slavery?* (London: Polity Press, 2015), Kindle edition, Kindle location 4126, 4397, 4542–4557, tables 4.1, 4.3.

35. Brenda E. Stevenson, *What Is Slavery?* (London: Polity Press, 2015), print edition, 130, 132, tables 4.1, 4.3.

36. Daniel F. Littlefield and Lonnie E. Underhill, "Slave 'Revolt' in the Cherokee Nation, 1842," *American Indian Quarterly* 3 no. 2 (summer 1977): 121–26,

https://doi.org/10.2307/1184177; Ethan Davis, "An Administrative Trail of Tears: Indian Removal," *American Journal of Legal History* 50, no. 1 (2008): 49–100,

http://www.jstor.org/stable/25664483; Wilcomb E. Washburn, "Indian Removal Policy: Administrative, Historical and Moral Criteria for Judging Its Success or Failure," *Ethnohistory* 12, no. 3 (summer 1965): 274–78, https://doi.org/10.2307/480522; Mary Hershberger, "Mobilizing Women, Anticipating Abolition: The Struggle against Indian Removal in the 1830s," *Journal of American History* 86, no. 1 (June 1999): 15–40, https://doi.org/10.2307/2567405; Stevenson, *What Is Slavery?*, Kindle edition, 5011–5017.

37. Stevenson, *What Is Slavery?*, Kindle edition, 2439.

38. This stipulation allowed these elderly people on the most labor-intensive agricultural units to seek some work redress by "choosing" another master. It also gave their children or loved ones greater opportunity to purchase and manumit them. Ibid.

39. George P. Rawick, *The American Slave: A Composite Autobiography*, vol. 2: *South Carolina, Parts 1 and 2* (Santa Barbara, CA: Greenwood Publishing, 1972), 22.

40. Daina Ramey Berry, *The Price for Their Pound of Flesh: The Value of the Enslaved, from Womb to Grave, in the Building of a Nation* (Boston: Beacon Press, 2017), Kindle edition, 11–32; Richard Sutch, "Slave Breeding" in *Dictionary of Afro-American Slavery*, ed. Randall M. Miller and John David Smith (Westport, CT: Praeger, 1997), 82–86.

41. United States Works Progress Administration, *Slave Narratives: A Folk History of Slavery in the United States from Interviews with Former Slaves, Arkansas Narratives, Part 1*, Kindle edition, Kindle location 3009. Hereafter *WPA Narratives (Arkansas, Part 1)*.

42. United States Works Progress Administration, *Slave Narratives: A Folk History of Slavery in the United States from Interviews with Former Slaves, North Carolina Narratives, Part 2,* Kindle edition, Kindle location 629–631. Hereafter *WPA Narratives (North Carolina, Part 2)*.

43. John Quincy Adams, *Narrative of the Life of John Quincy Adams, When in Slavery and Now as a Freeman* (Harrisburg, PA: Sieg, 1872), electronic edition as found on Documenting the American South, 5, https://docsouth.unc.edu/neh/adams/adams.html.

44. United States Works Progress Administration, *Slave Narratives: A Folk History of Slavery in the United States from Interviews with Former Slaves, Missouri Narratives*, Kindle edition, Kindle location 3130–3134. Hereafter *WPA Narratives (Missouri)*.

45. United States Works Progress Administration, *Slave Narratives: A Folk History of Slavery in the United States from Interviews with Former Slaves, Georgia Narratives, Part 1*, Kindle edition, Kindle location 1921–1930. Hereafter *WPA Narratives (Georgia, Part 1)*.

46. Ibid., 1198–1201.

47. United States Works Progress Administration, *Slave Narratives: A Folk History of Slavery in the United States from Interviews with Former Slaves, Texas Narratives, Part 4*, Kindle edition, Kindle location 2071–2073. Hereafter *WPA Narratives (Texas, Part 4)*.

48. Ibid., 2036.

49. Sojourner Truth and Olive Gilbert, *The Narrative of Sojourner Truth* (Boston: Author, 1850), as found on University of Pennsylvania Library's Celebration of Women Writers, https://digital.library.upenn.edu/women/truth/1850/1850.html#8.

50. United States Works Progress Administration, *Slave Narratives: A Folk History of Slavery in the United States from Interviews with Former Slaves, Arkansas Narratives, Part 5*, Kindle edition, Kindle location 135. Hereafter *WPA Narratives (Arkansas, Part 5)*.

51. Harriet Jacobs, *Incidents in the Life of a Slave Girl,* ed. Valerie Smith (New York: Oxford University Press, 1988), 58–59.

52. United States Works Progress Administration, *Slave Narratives: A Folk History of Slavery in the United States from Interviews with Former Slaves, Florida Narratives*, Kindle edition, Kindle location 1198–1201. Hereafter *WPA Narratives (Florida)*.

53. James Mellon, ed., *Bullwhip Days: The Slaves Remember* (New York: Grove Press, 1988), 136.

54. *WPA Narratives (North Carolina, Part 2)*, 636–639.

55. Frederick Douglass, *Narrative of the Life of Frederick Douglass, an American Slave. Written by Himself* (Boston: Anti-Slavery Office,1845), electronic edition, as found on Documenting the American South, 7, https://docsouth.unc.edu/neh/douglass/douglass.html].

56. Charles L. Perdue Jr., Thomas E. Barden, and Robert K. Phillips, eds., *Weevils in the Wheat: Interviews with Virginia Ex-Slaves* (Charlottesville: University Press of Virginia, 1976), 118.

57. United States Works Progress Administration, *Slave Narratives: A Folk History of Slavery in the United States from Interviews with Former Slaves, Texas Narratives, Part 2*, Kindle edition, Kindle location 618–619. Hereafter *WPA Narratives (Texas, Part 2)*.

58. The slaveowners treated them as if they had been common animals in this respect. *WPA Narratives (North Carolina, Part 2)*, 635–639.

59. Ibid., 784–785.

60. Ibid., 784–785.

61. United States Works Progress Administration, *Slave Narratives: A Folk History of Slavery in the United States from Interviews with Former Slaves*, Oklahoma Narratives, Kindle edition, Kindle location 356. Hereafter *WPA Narratives (Oklahoma)*.

62. United States Works Progress Administration, *Slave Narratives: A Folk History of Slavery in the United States from Interviews with Former Slaves, Texas Narratives, Part 1*, Kindle edition, Kindle location 3209. Hereafter *WPA Narratives (Texas, Part 1)*.

63. United States Works Progress Administration, *Slave Narratives: A Folk History of Slavery in the United States from Interviews with Former Slaves, Texas Narratives, Part 3*, Kindle edition, Kindle location 532–533. Hereafter *WPA Narratives (Texas, Part 3)*.

64. Frances Anne Kemble, *Women in Slavery: Journal of Residence on a Georgian Plantation, 1838–1839* (New York: Harper & Brothers, 1864), 226.

65. Basil Hall, "On a South Carolina Rice Plantation," in *A Documentary History of Slavery in North America*, ed. Willie Lee Rose (Athens: University of Georgia Press, 1999), 305.

66. *WPA Narratives (Texas, Part 2)*, 3272–3282.

67. *WPA Narratives (Florida)*, 1039–1054.

68. Ibid., 1079.

69. William Wells Brown, *Narrative of William Wells Brown, A Fugitive Slave in African American Slave Narratives, An Anthology*, vol. 2, ed. Sterling Bland Jr. (Westport, CT: Greenwood Press, 2001), 303.

70. Mellon, *Bullwhip Days*, 455.

71. *WPA Narratives (Georgia, Part 1)*, 705.

72. *WPA Narratives (Oklahoma)*, 1291.

73. United States Works Progress Administration, *Slave Narratives: A Folk History of Slavery in the United States from Interviews with Former Slaves, Alabama Narratives*, Kindle edition, Kindle locations 3608–3610. Hereafter *WPA Narratives (Alabama)*.

74. *WPA Narratives (Alabama)*, 1119–1120.

75. United States Works Progress Administration, *Slave Narratives: A Folk History of Slavery in the United States from Interviews with Former Slaves, South Carolina Narratives, Part 3*, Kindle edition, Kindle locations 1474–1475. Hereafter *WPA Narratives (South Carolina, Part 3)*.

76. Ibid., Kindle location 1474–1475.

77. *WPA Narratives (Alabama)*, 3292–3294.

78. Ibid., 548–550.

79. *WPA Narratives (Florida)*, 1205–1225.

80. Mellon, *Bullwhip Days*, 367.

81. *WPA Narratives (Alabama)*, 2892.

82. Mellon, *Bullwhip Days*, 429.

83. United States Works Progress Administration, *Slave Narratives: A Folk History of Slavery in the United States from Interviews with Former Slaves, South*

Carolina Narratives, Part 1, Kindle edition, Kindle locations 256–257. Hereafter *WPA Narratives (South Carolina, Part 1)*.

84. United States Works Progress Administration, *Slave Narratives: A Folk History of Slavery in the United States from Interviews with Former Slaves, Georgia Narratives, Part 1*, print edition, 75, http://memory.loc.gov/mss/mesn/041/041.pdf. Hereafter *WPA Narratives (Georgia, Part 1, print)*.

85. United States Works Progress Administration, *Slave Narratives: A Folk History of Slavery in the United States from Interviews with Former Slaves, Kentucky Narratives*, Kindle edition, Kindle location 23. Hereafter *WPA Narratives (Kentucky)*.

86. Account of Nancy Williams in Perdue et al., *Weevils in the Wheat*, 316.

87. *WPA Narratives (Alabama)*, 3299–3300.

88. United States Works Progress Administration, *Slave Narratives: A Folk History of Slavery in the United States from Interviews with Former Slaves, Virginia Narratives*, Kindle edition, Kindle location 221. Hereafter *WPA Narratives (Virginia)*.

89. *WPA Narratives (Arkansas, Part 5)*, 579.

90. See, for example, Jewel Lamas, "Female Circumcision: The History, the Current Prevalence and the Approach to the Patient," University of Virginia School of Medicine, April 2017, https://med.virginia.edu/family-medicine/wp-content/uploads/sites/285/2017/01/Llamas-Paper.pdf; Heather L. Sipsma, Peggy G. Chen, Angela Ofori-Atta, Ukwuoma O Ilozumba, Kapouné Karfo, and Elizabeth H. Bradley, "Female Genital Cutting: Current Practices and Beliefs in Western Africa, *Bulletin of the World Health Organization* 90, no. 2 (February 2012): 120–27, https://www.ncbi.nlm.nih.gov/pmc/articles/PMC3302551/.

91. Elizabeth Hyde Botume, *First Days amongst the Contrabands* (New York: Arno Press, 1969), 144–45.

92. Ibid., 147.

93. Ibid., 152.

94. Ibid.

95. Ibid., 148.

96. Lunsford Lane, *The Narrative of Lunsford Lane, Formerly of Raleigh, N.C. Embracing an Account of His Early Life, the Redemption by Purchase of Himself and Family from Slavery, and His Banishment from the Place of His Birth for the Crime of Wearing Colored Skin*, 2nd ed. (Boston: J. G. Torrey, 1842), electronic edition, as found on Documenting the American South, 10, https://docsouth.unc.edu/neh/lanelunsford/lane.html.

97. *WPA Narratives (North Carolina, Part 2)*, 1985–1986.

98. Bibb, *Narrative of the Life and Adventures of Henry Bibb*, 30–31.

99. Isaac Lane, *Autobiography of Bishop Isaac Lane, LL.D. with a Short History of the C.M.E. Church in America and of Methodism* (South Nashville, TN: Publishing House of the M.E. Church, 1916), electronic edition, as found on Documenting the American South, 49, https://docsouth.unc.edu/fpn/lane/lane.html#lane47.

100. Botume, *First Days amongst the Contrabands*, 152.

101. Mellon, *Bullwhip Days*, 428.

102. Lane, *The Narrative of Lunsford Lane*, 10.

103. Lewis and Milton Clarke, *Narratives of the Sufferings of Lewis and Milton Clarke, Sons of a Soldier of the Revolution During a Captivity of More than Twenty Years, among the Slaveholders of Kentucky, One of the So Called Christian States of North America* in *African American Slave Narratives, An Anthology*, vol. 1. ed. Sterling Bland Jr. (Westport, CT: Greenwood Press, 2001), 135.

104. *WPA Narratives (Arkansas, Part 5)*, 204–205.

105. Perdue et al., *Weevils in the Wheat*, 118.

106. *WPA Narratives (Texas, Part 2)*, 2872–2873.

107. Elizabeth Keckley, *Behind the Scenes, or, Thirty-Years a Slave, and Four Years in the White House*, ed. James Olney (1868; New York: Oxford University Press, 1988), 49–50.

108. For an exception, see United States Works Progress Administration, *Slave Narratives: A Folk History of Slavery in the United States from Interviews with Former Slaves, Arkansas Narratives, Part 6*, Kindle edition, Kindle location 862–863. Hereafter *WPA Narratives (Arkansas, Part 6)*.

109. United States Works Progress Administration, *Slave Narratives: A Folk History of Slavery in the United States from Interviews with Former Slaves, Georgia Narratives, Part 3*, Kindle edition, Kindle location 2582–2587. Hereafter *WPA Narratives (Georgia, Part 3)*.

110. Mellon, *Bullwhip Days*, 282–84.

111. *WPA Narratives (Alabama)*, 1853–1854.

112. *WPA Narratives (Georgia, Part 1)*, 987–989.

113. *WPA Narratives (Georgia, Part 3)*, 3302–3307.

114. Benjamin Drew, ed., *A North-Side View of Slavery, the Refugee; or the Narratives of Fugitive Slaves in Canada Related by Themselves with an Account of the History and Condition of the Colored Population of Upper Canada* (Boston: John Jewett, 1856), electronic edition, as found on Documenting the American South, 31, https://docsouth.unc.edu/neh/drew/drew.html.

115. Mellon, *Bullwhip Days*, 22.

116. United States Works Progress Administration, *Slave Narratives: A Folk History of Slavery in the United States from Interviews with Former Slaves, Arkansas Narratives, Part 7*, Kindle edition, Kindle location 74. Hereafter *WPA Narratives (Arkansas, Part 7)*.

117. *WPA Narratives (Alabama)*, 3298–3299.

118. *WPA Narratives (Oklahoma)*, 466.

119. *WPA Narratives (Florida)*, 57–62.

120. Perdue et al., *Weevils in the Wheat*, 129.

121. Caricature of a "broomstick-wedding," from a two-penny sheet by James Catnach, *The Marriage Act Displayed in Cuts and Verse* (London, 1822). The publication satirizes the proposed Marriage Act (known as the "Broomstick Marriage Act," "broomstick marriage" being a term for "sham marriage"). Outhwaite associates this term with the "effloresence of unregistered consensual unions" among the English and Welsh working class in the second half of the 18th century, citing a 1753 pamphlet mentioning "the Ceremonial of jumping over a Stick," and noting "Cathnach's illustrated two-penny-sheets of the 1820s carried charming drawings of broomstick

weddings." R. B. Outhwaite, *Clandestine Marriage in England, 1500–1850* (London, 1995), 139f," as found on Wikimedia Commons, 2020, https://commons.wikimedia.org/wiki/File:Catnach_broomstick-wedding_1822.jpg.

122. Regarding jumping the broom marriage traditions, see Alan Dundes, "'Jumping the Broom': On the Origin and Meaning of an African American Wedding Custom," *Journal of American Folklore* 109, no. 433 (summer 1996): 324–329, https://doi.org/10.2307/541535; Brenda E. Stevenson, *Life in Black and White: Family and Community in the Slave South* (New York: Oxford University, 1996), 228–29; Randal D. Day and Daniel Hook, "A Short History of Divorce: Jumping the Broom—and Back Again," *Journal of Divorce* 10, no. 3–4 (spring/summer 1987): 57–73, https://doi.org/10.1300/J279v10n03_05.

123. Tempie Herndon, in Norman R. Yetman, ed., *Voices from Slavery: 100 Authentic Slave Narratives* (Mineola, NY: Dover, 1999), 163; Ancestry.com, *1860 U.S. Federal Census—Slave Schedules*, http://search.ancestry.com/iexec?htx=View&r=an&dbid=7668&iid=NCM653_921-0217&fn=Jno&ln=Hearndon&st=d&ssrc=&pid=538067.

124. See also Yetman, *Voices from Slavery*, 164.

125. Mellon, *Bullwhip Days*, 428.

126. Yetman, *Voices from Slavery*, 164.

127. *WPA Narratives (Oklahoma)*, 1214–1221.

128. Thomas Chandler, *Water Cooler*, alkaline-glazed, slip-decoration stoneware, c. 1840 (High Museum of Art, Atlanta), https://high.org/collections/water-cooler/. The alkaline-glazed stoneware water jug is attributed to Thomas Chandler of Edgefield County, South Carolina, the leading site of stoneware production in the South.

129. *WPA Narratives (Georgia, Part 1, print)*.

130. *WPA Narratives (Alabama)*, 1291.

131. Mellon, *Bullwhip Days*, 384.

132. *WPA Narratives (Oklahoma)*, 1738–1742.

133. Keckley, *Behind the Scenes*, 41, 49.

134. *WPA Narratives (Alabama)*, 2845.

135. *WPA Narratives (Arkansas, Part 6)*, 489–492.

136. *WPA Narratives (Oklahoma)*, 3063.

137. *WPA Narratives (Arkansas, Part 6)*, 838.

138. *WPA Narratives (Texas, Part 2)*,1827–1829.

139. *WPA Narratives (North Carolina, Part 2)*, 142–143.

140. Botume, *First Days amongst the Contraband*, 221.

141. *WPA Narratives (Alabama)*, 4309–4310.

142. *WPA Narratives (Texas, Part 1)*, 835–839.

143. Keckley, *Behind the Scenes*, 50.

144. *WPA Narratives (Texas, Part 4)*, 1892.

145. Mellon, *Bullwhip Days*, 423–24.

146. *WPA Narratives (Arkansas, Part 5)*, 209.

147. Charles Ball, *Slavery in the United States: A Narrative of the Life and Adventures of Charles Ball, a Black Man, Who Lived Forty Years in Maryland, South Carolina and Georgia, as a Slave under Various Masters, and Was One Year in the Navy

with Commodore Barney, during the Late War (New York: John S. Taylor, 1837), 263–64.

148. Ball, *Slavery in the United States*, 264.

149. Ron Tyler and Lawrence Murphy, eds., *The Slave Narratives of Texas* (Austin: State House Press, 1997), 67.

150. Helen Tunnicliff Catterall, ed., *Judicial Cases concerning American Slavery and the Negro*, vol. 3: *Cases from the Courts of Georgia, Florida, Alabama, Mississippi, and Louisiana* (Washington, DC: Carnegie Institution, 1932), 398, 414, 419.

151. Frederick Law Olmsted, *The Cotton Kingdom: A Traveller's Observations on Cotton and Slavery in the American Slave States, 1853–1861* (Tucson, AZ: Mariposa Press, 2017), Kindle edition, 423.

152. *WPA Narratives (Oklahoma)*, 562.

153. *WPA Narratives (Georgia, Part 3)*, 3410–3411.

154. Moslie Thompson, in Mellon, *Bullwhip Days*, 99–100.

155. United States Works Progress Administration, *Slave Narratives: A Folk History of Slavery in the United States from Interviews with Former Slaves, South Carolina, Part 3*, print, 78, http://memory.loc.gov/cgi-bin/ampage?collId=mesn&fileName=141/mesn141.db&recNum=0. Hereafter *WPA Narratives (South Carolina, Part 1, print)*; Claudia Arzeno Mooney, April L. Hynes, and Mark M. Newell, "African-American Face Vessels: History and Ritual in 19th-Century Edgefield," Chipstone, 2020, http://www.chipstone.org/article.php/537/Ceramics-in-America-2013/African-American-Face-Vessels:-History-and-Ritual-in-19th-Century-Edgefield.

156. John James Audubon, "John J. Audubon Encounters a Runaway in Louisiana Swamps," in *A Documentary History of Slavery in North America*, ed. Willie Lee Rose (Athens: University of Georgia Press, 1999), 264.

157. Daniel and Mary Burton (Hunt) Marriage Record, May 13, 1866, Wilson County, TN as found on "Bureau of Refugees, Freedmen and Abandoned Lands, Miscellaneous records of various states, Freedmen's Marriage Certificates 1865 – 1869 Roll 2," Freedmen's Bureau Online, http://freedmensbureau.com/tennessee/marriages/tennmarrb2.htm.

158. Green and Lucy Coleman Marriage Record, August 27, 1865, Memphis, TN, as found on "Bureau of Refugees, Freedmen and Abandoned Lands, Miscellaneous records of various states, Freedmen's Marriage Certificates 1865–1869 Roll 2," Freedmen's Bureau Online, http://freedmensbureau.com/tennessee/marriages/tennmarrc2.htm.

159. Thomas and Jane Harris Marriage Record Record, April 28, 1866, as found on "Bureau of Refugees, Freedmen and Abandoned Lands, Miscellaneous Records of Various States Freedmen's Marriage Certificates 1865–1869 Roll 2," Freedmen's Bureau Online, http://freedmensbureau.com/tennessee/marriages/tennmarrh1.htm.

160. Thomas and Julia Henderson Marriage Record, June 4, 1866, Dyer County, TN, as found on "Bureau of Refugees, Freedmen and Abandoned Lands, Miscellaneous records of various states, Freedmen's Marriage Certificates 1865–1869 Roll 2," Freedmen's Bureau Online, http://freedmensbureau.com/tennessee/marriages/tennmarrh1.htm.

161. *WPA Narratives (Georgia, Part 3)*, 203–205.

CHAPTER 5

1. Steven Weisenburger, *Modern Medea: A Family Story of Slavery and Child-Murder from the Old South* (New York: Hill and Wang, 1998); Sara Haselhorst, "Margaret Garner's Story Has Resonated for the Past 164 Years. It's One She Never Got to Tell," *Cincinnati Enquirer*, August 3, 2020, https://www.cincinnati.com/story/news/2020/07/29/margaret-garners-story-has-resonated-decades-its-one-she-never-got-tell/5478537002/.

2. United States Works Progress Administration, *Slave Narratives: A Folk History of Slavery in the United States from Interviews with Former Slaves, Indiana Narratives*, Kindle edition, Kindle location 1750. Hereafter *WPA Narratives (Indiana)*.

3. Quote from Calvin Moye, as found in James Mellon, ed., *Bullwhip Days: The Slaves Remember* (New York: Grove Atlantic, 1988), Kindle edition, 153.

4. William Still, *The Underground Railroad (Complete Collection): Narratives, Testimonies, and Letters: The True Story of Hundreds of Slaves Who Escaped to Freedom* (Chicago: Musaicum Books, 2018), Kindle edition, Kindle location 8710.

5. Elizabeth Keckley, *Behind the Scenes, or, Thirty-Years a Slave, and Four Years in the White House*, ed. James Olney (1868; New York: Oxford University Press, 1988), 23–25.

6. Mary Ames, *From a New England Woman's Diary in Dixie in 1865* (Norwood, MA: Plimpton Press, 1906), electronic edition, as found on Documenting the American South, 64, https://docsouth.unc.edu/church/ames/ames.html.

7. Still, *The Underground Railroad*, Kindle location: 227.

8. United States Works Progress Administration, *Slave Narratives: A Folk History of Slavery in the United States from Interviews with Former Slaves, Arkansas Narratives, Part 5*, Kindle edition, Kindle location 202. Hereafter *WPA Narratives (Arkansas, Part 5)*.

9. United States Works Progress Administration, *Slave Narratives: A Folk History of Slavery in the United States from Interviews with Former Slaves, Oklahoma Narratives*, Kindle edition, Kindle location 3508. Hereafter *WPA Narratives (Oklahoma)*.

10. Sojourner Truth and Olive Gilbert, *The Narrative of Sojourner Truth* (Boston: Author, 1850), as found on University of Pennsylvania Library's Celebration of Women Writers, https://digital.library.upenn.edu/women/truth/1850/1850.html#8.

11. Octavia V. Rogers Albert, *The House of Bondage, or Charlotte Brooks and Other Slaves Original and Life-Like, As They Appeared in Their Old Plantation and City Slave Life: Together with Pen-Pictures of the Peculiar Institution, with Sights and Insights into Their New Relations as Freedmen, Freemen and Citizens* (New York: Hunt and Eaton, 1890), electronic edition, as found on Documenting the American South, 19–20, https://docsouth.unc.edu/neh/albert/albert.html.

12. Marne L. Campbell, *Making Black Los Angeles: Class, Gender and Community, 1850–1917* (Chapel Hill: University of North Carolina Press, 2016), 37.

13. Albert, *The House of Bondage*, 21.

14. Bills of Sale, February 6, 1826; October 7, 1828, Charles Ayer Papers, Barnwell District, S.C., Southern Plantation Records, Kenneth Stampp, ed., pp. 6, 14, 20, 49, 54, 67, National Humanities Center.

15. Bills of Sale to William Garrett, c. 1840, 1841, 1851, San Augustine County, Folder 21, San Augustine, Texas Papers, 1783–1937, Institute for the Study of the American West, Autry National Center, Los Angeles, California.

16. Tracie O. Afifi, Samantha Salmon., Isabel Garcés, Janique Fortier, Tamara Taillieu, Ashley Stewart-Tufescu, Gordon J. G. Asmundson, Jitender Sareen, and Harriet L. Macmillan, "Confirmatory Factor Analysis of Adverse Childhood Experiences (ACEs) among a Community-Based Sample of Parents and Adolescents," *BMC Pediatrics* 20, no. 178 (2020), https://doi.org/10.1186/s12887-020-02063-3; Celia Downes, :Foster Families for Adolescents: The Healing Potential of Time-Limited Placements," *British Journal of Social Work* 18, no. 5 (1988): 473–87, http://www.jstor.org/stable/23708954.

17. Simon and Eliza Adams Marriage Record, August 25, 1865, Memphis, TN, as found on "Bureau of Refugees, Freedmen and Abandoned Lands, Miscellaneous records of various states, Freedmen's Marriage Certificates 1865–1869 Roll 2," Freedmen's Bureau Online, http://freedmensbureau.com/tennessee/marriages/tennmarra.htm.

18. Caleb and Elizabeth Adams Marriage Record, August 30, 1865, Memphis, TN, as found on "Bureau of Refugees, Freedmen and Abandoned Lands, Miscellaneous records of various states, Freedmen's Marriage Certificates 1865–1869 Roll 2," Freedmen's Bureau Online, http://freedmensbureau.com/tennessee/marriages/tennmarra.htm.

19. James and Christine Anthony, September 11, 1865, Memphis, TN, as found on "Bureau of Refugees, Freedmen and Abandoned Lands, Miscellaneous records of various states, Freedmen's Marriage Certificates 1865–1869 Roll 2," Freedmen's Bureau Online, http://freedmensbureau.com/tennessee/marriages/tennmarra.htm.

20. United States Works Progress Administration, *Slave Narratives: A Folk History of Slavery in the United States from Interviews with Former Slaves, Tennessee Narratives*, Kindle edition, Kindle location 2682–2685. Hereafter *WPA Narratives (Tennessee)*.

21. United States Works Progress Administration, *Slave Narratives: A Folk History of Slavery in the United States from Interviews with Former Slaves, North Carolina Narratives, Part 2*, Kindle edition, Kindle location 2682–2685. Hereafter *WPA Narratives (North Carolina, Part 2)*.

22. Elizabeth Hyde Botume, *First Days amongst the Contrabands* (New York: Arno Press, 1969), 144–45.

23. Ibid., 164.

24. John W. Blassingame, ed., *Slave Testimony: Two Centuries of Letters, Speeches, Interviews, and Autobiographies* (Baton Rouge: Louisiana State University Press, 1977), 421.

25. Still, *The Underground Railroad*, 8677.

26. United States Works Progress Administration, *Slave Narratives: A Folk History of Slavery in the United States from Interviews with Former Slaves, South Carolina Narratives, Part 1*, Kindle edition, Kindle location 2753–2754. Hereafter *WPA Narratives (South Carolina, Part 1)*.

27. United States Works Progress Administration, *Slave Narratives: A Folk History of Slavery in the United States from Interviews with Former Slaves, Alabama Narratives*, Kindle edition, Kindle location 146. Hereafter *WPA Narratives (Alabama)*.

28. Blassingame, *Slave Testimony*, 715–16.
29. *WPA Narratives (Alabama)*, 4774–4779.
30. Ibid., 4790–4795.
31. Ibid., 4779–4784.
32. Ibid., 4801–4806.
33. Ibid.
34. Ibid., 4806–4809.
35. Moses Roper, in *African American Slave Narratives: An Anthology*, vol. 1, ed. Sterling L. Bland, Jr. (Westport, CT: Greenwood Press, 2001), 61–62.
36. *WPA Narratives (Alabama)*, 3592–3595
37. Ibid., 3632–3633.
38. Henry Lee Swint, ed., *Dear Ones at Home: Letters from Contraband Camps* (Nashville, TN: Vanderbilt University Press, 1966), 60.
39. Ibid., 212.
40. Ames, *From a New England Woman's Diary in Dixie*, 90.
41. Botume, *First Days amongst the Contrabands*, 163.
42. Charles L. Perdue Jr., Thomas E. Barden, and Robert K. Phillips, eds., *Weevils in the Wheat: Interviews with Virginia Ex-Slaves* (Charlottesville: University Press of Virginia, 1976), 33.
43. Harrison Beckett's autobiographical account found in United States Works Progress Administration, *Slave Narratives: A Folk History of Slavery in the United States from Interviews with Former Slaves, Texas Narratives*, Kindle edition, Kindle location 621–658. Hereafter *WPA Narratives (Texas)*.
44. Albert, *The House of Bondage*, 14–15.
45. Nat Love, *The Life and Adventures of Nat Love, Better Known in the Cattle Country as Deadwood Dick, by Himself* (Los Angeles: Nat Love, 1907), electronic edition, as found on Documenting the American South, 7–9, https://docsouth.unc.edu/neh/natlove/natlove.html.
46. United States Works Progress Administration, *Slave Narratives: A Folk History of Slavery in the United States from Interviews with Former Slaves, Missouri Narratives*, Kindle edition, Kindle location 78. Hereafter *WPA Narratives (Missouri)*.
47. Frederick Douglass, *Narrative of the Life of Frederick Douglass, An American Slave, Written by Himself* (Boston: Anti-Slavery Office, 1845), electronic edition, as found on Documenting the American South, 2, https://docsouth.unc.edu/neh/douglass/douglass.html.
48. Ames, *From a New England Woman's Diary in Dixie*, 139.
49. Harriet Jacobs, *Incidents in the Life of a Slave Girl,* ed. Valerie Smith (New York: Oxford University Press, 1988), 28–220, passim.
50. Botume, *First Days amongst the Contrabands*, 153.
51. United States Works Progress Administration, *Slave Narratives: A Folk History of Slavery in the United States from Interviews with Former Slaves, Georgia Narratives, Part 3*, Kindle edition, Kindle location 3057. Hereafter *WPA Narratives (Georgia, Part 3)*.
52. *WPA Narratives (South Carolina, Part 1)*, 3731.
53. *WPA Narratives (Arkansas Part 5)*, 204.

54. United States Works Progress Administration, *Slave Narratives: A Folk History of Slavery in the United States from Interviews with Former Slaves, Texas Narratives, Part 2*, Kindle edition, Kindle location 2317–2318. Hereafter *WPA Narratives (Texas Part 2)*.

55. Helen Tunnicliff Catterall, ed., *Judicial Cases concerning American Slavery and the Negro*, vol. 3: *Cases from the Courts of Georgia, Florida, Alabama, Mississippi, and Louisiana* (Washington, DC: Carnegie Institution, 1932), 460.

56. Perdue et al., *Weevils in the Wheat*, 44.

57. United States Works Progress Administration, *Slave Narratives: a Folk History of Slavery in the United States from Interviews with Former Slaves, Georgia Narratives, Part 2*, Kindle edition, Kindle location 1008–1009. Hereafter *WPA Narratives (Georgia Part 2)*.

58. United States Works Progress Administration, *Slave Narratives: A Folk History of Slavery in the United States from Interviews with Former Slaves, Kansas Narratives*, Kindle edition, Kindle location 33. Hereafter *WPA* Narratives (Kansas).

59. *WPA Narratives (Oklahoma)*, 557.

60. Peter Wheeler and Charles Lester, *Chains and Freedom: Or, The Life and Adventures of Peter Wheeler, a Colored Man Yet Living. A Slave in Chains, a Sailor on the Deep, and a Sinner at the Cross* (New York: E. S. Arnold, 1839), electronic edition, as found on Documenting the American South, 22, https://docsouth.unc.edu/neh/lester/lester.html.

61. Shirley Plantation Slave Record Book, 1857, n.p., Shirley Plantation Collection, 1650–1888, Colonial Williamsburg Foundation Library, Microfilm, Container 92, Folder 1, 1854–1864.

62. United States Works Progress Administration, *Slave Narratives: A Folk History of Slavery in the United States from Interviews with Former Slaves, Texas Narratives, Part 1*, Kindle edition, Kindle location 1379. Hereafter *WPA Narratives (Texas Pt. 1)*.

63. Thomas Wentworth Higginson, *Army Life in a Black Regiment and Other Writings* (New York: Penguin, 2002) Kindle edition, Kindle location 2720–2724.

64. Ron Tyler and Lawrence Murphy, eds., *The Slave Narratives of Texas* (Austin: State House Press, 1997), 61.

65. Ibid., 63.

66. Lane managed to save enough money to purchase himself and his family by 1842. Lunsford Lane, "The Narrative of Lunsford Lane, Formerly of North Carolina" in *African American Slave Narratives: An Anthology*, vol. 1, ed. Sterling L. Bland Jr. (Westport, CT: Greenwood Press, 2001), 95.

67. Mellon, *Bullwhip Days*, 49–50.

68. Ames, *From a New England Woman's Diary in Dixie*, 34.

69. Mellon, *Bullwhip Days*, 93.

70. Ames, *From a New England Woman's Diary in Dixie*, 47.

71. Botume, *First Days amongst the Contrabands*, 250.

72. Tyler and Murphy, *The Slave Narratives of Texas*, 54.

73. Ibid., 50.

74. *WPA Narratives (Arkansas Part 5)*, 101.

75. *WPA Narratives (Missouri)*, 613.

76. United States Works Progress Administration, *Slave Narratives: A Folk History of Slavery in the United States from Interviews with Former Slaves, Texas Narratives, Part 4*, Kindle edition, Kindle location 2041. Hereafter *WPA Narratives (Texas, Part 4)*.

77. Mellon, *Bullwhip Days*, 42.

78. *WPA Narratives (Texas, Part 1)*, 753–755.

79. *WPA Narratives (Alabama)*, 1217–1219.

80. *WPA Narratives (Oklahoma)*, 3784.

81. James W. C. Pennington, *The Fugitive Blacksmith; or, Events in the History of James W. C. Pennington, Pastor of a Presbyterian Church, New York, Formerly a Slave in the State of Maryland, United States* (London: Charles Gilpin, 1849), electronic edition, as found on Documenting the American South, 2–4, https://docsouth.unc.edu/neh/penning49/penning49.html.

82. Moses Grandy, *Narrative of the Life of Moses Grandy, Late a Slave in the United States of America* (London: C. Gilpin, 1843), electronic edition, as found on Documenting the American South, 10–11, https://docsouth.unc.edu/fpn/grandy/grandy.html.

83. Lunsford Lane, *The Narrative of Lunsford Lane, Formerly of Raleigh, N.C., Embracing an Account of His Early Life, the Redemption by Purchase of Himself and Family from Slavery, and His Banishment from the Place of His Birth for the Crime of Wearing a Colored Skin* (Boston: Lunsford Lane, 1842), electronic edition, as found on Documenting the American South, 7–8, https://docsouth.unc.edu/neh/lanelunsford/lane.html.

84. Ibid., 8.

85. Benjamin Drew, *The Refugee: The Narratives of Fugitive Slaves in Canada* (Boston: John P. Jewett, 1856), Kindle edition. Kindle location 3752.

86. *WPA Narratives (Arkansas Part 5)*, 221.

87. *WPA Narratives (Indiana)*, 1507.

88. Ames, *From a New England Woman's Diary in Dixie*, 64–65.

89. Botume, *First Days amongst the Contrabands*, 243.

90. Grandy, *Narrative of the Life of Moses Grandy*, 9.

91. *WPA Narratives (Texas, Part 1)*, 286.

92. Keckley, *Behind the Scenes*, 30.

93. Tyler and Murphy, *The Slave Narratives of Texas*, 61.

94. William Wells Brown, "Narrative of William Wells Brown, A Fugitive Slave," in *African American Slave Narratives: An Anthology*, vol. 1, ed. Sterling L. Bland Jr. (Westport, CT: Greenwood Press, 2001), 304.

95. Tyler and Murphy, *The Slave Narratives of Texas*, 63.

96. Emma Gerald Stevenson, interview by Brenda E. Stevenson, August 30, 1989, author's archive.

97. Drew, *The Refugee*, 1171.

98. Ibrahima Seck, *Bouki Fait Gombo: A History of the Slave Community of Habitation Haydel (Whitney Plantation) Louisiana, 1750–1860* (New Orleans: University of New Orleans Press, 2014), Kindle edition, Kindle location 2322.

99. Mellon, *Bullwhip Days,* 244; Delia Garlic, "Dem Days Wuz Hell," in United States Works Progress Administration, *Slave Narratives: A Folk History of Slavery*

in the United States from Interviews with Former Slaves, Alabama Narratives, 129, print, as found on Library of Congress, https://www.loc.gov/resource/mesn.010/?sp =135. Hereafter *WPA Narratives (Alabama, print)*.

100. Lewis Clark, *Leaves from a Slave's Journal of Life,* in *The Anti-Slavery Standard*, October 20, 27, 1842, ed. Lydia Maria Child, as found on Documenting the American South, 78–79, 83, http://docsouth.unc.edu/neh/clarke/support1.html. See also Lewis Clark, *Narrative of the Sufferings of Lewis Clark During a Captivity of More Than 25 Years, among the Algerines in Kentucky one of the So-Called Christian States of North America* (Boston: David H. Ela, 1845).

101. Keckley, *Behind the Scenes*, 38–39.

102. See, for example, Brenda E. Stevenson, *Life in Black and White: Family and Community in the Slave South* (New York: Oxford University Press, 1996), 253–54; "Navigating the Trauma of Slavery to the Descendants of Slavery," *The Panorama: Expansive Reviews from the* Journal of the Early Republic (June 5, 2017), http://thepanorama.shear.org/2017/06/05/navigating-the-trauma-of-slavery-to-descendants-of-the-enslaved/.

103. Pennington, *The Fugitive Blacksmith*, v.

104. The first captor of the Edmondson girls sold them in 1848 because they had tried to escape. They were to be sold as prostitutes. Their father did raise the money to purchase them with the help of the Methodist Episcopal Church, North. Pennington, *The Fugitive Blacksmith*, v–x; Perdue et al., *Weevils in the Wheat*, 236.

105. Louisa Picquet and Hiram Mattison, *Louisa Picquet, the Octoroon: Or, Inside Views of Southern Domestic Life* (New York: Author, 1861), electronic edition, as found on Documenting the American South, 34–35, https://docsouth.unc.edu/neh/picquet/picquet.html. Elizabeth Ramsay was probably about forty-five years old at the time, well past the age of a prime worker, particularly a concubine. Her slave owner, A. C. Horton indicated she was, however, still "as fine a washer, cook, and ironer as there is in the United States."

106. Still, *The Underground Railroad*, 9959.

107. *WPA Narratives (Oklahoma)*, 4557.

108. Albert, *The House of Bondage*, 20.

109. University of Virginia Commission on Slavery, *President's Commission on Slavery at the University Report to President Sullivan* (Charlottesville: University of Virginia, 2018), 23–24, https://slavery.virginia.edu/wp-content/uploads/2021/03/PCSU-Report-FINAL_July-2018.pdf.

110. Mellon, *Bullwhip Days*, 122.

111. Ibid., 219–20.

112. Swint, *Dear Ones at Home*, 55–56.

113. Mellon, *Bullwhip Days*, 121.

114. Annette Gordon-Reed, *The Hemingses of Monticello: An American Family* (New York: Norton, 2008), 11–13, 668–71.

115. Piquet and Mattison, *Louisa Picquet, the Octoroon*, 5.

116. Glenn Emery, "The Hanging of Celia," as found on the Jacksonville Historical Society: One City, Many Stories, https://www.jaxhistory.org/portfolio-items/the-hanging-of-celia/.

117. Jacobs, *Incidents in the Life of a Slave Girl*, 87–90.

118. Blassingame, *Slave Testimony*, 703–706.
119. Ibid.
120. Ibid., 706–35.
121. United States Works Progress Administration, *Slave Narratives: A Folk History of Slavery in the United States from Interviews with Former Slaves*, Maryland Narratives, Kindle edition, Kindle location 399. Hereafter *WPA Narratives (Maryland)*.
122. *WPA Narratives (Oklahoma)*, 2961.
123. Helen Tunnicliff Catterall, ed., *Judicial Cases concerning American Slavery and the Negro*, vol. 2: *Cases from the Courts of North Carolina, South Carolina, and Tennessee* (Washington, DC: Carnegie Institution, 1927), 284.
124. Ronald G. Shafer, "He Became the Nation's Ninth Vice-President: She Was His Enslaved Wife," *Washington Post*, February 7, 2021, https://www.washingtonpost.com/history/2021/02/07/julia-chinn-slave-wife-vice-president/. Shafer's story is based on the research of historian Julia Chinn's biographer, Amrita Chakrabarti Myers. Amrita Chakrabarti Myers, "The Erasure and Resurrection of Julia Chinn, U.S. Vice President Richard M. Johnson's Black Wife," as found on the Association of Black Women's Historians, March 3, 2019, http://abwh.org/2019/03/03/the-erasure-and-resurrection-of-julia-chinn-u-s-vice-president-richard-m-johnsons-black-wife/.
125. Catterall, *Judicial Cases concerning American Slavery and the Negro*, 2:281.
126. Ibid., 34.
127. Ibid., 326–27l, 332.
128. Jane Landers, *Black Society in Spanish Florida* (Urbana: University of Illinois Press, 1999), 136–56, passim.
129. Edward Dryer, Lyle Saxton, and Robert Tallant, eds., *Gumbo Ya-Ya: A Collection of Louisiana Folk Tales* (Boston: Works Progress Administration, 1945),155–56.
130. Catterall, *Judicial Cases concerning American Slavery and the Negro*, 3:452–53.
131. Swint, *Dear Ones at Home*, 73.
132. *WPA Narratives (Tennessee)*, 566–68.
133. Mellon, *Bullwhip Days*, 220.
134. George P. Rawick, ed., *The American Slave: A Composite Autobiography*, vol. 12: *Georgia Narratives* (Westport, CT: Greenwood Publishing, 1972), 292.
135. Rawick, *The American Slave*, 12:295.
136. Mellon, *Bullwhip Days*, 220.
137. Ibid., 121.
138. Rawick, *The American Slave*, 12:295; Catterall, *Judicial Cases concerning American Slavery and the Negro*, 3:243.
139. *WPA Narratives (South Carolina Part 1)*, 2771–2773.
140. See, for example, Ames, *From a New England Woman's Diary in Dixie*, 74; Botume, *First Days amongst the Contrabands*, 253.
141. Laura Towne, *Letters and Diary of Laura M. Towne: Written from the Sea Islands of South Carolina, 1862–1884*, ed. Rupert Sargent Holland (Cambridge, MA: Riverside Press, 1912), 121.

142. *WPA Narratives (Arkansas Part 5)*, 204.

143. *WPA Narratives (Oklahoma)*, Kindle location 441.

144. Jean Bradley Anderson, *Piedmont Plantation: The Bennehan-Cameron Family and Lands in North Carolina* (Durham, NC: Historic Preservation Society of Durham, 1985), 108.

145. *WPA Narratives (Georgia Part 1)*, 198–199.

146. John Michael Vlatch, "'Without Recourse to Owners': The Architecture of Urban Slavery in the Antebellum South," *Perspectives in Vernacular Architecture* 6 (1997): 151, https://doi.org/10.2307/3514369; Richard C. Wade, *Slavery in the Cities: The South 1820–1860* (New York: Oxford University Press, 1967), 16–23, 325–30.

147. Ibid., 151.

148. Tommy Bogger, *Free Blacks in Norfolk, Virginia, 1790–1860: The Darker Side of Freedom* (Charlottesville: University Press of Virginia, 1997), 121–22.

149. Lane, *The Narrative of Lunsford Lane*, 5.

150. Ibid.

151. Gina Haney, "Understanding Antebellum Charleston's Backlots through Light, Sound, and Action," in *Slavery in the City: Architecture and Landscapes of Urban North America*, ed. Clifton Ellis and Rebecca Ginsberg (Charlottesville: University Press of Virginia, 2017), Kindle edition, Kindle location 1588.

152. William Johnson, *William Johnson's Natchez: The Ante-Bellum Diary of a Free Negro*, ed. William Ransom Hogan and Edwin Adams Davis (Baton Rouge: Louisiana State University Press, 1951), 331.

153. *WPA Narratives (Georgia Part 1)*, 462–463.

154. Lane, *The Narrative of Lunsford Lane*, 5.

155. *WPA Narratives (Alabama)*, 3608–3611.

156. United States Works Progress Administration, *Slave Narratives: A Folk History of Slavery in the United States from Interviews with Former Slaves, Mississippi Narratives*, Kindle edition, Kindle location 844. Hereafter *WPA Narratives (Mississippi)*.

157. Perdue et al., *Weevils in the Wheat*, 97.

158. United States Works Progress Administration, *Slave Narratives: A Folk History of Slavery in the United States from Interviews with Former Slaves, Virginia Narratives*, Kindle edition, Kindle location 715. Hereafter *WPA Narratives (Virginia)*.

159. Ibid., 3204.

160. Ibid., 433–434.

161. *WPA Narratives (North Carolina Part 2)*, 486–487.

162. United States Works Progress Administration, *Slave Narratives: A Folk History of Slavery in the United States from Interviews with Former Slaves, Arkansas Narratives*, Kindle edition, Kindle location 509. Hereafter *WPA Narratives (Arkansas Part 1)*.

163. United States Works Progress Administration, *Slave Narratives: A Folk History of Slavery in the United States from Interviews with Former Slaves, South Carolina Narratives, Part 2*, 58. Hereafter *WPA Narratives (South Carolina Part 2)*.

164. United States Works Progress Administration, *Slave Narratives: A Folk History of Slavery in the United States from Interviews with Former Slaves, North Carolina Narratives, Part 1*, Kindle edition, Kindle location 2654–2665. Hereafter *WPA Narratives (South Carolina Part 2)*.

165. *WPA Narratives (South Carolina Part 1)*, 1303–1305.

166. *WPA Narratives (Georgia Part 1)*, 233.

167. Perdue et al., *Weevils in the Wheat*, 33–42.

168. George P. Rawick, ed., *The American Slave: A Composite Autobiography*, vol. 15: *North Carolina Narratives* (Westport, CT: Greenwood Publishing, 1972), 74, 395; Perdue et al., *Weevils in the Wheat*, 202–203.

169. Jacobs, *Incidents in the Life of a Slave Girl*, 69–70.

170. Albert, *The House of Bondage*, 66.

171. Perdue et al., *Weevils in the Wheat*, 185–86, 203, 287; Rawick, *The American Slave*, 12:33.

172. Perdue et al., *Weevils in the Wheat*, 185–86, 203, 287; Rawick, *The American Slave*, 12:33.

173. Jean Friedman, for example, asserts in *The "Enclosed Garden"*, that "the slave system and Afro-American culture circumscribed relationships beyond the family, and the subordinate position of women became clear in family culture and evangelical religious symbolism." Jean Friedman, *The "Enclosed Garden": Women and Community in the Evangelical South, 1830–1860* (Chapel Hill: University of North Carolina Press, 1985), 69. Betty Wood notes of the hierarchical structure of enslaved evangelists in their Savannah churches in *Women's Work, Men's Work* that while women were esteemed because of their great piety or age, "as in the other African American and biracial Baptist churches, the offices of pastor and deacon, with the formal authority they entailed, not least in the disciplining of congregations, were filled by men." Betty Wood, *Women's Work, Men's Work: The Informal Slave Economies of Lowcountry Georgia* (Athens: University of Georgia Press, 1995), 171. Important works that discuss the religious practices of the enslaved and the roles of women include Friedman, *The "Enclosed Garden"*, especially pp. 67–91; Margaret Washington, *"A Peculiar People"*, especially pp. 259–303; Cynthia Lyerly, "Religion, Gender and Identity: Black Methodist Women in a Slave Society, 1770–1810," in *Discovering the Women in Slavery: Emancipating Perspectives on the American Past*, ed., Patricia Morton (Athens: University of Georgia Press, 1997), 203–21; Brenda E. Stevenson, "Gender Conventions, Ideals and Identity Among Antebellum Virginia Slave Women," in *More Than Chattel: Black Women and Slavery in the Americas*, ed. Barry Gaspar and Darlene Clark Hine (Bloomington: Indiana University Press, 1996), 169–90. Of great importance to the continuing discussion of enslaved women's religiosity, identity formation/transformation, and community implications are general studies on slavery, religion, and community. Among the most important are Raboteau, *Slave Religion*; Mechal Sobel, *Trabelin' On: The Slave Journey to an Afro-Baptist Faith* (Princeton, NJ: Princeton University Press, 1988); Sobel, *The World They Made Together*, 180–203; Gomez, *Exchanging Our Country Marks;* Wood, *Women's Work, Men's Work*, especially chap. 8, 160–77; Sylvia Frey, "Shaking the Dry Bones: The Dialectic of Conversion," in *Black and White Cultural Interaction in the Antebellum South*, ed. Ted Ownby (Oxford:

University of Mississippi Press, 1993), 23–44. Also see Sylvia Frey's larger work *Water from the Rock: Black Resistance in a Revolutionary Age* (Princeton, NJ: Princeton University Press, 1991), 243–325; Eugene D. Genovese, *Roll, Jordan, Roll: The World the Slaves Made* (New York: Pantheon, 1974), 159–285; V. P. Franklin, *Black Self-Determination: A Cultural History of the Faith of the Fathers* (Westport, CT: Lawrence Hill, 1984), 29–67; John C. Willis, "From the Dictates of Pride to the Paths of Righteousness: Slave Honor and Christianity in Antebellum Virginia," in *The Edge of the South: Life in Nineteenth-Century Virginia*, ed. Edward Ayers and John C. Willis (Charlottesville: University Press of Virginia, 1991), 37–55; John W. Blassingame, *Slave Community: Plantation Life in the Antebellum South*, rev. ed., (New York: Oxford University Press, 1979), 130–48; Sterling Stuckey, *Slave Culture: Nationalist Theory and the Foundations of Black America* (New York: Oxford University Press, 1987), 3–97. Also see for general context purposes William Andrews, ed., *Sisters of the Spirit: Three Black Women's Autobiographies of the Nineteenth Century* (Bloomington: Indiana University Press, 1986), 1–22; Donald G. Matthews, *Religion in the Old South* (Chicago: University of Chicago Press, 1977); John Boles, *The Great Revival, 1787–1805: The Origins of the Southern Evangelical Mind* (Lexington: University of Kentucky Press, 1972); Jon Butler, *Awash in a Sea of Faith: Christianizing the American People* (Cambridge, MA: Harvard University Press, 1990).

174. Perdue et al., *Weevils in the Wheat*, 287.

175. Viewing the nineteenth-century Christian church, regardless of the race of its members, as a patriarchal entity, scholars generally have asserted the importance of enslaved leadership within Christian churches as a boost to African American manhood. Albert Raboteau, for example, notes that while it was certain that Whites as well as Blacks fell under the powerful preaching of eloquent "brethren in black, . . . more common was the day-to-day presence of the black minister in his community, slave or free, preaching funerals, weddings, prayer meetings, Sabbath sermons, with a force that uplifted blacks and proved the ability of black men." Raboteau goes on to argue that "the ineluctable tendency of the black evangelical ethos was in the direction of asserting 'manhood' rights, which were understood as a vital form of self-governance." Albert Raboteau, "The Black Experience in American Evangelicalism: The Meaning of Slavery," in *African American Religion: Interpretive Essays in History and Culture*, ed. Timothy E. Fulop and Albert J. Raboteau (New York: Routledge, 1997), 94. Charles Joyner notes, "To Christian slaves, the slave preachers were men of status." Charles Joyner, "'Believer I Know:' The Emergence of African-American Christianity" in *Religion and American Culture, A Reader*, ed. David G. Hackett (New York: Routledge, 1995), 193.

Jacqueline Jones asserts, however, that enslaved women, especially those who were older, "often gained influence [among other slaves] by virtue of the knowledge of herbal medicine, poisons, conjuring, and midwifery." Jacqueline Jones, "Status of Slave Women," in *Slavery and Freedom in the Age of the American Revolution*, ed. Ira Berlin and Herbert Gutman (Charlottesville: University Press of Virginia, 1983), 320. Betty Wood contends that enslaved women in the First African Church in Savannah "might have enjoyed a certain prestige and influence within the church by virtue of the age or piety." Wood, *Women's Work, Men's Work*, 171; see also Stevenson, *Life in Black and White*, 227–28.

176. For more information on enslaved women and childrearing, particularly within the context of moral and or religious socialization, see Wilma King, *Stolen Childhood: Slave Youth in Nineteenth-Century America* (Bloomington: Indiana University Press, 1995), 80–90; Thomas L. Webber, *Deep Like the Rivers: Education in the Slave Quarter Community, 1831–1865* (New York: Norton, 1978), 80–130, passim; Brenda E. Stevenson, "Distress and Discord in Virginia Slave Families, 1830–1860," in *In Joy and In Sorrow: Women, Family and Marriage in the Victorian South, 1830–1900*, ed. Carol Bleser (New York: Oxford University Press, 1990), 103–24; Stevenson, "Gender Convention, Ideals, and Identity Among Antebellum Virginia Slave Women," 174–80.

Scholars have noted the "social power" of Black female religious leaders within the growing historiography on this subject. The vast majority of these scholars have centered their analysis on the generations of Black religious women who came after the end of slavery. See, for example, the work of Evelyn Brooks Higginbotham in *Righteous Discontent: The Women's Movement in the Black Baptist Church, 1880–1920* (Cambridge, MA: Harvard University Press, 1993); Cheryl Townsend Gilkes, "The Roles of Church and Community Mothers: Ambivalent American Sexism or Fragmented African Familyhood?" *Journal of Feminist Studies in Religion* 2, no. 1 (spring 1986): 41–59, http://www.jstor.org/stable/25002029; Jualynne E. Dodson, "Power and Surrogate Leadership: Black Women and Organized Religion," *SAGE* 5, no. 2 (fall 1988): 37–52, https://www.proquest.com/scholarly-journals/power-surrogate-leadership-black-women-organized/docview/1300126123/se-2?accountid =14512; Stephen Ward Angell, "The Controversy over Women's Ministry in the African Methodist Episcopal Church during the 1880s: The Case of Sarah Ann Hughes," in *This Far by Faith: Readings in African-American Women's Religious Biography*, ed. Judith Weisenfeld and Richard Newman (New York: Routledge, 1996), 94–109; Judith Weisenfeld, "Introduction: We Have Been Believers: Patterns of Africa-American Women's Religiosity," in *This Far by Faith*, 1–2; Judith Weisenfeld, "'Who Is Sufficient for These Things?': Sara G. Stanley and the American Missionary Association, 1864–1868," *Church History* 60, no. 4 (1991): 493–507, https://doi.org/10.2307/3169030; and Nell Irvin Painter, "Representing Truth: Sojourner Truth's Knowing and Becoming Known," in *This Far by Faith*, pp. 262–99. "The large degree to which personal religious experience, the bonds of communities of faith, and sacred traditions all afforded African-American women access to varieties of power should not be underestimated," Weisenfeld asserts. While power is conventionally construed as derived from institutions and hierarchies, it is the case that African American women most often created and utilized power in ways that do not appear significant according to traditional standards. Weisenfeld relies on Jualynne Dobson's analysis to underscore her own point: "Despite the access to formal positions of religious leadership in most Christian churches, African-American women understood their power to rest *not* in these positions exclusively, but also in their overall impact on their communities, through their ability to mobilize people and financial resources, for example. Weisenfeld, "Introduction," in *This Far by Faith*, 3–4.

I certainly agree, but again the work of Dobson and Weisenfeld centers on Black women beyond the slavery era. The power that devout enslaved women derived from their obvious religiosity and religious leadership was to challenge prevailing White views of their moral depravity, and thus worthlessness, as women, Black women.

177. Raboteau, *Slave Religion*, 227–28.

178. Octavia V. Rogers Albert, *The House of Bondage, or Charlotte Brooks and Other Slaves* in *The Schomburg Library of Nineteenth-Century Black Women Writers*, ed. Henry Louis Gates (New York: Oxford University Press, 1988), 12–14. All subsequent references to the Albert's *House of Bondage* refer to this edition of the text, not the 1890 original. The rejection of Catholicism by some slaves who felt more comfortable with the praise and worship styles of Protestant camp meetings and its related ritual styles of some West African societies also is documented in the testimony of Elizabeth Ross Hite. Edward Dryer et al., *Gumbo Ya-Ya*, 242.

179. Clifton H. Johnson, ed., *God Struck Me Dead: Voices of Ex-Slaves* (Eugene, OR: Wipf and Stock, 1969), 121.

180. Albert, *The House of Bondage*, 70–71.

181. Perdue et al., *Weevils in the Wheat*, 34.

182. *WPA Narratives (Texas Part 1)*, 3293–3294.

183. *WPA Narratives (Georgia Part 3)*, 2762–2768.

184. Rawick, *The American Slave*, 15:133.

185. Johnson, *God Struck Me Dead*, 114.

186. Ibid., 169.

187. Ibid.

188. Ibid.

189. Ibid., 65–67.

190. Bethany Veney, *The Narrative of Bethany Veney, A Slave Woman* (Worcester, MA: George Ellis Press, 1889), electronic edition, as found on Documenting the American South, 7–8, http://docsouth.unc.edu/fpn/veney/veney.html.

191. Ibid., 8.

192. Perdue et. al., *Weevils in the Wheat*, 80.

193. Ibid., 33.

194. Mellon, *Bullwhip Days*, 187–88.

195. Ibid., 186–87.

196. Ibid. Many scholars have written on the textual importance of the slaves' religious songs. Two of the earliest in the "revisionist" school of slavery that dominated the 1970s, 1980s and 1990s are Lawrence W. Levine, "Slave Songs and Slave Consciousness: An Exploration in Neglected Sources," 1971, reprinted in in Timothy E. Fulop and Albert J. Raboteau, *African American Religion: Interpretive Essays in History and Culture* (New York: Routledge, 1997), 59–87; and James H. Cone, *The Spirituals and the Blues* (New York: Seabury Press, 1972).

197. Mellon, *Bullwhip Days*, 85.

198. Ibid.

199. Regarding African American slave religion and resistance, see notes 174 and 176 in this chapter.
200. Rawick, *The American Slave*, 15:1330.
201. Albert, *The House of Bondage*, 68–69.
202. Terry Alford, *Prince among Slaves: The True Story of an African Prince Sold into Slavery in the American South* (New York: Oxford University Press, 1977), 81–82.
203. United States Works Progress Administration, *Slave Narratives: A Folk History of Slavery in the United States from Interviews with Former Slaves, Tennessee Narratives*, Kindle edition, Kindle location 545–551. Hereafter *WPA Narratives (Tennessee)*.
204. Perdue et al., *Weevils in the Wheat*, 322.
205. Albert, *The House of Bondage*, 34.
206. Perdue et al., *Weevils in the Wheat*, 224.
207. *WPA Narratives (Missouri)*, 3125–3127.
208. Mellon, *Bullwhip Days*, 185.
209. Perdue et al., *Weevils in the Wheat*, 241.
210. Blassingame, *Slave Testimony*, 411.
211. Keckley, *Behind the Scenes*, 32–38.
212. Perdue et al., *Weevils in the Wheat*, 267.
213. "Plantation Life as Viewed by Ex-Slave Alice Green of Athens, Ga.," in Rawick, *The American Slave*, 12:35.
214. George P. Rawick, ed., *The American Slave: A Composite Autobiography*, vol. 2: *South Carolina Narratives* (Westport, CT: Greenwood Publishing, 1972), 131.
215. Perdue et al., *Weevils in the Wheat*, 150.
216. Johnson, *God Struck Me Dead*, 118–19.
217. Perdue et al., *Weevils in the Wheat*, 94. Here, Folkes is recalling what her mother told her about the female slave experience in antebellum Virginia.
218. For some discussion of the African influence on the "Christian" practices of enslaved southerners, see note 168 in this chapter.
219. United States Works Progress Administration, *Slave Narratives: A Folk History of Slavery in the United States from Interviews with Former Slaves, Arkansas Narratives, Part 6*, Kindle edition, Kindle location 164–165. Hereafter *WPA Narratives (Arkansas Part 6)*.
220. Rawick, *The American Slave*, 15:156–57.
221. Cited in Raboteau, *Slave Religion*, 238.
222. Ibid.
223. Towne, *Letters and Diary of Laura M. Towne*, 20.
224. *WPA Narratives (Maryland)*, Kindle location 348.
225. *WPA Narratives (Alabama)*, 1316–1317.
226. *WPA Narratives (South Carolina Part 1)*, 605–606.
227. *WPA Narratives (North Carolina Part 2)*, 2327–2328.
228. *WPA Narratives (Arkansas Part 5)*, 2507–2508.
229. Lane, *Autobiography of Lunsford Lane*, 11–12.
230. *WPA Narratives (Alabama)*, 1316–1317.

231. *WPA Narratives (Texas Part 1)*, 7.
232. Emily P. Burke, "Letter XVI," in *A Documentary History of Slavery in North America*, ed. Willie Lee Rose (Athens: University of Georgia Press, 1999), 325.
233. *WPA Narratives (Arkansas Part 6)*, 839.
234. United States Works Progress Administration, *Slave Narratives: A Folk History of Slavery in the United States from Interviews with Former Slaves, Kentucky Narratives*, Kindle edition, Kindle location 501–502. Hereafter *WPA Narratives (Kentucky)*.
235. *WPA Narratives (Alabama)*, 884.
236. *WPA Narratives (South Carolina Part 1)*, 501–502.
237. *WPA Narratives (Alabama)*, 1225–1227.
238. Ibid., 1802–1803.
239. Lewis and Milton Clark, *Narratives of the Sufferings of Lewis and Milton Clarke, Sons of a Soldier of the Revolution*, in *African American Slave Narratives, An Anthology*, ed. Sterling Bland (Westport, CT: Greenwood Press, 2001), 134–35.
240. Ibid., 135.
241. *WPA Narratives (South Carolina Part 1)*, 141–142.
242. Ibid., 501–502.
243. *WPA Narratives (Arkansas Part 6)*, 3569.
244. Regarding health care of enslaved peoples provided by slaveholders and enslaved family and community members, see Todd Savitt, *Medicine and Slavery: The Diseases and Health Care of Blacks in Antebellum Virginia* (Urbana: University of Illinois Press, 1978); Sharla Fett, *Working Cures: Healing, Health, and Power on Southern Slave Plantations* (Chapel Hill: University of North Carolina Press, 2002). Regarding the care of children, see King, *Stolen Childhood*, 876–949. Regarding the care of pregnant women and midwifery, see particularly Deidre Cooper Owens, *Medical Bondage: Race, Gender, and The Origins of American Gynecology* (Athens: University of Georgia Press, 2017), Kindle edition, Kindle location 918–1787.
245. United States Works Progress Administration, *Slave Narratives: A Folk History of Slavery in the United States from Interviews with Former Slaves, Florida Narratives*, Kindle edition, Kindle location 1429. Hereafter *WPA Narratives (Florida)*.
246. *WPA Narratives (Georgia Part 1)*, 487–490.
247. *WPA Narratives (Georgia Part 3)*, 1036.
248. *WPA Narratives (Alabama)*, 894. United States Works Progress Administration, *Slave Narratives: A Folk History of Slavery in the United States from Interviews with Former Slaves, South Carolina Narratives, Part 3*, Kindle edition, Kindle location 1474–1475. Hereafter *WPA Narratives (South Carolina, Part 3)*.
249. *WPA Narratives (Alabama)*, 3616–3617.
250. Ibid., 2572–2573.
251. *WPA Narratives (South Carolina Part 1)*, 2087.
252. Ibid., 3606.
253. Ibid., 420; *WPA Narratives (Arkansas Part 5)*, 1841.
254. *WPA Narratives (Missouri)*, 3614–3619.

255. Mellon, *Bullwhip Days*, 96.
256. Seck, *Bouki Fait Gombo*, 1613.
257. 257 Acct of deaths from Cholera, Negroes at Shirley [Plantation], 1849, n.p. Shirley Plantation Collection, 1650–1888, Colonial Williamsburg Foundation Library, Microfilm, Container 92, Folder 1, 1854–1864.
258. *WPA Narratives (South Carolina Part 1)*, 20.
259. *WPA Narratives (Indiana)*, 2087–2088.
260. Tallant, *Gumbo Ya-Ya*, 234.
261. Frances Anne Kemble, *Women in Slavery: Selections from Her Journal of Residence on a Georgian Plantation, 1838–1839*, Kindle edition, Kindle location 256.
262. Ibid., 183.
263. Ibid., 251.
264. Frederick Law Olmsted, "Medical Survey," in *A Documentary History of Slavery in North America*, ed. Willie Lee Rose (Athens: University of Georgia Press, 1999), 293–95.
265. *WPA Narratives (Arkansas Part 5)*, 643.
266. See, for example, Hill Carter's Shirley Plantation Farm Book, 1817–1865, September 3, 1846, Shirley Plantation Collection, 1650–1888, Colonial Williamsburg Foundation Library, Microfilm, Container 92, Folder 1, 1854–1864.
267. *WPA Narratives (Georgia Part 1)*, Kindle location 267; Savitt, *Medicine and Slavery*, 64–73.
268. *WPA Narratives (Oklahoma)*, 4053.
269. Botume, *First Days amongst the Contrabands*, 48; "Names and Naming: African," as found on Encyclopedia of African American Culture and History, Encyclopedia.com, 2019, https://www.encyclopedia.com/history/encyclopedias-almanacs-transcripts-and-maps/names-and-naming-african.
270. Botume, *First Days amongst the Contrabands*, 48.
271. *WPA Narratives (Arkansas Part 5)*, 1829.
272. *WPA Narratives (North Carolina Part 2)*, 374.
273. *WPA Narratives (Arkansas Part 6)*, 1276–1277.
274. For records of a southern physician who had a large slaveholding clientele that included these persons, see, for example, Account Book, 1825–1827, of the medical practice of Doctor Matt. C. Whitaker, of Halifax County, N.C., concerning, in part, Ricks Fort and African-American captors, Virginia Historical Society, Mss1 F7755a 13, as found on "Halifax County," Virginia Untold: The African American Narrative, http://digitool1.lva.lib.va.us:8881/R/R2CQ3LQLD6S9B2D4H1NINKRB8D8DL632GLYKQTIKMB5BSGVRX4-03654?func=results-jump-full&set_entry=000002&set_number=363008&base=GEN01-LVA01.
275. *WPA Narratives (Alabama)*, 892.
276. *WPA Narratives (Tennessee)*, 563–564.
277. Catterall, *Judicial Cases concerning American Slavery and the Negro*, 3:458.
278. Ibid., 407.
279. Catterall, *Judicial Cases concerning American Slavery and the Negro*, 2:321.

Notes   395

280. Catterall, *Judicial Cases concerning American Slavery and the Negro*, 3:415, also n. 1 on 415.
281. Catterall, *Judicial Cases concerning American Slavery and the Negro*, 2:331.
282. Hill Carter's Shirley Plantation Farm Book, 1817–1865, Shirley Plantation Collection, 1650–1888, Colonial Williamsburg Foundation Library, Microfilm, Container 92, Folder 1, 1854–1864.
283. Catterall, *Judicial Cases concerning American Slavery and the Negro*, 3:404.
284. Mellon, *Bullwhip Days*, 157.
285. Ibid., 153.
286. *WPA Narratives (Georgia Part 3)*, 590–591.
287. Ibid., 964–966.
288. Mellon, *Bullwhip Days*, 4–5.
289. United States Works Progress Administration, *Slave Narratives: A Folk History of Slavery in the United States from Interviews with Former Slaves, Kansas Narratives*, Kindle edition, Kindle location 1474–1475.
290. Truth and Gilbert, *The Narrative of Sojourner Truth*, 16–17.
291. Kemble, *Women in Slavery*, 308, 401, 500.

CHAPTER 6

1. Lyrics from Bob Marley, "Redemption Song," *Redemption Song* (UMG Recordings, Inc. Courtesy of Island Records under license from Universal Music Enterprises), https://youtu.be/yv5xonFSC4c.
2. Charles Ball, *Slavery in the United States. A Narrative of the Life and Adventures of Charles Ball, a Black Man, Who Lived Forty Years in Maryland, South Carolina and Georgia, as a Slave under Various Masters, and Was One Year in the Navy with Commodore Barney, during the Late War* (New York: John S. Taylor, 1837), 264–66.
3. "Archeology and African American Cemeteries," South Carolina Information Highway, Chicora Foundation, 2022, https://www.sciway.net/hist/chicora/grave matters.html#archeology; Michael Trinkley, *An Archaeological Survey of Long-Point Development, Charleston County, South Carolina: Palmetto Grove Plantation* (Columbia, SC: Chicora Foundation,1987), https://www.chicora.org/pdfs/RS8%20 %20Longpoint%20Palmetto%20Grove.pdf.
4. Michael E. Ruane, "An Archeological Dig Unearths the Earliest Slave Remains in Delaware," *Washington Post*, December 5, 2017, https://www.washing tonpost.com/news/retropolis/wp/2017/12/05/an-archaeological-dig-unearths-one-of -the-earliest-slave-remains-in-delaware/.
5. "The Young Woman from Harleigh Knoll," National Museum of Natural History, Smithsonian Institution, 2022, https://naturalhistory.si.edu/education /teaching-resources/written-bone/forensic-case-files/young-woman-harleigh-knoll.
6. Ball, *Slavery in the United States*, 264–65.
7. Ball, *Slavery in the United States*, 219.

8. Allan Anderson, "African Religions," *Encyclopedia of Death and Dying*, 2022, http://www.deathreference.com/A-Bi/African-Religions.html.

9. Benjamin Drew, *The Refugee: The Narratives of Fugitive Slaves in Canada* (Boston: John P. Jewett, 1856), Kindle edition. Kindle location, 593.

10. James Mellon, ed., *Bullwhip Days: The Slaves Remember* (New York: Grove Atlantic, 1988), Kindle edition, 41.

11. Edward Dryer, Lyle Saxton, and Robert Tallant, eds., *Gumbo Ya-Ya: A Collection of Louisiana Folk Tales* (Boston: Works Progress Administration, 1945), 234.

12. Mellon, *Bullwhip Days*, 41.

13. William Still, *The Underground Railroad (Complete Collection): Narratives, Testimonies, & Letters: The True Story of Hundreds of Slaves Who Escaped to Freedom* (Chicago: Musaicum Books, 2018), Kindle edition, Kindle location 4800.

14. John W. Blassingame, ed., *Slave Testimony: Two Centuries of Letters, Speeches, Interviews, and Autobiographies* (Baton Rouge: Louisiana State University Press, 1977), 650.

15. Ibid., 230–31.

16. Harriet Jacobs, *Incidents in the Life of a Slave Girl*, ed. Valerie Smith (New York: Oxford University Press, 1988), 220–23.

17. Elizabeth Hyde Botume, *First Days amongst the Contrabands* (New York: Arno Press, 1969), 166–67.

18. United States Works Progress Administration, *Slave Narratives: A Folk History of Slavery in the United States from Interviews with Former Slaves, Missouri Narratives*, Kindle edition, Kindle locations 3123. Hereafter *WPA Narratives (Missouri)*.

19. United States Works Progress Administration, *Slave Narratives: A Folk History of Slavery in the United States from Interviews with Former Slaves, Mississippi Narratives*, Kindle edition, Kindle locations 499–536. Hereafter *WPA Narratives (Mississippi)*.

20. Mellon, *Bullwhip Days*, 41.

21. Blassingame, *Slave Testimony*, 734.

22. Still, *Underground Railroad*, 10072.

23. United States Works Progress Administration, *Slave Narratives: A Folk History of Slavery in the United States from Interviews with Former Slaves, Georgia Narratives, Part 1*, print, 45. Hereafter *WPA Narratives (Georgia Part 1, print)*. https://www.loc.gov/resource/mesn.041/?sp=49.

24. James L. Smith, *Autobiography of James L. Smith, Including, Also Reminiscences of Slave Life, Recollections of the War, Education of Freedmen, Causes of the Exodus, etc.* (Norwich, CT: Bulletin, 1881), 30.

25. Charles L. Perdue Jr., Thomas E. Barden, and Robert K. Phillips, eds., *Weevils in the Wheat: Interviews with Virginia Ex-Slaves* (Charlottesville: University Press of Virginia, 1976), 289–90.

26. *WPA Narratives (Missouri)*, 3123.

27. *WPA Narratives (Mississippi)*, 844.

28. Perdue et al., *Weevils in the Wheat*, 289.

29. Warren R. Perry, Jean Howson, and Barbara A. Bianco, eds., *New York African Burial Ground Archeology Final Report* 1 (Washington, DC: Howard University,

2006), 250–87; Christopher Moore, "African Burial Ground in History," African Burial Ground, National Park Service, 2019, https://www.nps.gov/afbg/learn/history culture/african-burial-ground-in-history.htm.

30. Mellon, *Bullwhip Days*, 162.

31. *WPA Narratives (Missouri)*, 2067.

32. Albert J. Raboteau, *Slave Religion: The "Invisible Institution" in the Antebellum South* (New York: Oxford University Press, 2004), 230.

33. United States Works Progress Administration, *Slave Narratives: A Folk History of Slavery in the United States from Interviews with Former Slaves, South Carolina Narratives, Part 1*, Kindle edition, Kindle location 2357–2359. Hereafter *WPA Narratives (South Carolina Part 1)*.

34. Mellon, *Bullwhip Days*, 365–66. See also United States Works Progress Administration, *Slave Narratives: A Folk History of Slavery in the United States from Interviews with Former Slaves, Georgia Narratives, Part 3*, Kindle edition, Kindle location 2067–2069. Hereafter *WPA Narratives (Georgia Part 3)*.

35. "African Burial Ground," New York Preservation Archive Project, 2022, https://www.nypap.org/preservation-history/african-burial-ground.

36. "History of African American Cemeteries," South Carolina Information Highway, Chicora Foundation, 2022, https://www.sciway.net/hist/chicora/grave matters-1.html.

37. Austin Steward, *Twenty-Two Years a Slave, and Forty Years a Freeman: Embracing a Correspondence of Several Years, While President of Wilberforce Colony, London, Canada West (1857)*, in *African American Slave Narratives, An Anthology*, vol. 3, ed. Sterling L. Bland Jr. (Westport, CT: Greenwood Press, 2001), 711–12.

38. Mellon, *Bullwhip Days*, 162.

39. Ibid., 57.

40. Ibid., 217.

41. United States Works Progress Administration, *Slave Narratives: A Folk History of Slavery in the United States from Interviews with Former Slaves, Arkansas Narratives, Part 5*, print, 46–47. Hereafter *WPA Narratives (Arkansas Part 5, print)*.

42. Mellon, *Bullwhip Days*, 144–45.

43. Ibid., 217.

44. United States Works Progress Administration, *Slave Narratives: A Folk History of Slavery in the United States from Interviews with Former Slaves, Oklahoma Narratives*, Kindle edition, Kindle location 3420. Hereafter *WPA Narratives (Oklahoma)*.

45. Georgia Writers' Project, *Drums and Shadows: Survival Studies amongst the Coastal Georgia Negroes* (Athens: University of Georgia Press), Kindle edition, Kindle location 3866; Raboteau, *Slave Religion*, 68, 71–72.

46. Frederick Law Olmsted, *The Cotton Kingdom: A Traveller's Observations on Cotton and Slavery in the American Slave States, 1853–1861* (Tucson, AZ: Mariposa Press, 2017), Kindle edition, 348.

47. United States Works Progress Administration, *Slave Narratives: A Folk History of Slavery in the United States from Interviews with Former Slaves,*

Maryland Narratives, Kindle edition, Kindle location 70. Hereafter *WPA Narratives (Maryland)*.

48. Jacobs, *Incidents in the Life of a Slave Girl*, 222.

49. Olmsted, *The Cotton Kingdom*, 37. Olmsted noted the presence of the White witness. The law actually forbade Black people from officiating at funerals in Richmond as of 1832. Richard C. Wade, *Slavery in the Cities: The South, 1820–1860* (New York: Oxford University Press, 1964), 271.

50. Gina Haney, "Understanding Antebellum Charleston's Backlots through Light, Sound, and Action," in *Slavery in the City: Architecture and Landscapes of Urban North America* ed . Clifton Ellis and Rebecca Ginsberg (Charlottesville: University Press of Virginia, 2017), Kindle edition, Kindle location 1711–1715.

51. Smith, *Autobiography of James L. Smith*, 96.

52. "1860 Census: Population of the United States," United States Census Bureau, https://www.census.gov/library/publications/1864/dec/1860a.html.

53. Burke Davis, *The Civil War: Strange and Fascinating Facts* (New York: Fairfax Press, 1982), 215.

54. "Timeline of the Civil War," Civil War Glass Negatives and Related Prints, Library of Congress, https://www.loc.gov/pictures/collection/cwp/timeline.html.

55. Works that address Black women during the postemancipation, Reconstruction and Jim Crow eras include, but certainly are not limited to Jacqueline Jones, *Labor of Love, Labor of Sorrow: Black Women, Work and the Family from Slavery to the Present*, 2nd ed. (New York: Basic Books, 2010); Deborah White, *Too Heavy a Load: Black Women in Defense of Themselves, 1894–1994* (New York: Norton, 1999); Darlene Clark Hine and Kathleen Thompson, *A Shining Thread of Hope: The History of Black Women in America* (New York: Broadway, 199); Herbert Shapiro, *White Violence and Black Response: From Reconstruction to Montgomery* (Amherst: University of Massachusetts Press, 1988); F. G. Wood, *Black Scare: The Racist Response to Emancipation and Reconstruction* (Berkeley: University of California Press, 1968); Tera W. Hunter, *To 'Joy My Freedom: Southern Black Women's Lives and Labors after the Civil War* (Cambridge, MA: Harvard University Press, 1997); Elizabeth Regosin, *Freedom's Promise: Ex-Slave Families and Citizenship in the Age of Emancipation* (Charlottesville: University Press of Virginia, 2002).

56. Smith, *Autobiography of James L. Smith*, 96.

57. Perdue et al., *Weevils in the Wheat*, 110.

58. Tempie Herndon, in *Voices from Slavery: 100 Authentic Slave Narratives*, ed. Norman R. Yetman (Mineola, NY: Dover, 1999), 165.

59. Dora Franks, in *Voices from Slavery: 100 Authentic Slave Narratives*, ed. Norman R. Yetman (Mineola, NY: Dover, 1999), 127.

60. Ibid., 129.

61. *WPA Narratives (Mississippi)*, 499–536.

62. Franks, *Voices from Slavery*, 129.

63. *WPA Narratives (Mississippi)*, 499–536.

64. Josephine Allen of Florida, for example, noted that "most folks dem days got married by layin a broom on de floor an jumpin over it." United States Works Progress Administration, *Slave Narratives: A Folk History of Slavery in the United States*

from Interviews with Former Slaves, Florida Narratives, Kindle edition, Kindle location 57–62. Hereafter *WPA Narratives (Florida)*.

65. United States Works Progress Administration, *Slave Narratives: A Folk History of Slavery in the United States from Interviews with Former Slaves, Arkansas Narratives, Part 5*, 42–43. Hereafter *WPA Narratives (Arkansas Part 5)*.

66. For a discussion of the roles of the Freedmen's Bureau and Freedmen Aid and missionary societies freedmen marriage see, for example, Reginald Washington, "Sealing the Sacred Bonds of Holy Matrimony: Freedmen's Bureau Marriage Records," *Prologue* 37, no. 1 (spring 2005), http://www.archives.gov/publications/prologue/2005/spring/freedman-marriage-recs.html; Noralee Frankel, "From Slave Women to Free Women: The National Archives and Black Women's History in the Civil War Era," *Prologue* 29, no. 2 (summer 1997), http://www.archives.gov/publications/prologue/1997/summer/slave-women.html.

67. *WPA Narratives (Florida)*, 351–363.

68. Charlotte Forten Grimke, *The Journals of Charlotte Forten Grimke*, ed. Brenda E. Stevenson (New York: Oxford University Press, 1988), 402.

69. *WPA Narratives (South Carolina Part 1)*, 2984–2986.

70. *WPA Narratives (Florida)*, 1026–1028.

71. *WPA Narratives (Mississippi)*, 255–256).

72. Perdue et al., *Weevils in the Wheat,* 122.

73. Mary Reynolds, in George P. Rawick, ed., *The American Slave: A Composite Autobiography*, vol. 5, *Georgia Narratives* (Westport, CT: Greenwood Publishing, 1972), 236–46.

74. United States Works Progress Administration, *Slave Narratives: A Folk History of Slavery in the United States from Interviews with Former Slaves, Arkansas Narratives, Part 7*, 40. Kindle location 577. Hereafter *WPA Narratives (Arkansas Part 7)*.

75. United States Works Progress Administration, *Slave Narratives: A Folk History of Slavery in the United States from Interviews with Former Slaves, Arkansas Narratives, Part 3*, Kindle edition, Kindle location 3315–3320. Hereafter *WPA Narratives (Arkansas Part 3)*.

76. United States Works Progress Administration, *Slave Narratives: A Folk History of Slavery in the United States from Interviews with Former Slaves, Texas Narratives, Part 2*, Kindle edition, Kindle location 1307–1311. Hereafter *WPA Narratives (Texas Part 2)*.

77. *WPA Narratives (Georgia Part 3)*, Kindle locations 3125–3127.

78. *WPA Narratives (Texas Part 2)*, 2853–2855.

79. Ibid., 2748–2757.

80. *WPA Narratives (Florida)*, 57–62.

81. *WPA Narratives (Georgia Part 1)*, 2284–2286.

82. *WPA Narratives (Texas Part 2)*, 242–245.

83. *WPA Narratives (Georgia Part 3)*, 906–908.

84. Ibid., 461–463, 2399–2400.

85. Ibid., 655–663.

86. Ibid., 1051–1052.

87. Sumptuary laws, for example, existed in the colonial era and customarily throughout the antebellum period. See, for example, "An Act for the Better Ordering and Governing Negroes and Other Slaves In This Province," as found on Teaching US History, http://www.teachingushistory.org/pdfs/Transciptionof1740Slave-Codes.pdf.

88. Regarding physically appealing women forced into concubinage, see Brenda E. Stevenson, "'What's Love Got to Do With It?': Concubinage and Enslaved Black Women and Girls in the Antebellum South," *Journal of African American History* 98 no. 1 (winter 2013): 99–125, https://doi.org/10.5323/jafriamerhist.98.1.0099

89. United States Works Progress Administration, *Slave Narratives: A Folk History of Slavery in the United States from Interviews with Former Slaves, Arkansas Narratives, Part 6*, Kindle edition, Kindle location 2595–2599. Hereafter *WPA Narratives (Arkansas Part 6)*.

90. Easter Brown of Athens, Georgia, accused a Black woman of stealing her wedding dress. *WPA Narratives (Georgia Part 1)*, Kindle location 1320–1324.

91. *WPA Narratives (Georgia Part 3)*, 906–908.

92. Ibid., 661–663.

93. See, for example, Monica L. Miller, *Slaves to Fashion: Black Dandyism and the Styling of Black Diasporic Identity* (Durham, NC: Duke University Press, 2009), 77–136.

94. *WPA Narratives (Georgia Part 1)*, 2703–2705.

95. United States Works Progress Administration, *Slave Narratives: A Folk History of Slavery in the United States from Interviews with Former Slaves, Arkansas Narratives, Part 1*, Kindle edition, Kindle location 1925–1926. Hereafter *WPA Narratives (Arkansas Part 1)*.

96. *WPA Narratives (Georgia Part 3)*, 3125–3127.

97. *WPA Narratives (Texas Part 2)*, 242–245.

98. *WPA Narratives (Georgia Part 3)*, 655–663.

99. Ibid., 461–463.

100. *WPA Narratives (Florida)*, 57–62.

101. *WPA Narratives (Arkansas Part 6)*, 3163–3165.

102. United States Works Progress Administration, *Slave Narratives: A Folk History of Slavery in the United States from Interviews with Former Slaves, Arkansas Narratives, Part 2*, Kindle edition, Kindle location 841. Hereafter *WPA Narratives (Arkansas Part 2)*.

103. *WPA Narratives (South Carolina Part 1)*, 4106–4110.

104. *WPA Narratives (Georgia Part 3)*, 461–463.

105. *WPA Narratives (Arkansas Part 3)*, 3320.

106. Perdue et al., *Weevils in the Wheat*, 36.

107. *WPA Narratives (Texas Part 2)*, 2748–2757.

108. Ibid., 2748–2755.

109. Ibid., 2748–2757.

110. Ibid.

111. *WPA Narratives (Arkansas Part 3)*, 3315–3320.

112. *WPA Narratives (Texas Part 2)*, 158–161.

113. *WPA Narratives (Florida)*, 1323–1332.
114. *WPA Narratives (Georgia Part 1)*, 2414–2417.
115. *WPA Narratives (Arkansas Part 5)*, 23.
116. *WPA Narratives (Georgia Part 3)*, 1743–1745.
117. Ibid., 906–908.
118. *WPA Narratives (South Carolina Part 1)*, 4106–4110.
119. *WPA Narratives (Arkansas Part 7)*, 23.
120. *WPA Narratives (Georgia Part 3)*, 3125–3127.
121. *WPA Narratives (Arkansas Part 1)*, 1919–1926.
122. Perdue et al., *Weevils in the Wheat*, 126.
123. United States Works Progress Administration, *Slave Narratives: A Folk History of Slavery in the United States from Interviews with Former Slaves, Alabama Narratives*, Kindle edition, Kindle location 1157–1602. Hereafter *WPA Narratives* (Alabama).
124. Ibid., 1157–1602.
125. Delia Garlick [sp]; Year: *1930*; Census Place: *Montgomery, Montgomery, Alabama*; Roll: *2339778*; Page: *32B* Enumeration District: *006*; Image: *264.0*, as found on Ancestry.com. Delia Garlick [sp]. Year: *1940*; Census Place: *Montgomery, Montgomery, Alabama*; Roll: *m-t0627-00067*; Page *1B*; Enumeration District: *51-14*, as found on Ancestry.com. https://www.ancestrylibrary.com/discoveryui-content/view/118677169:6224?tid=&pid=&queryId=9a43a13e5fdb29da547d304f4511f32a&_phsrc=BHW387&_phstart=successSource. For 1940, please insert: https://www.ancestrylibrary.com/discoveryui-content/view/67512680:2442?tid=&pid=&queryId=9a43a13e5fdb29da547d304f4511f32a&_phsrc=BHW388&_phstart=successSource.
126. *WPA Narratives (Alabama)*, 1157–1602.
127. Harrison Beckett's autobiographical account found in United States Works Progress Administration, *Slave Narratives: A Folk History of Slavery in the United States from Interviews with Former Slaves, Texas Narratives, Part 1*, Kindle edition, Kindle location 621–658. Hereafter *WPA Narratives (Texas Part 1)*.
128. Thomas Wentworth Higginson, *Army Life in a Black Regiment and Other Writings* (New York: Penguin, 2004), Kindle edition, Kindle location 3756.
129. Herndon, *Voices from Slavery*, 165.
130. Ibid.
131. Emily P. Burke, "Letter XVI," *A Documentary History of Slavery in North America,* ed. Willie Lee Rose (Athens: University of Georgia Press, 1999), 327–28.
132. Herndon, *Voices from Slavery*, 291.
133. Susan Snow, in *Voices From Slavery: 100 Authentic Slave Narratives*, ed. Norman R. Yetman (Mineola, NY: Dover, 1999), 293.
134. These Mississippi counties include Jasper, Lauderdale, Jones, Newton, and Clarke.
135. http://search.ancestry.com/iexec?htx=View&r=an&dbid=7163&iid=4273831_00433&fn=Lear&ln=Snow&st; Year: *1870*; Census Place: *North East Beat, Jasper, Mississippi*; Roll: *M593_732*; Page: *548B*; Image: *433*; Family History Library Film: *552231*.
136. Snow, *Voices from Slavery*, 293.

137. Ibid., 293.

138. Ibid., 293.

139. Susan Snow; Year: *1880*; Census Place: *Meridian, Lauderdale, Mississippi;* Roll: *653*; Page: *11A*; Enumeration District: *090*.

140. Snow, *Voices from Slavery*, 293.

141. Dawn Keetley and John Pettegrew, eds., *Public Women, Public Words: A Documentary History of American Feminism*, vol. 3 (Lanham, MD: Rowman and Littlefield, 2005), 157–158; see also Catherine Clinton, "Bloody Terrain: Freedwomen, Sexuality and Violence During Reconstruction," *Georgia Historical Quarterly* 76, no. 2 (summer 1992): 313–32, http://www.jstor.org/stable/40582538.

142. Katie [Snow?]; Year: *1880*; Census Place: *Meridian, Lauderdale, Mississippi;* Roll: *653*; Page: *11A*; Enumeration District: *090*.

143. Susan Snow; Year: *1900*; Census Place: *Meridian Ward 4, Lauderdale, Mississippi*; Roll: *T623_815*; Page: *24A*; Enumeration District: *019*. Susan Snow; Year: *1910*; Census Place: *Meridian Ward 5, Lauderdale, Mississippi*; Roll: *T624_746*; Page: *8A*; Enumeration District: *048*. Susan Snow; Year: *1930*; Census Place: *Meridian, Lauderdale, Mississippi*; Roll: *1153*; Page: *20B*; Enumeration District: *008*. Susan Snow; Year: *1920*; Census Place: *Meridian Ward 5, Lauderdale, Mississippi*; Roll: *T625_882*; Page: *15A*; Enumeration District: *054*.

144. Snow, *Voices from Slavery*, 293.

145. Ibid.

146. See, for example, Paula Giddings's discussion of the violence Black women suffered when living alone in *When and Where I Enter: The Impact of Black Women on Race and Sex in America* (New York: William Morrow, 1996), 5–6.

147. Because the surviving 1890 census is only a partial one, information on these women could not be found for that year.

148. See note 133 in this chapter.

149. Daisy Allen; Year: *1920*; Census Place: *Meridian Ward 3, Lauderdale, Mississippi*; Roll: *T625_882*; Page: *5A*; Enumeration District: *049*, https://www.ancestrylibrary.com/discoveryui-content/view/84797057:6061?_phsrc=pjg27&_phstart=successSource&gsfn=Daisy&gsln=Allen&ml_rpos=1&queryId=1a54167e6694f7784b764a0636b3283f.

CONCLUSION

1. Lyrics from Bon Jovi, "American Reckoning," *Bon Jovi: 2020* (Island Records, 2020).

2. Robert Samuels was born on October 4, 1851, and died February 3, 1941. He was buried in the Washington Cemetery in Hempstead County, Arkansas. His story is found in United States Works Projects Administration, *Slave Narratives: A Folk History of Slavery in the United States from Interviews with Former Slaves, Arkansas Narratives, Part 6* (New York: Firework Press, 2015), Kindle edition, Kindle location 1170–1184. Entry for Robert Samuels, Ancestry.com. *U.S., Find a Grave Index, 1600s–Current* https://www.ancestrylibrary.com/discoveryui-content/

view/67611137:60525?tid=&pid=&queryId=4f15dd7dc1f93e3a24a65368dc8 91c23&_phsrc=BHW391&_phstart=successSource.

3. The WPA interviewer was directed to Bob and his amazing story by Mr. J. W. C. Smith. The 1930 Federal Census suggests that J. W. (C. M.) Smith was a thirty-three-year-old Black hotel waiter residing in Little Rock, Arkansas. See J. W. Smith; Year: *1930*; Census Place: *Little Rock, Pulaski, Arkansas*; Roll: *2339826*; *Page*: *15A*; Enumeration District: *0022*, or W. Conway Smith; Year: *1920*; Census Place: *Little Rock Ward 8, Pulaski, Arkansas*; Roll: *T625_79*; Page: *21B*; Enumeration District: *146*.

4. David Block, born approximately 1822 in Virginia, is listed as a Methodist minister in 1850. Block, who fought in the Civil War, received a pardon in 1865. He died in 1866. David Block; Year: *1850*; Census Place: *Washington, Hempstead, Arkansas*; Roll: *26*; Page: *208a*.

He is listed as a merchant in 1860 with seven enslaved people in Hempstead County, three females (thirty-two, twenty, and fifteen) all designated as mulatto and four males (ages thirteen, ten, two, and one month) also designated as mulatto. David Block; Year: *1860*; Census Place: *Ozan, Hempstead, Arkansas*; Roll: *M653_42*; Page: *705*; Family History Library Film: *803042*. David Block; *Eighth Census of the United States 1860—Slave Schedules*; Series Number: *M653*; Record Group: *Records of the Bureau of the Census*; Record Group Number: *29*. Block also is listed in the 1860 slave schedule as owning ten enslaved people in Poinsett County, Arkansas (six females, ages forty, twenty-seven, eighteen, eleven, five, and two, and for males, ages thirty-five, eight, six, and two). See *Eighth Census of the United States 1860—Slave Schedules*; Series Number: *M653*; Record Group: *Records of the Bureau of the Census*; Record Group Number: *29*. See also David Block; *Bonds, Inventories & Appraisements, 1826–1927*; Author: *Arkansas. Probate Court (Hempstead County)*; Probate Place: *Hempstead, Arkansas*.

5. Peggy S. Lloyd, "The Howard County Race Riot of 1883," *Arkansas Historical Quarterly* 59, no. 4 (2000): 355, https://doi.org/10.2307/40023190.

6. Gaines Landing is in Chilcot County, Arkansas. Robert Patrick Bender, "Skirmish at Gaines' Landing," *Encyclopedia of Arkansas*, October 6, 2020, https://encyclopediaofarkansas.net/entries/skirmish-at-gaines-landing-6663/ .

7. "Hernando de Soto: North American Journey," Georgia Historical Society, https://georgiahistory.com/education-outreach/online-exhibits/featured-historical-figures/hernando-de-soto/north-american-journey./

8. United States Works Projects Administration, *Slave Narratives: A Folk History of Slavery in the United States from Interviews with Former Slaves, Arkansas Narratives*, Kindle edition, Kindle locations 1170–1184. Hereafter *WPA Narratives (Arkansas Part 6)*.

9. Regarding Hernando de Soto's travels through Arkansas, which is most of what Samuels also chronicles, see Jeffrey M. Mitchen, "Hernando de Soto (1500?–1542)," *Encyclopedia of Arkansas*, January 13, 2017, https://encyclopediaofarkansas.net/entries/hernando-de-soto-1770/.

10. Hernando de Soto is believed by historians to have died from a fever on May 21, 1542, and buried in the Mississippi River. "Hernando de Soto: North American

Journey," Georgia Historical Society, https://georgiahistory.com/education-outreach/online-exhibits/featured-historical-figures/hernando-de-soto/north-american-journey/.

11. Boiling Springs is in Pope County, Arkansas. "Boiling Springs, Arkansas," *Go Historic*, April 23, 2022, gohistoric.com/places/55763-boiling-springs-arkansas.

12. Bob Samuels believes she eventually returned to Spain. *WPA Narratives (Arkansas Part 6)*, 1170–1184.

13. Regarding Blacks and Atlantic creoles of mixed race in the expeditions of Hernando De Soto see Matthew Restall, "Black Conquistadors: Armed Africans in Early Spanish America," *Americas* 57, no. 2 (2000): 171–205, https://doi:10.1353/tam.2000.0015; and Jane Landers, "Africans in the Spanish Colonies" *Historical Archaeology* 31, no. 1 (1997): 84–103, http://www.jstor.org/stable/25616520.

14. See, for example, H. Terry Childs and Charles H. McNutt, "Hernando de Soto's Route from Chicaca through Northeast Arkansas: A Suggestion," *Southeastern Archaeology* 28, no. 2 (2009): 165–83, http://www.jstor.org/stable/40713517; John R. Swanton, "Hernando De Soto's Route through Arkansas," *American Antiquity* 18, no. 2 (1952): 156–62, https://doi.org/10.2307/276540; and Jeffrey M. Mitchem, "The Parkin Site: Hernando de Soto in Cross County, Arkansas," *Central States Archaeological Journal* 46, no. 4 (1999): 164–65, http://www.jstor.org/stable/43144187.

15. *WPA Narratives (Arkansas Part 6)*, 1170–1184.

16. Gaines Landing, located at Chicot County, Arkansas, on the western bank of the Mississippi River. Don R. Simons, "Skirmish at Gaines' Landing (June 28, 1863)," *Encyclopedia of Arkansas*, July 13, 2022. https://encyclopediaofarkansas.net/entries/skirmish-at-gaines-landing-6938//.

17. The Arkansas River is a major tributary of the Mississippi River, and the sixth longest river in the United States. It traverses Arkansas, Oklahoma, Kansas, and Colorado. "History along the Arkansas River," *Legends of America*, December 2021, https://www.legendsofamerica.com/arkansas-river/.

18. Boiling Springs is in Pope County, Arkansas. "Boiling Springs Arkansas," *Go Historic*, gohistoric.com/places/55763-boiling-springs-arkansas.

19. The Ouachita River flows southeasterly through Arkansas into Louisiana. Arkadelphia is located on this river. It is the twenty-fifth longest river in the United States "Ouachita River," LakeOuachita.org, https://lakeouachita.org/ouachita-river/.

20. The Little Missouri River runs from the Ouachita Mountains southwesterly in Arkansas. Little Missouri River, Arkansas: The Natural State, https://www.arkansas.com/mena/outdoors-nature/little-missouri-river.

21. Wallaceburg is a hamlet in Hempstead County, Arkansas. David Sesser, "Wallaceburg, Hempstead County," *Encyclopedia of Arkansas*, November 20, 2020, https://encyclopediaofarkansas.net/entries/wallaceburg-hempstead-county-11382/.

22. Indian mounds in the area that have been located include, but are not exclusive to Mississippi County, Arkansas, Red River Parish, Louisiana, and Cherokee County, Texas. Ann M. Early, "Prehistoric Caddo," *Encyclopedia of Arkansas,* May 2, 2012, https://encyclopediaofarkansas.net/entries/prehistoric-caddo-548/; "Indian Mounds," *Encyclopedia of Arkansas,* August 28, 2020 https://encyclopediaofarkansas.net/entries/indian-mounds-573/; John Hedgecock, "Hernando de Soto vs the Tula Indians of Arkansas, *Central States Archaeological Journal* 45, no. 3 (1998): 118–19, http://www.jstor.org/stable/43144159.

The remainder of Bob's recollections regarding these travels include:

> Then they traveled on a trail from there to Washington turned into Washington and took a trail toward They crossed Little River at Ward's Ferry and crossed the Saline river. Traveling northwest they reached White Oak shoals where Indexis now and crossed over into what was Mexico and traveled to a place called Kawaki located where now is. After camping here for a while they came back into Arkansas to some point near Rando, crossed Red River at Dooley's Ferry, went to Coola Fabra(?) and back to Boiling Springs. [Here a gold mine was found and a quarrel ensued, and in a fight De Soto was killed] They carried his body overland and buried him in the Mississippi River between Grensville . . . and Vicksburg. Columbus and turned off to the right (Uncle Bob not sure of the name of this trail) and crossed what is known as Beard's Lake.

I was able to identify all these locations except "Kawaki" and "Coola Fabra." *WPA Narratives (Arkansas Pt. 6)*, 1170–1184.

23. Ibid.
24. Ibid.
25. Ibid.
26. Ibid.
27. Ibid.
28. David Block. *Eighth Census of the United States 1860—Slave Schedules*; Series Number: *M653*; Record Group: *Records of the Bureau of the Census*; Record Group Number: *29*.
29. See note 4 in this chapter.
30. *WPA Narratives (Arkansas Part 6)*, 1170–1184.
31. Record of Richard P. Samuels and Mary Ellen Harris, *Arkansas, U.S., Compiled Marriages, 1851–1900*, https://www.ancestrylibrary.com/discoveryui-content/view/778087:2548?tid=&pid=&queryId=6f47103b170487876f15685ff46ca01c&_phsrc=BHW392&_phstart=successSource.
32. Regarding freed people in Reconstruction and Jim Crow Arkansas, see Bobby L. Lovett, "African Americans, Civil War, and Aftermath in Arkansas," *Arkansas Historical Quarterly* 54, no. 3 (1995): 304–58, http://www.jstor.org/stable/40030945; Horace Nash, "Blacks in Arkansas during Reconstruction: The Ex-Slave Narratives," *Arkansas Historical Quarterly* 48, no. 3 (1989): 243–59, https://doi.org/10.2307/40022474; Chris W. Branam "'The Africans Have Taken Arkansas': Political Activities of African Americans in the Reconstruction Legislature," *Arkansas Historical Quarterly* 73, no. 3 (2014): 233–67, http://www.jstor.org/stable/24477452.
33. Lovett, "African Americans, Civil War, and Aftermath in Arkansas," 333.
34. R. G. Samuels in the 1940 US Federal Census. R. G. Samuels; Year: *1940*; Census Place: *Ozan, Hempstead, Arkansas*; Roll: *m-t0627-00140*; Page: *16B*; Enumeration District: *29-21*.
35. Richard Samuels did break away from the other four Black Republican lawmakers when he became part of the faction known as the Liberal Republicans. Lovett, "African Americans, Civil War, and Aftermath in Arkansas," 333–38; *Freedom's Lawmakers.*Eric Foner, ed., *A Directory of Black Officeholders during Reconstruction*, rev. ed. (Baton Rouge: Louisiana State University Press, 1996); Fay Hempstead,

A Pictoral History of Arkansas, up to 1890 (New York: N.D. Thompson, 1890), 603; Branam, "The Africans Have Taken Arkansas," 235–46.

36. Lovett, "African Americans, Civil War, and Aftermath in Arkansas," 342.

37. Richard Samuels served as County Clerk of Hempstead County, Arkansas from 1872 to 1874. "County Officers" (Hempstead County, Arkansas), Hempstead County Historical Society, https://hcb.wildapricot.org/County-Officers.

38. Record of Richard Samuels, May 25, 1896. United States, Bureau of Land Management. *Arkansas, U.S., Homestead and Cash Entry Patents, Pre-1908*, https://www.ancestrylibrary.com/discoveryui-content/view/21905:2070?tid=&pid=&queryId=f96cf1f8d4b0228785cb723cc5407504&_phsrc=BHW393&_phstart=successSource.

39. Record of Robert Samuels and Sarah Paxton. *Arkansas, U.S., County Marriages Index, 1837–1957*, https://www.ancestrylibrary.com/discoveryui-content/view/691670:2548?tid=&pid=&queryId=b73d85af2a4ac4bcb7174b09c468b499&_phsrc=BHW394&_phstart=successSource.

40. Robt G. Samuels; Year: *1880*; Census Place: *Ozan, Hempstead, Arkansas*; Roll: *46*; Page: *496B*; Enumeration District: *112*.

41. Robt G. Samuels, Year: *1900*; Census Place: *Ozan, Hempstead, Arkansas*; Roll: *60*; Page: *13*; Enumeration District: *0049*; FHL microfilm: *1240060*.

42. Lovett, "African Americans, Civil War, and Aftermath in Arkansas," 353–54.

43. "All Public Member Trees results for Emanuel O. Samuels," https://www.ancestry.com/search/collections/1030/?name=Emanuel+O._Samuels&birth=_Arkansas&father=Robert&mother=Sarah.

44. Bob and Sarah owned their farm, or at least did so by the turn of the century. Robt G. Samuels'; Year: *1900*; Census Place: *Ozan, Hempstead, Arkansas*; Roll: *60*; Page: *13*; Enumeration District: *0049*; FHL microfilm: *1240060*.

45. Lovett, "African Americans, Civil War, and Aftermath in Arkansas," 338; Brent E. Riffell, "Lynching," *Encyclopedia of Arkansas*, June 14, 2022. https://encyclopediaofarkansas.net/entries/lynching-346/.

46. Peggy S. Lloyd, "The Howard County Race Riot of 1883," *Arkansas Historical Quarterly* 59, no. 4 (winter, 2000), 354.

47. Lloyd, "The Howard County Race Riot of 1883," 353–87, passim.

48. Record of R. H. Samuels and Nannie Richman. *Texas, U.S., Select County Marriage Index, 1837–1965*, https://www.ancestrylibrary.com/discoveryui-content/view/2128479:60183?tid=&pid=&queryId=41101dedc5c25d87a9ff509d09574ddd&_phsrc=BHW396&_phstart=successSource.

49. Izadore D. Benson, Year: *1920*; Census Place: *Union, Jackson, Arkansas*; Roll: *T625_66*; Page: *30A*; Enumeration District: *71*.

50. Ella [Lela] Samuels, "Lawson-Harrison Family Tree," https://www.ancestry.com/family-tree/person/tree/53273068/person/13493804871/facts.

51. Lucy Hamilton; Year: *1920*; Census Place: *Ozan, Hempstead, Arkansas*; Roll: *T625_64*; Page: *25A*; Enumeration District: *103*.

52. Record of James Hamilton, National Archives at College Park; College Park, Maryland; Record Group Title: *Records of the Office of the Quartermaster General, 1774–1985*; Record Group Number: *92*; Roll or Box Number: *6*.

53. Record of Lillian Turner, Arkansas Department of Vital Records; Little Rock, Arkansas; *Death Certificates*; Year: *1919*; Roll: *2*.

54. It is indicated in the 1940 census that Bob Samuels's grandson, J. Lillian Turner, was employed as a farm worker on his grandfather's family farm. He is listed as an "unpaid family worker." He had completed six years of formal education. J. Lillian Turner; Year: *1940*; Census Place: *Ozan, Hempstead, Arkansas*; Roll: *m-t0627-00140*; Page: *16B*; Enumeration District: *29-21*.

So, too, was his brother, Howard. He had completed eight years of formal education. Howard Turner; Year: *1940*; Census Place: *Ozan, Hempstead, Arkansas*; Roll: *m-t0627-00140*; Page: *16B*; Enumeration District: *29-2*.

55. Record of Leila B. Samuels and Joe Armstrong, *Arkansas, U.S., County Marriages Index, 1837–1957*, https://www.ancestrylibrary.com/discoveryui-content/view/3124323:2548?tid=&pid=&queryId=6ec4ef41fa305e623d5e99972f0d55e7&_phsrc=BHW398&_phstart=successSource.

56. [B]obbie Samuels and Warren Wise, *Arkansas, U.S., County Marriages Index, 1837–1957*, https://www.ancestrylibrary.com/discoveryui-content/view/3288819:2548?tid=&pid=&queryId=64ee771d6397b333f1a98c937241fa38&_phsrc=BHW400&_phstart=successSource.

57. Sarah Samuels; Year: *1930*; Census Place: *Ozan, Hempstead, Arkansas*; Page: *8B*; Enumeration District: *0020*; FHL microfilm: *2339811*.

58. Ibid. John Samuels; Year: *1930*; Census Place: *Ozan, Hempstead, Arkansas*; Page: *8B*; Enumeration District: *0020*; FHL microfilm: *233981*.

59. Sarah J. Paxton Samuels, Arkansas Department of Vital Records; Little Rock, Arkansas; *Death Certificates*; Year: *1933*; Roll: *1*.

60. Record of Warren and Bobbie Wise, Arkansas Department of Vital Records; Little Rock, Arkansas; *Divorces*; Year: *1939*; Film Number: *2*.

61. Bobbie G. Samuel Wise. Arkansas Department of Vital Records; Little Rock, Arkansas; *Death Certificates*; Year: *1956*; Roll: *2*.

62. Robert Samuels, Arkansas Department of Vital Records; Little Rock, Arkansas; *Death Certificates*; Year: *1941*; Roll: *1*.

63. Henry L. Harden, Social Security Administration; Washington DC; *Social Security Death Index, Master File*. Henry Hardin; Year: *1940*; Census Place: *Corinth, Alcorn, Mississippi*; Roll: *m-t0627-02006*; Page: *8B*; Enumeration District: *2-4*.

64. Lucy Jefferson, Social Security Administration; Washington DC; *Social Security Death Index, Master File*.

65. Phillis Wheatley, "To the Right Honorable William, Earl of Dartmouth, His Majesty's Principal Secretary of State for North-America, Etc.,'" from *Poems on Various Subjects, Religious and Moral* (Walpole, NH: Thomas and Thomas, 1802), 50–51, as found on "To the Right and Honorable William, Earl of Dartmouth . . . ," Massachusetts Historical Society, 2022, https://www.masshist.org/database/821.

Index

abolition/abolitionists, 166; emancipation, 282–99; gradual international adoption of, 194; laws for, 169–70; Miles, M., as, 191; organizations, 168, 369n258; in state constitutions, 169
abortion, 267
Abbott, James, 228–29
absent black fathers, 3, 9, *10*, 23
Adahoonzou, 43
Adams, Eliza, 223
Adams, John, 32
Adams, Samuel, 242
Adams, Simon, 223
Adams, Victoria, 204
adultery: African marriages and, 49; Akan marriages and, 56; of Bibb, M., 191; of Igbo, 42, 43–44; Igbo marriages and, 58; polygamy and, 49; by priest, 140; in slave marriages, 216; Yoruba marriages and, 60
AFDC. *See* Aid to Families with Dependent Children
Africa: after emancipation, 295; slaves and slavery in before Atlantic trade, 41–44; slave trade to the Americas, 44–47, *56*. *See also specific locations, groups, and topics*
The African Background Outlined (Woodson), 15
African King, of Kongo, 124
African marriage, 47–63; of Ashanti, 55–57; of Fula, 50–53; of Igbo, 57–59; of Kongo, 62–63; of Mende, 53–55; of Poro, 54–55; of Sande, 53–55; in Senegambia, 50–53, *52*; of Serer, 50–53; of Temme, 53–55; of Wolof, 50–53; of Yoruba, 59–62, *61*
After Freedom (Powdermaker), 18
agency, of slaves, 22
Aid to Families with Dependent Children (AFDC), 4
Akan: freedom suit of, 169; marriages of, 55–57; naming practices of, 268; slave families of, 92, 93, 95, 96; in slave revolts, 156. *See also* Coromantees
Akan Queenmother *(ohemmaa)*, 55–56
Albert, James (Ukawsaw Gronniosaw), 42, 58–59
alcoholism: of Keckley's husband, 214; of rapists, 140; of slave children, 223
Alford, Deleso, 27
Allen, Daisy, 298
Allen, Josephine, 398n64
Allen, Walter, 8, 324n23
Ambundu, 82
American colonies: resistance in, 129–81; slave codes of, 96–117; slave

families in, 79–128; slave housing in, 118–23, *121*, *122*; slave labor in, 117–18; slave populations in, 84–91, *86*; slave recreation in, 123–26, *125*; slavery in, *80*, *83*
American Convention for Promoting the Abolition of Slavery, 369n258
An American Dilemma (Myrdal), 17
American Revolution: British colonies in, 165–66; fugitive slaves in, 160–75; resistance and, 160–75; spies in, 172
American Weekly Mercury, 133–34
Ames, Mary, 229, 232
Amistad (slave ship), 64, 74
ancestors: African marriages and, 48, 49; Igbo marriages and, 58–59
Anderson, Josephine, 209, 290
Anderson, Rod, *10*
Andry, Manuel, 158
Anglicanism, 82–83
Angola: Atlantic slave trade from, 44; Portuguese slave traders in, 82; slave families of, 94, 95, 96
antebellum period: courtship in, 202–7; domestic slave trade in, 36; elderly in, 270–71; food in, 263–70; medical care in, 263–70; procreation in, 197–202; religion in, 254–63; resistance in, 246–54; Samuels, Robert, in, 302; slave families in, 219–71; slave housing in, 247–50, *248*, *249*, *251*; slave marriage in, 185–217
Antelope (slave ship), 340n168
Antrobus, John, *280*
Apteker, Herbert, 149
Armistead, James, 172
Arnold, Benedict, 172
Ar'n't I a Woman? (White), 24
Arons, Charlie, 224
arson, for resistance, 139–41
Ashanti: African marriages of, 55–57; hard labor effects of, 274
Ashley, John, 169

Atlanta University Conference for the Study of Negro Problems (AU Conference), 13–14
Atlantic slave trade: African marriages before, 47–63; to Americas, 44–47, *46*; continued activity after legal ending of, 168–69, 349n97; legal end to, 169, 349n97, 370n259; slavery in Africa before, 41–44; violent capture in, 63–70, *64*, 82. *See also* Middle Passage
The Atlantic Slave Trade (Curtin), 346n68
Attucks, Crispus, 160–61
AU Conference. *See* Atlanta University Conference for the Study of Negro Problems
Audubon, John James, 216
L'Aurore (slave ship), 143
Ayer, Charles, 222

Baby Mamas, 7
Bacchus, Josephine, 267
Bailey, Harriet, 229
Baker, Georgia, 266, 277
Ball, Charles, 137–38, *148*, 176–77, 215, 273, 274, 276
Bamana: fugitive slaves, 147; marriages of, 94; slave families of, 92
Bambara: slave families of, 94, 95; in slave revolts, 157; thefts by, 143
baptism, 97–98, 101, 105, 255; courtship at, 204; indentured servants and, 361n48; manumission and, 173
Bara, 349n99
Barbadian Act of 1661, 100
Barbados, mulattos in, 76
Barber, Charley, 93, 265
Barber, Millie, 263
Bartee, Robert, 116
basket names, 268
Bastide, Roger, 12
Baumfree, Isabella (Sojourner Truth), 135, 198, 201, 221–22, 271
Beard, C., 244–45

Beauregard, Monsieur, 173
Beckett, Harrison, 228, 294
Bellamy Mansion, 250, *251*
Bendy, Edgar, 233
Bennett, Herman, 90
Ben Solomon, Job (Ayuba Suleiman Diallo), 52, 53, 76, *77*; on Middle Passage, 76
Berlin, Ira, 26
Berry, Daina Ramey, 27, 29
Berry, Fanny, 227–28, 229, 258, 269, 290, 292
Besi, 349n99
Betts, Ellen, 211
Betts, Sidney, 211
Beyond the Melting Pot (Glazer), 14
Bibb, George Mortimer, 372n2
Bibb, Henry Watson, 185–88, *192*, *193*, 372n2; to Canada, 188, 191; Christianity of, 188, 190–91; courtship of, 206; as fugitive slave, 187, 188, 189–90, 191; marriage of, 187–95; sale of, 190, 191; slave families of, 189–91
Bibb, James, 185
Bibb, Malinda, 187–95, *192*; courtship of, 206
Bibb, Mary Frances, 189–91, *192*
Biddy, Mary, 286
Bight of Benin: Atlantic slave trade from, 44; Igbo from, 347n75; Mexico and, 345n54; slave families of, 95
Bight of Biafra, 93–94; Atlantic slave trade from, 44; Mexico and, 345n54; slave families of, 95
Binns, Arrie, 204–5
Binns, Franklin, 204–5
bipolar disorder, 223
birth rates, of minorities, 7
Biscoe, Mary Scott DeValls, 269
The Black Family in Slavery and Freedom (Gutman), 21, 23–24
Black Folk Then and Now (Du Bois), 15
Black Metropolis (Drake and Cayton), 17–18

Black Power movement, 22
Black Society in Spanish Florida (Landers), 27
A Black Women's History of the United States (Berry, D., and Gross), 27
Blassingame, John, 21, 22–23, 24
Block, Almadene, 302
Block, David, 302, 304–5, 403n4
Boas, Franz, 15
Boggs, Susan, 224
Bogie, Dan, 205
Bolton, James, 209, 211
Bond, Bunny, 292
Bond, Mrs. Ed, 289
Bond, Sam, 289
bondspeople: born from sexual abuse, 185–86; earnings of, 374n39; Equiano as, 114; food for, 263; Freedmen's Bureau for, 285–86; as fugitive slaves, 144–45; funerals for, 280; from Gold Coast, 93; killing of, 91; mulattos, 141; resurrection for, 276; slave codes and, 101; slave housing for, 121–22; in slave revolts, 157, 158–59; of Washington, G., 150, 171–72
bondswomen: fugitive slaves, 145; Igbo, 89; marriage of, 215; Samuels, M., as, 304–5; sexual abuse of, 240
Bornou, 42, 59
Boston Massacre, 160–61, *161*
Botume, Elizabeth, 206, 214, 224, 232; on naming practices, 268
Bound in Wedlock (Hunter, T.), 29
bounty hunters, marronage and, 150
Bradford, Gamaliel, 112–13
Bradley, William, 178–80, *179*
Brady, Wes, 232–33
Branch, Jacob, 235–36
Brandum, Robin, 172
Brasseaux, Carl, 98–99
"Breakup of Black Families Imperils Gains of Decades," 6
breastfeeding, 267
Breen, T. H., 81

Bremar, Eliza, 244
Bremar, F., 244
Bridges, Francis, 200–201
Brinch, Boyrereau: on Middle Passage, 71, 73, 75; violent capture of, 65–66
British abolitionists, in Canada, 166
British colonies, 85, 91, 107; in American Revolution, 165–66; mixed-race in, 108; mulattos in, 108; octoroon in, 108; quadroon in, 108; slave codes of, 99–104; slave families in, 94, 95–96, 353n158; slave housing in, 118, 120; slave revolts in, 157–58; zambo in, 108
British slave traders, 44, 46, 47, 73, 84
Brooks, Susan, 277
Broomstick Marriage Act, 377n121
broomstick weddings, *199*, 208–11, *210*, 217, 286, 287
Brown, Betty, 233
Brown, Charles, 293
Brown, Elizabeth, 202
Brown, James, *317*
Brown, Jenny, *317*
Brown, John, *317*
Brown, Mary Frances, 261
Brown, Michael, 7–8
Brown, Nancy, *317*
Brown, Peggy, *317*
Brown, Peter, 197
Brown, William, 161
Brown, William Wells, 202, 236
Brown v. Board of Education, 7, 21
Bruson, Vinnie, 281
Bryan, Celia, 241
Bryan, Jacob, 240
Buckminster, Joseph, 161
Bull, Hannah Beale, 134
Bull, William, 118
burials. *See* funerals
Burke, Elizabeth, 295–96
Burke, Emily, 264
Burr, Seymour, 167
Bush, Barbara, 26
Butler, Pierce, 177, 201

Byrd, Sam, Jr., 160
Byrd, Susie, 29
Byrd, William, 118–19

Cade, John B., 21, 29
Caden, Minty, 176
Caden, Philis, 176
Cameron, Paul, 248–49
Campbell, William, 237
Canada: Bibb, H. to, 188, 191; British abolitionists in, 166; emancipation in, 165; fugitive slaves in, 165–66, 181, 219–20; race riots in, 165; refugees in, 165–66; slave families to, 219–20
Cannon, Billy, 200
"Can the Children Be Saved?," 6
Canuet, Cecilia, 153
Cape Coast Castle, 46, 67, *68*
Carabali, slave families of, 95
Carillo, Juana, 98
Carter, Hill, 269
Carter, John, 104
Carter, John Tasker, 171
Carter, Landon, 147
Carter, Robert, III, 170–71
Carter, Robert "King," 104, 147
Cartwright, Samuel, 147
Casenave, Joseph, 173
casta system, of Spanish, 108
castles, 46, 65, 67, *68*
Catholicism, 82, 90, 97, 98–99; in antebellum period, 255, 256; communion in, 259; funerals in, 281–82; resistance and, 136; slave rejection of, 391n178; in Spanish colonies, 87, 196
Catnach, James, 377n121
Cavelier, Rene Robert, 345n51
Cayton, Horace R., 17–18
cemeteries, of slaves, 273–82, *279*
Chambers, Douglas, 346n68
Chandler, Thomas, *212*
Chaplin, Joyce, 117
Charles II (King), 88
Charpentier, Jacques, 133

Chessier, Betty Foreman, 209
Chicago Tribune, 4
"Childhood's End," 6
children: of Samuels, Robert, 306–8. *See also* slave children
Chinn, Julia, 242
Christianity, 78, 84; in antebellum period, 254–63; of Bibb, H., 188, 190–91; marriage and, 345n60; Muslims and, 259; patriarchy in, 389n175; resistance and, 136, 138–39; resurrection in, 276; in Sierra Leone, 166; slaveholder influence on, 260–62; in slave recreation, 126; of Spear, Chloe, 112–13; of Wheatley, P., 111. *See also* baptism; Catholicism; Protestants; Quakers
Christomo, Thomas, 89
Church, Lewis (Lymas), *311–12*
Cinque, 74
Civil Rights Act of 1964, 21
civil rights movement, 19–26
clans, 335n46; African marriages and, 49
Clark, Gus, 287
Clark, Lewis, 237, 265
Clark Hine, Darlene, 27
Clay, Berry, 197
Clay, Edward Williams, 219, *220*
Clay, Henry, 32
Clinton, Henry, 168
clitorectomy, 205–6
Clotilda (slave ship), 66–67
Cochrane, Alexander, 176
Code Noir, 97, 98, 196
Cody, Pierce, 197
coffins, 278–80, 282
Cole, Julia, 288
Coleman, Green, 217
Coleman, Lucy, 217
Coles, Charles, 282
A Colored Man's Reminiscences of James Madison (Jennings, P.), 28
Colquitt, Martha, 292
Colquitt, Sara, 203

Committee on Equal Employment Opportunity, 21
common-law marriage, 17
communion, 253; in Catholicism, 259
Conceiving Freedom (Cowling), 28
concubines, 98, 240–45; Bibb, M., as, 191; marriage to, 245; slave children of, 241–42; in Spanish colonies, 244
Congo, Manuel, 91
conjurers, 230–31; medical care by, 268
Conrad, George, 216, 231
Cornwallis, Charles, 172
Coromantees, 93, 349n99; in slave revolts, 156
Cosby, Bill, 7
Cosby Show, 7
The Cotton Pickers (Homer, W.), *195*
courtship, in antebellum period, 202–7
Cowling, Camilla, 28
"Crack Babies," 6
Craig, Caleb, 224
Craven, Jackson, 297
Creoly, Jan, 91
critical fabulation, 29
Cross, Cheyney, 233, 265
cross-cousins: in Kongo African marriages, 62; in Senegabia African marriages, 52
Cruze, Rachel, 280
Cugoano, Ottobah, 67–68
Cullen, Anne, 114
Cullen, Susan, 114
cultural deprivation, 324n21
cultural deviance, 8, 324n23
cultural equivalence, 8, 324n23
cultural relativism theory, 15
cultural variance, 8, 324n23
culture of poverty, 18–19, 21
Cumby, Green, 215
Cunningham, Dinah, 258
Curlett, Betty, 290
Curtin, Philip, 346n68

Da Costa, Emilia Viotti, 12
Daniel, Matilda Pugh, 208

D'Auseville, Councillor, 172
Davenport, Carey, 232
Davidson, Elige, 201
Davis, Angela, 24
Davis, Campbell, 232, 235, 236
Davis, Carrie, 263, 264
Davis, Charles, 287
Davis, Philip, 170
Dawkins, Elias, 229
The Dawn of Freedom (Miles, T.), 27–28
Dawson, Molly, 204, 207, 215
day names, 268
Deagan, Kathleen, 89
Deetz, James, 119
De India y Zambiago, Albarazado, 109
DeLancy, Peter, 102
democracy, in slavery, 23
depression, 223
Derricotte, Ike, 289
de Soto, Hernando, 87, 302–3
Deutsch, Barry, *11*
Deveau, James, 144
Diallo, Ayuba Suleiman (Job Ben Solomon), 52, 53, *77*; on Middle Passage, 76
Digges, Elizabeth, 104
Diouf, Sylvianne, 136
disabled slaves, 235
Dismal Swamp Canal Company, 150–51
Dispossessed Lives (Fuentes), 28
divorce: in African marriages, 52–53; in Akan African marriages, 55; in Kongo African marriages, 63; in slaveholding families, 245
Dixon, Emily, 258
DNA analysis, 223, 346n68
Documents Illustrative of the Slave Trade to the Americas (Donnan), 346n68
domestic slave trade: in antebellum period, 36; reenslavement in, 174; of slave families, 221–22
Donnan, Elizabeth, 346n68

Douglass, Frederick, 116, 229
Douglass, Sarah, 260
Dowd, Maureen, 3
dowry: for Diallo, 52–53; in Igbo marriages, 57–58
Drake, St. Claire, 17–18
drapetomania, 147, 363n127
"Dressing forb Carnival" (Homer, W.), *125*
dropout rate, 7
Du Bois, W. E. B., 13, 14, 15
Duchon, Victor, 256
Dudrian, 349n99
Dukes, Willis, 287
Dunbar, Erica Nelson, 28
Dunham, Ann, 2, 3
Dunmore, Lord (John Murray), 161–62, 164, 176
Dunn, Richard, 27
Durant, Sylvia, 290, 292
Dutch colonies, 85, 90–91; religion in, 138; slave families of, 96; slave housing in, 120; slave recreation in, 124
Dutch slave traders, 44, 46, 47
Dykstra, Robert, 25
dysfunctional black families, 3; civil rights movement and, 19–26; compared with other groups, 325n24; Cosby on, 7; cultural deviance/variance of, 8; Moynihan Report on, 8–13, 22; slavery and, 8–13, 21–26; welfare queen of, 5–6

Eden, Bun, 240
Edings, Benjamin, 163
Edmondson, Emily Catherine, 238–39, 385n104
Edmondson, Mary Jane, 238–39, 385n104
Edwards, Minerva, 288
Efik, slave families of, 95
elderly slaves, 50; in antebellum period, 270–71; funerals and, 278; manumission of, 170; sale of, 98,

222; slave children and, 230; work by, 118. *See also* grandfathers; grandmothers
Eliason, Armistead C., 240
Elkins, Stanley, 12–13
Eltis, David, 103, 346n68, 348n82
emancipation, 282–99; in Canada, 165; families after, 284–85, 293; grandmothers after, 284; marriage after, 286–94, *291*, *295*; Samuels, Richard, after, 305; slave families after, 295–96. *See also* fugitive slaves
Embers, Hannah, 222
Encyclopedia of Black Women in America (Clark Hine and Penn), 27
endogamy, 50
Enslaved Women in America (Berry, D., and Alford), 27
Equiano, Olaudah, 43–44, 46, 47–48; on Igbo marriages, 57–59; on Middle Passage, 71–76; violent capture of, 68–69
Estavanico (Esteban the Moor), 89
Estes, Mary, 235
eugenics, 7
Evans, Eliza, 65, 211
Everett, Louisa, 202
Everett, Sam, 202
Ewe-Yoruba, 94
Ewing, Matthew, 258
Executive Order 10925, 21
exogamy, 50

Falconbridge, Alexander, 71, 72, 73
families: after emancipation, 284–85, 293; of Samuels, Robert, 301–8. *See also* dysfunctional black families; nuclear families; slave families
Farmer, Lizzie, 203
fathers: absence of, 3, 9, *10*, 23; discipline by, 232; after emancipation, 294; naming practices for, 2698; patrilineal societies, 92, 335n46; present, 23; restricted time with children by masters, 231; separated from slave families, 221, 223–24; in slave families, 221, 223–24, 231–32; as teachers, 232. *See also* patriarchy; *specific individuals*
female genital surgeries, 205–6
Ferguson, Leland, 121
Finding Charity's Folk (Millward), 27
Fitch, Timothy, 46, 73–74
Fito, Francis Phelipe, 116
Fitzpatrick, Sarah, 277
Five Families (Lewis, O.), 18
flat foot dance, 203
Flogging a Slave Fastened to the Ground (Mason, G.), *132*
Flowerdew Hundred, 82
Folkes, Minnie, 205, 206, 262
Fon-Ewe, 348n89; slave families of, 94
food: of Akan, 56; in antebellum period, 263–70; gardens for, 264–65; on Middle Passage, 71–72; of Poro, 54; of slaves, 121
food stamps, 2, 3
Forbes, John, 88
Ford, Sarah, 200
Foreman, Betty, 247–48
Fort Mosé (Gracia Real de Santa Teresa de Mosé), 87–89, 95
Fortune (slave ship), 84
Fortune, Rose, *180*, 180–81
Franklin, Benjamin, 111
Franks, Dora, 277, 285, 298
Frazier, E. Franklin, 14–18, 24
Frazier, Julia, 252
free blacks: elderly as, 271; emancipation and, 282–99; Miles, M., as, 191; slave families and, 174–75; slave trade of, 304; in Trinidad, 177; in War of 1812, 175–77. *See also* abolition/abolitionists; manumission
Freedmen Aid, 399n66
Freedmen's Bureau, 217, 223, 285–86, 297, 399n66
French colonies: bondspeople of, 101; colonies of, 85–87; failed attempt

at, 345n51; marronage in, 154; of Native Americans, 108; Negro Diocou in, 172; slave codes of, 97, 98–99; slave families of, 94; slave housing in, 120; slave recreation in, 125; slaves in, 195–96; white-on-black violence in, 131–33
French slave traders, 44, 46
Freyre, Gilberto, 12
Fuentes, Marissa, 28
fugitive slaves (refugees): advertisements for, 143, *146*, 147, 163, *179*; in American Revolution, 160–75; Bibb, H., as, 187, 188, 189–90, 191; at Boston Massacre, 160–61; in Canada, 165–66, 181, 219–20; from Carter, J. T., 170–71; drapetomania and, 147, 363n127; in Great Dismal Swamp, *130*, 144, 149–51; marronage of, 148–55; murder of, 148; Native American apprehension by, 151; punishment of, 147–48; slave families and, 144–45, 147, 219–20; in slave revolts, 158; in Spanish colonies, 152
Fula, 333n4; African marriages of, 50–53; Muslims, 47
funerals (burials): of Akan, 55; in Catholicism, 281–82; jazz, 281; of slaves, 156, 273–82, *274*, *280*
Furman v. Miller, 73
Furro, Broteer (Venture Smith), 46, 49; violent capture of, 64–65
Furro, Saugum, 64–65

Ga, 93. *See also* Coromantees
Gaffney, Mary, 277
Gambia, 95; Atlantic slave trade from, 44. *See also* Wheatley, Phillis
gardens, 264–65
Garlic, Delia, 236–37, 293–94
Garner, Margaret, 219–20
Garner, Robert, 219–20
Garrett, William, 222
Garrido, Juan, 87

Garrison, Madison, 190
Gates, Henry Louis, Jr., as Wolof, 333n2
Geggus, David, 346n68
Genovese, Elizabeth Fox, 24
Genovese, Eugene, 21, 23, 24
Gerald, Henry, 236
Gibbons, Joseph, 143
Gibbons, Sarah, 163
Gibbs, Georgianna, 209
Gilchrist, John, 116
Gill, Frank, 265
Gilliard, Jim, 208
Givin, Henry, *314*
Glazer, Nathan, 14–15
Godfrey, Abigail, 114, 162, *309*
Godfrey, Betsey, 162, *309*
Godfrey, Bridget, 114, 162, *311*
Godfrey, Bristol, *316*
Godfrey, China (Jane), 162, *316*
Godfrey, Edward, *316*
Godfrey, Elizabeth, 162, *309*
Godfrey, Hannah, *315*, *316*
Godfrey, Hester, 181
Godfrey, Isaac, 181
Godfrey, Jeffrey, 162, *309*
Godfrey, Jenny, 162
Godfrey, John, 114, *315*
Godfrey, Kate, 162, *311*, *315*
Godfrey, Kezia, 115
Godfrey, Lettius, 115, *314*
Godfrey, Lucy, 162, *312*
Godfrey, Matthew, 114, 115, 162
Godfrey, Ned, 162, *309*, *314*
Godfrey, Ned, Jr., *310*
Godfrey, Nelly, 162
Godfrey, Petter, *315*
Godfrey, Pleasant, 115, 116, *314*
Godfrey, Polly, *315*
Godfrey, Port, 162, *312*
Godfrey, Sally, *315*
Godfrey, Sam, 162, *312*
Godfrey, Sarah, 114, *312*
Godfrey, Sucky, *313*
Godfrey, Valentine, *316*

Godfrey, William, *313*
Godwin, Morgan, 126
Gold Coast, 45, 46, 348n89; African marriages in, 49; bondspersons from, 93; Mexico and, 345n54; slave families of, 93–94, 95
Gomez, Michael, 346n68
Gonzalez, Juan, 87
Goodwin, Richard, 328n90
Gordon, C. W. B., 284
Gracia Real de Santa Teresa de Mosé (Fort Mosé), 87–89, 95
Gragston, Arnold, 198
grandfathers: funeral for, 280–81; in slave families, 232. *See also specific individuals*
grandmothers: after emancipation, 284; medical care by, 266; naming practices for, 268; of Samuels, Robert, 301, 302–3, 304; in slave families, 229–30. *See also specific individuals*
Grandy, Charles, 200, 208
Grandy, Moses, 234, 235
Grathan, Nancy, 239
Graves, Mildred, 287
Graweere, John, 84
Graxales, Pedro, 89
Great Awakenings, 138–39
Great Dismal Swamp, *130*, 144, 149–51
Great Migration, 9
Green, Alice, 261
Green, Arthur, 293
Gresham, Harriet, 292
Greyhound (slave ship), 77–78
Gronniosaw, Ukawsaw (James Albert), 42, 58–59
Gross, Kali, 27
Grubb, Minerva, 258
Guinea: Atlantic slave trade from, 44; fugitive slaves, 144; Mexico and, 345n54
Guinea Bissau, 44
Gullah, 151–52, 268
Guro, slave families of, 95

Guthrie, Mary, 142
Gutman, Herbert, 21, 23–24
Gwin, Peter, 73

Hadnot, Mandy, 288
Haitian Revolution, 155, 242
Hall, Basil, 201
Hall, Felix, 193
Hall, Gabriel, 177, *178*
Hamilton, James, 307
Hampton, Wade, 252
Hannibal (slave ship), 73–74
Hardin, Henry, 308
Hardy, George H., 240
Harris, Caroline, 209
Harris, Jane, 217
Harris, Leslie, 90
Harris, Thomas, 217
Hartman, Saidiya, 29
Hausa, 42; Gronniosaw and, 58–59
Help Me to Find My People (Williams, H.), 28–29
Hemings, Elizabeth, 240
Hemings, Sally, 240–41
The Hemings of Monticello (Reed), 28
Henderson, Julia, 217
Henderson, Thomas, 217
Henry, Ida, 211
Herndon, Elizabeth, 210
Herndon, Exeter, 284–85
Herndon, George, 210
Herndon, Temple, 284–85, 298
Herskovits, Melville J., 16–17
Higginson, Thomas Wentworth, 231–32, 294
Higman, B. W., 25–26, 331n120
Hilton, Anne, 62
Hispaniola, 90
Hita, Maria de la Concepcion, 89
Hodell, Rody, 279
Hoffman, Frederick L., 13–14
Holden, Vanessa, 28
Homer, Bill, 213
Homer, Winslow, *125*, *195*
homosexuality, 192–93

hoodoo, 136, 262
Hooks, Rebecca, 266
Horn, Hazel, 301–2, 304
Horn, Molly, 290, 292
housing. *See* slave housing
Howard, Sarah J. Paxton, 306
Hullett (Captain), 116
Hunter, Caroline, 261
Hunter, Tera, 29

Ibn Said, Omar, 136, *137*
Ibrahima, Abdula Rahman, 259–60
Ibrahima Ibn Sori, Abdurahman, 30–32, 47
Igbo, 348n76, 348n92; adultery of, 42, 43–44; African marriages of, 57–59; from Bight of Benin, 347n75; bondswoman, 89; marriages of, 94; naming practices of, 268; slave families of, 93–94, 95, 96; yam festivals of, 138
incest, 240
indentured servants: baptism and, 361n48; in British colonies, 107; with fugitive slaves, 147
"The Indians and Negroes Massacreing the Whites in Florida," *196*
indigenous peoples. *See* Native Americans
indio, 89
Innes, Stephen, 81
Islam. *See* Muslims
Ivory Coast, 45, 95; Atlantic slave trade from, 44

Jacinto Rodriguez, Juan, 89
Jackson, Andrew, 147
Jackson, Mildred, 185
Jackson, Odee, 267
Jackson, Silas, 263
Jacobs, Harriet, 198, 241, 277, 282
James, James C., 242
James, John, 229
Javier, Francisco, 89
jazz funerals, 281

Jefferson, Lucy, 307
Jefferson, Thomas, 121; in American Revolution, 163; concubine of, 240; Hemings, S., and, 240–41
Jefferson, Vivian, 307
Jeffries, Isaiah, 255
Jelineau, Francis, 242–43, 245
Jennings, Edmond, 95
Jennings, Paul, 28
Jennison, Nathaniel, 170
Jezebel stereotype, 24, 329n112
Jim Crow, 9; Samuels, Robert, in, 303
Johnson, Anthony, 83–84, 101
Johnson, Ben, 213–14
Johnson, Charles S., 17, 18
Johnson, Jessica Marie, 28
Johnson, Lyndon, 19–20, *20*, 328n90
Johnson, Mary, 83–84, 101
Johnson, Nellie, 239–40
Johnson, Richard Mentor, 242
Johnson, William, 250, 276
Johnstone, Abraham, 126–28
Jones, Bill, 288, 290–91
Jones, Hannah, 212
Jones, Harriet, 290–91
Jones, Jacqueline, 24, 389n175
Jones, John, 144
Jones, Lewis, 277
Jones, Liza, 288
Jones, Marse, 201–2
Jordon, Lucindy, 204
Journal of Negro History, 15, 21
Judge, Ona, 28
jump the broomstick weddings, *199*, 208–11, *210*, 217, 286, 287

kanda, 62
Keckley, Elizabeth, 208, 211–12, 214, 221, 235, *238*; on religion, 261; sexual abuse to, 237
Kelley, Jenny, *311*
Kelley, Moses, *311*
Kelly, Rebecca, 242
Kemble, Frances, 201, 262; on elderly, 271

Kennedy, Hamp, 252
Kennedy, Johnson, 21
Kimbundu, 82–83; on *São João Bautista*, 341n2
King, Boston, 164–65, 368n236; in Sierra Leone, 166
King, Charlie, 217
King, Sylvia, 72, 93, 201–2
King, Violet, 163, 166, 368n236
King, Wilma, 27
Kingsmill Plantation, 119
Kirby, Edmond, 210
Kissi (Kishee): fugitive slaves, 143; from Sierra Leone, 93; slave families of, 93
Kitchen Ball at White Sulphur Springs, Virginia (Mayer), *186*, 189
Kite, Joe, 219–20
Kongo: African King of, 124; African marriages of, 62–63; naming practices of, 268; religion of, 136; on *São João Bautista*, 341n2; slave families of, 92, 93, 95; in slave revolts, 157
Kossuala (Cudjo Lewis), 60, 69–70; on Middle Passage, 71; violent capture of, 66–67
Ku Klux Klan, 297
Kulikoff, Allan, 25, 26, 92, 95, 330n115, 346n68

Labor of Love, Labor of Sorrow (Jones, Jacqueline), 24
Lafayette, Marquis de, 172
Lafayette, Pierce, 193
Landers, Jane, 27, 87, 95, 116, 244
Lane, Lunsford, 206, 207, 232, 234; on food, 264; on slave housing, 250, 252
Larken, Julia, 289–90
Larken, Matthew, 289–90
Lawal, Babatunde, 60
Lawson, Dave, 269
Lee, Jane, 222
Le Jau, Francis, 105, 126, 138

Lester, Charles, 231
Lester, Dinah, 231
Levin, Josh, 4
Lewis, Cudjo. *See* Kossuala
Lewis, Daurene, 181
Lewis, Lucy, 134
Lewis, Oscar, 18–19
Liberia, 32; Atlantic slave trade from, 44
Life in Black and White (Stevenson), 25, 330n118
Limba, 349n99
Lincoln, Abraham, 283
Lisbon, *88*
literacy, 9
Little, K. L., 54
Little Coke, 152
Littlefield, Daniel, 106
Lloyd, Nellie, 203
Lobato, Bartholomé, 98
Louisiana Purchase, 194
Louisiana Slave Code, 98–99, 351n122
Louis XVI (King), 97
Love, Nat, 228, *229*

MacIntosh, Susan, 289, 292
Mack, Chaney, 232
Maddox, Jack, 240, 246
Maddox, Rose, 240
Madison, Ambrose, 139
Madrid, Maria, 89
Malone, Ann Patton, 330n114
Mammy stereotype, 3–4, 24, 329n112
Mandingo, 89; fugitive slaves, 143; slave families of, 94, 95; in slave revolts, 157. *See also* Wheatley, Phillis
Mandinka, 333n4; marriages of, 50–53
Manfra, Jo Ann, 25
Mansfield, Lord, 78
Manson, Jacob, 200, 240
manumission: of Carter, Robert, III, 170–71; of elderly slaves, 170; laws, 168, 169–70; in Louisiana Slave Code, 99, 351n122; in Spanish colonies, 168

Many Thousands Gone (Berlin), 26
marriage: of Bibb, H., 187–95; Christianity and, 345n60; common-law, 17; to concubines, 242, 245; after emancipation, 286–94, *291*, *295*; religion in, 262–63; of Samuels, Robert, 306; in Senegambia, 50–53, *52*; of Spear, Chloe, 113; of Wheatley, P., 111–12. *See also* African marriage; divorce; polygamy; slave marriage
The Marriage Act Displayed in Cuts and Verse (Catnach), 377n121
"Marriage Fixes Everything" (Deutsch), *11*
marronage, 148–55; bounty hunters and, 150; in French colonies, 154; mulattos in, 131; after slave revolts, 158
Marshall, Adeline, 232
Marshall, Alice, 254
Marshall, James, 306
Marston, Benjamin, 165–66
Martin, John Sella, 224, 241–42, 277
Martin, Josie, 205
Maryland Society for Promoting the Abolition of Slavery and for Relief of Poor Negroes and Others Unlawfully Held in Bondage, 369n258
Mason, Biddy, 222
Mason, Christopher, 107
Mason, George, *132*
matriarchy, 9, 15, 24, 331n120
matrifocality, 25–26
matrilineal societies, 92, 335n46; Samuels, Robert, from, 302
Matthews, Samuel, 85
Maul, Ben, 129, 137–38
Maverick, Samuel, 40
Maxwell, Malindy, 268, 280–81
Mayer, Christian Friedrich, *186*, 189
Mbala, slave families of, 93
Mbiti, John, 48, 360n42
McClain, "Big Jim," 202
McCree, Ed, 270, 288, 289

McCree, Nettie, 288, 289
McCullers, Henrietta, 254
McCullough, Willie, 197, 199–200
McDonald, Dedra, 93, 98, 102, 155–56
McFarland, Harriet, 208, 229; on slave housing, 247
McGillivray, Lachlan, 143
McIver, Roderick, 88
McKinney, Warren, 292
McQueen, Don Juan, 116–17
McWhorter, William, 270, 288
medical care: in antebellum period, 263–70; on Middle Passage, 70; for pregnancies, 267; for slaves, 100, 132–33, 187
Mende: African marriages of, 53–55; on Middle Passage, 74; religion of, 136, 254; of Sierra Leone, 49, 53, 63–64, 93; slave families of, 92, 93; violent capture of, 63–64
Menefee, Frank, 205
Menendez, Ana Maria, 89
Menéndez de Aviles, Pedro, 87
Mennonites, 168
The Merikians, 177
mestizaje, 108
mestizo, 89
Metcalf, Deborah, 140
Mexico: loss of territory by, 194; slaves in, 89–90, 345n54
Middle Passage, 70–78; deaths during, 73, 340n168; illnesses from, 81; suicides on, 71, 73, 75
Midlo Hall, Gwendolyn, 94–95, 107, 346n68, 347nn75–76
Miles, Mary Elizabeth, 191
Miles, Tiya, 27–28, 85–87
Miller, William, 148
Millward, Jessica, 27
Mina, slave families of, 94
Mitchell-Kernan, Claudia, 324n23
Mixon, John, 65, 211
Mondongo, 349n99
monogamy: in African marriages, 49–50; in slave marriages, 81

Monroe, James, 159
Montandon, James E., 240
Moore, Fannie, 256–57, 259
Moore, Julia, 201
Moran, Thomas, *130*
Moravians, as abolitionists, 168
Morgan, America, 235
Morgan, Isaam, 279
Morgan, Olivia, 233
Morgan, Philip, 26, 353n158
Mormons, 222
Morocco, 44, 89, 93
Morris, Lewis, 102
Morrissey, Marietta, 26
Morrow, John, 304
Moses, Patsy, 266
Moss, Andrew, 223, 245, 259–60
mothers: breastfeeding by, 267; food from, 263; matriarchy, 9, 15, 24, 331n120; matrifocality, 25–26; matrilineal societies, 92, 335n46; naming practices for, 268; nursing by, 55; religion and, 256–58; in slave families, 226–29, *229*. *See also specific individuals*
Moye, Calvin, 221, 270, 279
Moynihan, Daniel Patrick, 9, 21, 23–24, 325n25
Moynihan Report, 8–13, 21, 22
Moyo, 349n99
mulattos, 354n188, 403n4; in Barbados, 76; bondspeople, 141; in British colonies, 108; after emancipation, 296; fugitive slaves, 144; Maddox, J., and, 240, 246; manumission of, 172–73; in marronage, 131; Samuels, Robert, and, 306; slave marriage of, 143; in Spanish colonies, 89, 97
murder: of American Revolution soldier, 172; by conjurers, 231; of fugitive slaves, 148; of incestuous brother, 240; for resistance, 139–41; in slave marriages, 215; in slave revolts, 157; of slaves, 236

Murray, John (Lord Dunmore), 161–62, 164, 176
Muslims: Christianity and, 259; Fula, 47; marriage of, 52–53; on Middle Passage, 76; resistance and, 136; resurrection for, 276; slavery by, 42, 47; Spanish and, 87
Myrdal, Gunnar, 17
The Myth of the Negro Past (Herskovits), 16–17

NAACP, 14
naming practices, in slave families, 268
Naranjo, José, 155
A Narrative of the Most Remarkable Particulars in the Life of James Albert Ukawsaw Gronniosaw (Gronniosaw), 59
Native Americans (indigenous peoples): African marriages with, 107–8; family dysfunction of, 325n24; fugitive slave apprehensions by, 151; in Great Dismal Swamp, *130*, 144, 149–50; Seminoles, 150, 154–55, 195; slaves of, 195
Ndongo, 79, 82
Neal, Tom Wylie, 268
The Negro American Family (Du Bois), 13
Negro Diocou, 172
The Negro Family in America (Moynihan), 23–24, 325n25
The Negro Family in the United States (Frazier, E.), 14–15, 17
Never Caught (Dunbar), 28
New Jersey Society for Promoting the Abolition of Slavery, 369n258
Newsweek, 6
New York Manumission Society, 168
New York Times, 3, 6, 7–8
Nichols, Christopher, 236
Nieu Amsterdam, 90, *91*
Norwood, Cary, 268–69
Norwood, Drew, 268–69

Nsundi: on *São João Bautista*, 341n2; slave families of, 93
nuclear families: on *Cosby Show*, 3; after emancipation, 298; family dysfunction of, 325n24; of Godfreys, 115; Moynihan Report and, 19, 24–25; patriarchy in, 3, 8–9; of slaves, 25–26, 99, 330n115, 353n164; Wheatley, P., from, 50. *See also* Obama
nursing, by mothers, 55
Ny-fond-lo-loo, 60

Obama, Barack, 1–3, *2, 4*
Obama, Barack, Sr., 2–3
Obama, Kezia, 3
Obama, Malia, 1–2, *2*
Obama, Michelle, 1–5, *2*; malicious characterization of, 3, 25, 330n113
Obama, Sasha, 1–2, *2*
obsessive-compulsive disorder, 223
octoroon, 354n188; in British colonies, 108
ohemmaa (Akan Queenmother), 55–56
Oliver, Solomon, 242
Olmsted, Frederick Law, 215–16, 281, 282
O-lo-loo-ay, 60
Oñate, Don Juan de, 90
"Out of the Mouth of the Ex-Slaves" (Cade), 21
Ovington, Mary White, 14
Owens, Wade, 203

"The Pain of the Absent Father" (Anderson, R.), *10*
Painter, Nell Irwin, 29
Palmer, Colin, 73
panic attacks, 223
Parker, Molly, 226
Parks, Annie, 264
Parton, Ellen, 297
Pati, 349n99
patriarchy, 15, 23; in Christianity, 389n175; family dysfunction of, 325n24; in nuclear family, 3, 8–9; semi-patriarchy, 329n111
patrilineal societies, 92, 335n46
Pattison, Jeremiah, 140
The Peculiar Institution (Stampp), 12
Peirce (Captain), 107
Penn, Rosalyn Terborg, 27
Pennington, James, 233–34, 237–39
Pennsylvania Society for Promoting the Abolition of Slavery, 168
Perkins, John, 102
Perry, Matilda, 260
Peters, John, 111–12
Petit Jean, 167–68
Philadelphia Negro (Du Bois), 13
Phillips, Oluwaseun Foluso, 59
Phillips, Thomas, 73–74
Phillips, U. B., 9–11
Phillis (slave ship), 70, 73–74
Picquet, Louisa, 239, 240
Pinkster festivals, 125
pipes: in marronage, 150; of slaves, 123, *123*
Pizarro, Francisco, 302
A Plantation Burial (Antrobus), *280*
Poe, Matilda, 213
Poems on Various Subjects, Religious and Moral (Wheatley, P.), 111
poisons, 139–40
police shooting, of Brown, Michael, 7–8
polygamy: adultery and, 49; in African marriages, 49–50; in American colonies, 105; in Igbo marriages, 57; in slave marriages, 81, 105, 201; in Yoruba marriages, 59, 60, 62
Ponce de Léon, Juan, 87
Pope, Alex, 292
Poro: African marriages of, 54–55
Port Royal Relief Association, 287
Portuguese colonies, 87
Portuguese slave traders, 41, 44, 47; in Angola, 82
post-traumatic stress disorder, 223
Powdermaker, Hortense, 18
Powhatan Confederacy, 80

Premero, Jan, 91
present black fathers, 23
Preston, Dickson, 116
The Price for their Pound of Flesh (Berry, D.), 29
procreation: African marriages and, 48; in American colonies, 103; in antebellum period, 197–202
promiscuity, 12
Prosser, Tom, 158–59
prostitution, 12; Edmondson girls and, 238–39, 385n104
Protestants, 81, 136; in antebellum period, 255–56
Providence (Rhode Island) Abolition Society, 168
Pueblo Revolt, 155
Pugh, Matilda, 211

quadroon, 239, 245, 354n188; balls, 244; in British colonies, 108; rape of, 240
Quakers: as abolitionists, 168; Miles, M., as, 191
queens, of Washington, DC, 193
A Question of Freedom (Thomas, W.), 28

Raboteau, Albert, 136, 360n42, 389n175
race riots, in Canada, 165
Race Traits and Tendencies of the American Negro (Hoffman), 13–14
Radcliffe-Brown, A. R., 58, 335n46
Rahhahman, Abduhl, *32*
Ramsey, Betsey (Betty), *316*
Ramsey, Cato, *316*
Ramsey, China (Jane), *316*
Ramsey, Elizabeth, 239
Ramsey, George, 115–16
Ramsey, James, *316*
Ramsey, Nelly, *316*
rape: by Ku Klux Klan, 297; of quadroon, 240; for resistance, 139–41; by slaves, 140–41
Raper, Robert, 134

Read, Thomas, 126
Reagan, Ronald, 4
redondos (round houses), 120
Reed, Annette Gordon, 28
refugees. *See* fugitive slaves
religion, 360n42, 388n173; in antebellum period, 254–63; in Atlantic slave trade, 137; in domestic slave trade, 137; in marriage, 262–63; resistance and, 135–39, *137*; slave families and, 255–56; social power in, 390n176. *See also* Catholicism; Christianity; Muslims; Quakers
resistance: American Revolution and, 160–75; in antebellum period, 246–54; marronage and, 148–55; with masking, 130–31; with murder, rape, and arson, 139–41; religion and, 135–39, *137*; slave families and, 129–81; War of 1812 and, 175–77; white-on-black violence and, 131–35, *132*. *See also* abolition/abolitionists; fugitive slaves; slave revolts
resurrection: for bondspeople, 276. *See also* emancipation
de Reus, Gerrit, 91
Revere, Paul, *161*
revolts. *See* slave revolts
Revolutionary War. *See* American Revolution
Reynolds, Mary, 209
Rice, Francis, 116
Richardson, David, 103, 346n68
Richardson, Martin, 204
Riddle, Pleasant, 229
Rigeley, Ida, 213
ring shout, 281
Riordan, Patrick, 154
The Rise of African Slavery in the Americas (Eltis), 348n82
Roberts, James, 166–67
Robin John, Ancona, 76–78
Robin John, Ephraim, 76–78
Robinson, Harriet, 281

Roll, Jordan, Roll (Genovese, Eugene), 21, 23
Rolling Stone, 6
Roper, Moses, 226
Ross, Amanda, 213, 264
Ross, Benjamin, 224
Ross, Harriet, 224
round houses *(redondos)*, 120
Rout, L. B., Jr., 90
Rowe, Katie, 221
Royal African Company, 73
Rudd, John, 221
Ruggles, Timothy, 165
runaway slaves. *See* fugitive slaves

Saint Malo, Juan, 154
Sambo personalities, 12
Samuels, Lucy, 306–8
Samuels, Mary, 302, 304, 306
Samuels, Richard (Dick), 302, 305, 306, 405n35
Samuels, Robert (Bob), 87, 301–8, 402n2, 407n54
Samuels, Sarah, 306, 307
Sanchez, Don Francisco Xavier, 116
Sande: African marriages of, 53–55; religion of, 136
São João Bautista (slave ship), 79, 341n2
Sapphire stereotype, 24, 329n112
Sarzain, Antoine, 158
Savage, Edward, *105*
Sayers, Daniel, 149
Scales, Porter, 206
self-emancipation. *See* fugitive slaves
Sells, Abram, 232
Seminoles, 150, 154–55, 195
semi-patriarchy, 329n111
Senegal, *51*, 136; Atlantic slave trade from, 44, *45*. *See also* Diallo, Ayuba Suleiman
Senegambia, 41, 348n82; African marriages in, 50–53, *52*; Mexico and, 345n54; slave families of, 93, 94, 95, 96

Senufo, 95
separation anxiety, 223
Serer, 333n4; African marriages of, 50–53
Las sergas de Esplandia, 89
Sewell, Alice, 197, 260, 277
sexual abuse: abortion for, 267; of Bibb, M., 190; bondspersons born from, 185–86; emancipation and, 296; religion and, 256; in slave marriage, 202–3; against slaves, 133, 187, 190, 237–40, 242–43, 246; by slaves, 140–41. *See also* concubines; prostitution; rape
sexual trafficking, 12
Shadow of the Plantation (Johnson, C.), 17
Shakespeare, Stephen, 115–16
Sharpe, Granville, 111
Shaw, Jimmie, 245
Sherman, William Tecumseh, 297
Sherrod, Benjamin, 134–35
Shields, Francis de, 166
A Shining Thread of Hope (Clark Hine and Thompson, K.), 27
ships. *See* slave ships
Shirley Plantation, 231
Sibly, Henry, 188–89
Sides, Mollie, 252
Sierra Leone, 94, 95, 348n82, 348n89; Atlantic slave trade from, 44; British abolitionists and, 162, 166; Christianity in, 166; Godfreys from, 162; Mende of, 49, 53, 63–64, 93
Las Siete Partidas, 97, 196
Simmons, Bill, 271
Singleton, Marrinda Jane, 261
Singleton, Tabitha, 244
Singleton, Teresa, 122
Skinner, Richard, 356n216
"Slandering the Unborn," 6
Slate, 4
slave castles, 46, 65, 67, *68*
slave children, *243*; as companions for white children, 233–34; deaths of,

Index 425

268; elderly and, 230; fear of being sold, 234; first jobs of, 232–33; funeral of, 274–76; hard work of, 234–35; maltreatment of, 235–37; medical care for, 267–68; religion and, 262–63. *See also specific individuals*

slave codes: of American colonies, 96–117; to avoid insurrections, 351n134; bondspeople and, 101; of British slave traders, 99–104; of French slave traders, 97, 98–99; of Spanish slave traders, 97–98

The Slave Community (Blassingame), 21, 22–23

Slave Counterpoint (Morgan, P.), 26

slave families, *227*; abolition for, 169–71; African ethnic origins of, 92–96; in American colonies, 79–128, 353n158; in American Revolution, 160–75; in antebellum period, 219–71; of Bibb, H., 189–91; breakup of, 220–26; to Canada, 219–20; children taken by masters, 231; courtship and, 206; domestic slave trade of, 221–22; after emancipation, 295–96; free blacks and, 174–75; fugitive slaves and, 144–45, 147, 219–20; housing for, 118–23, *121*, *122*; labor of, 117–18; mandatory migration of, 222–23; in marronage, 149–55; naming practices in, 268; parenthood in, 226–46; reconstitution of, 223–24; religion and, 254–63; resistance and, 129–81; separation of, 133–35, 293; in slave revolts, 155–60; in War of 1812, 175–77

slave housing: in American colonies, 118–23, *121*, *122*; in antebellum period, 247–50, *248*, *249*, *251*, 252

Slave Hunt (Moran), *130*

A Slave in the White House (Taylor, E.), 28

slave marriage, 22, 25, 29, 83–84, 89, 90, 94–117; adultery in, 216; in antebellum period, 185–217; courtship in, 202–7; jump the broomstick weddings, *199*, 208–11, *210*, 217, 286, 287; love in, 216–17; of mulattos, 144; murder in, 216; polygamy in, 81, 201; for procreation, 197–202; purchasing bride for, 200; rituals of, 208–17; sexual abuse in, 202–3; unhappiness in, 214–16. *See also specific individuals*

slave revolts, *159*; in British colonies, 157–58; in Haiti, 155, 242; Nat Turner's Rebellion, 252; punishment of, 157, 158; secrecy of, 155; slave families in, 155; in Spanish colonies, 155; of Turner, N., 252, 261

Slavery: A Problem in American Institutional and Intellectual Life (Elkins), 12–13

slaves and slavery: in Africa before Atlantic trade, 41–44; agency of, 22; in American colonies, *80*, *83*; cemeteries of, 273–82, *279*; democracy in, 23; dysfunctional black family and, 8–13, 21–26; economies of, 141–43; expanded territory for, 194; food of, 121, 122–23; freedom for, 28–29; in French colonies, 195–96; funerals of, 156, 273–82, *274*, *280*; hanging of, *148*; life expectancy of, 273–74; medical care for, 100, 132–33, 187; in Mexico, 89–90, 345n54; by Muslims, 42, 47; of Native Americans, 195; nuclear families of, 25–26, 99, 330n115, 353n164; number by state, 1820-1860, *320-21* ; Phillips, U., on, 9–11; pipes of, 123, *123*; as property, 100; rape by, 140–41; recreation of, 123–26, *125*; sale of, 133–34; sexual abuse against, 133, 187, 190, 237–40, 242–43, 246; sexual abuse by, 140–41; in Spanish colonies, 195–96; state percentages of households

with, 1860, 194, *319*; Tannenbaum on, 11–12; trade from Africa to the Americas, 44–47, *56*; in Trinidad, 25–26; West Africa slave trade map, *40*; White House by, 1; white-on-black violence on, 131–35, *132*. *See also specific individuals and topics*
slave ships: *Amistad*, 64, 74; *Antelope*, 340n168; *L'Aurore*, 143; *Clotilda*, 66–67; *Fortune*, 84; *Greyhound*, 77–78; *Hannibal*, 73–74; *Phillis*, 70, 73–74; *São João Bautista*, 79, 341n2; *Treasurer*, 79–80
slave trade: of free blacks, 304. *See also* Atlantic slave trade; domestic slave trade; *specific countries' slave traders*
Slave Women in Caribbean Society, 1650-1838 (Bush), 26
Smith, Ann, 131–32
Smith, Georgia, 256
Smith, James, 277–78, 284
Smith, Lou, 233
Smith, Nellie, 289, 292
Smith, Paul, 209
Smith, Robert Marion, 222
Smith, Samuel, *283*
Smyth, J. D., 149
sodomy, 91
Sojourner Truth's America (Washington, Margaret), 27
Sorrell, Ria, 264
Soso, 94
Soul Murder and Slavery (Painter), 29
Spanish colonies: bondspeople of, 101; *casta* system of, 108; Catholicism in, 87, 196; colonies of, 85, 87–90; concubines in, 244; fugitive slaves in, 152; indio in, 89; manumission in, 168; mestizo in, 89; mixed-race in, 108; mulattos in, 89, 97; slave codes of, 97–98; slave families of, 94, 95; slave housing in, 120; slave recreation in, 125; slave revolts in, 155; slaves in, 195–96

Spanish slave traders, 41, 44
Spear, Caesar, 113
Spear, Chloe, 63, 69; Christianity of, 112–13; marriage of, 113; on Middle Passage, 75–76
spies, in American Revolution, 172
Spratley, Benjamin, 170
Stampp, Kenneth, 12
Stanton, Lucia, 28
Staples, Robert, 8
Starke, Rosa, 199
Steele, Elmo, 208
Stephens, Alexander, 193
sterilization, 7, 324n19
Sterling, James, 145
Steward, Austin, 280
Stolen Childhood (King, W.), 27
suicide: of fugitive slaves, 147; on Middle Passage, 71, 73, 75; in slave revolts, 156; of slaves, 235
Sullivan, John, 167
sumptuary laws, 401n87
Surviving Southampton (Holden), 28
Susu, 349n99; slave families of, 95
Swedish slave traders, 44
Sykes, Amanda, 216
syncretic religion, 254

A Tale of Two Plantations (Dunn), 27
Tannenbaum, Frank, 11–12
Tanner, Obour, 109
Taylor, Adeline, 198
Taylor, Alan, 162, 176
Taylor, Elizabeth Dowling, 28
Taylor, Linda, 4–6, *5*
Taylor, Tishey, 266
Temme: African marriages of, 53–55; from Sierra Leone, 93; slave families of, 93
Thirteenth Amendment, 168, 283
Thomas, Jacob, 223–24
Thomas, William, 28
Thompson, John, 76–77
Thompson, Kathleen, 27
Thompson, Moslie, 216

Thornton, John, 82, 341n2
Thornton, Laura, 290
"Those Who Labor for my Happiness" (Stanton), 28
Toto, 124
Towne, Laura, 262–63
Trail of Tears, 195
Trammel, Nick, 304
Treasurer (slave ship), 79–80
Treaty of Paris, 103, 352n154
Trinidad: free blacks in, 177; slaves in, 25–26
Truth, Sojourner (Isabella Baumfree), 135, 198, 201, 221–22, 271
Tucker, M. Belinda, 324n23
Tucker, William, 81
Turner, J. Lillian, 407n54
Turner, Nat, 160; confessions of, 366n211; Rebellion of, 252, 261
Turner, West, 278

Underground Railroad, 191
Upson, Neal, 204, 279
Utye, Mary, 140

Veney, Bethany, 30, *31*, 257–58
Viaud, Pierre, 133
Virginia Abolition Society, 369n258
virginity, 205
Voice of the Fugitive, 191
voodoo, 136, 262; for medical care, 266
Voting Rights Act of 165, 21

Walker, Quock, 169
War of 1812, 154–55; resistance and, 175–77
War on Poverty, 19–20
Warren, Wendy, 107
Washington, DC, queens of, 193
Washington, Eliza, 288
Washington, George, 104; in American Revolution, 163, 166; bondspeople of, 171–72; fugitive slaves and, 144; Great Dismal Swamp and, 150; manumission by, 171; slave housing of, 119

Washington, Harry, 163
Washington, Margaret, 27
Washington, Martha, 28, 104, 171
The Washington Family (Savage), *105*
Washington Post, 6
Water Cooler, *212*
Watson, Elkanah, 134
Wax, Donald, 346n68
Wayles, John, 240
Webster, Nancy Watkins, 206
Weiss, John, 177
welfare queen, 4–6, *5*
Wells, Easter, 268
West, Kanye, 6–7
Wheatley, John, 39, 108–9
Wheatley, Phillis, 32–33, *33*, 39–41, 46, 50–52, 63, 69, *110*; Christianity of, 111; death of, 112; as Mandingo, 333n2; marriage of, 111–12; on Middle Passage, 70, 75; training of, 108–9; Wheatley, S., and, 110–11
Wheatley, Susanna, 108–11
Wheeler, Peter, 231
White, Deborah Grey, 24, 329n112
White, John, 225
White, Julia, 209
White, Mingo, 224–26
White, Selina, 225–26
White, Shane, 124
Whitefield, George, 126
White House, 1
white-on-black violence, 131–35, *132*
Whitey Plantation, 94
Whitfield, Francis, 190
Wicked Flesh (Johnson, J.), 28
Wilkinson, Willis, 116
Williams, Annie, 254–55
Williams, Heather, 28–29
Williams, Nancy, 205
Williams, Rose, 214–15
Willoughby, John, 164
Wilson, Lulu, 198, 233
witches, 216
Within the Plantation Household (Genovese, Elizabeth), 24

Wolof, 41; African marriages of, 50–53; Gates as, 333n2; marriages of, 94–95; slave families of, 92, 95. *See also* Wheatley, Phillis
Women, Race and Class (Davis, A.), 24
Women's Work, Men's Work (Wood, B.), 388n173
Wood, Betty, 388n173
Wood, Peter, 99
Woodson, Carter G., 15, 29
Works Progress Administration (WPA), 22, 294, 302, 307
Wormely, Ralph, 104
WPA. *See* Works Progress Administration
Wyatt, Thomas, 306

Wyley, Ann, 142

Yaka, 93
Yeardley, George, 82
Yellerday, Hillard, 200
Yombe, 93
Yoruba, 348n89; African marriages of, 59–62, *61*; Gronniosaw and, 58–59; religion of, 136; slave families of, 92, 94
Young, Annie, 239
Young, Clara, 258–59
Younger, Mary, 234–35

zambo, 354n188; in British colonies, 108

About the Author

Brenda E. Stevenson is the inaugural Hillary Rodham Clinton Chair in Women's History at the University of Oxford and the Nickoll Family Endowed Chair in History at UCLA. She is the author of the award-winning books *Life in Black and White: Family and Community in the Slave South* and *The Contested Murder of Latasha Harlins: Justice, Gender and the Origins of the L.A. Riots*. Her other books include *What Is Slavery?* and *Journals of Charlotte Forten Grimke*. She has been the recipient of research fellowships from Guggenheim, the Center for Advanced Studies of the Behavioral Sciences, the National Humanities Center, and the American Academy in Berlin, among others. In 2021, Professor Stevenson was selected by President Joseph Biden to serve on the Civil Rights Cold Case Review Board.

Ingram Content Group UK Ltd.
Milton Keynes UK
UKHW041405220623
423881UK00005B/42